A native of St. Louis, Missouri, Robert M. Seltzer is
an associate professor of history at Hunter College of the
City University of New York, where he teaches Jewish
history and is coordinator of the interdisciplinary program in Jewish studies. He taught previously in the department of Religious Thought at the University of
Pennsylvania. He holds degrees from Washington University, Yale University, the Hebrew Union College-
Jewish Institute of Religion, and Columbia University,
and has studied at Harvard University and the Hebrew
University in Jerusalem. He has published scholarly
papers on the rise of Jewish nationalism, on the eminent
Russian-Jewish historian Simon Dubnow, and on the history of the Jews in Eastern Europe.

Jewish People, Jewish Thought

Jewish People, Jewish Thought:

The Jewish Experience In History

ROBERT M. SELTZER

Macmillan Publishing Co., Inc.
New York

Collier Macmillan Publishers
London

Macmillan Publishing Co., Inc.
866 Third Avenue, New York, New York 10022

Collier Macmillan Canada, Ltd.

Library of Congress Cataloging in Publication Data

Seltzer, Robert M
  Jewish people, Jewish thought.

  Includes bibliographies and index.
  1. Judaism—History. I. Title.
BM155.2.S43   1980   296'.09   78–19102
ISBN 0–02–408950–8

Printing: 1 2 3 4 5 6 7 8   Year: 8 9 0 1 2 3 4

BM
155.2
.S43
1980

The author makes grateful acknowledgment to the following:

Bloch Publishing Company, for permission to quote from Abraham J. Mesch,
trans., *The Abyss of Despair* by Nathan Hanover, Bloch Publishing Co., 1950.
Copyright 1950 by Abraham J. Mesch.

David Higham Associates Limited, for permission to quote from David Goldstein, trans., *The Jewish Poets of Spain*, Penguin Books, 1971. Copyright 1965
by David Goldstein.

Solomon Grayzel, for permission to quote from *The Church and the Jews in
in the Thirteenth Century*, revised edition, Hermon Press, 1966. Copyright
1966 by Solomon Grayzel.

Harvard University Press, for permission to quote from H. St. J. Thackeray,
Ralph Marcus, and Louis H. Feldman, trans., *The Writings of Josephus* (The
Loeb Classical Library), 1926–1965. Copyright by Harvard University Press.
And for permission to quote from F. H. Colson, G. H. Witaker, and Ralph
Marcus, trans., *The Writings of Philo* (The Loeb Classical Library), 1929–
1965. Copyright by Harvard University Press.

Hebrew Publishing Company, for permission to quote from J. Clark Murray,
trans., *The Autobiography of Solomon Maimon*, East and West Library, 1954.
Copyright by the Hebrew Publishing Company.

Hebrew Union College-Jewish Institute of Religion, for permission to quote
from M. Tsevat, "God and the Gods in Assembly," in the *Hebrew Union*

To Cheryl

Preface

Like every distinctive heritage, Judaism must be understood as a creative response to ultimate issues of human concern by members of a group that has faced a unique concatenation of political, economic, and geographical circumstances. And the Jewish historical experience is more unusual than most. Standing both within and without the mainstream of Western culture, Judaism offers remarkable insights into the genesis and elaboration of powerful religious ideas and into the determined survival of a small, vulnerable people repeatedly forced to confront and adjust to conditions beyond its immediate control.

In this work, I have attempted to survey the Jewish historical landscape and orient the reader to its main features, opening up for him access to the rich scholarly literature on Jewish history, theology, philosophy, mysticism, and social thought that has been produced in the last century and a half. The subject of every section of every chapter involves the lifework of several researchers. Within the limits of the space available to me I have tried to provide a reasonably detailed introduction to a complex, ramified, and intellectually challenging field of humanistic learning.

The structure and contents of this book have been affected by the following considerations. First, I felt that it was necessary to include enough general historical background that the reader could glimpse the larger context in which each new phase of Judaism emerged out of previous phases. The separateness of Judaism has always been relative rather than absolute. The overall political and social milieu and the spiritual climate have shaped, sometimes subtly and sometimes conspicuously, the Jewish condition. Jewry has responded selectively and according to its own criteria of meaning and value to events affecting non-Jews as well; Judaism, at the same time, has exerted a reciprocal influence, direct or indirect, on the general course of historical development. It is always necessary to adjust the usual rubrics of history, such as ancient, medieval, and modern, to the particular contours of Jewish identity to define the changing subjective borders between Jew and non-Jew. Thus, it was a crucial transition when Judaism passed from being the only monotheistic civilization in a polytheistic world to being the monotheism of a minority living in lands where the state religions of the Christian or Muslim majority were spiritual descendants of Judaism; and it was another crucial transition when the secularization of European society set in motion a variety of contradictory redefinitions of the status and core of modern Jewish identity.

Second, I have tried to avoid falsifying the nature of Jewish history through oversimplification. The social profile and institutional structure of Jewry have been modified to such an extent in the course of centuries that no single definition of the Jews in a few words is possible, except that they are the continuation of previous Jewish generations. Emerging from a collectivity of seminomadic clans and tribes, the Jews during some periods were mainly peasants and fighters; in later periods they have been predominately urban artisans and merchants, sometimes widely scattered in small villages and towns, sometimes concentrated in a few geographical regions or in the major cities of the world. There have been centuries when Jewish identity was primarily an unquestioned matter of descent, and ages when proselytes have been enthusiastically sought or when positive Jewish loyalty involved a strong element of personal choice. Discrimination, hatred, and violence against Jews have marked certain epochs, alternating with times of relative security when there were some tangible, as well as psychological, advantages of belonging to the Jewish minority. For over 1,500 years Jewry was rooted in its original homeland (surely the return of a large proportion of modern Jews to that homeland is one of the most striking chapters in the history of any people), yet there is hardly any part of the world that has not seen one or more waves of Jewish settlement. Owing to the adaptability of Judaism, centrifugal tendencies of diaspora produced regional varieties of Jewish custom and culture—only to have other, centripetal, forces bring these separate Jewish ethnicities together into crucibles where new forms of Jewishness emerged. And in the course of history the Jewish people has had various, quite different political and intellectual elites: monarchs and ethnarchs, priests and sages, scholars and elected communal officials. The survival of the Jewish group has been the triumph of continuity over periodic, sometimes drastic, change.

Third, I have tried to indicate that the intellectual history of the Jewish people exhibits a complexity similar to that of its social history. The character of Jewish thought—whether it was innovative or conservative, whether it took a collective or individualistic form of expression—has been a function of the nature of Jewish society at the time, of the presence or absence of internal sectarian or political controversy, and of the roles that Jewish writers, sages, and intellectuals projected for themselves with respect to the people and God. Jewish intellectual history embraces periods of conscious encounter with the most sophisticated general modes of philosophical and scientific thought and eras of relative intellectual isolation when Jewish legal, theological, and mystical preoccupations do not correspond in any obvious way to those of adjacent cultures. In certain centuries some Jewish intellectuals have enthusiastically adapted rationalism to the defense of their faith, whereas their contemporaries or successors rejected rationalism as undermining religion and threatening the integrity of the Jewish tradition. I have tried to describe most of the principal modes of thought that have been called Jewish by Jews, so that the reader can gain an overall and representative conception of the sub-traditions of Judaism and their outstanding individual exemplars. But there is a unity with the diversity of Jewish thought. The Jewish intellectual heritage is not merely a sequence of writings produced by Jews, but a consideration of issues arising out of the biblical world view, augmented and reshaped by later concerns and partaking in a self-transforming unity of themes, symbols, and beliefs. The convictions that there is only one God who created the universe and who guides history, that He commands justice and mercy, and that Israel is His people provide the starting points and focus of Jewish religious thought throughout most of history and affect secular Jewishness in the modern world as well.

Above all, it has been the aim of this book to address itself to one of the greatest puzzles facing the modern student: that Jewish history is at the same time an account of a people and a religion—a very unusual people and a religion exactly like no other, both of which have to be understood according to their own dynamics and their own categories. The overarching unity of the societal and the ideational poles of Jewish historical experience seems to me to require that each be treated in some detail. Neither a history of the Jewish people that mentions only in passing the greatest Jewish thinkers nor a history of Jewish thought that is forced to omit much of the Jewish historical continuum, conveys the rich uniqueness of Jewish identity. A grasp of the interrelationship of these two levels of the common denominator "Jewish" should accompany the reader's exploration of particular phases and elements of Jewish history. It is crucial in an introductory survey to exhibit the interplay between the body and the mind of Judaism, because, in the long run, the social shaped the ideational and the ideational shaped the social in surprising ways.

A brief explanation of some specific choices I have made in the process of writing this book: For practical and historical reasons, I decided to present the Bible according to its traditional format, not according to the preliminary oral or literary phases that were absorbed into the final text. Familiarity with the Bible can not be taken for granted in a beginning study of Judaism, and a description of the contents of the principal biblical books—with historical explanations and flashbacks in passing—seemed useful. Moreover, it was the Bible as a whole, not its earlier components, that became the groundwork for the development of Judaism in subsequent periods. Second, I have tried to convey, when dealing with certain formative periods of Judaism such as the rise of monotheism and the religious ferment of the first century BCE and the first century CE, the awareness that limited and uncertain data make every reconstruction conjectural and a subject of considerable scholarly dispute. Third, I regret that limitation of space prevented more extended treatment of certain topics, but I wanted to concentrate on those intellectual movements, such as philosophy and mysticism, which, in the long run, represent the most self-conscious speculation on the truth of Judaism, and it was imperative that they be presented with adequate scope. Finally, a word on why I devoted so much attention to modern Jewish secular thought. I believe that Jewish secularism has features that differentiate it from secularism in general and make it a re-examination, from a new perspective, of the meaning of Jewish existence. Secular Zionism has been, of course, one of the most vital movements of modern Jewish renewal and its diagnosis of the Jewish predicament cannot be ignored. No one can describe Judaism, especially its recent trends, without assumptions and a position of his own, but I hope that mine are sufficiently inclusive and catholic not to distort unfairly any of the movements I have portrayed. It is my conviction, however, that the future of Judaism as a coherent world view, and therefore as an identity with continued personal relevance, involves philosophical and theological exploration of the kind indicated in the last chapter.

I would like to record my gratitude to those who have helped me during the years when this book was in preparation. The original plan for a history of Jewish thought was conceived by me and Rabbi Jack Bemporad, now of Dallas, Texas; I am grateful to him for memorable conversations and for materials on the Bible, Hellenistic Judaism, and Jewish philosophy. Although in the course of time the book took on a different character and all responsibility for the present version is mine, without the stimulation of his friendship and learning I would hardly have set out. I have had the benefit also of insightful comments and suggestions by Professors Matitiahu Tsevat, Joseph L. Blau, Martin A. Cohen, Eugene B. Borowitz, Rabbi Edward Schecter, Dr. Irving Levitas, and Philip Winograd, all of whom read part or all of the manuscript. I am indebted to several of my colleagues in the History Department of Hunter College: Professors Nancy G. Siraisi and Naomi W. Cohen for criticizing sections that fell into their purview, and my chairman, Professor Naomi C. Miller, for her constant encouragement and wise advice. A fellowship from the National Endowment for the Humanities in 1973–74 gave me the leisure to do research on various topics, and I was also fortunate to receive a grant from the National Foundation for Jewish Culture in 1972. At Macmillan, Charles E. Smith, Ron Harris, and above all, my editor, Kenneth J. Scott, have been exceedingly patient and helpful, despite the many delays I forced on them. The friendship and assistance of Rosalie Bachana were invaluable. Major typing and other responsibilities were handled by my sister, Frances Mendlow, and by Brenda Parnes and Nanci Kramer. Art research was done by Lucy Rosenfeld, who adroitly helped me choose pictures illustrative of each period of Jewish history and of its general environment. Only I should be blamed for mistakes of fact and interpretation and for errors of emphasis and omission. I cannot begin to recount the role of my wife in making possible the completion of this endeavor.

R. M. S.

Contents

PART TWO
From the Hellenistic Period to Late Antiquity

PART THREE
Middle Ages and Early Modern Times

Contents **xix**

LIST OF MAPS

LIST OF CHRONOLOGICAL TABLES

PART ONE

The Ancient Near Eastern Period

CHART 1. CHRONOLOGICAL LANDMARKS OF THE ANCIENT NEAR EASTERN PERIOD

General History	Israel and its Antecedents
c. 3100. Invention of cuneiform writing by the Sumerians in southern Mesopotamia.	
c. 2615–2175. Old Kingdom period of Egyptian history (building of the pyramids).	
c. 2360–2180. First large-scale territorial empire in Mesopotamian history: Sargon of Akkad.	
21st–19th centuries. Movement of Amorites and other barbarian peoples into the settled areas of Mesopotamia and Canaan.	21st–15th centuries. Middle Bronze Age in Canaan; probable origins of the patriarchal traditions of Israel.
2060–1950. Third Dynasty of Ur.	
1792–1750. Reign of Hammurabi of Babylon.	
	1678–1570. Canaan and Egypt ruled by the Hyksos; possible setting for the descent of Israel's ancestors to Egypt.
	1570–1304. New Kingdom or Empire period of Egyptian history; Egypt dominates Canaan.
1450–1200. Hittite empire in Asia Minor and Syria.	
	c. 1275–1250. Exodus of Israelites from Egypt.
13th–12th centuries. Wave of invasions in Syria and Palestine by Arameans, "Sea Peoples," and other groups.	c. 1250–1200. Israelite conquests in Canaan, leading to formation of a tribal alliance. Occasional inter-tribal leadership by judges.
1100 BCE	
	c. 1100. Early iron age; rise of Philistine league of cities along the seacoast.
	c.1050. Victory of Philistines over Israelites at Aphek.
	c. 1020–1000. Saul as first king of Israel.
1000 BCE	
969–936. Hiram I, king of Tyre in Phoenicia, ally of David and Solomon.	c. 1000–961. David, second king of Israel.
	c. 961–922. Solomon, third king of Israel.
	c. 922. Secession of northern tribes from the Davidic dynasty; split between northern kingdom (Israel) and southern kingdom (Judah).

General History	Israelite History	Israelite History
900 BCE	*Northern Kingdom (Israel)*	*Southern Kingdom (Judah)*
900–842. Ben Hadad I and rise of Aramean state of Damascus. Early 9th century. Resurgence of Assyria. 854. Beginning of temporary decline of Assyrian power west of Mesopotamia, permitting domination by Aram-Damascus over Israel.	875–842. Dynasty of Omri. Religious conflicts during reign of Ahab son of Omri, involving the prophets Elijah and Elisha. 842. Jehu overthrows the Omri dynasty, attacks worship of Baal in Israel.	873–849. Jehosaphat, king of Judah, allied with Israel and Tyre. 836. Overthrow of Ahab's daughter, Athaliah, in Jerusalem; restoration of Davidic dynasty.
800 BCE		
Early 8th century. Renewed Assyrian campaigns west of Mesopotamia. 745–727. Conquests of Assyrian king Tiglath-Pilesar IV, establishing permanent empire in Syria and Palestine.	785–745. Reign of Jeroboam II and revival of Israel; the prophets Amos and Hosea. 722. Siege and fall of Samaria; Assyrian deportations of northern Israelites; end of the northern kingdom.	734–715. Ahaz refuses to join anti-Assyrian alliance; Judah spared. c. 715–687. Reign of Hezekiah; the prophets Isaiah and Micah. 701. Assyrian siege of Jerusalem, reestablishing Judah's subservience to Assyria.
700 BCE		
625–605. Narbopolassar, the last Assyrian ruler; the Assyrian empire crumbles.	640–609. Reign of Josiah; resurgence of Judean independence; Deuteronomic movement of religious reform. Early period of the prophet Jeremiah.	

Chart 1. (con't)

General History	Jewish History
600 BCE	
Early 6th century. Division of the Assyrian empire between the Babylonians (ruled Mesopotamia and Syria-Palestine) and the Medes (in Iran and northern territories).	597. Babylonian siege of Jerusalem; first deportations of Judeans to Babylon. 587. Second Babylonian siege of Jerusalem. Fall of the city, destruction of the Temple, massive deportations to Babylon. Prophets of the exilic period: Ezekiel, Second Isaiah.
546–530. Cyrus the Persian overthrows the Median kings, puts an end to the Babylonian empire. Persian empire dominates the ancient Near East (to the 330s).	538. Cyrus's edict permitting the Judean exiles to return home. c. 515. Completion of the Second Temple in Jerusalem. Prophets Haggai and Zechariah. Judah a semiautonomous province of the Persian empire (to the 330s).
500 BCE	
490s–480s. Unsuccessful Persian efforts to conquer European Greece. 450s–430s. Periclean Athens. 431–404. The Peloponnesian Wars in Greece. 427–347. The philosopher Plato.	c. 450s–440s. New wave of return from Babylonia under Nehemia and Ezra; social and religious reforms in Judah.
400 BCE	
384–322. The philosopher Aristotle. 336–323. Reign of Alexander the Great; 334–331, Alexander defeats the Persians and conquers the Near East. 301. Beginning of the stabilization of Hellenistic kingdoms under Alexander's generals.	4th century. Possible crystallization of the Samaritan tradition. c. 333. Alexander's army occupies Judea and Palestine.

General History	Jewish History
300 BCE	
3rd century. Rise of Rome as the main power in Italy; Alexandria in Egypt as a major center of Hellenistic culture.	3rd century. Judea under the rule of the Ptolemies, the Hellenistic kingdom based in Egypt. Rise of the Jewish community of Alexandria and the first translations of parts of the Bible into Greek.
	201–198. Judea passes to the rule of the Seleucids of Syria, Mesopotamia, and adjacent areas.
200 BCE	
	175. Beginning of dominance by Hellenizing elements in Jerusalem.
175–163. Rule of Seleucid king Antiochus IV Epiphanes.	167. Antiochus IV converts the Temple to a pagan shrine; beginning of the Maccabean revolt.
	164. Temple retaken by the Maccabees, who purify and rededicate it.

CHAPTER 1

The History of Israel from Its Origins to the Sixth Century BCE

Thirty-two centuries ago, the Jewish people brought its root principle —a singular, imageless, invisible, commanding God—across the border from Near Eastern semidesert pasture land to the urban, agrarian civilization of Canaan. A tradition, like a personality, is a complex unity: a flow of elements received from previous generations, assimilated, and passed on; adapted to and combined with elements of other cultures; repeatedly filtered, censored, and refashioned; subjected to shifts of emphasis and the working out of new corollaries; preserved for long stretches in a state of apparent changelessness, yet periodically reformed according to new perspectives; always retaining a core of sameness on which it depends for potency, sustenance, and vigor. Of the living traditions in the world today, Judaism is one of the oldest—perhaps the very oldest. The two world religions branching off from ancient Jewish roots, Islam and Christianity, attained their own identities almost fourteen and nineteen and a half centuries ago, respectively. The Confucian tradition of China and the Buddhist of southern Asia date from about 2,500 years ago; the earliest Sanskrit hymns of Hindu India are thought to go back almost thirty centuries. As we shall see, there were far older peoples in the Near East, but they and their gods have disappeared or have been absorbed into quite different traditions.[1] Judaism remains the only religion arising in the ancient Near East and still immediately present in contemporary life.

7

Envoys from Canaan presenting gifts to the Pharaoh, from a fifteenth-century BCE tomb at Thebes. (Courtesy of the British Museum.)

Some Preliminary Definitions

The modern study of a tradition requires the use of neutral and un-committed terms, such as *Judaism*, which facilitate objectivity and distance, although perhaps obscuring the uniqueness of a people and the numinous, sacred quality that is the source of religion. In the ancient world, the Greek word *Ioudaïsmos* was occasionally used to describe the beliefs and practices of the Jews; Christianity has employed the term *Judaism* since the late Middle Ages in contrast to its own system of faith.[2] But only in the last 200 years has the word *Judaism* become prevalent among Jews. The more authentic term is *Torah*, which means teaching or instruction; *Torah*, in the narrow sense, comprises the sacred texts—the first five books of the Hebrew Bible, the Pentateuch—that form the core of Jewish learning; in the broad sense, *Torah* takes in the whole body of doctrines and laws derived from and read into these sacred texts. The earliest equivalents, before there existed a written Scripture, were such biblical expressions as "word of God," "knowledge of God," and "fear of God." The proper name for the Jewish people is *Israel* ("Hear, term is *redacted*) considerably later than when they were first set down in writing, and that, furthermore, these earlier sources often drew on traditions transmitted orally over many generations. (We will examine the composition of the final form of the biblical narrative later in the chapter.) When the Bible is correlated with external evidence, it is apparent that a great deal of reliable historical information can be gleaned from the text, but a cautious and critical attitude must be maintained on any single aspect of Israel's history.

Modern archeology has made available two kinds of data for this purpose: material remains and literary documents. The former shed light on such topics as the history of urban settlement in the Near East, the dating of conquests and destructions, the development of agriculture, crafts, and military techniques, the arrangement of trade routes, and so forth. These data, however, are mute and do not tell us what peoples were responsible for the artifacts uncovered or the waves of invasion revealed by excavation; these require interpretation by means of written evidence. Unfortunately, we have very few written sources from Israel in biblical times, except for short pieces of writing on pottery fragments. (The Israelites probably used for their documents perishable materials, such as parchment from animal skins.) Extensive literary materials have been found for some other peoples of ancient Mesopotamia, Anatolia, and Egypt, preserved on stone or clay tablets. (Clay tablets were an important writing material for cuneiform script.) Such sources—political, religious, and economic—provide insight into the development of languages, the spread of ideas, and the rise and fall of states and empires. Although documents so far discovered refer only occasionally to Israel (mainly in the later centuries of the biblical era), they do illuminate indirectly the history of Israelite society and the intellectual context in which the biblical tradition took shape.

In approaching the biblical narrative as a historical source, it is useful to distinguish between the record prior to the late eleventh century BCE and the subsequent period down to the sixth century BCE when the continuous narrative comes to an end. The earliest stories in the Pentateuch (the *Pentateuch* is the common term for the first five books of the Bible) are a selection of centuries-old traditions, much reworked later, on the formation of the people of Israel from the perspective of the divine intention. Although some of these materials tally with external sources, the fragmentary nature of the biblical record means that any account of the origins of Israel must remain, for the present, conjecture and only plausible at best. The two books that follow the Pentateuch (Joshua and Judges) describe the Israelite occupation of Canaan and allude to its mode of social organization during the almost two centuries that elapsed before the first Israelite kings; both historically reliable and legendary materials have been incorporated into these accounts. Only with the last four books of the narrative sequence, 1 and 2 Samuel and 1 and 2 Kings, did the editors make direct use of written sources close in time to the events described. Of course, these data also have to be weighed carefully, especially when they concern personal motives and political conflicts, but there is no reason to doubt that the individuals, groups, rebellions, and wars are not fully historical or that the underlying sociopolitical structures do not convey a reliable, albeit incomplete, picture of Israelite life during these centuries. The problem here is that the biblical authors, with quite special questions in mind (the religious significance of the rise and fall of the Israelite kingdoms), omit much that the modern historian would like to know. But again, it should be kept in mind that no other Near Eastern people left such a record, and that the significance of the biblical narrative for the religious heritage of Judaism and Western civilization, which will concern us in the following chapters, is immense.

The Rise of Civilization in the Near East

The beginnings of regular agriculture, the domestication of animals, and the first urban communities around 7000 BCE have been traced to the hills of western Iran and Anatolia (Asia Minor), to the shores of the Caspian Sea, and to Palestine. (One of the oldest cities yet discovered is Jericho in the Jordan River valley, settled in the eighth millennium BCE and surrounded by stone fortification walls in the 6800s.) The rise of civilization—the cumulative and conscious transmission of advanced culture—occurred about 3100 BCE in the south of Mesopotamia, the fertile lowlands between and alongside the Tigris and Euphrates rivers (modern-day Iraq). There the Sumerians, a people whose language has no clear relation to any known Near Eastern linguistic group, created highly organized city-states, a complex network of drainage and irrigation canals, and the first written script, the cuneiform system of wedge-shaped signs that became the medium for the diffusion of Sumerian mythology, science, and other cultural patterns to adjacent peoples. One or two centuries after the rise of Sumer, a second major center appeared in the Nile valley of Egypt, but Egyptian civilization remained for some time isolated from direct participation in the Mesopotamian orbit. In central Mesopotamia, one of the first groups to absorb the Sumerian innovations were the Akkadians, speaking the oldest Semitic language to attain written form by means of cuneiform script. (It should be noted that the term *Semitic*, like *Indo-European*, refers to a linguistic family with phonetic and grammatical similarities, not to any purported cultural or religious distinctiveness.) Akkadian and its later Babylonian and Assyrian dialects became the main international language of diplomacy and culture in the ancient Near East from the early second millennium until the sixth century BCE. During the 2000s BCE, Mesopotamian cities, previously dominated by Temple priesthoods, developed forms of kingship claiming wider hegemony, eventually leading to the formation of the first large empire in history by Sargon of Akkad (2360–2305 BCE).

At its height, the empire of Sargon and his descendants stretched from the Persian Gulf to the Syrian shores of the Mediterranean. Prefiguring a common pattern, this vast territorial state collapsed about 2200 BCE through internal dissension and barbarian invasion. Among the new arrivals in Mesopotamia were peoples from the Zagros mountains of Iran and a Semitic-language group called the Amorites (westerners). One portion of the Amorites settled down in the cities of Mesopotamia (Mari, Babylon, and other places) where they were soon integrated into Sumero-Akkadian civilization. (For several centuries these Amorites can be still identified through personal names.) Other Amorites moved into the Syria-Palestine area (ancient Canaan), in some cases retaining their separate clan or tribal structure. (We will later see that the earliest ancestors of Israel may have been among this Amorite population.)

The breakdown of the Akkadian empire was followed by a Sumerian revival under the Third Dynasty of the city of Ur. One of the best known of the following series of second-millennium Mesopotamian states was established in the eighteenth century BCE by Amorite rulers of Babylonia, especially the famous Hammurabi, who promulgated an important code of law. After the decline of the Babylonian kingdom, the center of political gravity shifted northward to the Hurrian kingdom of the Mitanni and then to the Hittite empire, whose heartland lay in Asia Minor.

Throughout most of the third and second millennia, Canaan was divided into small city-states populated by western Semitic groups and other peoples, such as Hurrians and Hittites. Many of these ancient cities (Aleppo in northern Syria, Byblos on the seacoast, Hazor in the northern part of what was to become the land of Israel, Jerusalem, and so on) enjoyed long histories under different ruling groups. The city of Ugarit on the northern coast of Syria is a major source of information for the society and religion of pre-Israelite Canaan, as a result of a large collection of fourteenth-century cuneiform documents discovered there by archeologists.

Off and on between 2600 and 1700 BCE, the Canaanite city-states maintained trade ties with Egypt. Canaan and Egypt became even more closely linked in the 1670s BCE when the Nile Delta and nearby regions were ruled by the *Hyksos* (an Egyptian term meaning "foreign rulers"), who also controlled Canaan. When the Hyksos were deposed in the 1570s, the new Egyptian dynasty founded an empire that dominated much of Canaan by means of military garrisons and local vassal kings. Fourteenth-

Ivory figure from Megiddo, thirteenth century BCE. (Courtesy of the Oriental Institute, University of Chicago.)

century Canaan, a highly stratified society comprised of a warrior nobility and a large population of oppressed peasants, is known from a collection of letters (the Amarna documents) found in the Egyptian capital of the time. In the early thirteenth century, the Egyptians clashed with the Hittite kingdom to the north, eventually dividing Canaan between them. The Egyptian hold on southern Canaan came to an end in a wave of invasions from almost every direction that inundated most of the Near East in the thirteenth century, an era of population movement and social chaos that brought the people of Israel into the agricultural and urban regions of Canaan.

The Earliest Stages of Israel's History, Before 1050 BCE

The second half of the book of Genesis describes a series of Israel's ancestors—the patriarchs Abraham, Isaac, and Jacob and their extended families—who stemmed from Mesopotamia but lived for some time in the land of Canaan before Jacob and his family eventually settled in Egypt. The biblical tradition relates that the patriarchs retained their ties for

Horned incense altar from Megiddo, tenth or ninth century BCE. (Courtesy of the Oriental Institute, University of Chicago.)

several generations with the city of Haran in northern Mesopotamia, where Isaac and Jacob returned to find wives. Archeological evidence indicates that these stories may have preserved authentic information about Amorite clans, widespread in Mesopotamia and Canaan after 2000 BCE, from which at least some of the later Israelites were descended. Names, the close equivalents of Abraham, Jacob, and one of Jacob's sons, Benjamin, crop up in materials found at Mari, an important city on the northern Euphrates up to the time of Hammurabi. Cuneiform documents found in the Hurrian-dominated city of Nuzi, east of the Tigris, allude to marriage and inheritance customs similar to those related in Genesis and at considerable variance from later biblical law. It would seem that the Bible preserves distinct memories of small, mobile, seminomadic clans that lived on the outskirts of the main urban areas of Canaan, moving around with their flocks and herds and temporarily settling down, purchasing a piece of land for a burial site (Gen., chap. 23), entering into generally peaceful ties with the local peoples but also ready, on occasion, to fight and pillage (Gen., chaps. 14 and 34).

Another link connecting the biblical traditions to the history of the second millennium BCE is the widespread use in Near Eastern sources of the term *Habiru* (or *Apiru*), which closely resembles the biblical word *Hebrew*. Mentioned in many documents from different areas and ranging from the late third millennium down to the twelfth century BCE, the *Habiru* were a social stratum living on the fringes of settled society, often as dependents of local rulers. *Habiru* figure prominently in the Amarna letters sent by Canaanite princes to the Egyptian Pharaoh in the fourteenth century BCE, imploring the Egyptian ruler for help in putting down troublesome groups threatening the Canaanite nobles' control of their cities. The patriarchal clans may have been part of this *Habiru* element in Canaan.

Close relations between Canaan and Egypt during the Hyksos period and the Egyptian empire that followed offer another point of contact between the biblical record and other second-millennium information. The biblical tradition that the ancestors of Israel came to reside in Egypt tallies with the mention of Semitic names in Egyptian documents and with the probable Egyptian origin of some Israelite names, such as Moses and Aaron. According to the Bible, Jacob and his family settled in Egypt on the invitation of the Pharaoh, after Jacob's son Joseph had risen to a high position in the Egyptian state. A career such as Joseph's, if historical, would have been possible under the Hyksos, although some scholars prefer the Empire period, which would leave a lesser gap between the descent into Egypt and the exodus from it. The Bible relates that the patriarchal clan, from which Israel was descended, settled in Egypt as free herdsmen who were later enslaved. Egyptian documents of the imperial

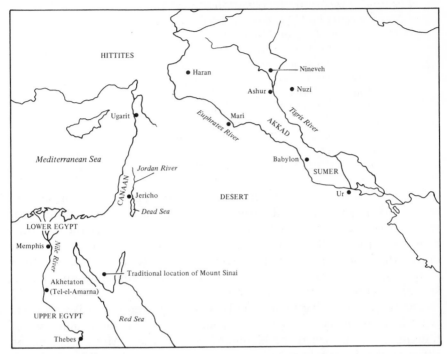

Ancient Near Eastern Places of Special Relevance to Early Israel. Canaan connects the two most ancient centers of civilization in the Near East: Mesopotamia and the Nile valley. The Bible associates the patriarchal ancestors of Israel with the Mesopotamian cities of Ur and Haran (see Gen. 11:31) and with brief stays in Egypt (Gen. 13:1), but Israelite religion was deliberately to reject major elements of the traditions of both.

centuries refer to *Apiru* as bondsmen in Egypt. The cities that, according to the Bible, the Hebrews helped build were indeed part of the construction program of the early thirteenth-century Pharaohs. There is no mention in Egyptian texts of a mass flight of hundreds of thousands of Hebrew slaves to the Sinai peninsula, but a much smaller group could have escaped from slavery in this way. The historical basis of the biblical exodus from Egypt may have involved a few thousand led by Moses, rather than 600,000 men with their families as described in the book of Exodus.

The exodus probably occurred around 1260 BCE, or sometime during the reigns of Sethos I (c. 1305–1290) or Ramses II (c. 1290–1224), who built the store cities referred to in Exodus 1:11. A stele in the name of the following Pharaoh, Merneptah (c. 1224–1211), refers to the presence in Canaan of the people of Israel. In light of the duration of Jewish history, Merneptah's declaration—the only mention of the name Israel yet discovered in ancient Egyptian sources—is singularly unprophetic:

> *The princes are prostrate, saying "Mercy!"*
>   *Not one raises his head among the Nine Bows.*
> *Desolation is for Tehenu; Hatti is pacified;*
>   *Plundered is the Canaan with every evil;*
> *Carried off is Ashkelon; seized upon is Gezer;*
>   *Yanoam is made as that which does not exist;*
> *Israel is laid waste, his seed is not;*
>   *Hurru is become a widow for Egypt!*
> *All lands together, they are pacified;*
>   *Everyone who was restless, he has been bound*
> *By the King of Upper and Lower Egypt; Ba-en-Re Mari-Amon; the Son*
> *of Re: Mer-ne-Ptah Hotep-hir-Maat, given life like Re every day.*[6]

Merneptah's campaign was the last Egyptian effort to retain control over Canaan. As mentioned earlier, archeological findings indicate that the lands of the eastern Mediterranean were shaken during the late thirteenth and the twelfth centuries BCE by invasions from the sea and the desert that threatened the Egyptian and Hittite realms, razed cities throughout Syria and Palestine,[7] and brought new ethnic groups, including the Israelites, into the cultivated lands.

The Bible relates that before the Israelites appeared in Canaan they had wandered for forty years in the wilderness to the south and east of Canaan, at a time when the kingdoms of Edom and Moab were taking shape in the Jordan highlands. Exactly how and when these Hebrews became united into Israel is a matter of dispute among modern scholars. The biblical narrative indicates that the seminomads absorbed a mixture of peoples ("a mixed multitude") who accompanied them from Egypt (see, for example, Ex. 12:38). It is possible that this force was later joined in Canaan by local *Habiru* bands and by descendants of the patriarchal clans who had not settled in Egypt. Nevertheless, the subsequent history of Israel and the grounding of its religion is not understandable without the as yet externally unverified episode at Mount Sinai, in which Israel, under Moses' leadership, achieved the focus of its identity through acceptance of the sovereignty of YHVH, a deity previously unknown to Canaan. As shall be explained in more detail later in the chapter, it was also crucial that the Israelites' relationship to this deity—a tie that the Bible frequently designates as a covenant—stipulated that no other god was to be accepted alongside Him as part of the only legitimate cult of the new social entity.

At present, archeological evidence for the Israelite conquest of Canaan is only partly consistent with the biblical account of this invasion as presented in the book of Joshua and the first chapter of Judges. Two cities said to have been conquered during the Israelite invasion, Jericho and Ai (see Josh., chaps. 6 and 8), were destroyed long before the thirteenth century, indicating that some elements of the biblical account are legendary. Furthermore, the narrative omits any record of the conquest of the historically important Israelite area around Shechem. But archeological findings do show that other localities were destroyed about the time and in the manner indicated by the biblical narrative. The first chapter of Judges notes that Israel occupied only part of Canaan and that the pre-conquest population survived in the agricultural valleys and plains. (The people later called the Phoenicians, who lived on the coast north of Palestine in modern-day Lebanon, were descendants of preconquest Canaanites; their cities revived in the tenth century BCE to play a prominent role in the commercial life of the Mediterranean.) During the twelfth century, along with the Israelites, other waves of invaders settled in the area, such as the Ammonites in Trans-Jordan, the Arameans in the Syrian hinterland, and elements of a group referred to in Egyptian sources as "Sea Peoples," including the Philistines, who occupied the southern coast of Canaan.

Between about 1200 and 1020 BCE, as the Israelites became a considerable portion of the settled population of the land, they had no permanent, central political leadership. Besides tribal and local elders, there appeared from time to time a hero known as a *shofet* (plural, *shoftim*, usually rendered in English as "judge"). Some of the *shoftim* may have adjudicated disputes, but their main role was leading the Israelite militia into battle against Canaanite kings and against Moabite, Midianite, and Ammonite invaders. The *shofet's* authority was neither absolute nor hereditary but charismatic: He was considered to be possessed of divinely bestowed abilities and strength. Many of the *shoftim* may have been local rather than national leaders, although on a few occasions most of the Israelite tribes assembled under them to fight to retain their share of Canaan.

Despite incursions from without and disunity within, these two centuries were a period of consolidation. The Israelite family, clan, and other groupings gradually crystallized into a system of twelve tribes that expressed the growing feeling of kinship among all who entered into the covenant with YHVH. (The biblical account of twelve original tribes descended from the twelve sons of the patriarch Jacob is a schematization of a lengthy process of unification, during which separate traditions of these groups became the common heritage of the whole people.) An early attempt to establish an Israelite monarchy failed, according to the Bible, on the grounds that YHVH alone was king of Israel (see Judg. 8.23 and chap. 9). The Israelites adopted the local language (in the Bible Hebrew is known as the Canaanite tongue), but cultural assimilation did not entail accepting the Canaanite pantheon of gods as legitimate partners of YHVH. Although the biblical narrative refers to worship of Canaanite gods among the Israelites, the early belief that this was wrong continued to play an important role in the later period. During the tribal era, YHVH

The Canaanite god Baal, thirteenth-century BCE Megiddo. (Courtesy of the Oriental Institute, University of Chicago.)

was worshiped at many local shrines; toward the end of the period a rallying point was established at Shiloh, where the Ark of the Covenant of YHVH was kept. (The Ark was a portable chest, symbolizing YHVH's presence in Israel.) Around 1050 the shrine at Shiloh was destroyed and the Ark taken as booty by the Philistines. The Philistines' monopoly of iron manufacture gave them a temporary military advantage over other peoples in the area, and they gradually began to extend their control inland from a league of five Philistine cities along the coastal plain. The beginnings of Israelite-Philistine strife can be seen in the stories about Samson included in the book of Judges. The Philistine victory over the Israelite militia at the battle of Aphek-Ebenezer in 1 Sam., chap. 4, which resulted in the ruin of the Shiloh sanctuary, was an important step in the intensified strife that led the Israelite tribes finally to accept a king.

From Tribal Society to Monarchy, 1050–922 BCE

A new international pattern emerged in the Near East in the second half of the eleventh century as the chaotic mixture of warring peoples gave way to more stable political structures. Independent states emerged in Syria and Palestine, including Hittite city-states in the north, several Aramean kingdoms in Syria, the Phoenician kingdom and the Philistine league on the seacoast, and the Israelite monarchy.

According to the biblical narrative, Samuel, a charismatic figure who was judge, priest, and seer, reluctantly agreed to anoint Saul as the first king of Israel in order to repel the Philistine threat. Despite several military successes against the Philistines and other foes, Saul was not able to turn the tide. After he fell in battle c. 1000 BCE (he committed suicide rather than be captured), the task of establishing a unified Israelite state fell to his former officer and sometime rival David, king of his own tribe of Judah after Saul's death and, about seven years later, accepted as king by the rest of the tribes.

It was David's army that turned back the Philistines and subdued most of the other peoples who lived east of the Jordan and in Syria, creating the first imperial state native to the area. The newly conquered city of Jerusalem, not previously held by the Israelites but located on territory between the northern tribes and Judah, became the seat of his court. To enhance its religious significance, David brought the Ark of the Covenant to Jerusalem and installed it there in a tent shrine. David's state survived two revolts, fueled, in part, by resentment of the old tribal leadership against the monarchical government with its professional army and central bureaucracy. After his death, the kingship passed to his son Solomon.

During Solomon's reign (c. 961–922 BCE), the Israelite territory was

The United Israelite Kingdom Under David and Solomon (10th century BCE). At its maximum the authority of David and Solomon was said to have extended northward to the Euphrates (1 Kings 4:24, Hebrew text 5:4). During the reign of Solomon's son, the realm was split into a northern and a southern kingdom.

22

Rock-cut stairway to water pool of Gibeon, probably from the period of the united monarchy of Israel (2 Sam. 2:13). (Courtesy of the University Museum, University of Pennsylvania.)

divided into administrative districts in order to facilitate collection of taxes and drafting of forced labor battalions from among Israelites and subject peoples. The new wealth was used to launch a royal building program, including military citadels, a palace, and a Temple in Jerusalem on the Canaanite-Phoenician architectural model to house YHVH's Ark. (The priesthood of this Temple was to trace its ancestry back to Aaron, Moses' brother, and played a prominent role in Israel's history later.) Retaining the empire David assembled, Solomon exploited its trade routes and natural resources. Relations with Phoenician Tyre and with Egypt were cemented through treaties and royal marriages. In the biblical narrative Solomon's reign was looked on as a period of prosperity and peace, and he became the prototype of the wise, cultured king. Nevertheless, by the end of his life the monarchy was overextended economically and politically, and afterwards, most of the conquered peoples and the northern population of Israel threw off the rule of Jerusalem. The circumstances of the breakup of the united Israelite kingdom after less than a century indicate a persistent tension between the earlier premonarchical ideal, including the sole kingship of YHVH, and the Davidic-Solomonic state. It was impossible for Israel to survive without a king, but burdensome royal taxation and other exactions were unpopular in the north. Furthermore, Solomon's toleration of the cults of other deities in Jerusalem (see 1 Kings, chap. 11) threatened to turn YHVH into a mere dynastic god, thus subverting the religious concept of an exclusive covenant between Israel and YHVH.

The leadership of the northern tribes, under the slogan "Back to your tents, O Israel," rejected Solomon's son Rehoboam and chose as king Jeroboam son of Nabat (Jeroboam I), a former royal officer who had earlier led an abortive revolt against Solomon. The northern kingdom, called Israel, comprised the larger, more strategic, and more populous part of the Israelite homeland. Judah, which kept the territory of the tribe of Benjamin north of Jerusalem, remained through its history loyal to the house of David. Furthermore, the disruption of the united monarchy did not destroy the common religious identity. Men and ideas usually moved freely across the frontier between the two states.

The Two Kingdoms, Israel and Judah, 922–722 BCE

The most consequential international political development in this period was the gradual end, beginning in the ninth century, of the overall power vacuum in the Near East as a result of the re-emergence of the ancient nation of Assyria in northern Mesopotamia. First, the Assyrians undertook almost annual military expeditions down the Tigris and Euphrates valleys to collect tribute; gradually, despite several periods of

Tunnel leading to a cistern outside the city wall of Gibeon. (Courtesy of the University Museum, University of Pennsylvania.)

temporary decline, Assyria expanded its control over one area after another. Under Tiglath-Pilesar (ruled 744–727 BCE) and his two successors Shalmaneser V and Sargon (these two ruled from 726 to 706), most of the independent Mesopotamian, Syrian, and Palestinian states were destroyed and the rest reduced to vassalage. Out of conquered territories the Assyrian monarchs built a vast empire, the first of a series that would dominate the Near East for many centuries.

Although Jeroboam I did not venture to establish a permanent capital, he built two royal shrines to compete with the Jerusalem Temple, one at Dan in the far north and a second at Bethel in the southern part of his kingdom. (He and the later northern kings were much criticized in the biblical narrative, which was edited from the perspective of Jerusalem, for having included in these shrines golden calves, possibly as the pedestals of YHVH's throne.) The first forty years of the northern kingdom was marked by war with the south, interrupted by a destructive Egyptian invasion. During this period, only two of the six kings of Israel were sons of previous kings; violent overthrows of the government by army officers took place frequently during the turbulent history of the northern state.

In the 870s the chronic political instability of the north was ended for a while by an army general, Omri, who founded the city of Samaria as the permanent capital of his realm and inaugurated a period of renewed international glory for Israel. By this time a strong rival had arisen: the Aramean kingdom of Damascus. Omri assembled against Aram-Damascus an alliance of Israel, Judah, and the Phoenician state of Tyre, cemented by a chain of royal marriages. Omri's son Ahab was married to Jezebel, the daughter of the king of Tyre; their daughter, Athaliah, became the wife of the future king of Judah. This arrangement was to create a historic religious crisis within the two Israelite kingdoms.

Under Omri, his son, and his grandsons (c. 875–842 BCE), Israel became one of the most powerful states in Syria-Palestine. The Aramean threat was stemmed. According to Assyrian records but ignored by the biblical writers, Ahab provided a large military force in a coalition of western kings that stopped the Assyrian march of conquest at Qarqar on the Orontes in northern Syria in 854. (Ahab is the first Israelite king whose name has been discovered in a contemporary document, though his father, Omri, is mentioned in Assyrian inscriptions and on a Moabite monument.) Remains of Ahab's building projects in the city of Samaria and elsewhere testify to the material splendor of his reign. However, the Bible's main interest lies in the internal unrest fanned by the prophets of YHVH against the government's support of another cult, besides that of YHVH, in Israel. During the monarchical period, the role of prophet

(Hebrew, *navi*) had become a principal channel for the revelation of YHVH's word; the prophets produced some of the most powerful critics of kings and society in Israel and Judah throughout much of the biblical era. (We will discuss the prophets in detail in the following chapter.) The ninth-century prophets Elijah, Elisha, and their followers protested Ahab's acts of royal despotism as subversive of YHVH's ideal for Israel and vigorously opposed the cult of the god of Tyre, Baal-Melkart, introduced into Samaria by Ahab's wife Jezebel. Soon after Ahab's death in battle, the dynasty was overthrown by Jehu, an army captain who exterminated Ahab's family together with the prophets of Baal in Samaria. A few years later, the priests of the Jerusalem Temple led a similar revolution in Judah against Ahab's daughter, Queen Athaliah.

The house of Jehu lasted five generations (842–748 BCE), the longest of any northern dynasty. Jehu and his son ruled during a half-century of military weakness for Israel, paying tribute to Assyria until the Assyrian rulers became preoccupied by threats on their northern borders. Then Israel and Judah fell under the domination of Aram-Damascus, but the renewed Assyrian campaigns in the west (802 and 796) weakened Aram, relieved pressure on Israel, and ushered in another resurgence for both Israelite kingdoms. Jehu's grandson Jehoash and great-grandson Jeroboam II were said by the biblical narrator to have restored their kingdom to the old Davidic borders (2 Kings 14:25). Jeroboam II's reign was a period of wealth and luxury, at least for the upper classes, but economic exploitation of the poor was severely criticized by a new phase of the prophetic movement, initiated by Amos and Hosea.

Soon after Jeroboam's death in 748, the Assyrian presence in Syria-Palestine took on a new character: the establishment of a permanent Assyrian empire. Four of the last five men to rule Israel after the death of Jeroboam II ascended the throne by killing their predecessors and then were faced with the dilemma of costly submission to Assyria or futile attempts at defiance. One of these regicides, Menahem son of Gadi (ruled 748–738), saved his kingdom by capitulating to Tiglath-Pilesar. Another usurper, Pekah son of Remaliah (736–732), joined with Aram-Damascus and other states to oppose Tiglath-Pilesar, with the result that between 734 and 732 the Assyrian ruler invaded the area and converted Aram and much of Israel into Assyrian provinces. One of the means the Assyrians used to insure the tranquility of their provinces was extensive deportation and resettlement, a policy soon applied to Israel. According to Assyrian sources, over 13,000 Israelites were exiled to northern Mesopotamia in 732. The new king of Israel, Hosea son of Elah (732–723), at first an Assyrian vassal, turned to Egypt for support. The Assyrian king, Shalmaneser V, attacked in 724, took Hosea prisoner, besieged and destroyed Samaria (probably in 722 BCE), exiled 27,000 more Israelites, and organized the remaining territory of the northern kingdom as another Assyrian province. (His successor, Sargon II, claimed to have inflicted the final defeat on Samaria.)

During the period of the two concurrent Israelite kingdoms, the south, usually overshadowed by the north, was internally more stable. Relations between the two monarchies were sometimes hostile, sometimes friendly. The reigns of the first three kings of Judah after Solomon (Rehoboam, 922–915; Abijah, 915–913; Asa, 913–873) were marked by intermittent fighting with the north, until the border was finally stabilized. Jehosaphat (873–849) cooperated with Ahab of Israel in various military campaigns, especially against Aram-Damascus. Jehosaphat's son reigned only briefly, and his grandson was killed in the Jehu revolution of 842, leaving Ahab's daughter Athaliah ruler in Jerusalem. She was overthrown in 836 and a scion of the Davidic dynasty restored to the throne. During the rest of the ninth century, a weak Judah, like Israel, suffered the domination of

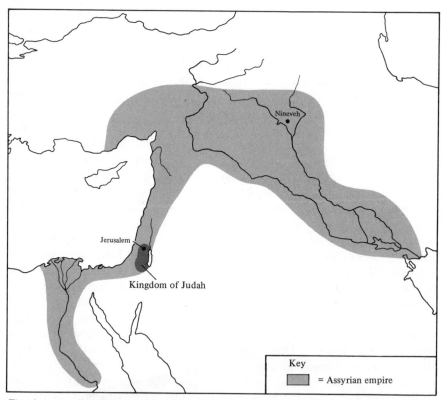

The Assyrian Empire in the Seventh Century BCE. In the 670s and 660s, when the Assyrian kings were campaigning in Egypt, their empire reached its greatest extent.

Aram-Damascus. When Aramean power declined, Judah remained subordinate to Israel.

A resurgence of Judah occurred during the reign of Uzziah (769–734), when the southern and northern states both enjoyed several decades of might and splendor. Judean military successes against neighboring peoples are mentioned in the Bible, and archeological findings indicate extensive royal construction around Jerusalem and the expansion of Judean settlements in the southern desert.

Of inestimable importance for Judaism was the survival of Judah during the Assyrian conquests in the late eighth century BCE. Ahaz (734–715) refused to join with Israel and Aram in a military alliance against Assyria, so that after extinction of the northern kingdom, Judah remained the sole center for the preservation and continuation of the Israelite tradition.

Judah Alone, 722–587 BCE

Throughout most of the seventh century BCE, Assyria dominated the Near East. Sennacherib (reigned 705–682) and Essarhaddon (681–670) added Babylonia and Egypt to their empire; the last powerful Assyrian ruler, Assurbanipal (669–627), was a patron of the arts and collector of old Mesopotamian literature. After Assurbanipal's death, Assyria began to crumble under the pressure of widespread revolt and the armies of the Babylonians and Medes. Toward the end of the century, the Babylonian ruler Narbopolassar (ruled 625–605) defeated the last Assyrian troops and gained for Babylon the position of leading power in Mesopotamia. His successor, Nebuchadnezzar II (605–562), controlled the Mesopotamian lowlands and all of Syria-Palestine. The highlands north of Assyria were ruled by the Medes, whose homeland was in Iran.

Judah had survived because Ahaz refrained from defying the Assyrians in the 720s, but his son, Hezekiah (probably reigned 715–687 BCE), participated in a new anti-Assyrian coalition during the early decades of his reign. As part of this attempted assertion of independence, he purged Jerusalem of non-Yahwistic symbols, including the Assyrian cults that his father had installed there as a sign of his submission. The biblical narrators relate that, from the time of king Asa of Judah in the late tenth and early ninth centuries, there had been recurrent efforts to eliminate the worship of deities other than YHVH and practices imitiative of their cults from Jerusalem. The religious consolidation of Hezekiah's early reign proved to be the beginning of an effective long-range reform: the "Deuteronomic" movement (the term will be explained later in the chapter) that was to become a potent force in the shaping of the Bible and of Judaism.

Detail from Assyrian relief showing the capture of the Judean city of Lachish by Sennacherib c. 701 BCE. (Courtesy of the British Museum.)

30

Hezekiah's defiance of Assyria, however, provoked a massive invasion in which many Judean cities were destroyed and Jerusalem besieged. In 701 Sennacherib was bought off with enormous tribute and the city remained inviolate. Although the Assyrians did not depose Hezekiah, his freedom of action was curtailed, and during the remaining years of his life and the almost fifty-year reign of his son Manasseh (687–640), the two Judean kings were docile Assyrian vassals. (Manasseh's acceptance of Assyrian and other cults in Jerusalem was viewed by the biblical tradition as an unforgivable sin against YHVH; he was considered by the redactors of the book of 2 Kings as one of the most wicked rulers of Judah's history.)

The decline of the Assyrian empire at the end of the seventh century made possible renewed political independence and cultural self-assertion of Judah. As the Assyrian armies were being defeated, Manasseh's grandson Josiah (ruled 640–609) annexed territories that had belonged to the former kingdom of Israel. He also sponsored the most extensive purge yet of Israelite worship: All rites now considered contrary to authentic Yahwist practice were suppressed, including local hill shrines dating from the tribal period. Jeroboam I's altar to YHVH at Bethel was destroyed and the system of Israelite sacrifices was centralized at the Jerusalem Temple. Around 622 BCE this reform program was climaxed and justified by the publication of a lawbook, the "Torah of Moses" (see 2 Kings 22:8, 23:25), which, as we shall see later, is considered by modern biblical scholars to be the core of the biblical book of Deuteronomy. (The movement responsible for editing this and several other biblical books is, therefore, usually called the Deuteronomic school.)

During Josiah's reign the international political situation remained fluid, as Assyria, Egypt, Babylonia, and Media jockeyed for power. Josiah was killed at Megiddo, in the north of Israel, trying to stop the Egyptians from coming to the aid of the remnant of the Assyrian army. The Babylonians and Medes soon destroyed the remaining Assyrian forces, and Judah was subsequently caught between Egyptian and Babylonian pressures. The Egyptians took Josiah's son Jehoahaz captive after a rule of only three months, replacing him on the throne with Jehoiakim, a second of Josiah's sons. When the Babylonian ruler, Nebuchadnezzar, defeated the Egyptians, Jehoiakim briefly switched to a pro-Babylonian orientation, but then rebelled. During the inevitable Babylonian invasion of Judah, Jehoiakim died and was succeeded by his son Jehoiachin, who opened the gates of Jerusalem to the Babylonians in 597 BCE. Nebuchadnezzar deported the king, his court, and a reputed 10,000 Jerusalemites to Babylon, leaving as regent in Jerusalem Zedekiah, a third son of Josiah. Encouraged by Egyptian promises and faith in the invulnerability of the holy city, a few years later the Judeans again defied Babylonia. In January 588 the Babylonian army appeared at Jerusalem; the city fell in July

587 BCE. Nebuchadnezzar ordered the Temple burned and the city destroyed. Zedekiah was blinded and most of the remaining Judean population exiled to Babylon.

The Babylonian Exile, 587–538 BCE

To oversee the few people left in Judah, almost all poor farmers, Nebuchadnezzar appointed as governor Gedaliah the son of Ahikam, a descendant of one of Josiah's officers who had favored a pro-Babylonian policy. In 582 Gedaliah was assassinated, leading to further deportations and flights from Judah, which ended the last shreds of Israelite political life there. For the next decades the Judean exiles in Babylonia become the main bridge for the survival of the Israelite tradition.

Our meager information about the lives of the captives indicates that the Babylonians did not enslave them or treat them with extreme physical cruelty. Settled in compact localities, they resumed their lives as farmers, craftsmen, and traders, with obligations of service and taxation to the state. In 561 BCE the former Judean king, Jehoiachin, was released from prison and awarded a pension by the Babylonian king, Evil-merodach (2 Kings 25:27–30), an event confirmed by Babylonian sources. We

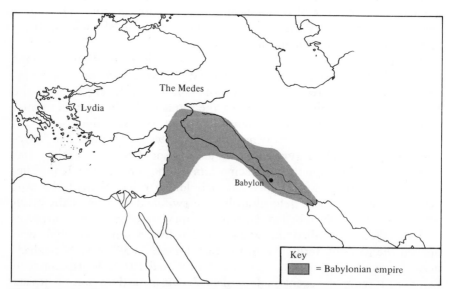

The Babylonian Empire in the Sixth Century BCE. The Babylonian empire was founded by Nabopolassar (625–605); during the reign of his son Nebuchadnezzar (605–561) Judah was conquered, Jerusalem destroyed, and many Israelites exiled to the area around Babylon.

do not know what the Judean king's function was among the exiles; their main leadership apparently consisted of elders and prophets.

The cultural impact of the Babylonian milieu on the Judeans can be seen in the adoption of Babylonian names, the Babylonian calendar, and the Aramaic language, which was becoming the main international language of Mesopotamia, Syria, and Palestine. Exile did not weaken their loyalty to YHVH. The Deuteronomistic historical books taught that the reason for the catastrophe was the persistent sin of worshiping foreign gods, especially by Israel's rulers. Far from being a proof of YHVH's weakness, conquest by the Babylonians was a confirmation of prophetic warnings of God's judgment; captivity was the just punishment of a people that had not fulfilled its covenantal obligations. But the exilic prophets also offered the consolation that YHVH would eventually cause the captives to return to their home and that the Temple would be rebuilt again on Mount Zion. Many scholars believe that much of the narrative and legal literature of Israel was assembled and redacted during this period in close to its final form. Because the Deuteronomic ideology insisted that the sole place for sacrificial offerings was the Jerusalem Temple, the exiles' worship consisted apparently of prayer, confession, fasting, honoring the Sabbath, and recitation of sacred texts. Although there is no direct

Left segment of the Assyrian relief of the capture of Lachish. (Courtesy of the British Museum.)

evidence, it can be inferred that during the Babylonian exile Israelite culture achieved a greater degree of self-awareness and a realization of the extent to which its monotheism was in sharp contrast with the polytheism of the general environment.

In 539 BCE, Cyrus, king of the Persians, took control of Mesopotamia and put an end to the Babylonian state. Having already overthrown the Median kings and conquered western Asia Minor, he brought under Persian rule the largest empire yet seen in Near Eastern history, an empire that stretched from Egypt and the Aegean shores of Asia Minor to eastern Iran. In 538, Cyrus gave the Judean exiles permission to return to Jerusalem and reconstruct YHVH's Temple. (The subsequent history of the Jewish people in Judea, where they created during the two centuries of Persian domination a commonwealth of a kind different than before 587, will be described in Chapter 3.)

Two Problems for Historical Reconstruction: The Rise of Israelite Monotheism and the Redaction of the Pentateuch

Radical monotheism, the principle that there exists but one God, is the contribution of biblical Israel to Western civilization. Israel was the first monotheistic people in the world at a time when polytheism was the norm. Monotheistic views can be found among individuals in other cultures too, often in the form of a postulated divine unity underlying the many gods that people worshiped. Israelite monotheism, however, was radical in that it arrived at the oneness of God by universalizing its own deity and denying the divinity of all other gods. As a result, the Israelite concept of God took on features not prominent in the more common, reflective monotheism just noted: Biblical religion accentuated to an unprecedented extent the moral element (it is frequently called, therefore, "ethical monotheism"). It emphasized human and divine freedom rather than preordained and fatalistic destiny, and it drastically altered the relationship between God and nature. (We will deal with these implications of biblical monotheism, which took many centuries to work out, in the next chapters.)

As there is no definitive information on how radical monotheism arose in Israel, scholars who have addressed themselves to this question sometimes seek to hypothesize one primary motive as the basis for the development of the mature monotheistic principle. Thus, E. A. Speiser, in his commentary to the book of Genesis, suggested that the beginnings of the distinctive world view of the Bible could well have stemmed from a disillusionment with Mesopotamian religion as early as the beginning of the second millennium BCE. Observing that Mesopotamian polytheism made for "chronic indecision in heaven and consequent insecurity on earth," as well as for preoccupation with divination and ritual appeasement of the gods, Speiser proposed that Israel's tradition began with the discovery by Abraham that a dependable and impartial criterion of universal justice can be attained only through a belief in a God with no rivals—a God who is, therefore, the sole supreme ethical will for humanity.[8]

More frequently, however, it is Moses rather than Abraham who is considered, in the words of W. F. Albright, the "principal architect of Israelite monotheism."[9] Albright notes that even before Moses there is evidence of a monotheistic tendency in the religious reforms of the fourteenth-century Egyptian Pharaoh Akhenaton, who promoted the cult of the solar disk, Aten, as the one god of Egypt. Other scholars have noted that Akhenaton, like all Pharaohs, was regarded as divine, that the status of the other gods in his system was not clarified, and that Akhenaton's memory was execrated in the next generation. Therefore, they doubt that there was any historical connection between this Pharaoh and Moses.[10] Yehezkel Kaufmann, the Israeli biblical scholar, supports the Mosaic origins of monotheism on the grounds that it was a unique jump to a different perspective by a revolutionary genius. As a result, Kaufmann argues, Moses inculcates in Israel a popular or folk monotheism that is opposed almost instinctively to the mythology and other features of paganism, an opposition that was the basis for later developments in biblical thought.

Dating a fully articulate theoretical monotheism to Moses, however, conflicts with biblical narratives of the tribal and monarchical periods that testify to an agonized struggle on the part of some Israelites to remain faithful only to YHVH in the face of other available and appealing deities. (See Josh. 24:15; 1 Kings 18:21.) It is more probable that radical monotheism is the product of a clash of cults and of religious concepts over the course of centuries, and is an idea that the redactors of the biblical text imposed on earlier, premonotheistic Israelite materials. A fruitful starting point, therefore, is the hypothesis that "monotheism was not the issue in the earlier period, monolatry was."[11]

Monolatry is the obligation to worship only one god, despite the admitted existence of other gods. Some have suggested that the original meaning of Deuteronomy 6:4, a summary proclamation of early Israelite religion, was "Hear, O Israel, YHVH our God, YHVH alone." (Later tradition interprets it "Hear, O Israel, YHVH our God, YHVH is one.") Monolatry was a feature of the covenantal relationship between Israel and YHVH, the origins of which preceded the conquest of Canaan: YHVH is the divine force who reveals his will to Israel's leaders, infuses its heroes with his spirit, protects his people in their wanderings, and guides them to victory. YHVH is Israel's sovereign; Israel is YHVH's possession. Hence the worship of any other deity was nothing less than

Thirteenth-century BCE stele from Beth-Shean: horned goddess and worshipper. (Courtesy of the University Museum, University of Pennsylvania.)

treason ("You shall have no other gods before me," Ex. 20:3). To be sure, there were other features of early Israelite religion that were also crucial for the development of monotheism: No images could be made of YHVH ("You shall not make for yourself a graven image, or any likeness of anything that is in the heaven above, or that is in the earth beneath, or that is in the water under the earth," Ex. 20:4); YHVH was not a member of the recognized pantheon of Mesopotamian, Egyptian, or

Canaanite gods; he was the deity of a people before being associated with a holy place (the Jerusalem Temple) or a dynasty (the house of David). Rather than symbolizing the cycle of nature, like some Canaanite deities, he was identified with redemptive events in Israel's experience, especially liberation from Egyptian slavery ("I am YHVH your God, who brought you out of the land of Egypt, out of the house of bondage," Ex. 20:2). These mighty acts of YHVH were used in the Bible to underpin such values as the mutual responsibility of Israelites for each other and the obligation to care for defenseless members of society. And, during the course of biblical history, additional functions were gradually attributed to YHVH, because they could not be left to other gods. YHVH, not the Canaanite god El, was the creator of the heavens and earth; YHVH, not Baal, was the source of rain and agricultural plenty; YHVH, not Asshur or Marduk, caused the Assyrian and Babylonian conquests and controlled the destiny of empires.

The most unambiguous statement in the Bible of radical monotheism is Isaiah 45:5: "I am YHVH and there is no other; besides me there is no God," a prophetic oracle dating from the Babylonian exile. Some scholars have suggested that the man who uttered this sentence "is the first Hebrew writer known to deny categorically the existence of other gods by the side of [YHVH] . . . similar denials in the Old Testament being demonstrably later than 500 BCE."[12] However, it does not necessarily follow that this particular statement that there is no God but YHVH signifies the beginning of the monotheistic principle. (Some scholars suggest that Isa. 45:5 was directed against Persian Zoroastrianism, which posited a good god in conflict with an evil being.) Following the seminal approach of Yehezkel Kaufmann, it would appear that the turning point to radical monotheism was the emergence of a concept of "idolatry": that entities customarily called gods are nonbeings in comparison to the God who rules the universe. Several decades before the Babylonian exile, the prophet Jeremiah stated, "Their idols are like scarecrows in a cucumber field, and they cannot speak; they have to be carried, for they cannot walk. Be not afraid of them, for they cannot do evil, neither is it in them to do good" (Jer. 10:5). Other utterances to this effect are found at least a century before Jeremiah (see Hos. 14:3 [Heb. text 14:4], Isa. 2:8).

The crucial moment in the emergence of Israelite monotheism, therefore, was the decision that "other gods" are "idols," the work of men's hands, artifacts of human culture—a decision that demotes these deities to a different ontological status from that of YHVH. YHVH was not "a god," but God, a being whose nature is unique, absolute, and ultimate.

From evidence now available, it is impossible to determine when this occurred. Most likely it was already articulated by the time of the eighth-century BCE prophet Amos, who went beyond a concern with idolatry to further implications of monotheism. Perhaps this step had been taken when Elijah and the prophets of YHVH in the ninth century BCE confronted the prophets of Baal with the cry "YHVH He is God; YHVH He is God" (1 Kings 18:39). As we saw, many eminent scholars would trace this insight to much earlier times. Part of the difficulty in pinning down the initial appearance of radical monotheism is that there may have been a considerable lapse of time during which the idea moved from a small group of YHVH worshipers to broader strata of the people.

A hypothetical reconstruction of the process by which monotheism was conceptualized begins with a position attributed to Jephthah in the tribal period. Assuming that the god Chemosh is as real as the god YHVH, Jephthah addresses the king of the Ammonites:

> So then, YHVH, the god of Israel, dispossessed the Amorites from before his people Israel; and are you to take possession of them? Will you not possess what Chemosh your god gives you to possess? And all that YHVH our god has dispossessed before us, we will possess. [Judg. 11:23–24.]

Similarly, David remarks that if he were driven away from Israel by Saul he would have to "serve other gods" (1 Sam. 26:19). YHVH could be worshiped only on the land occupied by Israel.

A second corollary permitting further development of monolatry into monotheism was the belief that the redemptive events of Israel's history showed that YHVH was far more powerful than any other god. In a song celebrating the miraculous salvation of the Israelites fleeing Pharaoh and his army during the exodus, the poet exclaims:

> *Who is like unto thee, YHVH, among the gods?*
> *Who is like unto thee, majestic in holiness,*
> > *terrible in glorious deeds,*
> > *doing wonders? [Ex. 15:11.]*

Faith in YHVH's triumphant majesty facilitated acceptance of the principle that YHVH was the supreme deity, that he had appointed other gods to govern the non-Israelite peoples of the world but retained for himself rulership of Israel and ultimate jurisdiction in the council of heavenly beings. Such a view may be implied in the following ancient biblical poem:

> *When the Most High apportioned the nations,*
> *When he set up the divisions of mankind,*
> *He fixed the boundaries of the people according to the numbers of*
> > *the sons of God.*
> *But YHVH's own allotment is His people,*
> *Jacob His apportioned property. [Deut. 32:8–9.]*[13]

In his article "God and the Gods in Assembly," Matitiahu Tsevat has proposed that a witness to the historic turn from monolatry to monotheism is Psalm 82:

> *YHVH stands in the divine assembly,*
> *He gives judgment in the midst of the gods.*
> *"How long will you judge unjustly,*
> *and show partiality to the wicked? (Selah).*
> *Give judgment to the poor and the orphan,*
> *vindicate the wretched and the destitute;*
> *Rescue the poor and the needy,*
> *deliver them from the hand of the wicked!—*
> *Without knowledge, without understanding they walk in darkness;*
> *the very foundations of the earth are shaken.—*
> *Once I had thought you to be gods,*
> *all of you sons of the Most High;*
> *Verily, however, you are now mortal like man,*
> *you will fall like any minister."*
> *Arise, O YHVH, judge the earth,*
> *for all the nations are indeed Your property!*[14]

Tsevat suggests that this poem describes a vision in which YHVH gives judgment on his divine vassals. The psalmist proclaims that YHVH condemns the other gods for perpetuating injustice on the earth and strips them of divine status and of immortality. (Immortality is the crucial dividing line between men and gods.) The poet implores YHVH to sweep away these phantoms and assert himself directly as the sole Judge of the world.

Radical monotheism was reached with the conclusion that "idols" have been endowed with supposed divinity by mere men, in contrast to the true God who is the Creator of heaven and earth and the Ruler of history, the God who will eventually be worshiped by all humanity:

And the idols shall utterly pass away. [Isa. 2:18.]—They were no gods, but the work of men's hands; wood and stone . . . Thou, O YHVH, art God alone. [2 Kings 19:18–19.]—Thus shall you say to them: "The gods who did not make the heavens and the earth shall perish from the earth and from under the heavens." [Jer. 10:11.]

Although the final redactors of the Pentateuch, and, indeed, of other biblical books, preserved various expressions testifying to a premonotheistic Israelite religion, for them monotheism is so self-evident that they assume early man knew of only one God and that history was not a progress from polytheism to monotheism, but a recurrent human propensity to fall away from monotheism to polytheism.

Clay cylinder from Baby-
lonia, with cuneiform text
concerning Nebuchadnezzar.
(Courtesy of the Metropolitan Museum of Art, pur-
chase, 1885.)

A related, though different, question for biblical studies is how the text of the Pentateuch, the Torah, which is the core document of the Jewish religion, reached its final form. Jews and Christians traditionally held the view that the Pentateuch, except for the last passage describing Moses' death, had been set down in writing by Moses before the Israelites began their conquest of Canaan. However, the Pentateuch does not actually claim to be entirely the work of Moses. (For example, Genesis does not open with the statement that to Moses was revealed the history of the world before his day and that he recorded the complete Torah in its definitive form.) The remark that Moses wrote "this torah" (this instruction) in Deuteronomy 31:9 and 31:24 may refer only to the chapters immediately preceding. As mentioned earlier, the weight of internal evidence has led most scholars to conclude that the Pentateuch is a composite work—that it underwent a period of gestation during which earlier materials were brought together into the present text. Duplicate versions of certain traditions are included in the final draft; alternative traditions were incorporated in some stories so as to leave traces of the constituent parts; contradictions and repetitions are found between the various bodies of law inserted in the narrative of Israel's wanderings in the wilderness.[15]

According to the classic analysis of the prehistory of the Pentateuch, as formulated by the German biblical scholar Julius Wellhausen in 1878, traces can be found of four prior documents, labeled J, E, P, and D by modern biblical scholarship. The J or Yahwist source, so-called according to its preference for the divine name YHVH when relating pre-Mosaic traditions, is thought to date from around the time of Solomon. The E or Elohist source (from the Hebrew *Elohim*, God) avoids using YHVH before the time of Moses in line with the thought expressed in Exodus 6:3 that the patriarchs had not known the name YHVH. The E source is perhaps from the eighth century BCE and reflects a northern, rather than a southern, milieu. The combined J and E material—consisting of tales describing the earliest history of mankind, the Hebrew patriarchs, Moses and the exodus, the wanderings of Israel in the wilderness —together form the backbone of the Pentateuchal narrative. The third or D source (the core of which is chaps. 5–26 and chap. 28 of Deuteronomy) is the only pre-Pentateuchal document that can be identified with a specific event: the religious reforms carried out by Josiah around 622 BCE in line with the discovery in the Temple of a lost "Torah of Moses." The Deuteronomic writings closely resemble the literary style of the prophet Jeremiah, who lived at that time, and Deuteronomy insists that sacrifices to YHVH should be offered only in one place of His choosing in the promised land—a ruling that tallies with an important feature of Josiah's reformation. As indicated earlier, it is likely that the Deuteronomic movement began during the reign of Hezekiah at the end of the preceding century and that it lasted well into the sixth century BCE, during which time several generations of "Deuteronomistic" writers edited the sequence of historical books that follows the Pentateuch: Joshua, Judges, 1 and 2 Samuel, and 1 and 2 Kings.

The fourth or P source is believed the work of a priestly group, whose special interests are apparent in the rituals, sacrificial laws, and other holy regulations contained in the laws of Leviticus and other places, in genealogical detail and other statistics such as the life span of a given individual, and in some of the narratives of Genesis, Exodus, and Numbers. Most scholars hold that the priestly writers were the final editors of the first four books of the Pentateuch and probably of the whole work, a task undertaken either during the Babylonian exile or in the fifth century BCE.

Positing these four literary sources does not, however, solve the problem of the origins of the biblical material, because the editors relied on historical and legal materials transmitted for many generations prior to their being written down. Moreover, it is no longer assumed, with Wellhausen, that the four documents represent successive stages in a single-line evolution of biblical ideas from primitive to advanced, culminating in the priestly editor whose beliefs reflected sophisticated Israelite religious conceptions after 587 BCE. The shaping of the four streams, J, E, P, and D, overlapped in time, so that the priestly stratum contains some of the earliest as well as the latest concepts in Israelite religious thought.

The study of the formation of the biblical text can be pushed back even further in time and made broader in scope through an approach known as form criticism, which seeks to isolate the types (forms) of composition that characterized the isolated, small units of tradition gathered together in the documents from which in turn the Pentateuch and other biblical books were constituted. Pioneered in the first decades of the twentieth century by Hermann Gunkel, form criticism has a sociological as well as a literary aim—reconstruction of the life setting of the earliest traditions: how they were used by the community in a concrete context, while still independent and oral sagas. For example, some of the stories in Genesis, before being selected for inclusion in the narrative sources, may have explained the significance of local shrines or other sacred sites. Other legends may have been associated with one segment of Israel before being absorbed into the tradition of the people as a whole. A few credal passages were possibly recited during Israelite religious celebrations, testifying to the beginning stages of the crystallization of biblical framework of ideas (e.g., Deut. 26:5–10, Josh. 24:3–13).

These and other modes of analysis lead to the conclusion that the relationship between the narratives and the events on which they are based is complex and indirect—that there were many links in the chain. Certain themes—primeval man, patriarchal wanderings, liberation from Egyptian bondage, covenant-making at Sinai, settlement in the promised land, apostasy and return to YHVH, the divine intent behind catastrophes and destruction—all gave rise to several versions reflecting different localities, tribes, groups of storytellers, religious functionaries, and lay intellectuals. During the centuries when the biblical material was elaborated and integrated, Israel was developing those aspects of its world view whose validity transcended the immediate historical and social conditions. The final biblical text in all its complexity emerges from a lengthy and considered exploration by Israelite religious thinkers of the meaning of their identity in the larger perspective, through a continual, intense, and forceful clarification of the contents of the divine will.

Appendix: A Brief Synopsis of the Tanakh, the Jewish Bible

Part One: Torah (Instruction)

The Torah is the Pentateuch or Five Books of Moses

Genesis. The creation of the universe and the origins of humanity (the "Primeval History"): stories of Adam and Eve, Cain and Abel, the flood, the tower of Babel, genealogies and other traditions concerning the early history of humankind. Tales of the patriarchal ancestors of the people of Israel: Abraham, Isaac, and Jacob (Israel). How Jacob's son Joseph is brought to Egypt, rises to a high position, is reconciled with the other sons of Jacob, and arranges for his family to settle there.

Exodus. The birth and youth of Moses, who is consecrated as God's messenger to bring the Israelites out of Egyptian slavery. After a prolonged confrontation with Pharaoh, the Israelites leave under Moses and his brother Aaron. Encamped at Mount Sinai, they receive divine instructions, which they promise to obey. Moses ascends the mountain to be given further ordinances.

Leviticus. Still at Mount Sinai, the Israelites receive additional commandments, many of which deal with priestly rituals and sacrificial offerings. Aaron and his children are consecrated as Israel's priesthood.

Numbers. The Israelites leave Mount Sinai for a period of wandering in the wilderness south of Canaan. Stories about this period are interspersed with the giving of other social and religious regulations.

Deuteronomy. At the end of forty years of wandering, Moses speaks to the Israelites on the plain of Moab across the Jordan River from Canaan, reiterating the divine instruction, reminding the people of its promise to be faithful, and supplementing previous ordinances with other laws and regulations. The Torah concludes with the death of Moses.

Part Two: Nevi'im *(Prophets)*

The *Nevi'im* are divided into Former Prophets, which are historical narratives, and Latter Prophets, which are oracles of the classical or literary prophets from the mid-eighth century BCE to the fifth century BCE.

FORMER PROPHETS:

Joshua.　The invasion of Canaan under Joshua, Moses' successor, leading to the division of the promised land between the twelve tribes of Israel.

Judges.　Stories of the period between the conquest and the rise of the monarchy, when the intertribal leadership consisted of heroic figures who led the people to victory over its enemies.

1 Samuel.　How the prophet-seer Samuel reluctantly accedes to the people's wish for a king to repulse the Philistines. Stories about Saul, the first king of Israel, and his lieutenant and rival David.

2 Samuel.　Events in the reign of David, who succeeds to the throne after Saul's death—especially David's adultery with Bathsheba, the revolt of his son Absalom, and David's renewed control of his kingdom and of the people of Israel.

1 Kings.　The last years of David's reign and that of his son Solomon, who builds the Temple in Jerusalem. After Solomon's death, the ten northern tribes secede from the rule of Jerusalem. Information and stories about the southern kingdom (Judah), which remains loyal to the house of David, and about the northern kingdom (Israel), which is ruled by a series of dynasties. The conflict between king Ahab of Israel and the prophet Elijah in the mid-ninth century BCE over the sole worship of the God of Israel.

2 Kings.　Further stories about Elijah, the prophet Elisha, and the overthrow of the house of Ahab. Information about the last kings of Israel down to the Assyrian conquest of 722 BCE and the subsequent history of Judah down to the Babylonian conquest of 587 BCE. (Later in this appendix we will describe the historical books of Ezra, Nehemiah, 1 Chronicles, and 2 Chronicles.)

LATTER PROPHETS:

Isaiah.　Oracles and a few narratives of the prophet Isaiah (late eighth century BCE). The second half of this book, chapters 40–66, contains oracles of a prophet (known as Second or Deutero-Isaiah) who lived just before the end of the Babylonian exile. Isaiah also probably contains the utterances of other prophets who lived after the return to Zion in 534 BCE.

Jeremiah.　Oracles, poems, and a few narratives of the prophet Jeremiah (last part of seventh century BCE and first part of sixth century CE).

Jeremiah lived during the last period of independent Judah, down to the fall of Jerusalem to the Babylonians.

Ezekiel. Oracles and a few narratives of the prophet Ezekiel (first half of sixth century BCE). Ezekiel lived in exile in Babylonia where his prophecies were delivered.

The Book of the Twelve—a collection of shorter prophetic books from different periods.

1. Hosea (a northern prophet of the second half of the eighth century BCE, a younger contemporary of Amos).
2. Joel (oracles, perhaps postexilic, concerning a day of divine retribution).
3. Amos (the first of the classical prophets, mid-eighth century BCE).
4. Obadiah (probably dating soon after the fall of Jerusalem in 587 BCE).
5. Jonah (unlike the other prophetic books, a tale about a prophetic figure, not a collection of oracles).
6. Micah (oracles of a Judean prophet of the late eighth century, a younger contemporary of Isaiah).
7. Nahum (an ode on the fall of the Assyrian capital at the end of the seventh century).
8. Habbakuk (probably from the last part of the seventh century).
9. Zephaniah (probably from the last part of the seventh century).
10. Haggai (narratives and oracles of a prophet who lived after the return from Babylonian exile, toward the end of sixth century BCE).
11. Zechariah (the first part contains allegorical visions of a prophet contemporary with Haggai; the last six chapters are probably from later in the postexilic period).
12. Malachi (usually considered the last prophet in the classical tradition, from the fifth century BCE).

Part Three: Ketuvim (Writings)

Works of various kinds that contain material from the earliest to the latest phases of biblical history.

Psalms. 150 poetical prayers and hymns.

Proverbs. Several collections of sayings and aphorisms, together with odes in praise of wisdom and related matters.

Job. A drama, mostly in poetry, on divine justice and human piety.

The five Megillot (*scrolls*)—short works of poetry or prose.

1. Song of Songs. A collection of love poetry.
2. Ruth. The story of a woman's faithfulness to the people and God of her adopted family, set during the period of the judges.
3. Lamentations. Dirges on the destruction of Jerusalem.

4. Ecclesiastes (*Koheleth*). Observations and reflections on the ironies and perplexities of life.

5. Esther. The story of an attempted persecution of the Jews of Persia and the events that led to their salvation, set in the capital of the Persian empire.

Daniel.   Tales about the sage Daniel and his friends in the royal court of Babylon during the sixth century BCE. Chapters 7–12 are apocalyptic visions dating from the second century BCE on the meaning and climax of history.

Ezra.   Accounts of the return of the Babylonian exiles at the end of the sixth century BCE and of the reforms promulgated by the priest and scribe Ezra in Jerusalem in the fifth century BCE.

Nehemiah.   Further narratives of the mid-fifth century BCE concerning the actions of Nehemiah, governor of Judah under the Persians, ending with the religious reconsecration of the people under the direction of Ezra.

1 Chronicles.   A summary of Israelite history through the reign of David, with emphasis on genealogy, on the Levites, and on David's successful undertakings.

2 Chronicles.   A continuation of 1 Chronicles; mainly the kings of Judah up to the Babylonian exile, based on the book of Kings but containing additional historical information not found there.

CHAPTER 2

The Biblical Heritage: Narratives, Law, and Pre-exilic Prophecy

The Bible and Ancient Near Eastern Literature

Religion begins with the experience of something uniquely holy, at once terrifying and fascinating, sublime and numinous. As a culture discerns symbols, metaphors, and analogies to identify and name the numinous, its deities provide a framework for understanding the most urgent matters of human concern: birth and death, the regularities and eruptions of nature, social solidarity and authority, personal solitude and the wish for forgiveness. Religion is man's effort to elicit meaning and value from confrontation with the holy. Through acts of worship he enters into formal communion with the divine; through myths and theology he seeks to explain the relation between the divine and the actualities of life. Proceeding one step further, religious literature collects, records, and organizes this lore and teaching, enabling man's positive response to the holy to be transmitted over the span of generations.[1]

The Bible—the surviving religious literature of ancient Israel—faces in two directions. It draws on the ideas and skills of three previous millennia of Near Eastern creativity and it opens new paths. No appreciation of the Bible can overlook the degree to which it reflects elements common to other cultures. The physical structure of the universe, taken for granted by biblical writers, characterizes ancient Near Eastern literature as a whole: The earth is a thin disk floating in the surrounding ocean; the heavens are a dome (the firmament) that holds back the "upper waters"

47

"Jehu son of Omri" presenting tribute to Shalmaneser III on the Black Obelisk from the Assyrian city of Nimrud. (Courtesy of the British Museum.)

unless its windows are opened to permit the rain to fall. Under the earth lies Sheol, the abode of the dead (see Ps. 88:3–12). In the heavens there meets a divine assembly where God announces his judgments (1 Kings 22:19). Although all humans descend to the underworld when life is over, the Bible mentions two who are raised up alive to join the celestial creatures in heaven (Enoch in Gen. 5:24 and Elijah in 2 Kings 2:11). Demonic spirits wander about in the world (Azazel in Lev. 16:8, the satyrs in Isa. 34:14), and even YHVH is capable of demonic behavior (Ex. 4:24). Like the gods in other ancient literatures, the God of Israel is portrayed in anthropomorphic terms: He walks in the garden of Eden "in the cool of the day" (Gen. 3:8); His bow appears in the sky after the rainstorm (Gen. 9:13); He sits on his heavenly throne surrounded by marvelous angelic beings (Isa. 6:1–2). Like other peoples, ancient Israel recognized the efficacy of magic (Ex. 7:11–12), acknowledged the power inherent in blessings and curses (Num., chaps. 22–24), and assumed the ability of some men to ascertain God's will through dreams, sacred dice, and oracles. (Second-millennium texts from the northern Mesopotamian city of Mari describe diviners who, like the biblical prophets, act as mouthpieces for the deities; the Bible mentions the prophets of Baal and Asherah in 1 Kings 18.) Like other religious writings, the Bible inculcates reverence for holy men (2 Kings 2:23–25), for kings (Ps. 2:6–7), and for priests (Num. 16). Common to Israelite and other ancient religions are sacrificial offerings, a preoccupation with ritual uncleanliness and purity, and atonement rites performed by priests set apart from the laity.

Many forms of biblical writing have parallels in the literature of other peoples. Genesis borrows details from the Mesopotamian epics of Atrahasis and Gilgamesh in connection with the legend of a world-wide flood. Biblical figures of speech are influenced by earlier Canaanite poetry, as is parallelism, a feature distinguishing poetry from prose in the Bible.[2] Biblical law shows many similarities with the legal collections of ancient Mesopotamia. Aspects of Hittite and Assyrian treaties between a king and his vassals are used to explicate the covenantal relationship between YHVH and Israel. Egyptian models are used for Psalm 104 and for a section of the book of Proverbs (22:17–23:11). As other ancient works are discovered in the future, it will become even more evident that the Bible is an integral branch of ancient Near Eastern literature as a whole.

Yet the differences are crucial and decisive, because the borrowings were transformed by Israelite monotheism. A few examples will indicate the scope of the reshaping that took place. (Others will emerge from our discussion of the biblical text in this and the next chapter.) Mythological themes retained in the Bible, such as the marriage of divine beings with human women, are abbreviated in the extreme and barely integrated into the narrative (Gen. 6:1–4). Biblical heroes are not worshiped as semidivine beings. In biblical religion the underworld is not a subject for religious speculation; indeed, the absence of a positive conception of personal immortality, other than through one's descendants, poses theological dilemmas resolved only at the end of the biblical period. The biblical cult includes no rites to placate ghosts or demons. There is no ancestor worship. The practice of magic is forbidden, as are consulting the dead, investigating the livers of sacrificial animals, observing the flights of birds, and other widespread forms of divination (see, for example, Deut. 18:10).

The Israelite wonder-worker derives his power not from knowledge of occult arts, but from direct divine intervention. Verbal revelation from God through the prophet is far more important in biblical Israel than in other ancient civilizations. The Bible has such a profound sense of the contrast between its view of the world and everyone else's, that much of the text is a sustained polemic, explicit or implied, against "idolatry," a category embracing all polytheistic religions and some of their most cherished beliefs about ultimate reality.

Compared to the epics of other peoples, the biblical narratives underwent drastic reorientation and simplification. Absent are myths of the birth of the gods, their rivalries and feuds, their sexual relations, their annual cycles of death and resurrection—all of which provide classic motifs in ancient literature. Biblical thought eliminates the notion, found in many pagan mythologies, of a primordial, inescapable Fate to which man and gods are subject, a Fate that can, at times, be manipulated through incantation, divination, and wisdom. Instead, the Bible is preoccupied with the moral condition of mankind, with the signs of divine providence and the wonders that accompanied the formation of Israel, and with the meaning of mundane, historical events in relation to the supreme and unconditioned will of a God not limited by destiny or Fate. Perhaps the overarching theme of the Bible is the tension between God's will and man's: between what should be (God's demands) and what actually is (man's failure, on the whole, to respond adequately to the divine expectations). As a result, the basic theological conceptions of sin and faith, holiness and redemption, justice and repentance are reworked and given new significance.

On reading the biblical narrative, one should keep in mind that it is a fabric woven of many threads of different ages and different textures.[3] As we saw in the previous chapter, the first four books of the Pentateuch were probably redacted by a school of priestly writers who added their cultic legislation, some marginal glosses, and a few narratives to much older sources written down early in the monarchical period. The typical style of the priestly sections is impersonal, ritualistic, and methodical. It has a vocabulary and interests all its own: "begettings," "be fruitful and multiply," genealogical continuity, the life span in years of a given person. The style of the "old sources," especially the J or Yahwist stratum, is concise, bold, and economical. The typical biblical tale is often compressed into forty sentences or less, and there are no lengthy descriptions of physical objects or people. J is a consummate master of the art of storytelling and a shrewd psychologist; the inner qualities of a personage are subtly indicated by a brief speech or action, the full meaning of which becomes clear only in retrospect. Some modern commentators speak of a characteristic "biblical irony" in the contrast between the immediate and the long-range significances of a detail, and between human action (J, especially, allows man considerable freedom of choice) and divine intention. The very act of selecting and assembling all these different elements, bringing together legends, genealogies, extracts from old poetry, information from royal chronicles, earlier works of literature, and later priestly accounts, infuses the old material with additional meanings. The parts must be understood from the perspective of the whole, as their original significance gains in richness by being placed in the larger context of a gradually unfolding divine plan for history. The following, necessarily brief and incomplete, discussion of the narratives will concentrate not on what the tales may have meant in their earliest phases, but on their meaning in the finished work, when monotheism became the controlling idea of the Israelite world view.

The Pentateuchal Narratives

As prologue and introduction to the Pentateuch, the priestly redactors in the sixth or fifth centuries BCE composed an account of the creation of the universe (Gen. 1:1–2:4) quite different from the ancient Near Eastern norm. The Babylonian creation poem "Enuma Elish," which is a reworking of older Sumerian motifs, traces the mystery of ultimate origins back to the primordial powers Tiamat (the salt water of the sea) and Apsu (the sweet waters). These two give birth to another pair of forces, which, in turn, engender further generations of gods, such as Anu, the god of heaven, and Ea, the god of running waters. When rest and inactivity give way to movement and energy, Apsu's sleep is disturbed and he plots the destruction of the gods. This plan is frustrated by Ea, who brings the sweet waters under control. Later Tiamat and an army of allied gods and monsters, together with her second husband, attack the younger gods. Marduk, the supreme god of Babylonia, slaughters Tiamat; from her corpse Marduk fashions the present cosmos and from the blood of her slain consort the god Ea makes man. Man is given menial work to lighten the administrative tasks distributed among the deities by Marduk, king of the gods.[4]

Similar motifs of YHVH's battle with primeval monsters are briefly mentioned in the Bible (Isa. 51:9, Job 26:12–13), but the opening of Genesis deliberately ignores them. There God forms the cosmos without any struggle, by means of an unexplained fiat: "Let there be light." The entities brought into being have no divine aspect: God is transcendent to nature, which exists only because of His creative will. The "abyss" (Hebrew *tehom*, etymologically related to *Tiamat*) is merely a descriptive term for the original state of the universe after a primary substance, unformed and watery chaos, came into being. The sun and moon, widely worshiped in the ancient Near East, are mentioned only as the "greater and lesser lights" that mark the passage of the day and year. The sea monsters, referred to elsewhere by name in biblical and Canaanite poetry, are alluded to in passing when the fish are created.

The opening chapter of the Bible indicates a carefully constructed hierarchy of created things that, somewhat like "Enuma Elish," moves from passivity to activity. The fixed entities brought into being on the first, second, and third days (light, the firmament of the heavens, the dry land with its vegetation, the seas) provide the abode for the objects created in the next three days: sun, moon, and stars, which move in set courses; then fish, birds, and animals, which move about independently but lack the higher freedom characteristic of man. In the Babylonian story, man is formed as a "lowly primitive creature, an earthly puppet" who toils so that the gods can rest and who builds and maintains temples to satisfy the divine needs. In Genesis, man, who is "God's image and likeness," is formed to be lord over the earth, the culmination of the stately order of creation. The manner in which man resembles God is not spelled out, but in Genesis 9:6 the same phrase returns in the context of the sanctity of human life.

The creation story concludes with God's resting from his work on the seventh day, a day made perpetually holy as the prototype of the later Israelite law of the Sabbath. Sabbath rest and worship (a biblical innovation in human civilization) is to be a reminder of creation. In the priestly account, God saw that what he made was good (at the climax that "it was very good"). How successfully man lives up to this ideal is the principal theme of the next ten chapters, an account of human beginnings that many scholars call the "primeval history."

The garden of Eden story (Gen. 2:5–3:24) opens with a different account of creation, part of the earlier J tradition. YHVH's first act is to water the dry ground; then he forms man from the dust of the earth. Having breathed life into him, God places man in an idyllic and delightful garden, together with the wild animals and the birds and with a female partner fashioned out of man's flesh and bone. YHVH forbids man and woman only the fruit of the "tree of the knowledge of good and evil." But the serpent, the "shrewdest of beasts," tempts the woman with the possibility of Godlike knowledge. When they eat the prohibited fruit, man and woman suddenly feel shame at their nakedness and try to hide from God. But YHVH confronts them and banishes man and woman to the world outside, where man must bring forth the produce of the soil through hard labor, and woman experiences the travail that accompanies childbirth and her special condition of desire for and domination by the husband.

This etiological tale seeks to explain the origins and reasons of the human situation: Man and woman move from a state of childlike simplicity to sexual awareness; they learn that they are to experience physical suffering and death. But they also acquire the beginnings of adult moral responsibility that comes through consciousness of the ability to do evil. (To do good implies deliberately refraining from doing evil.) Adam and Eve's disobedience of God's command is a free act of choice on their part. Having left the innocence of childhood, humanity becomes responsible for its sins and begins to live in a world of its own making, assuming some of the creativity previously characteristic only of God.

The nature of human freedom is further developed in the story of Cain and Abel (4:1–16). Cain, the farmer, becomes envious when his offering to God is rejected and that of his brother, the shepherd, is accepted. Although warned that the urge to sin can be mastered, Cain succumbs and kills Abel. When God confronts Cain with his deed, Cain lies and denies knowledge of Abel's death ("Am I my brother's keeper?"). Condemned to perpetual wandering on the earth that he had tilled, Cain, the first murderer, indicates how little control man has over his jealousy and passion.

The story of Cain and Abel is followed by genealogical lists (4:17–5:32), inserted by the priestly source, which provide continuity between the tales and relate ancient lore concerning the origins of the civilized arts, such as city building, metalwork, and music. A poetic fragment (4:23–24) indicates that human vindictiveness continues to grow, as Lamech boasts of his thirst for revenge, disproportionate "seventy-seven-fold" to the insult that provoked him. A fragmentary myth about the marriage of heavenly beings to human women (6:1–4) results in the reduction by God of man's life span. As the creation of humankind has turned out so badly ("every imagination of the thoughts of his heart was only evil continuously," 6:5), the stage is set for the tale of a world-wide flood.

The Mesopotamian flood story is found in several versions: a Sumerian account, the ninth tablet of the epic of Gilgamesh, and the Atrahasis epic. In these three works and in the Bible one man is singled out for instruction (Noah, Utunapishtim, Atrahasis); an ark is built and representatives of the various species of animals are brought on board; when the rains stop, birds are sent forth to learn if the waters have yet subsided. The ark finally settles on a mountain, where the survivors offer a sacrifice and receive a divine blessing.[5]

The biblical narrative (a fusion of J and P) ignores such details in the Mesopotamian versions as the gods' terror at the cataclysms accompanying the flood and their gathering afterwards, like flies, around the sacrifices. In the epic of Atrahasis the deluge is explained as a suggestion of the god Enlil, who is so disturbed by the tumult of mankind that he proposes to the other deities that the number of men and their noise be drastically reduced (perhaps an allusion to the perennial problem of overpopulation in Mesopotamia). In the Bible, the reason for the flood is man's wickedness and violence, which are polluting the earth. In the Mesopotamian version, Utunapishtim is eventually granted immortal life. Noah remains mortal.

When the flood is over and Noah, together with his family, is on dry land again, God sets out to rectify the ignorance that brought on the destruction. This time man is given laws: Murder is specifically prohibited and eating the flesh of animals is permitted. "Only you shall not eat flesh with its life, that is, its blood. For your lifeblood I will surely require a reckoning; of every beast I will require it and of man; of every man's brother I will require the life of man. Whoever sheds the blood of man, by man shall his blood be shed; for God made man in his own image. And you, be fruitful and multiply, bring forth abundantly on the earth and multiply in it" (9:4–7). In a priestly passage, God establishes a covenant with mankind through Noah, promising that this universal flood was unique and will never happen again. To symbolize the dependability of nature, God's bow, the rainbow that appears after the storm, is ordained as a perpetual sign of this covenant.

The primeval history now turns to the formation of the nations of the world out of Noah's offspring. In chapter 10, a genealogy traces the familial interrelationships of the peoples known to the biblical writers. The origin of the diversity of language is present by the J source in the story of the Tower of Babel (11:1–9). The inhabitants of the earth seek to achieve fame and prevent their dispersal by building a city and a tower to heaven. (The tower is perhaps an allusion to the famous zuggurat or pyramidal temple structure of Babylon, the Esagila—a sacred precinct the establishment of which is a theme of "Enuma Elish.") God disapproves of this plan, which to the biblical author signifies man's effort to put himself on a par with his Creator and refusal to acknowledge his own proper place in the universe. God confuses man's speech ("makes babble," a Hebrew word play on the name *Bavel*, Babylon), and the various linguistic-national groups are scattered over the face of the earth. Despite the origin of all humanity out of a common ancestor, divisiveness and the possibility of conflict have entered human life.

Another genealogical list (11:10–32) traces the line of descent from Shem, one of the sons of Noah, to the family of Abram (later renamed Abraham). In this transition the narrative shifts from human beginnings to Israelite origins: from the prehistory of the nations to the prehistory of a society called upon to embody a certain ideal, as though God was undertaking yet another new start by singling out one man through whom a people will be formed as a blessing to all the communities on earth (12:2–3). The remaining four fifths of Genesis consists of tales about four generations of Israel's ancestors, the patriarchs Abraham, Isaac, Jacob, and the twelve sons of Jacob. The narrative falls into two parts: from the time when Abraham leaves his native land in northern Mesopotamia until his death (12:1–25:18); from the birth of Jacob to the death of Jacob's son Joseph (25:19–50:26). (The E stratum is employed for the first time in these stories.)

The first group of stories, those that portray Abraham as the father of the future nation of Israel, establishes, first of all, Israel's claim to Canaan. Abraham erects altars in various localities, is blessed by Melchizedek (the priest-king of Jerusalem, 14:18–20), and buys a burial cave for himself and his family. Second, other tales trace Abraham's connections to the ancestors of the future Arameans (through his family in northern Mesopotamia), to the Moabites and Ammonites (through Abraham's nephew Lot), and to the desert tribes of the south (through his son Ishmael). Third, two main religious ideals are emphasized through accounts of Abraham's sense of justice and his faithfulness. The first is brought out in chapter 18. Having decided to destroy the wicked city of Sodom, YHVH asks,

> Shall I hide from Abraham what I am about to do, seeing that Abraham shall become a great and mighty nation, and all the nations of the earth shall bless themselves by him? No, for I have chosen him, that he may charge his children and his household after him to keep the way of YHVH by doing righteousness and justice . . . [18:17–19.]

This divine soliloquy sets the stage for Abraham's defense of the whole city, lest the innocent be swept away with the guilty. "Shall he who is the Judge of all the world not act with justice?" (18:25, Speiser's translation).

Abraham's trust in God, the second ideal quality on which the narrators focus, constitutes the opening and closing motif and is frequently reiterated in the tales about him. Well on in years (according to the priestly source, at the age of seventy-five), Abraham is instructed by God to set out for a land unknown to him toward a blessing that is but a distant promise (12:1–3). (Josh. 24:2 implies that by leaving the land of his fathers, Abraham was leaving idolatry.) In one of the few explicit statements describing Abraham's religious significance, the narrator remarks, "He put his trust in YHVH, who accounted it to his merit" (15:6, Speiser's translation). The continual tension in the Abraham stories is provided by the unspoken question of who will inherit the blessing of descendants as numerous as the stars in the heavens, with whom God will

maintain "an everlasting covenant." (In 17:1–14 the priestly stratum specifies that the covenant is symbolized by the sign of circumcision; chapter 15 contains the J version of the making of the covenant between
Abraham and YHVH.) Even before the Abraham stories begin, we are
told that his wife Sarai (later renamed Sarah) is barren (11:30). Because
she cannot conceive, Sarah gives to Abraham her servant Hagar, who
bears him Ishmael; Ishmael, however, is not to be the heir of the promise
and has his own destiny apart from the future Israel. When again a son
is promised, Sarah laughs in astonishment, for she is past the time of fertility (18:11). But Isaac is born and the covenant sustained. Suddenly,
Abraham is "tested," commanded by God to sacrifice Isaac on a mountain in the land of Moriah. (Many commentators believe that this is an
allusion to the mountain on which the Jerusalem Temple will be erected
centuries later.)

Genesis 22, the "binding of Isaac," is one of the most haunting episodes
of the Pentateuchal narrative. Elsewhere biblical law clearly indicates
that child sacrifice is abhorrent to Israel (Deut. 12:29–31), so that the
original message may have driven home the point that YHVH intensely
disliked the ritual slaughter of children practiced among neighboring
peoples and occasionally by Israelites who imitated this pagan rite (2
Kings 3:27, 2 Kings 16:2–4, 2 Kings 21:6). In its present context (Gen.
22), however, the story has been transformed into a supreme proof of
Abraham's faith. Were the knife to come down (verse 10), the promise
would be voided and the future Israel never exist. Abraham's single-
minded, unswerving trust in the divine purpose is vindicated when God
provides a ram to sacrifice in Isaac's stead (see verse 8), so that the continuation of the covenant is confirmed.

The stories of Isaac, which parallel several of those about Abraham and
repeat the divine promise of land and offspring (26:3–4 and 26:24), serve
to link the Abraham and Jacob cycles. Although Isaac dies at a ripe old
age after Jacob's children are born, of his later years we are told nothing
(35:22–27).

Whereas Abraham is presented in the narratives as a fully developed
figure, Jacob is portrayed through the various stages of life, and his character changes and grows accordingly. At the moment of birth, Jacob is
struggling to attain pre-eminence over his brother Esau. Jacob's life is
full of frustration, fear, and pathos: "Few and evil have been the days of
the years of my life . . ." (47:9).

A major theme in the Jacob stories is the deceiver who is deceived by
others. Jacob pries away his brother's birthright and deliberately mis-
leads his father in order to receive Isaac's blessing. Fleeing to his relatives
in northern Mesopotamia in order to escape Esau's vengeance (a second
version, by the priest source, has him sent there so he will not marry a

Canaanite woman), Jacob is deceived by his uncle Laban concerning a promised wife (29:25) and the division of their joint flocks (30:35). Jacob's magic, however, trumps his uncle, and Jacob's beloved wife, Rachel, deceives her father Laban while sitting on his idols. In the background of these stories the narrators indicate that divine providence is guiding events, inasmuch as God has determined that the promise to Abraham is to be carried on through Jacob, not Esau.

The Jacob narratives also contain several episodes in which the numinous breaks through into the foreground to punctuate the turbulent life of the hero. When Jacob first leaves home, he finds himself sleeping at the very gateway to heaven. Receiving confirmation of the divine promise, he sees in his dream a great stairway from earth to the heavenly realm on which messengers of God ascend and descend (28:1–17). Later he returns to this place (the future Israelite shrine of Bethel) to receive a divine blessing (35:9–12). Even more awesome is the cryptic encounter just before Jacob's reunion with Esau: East of the Jordan at the ford of the Jabbok River, Jacob wrestles all night with a divine being (32:24–32). His injury is used to explain why Israelites avoid eating a certain sinew of an animal's leg, but Jacob's struggle with the "man" is, above all, a test of fitness, resulting in the acquisition of a new name and completing his transformation from a devious to a forthright person. Jacob becomes Israel, "he who strives with man and God and prevails." After this story, Jacob and Esau are reconciled, but each of them goes his own way (chap. 33).

The last part of the patriarchal tales, extending from Genesis 37 to the end of the book, contains the story of Joseph and his brothers. Compared to the previous narratives, which are largely discrete episodes, the Joseph story (except for chap. 38) is a continuous flow of action. This novella, as it has been called, is a fusion of J and E passages with some marginal notes by P, but the skill of the redactor is such that the duplications do not detract from the unity of the story. (Two of the main inconsistencies are whether Reuben or Judah was the brother who tried to save Joseph, and was he sold to the Ishmaelites or to the Midianites.)

Young Joseph incurs the hatred of his brothers by tattling and by relaying dreams in which he sees his family bowing down to him. As a result, the brothers conspire to sell Joseph into slavery and they deceive Jacob about the supposed death of his favorite son (37:20, 37:31–33). The narrative follows Joseph's adventures in Egypt until, by virtue of a God-given ability to interpret dreams, he becomes second in authority to Pharaoh himself. At this point, the brothers are forced by famine to seek supplies in Egypt, putting them face to face with their former rival, whom they do not recognize. (This very famine is the theme of Pharaoh's dream that had brought Joseph to power.) The suspense comes to a head when Joseph, still harboring resentment but not motivated by retribution

Slaves making bricks, from a fifteenth-century BCE Egyptian tomb. (Courtesy of the Metropolitan Museum of Art.)

(see 50:15–26), tests his brothers by threatening to retain Jacob's beloved and youngest son, Benjamin. Not realizing that this Egyptian official is Joseph, but burdened by guilt and recognizing their responsibility, the brothers refuse to abandon Benjamin. Judah volunteers: "For your servant became surety for the lad to my father, saying, 'If I do not bring him back to you, then I shall bear the blame in the sight of my father all my life.' Now, therefore, let your servant, I pray you, remain instead of the lad as a slave to my lord; and let the lad go back with his brothers" (44:33–34). Moral regeneration and the transformation of character, adumbrated in the stories about Jacob, become even more clear in the Joseph story.

In the broader perspective, why must the family be reunited, rather than permanently divided, as in the earlier stories when Abraham and Lot, Isaac and Ishmael, Jacob and Laban, Jacob and Esau went their respective ways? Because the entire family now falls under the divine promise. Jacob is the father of an "assembly of tribes" (28:3, 48:34, Speiser's translation) who are to undergo the next step in the forging of their collective identity through sojourn in Egypt. Joseph arranges for them to settle in Egypt, but Jacob's body is to be buried alongside Abraham's and Isaac's, indicating that the link to Canaan is more important than the transient favor that the Hebrews enjoy with Pharaoh.

The patriarchal stories (indeed, all of biblical history) unfold, according to the narrators, on two planes: the mundane level of individual decision and the transcendent level of divine purpose. To the narrator it is evident that divine providence has watched over Joseph (39:2–3, 39:23, 45:7–8), saving him, his father, his brothers, and their households so that the family may be brought alive and whole into Egypt, in order that their descendants may be redeemed from another Pharaoh centuries later.

When the reader has reached the end of Genesis he is about halfway through the Pentateuchal narratives, since much of the remaining four books consists of legal and cultic instruction. At the beginning of Exodus a Pharaoh without gratitude to Joseph ("who knew not Joseph") enslaves the Hebrews, setting them to work in the fields and in the construction of his cities. Fearful of their potential power (they have become many thousands), Pharaoh orders all their male infants killed—actually the first step for the slaves' redemption. Because of this decree, the mother and sister of Moses, soon after his birth, hide him in a basket among the reeds of the Nile. There Moses is found by Pharaoh's daughter, who takes pity on the child, adopts him as her son, and appoints Moses' mother as his nurse. (Although similar tales are told of Sargon of Akkad and of Cyrus of Persia, this motif is used here to suggest that the future leader of liberated slaves must be reared not in slavery, but under conditions where he gains a different perspective.) When Moses grows up he acknowledges his ties with the Hebrew slaves and comes to their defense by killing an Egyptian taskmaster. However, when he rebukes an unjust Hebrew, he is rebuffed. Fearful of Pharaoh, Moses flees to a distant land; there he rescues the daughters of the priest of Midian, one of whom becomes his wife.

Soon afterwards, Moses becomes YHVH's messenger-prophet in an encounter with the numinous that is one of the longest sustained dialogues in the Pentateuch (3:1–7:13 is composed of material from J, E, and P). While tending the flocks of his father-in-law, Moses turns aside to view a marvel: a burning bush unconsumed by flames. God identifies the spot as holy ground and names himself the God of Abraham, Isaac, and Jacob, a God who sees (is aware of) the slavery of his people, and who commissions Moses to lead them to freedom. In answer to his request, God reveals the divine name *Ehyeh Asher Ehyeh* (3:14) based on the imperfect tense of the Hebrew verb "to be" and perhaps signifying "I am that I am," or "I will be what I will be," or "I will be there when I will be there," a few of the many interpretations that have been offered for this enigmatic phrase. Four times Moses confesses his inadequacy, showing himself a modest, reluctant leader who accepts his mission out of duty to man and God. Moses is told to return to Egypt, with his brother Aaron as mouthpiece, to confront Pharaoh with YHVH's demand that the people be allowed to leave in order to serve Him in the wilderness.

Pharaoh refuses: "Who is YHVH, that I should heed his voice and let Israel go? I do not know YHVH, and moreover I will not let Israel go" (5:2). The next section of the narrative heightens the contrast between the hitherto unknown deity (the one God), who claims the slaves as his own, and the ruler of an Egypt possessing vast riches, military power, and magical skills. Showing the impotence of the venerable gods of Egypt—Pharaoh was considered a god too—is one of the main themes of the plague stories, in which YHVH demonstrates his supreme power over nature (see 12:12). First, the waters of the Nile are turned to blood; then there appear, in sequence, a superabundance of frogs, gnats, cattle diseases, boils, hail, and locusts; in the penultimate plague absolute darkness descends on the Egyptians. (The old and later sources are combined in this narrative, drawing out the suspense and miraculousness.) Although Egyptian magicians are able to duplicate the first two plagues, they cannot reverse YHVH's wondrous acts and are forced to acknowledge that "This is the finger of God" (8:19 [Heb. 8:15]).

As before, the narrative presupposes two levels of causation: human freedom and divine providence. Pharaoh refuses to allow his valuable slaves to depart; he "hardens his heart," a biblical idiom for preparing to do evil (see 1 Sam. 6:6). Because the exodus is to be understood as a spectacular event transcending the regular order, God has informed Moses in advance: "Go in to Pharaoh; for I have hardened his heart and the heart of his servants, that I may show these signs of mine among them, and that you may tell in the hearing of your son and of your son's son how I have made sport of the Egyptians and what signs I have done among them; that you may know that I am YHVH" (10:1–2, J's version). (In the priestly explanation God tells Moses that he will not destroy Pharaoh and his people completely, so that "my name may be declared throughout all the earth" [9:15–16].) As their redemption draws near, the Israelites are instructed (chap. 12) to prepare for the ceremony of Pesah (Passover), the annual commemoration of the exodus. Having eaten the paschal lamb and marked their doorposts with its blood, the Israelites sit in their homes while the destroying angel smites "all the first-born in the land of Egypt, from the first-born of Pharaoh who sat on his throne to the first-born of the captive who was in the dungeon, and all the first-born of the cattle" (12:29). Now Pharaoh lets them go. Accompanied by a pillar of cloud by day and a pillar of fire by night, they set forth for Sinai. But Pharaoh and his servants change their minds: "What is this we have done, that we have let Israel go from serving us?" (14:5). The army of Egypt pursues them to "a sea" (usually mistranslated the Red Sea, but actually "a sea of reeds"). YHVH drives back the waters with a strong wind; the people of Israel pass through on dry land; the waters return to drown Pharaoh's

Head of a king, probably Ramses II, the most likely Pharaoh of the exodus. (Courtesy of the Metropolitan Museum of Art, Rogers Fund, 1934.)

horses, chariots, and horsemen. "Israel saw the great work which YHVH did against the Egyptians, and the people feared YHVH; and they believed in YHVH and in his servant Moses" (14:31).

The narratives of the exodus portray the Hebrews as an unformed, passive, and defenseless group whose liberation was the result of YHVH's initiative. Now they are to be forged into a collective entity worthy of redemption from physical bondage and spiritual ignorance. In the third

month after leaving Egypt, Israel camps before the holy mountain where
God had earlier appeared to Moses (Mount Sinai, sometimes Mount
Horeb, in the text). YHVH renews his promise to the patriarchs: An
obedient Israel will be his "treasured possession among all the peoples,"
consecrated to him as a "kingdom of priests and a holy nation" (19:5–6).
The people respond, "All that YHVH has spoken we will do" (19:8). In
a state of ritual purity they assemble at the foot of Sinai. Three days
later, amid fire, smoke, and the blasting of heavenly trumpets, God descends on the mountain and utters the Decalogue (the "Ten Words" or
Ten Commandments of Ex. 20:2–17). (The account of what occurred is
a conflation of various sources, which together envelop the happening
in a dramatic blur.) The awed people reaffirm their willingness to obey
God and ask Moses to carry on for them direct contact with the Holy.
"Moses drew near to the thick cloud where God was" (20:21) and receives a code of laws (chaps. 21–23). Preparations are made to confirm
the covenant; an altar is constructed and sacrifices presented to YHVH.
Moses, Aaron, Aaron's sons, and the seventy elders of Israel eat in God's
presence and behold a theophany (a divine self-manifestation) or, at least,
see the sapphire firmament under the divine throne (24:9–11).

After this ceremony, YHVH calls Moses up to the mountain to receive
the stone tablets to be placed in the Ark of the Covenant. Moses remains
on the mountain forty days in order also to be given instructions for
building a sanctuary, God's dwelling among the people (25:8). He learns
how to construct a portable tent of meeting (also called the Tabernacle),
with its altars, tables, and lamps, that is to accompany the Israelites in
their journeys through the wilderness. (The model is revealed to Moses
on the mountain in Ex. 25:10–27:21 and the Tabernacle is built in Ex.,
chaps. 35–39.)

A narrative interruption (Ex., chaps. 32–34) in this body of priestly
material on the tent of meeting relates a precipitous decline from the
people's earlier proclamation of faith in YHVH. While Moses is on the
mountain, the Israelites persuade Aaron to make the golden image of a
calf before which they exclaim, "These are your gods, O Israel, who
brought you up out of the land of Egypt" (32:4). (Perhaps originating
in a Judean polemic against the northern cult set up by Jeroboam I, the
Pentateuchal story views the golden calf as an idolatrous distortion of the
legitimate cult that is about to be instituted in Israel—a man-made symbol
accompanied by a made-up festival.) While the people are celebrating in
their encampment at the base of Sinai, Moses descends and shatters the
tablets inscribed by God, and YHVH orders the tribe of Levi to slay the
offenders. Moses intercedes with God for the people, receiving further
revelation of the divine nature: "YHVH, YHVH, a God merciful and
gracious, slow to anger and abounding in steadfast love and faithfulness,

keeping steadfast love for thousands, forgiving iniquity and transgression and sin, but who will by no means clear the guilty, visiting the iniquity of the fathers upon the children and the children's children, to the third and fourth generation" (34:6–7). A new set of tablets is given to Moses, and the people behold the radiance of his face when he comes to them from speaking directly to YHVH (34:35).

The entire fifty-three chapters from Exodus 25:1 to Numbers 10:10 (except for Ex. 32–34 and some of the material in Num. 10:11–36) are attributed by modern commentators to the priestly source and deal primarily with ritual laws: the various types of sacrifice, the holiness of the priesthood, and related cultic obligations. Their insertion at this point is appropriate because, according to the priestly ideology, the formation of Israel as a holy people requires a regular, orderly system of public worship for the expression of gratitude to YHVH and the atonement of sins. To administer these complex procedures, the tribe of Levi and one of its families, the sons of Aaron, are placed in charge. Installation of the priesthood and inauguration of their duties are described in Leviticus 8–10, which warns of the punishment in store for those who offer up "unholy fire" to God (10:1–2). Another theophany occurs when the initial sacrifices are completed:

> Then Aaron lifted up his hands toward the people and blessed them; and he came down from offering the sin offering and the burnt offering and the peace offerings. And Moses and Aaron went into the tent of meeting; and when they came out they blessed the people and the glory of YHVH appeared to all the people. And fire came forth from before YHVH and consumed the burnt offering and the fat upon the altar; and when all the people saw it, they shouted, and fell on their faces. [9:22–24.]

Although capable of accepting the covenant with enthusiasm, the people often regresses. The wilderness narratives are the education of Israel to be worthy of the one God. These stories are more difficult for the modern reader to follow than Genesis and Exodus, because duplicates have often not been fused and because they are interspersed with various bodies of legal material that tradition came to ascribe to this period.

The encampment at Sinai lasts almost one year. Before leaving the holy mountain, a census is taken and the tribes arranged in marching order (Num. 1–4). The people sets out in the second year after the exodus, on the twentieth day of the third month, having just celebrated the Passover. The next section of Pentateuchal narratives, covering almost thirty-eight years, is related in Numbers 10:11–36:13, its main theme being the difficult transformation of fearful slaves to disciplined warriors, faithful to YHVH and ready to take possession of the land promised to them. Various stories are inserted at different stages of the journey (some versions were already included earlier on the march from Egypt to Sinai), conveying the picture of a timid, "stiff-necked" people who only slowly and with constant setbacks prepare for the task ahead of them. A number of tales revolve around material complaints, such as lack of food and water (e.g., Num. 11:5), resolved when YHVH provides manna (a dew-like substance taking the place of bread) and flocks of quail (Ex. 16, Num. 11:4–9, 11:31–34), or when YHVH instructs Moses to make water gush from the desert rock (Ex. 17:1–7, Num. 20:3–12). While Israel is encamped at Kadesh-Barnea, in the Negev desert south of Canaan, YHVH instructs Moses to send spies to scout the land. The men return with a report that Canaan "flows with milk and honey" (an understandable exaggeration by a desert folk) but that its inhabitants are strong, even giants, and its cities well fortified. Only Caleb and Joshua encourage the people to advance. The Israelites complain that YHVH is leading them to a land where they will fall by the sword and their wives and children will be taken captive (Num. 14:1–3). YHVH therefore decrees that the whole generation of the exodus, except for Caleb and Joshua and those under twenty years of age, must die in the wilderness (14:26–35). Yet another type of revolt is directed against God's appointed leaders; the supremacy of Moses over other prophets and the primacy of the house of Aaron over the rest of the Levites is confirmed by stories of miraculous divine intervention in their behalf (Num. 12:6–8, chaps. 16–17).

After a long stay at Kadesh-Barnea, the people finally sets out for the territory east of the Jordan. Edom and Moab refuse Israel permission to pass through their lands, so the people bypasses these future neighbors and wins its first victories over the king of Arad in the Negev, over Sihon, the Amorite king of Heshbon, and Og, king of Bashan, in the plains beyond the Jordan north of Moab (Num. 21). At this point, the narrative introduces a cycle of stories (Num. 22–24) recapitulating a theme connected with the exodus: God's power over pagan magic. Fearful of the Israelite host, Balak, king of Moab, together with his elders and those of Midian, hires Balaam son of Beor, a Mesopotamian diviner, to curse Israel. Like the Egyptian magicians who were forced to suffer from divine plagues that they could not stop, Balaam is mocked by his own ass, who—unlike his master—sees an angel of YHVH barring the road from Mesopotamia to Moab (22:26–30). When Balaam stations himself on the height overlooking the Israelite camp, YHVH causes him to utter a series of blessings that prophesy the invincibility of Israel under YHVH's guidance and protection, its uniqueness and imperviousness to all occult forces and human enemies (see Num. 23:23). The narrative now returns to the Israelite camp with a tale of apostasy to a Moabite god, foreshadowing the later temptation to worship the gods of Canaan. The people's progress toward the promised land pauses again for a census (Num. 26), updating the census taken at Mount Sinai when the camp first set out a

The Aravah valley south of the Dead Sea, through which the Israelites passed according to the book of Numbers. (Photo by the author.)

generation earlier (Num. 1). A holy war against the Midianites (Num. 31) serves as a blueprint for the future campaign of conquest.

The final theme of the Pentateuchal narratives is the death of Moses, first presented in Numbers 27:12–23 and continued in Deuteronomy, chapters 31–34. Told of the divine decision that he must die before his people enters Canaan, Moses requests: "Let YHVH, the God of the spirits of all flesh, appoint a man over the congregation, who shall go out before them and come in before them, who shall lead them out and bring them in; that the congregation of YHVH may not be as sheep which have no shepherd" (Num. 27:16–17). YHVH instructs him to commission Joshua as his successor. After a lengthy final speech, which constitutes most of the book of Deuteronomy, Moses ascends Mount Nebo, views the promised land from afar, dies, and is buried by God in an unknown grave.

Moses is portrayed in the completed narrative as the initiator of three religious roles in later Israelite society: He establishes the office of judge, consecrates the priestly line of Aaron, and transmits God's word as a prophet. (No direct military role is ascribed to him; see Ex. 17:8–13.) He is endowed with the traits of an ideal leader: humility, integrity, and honesty (Num. 12:3, 16:15). Moses is "YHVH's servant," a title of honor for those who obey God's will and act justly (Ex. 14:31, Num. 12:7, Deut. 34:5). Yet even Moses has a moment when he fails to sustain his faith. The narrative refers vaguely to some sin of his, a reflection, perhaps, of the principle that even Moses is fallible and cannot bring his mission to fulfillment (see Num. 20:2–13 and 27:14). Although the messenger of YHVH to the people, he is pictured as also representing the people to God, pleading for them after their worst failures of nerve (Ex. 32:11–14, 32:31–32, 34:8–9, Num. 14:13–19). Moses rejects YHVH's offer to start over again with his offspring (as God had earlier started over with Noah's), demanding to be erased from God's record if He will not forgive Israel. Just as Abraham recalls to God his justice in the story of Sodom, Moses recalls to God his mercy: that YHVH is a patient God, although, to be sure, He remains the supreme judge and therefore the ultimate source of judgment and of law in ancient Israel.

Covenantal Law

A covenant (Hebrew, *berit*) is a solemn promise, creating a binding tie between two parties. In the biblical narrative, individuals covenant with each other (Jacob and Laban in Gen. 31:43–54, David and Jonathan in 1 Sam. 18:1–4), as do Israelite rulers and non-Israelite peoples (Josh. 9, 1 Kings 5:12) and a Judean king and his subjects (2 Kings 11:17). We have already referred to the stories of God's covenant with Noah and with Abraham; in 2 Samuel 7:16 God is depicted as making a covenant with David that his throne will be established forever. The pivotal event of the Pentateuchal narrative is the covenant established at Sinai between YHVH and Israel, a commitment considered so primary and inclusive that all biblical law is subsumed under its aegis.

In recent decades scholarship has become aware of the extent to which the biblical authors used ancient Near Eastern treaties as models for conceptualizing Israel's covenantal relationship to YHVH.[6] The literary format of the Israelite covenant with God has been traced to king-vassal treaties of the Hittites in the second millennium and of the Assyrians in the first millennium BCE. These Hittite and Assyrian political documents usually included the following features: a historical prologue describing the acts of benevolence that the ruler has already done for his vassal; the stipulations that the vassal agrees to accept, including the obligation not to enter into alliances with other kings; provision for the deposit of the treaty in a sanctuary and its periodic reading in public; lists of witnesses and of blessings and curses—blessings that will ensue if the vassal faithfully carries out his commitments, curses if he violates them. Each of the three main bodies of Israelite law in the Pentateuch has some of these elements in its manner of presentation.

The oldest collection of laws in the Pentateuch is Exodus 20:22–23:33, usually called the "Book of the Covenant" after the phrase in Exodus 24:7. (The duplicate body of laws in Ex. 34:10–28 is closely related.) The Book of the Covenant, thought by some scholars to be the legal corpus included in the original JE narrative, was perhaps compiled during the tribal period or just after the establishment of the monarchy. God's speech in Exodus 19:4–6 serves as its literary introduction, reiterating that He redeemed Israel from Egypt and bore them "on eagles' wings" to Sinai in order that they become a "kingdom of priests and a holy nation." The specific laws are the covenantal stipulations that Israel agrees to observe. The sacrificial meal of Exodus 24:9–11 is a formal ceremony of acceptance.

The legal collection of Deuteronomy 12–26 is the second corpus of Pentateuchal law, a revision of the Book of the Covenant and of other materials according to the ethical sensitivities and didactic rhetoric of the reform movement that reshaped biblical religion during the reign of Josiah in the latter part of the seventh century BCE. (We will discuss the ideology of this movement later in the chapter.) The Deuteronomic law is presented as a speech by Moses to the people in the plains of Moab just before his death, prefaced by a review of what God has done for Israel up to this point and by exhortations to remain faithful in the future (chaps. 1–11) and followed by a list of blessings and curses that will befall an obedient or a faithless people (chap. 28). Heavens and earth are called upon as witnesses, the narrators not caring to appeal to other gods to fulfill this task (Deut. 30:19, 31:28). The "Book of the Torah" in which the Deuteronomic covenant is written down is to be deposited in the Ark to be read before Israel every seven years (Deut. 31:10–13).

The third collection of laws and instructions is the priestly corpus stretching from Exodus 25 to Numbers 10, which includes a subsection (Lev. 17–26) usually called the Holiness Code because of the repeated use of such phrases as "You shall be holy, for I YHVH your God am holy." A list of blessings and curses for the Holiness Code is found in Leviticus 26. Most scholars date the present version of the priestly laws in the Pentateuch to the exilic or postexilic period, but the priestly tradition itself, from which these laws were culled, is certainly far more ancient.[7]

As with the narratives, the legal sections of the Pentateuch are difficult to date with precision because each of the three law corpora contain duplications, indicating that they were compiled from previously independent groupings of rules and instructions. All three probably had a long history before insertion into the narratives. The Book of the Covenant reflects the patriarchal, agrarian milieu of the first centuries of Israelite life in Canaan. Some of the Deuteronomic legislation may have been formulated in the northern kingdom before its destruction in 722 BCE. The priestly regulations have their roots in prehistoric notions of the holy and the profane widespread in the Near East. At several moments of Israel's history, during eras of political and social change, collections of legal decisions and religious commandments were compiled, using the model of a covenantal treaty to explain the nature of the people's obligations to God. Then these documents were incorporated into appropriate points in the Pentateuchal narrative.

Despite differences and contradictions in detail, the three legal corpora have much in common. All prohibit murder, robbery, incest, and adultery. Each requires respect for parents and strict justice in the courts. Each seeks to protect the rights of the stranger and provides remedies for the distress of the impoverished. A periodic liberation of Hebrew slaves and a seventh year of release for the soil and for debtors are envisioned. Certain localities are set aside as refuges for accidental and unpremeditated manslaughter. Destruction of idols and bans on sorcery and pagan methods of divination are stipulated. Observance of the Sabbath, the Passover, and the three pilgrim festivals is required. Tithes are to be given to priests and Levites; the first-born of animals and men belong to YHVH, and first-born sons are redeemed with special payments. Each code touches as well on many other areas of civil, criminal, and religious law. We will first survey some of the underlying features of Pentateuchal legislation as a whole, and then examine the significance of the covenantal form of biblical law and why these codes were placed in the Pentateuchal narratives of Israel's wanderings in the wilderness.

In the ancient Near East, law codes were compiled and published by Sumerian, Babylonian, Assyrian, and Hittite rulers to demonstrate their concern for justice and truth, to gain everlasting fame, and to ensure the favor of the gods.[8] These were not codes in the modern sense of comprehensive bodies of legislation that a local judge was obliged to consult in rendering a decision. They were reforms and amendments of customary law, demonstrating the ruler's concern for the underprivileged and for good government in his realm. It remains uncertain to what extent they influenced social behavior on a large scale. A similar question confronts the biblical historian: Does biblical law describe actual social arrangements prevailing in ancient Israel or is it an effort to reform and correct abuses? At least some of the laws (we will shortly note some examples) were the latter: attempts to ameliorate specific situations felt not to be fair or just, in order to construct a more equitable society that exemplified values espoused by the Israelite tradition. Like the narrative, Pentateuchal law is a mixture of fact and idealization.

The civil and criminal law of the biblical codes, especially that of the Book of the Covenant, draws extensively on the ancient Near Eastern collections mentioned above, either directly or via Canaanite legal works that have not yet come to light. However, borrowings are reshaped according to the distinctive features of Israelite religion. Thus, a fundamental concern of biblical law is the sanctity of the person. All three codes quote the old formula, "life for life, eye for eye, tooth for tooth, hand for hand, foot for foot, burn for burn, wound for wound, stripe for stripe" (Ex. 21:23–25, Lev. 24:19–20, Deut. 19:21). This injunction, called *lex talionis*, was a limitation of the right of vengeance (it prohibited taking a whole life for an eye), at a time when deliberately inflicted injuries were beginning to come under the aegis of state law. In Mesopotamian legislation *lex talionis* was a legal protection for freemen, preventing the nobility from escaping the consequences of violence with a financial payment. Biblical law goes a step further. Whereas Mesopotamian law retained a legal distinction between social classes in applying *lex talionis* and in other matters, biblical law extends the principle of punishment proportionate to the crime to all groups in society. Moreover, punishments in biblical law sharply distinguish between crimes against property and crimes against persons: A murderer cannot be let off with the payment of a fine. (This is the main instance where *lex talionis* was applied literally.) Kidnaping of a human being to enslave him is likewise punishable by death (Ex. 21:16). However, no crime against property warrants capital punishment. Another instance of the legal equality of all Israelites is the insistence that court procedure be thoroughly im-

partial and objective, regardless of the wealth or poverty of the plaintiffs
(Ex. 23:2–3, 23:9). Bribery of judges is particularly abhorrent, for "a
bribe blinds the officials and subverts the cause of those who are in the
right" (Ex. 23:8). The major exception to the freedom of the person in
biblical law is slavery. (In ancient western Asia the slave was a bonds-
man or an indentured servant, not the plantation type.) Biblical law
views slavery among Israelites as abnormal and temporary: All Hebrew
slaves were to be freed in the seventh year of their service, unless they
insisted on remaining with their masters (Ex. 21:1–6). Deuteronomy adds
further safeguards to the slave's situation: when liberated in the seventh
year, he is to be given the wherewithal to support himself (Deut. 15:12–
18); returning an escaped slave to his master is forbidden (Deut. 23:
15–16). The Holiness Code envisions the complete abolition of slavery
in Israel (Lev. 25:39–46).

A second major concern of Pentateuchal law is protecting the defenseless: the non-Israelite slave, the debtor, the poor, the "widow, orphan,
and stranger." Every seventh year, when the soil is to enjoy a Sabbath
and lie fallow, the poor may eat of what grows naturally (Ex. 23:10–11).
The forgotten sheaf and unpicked fruit are to be left for them (Deut.
24:19–22). Biblical law prohibits the collection of interest on loans to fellow Israelites (Ex. 22:25, Deut. 23:19–20). Deuteronomy legislates that
the debts of the poor shall be canceled every seventh year (Deut. 15:1–
11). Leviticus 25:8–12 gives every man a right in the forty-ninth or Jubilee year to return to ancestral property he has been forced to sell in the
interim. (It is not known how often this sweeping restoration of familial
property was carried out.) Biblical law insists that the same ruling should
apply to the native-born Israelite and the resident alien (Hebrew, *ger*),
the latter being a special social category with few legal rights in ancient
societies. "You shall not oppress a stranger; you know the heart of the
stranger, for you were strangers in the land of Egypt" (Ex. 23:9).

As befitting a people with strong patriarchal and tribal ties, all three
biblical codes are especially concerned to protect the dignity and purity
of the family, far more than their Mesopotamian models.[9] In contrast to
humane punishments for civil and criminal crimes, severe punishments are
enjoined against acts that tarnish the holiness of the family (incest, besti-
ality, sodomy) and for crimes against God (blasphemy and idolatry).
Pentateuchal law frequently appeals to the personal motives of the individual as a moral being; thus, all three codes, especially Deuteronomy,
attempt to put into practice the dictum that man is to be respected as the
"image of God." The rights of a personal enemy must be honored (Ex.
23:4–5); a neighbor's garment taken in pledge is to be restored before the
sun sets (Ex. 22:26–27); a creditor is not to enter the home of the debtor
to collect his pledge (Deut. 24:10–11); flogging is limited to forty
strokes, "lest, if one should go on to beat him with more stripes than these,

your brother be degraded in your sight" (Deut. 25:3). A captive woman must be allowed to mourn her parents before being taken as wife (Deut. 21:10–14). Trees are to be respected on military campaigns (Deut. 20: 19–20). Biblical authors were proud of the special features of Israelite law; according to Deuteronomy, when other peoples hear of Israel's laws and statutes, they will say, "Surely this great nation is a wise and under-standing people" (Deut. 4:6).

A distinctive feature of Pentateuchal legislation is the inclusion of both case law and unconditional demands. Each of the three corpora contains a list of categorical imperatives. The Book of the Covenant opens with the Decalogue, which is repeated, with slight differences, in Deuteronomy (Ex. 20:2–17, Deut. 5:6–21). Like the covenant with Noah, the Deca-logue is comprised of a few general rules that do not mention institu-tions of government or political and religious leadership but stipulate what it means in action, to be a son (in this case) of the Sinaitic covenant. An Israelite is to worship YHVH only, to make no visual images of Him, and to speak His name with reverence. He is to keep the Sabbath by re-fraining from work. (The Exodus text interprets the Sabbath as a remem-brance of God's rest after creating the universe; Deuteronomy interprets the Sabbath as a symbol of the exodus.) Human beings are commanded to honor their parents. They are to respect human life ("You shall not murder"), the sanctity of marital ties ("You shall not commit adultery"), and the property of others ("You shall not steal"). Honesty is required in public affairs ("You shall not bear false witness against your neighbor") and uncontrollable cravings and coveteousness are condemned. Leviticus 19, the counterpart of the Decalogue in the Holiness Code, contains simi-lar commands together with various other moral and ritual requirements. Although not as concise as the Ten Commandments, Leviticus 19 has some of the most sweeping admonitions in the Pentateuch, such as the commandment to love your neighbor and to love the stranger (Lev. 19:18, 19:34).

A further unique feature of Pentateuchal law is the fusion of civil and criminal law with cultic. All three corpora contain legislation on altars, sacrifices, holy days, and other sacral matters.

The dichotomy of the holy and the impure is universal to all ancient Near Eastern societies. As noted at the beginning of this chapter, early religion involved a notion of the sacred as a source of great danger because it is so immensely powerful. Biblical writers go to some length to indicate that supernatural danger radiates from YHVH alone, even attributing to Him certain harmful and destructive effects. (See, for example, 1 Sam. 6:19 and 2 Sam. 6:6–7 on the power inherent in the Ark of the Covenant, and Ex. 28:35, Lev. 16:13, and Num. 4:15 on dangers faced by the priests

Winged lion from the palace of the ninth-century BCE Assyrian King Ashur-nasir-apal II. (Courtesy of the Metropolitan Museum of Art, gift of John D. Rockefeller, Jr., 1932.)

in handling holy objects in the sanctuary.) Diseases and plagues are caused by God, and healing comes only from God, directly or indirectly through a "man of God" (e.g., Ex. 15:26, Num. 21:8, Deut. 32:39, 2 Chron. 16:12). In the priestly legislation, the impure or unclean is an impersonal, contaminating substance that adheres to things and people and can be removed only by rites exactly performed according to precedent. The main sources of defilement are dead carcasses of impure animals, the human corpse, *tsara'at* (usually, but incorrectly translated leprosy—actually a variety of skin diseases and fungus growths), and male and female sexual emissions, such as those connected with ejaculation, childbirth, and menstruation. Passage of time and immersion in water effect the removal of ritual uncleanliness. Pollution can also be transferred to an animal, such as a scapegoat, the animal then being sent off to die in the desert (Lev. 14:7, 16:10). The impure must be kept from contact with the vessels of the sanctuary, the offerings, the priesthood, the holy city, the holy land. A holy and pure God must be worshiped by a holy and pure people, so that holiness becomes the basis for the imitation of God in Leviticus 19, illustrating how, in the Bible, the notions of holiness and impurity gradually took on qualities of value rather than sheer power. Although ancient rituals involving demons and unclean forces were preserved in the cultic legislation, they were viewed as divine commandments rooted in God's will and ordained as part of the covenant, rather than as magical ceremonies or propitiatory rites for coercing the divine, which were to be kept secret by the priests from the laity.[10]

The system of sacrificial offerings is yet another inheritance from ancient Near Eastern culture preserved in Pentateuchal ceremonial law. Although the sacrifices of each society differed in detail, there are points of resemblance in that the gods are all presented with gifts of animals, cereal, drink, and perfume. The biblical text retains certain phrases referring to the sacrifices as food for the divine ("pleasing odor" and "bread of God") but nowhere is YHVH dependent for nourishment or efficacy on sacrifices, which became, in Israel, a tangible means by which the people maintained a continuous and uninterrupted relationship with Him. One category of sacrifice expressed thanksgiving, gratitude, and reverence: The gift was an act of submission, which the offerer hoped would find favor in God's eyes and gain for him God's blessing. A second category effected expiation through the blood poured out on the altar: Because blood, according to the Pentateuch, is the principle of life, the blood of an animal victim symbolically atoned for the guilt of the human offerer (Lev. 17:11 and many other places). All sin must be atoned for—especially unwitting sins and accidental states of impurity. Unless these sins are "covered" (the biblical word "to atone," *l'kapper*, literally means to cover), the wrath of the holy God may be aroused, with terrible results for the people. Although the priests had other duties, oracular and instructional, the task of making atonement for Israel and preserving its purity was a principal justification for the priestly prerogatives.

A third topic of Pentateuchal ceremonial law is the sacred calendar. The history of ancient Israel's holy days is a complex subject and one not fully solved, because of slight but significant differences between the various passages referring to them in the Bible.[11] Unique to Israel was the Sabbath, a joyful feast day consecrated solely to YHVH, a tithe on time, during which work was prohibited to man and beast. As noted earlier, the Sabbath is the only festival mentioned in the Decalogue, where it is linked with the two great themes of Pentateuchal theology: creation and redemption. (Whether there are pre-Israelite roots of the Sabbath remains a matter of scholarly controversy.)

It would seem that the other major festivals predate the existence of Israel and were gradually given a historical explanation appropriate to Israelite tradition, a process completed only in postbiblical times when several of the holy days acquired their most distinctive Jewish meanings. (It is common in the history of religion for old rituals to be carefully and conservatively maintained while their symbolic significance is reinterpreted in the course of time.) Passover probably originated in a spring celebration of nomadic herdsmen; its rites and customs, together with those of the first of the three agricultural festivals, the feast of Matzot (unleavened bread), were early reinterpreted as remembrances of the exodus from Egypt. (The fusion of the festivals of Passover and Unleavened Bread was probably spurred by the Deuteronomic reform that abolished private sacrifices, so that the paschal offering had to be made at the Temple and not, as previously, in the home.) All three Israelite agricultural festivals may have been adopted from Canaanite practices, but were transformed into occasions of pilgrimage to YHVH's sanctuary in order to celebrate his role in bestowing fertility on nature. The festival of Matzot marked the barley harvest, when bread made of new grain ("without leaven") was to be eaten for seven days. Seven weeks later came the festival of Shavuot (weeks), celebrating the wheat harvest. The fall agricultural feast, Sukkot (huts or booths), marked the ingathering of the fruit of the vineyards and other autumn crops. In the priestly code (Lev. 23:42–43) the custom of dwelling in temporary huts during that season is explained as a reminder that the Israelites had lived under God's protective care in the wilderness before entering the promised land.

In the early biblical calendar, Sukkot was the end of one year and the onset of the next (Ex. 23:16). In late pre-exilic times the start of the year was shifted to the spring. In the priestly calendar, which reflects this change, the seventh new moon was a memorial day, marked, like all new moons, by special sacrifices and trumpet blasts (Num. 10:10, 28:11–15, Lev. 23:24–25). The most important holy day for the priests was the tenth day of the seventh month, the fast of *Yom ha-Kippurim* (the Day of Atonement, now usually called Yom Kippur), when the sanctuary was ritually cleansed and the sins of priests and people expiated (Lev. 16). In postbiblical times, perhaps as late as the first century BCE or CE, the start of the year was again shifted to the fall: The seventh new moon became Rosh Hashanah ("the head of the year"), commemorating the creation of the universe and the kingship of God. The Day of Atonement became a season of solemn personal repentance for all Jews. (The second biblical pilgrimage festival, Shavuot, was reinterpreted as a celebration of the revelation at Sinai.)

Some modern biblical scholars have attempted to reconstruct ancient Israelite festivals not mentioned in the Pentateuch. Drawing on the form-critical approach, which suggests that certain biblical passages may have originally served as confessions of faith in cultic ceremonies, one theory proposes that Israel had an annual festival of covenant renewal when representatives of the people reaffirmed their loyalty to YHVH alone. A second theory suggests that the Jerusalem Temple celebrated a New Year rite akin to the Babylonian *Akitu* ceremony reenacting Marduk's conquest of the powers of chaos and his enthronement in the heavens together with that of the Babylonian king on earth. Among the evidence for this supposed Israelite New Year ritual are the many psalms in which God's kingship is the main theme (these psalms will be examined in the following chapter) and a few psalms extolling the king as God's adopted son and as bearing the dignity of a priest (2, 110). A third, even more extreme, hypothesis is that pre-exilic Israelite worship was influenced by Canaanite fertility rites, including the sacred marriage of god and consort thought to renew the fecundity of the earth after the dry season. These theories do point up how little historians know about the functioning of pre-exilic Israelite religion, since the redactors of the completed Pentateuch selected, summarized, and integrated old materials, probably censoring many practices no longer in harmony with mature radical monotheism. Regardless of whether these hypothesized rituals were prevalent in pre-exilic Israel (the evidence is dubious), the Pentateuchal legislation does not portray the cult as an acting out of myth, as an infusion of strength into the divine realm, or as a participation in the life of the deity, which were important aspects of pagan ritual. Israelite worship was the celebration of YHVH's continuous and uninterrupted power over creation and of the acts of redemption that led to his covenant with Israel.[12]

We have seen that Pentateuchal law is a combination of elements drawn from two widespread forms of ancient literature: legal collections periodically reaffirming justice in society and political treaties formalizing king-vassal ties. The covenant concept was used by the biblical writers to describe Israel's election by God and to base all law in God's will. It was noted in Chapter 1 that fundamental to the Israelite tradition was monolatry: the sole worship of YHVH, a "jealous" God who did not permit his followers to worship other deities. The covenantal idea captures with precision and rigor that YHVH alone was Israel's supreme sovereign and that, just as a vassal owes wholehearted devotion to his ruler, Israel is obligated to serve its God with undivided loyalty. Biblical law, as stipulations of that covenant, attempted to maintain the holiness of the people and the sanctity of its individual members.

The notion of covenantal law, a very early aspect of Israelite religion, had enormous long-range implications for Judaism. It is possible that some biblical legislation was Mosaic in origin, but much of it was formulated after the establishment of the kingdom and some, perhaps, after the destruction of Judah in 587 BCE. Laws were certainly introduced under royal auspices in ancient Israel (compare 1 Sam. 30:24–25 with Num. 31: 25–27), but the covenant principle meant that the administration of justice was supposed to reflect norms stipulated in advance by God, hence the significance of the redactors' insertion of all the legal corpora into the account of Israel wanderings before it entered Canaan. Even a tendency to glorify the king and the Davidic dynasty did not result in making the royal ruler a necessary intermediary between YHVH and Israel. The goal of civil and criminal law—the actualization of an objective and absolute standard of justice—was not to be subject to the personal wisdom and intelligence (or lack of it) of the king. Justice was an inescapable obligation imposed on Israelite society and its leaders by virtue of their covenant with YHVH, and the failure to carry out this duty could be the occasion of bitter denunciation by those claiming to be YHVH's spokesmen.

Israelite law was not the esoteric concern of a small group, as was the case frequently in the ancient Near East. Even the priests eventually inserted their sacral regulations into the Pentateuch in the form of divine edicts issued by prophetic revelation and not as esoteric analogies to events occurring in the heavenly regions. Law was in the public domain, to be known by all Israel and taught to them. Although no reasons were ascribed to many of the laws, the extent to which individual commandments were justified was unprecedented in ancient law codes. The study and interpretation of law becomes an important element of Judaism only after the Scriptures assume their final written form, but the potentiality for this later development is present in the Pentateuch itself.

Finally, the principle of covenantal law preserved the attitude, stemming from the beginnings of Israel's history, that the people was a moral entity responsible to God for the sins of its members. The law was a system of voluntarily accepted religious duties binding on the people as a whole, observance of which determined its future prosperity or suffering. The corporate nature of Israel meant that its identity was not contingent on any particular political structure, tribal, monarchical, or other. Even in

Ashur-nasir-apal II and his cupbearer; slab from the wall of the Assyrian ruler's palace at Nimrud. (Courtesy of the Metropolitan Museum of Art, gift of John D. Rockefeller, Jr., 1932.)

the period of the biblical kingdoms, however, the idea of a collective obligation of Israel to YHVH showed its radical potential in the prophets of the eighth to the sixth centuries, to be discussed next.

The Rise of Classical Prophecy

A third kind of literature in the Bible is the prophetic oracle. Although prophecy as a socioreligious role has its roots in early phases of Israel's existence, in the late eighth century BCE there appeared a series of prophetic figures who redefined Israel's relationship to YHVH and transformed the Israelite concepts of sin and faithfulness. As with any ancient document there are textual problems in the prophetic books of the Bible, including the probability of later additions and insertions. But, in contrast to the Pentateuch, which is a composite work built up around certain themes and assembled over several centuries, in the prophetic writings we are usually dealing with the thought of distinct and identifiable men who can be located reliably in Israelite history. Before turning to the outstanding prophets of the eighth century, we will briefly examine the previous development of prophecy and note some of the general characteristics of prophetic literature.

Introduction to the Role and Literature of Prophecy

Like all ancient societies, Israel had several ways of consulting God. In the patriarchal tales, the interpretation of dreams was Joseph's forte. In the Israelite cult, the casting of sacred dice (the *Urim* and *Thummim*) enabled the priest to determine God's will. The most important means, however, was the messenger-prophet (Hebrew, *navi;* plural, *nevi'im*), a man thought to have received a direct call to speak or act for God.

Prophets were not unique to ancient Israel; we have already noted that early second-millennium texts from the northern Mesopotamian city of Mari describe diviners who acted as mouthpieces of deities. Nevertheless, only in Israel did prophecy play an active role in shaping political events and only there did it produce an influential body of ideas and literature that decisively affect the history of religion.

The word *navi* came into use during the time of Samuel as a synonym for man of God and seer (1 Sam. 9:9). It has been suggested that the *navi* phenomenon appeared as part of an upsurge of Israelite religious-national feeling during the Philistine wars.[13] Knowledge of prophetic bands during this period is limited to descriptions of Saul's being caught up in the contagious elation of the *nevi'im*, impelled by a divine power to "become another man" (1 Sam. 10:5–6, 19:23–24). For a long time ecstatic behavior remained an aspect of prophecy and prophets were sometimes called crazy (2 Kings 9:11).

Prophetic madness inspired fear and awe; it was dangerous to provoke a prophet and advantageous to receive his help. Judging from legends and stories about the ninth-century prophets Elijah and his disciple Elisha, the people attributed miraculous powers to the *navi*. Elijah revived a dead child; divine fire consumed the men who came to arrest him; the Jordan parted to let him through; he was taken to heaven in a flaming chariot. Elisha also restored the dead to life; he had extrasensory perception, made bitter water healthful, rendered poisonous pottage fit to eat, fed many with a few loaves of bread, made an iron ax handle float, prescribed a cure for an ailment. Elisha's curses were especially effective. (The tales about these two *nevi'im* are contained in 1 Kings 17 to 2 Kings 13.)

What was unusual about Israelite prophecy was not, however, frenzied behavior, abnormal psychological states, and superhuman powers, but the coherence, clarity, and intelligibility of the oracles. As the prophetic movement developed, the rational aspect of prophecy became increasingly evident; the message, not the medium, was central. The late image of the supreme prophet in the Pentateuch attributes no ecstatic phenomena at all to Moses. (See especially Num. 12:6–8.) Indeed, the usual translation of *navi* as prophet is rather misleading, because the prophet did not foretell or predict future events; he issued a "word of YHVH," God's judgment on events taking place in the present.

From the inception of the monarchy, it would seem that the prophets, as a matter of course, expected to influence the political structure of society. Nathan, who rebuked David for adultery with Bathsheba and for planning the murder of her husband (2 Sam. 12:1–15), influenced Solomon's succession to the throne (1 Kings 1). Ahijah the Shilonite was associated with the rise and fall of Jeroboam I (1 Kings 11:29–39 and 14:1–16); and Jehu the son of Hanani, the demise of the house of Baasha (1 Kings 16:1–4). Elijah first humiliated and then massacred the prophets of Baal, whose cult was being promoted by Ahab and Jezebel (1 Kings 18:20–40); he appeared before the king to denounce the judicial murder of Naboth, arranged by Jezebel to allow Ahab to acquire a coveted vineyard (1 Kings 21). Elisha is described as the head of a prophetic commune, composed of men who lived, together with their families, under the prophet's charge, sharing his food, acting as his messengers, and publicizing his wonders. This movement played an important role in opposing the policies of the Omri dynasty and legitimizing Jehu's seizure of power (1 Kings 19:15–16, 2 Kings 9:1–13). After the program of Elijah and Elisha triumphed—that YHVH alone was the God of Israel—prophets continued to issue oracles critical of the rulers. Because of their intense conviction that they had to speak their conscience, it was impossible that all prophets would provide divine words favorable and flattering to the king. The potential for denunciation remained a feature of the prophetic role. Toward the end of the monarchical period, even though prophecy may have taken on more of a professional and cultic character, individual figures refused payment and proclaimed oracles demanding radical change. This growing diversity and the disagreement between what the Bible came to call "false" and "true" prophets of YHVH accompanied the onset of Israelite prophecy's classical phase.

Beginning in the mid-eighth century and continuing into the post-exilic period, the oracles of a small number of prophets, first in Israel and then in Judah, were collected and handed down to succeeding generations in written form. The Bible includes fifteen books, ranging from one to over sixty chapters in length and bearing the personal name of a prophet (although some, such as the book of Isaiah, contain the utterances of several men, as we shall see later). They are often known as "writing" or "literary" prophets, rather misleadingly, since the oracles were almost always delivered orally and written down by followers; the term "classical" refers to the pre-eminent position of these books in the history of Judaism, their literary excellence, and their seminal character. "Classical" also serves to distinguish them from "popular" prophecy, the *navi* as seer, wonder worker, healer, and apostle of YHVH, which preceded and continued to exist alongside classical prophecy for a long time.

Unlike popular prophets such as Elijah and Elisha, the classical prophets, by and large, did not prophesy to individuals: Their speeches were addressed to the people as a whole on its collective responsibility to YHVH. Classical prophets were not members of prophetic guilds or "men of God" consulted in everyday matters by the masses. Quite the contrary, they were unsolicited and unpopular preachers, not infrequently persecuted by the authorities. Widely misunderstood, they seem to have felt themselves failures. The preservation of the oracles of the pre-exilic classical prophets probably occurred because a dire catastrophe like that of which they warned was borne out by the Assyrian destruction of Israel in 722 and the Babylonian conquest of 587 BCE. Nevertheless, the early classical prophets did have an impact, and in the long run they were a vast influence on Judaism and Western civilization.

Classical prophecy deserves to be called literature also in that these prophets were skilled poets. Poetical improvisation before an audience was a common ancient practice, and Israel had a developed tradition of psalms and other forms that made available to the prophets many literary devices and techniques. Oracles were cast in the style of laments, riddles, decrees of judgment, dramatic dialogues, taunt songs, and combinations of these genres. The prophets exploited with great flexibility all the resources of poetical parallelism to draw out the meaning of a verse with ironical contrasts and dramatic crescendos. They employed simile, metaphor, wordplays, personification, and other figures of speech, transforming concrete aspects of the Israelite environment and social system into symbols of universal religious experience and aspiration. To be sure, there are some special difficulties in reading the prophetic literature. It is often difficult to determine where a single oracle begins and ends. Although there is also considerable repetition, it seems that the editors deliberately alternated oracles of weal and woe: condemnation, chastisement, and visions of doom, on the one hand; expressions of hope and reassurance, on the other hand. However, the structure of the prophetic book is also a result of the intuitive nature of the prophetic experience. Ideas were felt with overpowering certainty; the impulse to speak out was spontaneous

The Black Obelisk of the Assyrian ruler Shalmaneser III, ninth century BCE. (Courtesy of the British Museum.)

and irresistible. "The lion has roared; who will not fear? The Lord YHVH has spoken; who can but prophesy?" (Amos 3:8). The oracle was not a systematic discourse in theology, but an outpouring of impassioned reproof or consolation: the prophet's direct reaction to immediate social conditions from the viewpoint of YHVH's judgment on the people He has elected as His own.

Amos

The first of the classical prophets was a Judahite who gave perhaps his only public oracle at the royal sanctuary of Bethel in the northern kingdom around 750 BCE. Amos came from Tekoa, a village about 12 miles south of Jerusalem; according to the introduction of his book, he lived during the reigns of Uzziah of Judah and Jeroboam II of Israel. Amos's prophesying coincided with the last period of might and splendor in the northern kingdom, only a few decades before its extinction. Judging from Amos's denunciations, the traditional structure of Israelite society had been undermined by a century of war with Aram-Damascus and the emergence of an upper class of powerful and rich landowners who forced small farmers into debt, confiscated their property, corrupted the courts, and ignored the principle of Israelite brotherhood.

The only biographical narrative about Amos relates that the priest of Bethel accused him of conspiring against the king by a declaration that "Jeroboam shall die by the sword and Israel must go into exile away from his land" (7:11). (The closest parallel among Amos's oracles is 7:9.) The priest orders Amos to return to Judah and make his living as a prophet there. Amos's reply (7:14–15) indicates that he was not a professional prophet nor a member of their guilds: YHVH "took" him from his flock and sent him to Israel to prophesy.

The account of this episode interrupts a series of visions of impending doom (7:1–9, 8:1–9:4). First, Amos envisions a plague of locusts; he intercedes on behalf of the people, pleading with YHVH to relent. Then follows a fire that "devoured the great deep and was eating up the land" and a man standing by a wall, measuring its uprightness with a plumb line (a symbol for Israel's crookedness). Next, Amos sees a basket of summer fruit (a wordplay in Hebrew between *kaitz* [summer] and *ketz*, [end]) which indicates that "the end has come upon my people Israel," the text now shifting to a wail of lament for the piles of dead bodies left by the destruction. In the climactic vision YHVH stands ready to smash the holy altar: No one can escape Him, even by hiding in Sheol (the underworld) or at the bottom of the sea.

What has Israel done? According to Amos the people merit destruction and exile for the violation of everyday social morality by the upper classes. "They sell the righteous for silver and the needy for a pair of shoes—they that trample the head of the poor into the dust of the earth, and turn aside the way of the afflicted" (2:6–7). By exploiting the weak the rich lead lives of idle luxury: "They do not know how to do right, . . . those who store up violence and robbery in their strongholds" (3:10). There is no justice in the courts. "They hate him who reproves in the gate and they abhor him who speaks the truth, . . . you who afflict the righteous, who take a bribe . . ." (5:10, 12). The people's leaders are blind to God's condemnation; the speculators give short measures and care only for profit; the best are reduced to silence.

> *Woe to those who lie upon beds of ivory,*
> *and stretch themselves upon their couches,*
> *and eat lambs from the flock,*
> *and calves from the midst of the stall;*
> *who sing idle songs to the sound of the harp,*
> *and like David invent for themselves instruments of music;*
> *who drink wine in bowls,*
> *and anoint themselves with the finest oils,*
> *but are not grieved over the ruin of Joseph!* [6:4–6.]

For these crimes Israel will be granted no further reprieve, its altars and palaces will be destroyed, the survivors ignominiously carted off by a conqueror (3:14–4:3).

The innovation in Amos' prophecies is that social justice has been given decisive weight in determining national destiny.[14] Amos almost completely ignores idolatry and cultic sins (except for 2:7–8, 5:26, 8:14). The men whom Amos denounces fulfill their cultic duties, but YHVH is still not satisfied:

> *I hate, I despise your feasts*
> *and I take no delight in your solemn assemblies.*
> *Even though you offer me your burnt offerings and cereal offerings,*
> *I will not accept them,*
> *and the peace offerings of your fatted beasts*
> *I will not look upon.*
> *Take away from me the noise of your songs;*
> *to the melody of your harps I will not listen.*
> *But let justice roll down like waters,*
> *and righteousness like an ever-flowing stream.* [5:21–24.]

The cult does not ensure God's blessing or assuage his wrath, for YHVH is satisfied only by ethical behavior.

The book of Amos opens with a denunciation of the sins of six of Israel's neighbors, who will be punished for crimes against the defenseless Israelite population and for acts of betrayal and violence against each other. Were these oracles against Israel's enemies (a genre often found in the prophetic books) a device for capturing the attention of Amos' audience before turning (in 2:4 and following verses) to condemn his own people? YHVH, of course, is the God of all nations and all peoples: "Did I not bring up Israel from the land of Egypt, and the Philistines from Caphtor, and the Arameans from Kir?" (9:7). But to Israel YHVH has extended special instruction and concern, so that this people, above all, should know how to act rightly:

> *"You only have I known*
> *of all the families of the earth;*
> *therefore I will punish you*
> *for all your iniquities." [3:2.]*

By means of drought, blight, and plague, as well as through the words of the prophets, God has warned the people of his displeasure. But Israel ignores the lesson of these ominous events, and it commands the prophets not to prophesy (2:12). To epitomize the impending doom, Amos gives a new twist to what was apparently a concept from the cult or from the popular religion: the "day of YHVH," a day of divine judgment over Israel's foes.

> *Woe to you who desire the day of YHVH!*
> *Why would you have the day of YHVH?*
> *It is darkness and not light;*
> *as if a man fled from a lion,*
> *and a bear met him;*
> *or went into the house and leaned with his hand against the wall,*
> *and a serpent bit him.*
> *Is not the day of YHVH darkness, and not light,*
> *and gloom with no brightness in it? [5:18–20.]*

With foreboding Amos declares, "Prepare to meet your God, O Israel" (4:12) and sings a lament on the despoiled people "fallen, no more to rise" (5:2).

Amos is not, however, only a collection of oracles of doom. In the very nature of his demand there remains the possibility of change and hope, hence the oracle, "Seek me and live" (5:4–6). The concept of repentance ("to turn" or "to return" in biblical Hebrew) represents the assumption that man is free to change for the better. "Seek good, and not evil, that you may live; and so YHVH, the God of hosts, will be with you, as you have said." In the next verse Amos explains what this "good" means: "Hate evil, and love good, and establish justice in the gate; it may be that YHVH, the God of hosts, will be gracious to the remnant of Joseph" (5:14–15). Fundamental to classical prophecy is the conditionality of Israel's relation with YHVH. Were Israel to turn, then the God of justice would relent and his righteous judgment would be quite different from that chastisement of which Amos warns so vehemently.

Hosea

A slightly younger contemporary of Amos, Hosea prophesied in the northern kingdom during the reigns of Jeroboam II and succeeding kings, in the last decades before the Assyrian conquest. Whereas Amos is one of the easiest of the prophetic books for the modern reader, Hosea is difficult and disjointed, a torrent of threats, pleas, warnings, and promises. Hosea is concerned primarily with idolatry, almost not at all with social justice. Unlike Amos, Hosea ignores God's relation to the other nations. Hosea is, however, one of the most original figures in the prophetic tradition and he introduces themes that will be further developed in later books.

Hosea was the first prophet to make extensive use of adultery as a metaphor for Israel's infidelity to YHVH.[15] The prophet's unchaste wife is presented twice (chaps. 1 and 3) as an allegorical symbol for the people's religious defection. YHVH is the wronged husband; Israel is the adulteress who must be punished for ingratitude. The people pursues other "lovers," the Baals (Canaanite gods), attributing to them the agricultural fertility and other bounties that YHVH himself has bestowed. Hosea's children are given symbolic names. The first, "Jezreel," is named after the spot on which Jehu has massacred the family of Ahab (2 Kings 10:11), a violent deed of which the prophet presumably disapproves. The second, "Not-pitied," means that God can no longer love the people; the third, "Not-my-people," is an expression of God's total condemnation.

Despite this seeming rejection, however, God continues to care for his "wife": "YHVH loves the people of Israel, though they turn to other gods" (3:1). Thus Hosea's allegory of divorce is complemented with a vision of eventual restoration. Purified of fornication by a simple and chaste life "as at the time when she came out of the land of Egypt" and recognizing that survival depends on YHVH alone, Israel will be taken back and remarried. "I will betroth you to me for ever; I will betroth you to me in righteousness and in justice, in steadfast love, and in mercy. I will betroth you to me in faithfulness; and you shall know YHVH" (2:19–20). The names of Hosea's children will acquire positive meaning: Jezreel (Hebrew for "God sows") will stand for Israel sown anew in the earth; Not-pitied will be shown love; to Not-my-people YHVH will say: "You are my people," and Israel will say, "Thou art my God" (2:22–23, Heb. 2:24–5).

These basic themes are developed in the first three chapters and are reiterated later. Hosea denounces the corruption, decadence, and arrogance of priests, kings, and people, charging that "There is no faithfulness or kindness and no knowledge of God in the land" (4:1). Symptomatic of this ignorance is idolatry, which the prophet defines as worship of "the work of our hands" (14:3, Hebrew text 14:4). Hosea is the first biblical writer to employ this conception of idolatry as deification of the objects of man's making, a notion which, as we saw in the preceding chapter, is a crucial component of mature Israelite monotheism. The people's few moments of contrition have been insincere and superficial, for God demands profound change, not cultic propitiation. The whole nation must exemplify the virtue of *hesed:* steadfast love and unconditional loyalty. (*Hesed* is often translated as "mercy," but it has the connotations of faithfulness as well as love.) "For I desire *hesed* and not sacrifice, the knowledge of God, rather than burnt offerings" (6:6). Without the right knowledge, love, and loyalty, there will surely ensue disaster and exile: "For they sow the wind, and they shall reap the whirlwind" (8:7).

Nevertheless, YHVH remembers his fondness for his wild fruit (9:10), his trained heifer (10:11), his adopted son (11:1); he recalls his tender concern for Israel at the beginning of their life together in the exodus wanderings. In the divine soliloquy of 11:1–9, YHVH exclaims, "How can I give you up, O Ephraim! How can I hand you over, O Israel!" A sincere confession of sin will result in healing and the showering of God's blessings on his beloved children. In the expressions of hope that periodically relieve the gloom of his despair, Hosea develops the idea of the power of repentance to which Amos alluded. If Amos is the prophet of the implacable God of righteousness, Hosea is remembered principally as the spokesman of the bond of love between YHVH and Israel.

Isaiah

The first classical prophet to deliver his oracles in the southern kingdom was Isaiah the son of Amoz (First Isaiah), who prophesied for about forty years in Jerusalem, from 742 when Uzziah died (6:1), through the reign of Ahaz to 701 BCE, the fourteenth year of Hezekiah's rule (36:1). Isaiah is connected with two major historical events: first, Ahaz's refusal to join the kings of Israel and Damascus in a futile anti-Assyrian alliance that provoked the final Assyrian conquest of the north. (Isaiah approved of this policy of neutrality, for reasons that will shortly be explained.) Second, Isaiah is mentioned in connection with Hezekiah's defiance of Assyria, which led to the siege of Jerusalem in 701; the city did not fall because the Assyrian ruler was either bought off by Hezekiah or, perhaps, was forced to call off the invasion because of a plague in his army. (An account in 2 Kings 19–20 tells of Hezekiah's consulting Isaiah, a scene that is likely legendary because the oracle in it that YHVH will defend the city for his own sake and for the sake of his servant David eliminates the nuance of the prophet's position.)

The longest of all the prophetic scrolls, Isaiah contains much more than the prophecies of the historical Isaiah son of Amoz: Probably authentic messages of Isaiah are found in chapters 1–12, 17–23, and 28–33. Isaiah's poetry is among the most vivid, intense, and splendid in the prophetic books; he coins pointed, ironic proverbs, effectively uses similes from nature and city life, and draws imaginative visions, dignified and stately, of the utopian end of history. As with the other prophetic collections, oracles of chastisement and consolation alternate, so that a single section of Isaiah's poetry can move from one emotional extreme to the other.[16]

Like Amos, whom he closely resembles, Isaiah insists on the absolute priority of social morality. In chapter 1, the upper classes and the people —"rulers of Sodom" and "people of Gemorah"—are told that their sacrifices, holy days, and prayers are of no intrinsic value. When they lift up their hands to God, he sees blood stains on them—not the blood of their offerings but of their deeds. "Wash yourselves; make yourselves clean; remove the evil of your doings from before my eyes; cease to do evil, learn to do good; seek justice, correct oppression; defend the fatherless, plead for the widow" (1:16–17). Even when Israel honors God with their lips, "their hearts are far from Me, and their fear of Me is but a commitment of men learned by rote" (29:13). The upper classes expropriate land to form huge estates, pursue unbridled pleasure, exploit the weak through unjust laws and corrupt courts. Like Hosea, Isaiah conceives of God as feeling betrayed by a people he has carefully trained and guarded. In 5:1–7 he offers the parable of a vineyard that someone has planted and carefully tended, only to find that it bears unedible grapes. "The vineyard of YHVH of Hosts is the house of Israel, and the men of Judah are his pleasant planting; and he looked for justice, but behold, bloodshed; for righteousness, but behold, a cry!" (5:7, the English translation does not convey the play-on-words of the Hebrew). For all YHVH's solicitude, Israel has failed Him.

Isaiah repeatedly warns that the people ignores the chastisements sent by God to discipline it: plague, earthquake, a terrible nation from afar off that comes to ravage and take captives. The prophet considers himself yet another such warning: "Behold, I and the children whom YHVH has given me are signs and portents in Israel from YHVH of hosts, who dwells on Mount Zion" (8:18). In the 720s, Isaiah goes naked and barefoot three years, warning Egypt, Cush, and Judah of the futile outcome of their plans for defying Assyria (chap. 20). His sons receive symbolic names: "A-remnant-shall-return" (7:3, meaning in this context *only* a remnant) and "Speed-spoil-hasten-plunder" (8:1–4). A righteous and holy God is about to issue a verdict: "The Lord has taken his place to contend, he stands to judge his people" (3:13).

"The Holy One of Israel" is one of Isaiah's favorite terms for God. In chapter 6 the prophet explains how he was commissioned God's spokesman and messenger. "In the year that King Uzziah died I saw YHVH sitting upon a throne, high and lifted up; and his train filled the Temple." The attendant seraphim, heavenly beings with six wings, sing reverberatingly:

> *Holy, holy, holy is YHVH of hosts;*
> *The fulness of the earth is His glory.*

Isaiah is overwhelmed by his uncleanliness, but a seraph purifies his lips with a burning coal from the altar. "And I heard the voice of YHVH saying, 'Whom shall I send, and who will go for us?' Then I said, 'Here I am! Send me.'" An expression of Isaiah's pessimism at some point in his career pervades his account of the outcome of this encounter: "Make the heart of this people fat, and their ears heavy, and shut their eyes; lest they see with their eyes, and hear with their ears, and understand with their hearts, and turn and be healed." This ironic despair is a sign of his caring. In an oracle of approaching destruction in chapter 22, the prophet interrupts his picture of a forthcoming military disaster with the exclamation:

> *Look away from me,*
> *let me weep bitter tears:*
> *do not labor to comfort me*
> *for the destruction of the daughter of my people.* [22:4.]

The blindness of Israel's rulers is especially evident in their foreign policy where, according to Isaiah, they are unable to understand the true meaning of the international cataclysms that destroyed Samaria and Damascus and that reduced Judah and its neighbors to Assyrian vassalage. These terrible events are YHVH's "work"—His alone: "Ah, Assyria, the rod of my anger" (10:5), Assyria being a weapon of God's judgment. Instead of physical resistance to the conqueror, therefore, Isaiah demands absolute trust in God. This policy of nonresistance to worldly force is epitomized by the prophet's maxims: "If you will not have faith, surely you shall not be established" (7:9); "He who trusts feels no need to have things speed up" (28:16[17]); "In returning and rest you shall be saved; in quietness and in trust shall be your strength" (30:15). Isaiah's disregard for practical diplomatic and military maneuvering can be explained as a working out of classical prophecy's notion of repentance: Survival depended on a radical transformation of human ethical action and intention. Only a turning that produces justice and righteousness will satisfy the holy God. Shortsighted rulers look to armies and fortifications to resist the aggressor. Expecting defeat, people seek a last release in a moment of pleasure:

> *In that day the Lord YHVH of hosts,*
>   *called to weeping and mourning,*
>   *to baldness and girding with sackcloth;*
> *and behold, joy and gladness,*
>   *slaying oxen and killing sheep,*
>   *eating flesh and drinking wine.*
> *"Let us eat and drink,*
>   *for tomorrow we die."*
> *YHVH of hosts has revealed himself in my ears:*
>   *"Surely this iniquity will not be forgiven you till you die . . ." [22:12–14]*

Because Jerusalem was not destroyed in 701, there apparently grew up a legend that Isaiah had believed in the inviolability of Zion, that the holy city could never be conquered by Assyria; but the passages on which this legend is based, such as 2 Kings 19:32–34 and Isaiah 37:32–35, may be either later interpolations or else a response by the prophet to a specific situation and not a general statement that Jerusalem would never fall. The historical Isaiah seems to have felt that at most a "remnant will return, the remnant of Jacob, to the mighty God" (10:21). If Isaiah had faith in Zion at the end of his life it was a consequence of his view that Assyria was doomed. Assyria, "the rod of [God's] anger," believes he is the author of his victories, but "when YHVH has finished all his work on Mount Zion and on Jerusalem he will punish the arrogant boasting of the king of Assyria" who thinks that "by the strength of my hand I have done it, and by my wisdom, for I have understanding; I have removed the boundaries of peoples, and have plundered their treasures" (10:12–13). Assyria, representing blind self-glorification and vain pride, will be broken "upon my mountains," for no power can prevent God from accomplishing his purposes (14:25–27).

In the concept of the crushing of arrogance in the whole earth, Isaiah introduces into prophetic thought the notion of an end of idolatry everywhere. Indeed, Egypt and Assyria will eventually worship the one God of Israel. "In that day Israel will be third with Egypt and Assyria, a blessing in the midst of the earth, whom YHVH of hosts has blessed, saying, 'Blessed be Egypt my people, and Assyria the work of my hands, and Israel my heritage'" (19:24). The climax of this hopeful side of Isaiah's prophecy is an End of Days (*aharit ha-yamim*) when there will be no more war, and when Zion will be the center of God's universal rule, a place of law and justice for all nations:

It shall come to pass in the latter days
that the mountain of the house of YHVH
shall be established as the highest of the mountains,
and shall be raised above the hills;
and all the nations shall flow to it,
and many peoples shall come, and say:
"Come, let us go up to the mountain of YHVH,
to the house of the God of Jacob;
that he may teach us his ways
and that we may walk in his paths."
For out of Zion shall go forth the law,
and the word of YHVH from Jerusalem.
He shall judge between the nations,
and shall decide for many peoples;
and they shall beat their swords into plowshares,
and their spears into pruning hooks;
nation shall not lift up sword against nation,
neither shall they learn war any more. [2:2–4.]

As that End of Days draws near, Israel will be given a king who will strike down the ruthless and slay the wicked; "with righteousness he shall judge the poor, and decide with equity for the meek of the earth" (11:4, 32:1). From the house of David shall come forth such a prince:

King Jehu of Israel bowing before the Assyrian ruler, a detail from the Black Obelisk. (Courtesy of the British Museum.)

> *And the spirit of YHVH shall rest upon him,*
> *the spirit of wisdom and understanding,*
> *the spirit of counsel and might,*
> *the spirit of knowledge and fear of YHVH. [11:2.]*

In some of the Isaianic passages on the End of Days, the natural order will be transformed into a gentle harmony: "The wolf shall dwell with the lamb, and the leopard shall lie down with the kid, and the calf and the lion and the fatling together, and a little child shall lead them," a symbolic representation of the end of violence when no one hurts or destroys, "for the earth shall be full of the knowledge of YHVH as the waters cover the sea" (11:6–9, see also 9:2–7 [Heb. 9:1–6]). If these End of Days passages are indeed by Isaiah the son of Amos, then he would be the first in Israel, and perhaps in human history, to envision universal justice, brotherhood, and world peace.[18]

Micah

The last of the eighth-century classical prophets was Micah of More-sheth, from a village about 25 miles southwest of Jerusalem. The oracles of the book of Micah exhibit the usual alternation of prophecies of impending punishment and of eventual restoration; in this loosely connected material, themes already delineated in Micah's predecessors and in his slightly older contemporary, Isaiah, reappear with some new facets.

Like other classical prophets who insist on their independence, Micah denounces prophets who mold their oracles according to who pays them. "But as for me, I am filled with power, with the spirit of YHVH, and with justice and might, to declare to Jacob his transgression and to Israel his sin" (3:8). He castigates those who seize coveted property by force, cheat with false scales and measures, buy and sell decisions of the courts, and cause the end of trust between friends and family. His oracles are summed up in a scathing rebuke of Judah's rulers:

> *Hear, you heads of Jacob*
> *and rulers of the house of Israel!*
> *Is it not for you to know justice?—*
> *you who hate the good and love the evil*
> *who tear the skin from off my people,*
> *and their flesh from off their bones;*
> *who eat the flesh of my people,*
> *and flay their skin from off them,*
> *and break their bones in pieces,*
> *and chop them up like meat in a kettle,*
> *like flesh in a caldron. [3:1–3.]*

To the leadership of Judah, Micah announces: "Therefore, because of you, Zion shall be plowed as a field; Jerusalem shall become a heap of ruins, and the mountain of the house [of God] a wooded height" (3:12). This is the most extreme vision offered by the prophets of an unmitigated disaster about to befall Zion.

The first half of chapter 6 contains the prophet's recapitulation of the divine demands. After calling the people to a lawsuit, God asks how he has wearied them, considering that he brought them up from Egypt, and so on. The people inquires how its guilt can be propitiated, proposing an ascending series of lavish and precious offerings:

> *With what shall I come before YHVH,*
> *and bow myself before God on high?*
> *Shall I come before him with burnt offerings,*
> *with calves a year old?*
> *Will YHVH be pleased with thousands of rams,*
> *with ten thousands of rivers of oil?*
> *Shall I give my first-born for my transgression,*
> *the fruit of my body for the sin of my soul?*

The prophet answers that YHVH is not satisfied with sacrifices:

> *He has showed you, O man, what is good;*
> *and what does YHVH require of you*
> *but to do justice, and to love kindness [hesed],*
> *and to walk humbly with your God? [6:6–8.]*

This passage echoes Isaiah's criticism of arrogance. Chapters 4–5 of Micah, which begin with the citation of Isaiah 2:2–4, describe Jerusalem as the capital of a peaceful world under YHVH's suzerainty. Micah does not, however, proceed to Isaiah's vision of an end to idolatry throughout the world. His hope remains centered on Israel: "For all the peoples walk each in the name of its god, but we will walk in the name of YHVH our God for ever and ever" (4:5). Micah also picks up the Isaianic notion of a future remnant of Israel, which will reconstitute the nation, with YHVH its sole king, on Mount Zion. The triumphant "daughter of Zion" will then defeat its enemies and destroy all who hate Jacob (4:11–13, 5:9). Out of Bethlehem will arise a ruler who will deliver his brethren "and they shall dwell secure," a fleeting reference to Isaiah's concept of a just king in the End of Days (Micah 5:2–4 [Heb. 5:1–3]). The final statement of hope in Micah chapter 7 mentions Israel's confession of wrongdoing, as well as the rebuilding of its land with God's help, so that all nations shall fear and know YHVH, who will cast the sins of his people "into the depths of the sea" (7:19).

Early Classical Prophets: Conservative Radicals

Classical prophecy was a product of previous Israelite religion and a departure from it. The ability of these men to express immediate social tensions and to engage in open criticism of sacrosanct institutions was possible at a particular historical moment when prophecy was strong, having won a major victory championing the cause of YHVH against Baal, and when the written traditions of Israel had not been put in their final form. In the eighth century, the classical prophets were not confronted and limited by the completed Pentateuch, although some of its parts, narrative and legal, as well as certain later historical works, were in circulation. (The prophetic literature itself is an instance of this transition, inasmuch as the oracles were delivered orally but were preserved for posterity in scrolls or on tablets.) The prophets had a tradition of their own, contrary to the Pentateuchal materials, that Israel did not yet have a sacrificial cult in its early wilderness period (Amos 5:25 and Jer. 7:22). Ignoring the legendary stories of rebelliousness and moral weakness, the early classical prophets depicted the presettlement existence of the people as a time of intimacy with God, more like the religious atmosphere pervading the Genesis patriarchal narratives than that of the book of Numbers. (Perhaps the prophets were presenting a more accurate picture of the early religiosity of Israel, a point to which we will return later.) The prophets did not idealize the nomadic life as such; they were not primitivists. Rather, prophetic denunciations criticize the economic injustice and class differentiation of the later monarchy in contrast to the brotherhood and mutual aid that was the ideal of a people whose supreme sovereign was YHVH. But in formulating a call to "return," Amos, Hosea, Isaiah, and Micah, seemingly conservatives, were actually radical simplifiers, seeking to apply a clarified set of old values to the changed situation of their time.

In oracles demanding that the people fulfill its duties to a God with whom they stood in a unique relationship, these prophets advanced the notion of the conditionality of the YHVH-Israel tie to an unprecedented degree—unprecedented in that they called for a total rejection of idolatry in all its forms and for an immediate implementation of justice. Their emphasis on self-transformation, absolute faithfulness, and the end of arrogance on earth marked the beginnings of a change in the nature of religion that would have potent long-range consequences. Certainly there is precedent for these ideas in the Pentateuchal traditions—in such tales as those illustrating Abraham's trust in God, the moral change in Joseph's brothers, the humiliation of Pharaoh and the gods of Egypt, the laws protecting the widow, orphan, stranger, and slave. But in establishing the absolute priority of the moral over the cultic, the classical prophets moved one step further. (The early classical prophets avoided the term *covenant* in their oracles: Did it represent to them too limited and specific a set of stipulations, in view of the sweeping character of the repentance they envisioned?) Cult, Temple, land, and state were conditional, given by God to Israel, but revokable if the people did not live up to its task. The prophets did not conceive of a nation that could exist permanently without land or cult, but they saw these as secondary features of the religious life. This re-evaluation constituted the most revolutionary aspect of their thinking.

In assessing the classical prophets historically, one should keep in mind that the social sins which they lamented did not reflect a society in which all opposition to the establishment was choked off. Quite the contrary, behind Amos, Hosea, Isaiah, and Micah stood a turbulent prophetic stratum that had sought to shape the politics of Israel. Because politics and religion cannot be separated in ancient society, prophetic consciousness and advice to rulers was frequently tantamount to a claim for power. Not all prophets were troublesome to the authorities; kings had their court prophets, and sanctuaries had their cult prophets, who provided oracles satisfactory to the needs of the Israelite leadership, promising victory in war and assuring them that YHVH was indeed pleased with their sacrifices. (An early portrayal of "false" prophets who gave soothing oracles for payment can be seen in the story in 1 Kings 22, where they are juxtaposed to the prophet Micaiah the son of Imlah, who explains that a favorable oracle which the king of Judah received from these prophets was sent by God as a judgment to cause his downfall.) Perhaps some of the impetus to the acceptance of a fully formulated written version of YHVH's demands, attributed to Moses as the supreme prophet for all time, resulted from a desire to restrain the freedom of the condemnatory prophets to challenge the authorities and to criticize so sweepingly the economic and political arrangements prevailing in their society.

The classical prophets stood in a relationship to the prophetic movement as a whole like that of the philosophers Socrates and Plato, three centuries later in Greece, to the teachers of sophistic rhetoric: They saw themselves pursuing truth as against mere "opinion," even though it shattered hallowed conceptions. Amos, Hosea, Isaiah, and Micah were not leaders of a political movement, but they issued a political challenge. They spelled out specific sins of their times in a manner sufficiently general to constitute a world view and not merely judgments on persons. Given the distribution of social forces in late monarchical Israel, especially the interests of the large landowners and the priests, and given the tactical considerations of administering a state in a period dominated by the immensely powerful and rapacious Assyrian empire, there was little chance that the program of classical prophecy could be put into effect (as there was little chance that Plato's ideal republic could have been constructed in ancient Greece). The one concession that the Jehu dynasty had made to the prophetic movement, that YHVH alone was the God of Israel, had to be compromised when the Assyrian rulers required the installation of "idolatrous" symbols in Israel's sanctuaries as a sign of political submission (the probable meaning of 2 Kings 16:10–16).

What, then, was the impact of the early classical prophets? We noted

A stele from Khorsabad showing the Assyrian King Sargon II conferring with an officer. Sargon claimed to have completed the Assyrian conquest of the kingdom of Israel. (Courtesy of the British Museum.)

earlier that they are not mentioned in the historical narratives, except for a description of Isaiah at considerable variance from the spirit of his authentic utterances. It is also significant, in this regard, that the completed Pentateuch devotes considerable space to cultic legislation, the importance of which is not qualified according to the prophetic criticism of it. Yet there is indirect indication that other circles were being stirred by prophetic ideas at the end of the eighth century, perhaps those groups that preserved the utterances of Amos, Hosea, Isaiah, and Micah. (Indeed, Hosea is the only book of northern provenance in the Bible, although the Covenant Code, the E stratum of the Pentateuch, the tales about Elijah and Elisha, and other biblical materials were probably also northern in origin.) Stunned by the catastrophic destruction of the northern kingdom in 722, a reform movement coalesced in Judah during the reign of Hezekiah. Some modern scholars feel that it was composed of northern Levites, priests, and prophets; others maintain that it was a movement of nonpriestly scribal intellectuals in the royal court.[19] This Deuteronomic school represents an effort to construct a program based on the ethical and religious criticism of the eighth and seventh centuries, of which the classical prophets were the most extreme exemplars. During Josiah's reign, these men attempted to reform Judean society accordingly—a society far more complex than the simple tribal units of early Israel but still the Israel whose survival was thought to be justified by standards ultimately derived from its covenantal origins.

Last Stages of Pre-exilic Literature: The Deuteronomic School and Jeremiah

The long reign of Manasseh, who was completely submissive to his Assyrian overlords, represented, in the biblical tradition, the nadir of Judean idolatry. Apparently during that time the prophetic movement was repressed. The fading away and eventual destruction of Assyrian power in the second half of the seventh century BCE opened up, for a while, a possibility of renewed political independence and religious self-assertion by Jerusalem. For several decades Josiah was able to reimpose the rule of the Davidic dynasty on most of the land of Israel, and the reform forces in Judah could put their plans into operation. In the last decades before the Babylonian exile, classical prophecy revived to produce the first of a new series of major figures, Jeremiah of Anathoth, as well as the prophet Ezekiel (who will be discussed in the next chapter). Eventually, as we saw in Chapter 1, Judah was to be crushed and destroyed by the Chaldean rulers of the Neo-Babylonian empire, but both the Deuteronomists and the classical prophets continued after 587 BCE to shape the development of Judaism.

The Deuteronomic Ideology

The book of Deuteronomy contains the most articulate and developed theology in the Pentateuch, because its code of laws, to which we referred earlier, is prefaced by a long introduction (chaps. 1–11) and followed by a conclusion (chaps. 29–31) explaining in general terms the significance of the covenant. This speech, like the book of Deuteronomy as a whole, is attributed to Moses just before his death and the entrance of Israel into the promised land. (The English name of the book may stem from the Greek mistranslation of Deut. 17:18; "copy of the law" became "second law.") The basis of Deuteronomic thought is the monotheistic uniqueness of YHVH and the corresponding obligation of Israel to be unique. The heart of the covenantal bond between God and Israel is love.

God has chosen this nation to be his possession out of all the peoples of the earth (7:6, 14:2); therefore, Israel owes YHVH undivided loyalty, gratitude, and obedience. The land that God bestowed upon them is an undeserved gift (9:4–7). Love of God is to be the main motive of human action. In a passage that becomes central to postbiblical Judaism, the orator insists: "You shall love YHVH with all your heart and with all your soul and with all your might" (6:5). Israel is to obey all the commandments and avoid any taint of idolatry. Deuteronomic social legislation has a pronounced humanitarian character ("Justice, justice you shall pursue" 16:20), but the sanctions against idolatry are very strong. Israelites, even prophets who can accurately predict signs and portents, are to be put to death if they attempt to seduce their brothers from the sole worship of YHVH, so that this "evil be purged from [their] midst" (13:1–6).

The militant monotheism of Deuteronomy is closely related to its insistence that YHVH will select a single place in the holy land where sacrifices are to be offered him. (Jerusalem is not mentioned by name, but this choice is clear in the later Deuteronomistic works.) Centralization of the cult—one Temple, one altar, one priesthood—is the most radical innovation introduced into biblical religion by the Deuteronomic movement. All other local shrines were to be destroyed, entailing a purge from Israelite religion of old premonotheistic traditions associated with these sites, and hence a clarification and indoctrination of the monotheistic principle among the masses.

The Deuteronomic program de-emphasized, to a certain extent, the importance of sacrificial offerings in the daily life of the ordinary person, while accentuating the importance of the Jerusalem Temple for the nation as a whole. Whereas previously, Israelites had offered sacrifices to YHVH anywhere, as a regular part of the slaying of animals for meat, Deuteronomy permits secular slaughter for food in all Israel's settlements (12:20–23; compare Lev. 17:1–17). Special attention is placed on formal instruction: All Israelites are to meditate on the divine commands and to teach them to each new generation (6:7, 6:20–25). God does not demand that man learn the secrets of heaven or that he cross to the other side of the sea to obtain esoteric knowledge (30:11–14); He requires obedience here and now to the clear principles of the Torah book, containing a covenant made, the orator insists, not only with the generation under Moses, but directly with every generation through Israel's history. "Nor is it with you only that I make this sworn covenant, but with him who is not here with us this day as well as with him who stands here with us this day before YHVH our God" (29:14–15 [Heb. 13–14]).

Like the classical prophets, the Deuteronomists conceive that the future depends on Israel's behavior in the present. God will provide a faithful Israel with every kind of blessing; a disloyal Israel will be visited with drought and pestilence, panic and terror, defeat and exile. The freedom of choice that lies in man's hands is the subject of this passage which drives home the point with no ambiguity:

> See, I have set before you this day life and good, death and evil. If you obey the commandments of YHVH your God which I command you this day, by loving YHVH your God, by walking in his ways, and by keeping his commandments and his statutes and his ordinances, then you shall live and multiply, and YHVH your God will bless you in the land which you are entering to take possession of it. But if your heart turns away, and you will not hear, but are drawn away to worship other gods and serve them, I declare to you this day, that you shall perish; you shall not live long in the land which you are going over the Jordan to enter and possess. I call heaven and earth to witness against you this day, that I have set before you life and death, blessing and curse; therefore choose life, that you and your descendants may live, loving YHVH your God, obeying his voice, and cleaving to him; for that means life to you and length of days, that you may dwell in the land which YHVH swore to your fathers, to Abraham, to Isaac, and to Jacob, to give them. [30:15–20.]

Formed under the impact of the great disaster of 722 and further developed under the shadow of that of 587 BCE, the Deuteronomic ideology taught that the people fully deserved what occurred to them because of their failure to live up to the covenantal obligations. To show how this situation had come about, the Deuteronomic school undertook to assemble and rewrite the history of Israel in its promised land so as to justify God's judgment and place the blame for the vicissitudes of their nation squarely on the failings of the people and its leaders.

The Deuteronomistic History

The completed version of the sequence of biblical books that follow the Pentateuch—Joshua, Judges, 1 and 2 Samuel, and 1 and 2 Kings—was composed by Deuteronomic writers in the mid-sixth century during the Babylonian exile. As with the Pentateuch, these books contain two distinct strata: on the one hand, early legends, literary works, excerpts from royal chronicles; on the other hand, editorial comments and insertions using the distinctive terminology and formulas of the Deuteronomic movement. Sometimes the Deuteronomists themselves summarized a particular era; other times they put their ideas in the mouths of historical figures or added them to older speeches. The historical books are intended to be a balance sheet of Israel's religious behavior, the people's successes and failures (mainly failures) in constructing a society according to the principles of the covenant.

Each book has its own dominant mood, of either spiritual achievement or blindness, portraying a periodic ascent and descent of Israelite religious fidelity to YHVH. The book of Joshua, which relates Israel's conquest of Canaan and the land's division among the tribes, completes the story begun in Exodus. Israel enters the promised land under the leadership of Joshua. Like the exodus, the invasion is carried on amid wonders and miracles: The Jordan parts to let the Israelites pass through; the walls of Jericho fall down to the trumpet blasts of priests; the sun stands still at Gibeon to ensure a great victory. The mood of Joshua is military triumph and stalwart obedience. In Deuteronomic speeches in chapters 23–24, Joshua admonishes all Israel to keep the Torah of Moses and avoid Canaanite idolatry. He reviews the history of the people from when Abraham's forefathers dwelt beyond the Euphrates "and served other gods," to the time when YHVH gave Abraham's descendants full possession of Canaan. The people are "witnesses against themselves" that they have freely chosen to follow YHVH, rather than other gods (24:22). Reaffirming the covenant in the presence of Joshua at Shechem is the high point on which the book concludes, an act of commitment parallel to that at Sinai.

The book of Judges is the counterpart of the people's repeated failures of faith during the wilderness wanderings under Moses. The first chapter indicates that the Israelites were unable to occupy all of Canaan; this is explained as the result of their not uprooting all Canaanite idolatry (Judg. 2:2), as a test by God (2:20–23), and as a means for their further education (3:1–2). Stories incorporated into the book of Judges about heroes of this phase of the Israelite past not only mention practices contrary to Pentateuchal law, such as the use of images (17:3–4), but some of the actions of these mighty figures are quite dubious by later standards, such as Jephthah's sacrifice of his daughter to fulfill a vow to YHVH (11:29–40) or Samson's fatal attraction to Philistine women. Despite the Deuteronomists' emphasis on Israel's continued need for God's help, the ethos of the early material reflects staunch and fierce self-reliance. The Deuteronomic editors interpret the period as exemplifying the following cycle: Israel forsakes YHVH to worship Canaanite deities, kindling his anger. He allows them to be overrun by their enemies, so that, in their distress, Israel turns to him for help. Relenting, YHVH raises up champions who deliver the people from its foes, but after a respite, they relapse again into pagan practices (e.g., 2:6–23, 10:6–16).

Another important theme of Judges is persistent lawlessness, which even leads to fighting between Israelite tribes (12:1–6, chap. 20). The editors note, "In those days there was no king in Israel; every man did what was right in his own eyes" (17:6, 21:25, and elsewhere). Civil anarchy and military weakness set the stage for the formation of the kingdom, the subject of 1 and 2 Samuel, which reflect, in the final version, an ambivalence toward Israel's acquiring a king "like all the nations" (1 Sam. 8:5). On the one hand, a human king was a rejection of YHVH's sole kingship. The despotism frequently a feature of ancient kingship is also carefully noted in these biblical speeches. (See 1 Sam. 8:4–22, 10:19, chap. 12, and Judg. 8:23.) On the other hand, a king will provide the effective leadership lacking in the previous era, which is considered a cause for rejoicing (1 Sam. 11:14–15). Kingship was God's gift, but also a sign of Israel's lack of complete faith in God. Under Josiah, the Deuteronomic school enjoyed royal patronage and it respected the authority of kings as long as they obeyed the Torah (Deut. 17:14–20); for the Deuteronomists, the main issue was idolatry and justice, not the form of government per se.

In redacting the books of Samuel the Deuteronomists used several old literary sources: in 1 Samuel a number of works that conflict on some details; in 2 Samuel 11–20 a unified composition of great literary skill, one of the masterpieces of ancient literature. The early material in 1 and 2 Samuel can be considered to have several aims: justifying David's supplanting of Saul, substantiating David's selection by YHVH to found an eternal dynasty (2 Sam. 7:12–16), and explaining the transfer of power to Solomon.

These early materials present a consistent and subtle picture of the main figures of 1 and 2 Samuel and their interrelationships, a picture drawn with psychological nuance and artistic finesse. As in the Joseph story of Genesis, God remains in the background and human passions occupy the foreground, but the inner development of character is accompanied by a working out of divine justice. The judge and prophet Samuel stands in the line of succession with Moses and Joshua, a man totally consecrated to God, who proclaims the divine wrath when YHVH's will is ignored. Like Jacob, Saul and David are transformed in the course of the challenges and temptations that they encounter. Young David's popularity leads to Saul's increasingly insane jealousy, but Saul nevertheless dies in defense of his people. Saul's end is all the more heroic in that he knows, as a result of his visit to the witch of Endor and the statement of the shade of Samuel that she raises from the underworld, that the forth-coming battle will be his last (1 Sam. 28). Chapters 11–20 of 2 Samuel relate the intricate unfolding of the consequences of David's seduction of Bathsheba and the secretive royal murder of her husband. Expiation of this sin involves seduction and murder among David's own children and a revolt against him by his beloved son Absalom. Although David's forces suppress Absalom's defiance, the victory leads to the breaking of David's heart. David, the poet who had earlier lamented with great beauty the death of Saul (2 Sam. 1:17–27), can only cry out, "O my son Absalom, my son, my son Absalom. Would I had died instead of you, O Absalom, my son, my son!" (2 Sam. 18:33 [Heb. 19:1]). The story of the succession to the throne is concluded in the first two chapters of 1 Kings with the rise of Solomon—another tale of court intrigue, the settling of old accounts, and the expiation of old sins.

In the first part of 1 Kings, Solomon is portrayed as the ideally skillful king, a paragon of worldly learning and judicial wisdom. His greatest achievement, according to the Deuteronomists, was the establishment in Jerusalem of the house of YHVH, the place where God's name is now to be found (1 Kings 8:27–29). Chapter 8 contains a long Deuteronomistic speech by Solomon describing the Temple as a place where all men—including non-Israelites—will come to offer supplication and prayer. Solomon is said to exclaim: "But will God indeed dwell on earth? Behold, heaven and the highest heaven cannot contain thee; how much less this house which I have built" (verse 27). He prays that YHVH may grant justice to the king and his people, "that all the peoples of the earth may know that YHVH is God; there is no other. Let your heart therefore be wholly true to YHVH our God, walking in his statutes and keeping his commandments as at this day"—a typical Deuteronomistic sermon (verses 60–61).

According to the narrators, however, Solomon himself inaugurates a new phase of spiritual decline in Israel, by tolerating the worship of the gods of his foreign wives in the holy city (11:1–8). The kingdom is split into two parts: For the sake of God's servant, David, and God's holy city, Jerusalem, the Davidic dynasty retains the loyalty of Judah; the northern tribes follow a series of royal houses, all of which, in the Deuteronomic view, earn divine displeasure. The Deuteronomic structure of the books of 1 and 2 Kings consists in a careful synchronization of the dates of each ruler of the northern and southern kingdoms and a categorical judgment on each. Although briefly alluding to the political and military successes of a king, the narrators are primarily interested in his religious behavior. All northern rulers are condemned, at the very least, for not destroying the golden calves that Jeroboam I erected at his shrines. (It is noteworthy that no northern prophet before Hosea, not even Elijah, saw fit to denounce these symbols, which may possibly have

Assyrian soldier taking captives across a stream; alabaster sculpture from the palace of Sennacherib (705–680 BCE) at Nineveh. (Courtesy of the Metropolitan Museum of Art, gift of John D. Rockefeller, Jr., 1932.)

been, like the cherubim over the Ark of the Covenant in the Jerusalem Temple, merely a symbol of YHVH's throne.) Even rulers of Judah commended for combating foreign religious practices are criticized for tolerating ancient Judean high places and hilltop shrines that the Deuteronomic movement sought to eradicate. In addition to these editorial criticisms, further words of divine judgment are transmitted through the speeches of a series of prophets appearing throughout the book. Although the Deuteronomists believed that Israel as a whole was responsible to YHVH, they are preoccupied in these books with the guilt of kings, because royal religious policies were of paramount importance: A king who compromised Israel's exclusive allegiance to YHVH jeopardized the survival of the whole people (e.g., 2 Kings 17:21).

After the conquest of the northern kingdom by the Assyrians, the policies of Hezekiah, the first king to attempt the centralization of sacrifices in the Jerusalem Temple, win the Deuteronomists' approval. However, his successor, Manasseh, installed Assyrian and other pagan cults in Jerusalem and "shed innocent blood there." He was considered the worst royal apostate ever and a main reason why YHVH let Judah be destroyed by the Babylonians several generations later (21:16, 23:26–27). The principal bright spot in 2 Kings is the reign of Josiah, for he supported the destruction of all idolatrous practices, Israelite and foreign, in his realm (2 Kings 23). "Before him there was no king like him, who turned to YHVH with all his heart and with all his soul and with all his might, according to all the law of Moses; nor did any king like him arise after him" (23:25). The tale of the Babylonian siege and destruction of Jerusalem, the deportation of the people, and the plundering of the holy vessels of the Temple is followed by a brief sign of hope. About two decades later, a Babylonian ruler brings the king of Judah out of prison and treats him kindly, an event that indicates to the redactors that YHVH's affection for Israel had not ended and that his promise to his servant David, and to his servants Moses and Abraham, had not been forgotten.

Jeremiah

The oracles of four prophets have been preserved from the late seventh and early sixth centuries BCE: three short books attributed to Nahum, Zephaniah, and Habbakuk, and the much longer book of Jeremiah. Nahum's ode of divine vengeance on Nineveh, the Assyrian capital, depicts the plundering of the city, the flight of its inhabitants, and the exultation that everywhere greets the oppressor's fall. Zephaniah, also dating from the early years of Josiah's reign, urges Israel to repent of sins prevalent in Manasseh's time; the prophet proclaims God's wrath over other nations, especially Assyria, and promises comfort to the remnant of Israel and to other peoples who serve YHVH wholeheartedly. Habbakuk prophesies that YHVH is even now raising up another great empire, Chaldean Babylon, and asks God how long such devastation and violence will continue and why He is silent when the wicked swallow up the righteous (1:13). The response, an assurance that divine justice will come to pass in due course, includes a verse that will be of great importance later: "The righteous shall live by his faith" (2:4).[20]

Jeremiah the son of Hilkiah, from the village of Anathoth about two miles northwest of the old city of Jerusalem, began to prophesy in the thirteenth year of Josiah's reign and was a highly controversial figure in Jerusalem during the reigns of Jehoiakin and Zedekiah, the last kings of Judah. It is not clear how much, if any, of Jeremiah's career preceded the Deuteronomic reform of the 620s, to which he seems to refer in 11:1–8. Jeremiah's relationship to the Deuteronomic movement is a matter of scholarly dispute. The Deuteronomists edited his book, adding or reshaping some of the prose orations, but not Jeremiah's poetic oracles. He probably approved of the Deuteronomic program but, in the spirit of classical prophecy, criticized the limited and half-hearted implementation of social justice. (See, for example, Jeremiah's scathing indictment in 34:8–22 of only a temporary freeing of slaves carried out during the siege of Jerusalem in 588–87.[21])

The book of Jeremiah is unusual in its extensive biographical and autobiographical passages; Jeremiah is one of the first men in history who is knowable as an individual, rather than through a legendary haze. Although the materials do not permit a full account of his life, they do provide plausible information about his ideas, feelings, and reactions to events. Jeremiah was from a priestly line of descent; apparently his family descended from Abiathar, David's priest, who had been banished to a provincial estate in Anathoth by Solomon (1 Kings 2:26); his family in Anathoth became hostile to him, but he continued to feel responsible for his patrimony there, even though he was certain that Judah would be destroyed (Jer. 11:21, 12:6, 32:6–15). Denounced by other prophets, persecuted by the authorities, and nearly put to death, Jeremiah was also consulted by the king and protected by prominent people. He had a scribe, Baruch, who wrote down his prophecies (36:1–19). Jeremiah remained in Jerusalem during the siege of 588–87 and survived the fall of the city. Put in the custody of the Babylonian-appointed governor, Gedaliah the son of Ahikam, who was himself from a family that had always treated Jeremiah with great respect, the prophet was forced against his will to flee to Egypt with a group of Judean refugees after Gedaliah's assassination. There he disappears from our purview, still berating his audience for their sins (chaps. 41–44).

The book of Jeremiah contains six poems that are often called his "confessions," because they take the form of complaints to God about his condition, sometimes answered by a divine reassurance. (The main confessions are 11:18–20, 12:1–6, 15:10–20, 17:14–18, 18:18–23, 20:7–12; also in this vein is 20:14–18.) These poems and other incidental verses express emotions ranging from self-pity and misery to tenderness and pathos at the thought of his suffering people. Jeremiah's ability to express the inward dimension of the prophetic experience contributed much to the prophetic role, as a model of the true servant of God, becoming the prototype of the faith that the prophet demanded in later biblical thought.

In his oracles, Jeremiah covers the range of themes already described. In the distant past of Israel's desert wanderings, God had tender solicitude for his "bride" (2:1–3). Using Hosea's imagery, Jeremiah insists that Israel had turned to "harlotry"; it runs after other "lovers," the Baals, and merits God's divorcing her (3:1–10). Like Hosea, Jeremiah castigates the people's idolatry (2:11–13 and many other passages, some of which may have been inserted by the Deuteronomists). Borrowing Isaiah's figure of speech, Israel is God's "vine," grown up to be worthless (2:21). Jeremiah offers his own metaphors as well: YHVH, the fountain of living waters (2:13, 17:13); Israel looking for the way but spurning the "ancient paths" (6:16, 18:15). For Jeremiah, as for the other prophets, true "knowledge of God" is love, justice, and righteousness (9:23–24); justice is especially demanded of the king and the upper classes, who are in a position to actualize it (22:3, 22:13–17, 34:8–22). Like Amos and others, Jeremiah denies the absolute value of the cult (6:20, 7:21–23): What God wants is faithfulness and obedience. Like Isaiah, Jeremiah has moments of despair when he views the people as incapable of change (13:23), but he never loses hope and persists in trying to convince them to repent.

His earlier prophecies, however, are more conditional than his later ones, when the Bablyonian menace became obvious. The gist of an oracle delivered in the courtyard of the Temple at the turn of the sixth century was that God would not refrain even from destroying his house, which the people considered invulnerable. (Jeremiah's Temple speech is narrated in chap. 26 and cited in a fuller version in 7:1–15.) The "false" prophets have assured the people that God would never forsake Zion, and the patriotic inhabitants of Jerusalem expected YHVH to thwart Nebuchadnezzar's siege at the last possible moment, as He had Sennacherib's in 701 BCE. Jeremiah disagrees. Following Micah, he prophesies: "I will make Jerusalem a heap of ruins, a lair of jackals, and I will make the cities of Judah a desolation without inhabitant" (9:11). According to the narrative of Jeremiah's Temple oracle, when the mob was just about to lynch the prophet, his defenders quoted as precedent Micah's utterance that "Zion shall be plowed as a field" (26:18, compare Micah 3:12). The point of both prophets' judgments is that in order to teach the people a lesson, YHVH will not hesitate to destroy the holy land, the city, and his house, all of which have been given only conditionally to Israel.

Early in the reign of Zedekiah, Jeremiah explains that complete submission to Nebuchadnezzar is the only correct policy, because YHVH has given all the lands of the earth to the "king of Babylon, my servant" (27:6). In 598 BCE, Jeremiah had written a letter to the first group of Judeans exiled to Babylon, telling them they should not expect a speedy return, but should instead prepare for a long stay: "Build houses and live in them, . . . seek the welfare of the city where I have sent you into exile and pray to YHVH on its behalf" (29:5–7). When the siege of 588–87 begins, Zedekiah inquires of Jeremiah what is God's will. The prophet replies with the oracle, "I myself will fight against you" (21:5). Like Deuteronomy 30:15–20, Jeremiah offers the people a choice between life and death, but life is surrender to the Babylonians and death is remaining in defiance, for YHVH has said, "I have set my face against this city" (21:8–10). During a brief respite, when the Babylonians direct their attention to stopping an Egyptian force which had come to help the Judeans, Jeremiah insists that the enemy will surely return, capture the city, and burn it to the ground (37:6–10). Accused of undermining the defenders' will to resist, Jeremiah is thrown into a pit and left to die, but he is rescued with the connivance of the king. Once again the king asks for an oracle, and the answer remains that Jerusalem should be surrendered (38:14–28).

The apparent harshness and finality of Jeremiah's oracles of judgment must be seen in the context of the prophet's agony at the suffering of his people. Although he must make himself "an iron pillar and bronze walls" in opposition to everyone (1:18), he insists that he and his God love Israel and cannot bear to see their pain.

> *Hear and give ear; be not proud,*
>   *for YHVH has spoken.*
> *Give glory to YHVH your God*
>   *before he brings darkness,*
> *before your feet stumble*
>   *on the twilight mountains,*
> *and while you look for light*
>   *he turns it into gloom*
>   *and he makes it deep darkness.*
> *But if you will not listen,*
>   *my soul will weep in secret for your pride;*
> *my eyes will weep bitterly and run down with tears,*
>   *because YHVH's flock has been taken captive.*
>   *[13:15–17; see also 8:21–9:1 (Heb. 8:21–23).]*

And now YHVH must give "the beloved of [his] soul" into the powers of her enemy (12:7).

The Deuteronomistic editors of the books of Kings explain the fall of Jerusalem and the destruction of the Temple as a punishment for the burden of sins laid on Israel by Manasseh's generation. Jeremiah acknowledges the guilt of Israel's forefathers (14:20) but insists that a man is responsible only for his own wrongdoing and not that of his ancestors (31:29–30). Why should the people surrender to the Babylonian army in 587 BCE? Because salvation was conditional on a new attitude, epito-

Enameled brick panel from the Procession Street in Babylon, built by Nebuchad-nezzar (605–562 BCE). (Courtesy of the Metropolitan Museum of Art, Fletcher Fund, 1931.)

mized by the Deuteronomic phrase *the circumcised heart* (used by Jeremiah in 4:4). The circumcised heart meant a mind eager to do only the good (the heart being the seat of thought in the Bible). Jeremiah's attitude to the political events of his day was that the people had to undertake a thorough ethical reform to merit God's aid. From his point of view, Judah's "return" (an allusion to the Deuteronomic reform?) had so far not been in good faith, "but in pretense" (3:10). YHVH was not satisfied if the people merely swore enthusiastically to obey the covenant; He wanted a drastic re-creation of the moral self. Jeremiah refers to the stereotyped formula of a "seventy year" duration of divine punishment (25:11), but restoration after that period still involves self-transformation (29:10–14). Like Isaiah, who had rejected the pursuit of foreign alliances against Assyria, Jeremiah asserts that in his day sub-mission to Babylonia is evidence of total faith in God. Reliance on YHVH alone is a necessary first step to true repentance, a naked trust in God that must be acted on by man in the immediate historical situa-tion.

The hopeful side of Jeremiah's conception of faithfulness can be seen in his prophecies of consolation. Deuteronomy's promise that God will circumcise their hearts so that they will love him and live (Deut. 30:6) is developed by Jeremiah into the concept of a new covenant engraved on Israel's heart (31:31–34). The fall of Jerusalem is a mere episode in the course of God's relation to the people, not the end of that tie, for the true covenant is eternal, like the laws of nature (31:35–36, 50:4–5). In the depths of the siege, Jeremiah envisions the eventual cleans-ing of the people and God's forgiveness (33:7–8). Despite all that has happened, "They shall be my people and I will be their God" (32:38).

The exiles are undergoing a purgation that will lead to their truly knowing God (24:7). The remnant will be gathered up and restored (23:3–4,
30:1–3, and elsewhere). They will be returned to the land that God gave
them, over which a righteous king will wisely rule (23:5–8, 33:14–26).
This picture of a fully realized covenant is presented against the background of an end to idolatry in the earth, characteristic of classical
prophecy. All nations shall gather in Jerusalem to honor YHVH's
name; "they shall no more stubbornly follow their own evil heart"
(3:17). The nations will admit that their idols are "lies" and "worthless
things" (16:19–20), for they shall be told that "the gods who did not
make the heavens and the earth shall perish from the earth and from
under the heavens" (10:11).

For all their differences, Deuteronomy and Jeremiah together constitute an important step in the development of biblical thought and
the refinement of radical monotheism. The last half century of Judah's
existence was one of the great ages of biblical literature. (To be sure,
prophecy continues for some time to draw its vitality from direct
delivery in public and the Pentateuch was probably not yet completely
redacted.) Jeremiah supervised the writing down of some of his major
oracles; those of the next classical prophet, Ezekiel, have a pronounced
bookish quality. The Deuteronomic orations, rather than being oral
materials transcribed into the written medium, were probably composed
in writing to be read aloud repeatedly and studied carefully.[22] As yet
unnoticed in the Near East as a whole, an unusual religious tradition was
approaching its mature form, a religion based on a keen repudiation of
some of the key features of ancient religiosity long taken for granted
almost everywhere.

Summary: A National Epic of Self-criticism

Earlier, in discussing the first chapter of Genesis, we noted that the
biblical conception of God went hand in hand with the elimination of
much ancient mythology, such as the birth of the gods, their struggles
with each other, and their erotic entanglements. In place of deities
who symbolized the forces of human and vegetative fertility or who
resided in the storm and ocean or in the sun, moon, and stars, the Bible
presupposes a single deity, supreme over all nature and distinct from
it, whose creative will was not bound by a preordained pattern of cosmic
fate that could be manipulated by magic or consulted by divination,
but never overcome. Quite the contrary, the biblical world view attributes to God total freedom, physical nature being derivative from
him and subject to his control. The only necessity in the Bible is moral:
"Shall not the Judge of all the earth do justly?" (Gen. 18:25). Polytheistic

religions knew of benevolent gods devoted to fairness, moderation, and righteousness, but their effective authority was limited by their being part of a pantheon, together with other deities whose wills could conflict with theirs. The biblical postulate of a sole, transcendent divine will clarified and strengthened the principle of one universal moral standard, which gave coherence and purposiveness to Israelite and to universal history.

The great themes that produced some of the magnificent epic poetry of antiquity are not the subject of the biblical narrative: the descent into the underworld to bring a god back to the realm of the living (the Canaanite epic of Baal), a journey across the world in search of the secret of immortality (Gilgamesh), the wrath of a great hero and his vengeance upon the death of his friend (the Iliad), the wanderings of a certain cunning and wise man who returns home to rescue his wife from mercenary suitors (the Odyssey), a just matricide and its expiation (the *Oresteia* trilogy of Aeschylus). Instead, we have a series of tales in which the world, created by God to be good and containing one creature in God's image, turns out full of violent, murderous, and self-glorifying men. This state of affairs, in turn, leads to the formation of a people nurtured by God, capable of producing a few individuals of satisfactory spiritual stature, but in the main those that are obtuse, unfaithful, and frequently backsliding from their divinely given task. That the Bible should idealize some of Israel's ancestors is not unusual: All peoples endow those who are felt to be decisive in shaping their history with remarkable traits, such as wisdom, beauty, strength, and goodness. What calls for explanation is that the narrative and prophetic books of the Bible concentrate to such an extent on human failure and on the shortcomings of the people whose emergence they are chronicling.

It was not the case, after all, that the Israelites were so abnormally wicked. The social corruptions denounced by the classical prophets were common in ancient societies, and there were Israelites in every generation tenaciously faithful to the tradition's demand that they be loyal only to YHVH. Why the religion of Israel became so different from that of its neighbors cannot be recovered historically, but a partial answer would seem to lie in its origins, together with the challenges of later geographical and historical circumstances.

In the ancient Near East many peoples invaded, from time to time, the settled, agricultural areas of civilization—the Amorites, the Hittites, the Arameans, the Ammonites, Moabites, Edomites, Philistines, to mention only a few—sometimes holding on to their previous cults but always adopting the worship of gods long associated with the lands of their conquest. The Israelite tradition insisted that it was wrong for the people of its covenant to seek solutions to the painful problems of life and death in these hallowed symbols of pagan holiness. Israel came from without Canaan, but could have chosen to forget this in the course of time, as did many conquering groups. Other nations had a few brief periods of military power and splendor, leading them to revere the memories of certain generals and kings, but national pride in David and Solomon did not prevent Israelite writers from subjecting them to sharp criticism or even from indicating that Aaron and even Moses had their moments of failure. Other peoples fought holy wars, but in Israel the "day" of its God was transformed, in the prophets, into a day of doom on his most fervent worshipers because of their religious and moral faults. Quite naturally, some Israelites worshiped Baal and Asherah, the star gods and the desert satyrs, but there was always a "remnant" who combated this tendency and who vehemently insisted that the ethical and religious ideals of patriarchal and tribal times be applied to agricultural and urban society of a later period.

Once Israel settled down in Canaan, the very exclusivity of YHVH's jealous exclusiveness acted as a filter, not a barrier to the absorption of elements of the high culture of the ancient Near East. A puritanical desert people and its stern deity claimed as their own such already ancient holy places as Shechem, Bethel, and Jerusalem, and took over those items they found useful from the legal codes of Lipit-Ishtar and Hammurabi, or from the epics of Atrahasis and Gilgamesh. Hosea used the Canaanite fertility imagery of divine marriage to describe the tie between YHVH and his people; the Deuteronomic school borrowed the terminology of Assyrian vassal treaties to define Israel's covenant with YHVH. All these materials were put to work in bringing out what may have been implicit and potential to begin with, but which, in the process of being made explicit and overt, drastically reoriented the Israelite religious tradition. In the dynamic of biblical thought, the religious takes on ethical meaning and a universal perspective: The concept of the holiness of a people comes to entail a just society, and the prohibition of visual images of YHVH leads to the idea of an end to idolatry on earth. The Israel-YHVH covenant is charged with a love that brings the prophetic duty of denunciation, because the urgency to proclaim disaster expresses the prophet's concern that the people's survival depends on wholehearted repentance. The working out of these notions by certain Israelite intellectuals accounts for the Israelite national epic being the story of God's attempt to teach man how to follow Him and man's attempt to do so. Despite its criticism of human behavior, often realistic and sometimes exaggerated, the Bible is an expression of hope and confidence that the ideal can be realized by man.

The survival of the Israelite tradition belies its emphasis on backsliding and stiff-neckedness (not that these qualities do not reflect some historical realities). It obscures the determined thread of obedience to YHVH through the biblical period. And obedience was viewed as elevation, not abasement, because of what was asked of true servants of

YHVH: only justice, mercy, and love. Similarly, the self-preoccupation of Israel with its own history was the very path that led to the universalism in the Bible: a glimpse of what Israelite monotheism could mean on a vaster scale than a single land or one people. The prophetic vision of an ideal future, slowly being developed in the last period of Israelite monarchy, foretold an international order of justice that would end war between nations—the universal triumph of righteousness and perpetual peace.

In the last analysis, therefore, the national epic of ancient Israel is not an exoneration of the people but of its God. Their defeats in battle are the victory of a God who has promised to defend those he has elected—but not if they do not act justly. According to the Bible, these military and other disasters are rooted in Israel's guilt, not YHVH's impotence, for how could the one God be defeated except by the only creature He has endowed with freedom to resist him? The biblical epic is the first answer to an issue running through the totality of Jewish thought: God's justice in contrast to a mundane, everyday reality filled with violence, evil, and suffering.

CHAPTER 3

The Biblical Heritage: Later Developments and Other Streams of Thought

Early Jewish history, as examined in the first two chapters, can be divided into three phases. First, the long stretches of the second millennium BCE when the ancestors of Israel lived on the territorial and social fringes of settled Near Eastern civilization. Traditions from these centuries include those about the seminomadic patriarchal clans of Genesis, the Hebrews of the opening chapters of Exodus, and the desert folk under Moses' leadership when Israel as a self-conscious socioreligious identity came into being. The second phase comprises the two centuries when Israel was a tribal alliance in Canaan, united by common worship of YHVH and a sense of common kinship. The movement of Israel from the fringe to the agricultural heartland took place when other peoples were also invading Canaan and nearby areas and were evolving political institutions for these conditions. The appearance of new states during the twelfth and eleventh centuries BCE was possible because no imperial powers dominated the Near East at that time. The third phase of ancient Jewish history is the five centuries when the people of Israel were organized as kingdoms actively participating in the international diplomatic and military arena. With the rise of Assyria and its imperial successors, however, the political independence of smaller states became circumscribed and eventually impossible, as evidenced by the demise of the two Israelite monarchies in 722 and 587 BCE.

In this chapter a fourth phase of Jewish history begins. Israel is a semiautonomous collectivity without political independence in a Near East ruled by vast empires: the Babylonians and Medes, the Persians, the Hellenistic kingdoms. Israelite survival, despite defeat and exile, can be attributed, more than to any other single factor, to its unique form of monotheism—the thread linking this period with the previous, and the source of new developments in the crystallizing world view of ancient Judaism.

Political Background, 600 to 200 BCE

The Neo-Babylonian empire that had assumed hegemony over Mesopotamia and Syria-Palestine under Narbopolassar (626–605) and Nebuchadnezzar (605–561) survived little more than two decades after the latter's death. A usurper, Nabonidus (555–539), spent much of his reign in an oasis in northern Arabia. Babylonia fell almost without a struggle to Cyrus the Great of Persia (ruled 550–530), who created an ever vaster empire stretching from the borders of India to the Mediterranean. From the end of the sixth century BCE on, the horizons of Jewish history expand beyond Mesopotamia, Canaan, and Egypt to include the Iranian highlands (the homeland of the Achaemenian dynasty of Persia) and western Asia Minor and European Greece (the homeland of Hellenic civilization).

The Persian state proved to be the best organized, as well as the most extensive empire yet in the Near East. Cambyses, the son of Cyrus, conquered Egypt in 525. A period of revolt and confusion followed his death, but the empire was soon pacified and strengthened by Darius I. Divided into twenty large districts and administered from royal residences in Persepolis, Susa, Ecbatana, and Babylon, possessing efficient postal and security services and an army composed not only of Persians but of local mercenary troops (including Judeans and Greeks), the Persians successfully kept in a state of political apathy most of the peoples they conquered. Early in the fifth century, however, the Persians encountered difficulties with the Greeks: After repressing a revolt of the Ionian Greeks in Asia Minor, Darius launched an invasion of European Greece, repulsed at the battle of Marathon (490); a second expedition by his son Xerxes also resulted in Greek victories (480–479), which made possible the great age of Athens under Pericles in the later fifth century BCE.

The religion of the Achaemenid rulers was a near-monotheistic dualism developed out of ancient Iranian mythology as propounded by the sixth-century BCE reformer and sage, Zoroaster—dualism because Zoroastrianism viewed history and the world as a cosmic struggle between two contend-

Relief from the stairway of the palace of the Persian kings at Persepolis, fifth or fourth century BCE. (Courtesy of the Metropolitan Museum of Art, Harris Brisbane Dick Fund, 1934.)

ing primal spirits, one good and one evil. Gradually over many centuries, a Zoroastrian Scripture, the Avesta, came into being which included hymns thought to contain some of Zoroaster's teachings. The Zoroastrian tradition, beginning to take shape in the Achaemenid period of Persian history, would exist in close proximity to Jews for many centuries. No attempt was made by the Persians to impose their culture on the empire as a whole. The Persian rulers of the sixth to fourth centuries BCE extended full religious toleration and autonomy to other cults within their realm.

It will be recalled from Chapter 1 that Cyrus permitted the Judean exiles in Babylon to return to the holy land and reconstruct the sanctuary; the costs for the restoration of the Temple were subsidized by the royal treasury. The Bible preserves the following version of his decree:

> Thus says Cyrus, king of Persia: YHVH, the God of heaven, has given me all the kingdoms of the earth, and he had charged me to build him a house at Jerusalem, which is in Judah. Whoever is among you of all his people, may his God be with him, and let him go up to Jerusalem, which is in Judah, and rebuild the house of YHVH, the God of Israel—he is the God who is in Jerusalem; and let each survivor, in whatever place he sojourns, be assisted by the men of his place with silver and gold, with goods and with beasts, besides freewill offerings for the house of God which is in Jerusalem. [Ezra 1:2–3.]

Several ten thousands of Judahites in Babylonia made the four months' journey of 800–900 miles back to Zion. (Many others remained in the east.) Unlike the Assyrians, who had settled other peoples in the northern part of Israel after 722 BCE, the Babylonians left Jerusalem and its environs unpopulated. After a delay of almost two decades, the construction of the (Second) Temple was begun:

> And all the people shouted with a great shout, when they praised YHVH, because the foundation of the house of YHVH was laid. But many of the priests and Levites and heads of fathers' houses, old men who had seen the first house, wept with a loud voice when they saw the foundation of this house being laid, though many shouted aloud for joy, so that the people could not distinguish the sound of the joyful shout from the sound of the people's weeping. . . . [Ezra 3:11–13.]

Neighboring groups offered help in the rebuilding, but were rebuffed (Ezra 4:1–6; we will return to this episode later). The Temple was completed around 515 BCE, the sixth year of the reign of Darius.

Along with those who returned came two members of the Davidic dynasty, Sheshbazzar, probably the first governor of Judah, and Zerubbabel, who may have been his successor. (The sources also mention Joshua the son of Jehozadak as High Priest at that time.) There are hints in the Bible that an attempt may have been made to crown Zerubbabel king of Judah, but hopes for the restoration of the monarchy were quickly crushed and the Davidic line has no political power in Judah thereafter. A Persian administrator insured the tranquility of the area and supervised the collection of taxes. Internal affairs were left in the hands of the Temple priesthood, in cooperation with local landowners.

How the postexilic hierocracy (priestly rule) was arranged is not clear, since we possess no historical information in the Bible from the rebuilding of the Temple until the mid-fifth century, when two leaders of a second wave of Judahites returned to Zion and introduced major reforms. The first, Nehemiah, was a royal officer appointed by the Persian king as governor of Judah. Given permission to rebuild Jerusalem, which was still largely deserted, Nehemiah encountered considerable opposition from some of the gentry and the governor of Samaria. The book of Nehemiah, containing an autobiographical account of his undertakings, relates: ". . . half of my servants worked on construction, and half held the spears, shields, bows, and coats of mail; and the leaders stood behind all the house of Judah, who were building on the wall. Those who carried burdens were laden in such a way that each with one hand labored on the work and with the other held his weapon" (Neh. 4:16–17). Nehemiah also undertook sweeping social reforms, forcing landowners to return confiscated property and cancel debts owed them by the peasants, in the spirit of biblical legislation on the Sabbatical and Jubilee years. The second of the fifth-century Judahite reformers was Ezra, a priest and scribe "skilled in the law of Moses." Ezra came to Jerusalem either at the time of Nehemiah or a few decades later. (The biblical chronology is inconsistent.) The character and significance of the local opposition that Nehemiah encountered, as well as the innovations that Ezra introduced, will be discussed at the end of the next section.

After the period of Nehemiah and Ezra, Judah constituted a temple city, an urban center that, together with the surrounding countryside, was dominated by a priestly establishment. (There were a number of such hierocratic enclaves in the Near East in Persian and later times, especially in Asia Minor.) The civil and religious life of Judah was guided by a High Priest of the family of Aaron (Moses' brother) and Zadok (David's priest), together with other cultic officials, the Levitical orders of singers and Temple assistants, and lay scribes (*sofrim*, sing. *sofer*). Unfortunately, no historical narratives have survived in the Bible from the late Persian period. The Bible contains the first and second books of Chronicles (originally a single work) written in the early fourth century BCE, which cover the reigns of the kings of Judah from David to the Babylonian exile and emphasize the centrality of the Temple and the importance of the Levites; the biblical books of Ezra and Nehemiah may also have been composed by the same authors. Archeological findings do provide some information about Judah during the missing years. The presence of Greek coins and pottery during the fifth and fourth

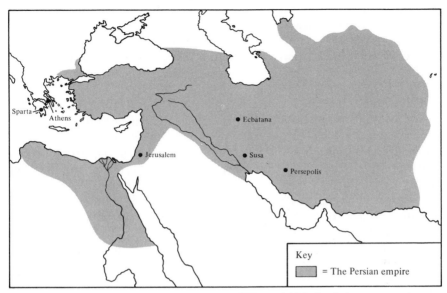

The Persian Empire c. 500 BCE. Between the 550s and 331 the Achaemenian dynasty ruled a domain extending from India to the Mediterranean, of which Judea was a small segment.

centuries indicates the increasing spread of Greek influence throughout the Near East and in Judah.

A major turning point in the political history of the Near East occurred in the 330s BCE, when the Persian empire was conquered by an army of Greeks and Macedonians. European Greece, torn by the Peloponnesian wars from the 430s to 401, was ripe for control from without. Beginning in the 350s, Philip, king of Macedonia to the north, was able to dominate Greece militarily and politically. His son, Alexander the Great (born 356, ruled 336–323 BCE), launched an invasion that was to result in the greatest conquests yet by one man. In 334 Alexander crossed the Hellespont and dealt crushing defeats to the Persians (333, 331), leading to the annihilation of the Persian state, as well as to the conquest of Egypt and of large areas of western India. Alexander's conquests are considered the end of the Ancient Near Eastern and the beginning of the Hellenistic era. As with every historical watershed, there is a danger of oversimplifying the break between Near Eastern history before and after Alexander. We noted already that Greek merchants penetrated the Near East long before; many thousands of Greeks served in the Persian army which Alexander defeated. Moreover, ancient Near Eastern cultural and social patterns did survive, especially in the villages and countryside. (That "Hellenistic" civilization was a blend of Greek and Near Eastern elements in the context of continuing social change throughout the area has led to the use of that term, in contrast to the classical, "Hellenic" Greek culture of the period before Alexander.) The impact of the Greek language, literature, and ideas on Jews and Judaism will be an important topic later in this chapter and subsequently.

Following Alexander's sudden death in 323 BCE at Babylon, there ensued two decades of war between the generals of his armies until three major Hellenistic states took shape: the Antigonid dynasty of Macedonia, the Ptolemies in Egypt, and the Seleucids in northern Syria, Mesopotamia, and Iran. The Ptolemies, from their capital at Alexandria in the Nile delta, in the third century BCE controlled coastal areas of Asia Minor and Libya, some of the Aegean islands, and parts of southern Syria and Palestine. Judea fell under their rule. (Henceforth we will use the term *Judea* rather than *Judah*, *Jew* rather than *Judahite*.) The Ptolemies did not interfere with the religious autonomy and the priestly control of Jerusalem. Information about the early Hellenistic period in Judea is quite limited, although some stories and data are related in *The Jewish Antiquities* of Josephus, a Jewish historian of the first century CE. Some Judeans, members of the Tobiad family closely associated with the Jerusalem hierarchy and owning large estates in the trans-Jordan, rose high in the Ptolemaic administration. Toward the end of the century,

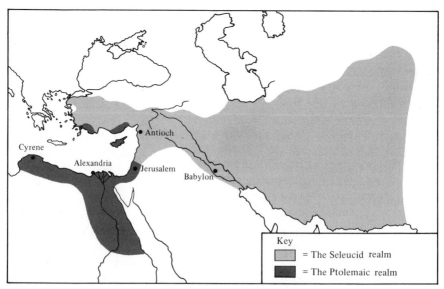

The Ptolemaic and the Seleucid Realms in the Mid-Third Century BCE. Of the two largest states carved out of Alexander the Great's conquests, the Ptolemies ruled Judea until the beginning of the second century BCE and the Seleucids thereafter until the Maccabean revolt.

the leadership of Judea was split between pro-Ptolemaic and pro-Seleucid groups. In 198 BCE, Judea came under Seleucid rule. How this affected Judean politics and religion will be the subject of a later section of this chapter, after we have completed a survey of the religious thought of the other books of the Bible.

Exilic and Postexilic Prophecy

We stopped our account of classical prophecy in the last chapter with Jeremiah; two major and several minor prophetic figures carry the history of the movement into the fifth century BCE, when prophecy subsides as an intellectual force. Previous ideas and themes are reiterated, but there is a greater emphasis on consolation for the suffering of the people, on the End of Days, and on cultic and social restoration in an age of growing priestly predominance.

Ezekiel and Other Exilic Books

Ezekiel, the son of Buzi the priest, was among the first wave of exiles deported to Babylon by Nebuchadnezzar in the 590s. Several prophets addressed the exiles in places of their resettlement; for Ezekiel this was the Babylonian village of Tel Aviv by the Chebar canal (3:12–15). Other prophets in exile were optimistic about an early return to Zion, whereas Ezekiel, like Jeremiah, expected Jerusalem to fall to Nebuchadnezzar and that considerable time would elapse before the exiles would be restored. Ezekiel's dated prophecies extend from the fifth year of king Jehoiachin (593 BCE, 1:2) to the twenty-seventh year (571 BCE, 29:17). It seems that Ezekiel remained in Babylonia during his entire prophetic career.

The literary style of Ezekiel is significantly different from that of the pre-exilic prophets. He reports more extended and detailed visions and makes more use of elaborate symbolic acts and allegories. Ezekiel's account of his consecration as a prophet is prefaced with a description of God, "a likeness as it were of a human form" glowing like bronze from the waist up and like fire from the waist down, surrounded by an encircling, luminous radiance like the rainbow (1:26–29). God is seated on a throne, which stands on a firmament supported by four winged cherubim, each with the faces of a man, lion, ox, and eagle, and each accompanied by an intricate, omnidirectional wheel studded with eyes. (This description will provide a key text for later Jewish mysticism.) Ezekiel's symbolic acts include enactment (before the actual event) of the Judean king's going into exile in 587 BCE (12:1–20), and a refusal to mourn the death of his wife, a symbol of accepting as deserved the destruction of Zion (24:15–27). Despite the concreteness of his visual presentations, Ezekiel lacks the poetic spontaneity of his predecessors; his allegories, mostly in prose, are labored and meticulously explained (e.g., chap. 17, chap. 23). Single-minded and consistent, Ezekiel firmly reiterates his main ideas and underscores the maxims that he wishes to drive home.

For Ezekiel, the entire history of the people, from before the exodus from Egypt to the present, has been one continual rebellion against God. Such wickedness fully deserves punishment. Ezekiel describes the idolatry found in the Temple precincts in such picturesque detail that some interpreters feel he invented these bizarre descriptions of public sinfulness to justify God's destruction of the holy place and departure from his sanctuary (chaps. 8–11).[1] After 587, Ezekiel's main concern was keeping up the exiles' spirits. The people ask, "How then can we live?" Against this despair, Ezekiel prophesies, "As I live, says the Lord YHVH, I have no pleasure in the death of the wicked, but that the wicked turn from his way and live; turn back, turn back from your evil ways; for why will you die, O house of Israel?" (33:11). Like Jeremiah, Ezekiel denounces the proverb that the fathers have eaten sour grapes and the children's teeth shall be set on edge. On the contrary, "the son shall not suffer for the iniquity of the father, nor the father suffer for the iniquity of the son; the righteousness of the righteous shall be upon himself, and the wickedness of the wicked shall be upon himself" (18:19–20; see also Ezek. 33:12–16 and Jer. 31:29–30). Each man is responsible for his own sins; even the greatest spiritual heroes, Noah, Daniel, and Job, will save only themselves by their righteousness (14:12–20). The fate of Jerusalem may have been sealed long before, but God's decree for the next generation depends on its own actions, and is not sealed. The heart of Ezekiel's later oracles is that God is surely going to restore the people. Responding to the fear that "our bones are dried up, and our hope is lost," he offers an allegory of a valley of dry bones, brought together and infused with new life (chap. 37). Judah and Ephraim (the northern Israelites) will be gathered up and resettled on the holy soil; they will again live under a Davidic king and under God's just rule (11:16–21 and the allegory in 17:22–24). YHVH will do this to vindicate the holiness of his great name, which has been profaned among the nations (36:22–23).

The prophet's extended blueprint for a rebuilt Temple begins with a vision in which an angel measures each dimension of the holy place, after which Ezekiel sees the God of Israel returning to infuse the house once more with His glory (chaps. 40–43). In following chapters, Ezekiel describes the restored Israelite commonwealth, organized to make impossible the former sins against God. A geometrical strip of territory will be given to each of the twelve tribes, six tribal patrimonies to the north and six to the south of Jerusalem. In the Temple the priests of the family of Zadok, aided by Levites, will offer sacrifices, and they will teach the people to distinguish between sacred and profane, clean and unclean

(44:23). Ezekiel's depiction of the End of Days develops, in much more concrete detail than previous classical prophecy, God's vengeance on the nations who have exulted in the fall of Judah and have viewed YHVH with scorn (chap. 25 and other places). "Gog of the land of Magog, the chief prince of Meshech and Tubal" (a mythic figure) will come with a mighty army to fall on defenseless Judah, only to find his demise in a great earthquake. After this victory, God's greatness and holiness will be acknowledged by all nations (chaps. 38–39).

Ezekiel straddles the prophetic and the priestly sectors of Israelite religion: He is a man with a priestly point of view, concerned with expiation, ritual uncleanliness, and cultic purity, who has adopted prophecy as a form of experience and communication. Ezekiel is as closely related to Leviticus as Jeremiah is to Deuteronomy. (There is a close

Bas-relief from Susa, one of the Persian capitals.

affinity between Ezekiel and the P source of the Pentateuch.) For this reason some of the main themes of classical prophecy are muted: He denounces Israel's sins, but there is no overwhelming urgency for justice. He ignores the ills of society, concentrating on the individual good man and the individual evil man. Unlike earlier classical prophets, Ezekiel does not question the absolute value of sacrifices, but confirms that YHVH demands the people's contributions and the best of their offerings (20:40). Ezekiel is an important step in the articulation of the priestly ideology that prevailed in Judean Jerusalem during the Persian and early Hellenistic periods.

Probably dating from immediately after the fall of Jerusalem are the short prophetic book of Obadiah (Obadiah 1:1–9 is similar to Jer. 49:7–22) and five poems of national mourning, which have been collected in the book of Lamentations. In Lamentations the poet describes the agony of the siege of Zion and the city's bitter fate. He advises penitence, humble acceptance of abuse, and patient waiting for God's forgiveness (3:22–33); he implores YHVH to exercise his just vengeance on Zion's enemies (3:64–66, 4:21–22). The book of Psalms contains one poem from the Babylonian captivity, lamenting the loss of the holy city and longing for return:

> *By the waters of Babylon*
> *there we sat down and wept,*
> *when we remembered Zion.*
> *On the willows there*
> *we hung up our lyres.*
> *For there our captors*
> *required of us songs,*
> *and our tormentors, mirth, saying,*
> *"Sing us one of the songs of Zion!"*
> *How shall we sing YHVH's song*
> *in a foreign land?*
> *If I forget you, O Jerusalem,*
> *let my right hand wither!*
> *Let my tongue cleave to the roof of my mouth,*
> *if I do not remember you,*
> *if I do not set Jerusalem*
> *above my highest joy! [137:1–6.]*

Isaiah 40–66

The second half of the book of Isaiah contains oracles of a prophet who addressed the exiles during the period when Cyrus was vanquishing the

Babylonian army, occupying the city of Babylon, and supplanting the Neo-Babylonian empire with the Persian. This unnamed exilic prophet is now called Deutero-Isaiah, or Second Isaiah. (Differences between chaps. 40–55 and 56–66 have led many scholars to hold that the second half of Isaiah includes compositions by at least two prophets, the second dating from after the return to Judah and the rebuilding of the Temple; however, these twenty-seven chapters are sufficiently consistent to warrant their being treated together in one discussion.) Deutero-Isaiah refers to Cyrus by name, calling him God's shepherd and "anointed" (44:28, 45:1); he alludes to a ruined and deserted Jerusalem, speaks of the exiles' suffering at the hands of the Babylonians, and is concerned with the prospects of their immediate restoration to Zion. The literary style of Second Isaiah differs considerably from that of Isaiah the son of Amoz (First Isaiah). First Isaiah's oracles are terse, compact, stately, and restrained; Second Isaiah's are flowing and lyrical, full of passionate, dramatic personification of nature and community, often drawn out over a series of verses. Ideas asserted by First Isaiah and other pre-exilic prophets are developed at length by Second Isaiah as he strives to persuade his audience to be faithful in its exilic situation. The extent of his theological explicitness makes the author (or authors) of the second half of the book of Isaiah a culmination of prophetic monotheism.

The opening motif of Deutero-Isaiah, repeated at intervals throughout, is consolation: that the time of destruction is at an end. "Speak tenderly to Jerusalem, and cry to her that her warfare is ended, that her iniquity is pardoned" (40:2). Israel has been punished for her former sins, which are now forgiven; a new redemption is about to occur, a glorious exodus from Babylonian captivity. God will make a highway through the desert to Zion, on which the exiles will return with YHVH himself guiding them (40:3–5, 40:10–11, 41:17–20). Like Jeremiah and Ezekiel, Second Isaiah assures the people that the next generation does not have to suffer for the sins of its ancestors; God has "swept away your transgressions like a cloud and your sins like mist" (44:22) and purified the people "in the furnace of affliction" for the sake of his name (48:9–11).

To demonstrate that no obstacles stand in the way of the people's deliverance, the prophet adduces arguments to confirm YHVH's uniqueness. A visionary lawsuit is brought against the supposed other gods. In YHVH's defense the prophet reminds the people that He is the omnipotent creator who transcends nature and history and who has foretold through the prophets His former works (44:7–8). The great new work being promised is the raising up of Cyrus. All nations will be put in Cyrus's power; he will be given the treasures of the earth, and Jerusalem and its Temple will be rebuilt (44:24–45:4). At the climax of the defense comes the proclamation:

I am YHVH, and there is no other,
besides me there is no God; . . .
I form light and create darkness,
I make peace and create evil,
I am YHVH, who do all these things. [45:5–7.]

In their behalf the nonexistent other gods can produce no witnesses: "Behold, they are a delusion; their works are nothing; their molten images are empty wind" (41:29). On YHVH's behalf Israel is his witness that "I am God . . . there is none who can deliver from my hand" (43:10–13). The notion of Israel as God's witness on earth in the face of the pagan nations will have a long, consequential history in Jewish and Christian theology.

Besides the metaphor of witness, the prophet has a second metaphor he uses even more extensively for Israel's religious role: the "servant of God." The meaning of this concept in Isaiah 40–53 has raised controversy for centuries, especially in the so-called servant poems (42:1–4, 49:1–6, 50:4–11, 52:13–53:12). The portrayal of a "servant" suffering for the sake of others in chapter 53 has been interpreted by Jews as referring to the Jewish people or to the messianic king who will redeem them and by Christians as referring to the Christ. It would seem that the servant is a complex and fluid personification, which the prophet employs for Israel in its ideal aspect (see 41:8–10 and Jer. 30:10; in Isa. 46:27–28 this term is applied to the people). The servant of Second Isaiah describes a role: sometimes Israel as a whole and sometimes the humble and contrite in Israel. We might understand the figure of the servant according to the analogy that the servant is to the nation as the nation—ideally—is to the peoples of the earth. The servant is a personification of the role of the prophet, based especially on the model of Jeremiah. Chosen by God to be a prophet to the nations (Jer. 1:4–5), the prophet suffers persecution and questions God's just treatment of him, but remains faithful to his mission. Second Isaiah's servant is "despised and rejected by men; a man of sorrows and acquainted with grief" (53:3). He patiently endures humiliation: "I gave my back to the smiters, and my cheeks to those who pulled out the beard; I hid not my face from shame and spitting" (50:6). But he does not waver in his prophetic task "that I may know how to sustain with a word him that is weary" (50:4). He trusts in God, who will vindicate him at the end. The servant's function is twofold: The medium for Israel's repentance and restoration (49:5), he also is to be "a light to the nations, that My salvation may reach to the end of the earth" (49:6). Second Isaiah's message of consolation extends the meaningfulness of Israel's suffering to the perspective of all the nations of the earth, who will recognize that the servant "bore the sin of many and made intercession for the transgressors" (53:12). He will persist in his task "till he has established justice in the earth, and the coastlands wait for his law" (42:4).

While developing the figure of the servant, Deutero-Isaiah introduces another personification also to symbolize national redemption and universal salvation. Zion, the city of God, is the abandoned mother whose children are about to return (49:14–26 and 54:1–17). Jerusalem will again be a beautiful bride adorned with precious stones, its walls too narrow to contain the assembled people. The nations of the world shall march toward Jerusalem's light; "kings shall be your foster fathers and their queens your nursing mothers" (49:23). The rebuilt Jerusalem shall herald the world's spiritual unification, for all mankind shall know that it is YHVH who ransomed Israel and reigns in Zion. Foreigners who give their allegiance to YHVH, who keep the Sabbath and hold fast to the covenant, are also counted among God's servants: "Their burnt offerings and their sacrifices will be accepted on my altar; for my house shall be called a house of prayer for all peoples" (56:1–8). The prophetic notion of the welcome to be accorded all those among the nations who spontaneously acknowledge YHVH of Hosts lays the groundwork for Jewish proselytism beginning in the last two centuries BCE.

In the latter part of Second Isaiah's oracles (or those of a Third, postexilic "Isaiah," according to many scholars), it becomes apparent that Cyrus and "the nations" are not about to acknowledge YHVH and that Israel has yet to be spiritually perfected. The prophet returns to the more traditional themes of chastisement and judgment. Israel still requires censure and rebuke: Its leaders are blind and greedy; scoffers occupy themselves with superstitious worship of spirits and eat the flesh of abominable things (56:9–57:13). Returning to the primacy of morality, the prophet answers the question, "Why have we fasted, and thou seest it not?" with the insistence that repentant fasting is to loose the fetters of injustice, feed the hungry, and satisfy the needs of the afflicted (58:6–7). Those who ask about the delay of justice and deliverance are reassured that God's covenant with Israel is eternal (59:21), and that a new, joyful Jerusalem and a "new heaven and a new earth," free of disease and violence, will come to pass (65:17–25, 66:22, and other places). Toward the end of Isaiah there are, however, terrifying images of God's warfare with his enemies, when he alone treads the wine press, stamping in his wrath on the peoples, sprinkling their lifeblood on his garments. "For behold, YHVH will come in fire, and his chariots like the stormwind, to render his anger in fury, and his rebuke with flames of fire" (66:15). But Israel shall find delight on God's holy mountain; the nations of the world will be gathered up to Zion, where they will abhor the memory of those who have transgressed against God. "From new moon to new moon, and from Sabbath to Sabbath, all flesh shall come to worship before me, says YHVH" (66:23).

The tendency in exilic and early postexilic prophecy to turn away from the mundane world to God's final retribution on evil—an overriding concern for eschatology (from the Greek, *eschaton*, end)—is even more apparent in the last group of prophets datable to Judah under the Persians.

Postexilic Prophets

Although prophecy continued at least three quarters of a century after Second Isaiah, we possess only a few prophetic works from these years. In 520 the prophets Haggai and Zechariah addressed the returned exiles, who had rebuilt their homes but not yet laid the foundations of the Temple. Haggai encouraged the Judean governor, the High Priest, and the rest of the people to begin work on YHVH's house, promising divine blessings on the people and the sanctuary. Suggesting that YHVH was about to bring an end to Persian rule, Haggai and Zechariah hinted at a restoration of the Davidic kingdom through Zerubbabel. In eight allegorical visions symbolizing God's judgment on the idolatrous nations and the glorious age to follow, Zechariah prophesied that Zerubbabbal will be recognized as ruler "Not by might, nor by power, but by my spirit, says YHVH of hosts" (4:6). As mentioned earlier, the Persian empire was only temporarily shaken by a succession crisis; Darius put down all opposition, welded his realm together more strongly than ever, Zerubbabel disappeared from history, and the brief dream of an independent Judah under a Davidic prince faded, leaving the priesthood in charge of the people.

Probably composed during the postexilic period are the oracles of Joel, Isaiah 24–27, the last six chapters of Zechariah (usually called Deutero-Zechariah because they are from a different hand), and Malachi. Except for Joel and possibly Malachi (which means "my messenger" and may not be a proper name), these oracles are anonymous. Absence of specific historical allusions makes much of this material impossible to date exactly; there are scholars who argue for a pre-exilic provenance for all these works except Haggai, Zechariah 1–8, and Malachi. But a new tone to some old themes indicates a development in the direction of much later biblical writing.

The "day" of YHVH appears prominently in postexilic prophecy. In Joel, a devastating locust plague occasions the call for penitence, fasting, and prayer. The End of Days brings the spread of ecstatic prophecy everywhere (2:28–29 [Heb. 3:1–2]) along with terrifying heavenly portents (2:30–31 [Heb. 3:3–4]). Joel and Zechariah 9–14 echo Ezekiel's vision of a last battle against pagan hordes, the armies of the nations that will assemble before Jerusalem: "Multitudes, multitudes, in the valley of decision!" (Joel 3:14 [Heb. 4:14]). Deutero-Zechariah presents a series of enigmatic oracles referring to the shattering of Israel's enemies (9:1–6 and elsewhere), the coming of a victorious king in Judah "humble and riding on an ass" who rules the world peacefully (9:9–10), and the elevation of Jerusalem to a center of worship for all men. "On that day living waters shall flow out from Jerusalem, half of them to the eastern sea and half of them to the western sea; it shall continue in summer as in winter. And YHVH will become king over all the earth; on that day YHVH will be one and his name one" (Zech. 14:8–9). Isaiah 24–27 contains an even more cataclysmic view of the future: "The earth is utterly broken, the earth is rent asunder, the earth is violently shaken. The earth staggers like a drunken man, it sways like a hut; its transgression lies heavy upon it, and it falls, and will not rise again" (24:19–20). As God judges the world, the righteous survivors, God's faithful people, sing hymns of thanksgiving. "On this mountain YHVH of hosts will make for all peoples a feast of fat things, a feast of wine on the lees . . . And he will destroy on this mountain the covering that is cast over all peoples, the veil that is spread over all nations. He will swallow up death forever . . . (25:6–9). (See 26:19 for another allusion to the later doctrine of the resurrection of the dead.)

Malachi reflects the confused social conditions in Judah just before Nehemiah and Ezra. The prophet castigates the priests for improper sacrifices (1:6–2:9) and the people for marriage with pagan women (2:11) and remissness in the payment of tithes (3:6–12). He prophesies an approaching judgment, when God "will be a swift witness against the sorcerers, against the adulterers, against those who swear falsely, against those who oppress the hireling in his wages, the widow, and the orphan, against those who thrust aside the sojourner, and do not fear Me . . ." (3:5). Malachi concludes by calling on the people to remember the statutes and precepts of the Law of Moses and foretells that Elijah will return before "the great and terrible day of YHVH" to reconcile fathers to sons and sons to fathers, lest God "smite the land with a curse."

A pessimistic and despairing mood pervades many postexilic oracles. Ezekiel and Second Isaiah had promised great acts of divine salvation, which had come to pass only in part and on a small scale. There is a loss of confidence in man's ability to repent and change. Immediate hopes are deferred to a final, eschatological judgment when the few will see the many being destroyed by God himself. The desire to escape from history, evident in these writings, makes them a precursor and source for the apocalypticism that appears in Judaism later, at the beginning of the second century BCE.

The End of Classical Prophecy and the Consolidation of the Hierocracy

The emotional tone of postexilic prophecy changed, because the post-exilic social situation was so different from that before 587. The royal court was gone; Jerusalem was impoverished and sparsely settled; the priests directed a much simpler society reduced to clan and family ties and to peasant and landlord classes. Judah consisted of a small area around the holy city little more than 24 miles across, since the old Israelite territories to the north and south were occupied by other peoples. The pre-exilic prophets had been part of a nation that, at certain strategic moments, could make political choices of considerable scope. Now, in exchange for toleration and support of the Temple, the leadership was dependent on the Persian government and answerable to its dictates. Political passivity is reflected in the mood of withdrawal that can be detected in the late prophetic writings.

Ezra and Nehemiah, in the mid-fifth century, brought about a revival of spirits and a new start. Both Nehemiah and Ezra came from Babylonia with the permission, perhaps also because of the instigation, of a Persian government concerned to combat anarchy in a strategic region. Nehemiah improved the condition of the peasantry and re-established Jerusalem as an urban center. Ezra's reforms aimed to strengthen the religious identity of the Judahites, revitalize their morale, and prevent the dissolution of biblical monotheism.

One of Ezra's most controversial measures was a campaign to force the Judahites to give up their "foreign" wives (Ezra 9–10, see also Neh. 13: 23–27 and Mal. 2:10–16). This probably reflected a fear of religious syncretism, the mixing of Israelite and pagan religious customs. Evidence of such syncretism can be gleaned from a group of letters in the Aramaic language sent to Jerusalem toward the end of the fifth century BCE by a community of Judahite soldiers in the Persian army stationed on the island of Elephantine in the Nile, who had a temple where they worshiped other gods alongside YHVH. (The letters mention Anath-yahu, Anath-bethel,

Aramaic papyrus from the Jewish military unit at Elephantine in Egypt, fifth century BCE. (Courtesy of the Brooklyn Museum, Bequest of Miss Theodora Wilbour.)

Herem-bethel, and Ishum-bethel, deities which are either a continuation of premonotheistic popular polytheism or a decline as a result of the group's isolation from monotheistic leadership.) Ezra's purge may have been an attempt to reverse such syncretism in the holy city. However, it also suited the religious mood of the Jerusalemites at the time. According to speeches attributed to Ezra (Ezra 9 and Neh. 9:6–37), the Judahites of this day thought of themselves as the sole remnant of ancient Israel in the holy land, with one last chance to atone for the guilt of their ancestors and demonstrate that they were worthy of God's favor. Separation from surrounding peoples was a consequence of a desire to strengthen national continuity and cultic holiness. (The Pentateuchal prohibition against intermarriage with Canaanites, Deut. 7:3, would have been felt to apply directly to such a repentant group.)

The hopes of classical prophecy, above all Second Isaiah, that the whole earth would soon worship YHVH, must have seemed remote indeed. The Judahites' rebuff of help from their neighbors around 520 BCE in restoring the Temple cult was in sharp contradiction to that idea, then only a vision and not a practical program. To the extent to which this rebuff was ideological rather than personal and political, it can be explained as a consequence of the self-image of the Judahites trying to retain their historical roots. The opposition that Nehemiah encountered in the following century came from the north (see Neh., chaps. 4–6). According to the biblical narratives, the northerners were not offspring of the tribes of Israel but a new population brought in by the Assyrians after 722 (2 Kings 17:24–41). (Substantiating the veracity of the biblical account is the fact that the northerners preserved no pre-exilic literature apart from the writings retained in Jerusalem.) Sometime after Ezra, perhaps in the late fourth century BCE, the neighboring people identified themselves as Samaritans (from the biblical place-home Samaria) and accepted the Pentateuch as their sacred book. Claiming to be Israelites by origin but insisting that the sole place where YHVH intended to be worshiped was Mount Gerizim near Shechem, not the Temple Mount in Jerusalem, the Samaritans were the first Judaizers who formed a separate religion, apart from Judaism, based on the Jewish Scriptures. A sizable Samaritan population existed in the first centuries CE; a handful has survived to the present.

The rejection of nearby peoples who wanted to worship YHVH at the Temple and Ezra's efforts to force the Judahites to divorce their foreign wives were symptomatic of a certain phase in the transformation of ancient Judaism. Earlier, in the pre-exilic period, assimilation of gentiles into Israel probably took place naturally and on an individual basis. The book of Ruth, set in the time of the judges, depicts its heroine as becoming an Israelite merely by declaring to her mother-in-law Naomi, "Where you go I will go, and where you lodge I will lodge; your people shall be

my people, and your God my God" (1:16). (That the author approved
of this action is indicated by the end of the book, where Ruth is identified
as the great-grandmother of King David; there are some scholars who
believe that Ruth represents a postexilic polemic against Ezra's stand on
divorcing foreign wives.) The Deuteronomic reform, with its concern
for the immediacy of the covenantal commitment to each successive
generation since Sinai, made ad hoc conversion difficult, if not impossible,
especially for large numbers, and the postexilic priesthood placed considerable emphasis on genealogical purity. Later in the Hellenistic era
formal conversion—even forced conversion—brought many thousands of
gentiles into the Jewish people. But the religious atmosphere of the period of restoration militated against both the earlier absorption of non-
Israelites and the later proselytism.[2]

The most decisive act undertaken by Ezra was an assembly in Jerusalem (Neh. 8–10) where the "Book of the Law of Moses which YHVH
had given to Israel" was read and explained to the people. A few days
later the Judahites "stood and confessed their sins and the iniquities of
their fathers," making a "firm covenant" to do all the commandments,
ordinances, and statutes of their God. Many modern historians feel that
it was at this moment when the Torah book, the Pentateuch in close to
its final form, became the unchallenged norm of Israel's religion and
when Judaism took its single most important step to becoming a religion
of Scripture, indeed, the first scriptural religion.

The consolidation of the hierocracy in Jerusalem is probably connected to the disappearance of the prophetic tendency. Perhaps completion of the Torah, which placed supreme authority in the hands of the
Aaronide priests, undermined the independent public function of the
prophets, since the authoritative word of God was now embodied in
recorded revelations ascribed to Moses. The canonization of the Pentateuch (from the Greek *kanon*, fixed rule) was a key stage in a long-range
historical process, a process that began with the writing down of the first
narratives and law codes in the early monarchy and with the compilation
of Deuteronomy in the seventh century. This process would be concluded at the end of the first century CE when the final list of biblical
books would be fixed. The Pentateuch served as the hierocracy's constitution. In the absence of a Joshua or a David, the descendants of Aaron
were clearly in charge of the primary Jewish institution, the Temple.
(As we saw in the previous chapter, the priestly stratum of the Pentateuchal narratives confirms the authority of the priests in no uncertain
manner.) Assisting the priests were the Levitical guilds and a class of
scribes or sages whose subsequent history is of immense importance for
the development of postbiblical Judaism. However, these two groups, the
Levites, who were probably in charge of Temple music, and the scribes,
had already produced or compiled significant bodies of writing: Psalms

and Proverbs. We will now examine these two collections and several other books, written in postexilic times, which further develop central issues in the biblical world view.

The *Ketuvim* (Other Biblical Writings) on Faith, Retribution, and Chance

A wide variety of literary works, dating from different periods of Israel's history, is found in the third section of the Bible according to Jewish arrangement, the *Ketuvim* (writings) or Hagiographa. We have already referred to the sequence of history books written in the postexilic period (1 and 2 Chronicles, Ezra, and Nehemiah) and have mentioned Lamentations and Ruth. As a bridge between earlier and later phases of biblical religion stand the large collections of Psalms and Proverbs and the book of Job. Some of the ideas already examined are also found in these works: YHVH's actions in nature and history (the theme of many communal psalms), the principle of divine retribution (there are close affinities between the Deuteronomic school and Proverbs), the experience of God's revelation (the climax of Job). But much of the material in these three large books, and in the smaller works to be surveyed later in the chapter, conveys a more intimate dimension of Israelite religiosity. Composed for the use and guidance of the ordinary man, they give insight into the individual's needs, the ideal personal life, and the issue of unmerited suffering in relation to divine justice as posed by the biblical tradition.

The writings now to be examined stem from two professional roles that we have not yet considered: the lyric poet and the teacher of wisdom. Unlike a prophetic oracle, in which poetry is presented as a direct statement of God's will, the lyric poem conveys the author's own state of mind and feeling in response to the events of history and the problems of human existence—a continuum of doubt, despair, gratitude, and trust in God. Similarly, the teacher of wisdom offers advice on the conduct of a good life and reflections on God's relationship to the world in a more directly philosophical manner than do the narrative and prophetic literatures. A combination of these two human points of view, the poet's and the sage's, leads to a challenging criticism of fundamental assumptions of earlier biblical thought and eventually to a reorientation of Jewish theology in late biblical and early postbiblical times.

Psalms

The principal collection of religious lyric poetry in the Bible is the book of Psalms (often called the Psalter), consisting of 150 poems, most of which are prayers addressed to God. The psalms are usually divided into three main types, according to content and form: hymns, laments, and thanksgiving songs. (There are also a number of more narrow categories, such as psalms praising YHVH as king of the world, songs recited in behalf of the king, psalms in honor of Jerusalem and the Temple, history poems, and psalms of confidence in God.) The titles of about half mention King David, indicating not that he wrote them but that he was considered the patron of this kind of poetry. (Some of the psalms are attributed to professional Temple guilds.) Since about one third of the psalms refer to Mount Zion or the Temple, it is generally assumed that they accompanied communal and individual worship there.[3]

On the whole, the religious tradition of the Psalter seems to be separate from—and in part chronologically prior to—classical prophecy.[4] Unlike classical prophecy, the psalms do not refer to social injustice as the cause of Israel's suffering nor do they explain that the nation's enemies have been sent by God to punish Israel for not living up to the covenant. Whereas the prophets reacted directly to the momentous events of their time, the psalms contain no historical allusions to occurrences after the period of the judges. (The exception is Psalm 137, set in the Babylonian exile.)

Intended for as many specific events as possible, the psalms employ a common fund of images, formulas, and concepts. The suppliant refers to himself as innocent, poor, destitute, needy, pious, meek—broad terms referring not to social classes but to roles in which the community and the individual appeal to God. The suppliant's enemies are workers of iniquity, the arrogant, and the proud—men who trust only in themselves, do not fear God, and who plot against the weak. The lack of historical immediacy, the generality of the emotions expressed, and the applicability of most psalms to a variety of occasions contributed to making the book a constant source of inspiration to later generations.[5] The Psalter can therefore be read on two levels: A source for the early stages of certain crucial biblical ideas, it is also one of the most influential biblical legacies for personal spirituality in Western civilization. The following summary of motifs in Psalms deals, first, with the nature of divine activity in the world and, second, with the perils and joys experienced by the righteous man.

Depictions of nature are used frequently by the psalmists as a manifestation of the power of God, the Creator. The perpetual harmony of the heavens is God's handiwork (19:1–6); awesome phenomena, such as the thunderstorm, demonstrate God's might (18:7–15, 29:3–9); the plenitude of plants and animals on earth reveals his beneficence (104:14–18). Only God's will prevents the world from reverting to chaos (93:1). The psalmist calls on the heavens and earth to rejoice in YHVH's kingship,

Processional frieze from the Persian capital of Persepolis. (Photo by the author.)

the sea and fields to roar their praises of him (96:11–12). Descriptions of nature in the psalms are among the most majestic in the Bible, but nature is never portrayed for its own sake, only as a means of proclaiming the divine sovereignty.

A major theme of Psalms is the kingship of YHVH. As in the prophets, God's role as ruler entails his acting as cosmic judge, for "righteousness and justice are the foundation of his throne" (97:2 and elsewhere), and psalms that celebrate God as king frequently call on the nations of the world to acknowledge his rule publicly, for he alone determines their destinies.

> *Come, behold the works of YHVH,*
> *how he has wrought desolations in the earth.*
> *He makes wars cease to the end of the earth;*
> *he breaks the bow, and shatters the spear,*
> *he burns the chariots with fire!*
> *"Be still and know that I am God.*
> *I am exalted among the nations,*
> *I am exalted in the earth!"* [46:8–10.]

Although in the psalms God's direct rule over the peoples of the earth is not specifically tied to the End of Days, as in the prophets, later generations would read eschatological meaning into these fervent expectations of the divine kingdom.

God's ultimate reputation among the nations requires that he defend Israel from its foes; although YHVH is the ruler of the world, only Israel pays him homage. Foreign peoples who threaten the king or Zion must be defeated so that they will learn that YHVH alone is the Most High:

> *Pour out thy anger on the nations*
>   *that do not know thee,*
> *and on the kingdoms*
>   *that do not call on thy name!*
> *For they have devoured Jacob,*
>   *and laid waste his habitation.* [79:6–7.]

Asking God's help for Israel, the poet reminds YHVH what He has done for his people in the past and extols His everlasting, steadfast, and dependable love (*hesed*). (See Psalms 107, 118, 136, 146.) Psalm 85, probably a prayer for deliverance from famine, ends with a prophetic oracle of assurance that Israel's fidelity to God will certainly merit a divine response:

> *Steadfast love and faithfulness will meet;*
>   *righteousness and peace will kiss each other.*
> *Faithfulness will spring up from the ground,*
>   *and righteousness will look down from the sky.* [85:10–11.]

The psalms constantly reiterate that God's creative might and justice ensure that the nation that worships him cannot fail to be delivered.

The Psalter constitutes a guidebook for the spiritual life of the individual, providing him with the opportunity to confess his failings, proclaim his good intentions, and affirm his trust in divine providence. The suppliant frequently complains that he is threatened by many and violent enemies who spread lies about him or who falsely accuse him of crimes; an object of scorn and dishonor, the victim claims that he has no one but God to save him (109, 142). In some laments, the suppliant prays principally for health (38, 39, 102, 116). Because of his iniquities, God has sent a sickness; heartfelt and sincere prayer will certainly convince God to heal him (107:17–20). YHVH is frequently reminded that dying is the extinction of man's opportunity to worship: "The dead do not praise YHVH" (6:5, 88:3–12). (Although a disregard for ancient mythology concerning the underworld [Sheol] is evident in the narrative and prophetic books, this feature of Israelite religion is clearly spelled out in the psalms.) Reflection on human finitude also figures in meditations on the brevity of human life in contrast to God's eternity:

> *For a thousand years in thy sight*
> *are but as yesterday when it is past,*
> *or as a watch in the night. . . .*
> *The years of our life are threescore and ten,*
> *or even by reason of strength fourscore;*
> *yet their span is but toil and trouble;*
> *they are soon gone, and we fly away. [90:4, 10.]*

The psalmists accept the physical limits of man's existence and the inevitability of death, but express astonishment at the gap between divine
justice and human reality. YHVH must certainly come to aid the
helpless, needy, and oppressed (145:14–20, 146:5–9). Wondering why
YHVH's deliverance is delayed, the poet asks how much longer must he
wait (6:3, 12:1–2, 22:1–2), how long will God hide himself (10:1, 89:46).
He demands that God end his silence (83:1, 109:1), that he awake (7:6,
44:23), that he rise up and issue judgment (94:1–2). Giving in to despair,
the author of Psalm 73 observes:

> *Behold, these are the wicked;*
> *always at ease, they increase in riches.*
> *All in vain have I kept my heart clean*
> *and washed my hands in innocence.*
> *For all the day long I have been stricken,*
> *and chastened every morning. [73:12–14.]*

Psalms that raise the issue of divine retribution conclude by expressing
renewed faith in God's goodness. (The exception is Psalm 88.) In the
poem just quoted, after the author complains that the evil prosper and
that his own moral innocence has only brought him misery, he nevertheless ends by affirming,

> *Whom have I in heaven but thee?*
> *And there is nothing upon earth that I desire besides thee.*
> *My flesh and my heart may fail,*
> *but God is the strength of my heart and my portion for ever. [73:25–26.]*

A striking characteristic of psalm imagery is the variety of metaphors
expressing faith in God: Shield, Tower of Strength, Stronghold, Refuge,
Shelter, Rock. The psalmist hides in the shadow of God's wings from
attacks by the wicked (17:8–9). Even if the earth be shaken by convul-
sions, with God as his champion he will not be afraid (46:2–3). God
represents security in a dangerous, unstable world. Men betray their
friends (41:9, 55:12–14), rulers act unjustly (118:9), parents abandon
their children (27:10), but God cannot but be righteous (56:10–11). Part

of the psychological legacy of the Psalms is that dependence on God means independence from men.

The quintessence of this trustful attitude can be seen in the psalms of confidence, containing no hint of lament or petition. The twenty-third psalm depicts God as a shepherd, guiding the poet in straight paths through a fearsome valley, after which he can sit tranquilly even in the presence of his enemies. Even more blissful is the tiny 131st psalm:

> *O YHVH, my heart is not lifted up,*
> *my eyes are not raised too high;*
> *I do not occupy myself with things*
> *too great and too marvelous for me.*
> *But I have calmed and quieted my soul,*
> *like a child quieted at its mother's breast;*
> *like a child that is quieted is my soul.*

The psalms contain some of the most inward descriptions of biblical faith, emphasizing the contrition and remorse felt by the sinner in his search for God's mercy, and the goodness and truthfulness of the man worthy of admission to God's presence (e.g., 24:4, 51:17). Confidence in God's justice, trust in His might, assurance that YHVH will support the individual in an hour of need are essential convictions of biblical piety—and raise major theological dilemmas in every phase of later Jewish thought.

Proverbs

Wisdom is human intelligence applied to understanding the ways of the world—traditional advice that has been refined and tested by the sages, as well as critical reflection on commonly held beliefs about life's ultimate mysteries. Cosmopolitan rather than national, directed toward the individual rather than society, wisdom literature formed a distinct tendency within Israelite culture and that of the ancient Near East as a whole. Ranging from pithy sentences to elaborate poetic addresses, biblical wisdom focused on man as man, rather than as Israelite. The meaning of the people's historical destiny, the atonement effected by the Temple and the sacrificial cult, the prophetic denunciation of idolatry and social injustice, were not matters of professional concern to the teachers and sages who relied on observation of the regularities of everyday life, not on revelation, as their source of truth. The characteristic terminology and attitudes of the wisdom tradition probably influenced the narrative and prophetic literatures, such as the Joseph story, Deuteronomy, and Jeremiah. But only slowly and gradually did radical monotheism penetrate wisdom literature and bring it into closer agreement with the Pentateuch and classical prophecy.[6]

At first the term wise (*ḥaḥam*) in the Bible connoted ability and shrewdness. The skillfulness of the craftsman, the soldier, and the musician makes them "wise" (e.g., Ex. 28:3, Isa. 10:13, Jer. 9:17). Solomon's knowledge of trees and animals, Joseph's tact, even Jonadeb's craftiness constitute their "wisdom" (1 Kings 4:29 [Heb. 5:9], Gen. 41:33, 2 Sam. 13:3). The opposite of *wise* was *fool*. Gradually the dichotomy of wise versus fool is brought together with the dichotomy of righteous versus wicked, and the idea of wisdom takes on greater moral and theological content.

Although fables, riddles, aphorisms, and other typical modes of conveying wisdom are scattered throughout the Bible (1 Sam. 24:13 [Heb. 24:14], 1 Kings 20:11, Judg. 9:8–15 and 14:14, Ezek. 16:44), the main collection of didactic materials from ancient Israel is the book of Proverbs, ascribed to Solomon, the wise king. (Solomon was the honorary author of wisdom in the Bible, as was David for religious poetry and Moses for law.) Like Psalms, Proverbs was probably put in final form in the postexilic period, from materials, some of pre-exilic origin, that were accumulated over several centuries.[7]

A chief aim of Proverbs is to inculcate wisdom as the means to social tranquility and a happy life. Perhaps the most reiterated teaching is that the intelligent man listens to advice and accepts rebuke (13:1, 15:5, 15:32, etc.). Youth are exhorted to lead productive and sensible lives by mastering their impulses. The wise man plans ahead and avoids impetuous behavior (14:15–17); he cultivates calm speech and patience (15:28); he avoids gossip and slander (11:13). Many proverbs emphasize the value of hard work and diligence (10:4–5) and warn against fornication, excessive sleep, and too much wine (20:13, 23:26–35). Servants and children should be firmly disciplined, so that the former will not be spoiled and the latter will learn to respect their elders and acquire good habits (13:24, 19:18, 22:6, 29:19). The wise man is honest in business affairs, kind to the poor, loyal to friends; he does not insist on revenge against enemies and he avoids cruelty to animals (11:1, 12:10, 14:21, 18:24, 24:29). When serving as judge, he renders impartial decisions; when acting as witness, he gives accurate testimony (14:5, 24:23–25). Riches are desirable, but not greed or covetousness, for calmness and peace are higher values: "Better is a dry morsel with quiet than a house full of feasting with strife" (17:1). God delights in the sober, humble, restrained, and sincere; he dislikes the liar, the arrogant, the cruel.

A few maxims of the book of Proverbs are realistic comments on life. ("Wealth brings many new friends, but a poor man is deserted by his friend," 19:4.) Several emphasize God's intimate knowledge of men's hearts. ("The eyes of YHVH are in every place, keeping watch on the evil and the good," 15:3.) More usually the proverbs treat divine justice as an inexorable law of retribution operating in human affairs: "He who digs a pit will fall into it, and a stone will come back upon him who starts it rolling" (26:27). Because a good deed is wise, it brings happiness and success; because an evil deed is foolish, it leads to failure and ruin. In God's universe the righteous and the wicked receive what they deserve—eventually. It is a matter of enlightened self-interest, therefore, to be blameless and upright. "The teaching of the wise is a fountain of life, that one may avoid the snares of death" (13:14).

The most extensive effort in Proverbs to establish wisdom as a religious concept is found in the discourses of chapters 1–9, the section of the book probably written last. A gift from YHVH, wisdom guards the man of integrity from evil ways. Humble and reverent obedience to YHVH is the beginning of knowledge (1:7, 3:5–8). He is wise who accepts the sufferings with which God disciplines him, "for YHVH reproves him whom he loves, as a father the son in whom he delights" (3:12). The man who has gained wisdom possesses something better than silver, gold, and jewels: "She is a tree of life to those who lay hold of her; those who hold her fast are called happy" (3:18). In several passages wisdom is personified as a woman promising the reader insight and counsel, and warning that those who ignore her will suffer calamity and anguish (1:20–33, 9:1–12). In Proverbs 1–9, wisdom is not just a human skill and acuteness, but a primary attribute of YHVH and the supreme goal for men. Present when the universe was created, wisdom rejoiced when God established the heavens, assigned limits to the seas, and marked off the foundations of the earth, preparing it for habitation by humanity (8:22–31, also 3:19–20). The link between God and humankind, wisdom enables the mind to know that it is firmly rooted in a coherent and ethically ordered world.

Job

In the book of Job, one of the universally acknowledged masterpieces of world literature, the optimistic, conventional piety of Proverbs is sharply attacked. The prologue (chaps. 1–2) poses the issue of whether men will be pious and virtuous without reward from God. In a poetic drama of extraordinary intensity (chaps. 3–31) the focus shifts to the existence of blatant injustice and of undeserved suffering in the world. At the end of the book are God's address to Job and Job's response (38:1–42:6), and a brief epilogue (42:7–17). Although Job incorporates various styles of biblical writing (wisdom, lament, prophecy, narrative), in its totality the book is unique. Many scholars believe that the prologue and epilogue may have been composed before the poetic speeches. (Job is mentioned as a legendary wise man in Ezek. 14:14.) However, the various sections complement each other and form a coherent presentation of the question of the relation of suffering to piety, ending with a resolution of the hero's religious dilemma and restoration of his faith.[8]

In the prologue, Job is introduced as a prosperous patriarch of the land of Uz (the steppes southeast of Judah), a man "blameless and upright, who feared God and turned away from evil." One day, God speaks with the Accusing Angel (*ha-satan* in Hebrew, from which comes the later term *Satan*), whose role was to question the sincerity of men's religious behavior. The angel asks whether Job's piety was truly unselfish and disinterested, inasmuch as God had lavished him with blessings. In order to find out, God places Job in the Accuser's power. Job's flocks and herds, his servants, and his ten children are destroyed, but Job reaffirms his faith: "Naked I came from my mother's womb, and naked shall I return; YHVH gave, and YHVH has taken away; blessed be the name of YHVH" (1: 21). Once again the Accuser appears before God and receives permission to test Job, this time causing his body to be covered with painful sores. When Job's wife asks why he does not curse God, Job rebukes her: "Shall we receive good at the hand of God and shall we not receive evil?" (2:10). Job's conduct thus vindicates God's original judgment. Also the prologue assures the reader that Job's sufferings are not deserved, an important consideration in view of Job's speeches of complaint later. The introductory prose section ends with the arrival of three friends, Eliphaz, Bildad, and Zophar, to comfort him. Appalled at his condition, for seven days they sit in silence. Job finally begins the poetic dialogue by "cursing the day of his birth." Had he died then, he would have been spared his present misery and bitterness of soul. He envies those who are at rest in the grave (chap. 3).

Eliphaz, the first of the friends to speak, responds that Job had often instructed and consoled others, but that now he himself was lacking in patience. Never do the upright perish from adversity; only the wicked resent the actions of divine providence. A mortal cannot be more righteous and pure than God; if Job would accept his suffering as a divine chastisement, he could look forward to future blessings. "Happy is the man whom God reproves" (chaps. 4–5). Job replies that he is impatient because his torments are truly unbearable; how could he have sinned to such an extent that God should treat him like a monster needing to be subdued? He prefers death to such agony (chaps. 6–7).

Bildad criticizes Job's implication that he, not God, is in the right: God cannot be unjust; Job's children probably died because they had sinned. It is an ancient, dependable teaching that retribution awaits the evildoer, and if Job is righteous, in the end God will reward him (chap. 8). Job retorts that the forces of nature indeed testify that God is all-powerful—so much so that he destroys innocent and guilty alike. More calmly, Job inquires, for what secret purpose could God have intended these sufferings? Why did God give him life in the first place? He requests a moment of relief before entering the blackness of death (chaps. 9–10).

Zophar disputes Job's protestations of innocence. Divine wisdom is beyond man's grasp. If Job will be penitent, God will grant him brighter days (chap. 11). Job agrees that the great catastrophes that befall rulers and nations imply that God is unlimited in might. But his friends speak falsely of God with their "proverbs of ashes" and "defenses of clay." Job calls God to judgment: "Behold, I have prepared my case; I know that I shall be vindicated." Why does God hide himself and treat Job like an enemy? Surely human life is short; death is certain; man's hope is cut off (chaps. 12–14). In the first cycle of speeches neither Job nor his friends question the principle that sufferings are a sign of God's displeasure. The friends try to convince Job of his guilt by praising God's goodness, justice, and knowledge. Job is certain that he has not sinned in proportion to his punishment. God, being God, knows that he is blameless; hence Job confronts God with the charge of injustice.

In the second cycle of speeches (chaps. 15–21), the friends dwell on the fate that befalls the sinner: the impermanence of the sinner's happiness and wealth, the woes and terrors decreed for him by God. Job is accused of insincerity, arrogance, even of impiety (15:4). He becomes conscious of his isolation not only from God but also from men; abandoned by acquaintances and family, he is an object of mockery and abhorrence. Faith in his innocence is the single support remaining to him (chap. 19). At times Job is defiant: He condemns, in its entirety, the justice of God's rule in the world; because the wicked are secure, they prosper and die in peace (chap. 21). Elsewhere, Job affirms that he has a Witness in heaven who will vindicate him (16:19) and that he knows that his Redeemer lives (19:25).

In the third cycle of speeches, Eliphaz describes the sins Job has probably committed: cruelty, avarice, abuse of power (22:6–20). Job should become reconciled with God, who will surely hear and save him. Bildad reiterates that all humans are imperfect in God's eyes (chap. 25). Beginning in chapter 27, Job summarizes his case (27:1–6, chaps. 29–31), and he swears a lengthy oath (chap. 31):

> If I have walked with falsehood . . . if my heart has been enticed by a woman and I have lain in wait at my neighbor's door . . . if I have rejected the cause of my manservant or my maidservant . . . if I have withheld anything that the poor desired or have caused the eyes of the widow to fail . . . if I have seen anyone perish for lack of clothing . . . if I have made gold my trust . . . if I have rejoiced because my wealth was great . . . if I have rejoiced at the ruin of him that hated me. . . .

If these charges were true, then his punishment would be just. Because they are not, God must tell him why he suffers.

The argument between Job and his friends has ended in deadlock. Suddenly Job is granted a theophany (a self-manifestation of God). The divine voice comes to him "out of the whirlwind." Job is told that he speaks "without knowledge" (38:1–2) and is asked, "Where were you when I laid the foundation of the earth?" (38:4). Where was Job when God fixed the limits of the sea? Does Job know how God causes the dawn to rise? Has Job walked in the recesses of the deep or seen the gates of death? Has he visited the storehouse of the snow, the hail, the winds? The voice from the whirlwind turns from the wonders of inanimate nature to those of the animal world. Can Job provide food for the lion and his young? Does he know where the mountain goats give birth? What of the wild ox, the ostrich, the hawk, the vulture: Do they owe their freedom, nourishment, and strength to Job? The climax comes in chapter 40: "Will the reprover enter suit against the Almighty? Let him who admonishes God give answer." If Job has the knowledge and power to govern the world, he should "tread down the wicked where they stand." Only then will God acknowledge that "Your own right hand can give you victory" (40:14). Job responds, "I am of small account, what shall I answer thee?" (40:4). "I know that thou canst do all things, and that no purpose of thine can be thwarted" (42:2). He repents "in dust and ashes" (42:6).

The prose epilogue of the book (42:7–17) rounds off the story, without retracting the essential point that Job was innocent of sin. God instructs him to offer a sacrifice in behalf of Eliphaz, Bildad, and Zophar, for "they have not spoken of me what is right, as my servant Job has" (42:7). YHVH restores his fortune, giving him "twice as much as he had before." Job is reunited with his family; he has ten children to replace those he has lost. After living a long life, "Job died, an old man, and full of days." But the author indicated clearly that Job's argument—the righteous can suffer unjustly and the wicked prosper—is not to be denied.

The book of Job is one of the most problematic portions of the Bible and has called forth a variety of interpretations. A major difficulty in understanding the meaning of the book is what insight leads Job to submit so humbly to God at the end. (It should be kept in mind that Job is not the author, but the principal character.) There are important and subtle differences between the various modern scholarly views, but they usually revolve around two aspects of God's speech from the whirlwind. First, that the divine voice does not answer Job's complaint directly, but instead describes the wonders of creation, pointing to natural occurrences that surpass the limits of human understanding. Second, that Job does indeed receive an answer.

One widely held view is that the climax of the book teaches that God's purposes and ways are mysterious and unfathomable, hidden from his creatures. Given the difference between infinite God and finite man, theodicy is not possible. (Theodicy is the theological justification of God's goodness in relation to his omnipotence.) Walther Eichrodt writes, "In the speeches of God in the book of Job, this God of men's construction [the traditional theodicy of the friends] is opposed to the incomprehensibly wonderful Creator God, who cannot be caught in a system of reasonable purposes, but escapes all human calculation."[9] Also taking note of the preoccupation with the beauties of nature in the speech from the whirlwind, but drawing a less extreme conclusion, is Robert Gordis, who suggests that the author implies that there is an analogy between the harmonious order of the natural world and the moral order. "What cannot be comprehended through reason must be embraced in love."[10] Several scholars have turned to an earlier chapter of the book for the key to the divine speeches (chap. 28, especially 28:28). A righteous man cannot know why he suffers and the wicked prosper, because men's wisdom is not God's. YHVH keeps his cosmic wisdom from human beings, giving them instead a "fear of God" as their own precious and proper concern.[11]

The second aspect of the speech of the voice from the whirlwind is that it takes the form of a theophany. Martin Buber writes, "But how about Job himself? He not only laments, but he charges that the 'cruel' God had 'removed his right' from him and thus that the judge of all the earth acts against justice. And he receives an answer from God. But what God says to him does not answer the charge; it does not even touch upon it. The true answer that Job receives is God's appearance only, only this, that distance turns into nearness, that 'his eye sees him,' that he knows Him again. Nothing is explained, nothing adjusted; wrong has not become right, nor cruelty kindness. Nothing has happened but that man again hears God's address."[12] According to this position, the answer to Job's dilemma is found in religious experience, not in theological speculation. Rather than a theoretical solution to Job's problem, there is an ineffable self-manifestation of deity to the individual in his particularity. In H. H. Rowley's interpretation, "All his past experience of God was as nothing compared with the experience he has now found. He therefore no longer cries out to God to be delivered from his suffering. He rests in God even in his pain."[13] If the theophany is made central, then the book of Job can be seen as a large-scale psalm of lament, like Psalm 73 described earlier, in which accusation and doubt are resolved by an experience of reaffirmed faith and trust.

A quite different interpretation has been proposed by Matitiahu Tsevat in his essay, "The Meaning of the Book of Job."[14] Tsevat suggests that the content of God's speech is intended to convey a picture of the universe deliberately at variance with that held previously by Job and the friends. In the friends' insistence that Job's suffering meant he had sinned, and in Job's demanding a specific reason why he, in his innocence, should suffer, both sides had presumed the reality of reward and punishment in the cosmos. Perhaps, however, the voice from the whirlwind is asserting that there is no such law of retribution and that nature is neutral to man's moral action. The sun rises on the righteous and sinner alike (28:13, 15). Rain falls on the desert, whereas it could have been directed only to the cultivated land where it is needed by men (38:26–27). Wild animals do not observe the tenets of human morality (38:15–16). Accordingly, God's speech can be construed to imply that material prosperity and misfortune do not constitute divine recompense or chastisement. Tsevat proposes that only the concept of a cosmic order that does not operate according to a built-in principle of moral retribution makes possible the selfless piety that was the first issue posed by the book of Job. "It would be a grave error to interpret [the book's] denial of divine retribution as constituting a legitimate excuse for man from his obligations to establish justice on earth. Justice is not woven into the stuff of the universe nor is God occupied with its administration, but it is an ideal to be realized by society."[15] The author of Job may be denying one fundamental assumption of the narrative and prophetic books of the Bible, but his denial is consistent with another, even more fundamental assumption: that it is up to man to carry out God's commandments and that this primary task must be done in society and actualized in the course of history. A principle of automatic reward and punishment would, in fact, be a form of coercion, leaving no special realm in which man could exercise his moral freedom by doing the good from purely disinterested motives.[16]

Most interpreters agree that the ultimate theme of the book is the nature of the righteous man's faith in God. As Leon Roth states, "The book of Job turns on the question of the nature of religion: Can man serve God for nought? . . . When Job says, 'Though he slay me, yet will I trust in Him' (13:15), he vindicates both himself and God."[17] The book reaffirms Job's trust in God—and God's trust in Job. In teaching that piety must be unselfish and that the righteous sufferer is assured not of tangible reward but of fellowship with God, biblical thought about justice, retribution, and providence reaches a climax—and a limit. One alternative that the author of Job did not consider was that the sufferings of the innocent might be compensated in a future life. As we shall see later, the problem of theodicy is resolved through just this means in postbiblical Judaism.

The Literary Revival in Judea During the Later Persian and Early Hellenistic Eras; The Song of Songs

As with many books of the Bible, dating the *Ketuvim* presents difficulties that may never be fully resolved. It is generally held that many of the psalms and the shorter maxims of Proverbs are pre-exilic, but that sections of both were composed after the return to Zion when the ma-

Head of Zeus Ammon, an example of the fusion of Hellenistic and Egyptian religious traditions in the late Ptolemaic or
early Roman period. (Courtesy
of the Brooklyn Museum.)

terial was selected and the books compiled. The date of Job, because of
its uniqueness in Israelite literature, is even more uncertain: Although
there are scholars who hold to a pre-exilic or exilic provenance, the
majority locate Job in the fifth or fourth centuries BCE.[18]

In the period after Ezra and Nehemiah a literary renaissance took place
in Judea. Some historians feel that this new age shows the stimulus of
Hellenistic culture and the resulting emergence of a sophisticated and
cosmopolitan Judean upper class in the third century BCE. (Attempts to
prove the influence of Greek drama on Job have generally not been
accepted.) A biblical work compiled either late in the Persian period or
under the impact of Hellenism (probably the former) is the Song of
Songs, a collection of about two dozen love poems of varying lengths.
As with Psalms and Proverbs, an ancient stratum underlies the Song of
Songs, but there are passages containing a few Persian and Greek loan
words. Although the Song of Songs (the superlative or finest of songs)
was included in the biblical canon because it lent itself to an allegorical
interpretation as the love bond between Israel and God, on a literal and

secular level these eight chapters of verse celebrate the beauty of youth, erotic yearning, and the pleasures of springtime; their courtly or pastoral figures of speech are sensual, passionate, and elegant. A famous lyric on love's longing for fulfillment is found in chapter 8:

> Set me as a seal upon your heart,
>   as a seal upon your arm;
> for love is strong as death,
>   jealousy is cruel as the grave.
> Its flashes are flashes of fire,
>   a most vehement flame.
> Many waters cannot quench love,
>   neither can floods drown it.
> If a man offered for love
>   all the wealth of his house,
>   it would be utterly scorned. [8:6–7.]

A more certain setting in Hellenistic Judea can be attributed to the wisdom books of Ecclesiastes and Ben Sira and the second half of the book of Daniel, all of which were written in the third and early second centuries BCE. These three books, together with several tales dating either from the Persian or Hellenistic periods, will complete our discussion of the late development of biblical literature and thought.

Ecclesiastes

Even further removed than Job from the certain and secure faith of Proverbs is the book of Ecclesiastes (*Koheleth* in Hebrew), written by a sage who presents himself in the literary guise of "the son of David, king in Jerusalem."[19] (Posing as Solomon, particularly honored by the wisdom literature, is especially appropriate because the author of Ecclesiastes claims to have exhausted all the resources of wisdom and luxury in his quest for the meaning of life.) In form the book stands between Proverbs and a philosophical treatise: some continuous sections, many short paragraphs, and a few groups of isolated aphorisms. In the wisdom tradition, the author of Ecclesiastes is concerned not with the nation but with the individual, and he speaks in general terms about the experience of man as such, not of the Jew. Ecclesiastes, however, stands in the greatest contrast to the impersonal and conventional tone of the book of Proverbs. He observes the world with a cool, almost cynical detachment and a skepticism verging on despair and fatalism. Somber, melancholy, and resigned, this work may perhaps be a symptom of a profound religious crisis affecting a circle of upper-class Jerusalemites in the mid-third century BCE, as old forms of religiosity lost their hold and new forces and ideas were in the early stages of appearance.

The opening theme of Ecclesiastes, frequently reiterated, is the emptiness of human effort. Human toil is incommensurate with its gain: "All is vanity." (Vanity is the usual rendering of the Hebrew *hevel*, more narrowly, breath, steam, vapor, and, by extension, anything insubstantial and ephemeral.) The endless chain of natural phenomena—the rising and setting of the sun, the constant circuit of the winds, the flow of water from rivers to never-filled sea and back again—produce in the author not awe and wonder, but weariness and futility. The natural world is indeed permanent, but human existence moves in a perpetual circle where, paradoxically, there is nothing new and yet no remembrance (1:2–11). A season and a time exists for every extreme: birth and death, breaking down and building up, weeping and laughter, silence and speaking, love and hate, killing and healing (3:1–9). Where can the individual find permanent value? Not in wisdom, as Proverbs 1–9 had affirmed. The author, himself a sage, does not entirely deny its usefulness: "Wisdom is better than might" (9:16–18), and it is certainly better than folly. But increased knowledge frequently means increased pain (1:18). Baffled by the stream of events, man is not the master of his destiny. At bottom, wisdom is "vanity and a striving after wind" (1:14, 1:17). Physical pleasure is equally unsatisfying, transient, and empty; riches are a source of anxiety and who knows whether one's heir will be a wise man or a fool? (2:18–19). Besides, death obliterates everything. "As he came from his mother's womb he shall go again, naked as he came, and shall take nothing of his toil, which he may carry away in his hand" (5:15 [Heb. 5:14]). Ecclesiastes offers only one consolation: that God may give the individual a few moments of happiness, which a wise and temperate man should seize while he may. "Behold, what I have seen to be good and fitting is to eat and drink and find enjoyment in all the toil with which one toils under the sun the few days of his life which God have given him, for this is his lot" (5:18 [Heb. 5:17], also see 2:24–25, 8:15, 9:7). But when, or even whether, one is awarded these occasions is unpredictable, uncertain, and chance.

Ecclesiastes does not deny God's power and majesty, but his is a distant deity, far removed from daily life: "God is in heaven and you are on earth" (5:2 [Heb. 5:1]). God's actions are unfathomable; the preordained pattern of the universe is incomprehensible and cannot be changed. "I know that whatever God does endures forever; nothing can be added to it, nor anything taken from it; God has made it so, in order that men should fear before him" (3:14; see also 7:14, 7:24, 8:16–17). Impervious to rational comprehension, human destiny is full of unexplainable reversals.

Again I saw under the sun the race is not to the swift, nor the battle to the strong, nor bread to the wise, nor riches to the intelligent, nor favor to the men of skill; but time and chance happen to them all. For man does not know his time. Like fish which are taken in an evil net and like birds which are caught in a snare, so the sons of men are snared at an evil time, when it suddenly falls upon them. [9:11–12.]

Like Job, Ecclesiastes asserts that divine providence is not evident in life. Evil men frequently live long and prosper; the righteous perish prematurely (7:15, 8:10, 8:14). Sensitive to the prevalence of injustice, Ecclesiastes draws his most bitter conclusion:

Again I saw all the oppressions that are practiced under the sun. Behold, the tears of the oppressed, and they had no one to comfort them. . . . I thought the dead who are already dead more fortunate than the living who are still alive; but better than both is he who had not yet been, and has not seen the evil deeds that are done under the sun." [4:1–3, also 3:16, 5:8 (Heb. 5:7).]

Whereas Job protested the absence of retributive justice in the world, Ecclesiastes counsels resignation. In view of the hazards of living in an evil age, he calmly advises: "Be not righteous overmuch, and do not make yourself over-wise; why should you destroy yourself? Be not wicked overmuch, neither be a fool; why should you die before your time?" (7:16–17).

Shrewd, frank, even bold in his own way, Ecclesiastes is devoid of such fundamental biblical attitudes as the feeling of moral outrage, the experience of revelation, the call for repentance, an unquestioned or a rediscovered trust in God. The lack of absolute value in human existence could be resolved by the conception of immortality, a personal encounter with the divine in a realm beyond death. Although Ecclesiastes seems aware of this idea (3:17), it is rejected.

For the fate of the sons of men and the fate of beasts is the same; as one dies, so dies the other. They all have the same breath, and man has no advantage over the beasts; for all is vanity. All go to one place; all are from the dust, and all turn to dust again. Who knows whether the spirit of man goes upward and the spirit of the beast goes down to the earth? [3:19–21.]

Perhaps Ecclesiastes' insistence that one not harbor illusions about reality blocked his adhering to the notion of eternal life, most likely beginning to be accepted by the Jewish masses in his time. Only the last few sentences of the book, an epilogue most scholars believe was added by another hand, allude to contact with God beyond the limits of earthly existence. After commending Ecclesiastes' efforts to write "words of truth," the editor softens the despairing impact of the book: "The end of the matter; all has been heard. Fear God, and keep his commandments, for this is the whole duty of man. For God will bring every deed into judgment, with every secret thing, whether good or evil" (12:13–14).

Ecclesiastes has been called the strangest book to be included in the Bible, for the author's skeptical and pessimistic fatalism is without parallel among biblical writers. What environment and which influences could have contributed to such an attitude? Scholars have pointed to similar moods in the literature of the ancient Near East, such as the acceptance of human limitations and personal resignation in the face of death at the end of the Gilgamesh Epic. Almost all interpreters agree that there is some Greek influence on Ecclesiastes—for example, in the cyclicality of existence—though not that of any specific philosophical school. Elias Bickerman suggests that the author was a Jerusalemite affected by the intellectual atmosphere of third-century Hellenism, a man who lost his childhood faith but could not forge a positive philosophical position of his own. Living in a period of cosmopolitan, secular enlightenment, but also a time when many pagans worshiped the god Luck (Fortuna, Tyche), Ecclesiastes attacked the conventional religious morality of his own tradition without being able to offer a cogent alternative. Ecclesiastes was a "Job who failed in the test." Martin Hengel also views Ecclesiastes as a man of the third-century enlightenment who, with great independence of mind and originality, criticized the well-to-do Hellenistic middle-class ideal and style of life but could no longer make sense of traditional wisdom and piety. Another scholarly view, that of Georg Fohrer, sees Ecclesiastes as a deliberate attack on the theology of wisdom instruction and on the sages' presumption to formulate a doctrine of retribution; for all their differences, Job and Ecclesiastes addressed themselves to the same question.

Why is Ecclesiastes in the Bible? There was considerable controversy over including it until the end of the first century CE. Robert Gordis feels the supposed Solomonic authorship tipped the scale but that the book exerted an intrinsic fascination; moveover, the inclusion of some conventional pieties, such as in the epilogue, also made Ecclesiastes more palatable. R. B. Y. Scott suggests that Ecclesiastes was accepted in stages, first as part of the wisdom movement, which grew in importance after the canonization of the Pentateuch, and later when these wisdom works were brought together in the *Ketuvim* and the *Ketuvim* were absorbed into the Scriptures.

A final aspect should be noted. The very negativity of Ecclesiastes' message had a positive significance, perhaps intentional, perhaps not. By showing that the usual pursuits of men—fame, wisdom, riches—are vain and empty, Ecclesiastes enhanced the value of contemplating heavenly matters. Most likely that was the message that reached later generations.[20]

Ben Sira

A wisdom book in the style of Proverbs written slightly later than Ecclesiastes and not included in the Bible is Ben Sira (sometimes entitled Sirach or Ecclesiasticus).[21] The author, Jeshua (Joshua) ben Sira, was a historical personage who lived in Jerusalem at the beginning of the second century BCE (see 50:27), where he was probably a teacher of upper-class youth. Like Proverbs, his book contains exhortations on such virtues as humility, honesty, moderation, prudence, charity, patience. Various other aspects of the life of the cultured individual are also touched on, such as consulting physicians (38:1–15), training servants (33:24–31), appreciating music at banquets (32:1–6).

Unlike Ecclesiastes, Ben Sira maintains faith in man's free will and in

Alabaster head of Alexander the Great, from second-century BCE Egypt. (Courtesy of the Brooklyn Museum, Charles Edwin Wilbour Fund.)

God's mercy and justice. But there are signs of a deliberate effort to integrate the wisdom tradition with the traditions of the Pentateuch, history books, and prophets. The last section contains several odes in praise of the spiritual heroes of Israel's past (chaps. 44–49), culminating in a description of the holy splendor of the High Priest as he stands in his sacred vestments at the Temple altar in Ben Sira's day (chap. 50). Chapter 36 contains a prayer in which the author expresses the hope that pagans will learn that there is no God but Israel's. Especially important is a change in the meaning of wisdom evident in the book. In chap. 24, wisdom, personified as a woman, is defined as Israel's covenantal law, the law that Moses transmitted to be the people's heritage. Ben Sira viewed wisdom not only as "fear of God" but as a synonym for *Torah;* the Creator of the universe decreed that wisdom make its home in the tents of Israel (verse 8).

Equating wisdom with Torah will prove to be a consequential development in Jewish thought. Reason and revelation, as they are later called, become fused. Although, on the one hand, wisdom becomes locked to the written text of Scripture as it never was in ancient Israel, on the other hand, the text is freed from the limitations of a literal reading. If the Torah book is wisdom, then Torah can be subjected to constant and ever-expanding interpretation, for wisdom is a process of thinking and reflection, as well as a received body of formulated truths. In late biblical Judaism the sage's intellect and experience are beginning to be applied to past revelations in the canonized Scriptures as a source of present guidance.

Indicative of the coming together of cosmopolitan wisdom and the national tradition of ancient Israel is the opening of the book of Psalms, where the wise man is he who takes joy in Torah:

> *Blessed is the man*
> *   who walks not in the counsel of the wicked,*
> *nor sits in the seat of scoffers;*
> *   but his delight is in the Torah of YHVH*
> *   and on his Torah he meditates day and night.*
> *He is like a tree*
> *   planted by streams of water,*
> *that yields its fruit in its season,*
> *   and its leaf does not wither.*
> *In all that he does, he prospers. [1:1–3.]*

The Tales of Jonah, Esther, and Daniel

The literary revival of late Persian and early Hellenistic times also produced a reinvigoration of the biblical art of storytelling. Of the tales about Jewish heroes circulating in the last centuries BCE, several with diverse religious messages were selected for inclusion in the biblical canon.[22] The stories to be discussed here are, like modern historical novels, placed in settings earlier than the lives of their authors and written to entertain as well as instruct. Along with the serious purposes the authors had in mind, there are lighter tones, satirical and humorous, which poke fun at pagan and Jewish pomposity.

The book of Jonah, probably written in the late fifth or in the fourth century BCE, is a tale of a man commanded by God to go to Nineveh and denounce its violence and wickedness.[23] (Nineveh was the capital of the Assyrian empire that had destroyed the northern kingdom in 722.) Instead, Jonah boards a ship in the opposite direction. God does not let him escape. Jonah is brought back to shore in the belly of "a great fish" and makes his way to that city where he cries, "Yet forty days and Nineveh shall be overthrown!" (3:4—the entire content of his message). But amazingly the people of Nineveh understand; by decree of king and nobles, the population and animals of the city pray to God, for, "Who knows, God may yet repent and turn from his fierce anger, so that we perish not?" When the divine punishment is indeed revoked, Jonah is displeased. "I pray thee, YHVH, is not this what I said when I was yet in my country? That is why I made haste to flee to Tarshish; for I knew that thou art a gracious God and merciful, slow to anger, and abounding in steadfast love, and repentest of evil" (4:1–2, compare Ex. 34:6). The point of the tale is the compassionate and forgiving nature of God, who wishes men to change so that his just decree of destruction may be averted, precisely the attitude of classical prophecy at its height (see Jer. 18:7–8).

Notable in Jonah is the author's open-minded and sympathetic picture of the pagans whom he describes, and their respect for YHVH, the God of heaven. When the sailors discover, by casting lots, that Jonah's presence on board is the reason why God has sent a mighty sea storm, they nevertheless "rowed hard to bring the ship back to land" before they finally threw Jonah overboard to save themselves, and they then prayed to YHVH and revered him (see 1:13–16). The repentance of the people of Nineveh is exemplary. The antihero is the blunt and stubborn Jonah, who sulks in the hot sun east of the city. To teach him the message God causes a plant to grow so as to provide shade, and then sends a worm to kill it. Quite faint, Jonah announces that it is better for him to die than live; but YHVH responds, "You pity the plant, for which you did not labor, nor did you make it grow, which came into being in a night, and perished in a night. Should I not pity Nineveh, that great city, in which there are more than a hundred and twenty thousand persons who do not know their right hand from their left, and also much cattle?"

The book of Esther explains the origins of festival of Purim, commemorating Jewish salvation from a threat of persecution and destruction.

Mosaic from Susa showing Hellenistic influence: the triumph of Bacchus.

The tale is set in the Persian court of Ahasuerus, "the Ahasuerus who reigned from India to Ethiopia over one hundred and twenty-seven provinces." An odd set of circumstances leads the king to marry Esther, niece of Mordecai, a Judean exile, although Esther hides her Jewishness from her royal husband. The villain is Haman, chief courtier of the realm, who plots to kill the Jews because Mordecai will not do him obeisance. A fortunate combination of Esther's cleverness and tact, together with luck, foils Haman. He is hanged on the very gallows that he had built for Mordecai; the day he chose by the casting of lots (*purim*, "dice") for the slaughter of Jews becomes the day on which they successfully defend themselves, with royal permission, against attackers throughout the empire. At the end of the book, Mordecai is, elevated to the rank of king's favorite, in place of Haman.

The author, who may have lived in the Hellenistic period, carefully sets the stage for the various twists and turns that complicate the plot of the story, and then bring it to a satisfactory conclusion. Esther becomes queen because Ahasuerus's wife refused to appear before his guests at a state banquet, causing him to divorce her. Because Ahasuerus had insomnia one fateful night and had read to him the "book of memorable deeds," he discovers that Mordecai had never been suitably rewarded for preventing the king's assassination; when Haman is asked "What shall be done to the man whom the king delights to honor?" he thinks "Whom would the king delight to honor more than me?" and advises royal honors—which Haman is forced to provide to Mordecai (chap. 6). When Esther finally dares broach the subject of the impending demise of her people at a private banquet for the king and Haman, the "king rose from the feast in wrath and went into the palace garden; but Haman stayed to beg his life from Queen Esther, for he saw that evil was determined against him by the king. And the king returned from the palace garden to the place where they were drinking wine, as Haman was falling on the couch where Esther was; and the king said, 'Will he even assault the queen in my presence, in my own house?'" (7:7–8). Chance and coincidence seem to rule, but providential factors underlie the apparent happenstance. After the decree against them becomes known, the Jews mourn and fast (4:1–3), and Mordecai states to Esther, "If you keep silent at such a time as this, relief and deliverance will rise for the Jews from another quarter" (4:14), that is, God will make other arrangements. The outcome of the tale is that the seemingly absurd events that led to Esther's marriage to Ahasuerus have placed in the midst of the court the very person who can defend the Jewish people at a time of great danger.[24]

Inasmuch as Haman was supposedly able to recruit widespread support for his projected slaughter of the Jews, the book of Esther indicates the tensions and violence that were to imperil Jewish existence in the dispersion: "Then Haman said to King Ahasuerus, 'There is a certain people scattered abroad and dispersed among the peoples in all the provinces of your kingdom; their laws are different from those of every other people, and they do not keep the king's laws, so that it is not for the king's profit to tolerate them'" (3:8). But Esther also contains a hint of the spread of the Jewish way of life to others (8:17), reflecting new possibilities opening up for Judaism in this international setting.

The first six chapters of the book of Daniel contain a series of tales set during the Babylonian exile in the courts of the sixth-century BCE rulers Nebuchadnezzar, Balshazzar, and Darius. (It is most likely that these stories were written in the early Hellenistic period.) Daniel is a Jewish sage selected for training in the language and wisdom of the Chaldeans, together with his friends Hananiah, Mishael, and Azariah. Despite their roles as advisers to gentile rulers and despite various plots hatched against them by pagan courtiers, the four young men remain faithful to their religion. God rescues them from their ordeals and the pagan kings come to acknowledge the power and truth of the God of heaven.

In chapter 1, the four men avoid defilement by gentile food and wine, thriving on a diet of vegetables and water. In chapter 3, when Hananiah, Mishael, and Azariah (called by their Babylonian names, Shadrach, Meshach, and Abednego) refuse to worship a giant idol erected by Nebuchadnezzar, they are thrown into a burning fiery furnace. Later, when the door of the furnace is opened, the "hair of their heads was not singed, their mantles were not harmed, and no smell of fire had come upon them" (3:27). In chapter 6, jealous courtiers conspire against Daniel ("We shall not find any ground for complaint against this Daniel unless we find it in connection with the law of his God"), by persuading the king to issue an edict that for thirty days no petition is to be offered to anyone else but Darius. Daniel continues to pray to his God at the open windows of his house facing Jerusalem. Thrown into a den of lions, Daniel emerges untouched, but the lions gobble up Daniel's enemies who are tossed in by order of the king.

Like Esther, Daniel satirizes the pompous ceremonies of the pagan court.

> King Nebuchadnezzar made an image of gold, whose height was sixty cubits and its breadth six cubits. He set it up on the plain of Dura, in the province of Babylon. Then King Nebuchadnezzar sent to assemble the satraps, the prefects, and the governors, the counselors, the treasurers, the justices, the magistrates, and all the officials of the provinces to come to the dedication of the image which King Nebuchadnezzar had set up. . . . And the herald proclaimed aloud, "You are commanded, O peoples, nations, and languages, that when you hear the sound of the horn, pipe, lyre, trigon, harp, bagpipe, and every kind of music, you are to fall down and worship the golden image that King Nebuchadnezzar has set up; and whoever does not fall down and worship shall immediately be cast into a burning fiery furnace. Therefore, as soon as all the peoples heard the sound of the horn, pipe, lyre, trigon, harp, bagpipe, and every kind of music, all the peoples, nations, and languages fell down and worshiped the golden image which King Nebuchadnezzar had set up. [3:1–7.]

But the wisdom of the Jewish sages and their miraculous salvation lead the gentile kings to praise the Jewish God, the God of heaven whose "kingdom is an everlasting kingdom" (4:34–37; also see 2:47, 3:28–29, 6:25–27). In one of the stories, Daniel advises his monarch in the spirit of classical prophecy, "Therefore, O King, let my counsel be acceptable to you; break off your sins by practicing righteousness and your iniquities by showing mercy to the oppressed, that there may perhaps be a lengthening of your tranquility" (4:27).

Chapters 2, 4, and 5 of Daniel, in which the kings receive divinely inspired dreams and visions that only the Jewish sages can interpret, intimate a new kind of Jewish oracular literature: apocalyptic revelations of the rise and fall of great empires. In chapter 5, Belshazzar is seated with his lords at a great feast and commands that the vessels of gold and silver that Nebuchadnezzar had taken from the Jerusalem Temple be brought for them to drink from. On the wall before him the fingers of a man's hand appear, writing mysterious words that only Daniel can understand: "MENE MENE, TEKEL UPHARSIN." Daniel explains, "MENE, God has numbered the days of your kingdom and brought it to an end; TEKEL, you have been weighed in the balances and found wanting; PERES, your kingdom is divided and given to the Medes and Persians" (5:25–28). Events in Judean history in the first four decades of the second century BCE were to give a sharp impetus to this kind of visionary writing.

First Confrontations with Hellenism

The intersection of Jewish and G_eek civilizations was to be of momentous importance to the history of Western religion, theology, and philosophy through the Middle Ages and beyond. The first traces of Greek influence can already be detected in the later literature of the Bible, for Ecclesiastes had some general acquaintance, at least, with Greek ideas. The spread of Hellenism after Alexander's time was facilitated by the migration of tens of thousands of Greeks and Macedonians into the conquered areas. Greek culture flourished from Italy and Sicily to Bactria in central Asia. The metropolis of Alexandria in Egypt and the Hellenistic cities in Asia Minor, the Aegean, and elsewhere soon eclipsed Athens and the older centers of classical Greek culture. The Seleucid kings were particularly assiduous in encouraging the establishment of new cities and the conversion of old urban centers into cities with typical

A gold coin of Alexander the Great, deified. (Courtesy of the Seattle Art Museum.)

Greek institutions, such as an assembly of citizens, elected magistrates, educational-athletic centers (the *gymnasium*), and civic cults honoring Olympian gods and local deities. These Hellenistic cities were a key force in spreading the Greek language, dress, material culture, and modes of thought to the upper and middle classes of the Near East, so that Greek soon replaced Aramaic as the international language of commerce and diplomacy. The cultural style of the entire area was thus drastically transformed, affecting a significant segment of the inhabitants of Jerusalem, as well.

The Judean Hellenophiles and the Maccabean Revolt

In 198 BCE, after two decades of constant fighting, Judea pased into the control of the Seleucid king Antiochus III (ruled 223–187). Just as he was on the verge of establishing the Seleucids as the dominant power in the Near East, the Romans defeated him at Magnesia in Asia Minor (190 BCE), leading to the loss of much Seleucid territory, but not Judea. The change from Ptolemaic to Seleucid rule did not affect political conditions in Jerusalem during the lifetimes of Antiochus III and his son Seleucus IV. However, when Antiochus III's second son Antiochus IV Epiphanes ("god manifest") occupied the throne in 175, arrangements in Judea were soon altered. The High Priest Onias III was deposed and replaced by his brother Jason, who received permission from the Seleucid king to introduce Greek institutions into Jerusalem, such as a *gymnasium* for the training of future citizens of the city in the Hellenistic manner.

About three years after Jason's appointment, a second group of Jerusalem Hellenophiles prevailed on Antiochus to give the High Priesthood to a certain Meneleus; unrest and protests broke out, but were suppressed. Between 171 and 169 Antiochus IV almost succeeded in conquering Egypt until Roman pressure forced him to withdraw. During his Egyptian campaign a rumor reached Jerusalem that he had died; the former High Priest Jason attempted to regain control of the city with an armed force. Antiochus rushed soldiers to Jerusalem in support of Meneleus, but the turmoil continued. Thinking that a rebellion had broken out, Antiochus ordered the abolition of Jewish law in Judea. A new citadel was built in Jerusalem in which to station a pagan garrison, and an altar and statue of the Olympian Zeus was set up in the Temple. In December 167 BCE, sacrifices were commenced according to the new ritual. Seleucid agents and Jewish Hellenizers went into the countryside to force the people to demonstrate their loyalty to the regime by eating pork, refraining from circumcision and the Sabbath, and turning over their Torah scrolls for destruction.

The motives of Antiochus (quite unlike the usual tolerant attitude of pagan rulers) and those of the Jewish Hellenizers who supported the per-

Seleucid coin depicting Antiochus IV Epiphanes. (Courtesy of the American Numismatic Society.)

secutions (some of whom were priests) have been a matter of much scholarly dispute.[25] There is no indication that Antiochus prohibited the Jewish religion throughout his realm; he was probably trying to strengthen his hold on a strategic border province by backing an element of the Judean population that had showed itself willing to integrate Judea more closely into the Seleucid kingdom. He also stood to gain treasures and needed monies confiscated from the Temple. (Near Eastern sanctuaries, because of their holiness, often served as depositories for the wealth of those who worshiped there and contained many valuable gifts of thanksgiving.) In other circumstances, some Jews took to a Hellenic style of life without becoming pagan; it would seem that various competing Jewish groups wanted to transform Jerusalem into a typical Greek city (2 Macc. 4:9), where they would have greater power locally and closer contact with similar classes in other Hellenistic cities. In any event, all Judean Jews were faced with the choice of whether or not to collaborate. Some complied, but a great national-religious upsurge catalyzed. Chapters 6 and 7 of 2 Maccabees relate stories of Jews tortured by the government for refusing to eat pork and sacrifice to the king's god. The persecutions of the early 160s produced the first martyrs in history: men who willingly accepted death rather than violate the injunctions of their religion. (The Greek root of *martyr* means "to bear witness.")

The first resistors refused to fight on the Sabbath and were slaughtered (1 Macc. 2:29–38); the next stage of Jewish opposition was the emergence of a guerilla army under Mattathias, a priest from the town of Modein, which fought defensively on the Sabbath as well as aggressively on the weekdays (1 Macc. 2:41). When Mattathias died, the leadership of the armed revolt was taken over by his son, Judah the Maccabee (possibly meaning Judah the Hammer). After several victories over Seleucid troops and having cut off the main road from the seacoast to Jerusalem, the Maccabean fighters occupied the Temple Mount in 164 BCE. In December of that year the Temple was purified and reconsecrated. An eight-day festival (Hanukkah, rededication) was instituted. Soon afterward, the Seleucid government gave up the policy of religious repression, but could not put down the Maccabean revolt, as we shall see in the next chapter.[26]

Daniel 7–12 and the Rise of Apocalypticism

The tense atmosphere and the shock during the three years when the Temple was a pagan shrine and Judaism banned, is reflected in the final six chapters of the book of Daniel. (The last of the visions can be dated to 165 or early 164 BCE, just before the Temple was cleansed; in 11:40–45 the author predicts that Antiochus's final defeat would take place in the land of Israel, whereas he actually died in the spring of 163 fighting on the eastern frontier of the Seleucid realm.) The religiosity that lay behind these chapters of Daniel was part of a reaction against the overt Hellenization of the previous decades and the current persecutions, but it was a form of thought which was, nevertheless, considerably affected by Hellenistic civilization.[27]

The second half of Daniel builds on two themes in the first half: that the Jew must be faithful to God in the midst of temptation and trial, and that God defends loyal servants ready to die rather than violate the commandments. In the final six chapters the sage (or group of sages whose writings have been brought together by an editor, according to some scholars) relays the contents of visions that he has experienced in connection with the desecration of the Temple in 167 and the erection of the "abomination of desolation" (Antiochus's pagan altar). Daniel 7–12 marks the first appearance in Judaism of a tendency known as apocalypse (from the Greek *apocalyptein*, to uncover or disclose), which purports to disclose God's secret plan for all of history.

Chapter 7 relates a dream in which Daniel sees four great beasts, the last of which has ten horns. Between the eyes of the ten-horned animal sprouts an eleventh horn with "eyes like a man and a mouth speaking great things" (7:8). Daniel witnesses the divine tribunal in heaven sitting in judgment. There presides "One that was Ancient of Days . . . His raiment was white as snow, and the hair of His head like pure wool; His throne was fiery flames, its wheels were burning fire" (7:9). An angel explains to Daniel that the beasts in his dream symbolize the four great empires of history, the horns being various kings. (The empires to which Daniel alludes are the Babylonian, Median, Persian, and Hellenistic.)

When judgment falls on the last of the pagan rulers (Antiochus IV), dominion over the earth will be given to "the people of the saints of the Most High" (the Jews). The climax of history is to be a fifth empire: an everlasting kingdom of the people of the one God.

Chapter 8 is a second apocalyptic vision: First there appears a powerful ram (the Median-Persian empire), followed by a he-goat (Alexander the Great) who destroys the ram and sprouts horns representing various Hellenistic kings. After the last of these rulers does terrible things (another reference to Antiochus IV), he will be broken "not by human hand" (8:25). Chapter 9 contains a long prayer in which Daniel pleads for God's mercy towards his sinful people and requests an explanation for Jeremiah's prophecy that seventy years must pass before the end of the desolation of Jerusalem (Jer: 25:11 and 29:10). In reply, the angel Gabriel explains that seventy weeks of years (seventy times seven, or 490 years) must pass to atone for Israel's iniquities, the last of these "weeks" being a time of appalling crisis until the decreed end comes up on the king who has desolated Jerusalem (Antiochus IV).

In the longest and most detailed apocalyptic vision (chaps. 10–12), Daniel falls into a trance on the banks of the Tigris. A celestial being summarizes for him the wars and struggles for power that will take place in the future. Even though there will occur "a time of trouble such as never has been since there was a nation until that time," Daniel's people, with the help of the angel Michael, will be delivered. The sage is promised that Jewish martyrs dying during these final tribulations will awaken to eternal life (12:2–3). Daniel's prophecies are to be "shut up and sealed until the time of the end . . . but those who are wise shall understand" (12:9–10).

The apocalyptic literature, an early instance of which has just been described, can be considered a renewal and continuation of the prophetic tradition. Like prophecy, apocalypse is a revelation of God's warning of judgment and promise of salvation. But apocalypse differs in several crucial respects from classical prophecy and is a transformation in the form and content of revelatory experience in ancient Judaism.

First, the classical prophets proclaimed their messages in public; the apocalyptists made theirs available privately through writings attributed to biblical heroes of the distant past. (As we have seen, the author of Daniel projects his visions back into the time of the Babylonian exile.) Although other biblical books used this pseudonymous device, the classical prophets notably did not conceal their identity behind pen names. Perhaps the priestly establishment did not encourage the spontaneous and unpredictable issuance of divine pronouncements; already postexilic prophecy after Haggai and Zechariah was anonymous, though not pseudonymous. (It may be significant that apocalypse appeared with the weakening of the Aaronide hierocracy during the crisis of the 170s and

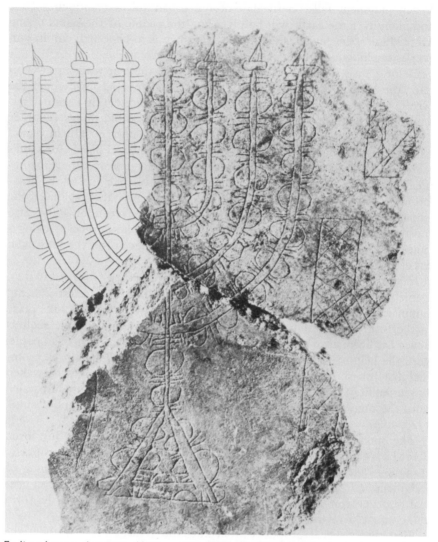

Earliest known depiction (first century BCE) of the menorah, incised on a plaster wall opposite the Jerusalem Temple. (Religious News Service photo.)

160s.) Furthermore, now that Judaism had a fixed body of authoritative ancient texts, the apocalyptic visionaries may have found it more effective to present their personal revelations in the form of old writings kept secret until a time of desperate need.

A second, even more crucial difference between classical prophecy and apocalypse is their respective attitudes to history. The classical prophets addressed their own age directly, calling for immediate political and ethical choices that could affect the impending divine judgment. For them, the future remained open, in that God's decision could be changed if man repented. But the apocalyptist views history as a closed and unified process, seeing his own age as the last link in a long chain of momentous events unfolding in preordained sequence. The visions of Daniel imply a tripartite division of world history. First, there was the period up to the Babylonian exile, which saw the formation of Israel, its settlement in Canaan, and the destruction of its kingdoms and Temple. The second period, slightly overlapping the first, was the time of the four world empires, the rise and fall of which Daniel foretells. (These apocalyptic prophecies are technically *vaticinia ex eventu*, "predictions after the event," since the true author lived after rather than before the historical facts to which he alludes.) The third period, slightly overlapping the second, is eschatological and ultimate: the climax of history. Unlike the eschatological promises of classical prophecy that envisioned an End of Days in the distant future, the apocalyptist believes that the goal is at hand: almost here is the end of pagan domination, the complete salvation of Israel, the final manifestation of God's kingdom on earth. The apocalyptic visionary offers a much broader panorama of the rise and fall of vast empires but his interest in the mundane and everyday is much less than prophecy's. His eye is focused on another world.

A third difference between classical prophecy and apocalyptic involves their closeness to the heavenly realm. The classical prophets (except for Ezekiel) were reticent in their reports of what they saw during their trances; their main task was to communicate the oral command they had been told to deliver, rather than to present a visual description of the divine court. The apocalyptist, however, describes his visits to the heavens in detail, mentioning the angels by name and reporting on the palaces, throne room, and celestial courtiers surrounding the divine King. The mysterious symbolism and the emphasis on eschatology indicate a certain tie with late postexilic prophecy, but apocalyptic thought is indebted, as much if not more, to the wisdom tradition of the Hellenistic age. (It should be noted that "Daniel" is a sage, not a prophet, just as the book is included in the *Ketuvim*, not the *Nevi'im*.)

The most important point of contact between apocalypse and wisdom is the idea of a predetermined cosmic order. It was the concept of a cyclical pattern inaccesible to human understanding that led to Ecclesiastes's musings on the vanity of human effort. Apocalypse translates this order into God's providential plan for history. In Daniel, the perplexing changes and painful crises of historical time are not the work of chance and contingency; they have been decreed by God from the very beginning. In this way recovering the Bible's repudiation of Fate, Daniel passes through despair to regained hope: God is about to shatter the power of the last pagan tyrant; "the people of the saints of the Most High" will soon be delivered. At last God will explicitly assume that sovereignty which prophets and psalmists proclaimed.

The apocalyptist's preoccupation with ultimates did not stop with history. God's power could not be limited even by the existence of death, so that apocalyptic eschatology is personal as well as historical. Man was also a citizen of an entirely different dimension. Chapter 12 of Daniel is the first place in the Bible to refer unambiguously to the resurrection of the dead, "some to everlasting life and some to shame and everlasting contempt" (12:2). At the End of Days the righteous "who sleep in the dust of the earth" will return to life to "shine like the brightness of the firmament . . . like the stars, forever and ever" (12:3). (This simile is doubly appropriate: The apocalyptist has his visionary eye on the realm "above the sun" where Ecclesiastes, for whom "there is nothing new under the sun," had not looked for an answer.) The problem of theodicy and the lack of divine retribution, the painful question of Job, is resolved by Daniel through a life beyond death, where the wicked are punished and the righteous enjoy the uninterrupted bliss of the divine presence. (The future development of Jewish apocalyptic literature will be discussed in Chapter 5.)

The Modernity of the Bible and the Coalescence of Early Postbiblical Judaism

The recovery of the history and civilizations of the ancient Near East has brought the biblical books alive again to the modern reader as grounded in their particular times and place. For all the manifold and multiform nature of these writings, many people feel a special affinity to the simplicity and directness that lies at the core of biblical thought. The Bible treats of man's life on earth, his search for security in a world threatened by chaos and destruction, and his share in determining the outcome of each historical moment. At its height, classical prophecy addressed itself to contemporary events as determinative of future blessing or curse, projected an ultimate, ideal goal that was not in a realm beyond history (as in apocalypse) but was an overcoming of exploitation and conflict within humankind, and prophecy gave to social ethics an urgency that does not return to Western consciousness until recently. The realism of the biblical narratives, the despair of Ecclesiastes, and the anguish of Job also speak to modern man with special sharpness and poignancy. In twentieth-century theology, the notions of a transcendent judgment on human affairs, the witness to God of a moral and faithful life, respect for nature and for the sanctity of man, also derive renewed vigor from a reacquaintance with their biblical roots.

In the Hellenistic world and afterward the biblical writings became "the Bible," an authoritative work presenting a compelling, universal framework for religious faith and action. The continuation of Jewish thought had to take different forms, because the text of the Bible could not be revised and added to, as the earlier compilers and redactors did. Instead, the Bible was to be the source of tens of thousands of discrete quotations, fragments of divine wisdom and knowledge applied to situations often quite unlike their original context. The underlying biblical ideas also developed, controlling the way the text is interpreted, but they too changed as a result of having encountered new cultural and social environments.

The faint outlines of early postbiblical Jewish thought can be seen in late biblical literature: a coming together of various strands and tendencies to form new approaches to what the prophets called "the knowledge of God." Torah becomes Israel's wisdom, as Jewish exegetes and religious philosophers will never cease to point out, making possible the derivation of new levels of meaning from the sacred text. A synthesis of cosmic, preordained wisdom and the experience of prophecy produces apocalyptic revelations, such as Daniel, in which the whole course of history is seen as a divine plan guaranteeing the final triumph of goodness and holiness. The piety of Psalms and the advice of Proverbs provide the basis for a closer fusion of the symbols of individual, national, and cosmic religiosity in Judaism. The problem of theodicy is partly resolved with the emerging belief in personal immortality: Injustice and suffering will be recompensed on another plane of existence, because the God of Israel rules over death too; YHVH finally conquers the underworld of Sheol as, surrounded in apocalyptic visions by celestial courtiers, angels, and palaces, He now explicitly presides over a heavenly realm largely ignored in the earlier phases of biblical religion.

While these new orientations were just emerging—biblical commentary, a religious law for the individual, cosmic speculations of an apocalyptic or a philosophical kind, a World to Come in which each righteous person has a share—the Jews remained the only completely monotheistic nation in a Hellenistic world where popular religion was still polytheistic. Self-conscious Jewish opposition to paganism was heightened by the successful conclusion of the Maccabean revolt. The following anecdote, concerning a Jewish soldier in a Hellenistic army, has been recorded in the name of the Greek historian Hecateus of Abdera; some modern scholars think the source may have been forged by a Jewish writer in the early second century BCE, but even so, the story conveys an important facet of the complex interaction between Jew and paganism in the milieu we shall describe in future chapters. Hecateus (or Pseudo-Hecateus) relates:

> When I was on the march toward the Red Sea, among the escort of Jewish cavalry which accompanied us was one named Mosollamus, a very intelli-

gent man, robust, and, by common consent, the very best of bowmen, whether Greek or barbarian. This man, observing that a number of men were going to and fro on the route and that the whole force was being held up by a seer who was taking the auspices, inquired why they were halting. The seer pointed out to him the bird he was observing, and told him that if it stayed in that spot it was expedient for them all to halt; if it stirred and flew forward, to advance; if backward, then to retire. The Jew, without saying a word, drew his bow, shot and struck the bird, and killed it. The seer and some others were indignant, and heaped curses upon him. "Why so mad, you poor wretches?" he retorted; and then, taking the bird in his hands, continued, "Pray, how could any sound information about our march be given by this creature, which could not provide for its own safety? Had it been gifted with divination, it would not have come to this spot, for fear of being killed by an arrow of Mosollamus the Jew." [Josephus, *Against Apion* I, 201–204.]

The Jews and their Scriptures were beginning to impinge on the pagan world to a degree that had not been possible previously. Armed with the idea of bearing witness to the one God and the expectation that paganism was finished, a highly unusual people and their religion were not going to be ignored, nor were they going to let themselves be ignored.

PART TWO

From the Hellenistic Period to Late Antiquity

CHART 2. HELLENISTIC AND ROMAN ERAS.

A. FROM THE MACCABEAN REVOLT TO THE REDACTION OF THE MISHNAH

General History	Jewish History
163. Beginning of civil wars between claimants to the Seleucid throne, eventually leading to the decline of the Seleucid state.	163–140. Continuation of the Maccabean struggle against the Seleucids, despite the end of the religious persecutions.
	161. Judah the Maccabee is killed and his brother Jonathan becomes leader of the Maccabean forces.
146. Imposition of Roman control on Greece and Macedonia.	140. Jonathan is killed; an assembly in Jerusalem recognizes his brother Simon as High Priest and ethnarch of independent Judea, these offices to be hereditary in the Hasmonean family thereafter.
	134–104. Rule of John Hyrcanus, Simon's son.
	104–103. Rule of Judah Aristobulus, John Hyrcanus's son.

100 BCE

General History	Jewish History
	103–76. Rule of Alexander Janneus, John Hyrcanus's second son. Extension of Judean control over most of Palestine and Trans-Jordan. Civil war between John Hyrcanus and the Pharisees.
	76–67. Rule of Salome Alexandra, wife of Alexander Janneus. She makes peace with the Pharisees.
65. Pompey's victory over the king of Pontus leaves all of Asia Minor and Syria in Roman hands.	67–63. Struggle between Salome's two sons for the throne of Judea.
48. Julius Caesar defeats Pompey and becomes the most powerful political figure in Rome.	63. The Roman general Pompey supports Hyrcanus and captures Jerusalem for him. Hyrcanus becomes High Priest; his advisor Antipater becomes administrator of Judea.
44. Assassination of Julius Caesar.	
42. Mark Anthony and Octavian defeat the anti-Caesar party at Philippi; Anthony takes control of the eastern half of the Roman empire, Octavian of the western.	40. The Parthians invade Judea; Antipater's son Herod flees to Rome, where he is recognized as king of Judea.
	37. With the help of a Roman army, Herod recaptures Jerusalem and regains control of Judea.
31. Octavian defeats Anthony at Actium; end of the Roman civil war. Octavian (Augustus) becomes emperor.	37–4. Reign of Herod as Roman client king of Judea.
	4 BCE. Division of Herod's kingdom between three of his sons.

1 BCE

General History	Jewish History
1 **CE**	
	6 CE. The Roman government assumes direct rule in Judea.
14–37. Tiberius, Roman emperor.	Early first century CE. Death of the sages Hillel and Shammai.
	c. 20 BCE–c. 50 CE. The philosopher Philo of Alexandria.
	26–36. Pontius Pilate is the Roman governor of Judea.
37–41. Gaius Caligula, Roman emperor.	c. 30. Crucifixion of Jesus of Nazareth.
41–54. Claudius, Roman emperor.	66–70. Jewish revolt against Rome, ending in Roman reconquest of Judea and the destruction of Jerusalem and of the Second Temple.
54–68. Nero, Roman emperor.	
69–79. Vespasian, Roman emperor.	
79–81. Titus, Roman emperor.	74. Fall of Masada, the last rebel stronghold.
81–96. Domitian, Roman emperor.	
96–98. Nerva, Roman emperor.	70s. The rabbinic council, the Sanhedrin, reassembles in the town of Yavneh.
98–117. Trajan, Roman emperor.	
100 **CE**	
114–117. Trajan invades Parthian Mesopotamia but is forced to retreat.	114–117. Revolt of Jews in Egypt, Cyrene, Cyprus.
117–138. Hadrian, Roman emperor.	132–135. Jewish revolt in Judea under Simon bar Kokhba.
	135. Beginning of a period of severe anti-Jewish persecutions in Palestine; martyrdom of Rabbi Akiva and other scholars.
138–161. Antoninus Pius, Roman emperor.	140s or 150s. End of the persecutions; the Sanhedrin reassembles in the Galilee.
161–180. Marcus Aurelius, Roman emperor.	c. 170–217. Judah I is patriarch (*Nasi*) of the Sanhedrin and recognized leader of the Jewish people in the Roman empire. Under his auspices is redacted the Mishnah, the basic code of rabbinic law.
180–192. Commodus, Roman emperor.	

Chart 2. (con't)

B. JEWS UNDER ROMAN AND PERSIAN RULE, THIRD TO SIXTH CENTURIES

Roman History	Jews in the Roman Empire	Jews in the Persian Empire	Persian History
200 CE			
193–235. The Severan dynasty of emperors; beginning of a period of economic and social troubles.		Early 3rd century. Rise of the Babylonian scholar class; the official head of the Jewish community in Persia, the exilarch, encourages the establishment of rabbinic academies in central Babylonia.	
	225–255. The seat of the patriarchate is moved to the Galilean city of Tiberias. Rabbinic learning continues to flourish in the Galilee, despite the general crisis.		226–240. Ardashir I, first ruler of the Sassanian dynasty, overthrows the Parthians and seeks to revive ancient Persian power and the Zoroastrian religion.
235–283. Height of political disorder and economic decline; frequent fighting between contenders for rule of the empire.			240–271. Shapur I confirms the religious autonomy of the Jews.
284–305. The Emperor Diocletian re-establishes order and reforms the Roman administration; widespread persecution of Christians.		Second half of 3rd century. Adjustment to Sassanian policies and continued development of rabbinic Judaism in Babylonia.	
300 CE			
306–337. The Emperor Constantine makes Christianity a legal religion.	Early 4th century. First restrictions on Jewish legal rights.	4th century. Rabbinic learning continues to flourish; major scholars include Abbaye and Rava in the first half of the century.	309–379. Shapur II, Sassanian ruler. Prolonged wars with the Romans. Persian power at a zenith toward the end of Shapur II's reign.
325. Church council of Nicea.			

Roman Empire	Jews in the Roman Empire	Jews in the Persian Empire	Persian History
361–363. Reign of Emperior Julian the Apostate; he unsuccessfully tries to reverse the Christianization of the empire. 340–397. Ambrose, bishop of Milan. 340–420. Jerome, translator of the Bible into Latin. 354–430. Augustine of Hippo. 379–395. Reign of the Emperor Theodosius I. Christianity fully the official religion of the empire. At his death the division between the western and eastern parts of the empire becomes permanent.	Middle 4th century. Redaction of the Jerusalem (Palestinian) Talmud is under way in the Galilee.	Late 4th century. Beginning of collection of materials to become the Babylonian Talmud, under R. Ashi at Sura.	339. Beginning of persecution of Christians, suspected of ties with the Romans.
400 CE			
The Western Roman Empire. 5th–6th centuries. Waves of barbarian invasions in Europe and North Africa (the Visigoths, Vandals, Huns, Ostrogoths, Lombards, Franks). 410. Sack of Rome by the Visigoths. 455. Sack of Rome by the Vandals.	420s. Death of the patriarch Gamaliel VI; the office of patriarch is abolished by the Roman government.		First half of 5th century. Toleration, then renewed persecution of Christianity in Persia. 485. Beginning of several decades of political-religious ferment (the Mazdak movement).

Chart 2. (con't)

Roman Empire	Jews in the Roman Empire	Jews in the Persian Empire	Persian History
475–476. Romulus Augustus, the last Roman emperor in the West.		c. 455–475. Persecutions of Jews; synagogues and academies closed.	
The Eastern Roman Empire. 408–450. Reign of Theodosius II; preparation of the first major code of Roman law.		c. 500. Re-establishment of Jewish institutions; redaction of much of the Babylonian Talmud.	
Christianity. 5th–6th centuries. Creedal controversies over the nature of Christ (Arian and Monophysite heresies).			
500 CE			
The West. 529. Establishment of the Benedictine monastery of Monte Cassino in Italy. 590–604. Pope Gregory the Great.	c. 600. Pope Gregory defines papal policy toward the Jews.	520s. The king of Himyar in southwestern Arabia converts to Judaism; Himyar is subsequently conquered by Christians and, later in the century, by Persians.	531–578. Khosrau I, the Sassanian ruler, reorganizes the Persian state.
The East. 527–565. The Emperor Justinian reconquers parts of the western Mediterranean. (They are lost after his death.) Publication of the Justinian Code of Roman law.	530s. Beginning of new restrictions on Jewish rights in Roman law.	6th century. Babylonian sages (the *Saboraim*) add comments and notes to the text of the Babylonian Talmud. 589. Traditional date for the beginning of the Geonic period.	589–628. Rule of Khosrau II, last major king of the Sassanian dynasty.

Arabia. c. 570. Birth of Muhammad. |

CHAPTER 4

The Hellenistic Diaspora and the Judean Commonwealth to 70 CE

The political geography of the Near East underwent two major shifts during the period to be studied in this chapter. The Hellenistic dynasties founded by Alexander the Great's generals in the early third century had, by the mid-second century, passed their prime. Weakened by military defeats, native revolts, and dynastic strife, the Macedonian rulers lost one outlying region after another to a new set of states, including the Parthians in Iran (who later occupied Mesopotamia also), the kingdoms of Pergamum, Pontus, and Armenia in Asia Minor, the Nabateans in Trans-Jordan and adjacent semidesert areas, and Judea after the Maccabean revolt. Only about a century was to elapse until the fragmentation of the Near East was put to an end by Rome. The last great empire of ancient times was already the single most powerful Mediterranean state after crushing Carthage in 202 BCE, leaving Rome in complete control of the West. The East was to fall under its domination in stages: first, when Rome undermined the Seleucids through support for smaller states breaking away from their rule; then by conversion of these kingdoms into Roman protectorates; finally by the imposition of direct Roman rule. In 148 BCE Macedonia was to become a Roman province and the city-states and leagues of mainland Greece taken under Roman supervision. In 133 the kingdom of Pergamum was to pass into Roman hands, followed by other parts of Asia Minor. Syria was to be annexed in 64 BCE by the Roman general Pompey, who was to make Judea a Roman dependency

Coin of Herod Antipas, 39–40 CE. (Courtesy Jewish Museum, New York.)

two years later. When the Roman empire reaches its maximum eastern borders in the first century CE, the only area of large Jewish settlement left outside its control is Parthian Babylonia.

After the end of the biblical period and with the large-scale settlement of Jews outside their original homeland, the narration of Jewish history presents a special problem that we have postponed to this chapter. The growing importance of the diaspora (from a Greek word meaning scattering or dispersion) makes it impossible to give a uniform chronological framework to the social and political development of the Jewish people. Although there are features common to the Jewish diaspora experience as a whole, each area of the diaspora has a separate historical pattern in relation to its immediate environment. Judea remains the heartland of the Jewish people throughout the Hellenistic and Roman eras, but before we study the rise and fall of the monarchy established by the Maccabees, we must move backward to survey the emergence and nature of the Jewish dispersion from the time when it became a significant factor in Jewish life.

The Expanding Diaspora

The first permanent Jewish diaspora was the settlement in Babylon created by Nebuchadnezzar's deportations from Judah in the 590s–580s. (The Israelites exiled by the Assyrians in the 720s did not long survive

as a separate group.) Although Babylonian Jews returned to Jerusalem in
several waves during the Persian period, a sizable Jewish population continued to reside in Mesopotamia, and, as we shall see in later chapters,
played an influential role in Jewish intellectual history beginning in the
third century CE. In Egypt Jewish settlements were established by refugees fleeing the Babylonians and by Jewish soldier contingents brought
there later by the Persians. These exilic and postexilic communities were
a modest prelude to the remarkable expansion in the numbers and distribution of diaspora Jewry that occurred in the Hellenistic era.

Tombstone from the Jewish catacomb of Vigna Randanini, Rome, second or third
century CE. (Courtesy Jewish Museum, New York.)

Diasporas were a common feature of the Hellenistic-Roman world. In the fourth century BCE, colonies of Egyptian, Syrian, and Phoenician merchants were frequent in the seaports of Greece and Italy. After the conquests of Alexander the Great, Greeks and Macedonians constituted an immense diaspora throughout the Near East. Ethnic resettlement and religious diffusion went hand in hand, as settlers brought with them ancestral cults and won for their gods new worshipers among the local population. Although not unique, the Jewish diaspora was outstanding in its ability to preserve and perpetuate its identity at considerable distance from the homeland and over large stretches of time.

Several factors guided the spread of the Jewish dispersion in Hellenistic times, of which the political history of the Mediterranean basin was the most important. During Ptolemaic rule in Judea, large-scale Jewish settlement in Egypt began. Under the first Ptolemies, Jewish captives, when freed, established communities throughout the country. The Ptolemies brought in Jewish soldiers and their families, and other Jews migrated from Judea to Egypt probably for economic reasons. At its height, Egyptian Jewry in Hellenistic times was highly diversified: There were peasants and shepherds, Jewish generals in the Ptolemaic army, and Jewish officials in the civil service and police. At Leontopolis, an Aaronide priest from Jerusalem founded a small temple with a sacrificial cult modeled on that of Jerusalem. (This shrine survived for over two centuries until just after 70 CE, but it does not seem to have been an important place of worship for Egyptian Jewry as a whole.) Alexandria, the capital of the Ptolemies and the intellectual center of Hellenistic civilization, became one of the most populous Jewish communities in the world between the third century BCE and the end of the first century CE. Numbering several hundred thousand at least, Alexandrian Jewry included wealthy merchants, bankers, and shippers at one end of the social spectrum and masses of Jewish artisans and shopkeepers at the other. The Ptolemies also founded Jewish colonies in the cities of Cyrenaica (modern-day Libya). The Falashas, black Jews of Ethiopia, may stem from Egyptian-Jewish contacts during Hellenistic and Roman times.

The northern diaspora arose when the Seleucids took control of Judea after 200 BCE. Around 210–205, the Seleucid king Antiochus III moved several thousand Jewish soldiers and their families from Babylonia to Asia Minor. Within two centuries, large Jewish communities were to be found in Antioch and Damascus, in the Phoenician ports, and in the Asia Minor cities of Sardis, Halicarnassus, Pergamum, and Ephesus. By the turn of the Common Era, Jews lived on most of the islands of the eastern Mediterranean, such as Cyprus and Crete, in mainland Greece and Macedonia, on the shores of the Black Sea, and in the Balkans. Jewish inscriptions from the early centuries CE have been found in the Crimea and in modern Romania and Hungary.

When the Roman presence was felt in the Near East, the growth of Jewish settlement further west ensued. By the mid-first century BCE, the Roman statesman Cicero, in his speech in defense of Flaccus, insinuates that the Jews were a troublesome element among the Roman masses. Large numbers of Jews were brought to Rome as slaves by Roman generals campaigning in Judea. Ransomed by other Jews and augmented by a steady stream of voluntary migrants, they swelled the Roman-Jewish community, despite occasional governmental effort, on one pretext or another, to reduce their numbers. According to satirical remarks in the Latin poets, most Roman Jews were poor and some were beggars, but there were Jewish storekeepers, craftsmen, and actors in Rome and visiting Jewish diplomats, merchants, and scholars.[1] In the later Roman empire, cities in southern Italy became important Jewish centers and large settlements appeared in western North Africa and in Spain. Jewish groups were found in Gaul (modern-day France) and in the Roman garrison towns on the Rhine. A remark attributed to the Greek geographer Strabo, partly true in his time (the first century BCE), was certainly characteristic of the Roman empire at its height: "This people has already made its way into every city, and it is not easy to find any place in the habitable world which has not received this nation and in which it has not made its power felt" (Josephus, *Antiquities* XIV, 115).

The Hellenistic and Roman states helped the spread of the diaspora by assembling the lands surrounding the Mediterranean into integrated economic and political units, which facilitated the relatively easy movement of trade, peoples, and ideas. These large imperial systems also created a propitious legal and political climate for Jewish settlement within pagan cities. The Hellenistic cities, despite typical Greek institutions of self-government, were not politically independent, as had been the earlier Greek city-states, so that foreign groups could now obtain rights of residence from the authorities higher up, if need be. In Alexandria, Jews became so well integrated, socially and economically, that they aspired to legal equality. A bitter dispute broke out between Alexandrian pagans and Jews in the late 30s of the first century CE, coinciding with the attempt by the Roman emperor Gaius Caligula to force all inhabitants of the empire to worship him; the pagans used the Jewish refusal to follow suit as a pretext for violent anti-Jewish riots. Although the rights and privileges of Alexandrian Jews were confirmed by the next emperor, Claudius, he drew the line at exempting them from the special taxes that fell also on the non-Hellenized native population, Nevertheless, many individual Jews did acquire full citizenship rights in Hellenistic cities. The Jews as a whole did not, because they could not participate in the pagan cults so important in the life of the city and because of the biblical Sabbath and food laws. Thus, for example, Jews did not have to appear in pagan courts on the Sabbath and other holy days; they received a money payment, in lieu of the pagan olive oil prohibited by Jewish religious law, as their share of the government distribution of foodstuffs. These and other special provisions, such as the right to send annual contributions to the Jerusalem Temple, were occasionally violated by the authorities, but the Jewish communities were usually able to appeal successfully to Rome for confirmation of their perogatives. Throughout the diaspora, Judaism was a fully licit religion, legally absolved from the emperor worship that the Romans encouraged among provincial pagans.[2]

Each local Jewish community collected and administered its finances, established places for study, worship, and burial, provided material help

Oil lamp from Palestine, with decorative menorah design, probably third century CE. (Courtesy Jewish Museum, New York.)

to indigents, especially widows, and maintained law courts to adjudicate disputes between Jews. There was no single legal term or uniform structure describing the voluntary associations that Jews formed in the Hellenistic and Roman cities. The Alexandrian community was called a *politeuma* (a community, a Greek term akin to *polis* or city-state), headed for a while by one administrative-judicial figure and later by a council of elders. In contrast, Roman Jewry was divided into many independent societies or synagogues, each with its own religious and civil officers.

Perhaps more than for any other reason, the diaspora survived and flourished because of the canonization of the Scriptures. By Hellenistic and early Roman times, the Scriptures had assumed their final form and became the basis for popular Jewish education. Through the Bible, the Jews retained a common identity as a people covenanted with God and obligated to fulfill his commandments. The Bible as interpreted by the Jews maintained Jewish monotheism in self-conscious distinction from other religious traditions, preserved the Jews from the natural assimilatory pressures of diaspora conditions, and drew a sharp line between them and their neighbors. Scriptural monotheism also stimulated a widespread effort by Jews to gain converts. Proselytism is mentioned often in ancient sources, Jewish and pagan. In the chaotic, cosmopolitan, and relatively open society of Hellenistic and Roman times, as local traditions weakened, foreign cults were sought out for their spiritual insights and sociopsychological benefits. Jewish worship of the one, invisible God and Judaism's distinctive ethical and ritual practices attracted interest on every level of society—hostile interest but also admiration. Besides full proselytes who identified themselves completely with the Jewish people, others (sometimes called *sebomenoi* or "God-fearers") worshiped the Jewish God and followed a few Jewish observances, especially the Sabbath, without merging into Israel. Descendants of *sebomenoi* often became Jews, and this group also provided a fertile ground for early Christian missionaries.

The language—including the language of prayer—of Judaism in the Hellenistic-Roman diaspora was predominately Greek. (Even the burial inscriptions of the Roman Jews and their personal names were mainly Greek, less frequently Latin, seldom Hebrew.) Until 70 CE the Temple in Jerusalem provided a central focus for the diaspora. The collection and transport of monies for its support was a major, somewhat hazardous, undertaking. The courtyards of the Temple at festival times were filled with Jewish pilgrims. That the diaspora continued to thrive after the fall of the monarchy and the destruction of the Temple indicates the intensity of Jewish participation in local Jewish communal institutions, but, nevertheless, Judea remained an important source of ideas and leadership for the internationalized Judaism of the Hellenistic period before and after 70. It was only in the fifth century CE, when Jewish life finally declined in Palestine, that the Jews become almost entirely a diaspora people.

Judea After the Maccabean Revolt

The political history of the Jews in Judea from the 170s BCE to 70 CE is known in some detail. A few remarks about the historical sources are necessary because, even though this period is better documented than any other in ancient Judaism, crucial gaps remain in our knowledge. The account given in 1 Maccabees covers events down to 135 BCE. Supplementing 1 Maccabees and carrying on where it leaves off are the writings of the Jewish historian Josephus Flavius (born about 37 CE and died after 100). A well-connected, upper-class Judean, Josephus participated in the Jewish revolt against Rome that broke out in 66 CE, but ended up on the Roman side. After the war, he lived in Rome where, under the patronage of the emperor, he published two works on Jewish history. *The Jewish War*, written by him in Aramaic in the 80s and translated into Greek with the help of assistants (only the Greek survives), seeks to dissuade the Jews in the East from blaming the Romans for the destruction of the Jewish commonwealth and of the Jerusalem Temple. *The Jewish An-*

Hasmonean coins. In place of portraits, ancient Jewish coins use such motifs as a cornucopia, a star with rays, a palm tree, or an anchor. (Courtesy American Numismatic Society.)

tiquities, published in the mid-90s, is a lengthy summary of the entirety of Jewish history, paraphrasing the biblical narrative and drawing on various (lost) works for the postbiblical period. The *Antiquities* seeks to enlighten non-Jews about Judaism and to counter the charge that the Jews were not an ancient people.[3] Both 1 Maccabees and Josephus's writings are selective and tendentious, but when allowance is made for bias, valuable data can be extracted. Additional information on Jewish history of this period is provided by archeological findings, such as coins, inscriptions, and the remains of buildings and other structures in Judea and elsewhere. Greek and Roman historians occasionally remark on the Jews, but their statements are useful mainly as an indication of pagan attitudes toward Judaism. (The considerable religious literature, Jewish and Christian, surviving from this period will be described in the next chapter.)

From Temple State to Theocratic Monarchy

The Maccabean revolt that began as a defensive struggle to save monotheism proved to be a historic turning point, because several centuries of submission to pagan rulers gave way to a new activism with many ramifications, political and religious. Fighting continued even after the religious persecutions ceased, for the revolt released pent-up tensions within Judea and smoldering Jewish-pagan hostility in adjacent areas. The Maccabees warred on three fronts: against Seleucid army contingents sent to pacify the country; against Jewish Hellenizers whose prestige had been badly damaged by the desecration of the Temple; against pagans who attacked Jews in many cities of northern Trans-Jordan, western Galilee, the coastal plain, and the Idumean district south of Jerusalem. The Seleucids were defeated; the Jewish Hellenizers harassed, expelled, or killed; the besieged Jews in pagan cities rescued. Despite several reversals, the momentum of the Maccabean insurgency could not be stopped.

It will be remembered that the first success of the revolution was the recapture of the Temple in 164. The following year Antiochus IV was killed while fighting the Parthians in Babylonia, and his successor appointed a Judean High Priest from among the old ruling families, a man acceptable to some of the pietists in the Maccabean army who then withdrew from the struggle. But the revolutionary forces regrouped in the countryside and, in 161, Judah the Maccabee won his most spectacular victory by defeating the Seleucid general Nicanor. A few months later Judah was killed. The rebels retreated to the Judean desert under Judah's brother Jonathan, and the Seleucids took advantage of the lull to surround Jerusalem with a ring of fortresses, but the situation remained fluid because Jewish support for the Seleucids was minimal. Even the High Priest appointed by them ran into trouble with the pietists before he died in 159. By the mid-150s, the Maccabean insurgents were out in the open, attacking Jewish Hellenists and consolidating their support among the populace. Jonathan was soon able to take advantage of a power struggle for the Seleucid throne. In 152 the Seleucid king Demetrius I acknowledged Jonathan's military control of most of Judea and allowed him to occupy all of Jerusalem except the citadel; his rival then recognized Jonathan as High Priest. Further concessions followed: In 150 Jonathan was officially appointed provincial governor; in 145 he and his men were brought to Antioch to repress riots against a claimant to the Seleucid throne. By this time, the Maccabees had already won diplomatic recognition from Rome. When Jonathan was taken prisoner by guile in 142 and put to death, Simon, Judah's last surviving brother, became leader of the revolution, extracted cancellation of all taxes to the Seleucid regime, and assumed control of the Jerusalem citadel. In 140, Simon's authority was confirmed by his own people. "A great assembly of the priests and the people and the rulers of the nation and the elders of the country" met in Jerusalem to ratify the *fait accompli* of the previous decades—even though Simon had a shaky claim, at best, to the supreme priestly office and none at all to the Davidic throne:

> And the Jews and their priests decided that Simon should be their leader and High Priest forever, until a trustworthy prophet should arise, and that he should be governor over them and that he should take charge of the sanctuary and appoint men over its tasks and over the country and the weapons and the strongholds, and that he should take charge of the sanctuary, and that he should be obeyed by all, and that all contracts should be written in his name, and that he should be clothed in purple and wear gold. [1 Macc. 14:41–43.]

The new Hasmonean dynasty (so-called from the name of one of the ruling family's ancestors) was a continuation, yet a transformation, of the previous leadership system, as the new political order was of the earlier Temple state. Because Hasmonean religious authority resided in the High Priesthood, Judea was still a theocracy, a society ruled by God's law and administered by His priestly deputy. But the Hasmoneans were also commanders of the Judean army (which had not existed previously) and were the recognized ethnarchs (leaders of the *ethnos*, the people). Paradoxically, the High Priesthood took on these additional, secular functions when the converse was occurring among the populace: a movement toward more active participation in the political and religious life of Judea by groups outside the Temple establishment and the priestly class. The history of the three generations of Hasmoneans who ruled Judea beginning with Simon was, therefore, a time of unprecedented opportunity but also of growing civil conflict.

When Simon was murdered in a palace intrigue (135 BCE), his son John

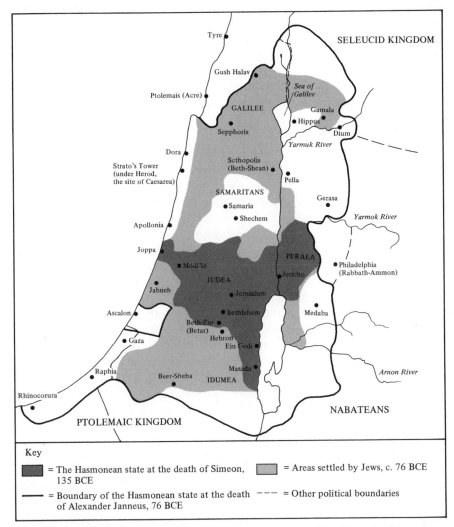

Key

![The Hasmonean state at the death of Simeon, 135 BCE]
= The Hasmonean state at the death of Simeon, 135 BCE

= Areas settled by Jews, c. 76 BCE

——— = Boundary of the Hasmonean state at the death of Alexander Janneus, 76 BCE

– – – = Other political boundaries

The Hasmonean State in the Second and First Centuries BCE. After the Maccabean revolt, Judea became politically independent for the first time in over four centuries and gradually conquered most of Palestine and Trans-Jordan.

Hyrcanus became High Priest and ethnarch. Early in his reign, the Seleucids besieged Jerusalem. Although the city did not fall, John Hyrcanus was forced to relinquish some territory and to accompany the Seleucid king in an unsucessful campaign against the Parthians. After this temporary setback, the political independence of Hasmonean Judea was not threatened again for over half a century. Hyrcanus conquered large areas in Trans-Jordan, Idumea (biblical Judah south of Jerusalem, which had been occupied by the Edomites in postexilic times), and Samaria, where he razed the Samaritan Temple on Mount Gerizim. His son, Judah Aristobulus (reigned 104–103), completed the conquest of the Galilee. Hyrcanus's second son, Alexander Janneus (ruled 102–76 BCE), campaigned in every direction, annexing almost all of the Hellenized cities of coastal Palestine and northern Trans-Jordan. Under Alexander Janneus the Hasmonean state was at its maximum extent. But by then ideological tensions had reached a critical point.

What factors, religious and political, fueled these tensions? We can speculate that the theocratic ideology of the time saw the expansion of Judea as an actualization of the biblical promise that the holy land was given to Israel so that God's laws could be followed there without contamination by paganism. Although the Hasmoneans at first expelled pagans and resettled Jews in their place, they soon turned to a policy of forced conversion—successful mass conversion, because the Judaized Idumeans and Galileans produced some of the most loyal Jewish elements in the following centuries. At the same time, the achievements of the Hasmoneans propelled them in the direction of becoming typical Hellenistic monarchs. Alexander Janneus called himself king, employed Greek mercenaries in his army, and surrounded himself with an increasingly Hellenized court. The religious upsurge of the Maccabean revolt was, therefore, channeled into movements highly critical of the Hasmoneans. Denunciations of the new Temple establishment and of Hasmonean legitimacy had surfaced even before the reign of Alexander Janneus (we will examine these groupings, the Essenes and Pharisees, in the next chapter), but the turbulence reached a height in a prolonged civil war against Janneus, during which his opponents even turned to a Seleucid king for help. When the Hasmonean ruler was able finally to regain control of his realm, he crucified (not a legal form of Jewish capital punishment) several hundred of his Jewish enemies. Thousands more fled the country. Only after Janneus's death, when his wife, Salome Alexandria, ruled Judea (she was queen from 76 to 67 BCE), did civil strife subside. The ousted forces were reconciled, took their revenge on hated courtiers of the former king, and the country enjoyed a decade of peace and tranquility. How the Hasmonean kingdom would have evolved on its own under Salome Alexandra's successors is a moot question, because by then the Romans were directly involved in Judean political affairs.

In the 60s the Roman general Pompey concluded his wars against the king of Pontus in northern Asia Minor. After putting an end to the remnants of Seleucid rule and annexing Syria to the Roman empire, he turned his attention to Judea, where a struggle for the throne had broken out between Salome's sons, Aristobulus II and Hyrcanus II, a conflict that provided a suitable pretext for Roman intervention. The rivals were

Roman statuary found at Caesarea, the port city built by Herod. (Photo by the author.)

ordered to present their claims before Pompey in Damascus. (A third group of Jews also appeared who rejected both candidates, preferring, perhaps, to sever the connection between the civic and priestly offices.) Pompey opted for Hyrcanus. Aristobulus fled to Jerusalem pursued by the Romans, and was forced to surrender. The city gates were opened to the Romans, but Aristobulus's followers continued to hold the Temple Mount. In 63 BCE, after a siege of three months, Pompey occupied the Temple and turned it over to Hyrcanus. (Its sanctity was respected by the Roman general.) Pompey exiled Aristobulus and his children to Rome; he recognized Hyrcanus as High Priest but not as king, reduced the size of Judea, and required an annual tribute. The Hellenistic cities conquered by the Hasmoneans became independent again, under Roman supervision. According to the new arrangement, the most powerful figure in Judea was not Hyrcanus, but his Idumean adviser Antipater, placed in charge of the administration of the Jewish commonwealth. Judea was now a vassal state of Rome.

Judea Under Herod and the Romans

The forties and thirties of the last century BCE were the final stages of a prolonged period of political instability in the Roman republic that eventuated in the centralization of power in the hands of one man, the emperor. The conflict between Pompey and Julius Caesar ended with Caesar's victory and Pompey's death in 48 BCE. After Caesar's assassination four years later, the empire was temporarily divided between Mark Anthony and Octavian, an arrangement that ended with the triumph of Octavian, now surnamed Augustus, the unchallenged first citizen (*princeps*) and military commander of an empire that dominated the entire Mediterranean basin from the Atlantic to the Parthian border. During the power struggles in the top echelon of the Roman state, Antipater and his sons made themselves helpful to whichever Roman leader happened to control the Near East, shifting sides when necessary but always showing themselves dependable supporters of the Roman cause.

Placed in power by Pompey, Antipater was able to render Caesar useful assistance, especially in the capture of Egypt. As a result, Caesar confirmed Hyrcanus as High Priest and Antipater as administrator of Judea, and he returned to their control some of the territories earlier taken away. When Julius Caesar was killed in 44, Antipater and his sons won the support of Cassius, a leader of the republican conspiracy, who briefly took control of Syria. Although Antipater was poisoned the following year, his sons Herod and Phasael remained in charge of Judea. In 42, when Mark Anthony and Octavian defeated Cassius and Brutus at the battle of Philippi, Mark Anthony, now the ruler of the eastern half of the empire, reaffirmed Herod and his brother as tetrarchs of Judea. (*Tetrarch* is a subordinate ruler.)

The Hasmoneans, however, had not given up hope of returning to power. In the middle 50s, Aristobulus II and his sons had escaped from Rome and had attempted unsuccessfully to regain the throne. In 40 BCE, one of these sons, Antigonus, gathered a force that invaded Judea, and with the aid of the Parthians, briefly took control of the country. Herod fled to Rome, where Octavian and Anthony arranged for the Roman Senate to proclaim him king of Judea. With a Roman army, Herod reconquered Judea between 39 and 37. After a five-month siege Jerusalem fell; the city was pillaged but the Temple was not touched. When Octavian defeated Anthony at Actium (31 BCE), Herod's kingship was reconfirmed. Reigning from 37 to 4 BCE, Herod was officially "an ally and friend of the Roman people," a client king maintained in power by the Romans because he was able to preserve order and security in the region. Accordingly, the Emperor Augustus enlarged Judea to include most of Palestine and gave Herod additional eastern areas to police against brigands and populate with dependable settlers. Throughout his reign, Herod needed to balance potentially conflicting forces: Jews, pagans, and Romans. He had to keep his Jewish subjects under control, retain the good will of the pagan population of his realm, and avoid any action counter to Roman interests.

Statue of the Roman Emperor
Augustus. (Courtesy of ENIT.)

Among the Jews, Herod could claim no religious authority. As his
family sprang from Idumean converts, he could not officiate as High
Priest, although he appointed and dismissed men from this office at will.
From time to time, Herod used his influence to protect Jewish rights in
the Asia Minor diaspora and he maintained close ties with the Jewish lead-

ership in Alexandria. By marrying Miriamne, Hyrcanus II's granddaughter, Herod connected himself with the Hasmonean dynasty; later, fearful of palace intrigue, he executed Miriamne, her mother, and her two sons. (Indicative of his status vis-à-vis the Romans, these executions had to be ratified by the Roman authorities.) Herod also posed as Hellenistic king, sending munificent gifts to pagan temples in various Greek cities and helping to finance the Olympic games. An ambitious builder, he founded several new cities in his kingdom, of which Caesarea, soon the main seaport of Palestine, was the most important. He also constructed or remodeled a string of fortresses, including Masada, perched on the top of a mountain in the Judean desert overlooking the Dead Sea. In Jerusalem he erected a sumptuous palace and he arranged for the rebuilding, on a very grand scale, of the Temple and its courtyards. (The present-day Western or "Wailing" Wall was part of the huge platform on which the Herodian Temple complex stood.) While the Herodian Temple became one of the architectural wonders of the eastern Mediterranean and enhanced the prestige of Judaism, it was both vulnerable to imperial manipulation and a volatile symbol of Jewish opposition to pagan hegemony. Not long before his death, Herod mounted over the Temple gate a golden eagle, which became an object of resentment and protest. Although Herod usually avoided such paganistic affronts to Judaism in the holy land, he brutally put down any sign of opposition. Only a façade of independence and splendor, the precarious Herodian arrangement in Judea did not long survive his death.

According to Herod's last will, confirmed by Augustus, in 4 BCE his territory was divided between three of his sons, two of whom received northern areas and the title *tetrarch* and the third of whom, Archeleus, was made ethnarch of Judea, Idumea, and Samaria. After complaints of mismanagement by Jews and Samaritans, Archeleus was deposed by Augustus in 6 CE in favor of direct Roman rule through an official (first a prefect, later a procurator) in charge of the Roman auxiliary troops stationed there, the collection of taxes for Rome, and the administration of criminal justice. Although in 4 BCE and in 6 CE the Romans repressed uprisings by Jewish groups, during the first four decades of the Common Era, anti-Roman protest was occasional and nonviolent, and the early prefects and procurators were usually careful to respect Jewish religious practices. However, episodes involving the installation of pagan symbols in Jerusalem and the expropriation of Temple funds occurred under the procurator Pontius Pilate (26–36 CE), noted for the harshness with which he put down any sign of defiance against Roman rule. An especially serious crisis threatened to erupt into violence when the Emperor Gaius Caligula (37–41) ordered a statue of himself placed in the Temple, but con-

Well-preserved Roman theater at Beth-Shean, c. 200 CE. (Courtesy of the Israel Government Tourist Office.)

frontation was averted by deliberate administrative procrastination and his timely assassination.

Caligula's successor, the emperor Claudius, briefly reverted to the Herodian arrangement, by making Agrippa I, a personal friend and a descendant both of Herod and of the Hasmoneans, king of Judea. Agrippa went out of his way to attract Jewish enthusiasm but his brief reign (41–44) was only a temporary interruption of direct Roman rule. Procurators in the following two decades were either inept or overtly hostile to the Jews. Economic conditions declined. (Thousands were probably thrown out of work when the rebuilding of the Temple was completed.) Security collapsed as anti-Roman terrorists (the *sicarii*, from the word *sica* or dagger) assassinated Jews favorably disposed to the Roman regime. The bodyguards of wealthy Jerusalem families clashed in the streets. Prophets proclaimed the end of the world, or the end of Roman domination. Open rebellion broke out in 66.

The Roman-Jewish War of 66–70 CE

The immediate cause of hostilities was a conflict over the respective rights of Jews and pagans in Caesarea, headquarters of the Roman admin-

Jewish coins issued during the first revolt against Rome, 67 CE. (Courtesy of the American Numismatic Society.)

istration of Judea. The procurator Florus took a determinedly anti-Jewish position, which he followed up by permitting his troops to pillage in rioting Jerusalem and to crucify a number of eminent Jews. After his return to Caesarea, pro-Roman Jews and the small Roman garrison in Jerusalem were slaughtered, and sacrifices in behalf of the emperor and the Roman people were halted (August 66), an action tantamount to a declaration of war. In October, the governor of Syria marched to Jerusalem with a legion. Commencing a siege of the Temple, he met vigorous resistance and retreated to the seacoast. In the same mountain passes where the Maccabees had won their first victories over the Seleucids, the rebels mauled the Roman forces. In the wake of this success, which left Judea free of Roman soldiers, a provisional government was set up and commanders appointed for the various districts of the country. At the end of 66 there were clashes between Jews and pagans in many cities and towns of Palestine.

In 67 the Emperor Nero put in charge of pacifying Judea an experienced general, Vespasian, who assembled a large army in the north. Sepphoris, the main Jewish city of the Galilee, refused to join the revolt, and the rebels were not able to make a stand against Vespasian's legions in the Galilean lowlands, but the fortress of Jotapata held out for 47 days. When the town fell, the Romans slaughtered most of its population. By the end of 67 Jewish resistance in the Galilee and northern Trans-Jordan was crushed.

During the winter of 67–68, the moderate government in Jerusalem was overthrown by extremists: the Zealots. Suspected pro-Romans were arrested, some killed. Militant anti-Roman groups poured into Jerusalem, occupying different parts of the city, sometimes fighting against each other. In March 67, Vespasian subjugated southern Trans-Jordan, west-

Air view of Masada; in the background is the Roman camp at the base of the mountain. (Courtesy of the Consulate General of Israel.)

ern Judea, and Idumea, as well as Samaria and the city of Jericho. Left in rebel hands were only Jerusalem and its environs and several Herodian fortresses in other parts of the country. In June 68, the Roman military effort was suspended when Nero committed suicide. (Revolts had broken out against him in Spain and Gaul.) During the next twelve months Roman armies in various parts of the empire elevated three generals to the throne; in July 69 the eastern legions proclaimed for Vespasian. Before leaving for Rome, Vespasian appointed his son Titus as head of the Judean campaign, with a huge army of four legions and many auxiliary troops. A few days before Passover, April 70, Titus set up camp outside the walls of the holy city.

The siege lasted from April to September, every section of the city being taken with great effort and loss of life. In late May the Romans occupied the newer part of Jerusalem, north of the Temple. When the Roman siege machinery was destroyed by the rebels, Titus built a wall to isolate the city from the countryside. By the end of July the Romans had occupied the citadel adjacent to the Temple. On August 6, sacrifices were suspended. A week later the porticos surrounding the Temple courtyards were burned. During the fighting on August 28 (the ninth day of the Hebrew month of Av), the Temple went up in flames. It took the Romans an additional month to capture the upper city west of the Temple. After all resistance ceased, Titus ordered Jerusalem razed, except for the towers of Herod's palace.

The middle terrace of Herod's palace at Masada, probably a platform for a semi-circular columned building; the Roman army camp can be seen below. (Courtesy of the Consulate General of Israel.)

During the rest of the year, Titus arranged celebrations in various Near Eastern cities, highlighted by throwing Jewish prisoners to wild animals and forcing them to fight in gladiator shows. In 71 Titus and Vespasian crowned their victory with a triumphal procession in Rome, in which Temple ritual objects and rebel leaders were exhibited. (The commemorative arch of Titus, with its relief showing the Temple menorah, still stands in the Roman forum.) It took the Romans several more years to capture the remaining fortresses. Masada, the last to hold out, fell in April 74. When the Romans breached the wall on top of the mountain, they found that the defenders had committed suicide rather than be taken captive.

How does the Roman-Jewish war compare to the Maccabean revolt? There are sufficient similarities between the two conflicts to indicate that the Jewish people and its religion had evolved considerably in the intervening 230 years.

In both wars the Jews opposed imperial powers, but the Maccabees were fighting a declining Seleucid state, about to be torn apart by regional uprisings, dynastic struggles, and outside enemies. The Roman empire of the mid-first century CE was in full ascent, temporarily embarrassed by political confusion at the center, but with immense military resources to put down a local rebellion. An independent Jewish state in the Near East in the first century CE was not a realistic possibility.

Both conflicts revealed pent-up tensions in Judean society. In Maccabean times resentment was focused against the Jerusalem Hellenizers who treated the Temple (and the Jewish religion) as their personal property. In the first century CE, Roman rule was, to be sure, disliked among much of the populace on whom the burden of tribute and taxes mainly fell. But there were material benefits to be had by the cooperative and the submissive, especially by large-scale landowners and tax farmers. Agrippa II, to whom the Romans had given the purely honorary title of king, argued at the outbreak of the revolt that, despite legitimate complaints against the procurator, no administrative corruption justified rebellion. In the early days of the uprising, the mob burned down his palace; at the same time

Archeological photo of a hoard of Jewish coins from the revolt, found at Masada. (Courtesy of the Consulate General of Israel.)

Arch of Titus, erected in the Roman forum in commemoration of the capture of Jerusalem in 70 CE. (Courtesy of ENIT.)

they destroyed the archives where the moneylenders' bonds were kept. Later, when the moderate leadership fell, the Zealots selected a new High Priest by lot, ignoring the small group of wealthy families that had monopolized this office since Herod. Despite internal Jewish hostilities vented in both historical situations, however, there was a crucial difference between the Jewish pro-Seleucids and the Jews who accepted the Roman presence. As a result of Antiochus' desecration of the Temple, the Hellenizers of Maccabean times became a despised and isolated minority, their religious motives thoroughly discredited. Although the Roman administration was by no means innocent of stirring up religious trouble, monotheism as such was not the issue during the war of 66–70 CE.

To what extent was the Roman-Jewish war a national conflict? The Jewish people of the first century CE was far more heterogeneous than that of two centuries earlier. The wave of conversions in Judea and the diaspora had resulted in a Jewish people composed of such diverse groups as Idumeans, Galileans, Hellenized Jews of the diaspora in Egypt, North Africa, Syria, Asia Minor, Greece, Rome, and elsewhere, in addition to the large settlement in Parthian Babylonia outside the borders of the Roman empire. The ruling family of the kingdom of Adiabene in northern Mesopotamia, who converted to Judaism in the first century CE, had built palaces for themselves in Jerusalem and fought actively among the

Relief from the Arch of Titus, showing the menorah and other holy objects taken from the Jerusalem Temple. (Courtesy of the Zionist Archives, New York.)

rebels during the war. According to the New Testament, "there were dwelling in Jerusalem Jews, devout men of every nation under heaven" (Acts 2:5). Jews thought of themselves as one nation, not in the modern secular sense, but as one nation because they worshiped the one God, creator of the universe and its sovereign, who had guided the patriarchs, revealed himself to Israel, and promised to protect his people if they adhered faithfully to the laws of his covenant with them and if they made his Name holy on earth.

In the war of 66–70 it was possible for Jews supporting the struggle and Jews opposed to it all to be pious members of the Jewish nation, as defined above. One could believe enthusiastically that the uprising was a realization of biblical promises and prophecies, or one could be equally convinced of the truth of these prophecies and not perceive the war as the decisive confrontation between Judaism and paganism. In order to see how this complex situation developed, we must know more about the religious movements within Judaism in the first century, the subject of the next chapter.

CHAPTER 5

Varieties of Judaism in the Late Second Temple Period

Absorption of all the lands around the Mediterranean into the Roman empire was the culmination of an integrative process taking place over several centuries, at least since the time of Alexander the Great. Despite incessant war and fluctuating political borders, a cosmopolitan, international milieu provided an overall framework for the Hellenistic kingdoms founded by Alexander's generals and later for those states, such as Judea, that gained independence in the second century BCE. Ideas freely circulated and interacted in a Hellenistic *ecumene* (from the Greek term for *inhabited world*) whose continuity was not interrupted by Roman conquest.

The Greek tradition was not the only component of this Hellenistic civilization: Several native cultures and religions reasserted themselves after a period of apparent submergence, including Persian dualism, Babylonian astral worship, and Jewish monotheism. Survival of old habits and languages (Egyptian, Aramaic, and other tongues) was more common in the countryside, whereas overt adaptation to Hellenic forms was most prevalent in the urban environment. Hellenistic and Roman cities proved to be challenging, fertile settings for the proliferation of the resurgent, now Hellenized Eastern traditions. (*Eastern* refers here to areas occupied by the ancient civilizations of the Near East, in contrast to the old Greek world around the Aegean and in the Latin West.)

195

Section of the Dead Sea Scroll containing hymns of thanksgiving. (Courtesy of the Zionist Archives, New York.)

Urban religiosity during the Hellenistic-Roman era was marked, first, by a trend toward syncretism or theocrasy: the mixing and fusion of deities of Western and Near Eastern origin, so that, for example, Hadad of Damascus was equated with the Olympian Zeus and the Phoenician Astarte with the Greek Aphrodite. Second, the Hellenistic era already saw the appearance of voluntarily organized private associations for the worship of foreign gods, such as the Egyptian Isis and the Persian Mithra, a migration of cults that continued in Roman times. Third, there was a pronounced yearning for individual salvation and assurance of immortality, gratified by participation in semisecret rituals that are usually called mystery religions. Fourth, apparent in the philosophies of the period but also in the religions, was a striving for inner freedom and emotional self-sufficiency through an internalized code of behavior as a guide for coping with the loneliness and anonymity of the large cities of the Mediterranean.

How was Judaism affected by this milieu? The imageless God of the Jews was not very amenable to syncretistic identification with other deities, nor were the Jewish Scriptures compatible with the mythologies of pagan peoples. (There were certain exceptions, especially in the realms of artistic decoration and magical incantations.) Other aspects of Hellenistic religiosity exerted their effect on Judaism both in the diaspora and in Judea. If we define Hellenization in the broadest sense as adaptive adjustment to the complex intellectual horizons, social conditions, and psychological stresses of that age, then most of Judaism became Hellenized to some degree beginning in the third and second centuries BCE. This adjustment took the form of increased openness to Greek thought among some strata of Jewry and decisive rejection of it (equally affected by its very presence) among others. The result was a remarkably broad range of Jewish religious tendencies. In this chapter we will first study the impact of Greek philosophy on diaspora Jewry and then survey the religious situation in Hasmonean, Herodian, and Roman Judea. Out of partly Hellenized Judea would come two movements that predominate toward the end of this period: rabbinic Judaism, about to reshape the Jewish people in a new mold, and Christianity, through which the Judaic heritage became an intrinsic component of Western civilization.

Diaspora Judaism and Greek Philosophy

The word *philosophy*, the basic terminology of philosophy, and the philosophical method originated in ancient Greece. The philosopher, "one who loves wisdom," was the thinker who sets out to investigate the nature of things, in contrast to the man who believes that he already possesses wisdom—although, to be sure, a variety of well-defined conceptions of wisdom emerged from early philosophical speculation. Beginning in the sixth century BCE, Greek thinkers began to develop diverse explanations for the origins and ultimate constituents of the world—explanations that differed strikingly in their abstract and speculative approach from ancient Near Eastern and Greek myths and sagas. Even though early philosophy is indebted to Greek religion for some of its fundamental assumptions and concerns, its greatest originality lay in a scientific interest in the elements of nature and the causes of change. The first stages (only fragmentary writings from which have survived) were characterized by a search for an underlying universal, impersonal principle (water according to Thales [flourished c. 585 BCE], the Indeterminate according to Anaximander [fl. c. 570], air according to Anaximines [fl. c. 550]), or by an inquiry into the principle of intelligibility behind the flux of nature (number according to Pythagoras [fl. c. 530], *logos* or rational order according to Heraclitus [fl. c. 500], unchangeable Being according to Parmenides [born c. 516], indivisible "atoms" according to Democritus [born c. 460]). In the fifth century BCE there appeared a class of professional teachers of rhetoric (the Sophists) who applied the critical spirit of philosophy to the conventions of Greek society in a relativist and individualistic manner. A pivotal figure in the growing philosophical tradition was Socrates (469–399 BCE), known, above all, for his vigorous exposing of unexamined pretensions to knowledge, his acute and probing questioning, and his concern to restore, against the Sophists, the primacy of the good as the highest type of human self-understanding. Pre-Hellenistic Greek philosophy culminated in Socrates' student Plato (427–347) and Plato's student Aristotle (384–322), whose systems have long been regarded as among the greatest intellectual achievements of all time.

Drawing especially on Pythagoras and Socrates, Plato formulated his views in a series of dramatic dialogues of extraordinary originality. Among Plato's most influential doctrines are the theory of Ideas or Forms, transcendent, eternal universals or patterns, which are the object of true rational knowledge and in which the particular entities perceived by the senses "participate"; the tripartite division of the soul (appetitive, spirited, and rational), of which the rational is potentially immortal; the portrayal of an ideal society, in which harmonious balance is achieved among the various classes, each excelling in a different virtue. In his later dialogues Plato developed a comprehensive theory of being, which formed the basis for Aristotle's encyclopedic synthesis. More empirical and prosaic than Plato, Aristotle organized into a methodical and disciplined system the fundamentals of mathematics, logic, physics, biology, politics, and art, as well as the basic categories of being and change as such, all this culminating in a conception of an eternal Unmoved Mover and Cause of causes, the contemplation of which was man's final good. (The philosophies of Plato and Aristotle were to have immense impact on Jewish

Fourth-century CE mosaic of Plato and his disciples, now in the Museo Nazionale, Rome. (Editorial Photo Archives, Inc.)

thinking later, and a summary of Aristotelianism will be given in Chapter 8 in connection with medieval Jewish philosophy.)

After Alexander's conquest of the Near East, Greek science, medicine, and mathematics enjoyed over a century more of brilliant achievement before they began to stagnate, eventually acquiring in Western civilization an almost canonical status during late antiquity and the Middle Ages. Of the schools of philosophy that emerged in response to the wider horizons and greater individualism of the Hellenistic milieu, the Stoics were especially influential. Stoicism sought to mold man's character through the ideal of a virtuous sage who attains tranquil strength of mind and the ability to overcome the disturbances of the passions by conducting his life in conformity with the "laws of nature." A philosophy of pantheistic monotheism (pantheism identifies God with material nature), Stoicism conceived of the cosmos as a living embodiment of the divine Mind and viewed the various deities that the common people worshiped as separate manifestations of a divine Logos (Reason) immanent in the laws of nature and in the mind of man. To bring the classical texts of ancient Greece—the Iliad and the Odyssey—into harmony with their viewpoint, the Stoics interpreted them as allegories, each element being treated as a symbol or metaphor representing a pure philosophical truth.

Among the other Greek philosophies available to the Hellenistic Jews of the last three centuries BCE were the teachings of the Epicureans (a school that, like the Stoics, offered a way of life leading to complete inward detachment, but with an emphasis on overcoming anxiety and the fear of death, fate, and injurious divine intervention) and a revival of ancient Pythagorean doctrines, including those dealing with the esoteric significance of numbers. Various Platonic notions, reinterpreted in an extremely religious, even mystical way, were increasingly absorbed into Stoicism and Neo-Pythagoreanism. (By the third century CE, this last tendency was to coalesce into the philosophical tradition of Neo-Platonism, of great importance for medieval religious thought, Jewish included.) As a result, Jews who plunged into the study of Hellenistic wisdom and learning and who mastered its models of reasoned argumentation and effective rhetoric as well as its doctrines of logic and ethics, of the ideal state and the ultimate nature of reality—or even Jews who merely absorbed some of its more popular features indirectly—found themselves confronted by intellectual resources and challenges of a quite different character than the ancient Near Eastern mythology in reaction to which Judaism had first developed.

As mentioned earlier, all branches and forms of Judaism were affected in some degree by the spiritual concerns and social pressures of the Hellenistic environment (the Greek language and culture penetrated Judea as it did the other lands of the Near East), but the greatest overt borrowing from Hellenism occurred among the Jews of the Mediterranean diaspora, especially the metropolis of Alexandria. Alexandrian Jewry produced an extensive body of writings in the Greek language, some surviving only in quotations, but other works having been preserved in almost complete form by the Christian Church.

The earliest important achievement of Alexandrian Jewry was the translation of the Bible into Greek, known as the Septuagint (from the Latin for *seventy*, according to a legend that the Septuagint Pentateuch was the work of seventy-two divinely inspired scholars). The Septuagint Pentateuch was probably translated during the third century BCE and the Prophets and Hagiographa in the following century.[1] Inasmuch as the Hebrew canon was still partly in flux, the Septuagint contains books and sections of books eventually not included in the Jewish Bible,

Fresco from the synagogue of Dura-Europas, third century CE. The figure wears a Roman-style toga and reads from a Torah scroll. (Courtesy of the Union of American Hebrew Congregations.)

works originally written in Hebrew (Ben Sira) and other works composed directly in Greek by Hellenistic-Jewish writers. (Material retained in the Septuagint but not in the Hebrew Old Testament is called the Apocrypha.[2]) In view of the considerable differences between Greek and Hebrew grammar and vocabulary, the Septuagint was a remarkable achievement, laying the groundwork for correlation of key biblical concepts such as "Torah," "soul," "salvation," and "sin" with Greek counterparts frequently possessing quite different connotations. For several centuries the Septuagint was the biblical text used and expounded by Greek-speaking Jews throughout the Mediterranean. (In the second century CE other translations, more literal and faithful to the Hebrew, although less elegant in Greek style, were composed.) The Septuagint facilitated Jewish and Christian proselytism and has been called one of the most important translations ever made, because through it the Bible first became an essential element of the Western tradition.

Apart from the Septuagint, Hellenistic-Jewish literature includes epic poems and tragic dramas on biblical themes, of which only a few passages have been preserved; historical works (1 and 2 Maccabees on the Maccabean revolt, 3 Maccabees on a supposed persecution of the Jews of Egypt in the mid-third century BCE, the *Letter of Aristeas* containing the legend of how the Septuagint was translated); imitations of pagan prophecies, which denounced idolatry and praised Jewish monotheism (the Jewish core of the Sibylline Oracles); and several treatises showing the growing impact of Hellenistic philosophy on Jews (the Wisdom of Solomon in the Apocrypha, 4 Maccabees, and the writings of Philo of Alexandria).[3]

How did Hellenistic-Jewish writers appropriate Greek philosophical themes for the defense of their religion? Belief in one God was a connecting link. In the *Letter of Aristeas*, the Jewish author puts in the mouth of a pagan the statement that the Jews "worship the same God—the Lord and creator of the Universe—as all other men, as we ourselves, O king, though we call him by different names, such as Zeus or Dis" (line 15).[4] In the same work, the High Priest of the Jerusalem Temple explains to his gentile guest that Moses "proved first of all that there is only one God and that his power is manifested throughout the universe, since every place is filled with his sovereignty and none of the things which are wrought in secret by men upon the earth escapes his knowledge" (line 132). It was a widespread assumption among Hellenistic-Jewish intellectuals that the Greek philosophers had acquired their ideas, especially of the one God, from Moses. What distinguished the Jewish God from the deities of the Hellenistic masses was that no image could be made of him, and criticism of pagan idolatry was a common theme of Hellenistic-Jewish literature. The author of the *Letter of Aristeas* asserts that "All mankind except ourselves believe in the existence of many gods, though they themselves are much more powerful than the beings whom they vainly worship. For when they have made statues of stone and wood, they say that they are the images of those who have invented something useful for life and they worship them, though they have clear proof that they possess no feeling" (lines 134–35). For Hellenistic-Jewish writers, idolatry, especially the representation of gods as animals, was a reprehensible deceit and a source of vice, "the beginning and cause and end of every evil" (Wisdom of Solomon 14:27).

If worship of idols was the most objectionable feature of pagan religion to the Jewish thinkers, the most criticized feature of Judaism among pagans was the Jewish law, which isolated the Jews from full social intercourse with the larger world. A philosophical defense of the rationality of the Jewish law was therefore necessary. In the *Letter of Aristeas* the High Priest explains,

> Now our Lawgiver being a wise man and specially endowed by God to understand all things, took a comprehensive view of each particular detail, and fenced us round with impregnable ramparts and walls of iron, that we might not mingle at all with any of the other nations, but remain pure in body and soul, free from all vain imaginations, worshipping the one Almighty God above the whole creation. [Line 139.]

The author proceeds to apply the allegorical method of the Stoics to a defense of the Jewish laws concerning unclean and clean animals. By distinguishing between wild, carnivorous animals which "tyrannize" over the others and tame animals which feed only on grain, the biblical lawgiver "gives a sign by means of [these laws] that those, for whom the legislation was ordained, must practice righteousness in their hearts and not tyrannize over any one in reliance upon their own strength nor rob them of anything, but steer their course of life in accordance with justice, just as the tame birds, already mentioned, consume the different kinds of grain that grow upon the earth and do not tyrannize to the destruction of their own kindred" (line 147). He concludes that

> nothing has been enacted in the Scripture thoughtlessly or without due reason, but its purpose is to enable us throughout our whole life and in all our actions to practice righteousness before all men, being mindful of the Almighty God. And so concerning meats and things unclean, creeping things, and wild beasts, the whole system aims at righteousness and righteous relationships between man and man. [Line 168.]

The impact of Stoic ethical theory on Judaism is especially apparent in 4 Maccabees, an address on the theme that "Inspired Reason" triumphs over the passions by facilitating the repression of physical appetites and the attainment of temperance.[5]

Accordingly, when we feel a desire to eat water-animals and birds and beasts and meats of every description forbidden to us under the Law, we abstain through the predominance of Reason. For the propensions of our appetites are checked and inhibited by the temperate mind, and all the movements of the body obey the bridle of Reason. [1:34–35.]

Martyrdom is the most extreme instance of self-control for the sake of a higher end, and the author of 4 Maccabees describes with much dramatic detail the refusals of the aged Eleazar and of the widow and her seven sons to obey Antiochus IV Epiphanes' command that they eat pork. Eleazar declares,

Were our Law, as you suggest, not truly divine, while we vainly believed it to be divine, not even so would it be right for us to destroy our reputation for piety. Think it not, then, a small sin for us to eat the unclean thing, for the transgression of the Law, be it in small things or in great, is equally heinous; for in either case equally the Law is despised. And you scoff at our philosophy, as if under it we were living in a manner contrary to Reason. Not so, for the Law teaches us self-control, so that we are masters of all our pleasures and desires and are thoroughly trained in manliness so as to endure all pain with readiness; and it teaches us justice, so that with all our various dispositions we act fairly, and it teaches us righteousness, so that with due reverence we worship only the God who is. Therefore do we eat no unclean meat; for believing our Law to be given by God, we know also that the Creator of the world, as a Lawgiver, feels for us according to our nature. [5:18–26.]

Despite extensive use of Stoic formulas, however, the author of 4 Maccabees does not depict the martyrs as self-sufficient Stoic sages, but as God-fearing Jews who die heroically from the tortures inflicted on them and are "gathered together unto the place of their ancestors, having received pure and immortal souls from God" (18:23–24). The "Reason" that the author extols is inspired by God and not inherent in the cosmos; the righteousness that he praises is obedience to the revealed legislation of the Torah.

Of all the doctrines of Stoic philosophy, one most amenable to synthesis with biblical thought was the concept of a divine wisdom that pervades the universe and directs man to spiritual well-being. Already present in the book of Proverbs, the notion of wisdom as a principle of order manifest in the world is developed further by the Wisdom of Solomon.

For it is [God] who gave me unerring knowledge of what exists, to know the structure of the world and the activity of the elements; the beginning and end and middle of times, the alternations of the solstices and the changes of the seasons, the cycles of the year and the constellations of the stars, the natures of animals and the tempers of wild beasts, the powers of spirits and the reasonings of men, the varieties of plants and the virtues of roots; I have learned both what is secret and what is manifest, for wisdom, the fashioner of all things, taught me. [7:17–22.]

According to the Wisdom of Solomon, wisdom instructs man in the cardinal virtues of Platonic philosophy (self-control, prudence, courage, and justice) and inspires the pious to become prophets and friends of God (8:17; 7:27). Wisdom is "more mobile than any motion, . . . a breath of the power of God, and a pure emanation of the glory of the Almighty; . . . a reflection of eternal light, a spotless mirror of the working of God, and an image of his goodness" (7:24–26). Wisdom is the divine agent by means of which God guides not only nature but history: Chapters 10–19 review major episodes in Genesis and Exodus, showing that the experience of the righteous illustrates God's providential control of the universe. Israel's history demonstrates that the universe works according to a pre-established and wise arrangement that God implanted in the elements at creation.

The acquisition of wisdom also leads to eternal life. The Wisdom of Solomon alludes to the typically Greek contrast between body and soul (8:19, 9:15), and presupposes a conception of immortality much closer to the notion of the liberation of the spirit from the fetters of matter than to the belief in a resurrection of soul and body together that became the norm in Judaism later. An even more conspicuous instance of the impact of this and other Hellenistic ideas on Judaism will be found, however, in the writings of Philo of Alexandria.

Philo

Philo Judaeus, as he is called, was, as far as we know, the most important Hellenistic-Jewish thinker to correlate the Bible and Greek philosophy. The writings of Philo's Hellenistic-Jewish predecessors have survived as quotations in later books or in the form of treatises, such as 4 Maccabees and the Wisdom of Solomon, which reflect only indirectly the influence of Greek ideas. Philo represents the intersection of three intellectual milieus. He brought to the study of Greek philosophy and literature a firm devotion to biblical monotheism and to the Jewish people. He brought to the interpretation of the Bible a substantial education in Greek thought. And he undertook both these endeavors in at the turn of the Common Era, when Hellenistic religion was increasingly preoccupied with personal salvation through direct communion with a transcendent deity. Although Philo was not a systematic philosopher,

First- or second-century BCE Alexandrian Jews, from a sixth-century CE mosaic in the church of San Vitale, Ravenna. (Editorial Photo Archives, Inc.)

he had a coherent point of view, making him perhaps the first true theologian and the first great mystic in the Jewish tradition.[6]

Of his biography we know relatively little. Philo participated in a delegation of Alexandrian Jews who journeyed to Rome in 40 CE, seeking to dissuade the Emperor Gaius Caligula, who took quite seriously his imperial self-deification, from installing a statue of himself in the Jerusalem Temple. Since Philo remarks in his account of that mission that he was already elderly, it is assumed that he was born around 20 BCE and died a few years after the trip, perhaps about 50 CE. He belonged to a wealthy, influential family; his brother, a prominent banker, was a leader of Alexandrian Jewry, a confidant of the Herod Agrippa who became king of Judea between 41 and 44 CE, and a friend of Claudius, who succeeded Caligula as Roman emperor. One of Philo's nephews married King Herod Agrippa's daughter; another nephew, the apostate Tiberius Julius Alexander, was Roman governor of Judea and of Egypt and a general in the Roman army during the siege of Jerusalem in 70 CE.

From childhood on, Philo acquired a thorough and extensive knowledge of Greek poetry, history, and philosophy. He was at home in the theater and the athletic stadium. He wrote in fluent Greek—an outstanding exemplar of the Hellenistic ideal that through training a member of a non-Greek people could become a Hellene. Of his Jewish education we know little, except that it centered on the meticulous study of the Septuagint. (Many scholars consider it unlikely that he knew much, if any, Hebrew.) Despite his Hellenism, Philo was a devout Jew who saw in Judaism the finest presentation of religious truth and the best philosophy. He made at least one pilgrimage to the Temple in Jerusalem, participated actively at times in Jewish communal affairs in Alexandria, and probably lectured frequently in public on his religious views. Almost all his surviving writings are allegorical expositions of Scripture.

We saw earlier that the *Letter of Aristeas* applied the allegorical method of the Stoics to the biblical food laws. Fragments of Aristobulus, an Alexandrian Jew of the second century BCE, indicate that he also viewed the Pentateuchal stories as symbols of philosophical principles. It would seem that this approach was popular in some circles of Alexandrian Jewry: Philo warns against the temptation to disregard the duty of concrete observance because one has grasped the allegorical significance of a Jewish ceremony. The literal and the allegorical meanings were both necessary, the first being the "body," the second the "soul" of Scripture. In one of his writings, Philo describes a Jewish monastic sect, the Therapeutae, who lived outside Alexandria and devoted themselves to allegorical exegesis of the Bible:

> They read the Holy Scriptures and seek wisdom from their ancestral philosophy by taking it as an allegory, since they think that the words of the literal

text are symbols of something whose hidden nature is revealed by studying the underlying meaning. They have also writings of men of old, the founders of their way of thinking, who left many memorials of the form used in allegorical interpretation and these they take as a kind of archetype and imitate the method in which this principle is carried out. . . . For these people [the rational soul], looking through the words as through a mirror, beholds the marvellous beauties of the concepts, unfolds and removes the symbolic coverings and brings forth the thoughts and sets them bare to the light of day for those who need but a little reminding to enable them to discern the inward and hidden through the outward and visible. [*On the Contemplative Life*, 28, 78.]

Unlike the work of most ancient thinkers, perhaps three fourths of Philo's writings have survived. The bulk fall into two series. The Exposition of the Law and The Allegorical Interpretation. The Exposition, possibly composed for non-Jews sympathetic to Judaism, defends the excellence and rationality of the Mosaic legislation; through its fulfillment one becomes a loyal citizen of the cosmos, "regulating his doings by the purpose and will of Nature." This series of treatises begins with Philo's interpretation of the creation story of Genesis, continues with portraits of the patriarchs as "living exemplifications" of the divine laws (only the philosophical biographies of Abraham and Joseph have survived), and then proceeds to the Pentateuchal legislation, which is shown to have been designed by Moses under divine inspiration, according to a pattern directly revealed by God in the Decalogue. The Exposition concludes with a treatise on the Law in relationship to the Greek philosophical virtues and a treatise on divine rewards and punishments, including those mentioned specifically in Leviticus and Deuteronomy. (Philo's biography of Moses as the ideal figure for the revelation of the divine law is often linked to this group of writings.)

The Allegorical Interpretation consists of eighteen treatises on verses in chapters 2 through 20 of Genesis, in which Philo concentrates on their esoteric and mystical meaning. Only a few parts of a third series, "Questions and Answers on Genesis and Exodus," have been preserved in Armenian translation. Four purely philosophical essays have also survived, as well as the description of the Therapeutae (*On the Contemplative Life*) previously quoted. Philo also wrote two historical narratives: *Against Flaccus*, critical of a Roman governor of Egypt for encouraging anti-Jewish riots there during the reign of Caligula, and *Embassy to Gaius*, describing Philo's visit to the imperial court in Rome.

The contrasts between body and soul, spirit and matter, the mind and the senses pervade Philo's thought and are among his most conspicuous debts to the Greeks. In the following passage God is conceived as the Mind of the universe.

Moses, both because he had attained the very summit of philosophy, and because he had been divinely instructed in the greater and the most essential part of Nature's lore, could not fail to recognize that the universe must consist of two parts, one part active Cause and the other passive object; and that the active Cause is the perfectly pure and unsullied Mind of the universe, transcending virtue, transcending knowledge, transcending the good itself and the beautiful itself; while the passive part is in itself incapable of life and motion, but, when set in motion and shaped and quickened by Mind, changes into the most perfect masterpiece, namely this world. [*On the Creation*, 8.]

God is a Oneness beyond the ability of the finite human mind to grasp. Philo's conception of God is a fusion of Greek and Jewish elements. Using Greek philosophical terms to emphasize the self-sufficiency and immutability of God, he retains the biblical notions of God's creativity and providential concern for every particular thing in the world. God is the infinite and ultimate One whose very nature it is to exist. Indeed, God is Being itself, a notion for which Philo finds justification in the Septuagint rendering of such biblical verses as "I AM has sent thee," "I AM THAT I AM," "The Lord is One." What can be asserted of God is that He is superior to everything in the world and to all human categories. What must be denied is that God is in any sense compound, that He is in need of anything, that He is limited by time or place. "God fills all things; He contains, but is not contained" (*On the Confusion of Tongues*, 136). Because God's nature is entirely perfect and utterly indescribable, nothing can be positively asserted of His essence—other than that He exists.

But how do we know that God exists? Philo employs the argument that the benevolent orderliness of nature surely indicates a divine designer:

We see then that any piece of work always involves the knowledge of a workman. Who can look upon statues or painting without thinking at once of a sculptor or painter? Who can see clothes or ships or houses without getting the idea of a weaver and a shipwright and a housebuilder? And when one enters a well-ordered city in which the arrangements for civil life are very admirably managed, what else will he suppose but that this city is directed by good rulers? So then he who comes to the truly Great City, this world, and beholds hills and plains teeming with animals and plants, the rivers, spring-fed or winter torrents, streaming along, the seas with their expanses, the air with its happily tempered phases, the yearly seasons passing into each other, and then the sun and moon ruling the day and night, and the other heavenly bodies fixed or planetary and the whole firmament revolving in rhythmic order, must he not naturally or rather necessarily gain the conception of the Maker and Father and Ruler also? For none of the works of human art is self made, and the highest art and knowledge is shown in this universe, so that surely it has been wrought by one of excellent knowledge and absolute perfection. In this way we have gained the conception of the existence of God. [*The Special Laws* I, 33–35.]

The argument from design implies that God, although transcendent in relation to the created world, is immanent within the order of nature. In developing this notion, Philo uses Plato's doctrine of Ideas or Forms —the patterns of things in the phenomenal world—and the Stoic notion of an indwelling divine Reason, a Logos that endows the world with intelligibility. Through these concepts God is shown to be above the world and yet a force pervading it, tranquil and yet active. For Philo, the Ideas (or Powers as he usually calls them) are God's thoughts prior to creation and subsequently the instruments by which God imposes regularity on matter. Philo interprets Moses' request to see God's glory (Ex. 33:18) as his desire to discern these divine Powers. God is said to tell Moses that one cannot physically apprehend these Powers, but can see only the result of their working. Just as men use seals to stamp impressions on wax, God's Powers supply structure to created being. "Some among you call them not inaptly 'Forms' or 'Ideas,' since they bring form into everything that is, giving order to the disordered, limit to the unlimited, bounds to the unbounded, shape to the shapeless, and in general change the worse into something better" (*The Special Laws* I, 45–50).

Inasmuch as Philo is interested not in nature itself but in God's relation to the world, the most important divine Powers, in his view, are goodness and sovereignty. *Theos*, the Septuagint translation of Elohim, symbolizes God's creative and merciful Power; *Kyrios*, the translation of the divine name YHVH, represents his ruling and punishing Power. The supreme Idea, the "Idea of Ideas" that unifies all the divine Powers, is the Logos, which emanates from God like light from the sun. The Logos is an aspect of God and yet is conceptually distinct from God's transcendent being—in effect, it is the highest intermediary between God and the world. Drawing on the concept of wisdom in Proverbs and in the Wisdom of Solomon, Philo praises the Logos as "the first born son" of God (see Prov. 8:22), the "image of God" (see Gen. 1:26), the divine "cupbearer," God's "chief messenger" and highest angel. The Logos is the immaterial agency through which God's activity is manifest in the world. Embodied in the Torah, the Logos is God's Law for men to live by.

Logos is immanent not only in the cosmos and in Torah, but in man himself. Through his body and the lower faculties of his soul, man belongs to the realm of the senses; the human mind, the highest faculty of the soul, is akin to God, being made in the image of the divine Logos. In the supersensual world of truth, the two most important realities are God and the rational part of the soul.

> For the heavenly element in us is the mind, . . . and it is the mind which pursues the learning of the schools and the other arts one and all, which sharpens and whets itself, and trains and drills itself strong in the contemplation of what is intelligible by mind. [*On the Giants*, 60.]

The "practical life," which is necessarily immersed in the tasks and duties of the everyday, is but "a prelude to a more advanced contest," the pursuit of "a quite different way of life [the contemplative life] whose delight is in knowledge and study of principles alone" (*On Flight and Finding*, 36–37). Contemplation, however, is not for the sake of empirical knowledge but a means to attain one's true destiny. On the earth, human souls are "sojourners" and "pilgrims" in a foreign country, destined to return eventually to their native land, "the heavenly region where their citizenship lies" (*On the Confusion of Tongues*, 78). Philo's attitude toward scientific investigation and philosophy is ambivalent. To be sure, conjecture and theorizing are valuable.

> Nothing is better than to search for the true God, even if the discovery of Him eludes human capacity, since the very wish to learn, if earnestly entertained, produces untold joys and pleasures. . . . For the very seeking, even without finding, is felicity in itself, just as no one blames the eyes of the body because when unable to see the sun itself they see the emanation of its rays as it reaches the earth, which is but the extremity of the brightness which the beams of the sun give forth. [*The Special Laws* I, 36–40.]

Through science and philosophy the individual can prepare to meet God, but clear apprehension of the divine light cannot be won by human effort alone. In the final analysis, every virtue is a gift of God, freely given: Active intrusion of the divine into the individual's mind is necessary for salvation.

Philo's theory of mystical encounter with God is shaped by the biblical notion of prophetic inspiration and by the Hellenistic quest to flee the "prison of the body" and "bondage to the flesh," with the Hellenistic influence predominating. The soul dwells in the body as in a tomb, and the goal of life is liberation. When God tells Abraham to leave his country, kindred, and father's house, Philo explains that this signifies that one should strive to escape the chains of corporeality and sensuality, humbly admit his worthlessness and recognize his creaturely dependence on divine help. "For Abraham . . . drew near and said, 'Now I have begun to speak to the Lord, and I am earth and ashes' (Gen. 18:27), since it is just when he knows his own nothingness that the creature

should come into the presence of his Maker" (*Who Is the Heir*, 30).
If one is prepared to receive divine grace, a moment of mystical exaltation may be had even in the body. This state (which Philo claims to
have experienced) he calls "sober intoxication," an ecstatic rapture of
the soul seized by God. "Now when grace fills the soul, that soul thereby
rejoices and smiles and dances, for it is possessed and inspired, so that
to many of the unenlightened it may seem to be drunken, crazy, and
beside itself" (*On Drunkenness*, 146). The most esoteric level of Philo's
allegorical interpretation of the Pentateuch is that Moses, in cryptic and
mysterious language, describes the universal human condition and man's
path to salvation. The soul descends into the world where it is captured
by the wiles of the senses and of physical pleasure. But the soul gradually
extracts itself from the body through learning and wisdom, which ready
it for God's entrance into the mind. Only at death, when the elements
of which man is composed "disunite," and the "shell-like growth which
encased him" is stripped away, does the soul, "laid bare," attain a permanent state of immortal bliss (*On the Virtues*, 76).

There is almost no trace of messianic eschatology in Philo's Judaism.
The name Israel he interprets as "the man or people" who "sees God."
To be sure, the best of the Greeks and barbarians acknowledge "the
supreme Father of gods and men and the Maker of the whole universe,"
but it is the Jewish people alone which actually chooses the service of
the Uncreated and Eternal One.

> For Moses alone, it is plain, had grasped the thought that the whole nation
> from the very first was akin to things divine, a kinship most vital, and a
> far more genuine tie than that of blood, and, therefore, he declared it the
> heir of all good things that human nature can contain. [*On the Virtues*, 79.]

It follows that Philo was very receptive to proselytes.

> Having laid down laws for members of the same nation, [Moses] holds
> that the incomers [proselytes] too should be accorded every favor and con-
> sideration as their due, because abandoning their kinsfolk by blood, their
> country, their customs, and the temples and images of their gods, and the
> tributes and honors paid to them, they have taken the journey to a better
> home, from idle fables to the clearer vision of truth and the worship of the
> one and truly existing God. [*On the Virtues*, 102.]

Drawing on the imagery and vocabulary of the Greek mystery cults (he
scorned the mystery cults themselves as mythological fables and occult
delusions), Philo describes Judaism as a sacred legislation and inspired
teaching that introduces its initiates into true and holy mysteries—those
most beautiful of all possessions, "the knowledge of the Cause and of

virtue, and besides these two, of the fruit which is engendered by them both" (*On the Cherubim*, 48).

Exploring potentialities of Jewish monotheism through the medium of Greek thought, Philo introduced into Jewish theology several striking departures from biblical thinking, especially a dualism of body and soul and an ascetic deprecation of the physical world. (Although advocating a frugal life of strict self-control, he did disapprove of excessive mortification.) Few of Philo's ideas were directly absorbed into Judaism during the next few centuries. The Alexandrian Judaism for which Philo is the spokesman was soon to be decimated by pogroms and war. His mode of thought was carried on by Christians, who preserved his writings because the allegorical method and some of his ideas, especially the Logos, were useful for explicating Christian doctrine. Philo also represents an important stage in the emergence of the Neo-Platonic school of philosophy in late antiquity, which held that the cosmos was a hierarchical continuum of grades of being, emanating out of the One into the lower levels of reality; this Neo-Platonism was later to have considerable impact on Christian and Jewish thought.

Even though Philo had little direct impact on Judaism, the problem he faced—how to integrate Greek philosophy and Jewish teaching in a single conception of ultimate truth—returned in full force to confront Jewish thinkers in the Middle Ages. Like Philo, they used allegory (though of a different sort); like Philo, they interpreted the God of Judaism in Greek philosophical categories and remolded Greek assumptions about God, man, and world from the perspective of scriptural faith. Philo was also a precursor of the monotheistic mysticism that reached its Jewish fruition in the Kabbalah during the medieval and early modern periods. However, medieval Jewish philosophy and mysticism would arise only after Judaism had been substantially transformed as a result of movements already active in Judea before Philo's lifetime.

Religious Groupings Within Judean Judaism

During the last two centuries BCE and the first century CE Judea was the scene of a religious ferment out of which came new formulations of belief, new patterns of organization, and new styles of personal holiness, which would decisively affect the religious traditions of the Near East and Europe—Jewish, Christian, and eventually Muslim—for many centuries.

The main written sources for Judean Judaism in the Late Hellenistic and early Roman period are the following: 1 and 2 Maccabees and the books of Josephus that narrate the history of Judea in the period between

Caves near Qumran where the Dead Sea Scrolls were found. (Courtesy of the Consulate General of Israel.)

the Maccabean revolt and the Roman-Jewish war; rabbinical text from the late second to the sixth centuries CE, which preserve oral traditions from the earlier period; the New Testament, which refers to Jewish religious movements of the first century CE; certain Jewish religious works not accepted into the canon of the Hebrew Bible but preserved by various Christian communities, and works discovered recently in the Judean desert (the Dead Sea Scrolls). Difficulties arise with the use of all these sources. The authors of Maccabees and Josephus mention religious groups only when they directly affect political events. Information on Judaism before 70 CE in rabbinic writings and the New Testament is filtered through the interests and outlooks of rabbinic Judaism and Christianity in later times. The noncanonical works are probably not representative of the major movements of the time, but of extremist and minority tendencies. As a result, scholars have at their disposal considerable information about Judaism during the period under discussion, but crucial gaps and problems of interpretation remain.

A first area of difficulty arises from a lack of firsthand knowledge about the workings of Jewish religious institutions. In the Hellenistic and Roman eras, the sanctity and splendor of the Jerusalem Temple had won international renown. Surrounded by a complex of buildings and courtyards, staffed by Aaronide priests administering the sacrifices and by Levitical guilds of musicians and Temple assistants, supported by a half-shekel tax collected from all Jews, the Temple was the goal of pilgrims from throughout Judea and the diaspora. Meeting in one of its chambers was the Sanhedrin, a supreme legislative-judicial assembly, but whether at that time the Sanhedrin was controlled by the chief priests or whether nonpriestly legists played a predominant role in its proceedings remains a matter of scholarly dispute. Also unclear is the degree of authority that the Sanhedrin exerted over provincial and local courts and in the diaspora, and what role the Judean king or the Roman administration played in the decisions of the Judean legal system. We have no direct knowledge whether local Jewish courts adjudicated on the basis of ad hoc, spontaneous inferences from Scripture or whether they had a systematized body of traditional law to supplement biblical precedents. Judea in the first century CE had a network of educational institutions, ranging from elementary to advanced, but the full extent of what was taught in them is unknown. Especially important is the character of the synagogue at this time. Already the synagogue had become the main focus of religious life for most Jews, having apparently developed out of the local assembly. (The Hebrew term *bet ha-knesset*, house of assembly, indicates that the community rather than the building itself is historically prior; the Greek term *synagogue* also refers originally to the congregation rather than the place where it assembled.) The synagogue was a center of communal prayer and learning where the Bible was read, translated into vernacular Aramaic, and interpreted. But the relation of synagogue leadership to the various religious groupings during this period remains a problematic area for historical reconstruction.

A second area of uncertainty has to do with the origin and development of the various religious movements shortly to be described. Lack of sufficient data means that any account of the rise of a grouping and the changes it underwent remains speculative. For example, 1 Maccabees 2:42 and 7:13 mention the Hasideans (from the Hebrew *ḥasid*, a pious person). The Hasideans were among the first to oppose the Jewish Hellenizers in 167 BCE; many were martyred by Antiochus Epiphanes. They supported the Maccabees; once religious persecution ceased, they withdrew from the Maccabean army and accepted the High Priest appointed by the Seleucids but eventually the Hasideans quarreled with him too. Here information stops. It has been suggested that the Hasideans represent the beginnings of the Essenes or of the Pharisees, but no definitive answer is yet possible.

With these difficulties in mind, we will now survey the main groups within Judean Judaism during this crucial formative period, limiting ourselves to a summary of the most reliable though, unfortunately, incomplete data.

Sadducees and Pharisees

According to Josephus, the three principal Jewish "philosophies" in the first century BCE and first century CE were those of the Sadducees, Pharisees, and Essenes. As we shall see in the following section, the Essenes separated themselves from society at large, whereas the Sadducees and the Pharisees were bitter rivals for the support of the people. Josephus relates that the two groups disagreed on the principle of immortal life, the Sadducees rejecting the belief that the soul survived death and the Pharisees holding that the soul of the good after death passes into another body. They also had different views on fate and free will, the Sadducees denying that there was a determinative fate and the Pharisees affirming fate and free will. (By fate Josephus may have meant divine providence.) The crux of their conflict, however, was not general theology but the nature and source of Jewish law.

The term *Sadducee* is apparently derived from the Hebrew name Zadok, a priest of Jerusalem during the time of the biblical kings David and Solomon (1 Kings 2:35). (In Ezekiel 40:46, 43:19, and elsewhere the Jerusalem priests are called sons of Zadok.) In post-Maccabean times the Sadducees seems to have been mainly upper-class Judeans who supported the priesthood as the supreme religious authority in Judaism and adhered, in this regard, to the literal meaning of the Pentateuch. The term *Pharisee* is more difficult to explain; it comes from the Hebrew *parush*, meaning separated. Some scholars surmise that it was applied to the Pharisees because they separated themselves from the masses for the sake of holiness; others suggest that this name was given them by opponents who charged they had separated themselves from the Sadducean interpretation of Scriptures. The Pharisees were men skilled in law and jurisprudence who possessed (according to the New Testament) in addition to the Bible, a body of unwritten "traditions of the fathers" (Gal. 1:14, Phil. 3:5, Matt. 23:2–4). Josephus explains that they had a reputation as "exact exponents of the law":

> The Pharisees have passed down to the people certain regulations handed down by former generations and not recorded in the laws of Moses, for which reason they are rejected by the Sadducean group, who hold that only those regulations should be considered valid which were written down, and that those which had not been handed down by former generations need not be observed. [*Antiquities* XIII, 297.[7]]

The Pharisaic tradition is the most important strand of what becomes after 70 CE rabbinic Judaism. (The term *rabbi*, master, comes into use as a title after the destruction of the Temple.) Rabbinic literature has preserved several accounts of disputes between Pharisees and Sadducees over points of law. Apart from these controversies, the term Pharisee is not widely used in rabbinical sources where the preferred term is sages (*hakhamim*, singular *hakham*).

According to rabbinic writings, the Pharisaic sages first appear in history as "the men of the Great Assembly." (Unfortunately we know almost nothing of this body; modern theories about when it flourished range from the time of Ezra in the mid-fifth century BCE to that of the Maccabees in the mid-second century BCE.) Subsequently there was a chain of five generations of "pairs" (*zugot*) of outstanding Pharisees, leaders of the Pharisaic supreme court up to the beginning of the first century CE. Josephus, who does not refer either to the Great Assembly or the pairs, first mentions the Pharisees as having been closely associated with the Hasmonean ruler John Hyrcanus. When the Pharisees challenged his priestly legitimacy, John Hyrcanus decided to favor the Sadducees. During the civil war of the reign of Alexander Janneus, the Pharisees were among the king's enemies and a large number were executed. Restored to power by Salome Alexandra, the Pharisees exacted retribution on the Sadducees. In a Jewish commonwealth, authority to interpret religious law was a political issue of considerable magnitude.

According to Josephus there were about 6,000 Pharisees during Herod's reign. Soon after his death one segment of the Pharisees, adamantly opposed to Roman rule, separated to become a "fourth philosophy" (to be discussed in the next section). The rest were, apparently, willing to accept the loss of Judean political independence. By the second or third decade of the Common Era they, in turn, had become divided into two "houses" (schools of thought) founded by the last of the "pairs," Hillel and Shammai. Rabbinic writings portray Hillel as one of the greatest of the early sages, a man responsible for important legal decisions, for introducing the use of hermeneutic or interpretative rules to extend biblical laws to new situations, and for incisive ethical maxims. To Hillel is ascribed one of the earliest formulations of the Golden Rule: "Do not do unto others as you would not have them do unto you." Hillel is said to have taught: "Be of the disciples of Aaron, loving peace and pursuing peace, loving your fellow-creatures and drawing them to the Torah"; "Do not judge your fellowman until you have come into his position"; and the interlinked series of rhetorical questions, "If I am not for myself, who will be for me? If I am for myself alone, what am I? If not now, when?"⁸ Hillel was said to be very patient in winning proselytes over to Judaism, whereas his rival, Shammai, more conservative and severe, was less hospitable in this regard. Their respective disciples, the "school of Hillel" and the "school of Shammai," disagreed on several hundred specific details of Jewish law until the views of the Hillelites generally prevailed after 70 CE.

Rabbinic traditions of the first century CE also mention Pharisaic brotherhoods as constituting what scholars call a "table fellowship," a group that adheres to a uniform definition of the Jewish food laws and participates in common meals, probably accompanied by prayer and learned discussion. (Another instance of a table fellowship, the Essenes, will be described in the following section.) If these fellowships are a feature of the Pharisaic movement as a whole, this information tallies with traditions cited in the name of specific Pharisees before 70 CE, which deal mainly with matters of personal piety, such as eating food that had been correctly tithed, following the rules of ritual purity, and carefully observing the Sabbath and the festivals. On the matter of ritual purity it would seem that the Pharisees accomplished two significant changes. They liberalized the laws as applied to the common people, making biblical obligations less onerous in the urban milieu. At the same time, they democratized Jewish piety by extending to all Jews various commandments that had previously been observed only by the priests.

The description of the Pharisees up to this point has avoided an issue on which there is great disagreement among historians: Were the Pharisees the dominant group in Judean Judaism before 70 CE or were they a minority with only limited impact on society in this period? At least three scholarly positions are taken on this controversy. Closest to the traditional rabbinic view but held by some eminent modern scholars is that the Pharisaic sages are the direct continuation of the scribes mentioned in connection with Ezra in the mid-fifth century BCE, a professional class that preserved, interpreted, and applied the oral traditions that supplemented the written biblical legislation. (The concept of a two-fold Torah, consisting of laws written down in the Bible and of laws orally transmitted from ancient times, was an important theme of rabbinic thought after 70 CE.) A second view holds that the Pharisee was a new kind of scribal intellectual who rose to prominence in the wake of social unrest and the decline of priestly prestige during the Maccabean upheavals. According to this position, the Pharisees used the concept of an Oral Torah to justify their authority against the Sadducees, who continued to support the supremacy of the priests, in which case the Pharisees are a broadly based movement controlling the Judean legal system and the Sanhedrin from Maccabean times on, except for a few brief periods of Sadducean domination. A third view argues that the Pharisees were only one of various tendencies in Judean life that aspired to leadership before 70 CE—that they were a rather small group of religious intellectuals beginning to develop the principles that came to fruition in rabbinic Judaism. This third position holds that the rabbinic traditions to the effect that the Pharisees instructed the priests in the internal management of Temple affairs are pious exaggerations of Pharisaic power and that Josephus's statement that the Pharisees enjoyed the support of the Judean masses reflects the situation only after the Roman-Jewish war; accordingly, therefore, the Sanhedrin must have been firmly in the hands of the chief priests and the local courts must have remained under the control of non-Pharisaic scribes until the postwar reconstruction.[9]

This crucial difference of opinion has not been resolved, but the profound change in Judaism of which the Pharisees were at least a symptom and possibly the major agent is quite discernible. The hereditary priestly caste, whose authority stemmed from the Pentateuch, was giving way to a leadership based on learning, knowledge, and wisdom. Scribes and sages were drawn from all levels of society: priests, Levites, lay Jews, proselytes. The sources indicate that the most important relationship between Pharisaic sages was that of teacher to student. The sage's reputation among his peers was based on learning transmitted orally from him to his disciples and on his ability to apply these teachings to specific situations. Pharisaic maxims and parables from this period deal with such subjects as fairness and honesty in judging, ethical responsibility, serving God not for the sake of reward, the sureness of divine retribution, love of the fellowman and the duty of bringing him closer to the life of Torah. The Pharisaic sages were not prophets—they believed that prophecy had come to an end. On the contrary, they resembled the philosophical sages of the Hellenistic world who sought to enlighten and guide students in right living. (Josephus compares the Pharisees to the Stoics in his autobiography, *Life*, 12.) Although some of the Pharisaic sages were reported to have briefly ascended in their lifetimes to the highest heavens—a mystical experience of which little is known—the core of Pharisaic Judaism was a rational mode of thought, which developed into the rigorously logical Torah interpretations of the later rabbis (according to their system of hermeneutic logic). The content of the Pharisaic sage's teaching was a Torah wisdom inexhaustibly and endlessly inspiring—in their eyes, the divine blueprint for creation, the ideal human life in This World and the pathway to eternal life in a World to Come. (The later rabbinic understanding of these concepts will be explained in greater detail in Chapter 6.)

Essenes and Revolutionists

The heart of the dispute between Pharisees and Sadducees was over the religious leadership of the entire people. There were, however, other groupings that withdrew from the general society into small holy communities, rejecting as illegitimate the priests who controlled the Temple in Hasmonean and Roman times. These were the Essenes, who, according to Josephus, believed in "unalterable fate" and the immortality of the soul. (It is possible, though by no means certain, that the word Essene may derive from an Aramaic cognate of the Hebrew *hasid*, pious, which might indicate a historical connection with the Hasideans mentioned earlier.) The Essenes were separatist associations or brotherhoods in the towns of Judea, and also in rural communes, where members engaged in agricultural and artisan labor and in the study of holy books. Living according to a rigorous and highly disciplined ideal of ritual purity and religious perfection, the Essenes resembled a monastic order; indeed many were celibate but there was at least one group that permitted marriage for the sake of procreation.[10]

Admission to the Essene order took place only after several periods of probation and preparation. Initiates had to swear obedience to the rules and leadership of the community and promise to keep secret its special doctrines, discipline being enforced by the expulsion of lax members after a vote of the council. Among the inner circle property was jointly owned; food, clothing, and other necessities were administered by overseers or guardians. Essene rituals included wearing of white garments, frequent ritual baths, and daily communal meals accompanied by prayer and recitation of Scripture. Josephus relates that the Essenes numbered about 4,000 in the first century CE and that Essene "prophets" or holy men were held in high regard by the masses and the kings for the accuracy of their predictions and for their medicinal lore.

The Essenes have been the subject of much discussion among scholars in recent decades since material has come to light on an Essene-like group that lived between 150 BCE and 68 CE in the Judean desert near the Dead

Excavations of the communal buildings at Qumran. (Courtesy of the Consulate General of Israel.)

Sea.[11] In 1947 Arab shepherds discovered a group of documents (the first of the so-called Dead Sea Scrolls), which were subsequently traced to eleven caves not far from Jerusalem where the desert climate had preserved them for almost 2,000 years. The Dead Sea Scrolls include communal rule books, hymns, and biblical commentaries—all previously unknown to scholars—as well as biblical manuscripts and several hundred fragments of other writings. (The scrolls will be described further in the next section.) Nearby was uncovered the remains of a community that flourished from about 130 BCE to the Roman-Jewish war, with the exception of three decades toward the end of the first century BCE when the site was temporarily abandoned. The ruins found on a cliff north of the Wadi Qumran (a *wadi* is a desert watercourse occasionally filled by torrential rain) include a tower, assembly chamber, kitchen, writing room, and workshops. (The members apparently slept in tents, caves, or upper floors of the buildings.) An elaborate arrangement of cisterns insured an adequate supply of water. The community's cemetery contained about a thousand burials. Qumran was, therefore, the headquarters of a well-organized settlement for about two centuries, which, at its height, numbered about 200. The Dead Sea Scrolls are probably the remains of their library, hidden during the Roman-Jewish war when Qumran was destroyed by Roman soldiers.

If Qumran was an Essene brotherhood and the Dead Sea Scrolls a collection of Essene writings, then the movement was less quietistic and philosophical than Josephus intimates. The Scrolls depict a priest-dominated group who considered the Temple to be controlled by wicked and corrupt men who had usurped power not rightfully theirs. From still obscure references in these writings, Qumran seems to have been founded by a priestly "Teacher of Righteousness," who was persecuted by a "Wicked Priest." (Various theories have been offered by scholars as to whom these men were; the Teacher of Righteousness is an unknown Aaronide priest and his enemy may have been one of the Hasmonean rulers, probably Jonathan or Simon.) The community looked with great hostility on the *Kittim* (probably the Romans). The Qumran sect considered itself the true heir of the Mosaic covenant and of the divine promises in the Scriptures. Members of the order had been saved from the domination of evil powers in order to settle in the wilderness as a holy society under the leadership of true priests until they could return to a purified Temple. As Men of the Covenant (sometimes Men of the New Covenant), they also constituted the elect in that God had predetermined the outcome of each individual's decision to join the holy community (the Sons of Light) or to remain with the outside forces hostile to God (the Sons of Darkness). Eventually the Sons of Light would issue forth in ritual combat under the triumphant leadership of their divinely inspired leaders to re-establish the remnant of Israel in the promised land and to witness the victory of God over the whole earth.

Present also in the Judean desert were individual charismatics probably not formally affiliated with the Essenes but whose way of life resembled the ascetic practices of that movement. In the twenties of the first century CE there was John the Baptist, "clothed with camel's hair, a leather girdle around his waist, and eating locusts and wild honey." According to the New Testament John preached a "baptism of repentance for the forgiveness of sins."[12] Another such holy man was Bannus, for three years young Josephus's mentor, "who dwelt in the wilderness, wearing only such clothing as trees provided, feeding on such things as grew of themselves, and using frequent ablutions of cold water, by day and night, for purity's sake" (Josephus, *Life*, 11–12). Several charismatic figures attracted a mass following that provoked armed repression by the Romans. In the forties of the first century a certain Theudas declared himself a prophet and persuaded crowds to follow him to the Jordan River, which was to part to let them through.

Roman cavalry sent by the procurator slaughtered many of Theudas's supporters and took the rest prisoner; Theudas was beheaded. (*Antiquities* XX, 97–99 and New Testament, Acts 5:36.) A decade later an "Egyptian false prophet" led his group to the Mount of Olives outside Jerusalem, proposing to force his way into the city, overpower the Roman garrison, and set himself up as ruler of the people. Again the procurator sent troops who killed part of the mob and dispersed the rest; the leader, however, escaped. (*War* II, 262–63 and Acts 21:38.) In the turbulent ideological atmosphere of first-century Judea, Romans did not find it easy to distinguish between pacific holy men who predicted a miraculous transformation of human existence and determined insurgents who called for violent rebellion.

No account of Jewish religious movements of the first century CE would be complete without mention of the fighters for the liberation of Judea from foreign domination, but once again the evidence for their ideology is tantalizingly incomplete. It seems that there never was a unified revolutionary movement during this time and no single, dominant messianic doctrine. Until 50 CE most Judeans acquiesced in direct Roman rule: Overt opposition was limited to generally peaceful demonstrations against sporadic threats to Jewish monotheism. There was, however, a revolutionary group that had a continuous history throughout most of the century. When direct Roman rule was instituted in Judea in 6 CE, Judas the Galilean and Zadok the Pharisee urged the people to refuse to pay taxes to the empire. According to Josephus, they established a "fourth philosophy" alongside the Sadducees, Pharisees, and Essenes:

> This school agrees in all other respects with the opinions of the Pharisees, except that they have a passion for liberty that is almost unconquerable, since they are convinced that God alone is their leader and master. They think little of submitting to death in unusual forms and permitting vengeance to fall on kinsmen and friends, if only they may avoid calling any man master. [*Antiquities* XVIII, 23.[13]]

Because Josephus usually calls the revolutionists "bandits," it is significant that he designates Judas a "sophist," implying perhaps that he was a teacher of Torah. Around 46 CE two of Judas's sons were crucified by a Roman procurator and in 66, at the start of the revolt, another son (or grandson), Menahem, seized the Dead Sea fortress of Masada. Menahem was assassinated in Jerusalem during the war by rebels who resented his royal pretensions. His contingent on Masada did not participate in the general fighting but remained there under the leadership of a relative, Eleazar ben Jair, until 74 CE when they committed mass suicide on the eve of the Roman capture of the mountain-top stronghold.

Some of the "fourth philosophy" escaped after the war to Egypt and Cyrene where they continued to refuse to acknowledge Caesar's lordship despite terrible tortures.[14]

There is little reason to believe that the emergence of the "fourth philosophy" was the main factor leading to the outbreak of hostilities, which should rather be traced to the deterioration of political and social conditions in Judea beginning in the late 40s, to the incompetence and insensitivity of the later Roman procurators, and to widespread economic hardship. Once the war broke out, a wide range of positions, moderate and radical, surfaced. In the winter of 67–68 CE a group known as the Zealots emerged in Jerusalem with a following from among the lower echelons of the priesthood. Another force, made up in part of freed slaves, coalesced around Simon bar Giora, an energetic and disciplined military leader who may have had royal ambitions. Except when these and other insurgent factions united in the face of an immediate Roman attack, they were usually at odds with each other, sometimes to the point of bloodshed.[15]

What religious beliefs fueled the uprising? The moderates may have envisioned only resistance to pagan pogroms and defensive preparations leading to negotiations with the Romans for reforms in the provincial administration that would respect more carefully the sanctity of Jewish institutions. But there was precedent in the Scriptures for a variety of more radical religious positions. We have no writings that can be explicitly identified with any of the extremist groups, but we may surmise that some of them hoped to emulate the Maccabean victories over the Seleucids and free the holy land from pagan rule. Coins issued in Jerusalem during the war are inscribed according to the year of the "redemption of Zion." Others, especially the Zealots, probably believed that purifying the Temple from pollution by gentiles and instituting a more equitable regime insured that God would help them to victory. A few, perhaps including Simon bar Giora, may have had a more explicit messianic hope: that a holy war against Rome would hasten the advent of God's kingdom of justice and truth on earth, according to Daniel 7:13–14 and other biblical prophecies. The emotional climate was certainly conducive to such eschatological expectations, for, as we shall see in the next section, the first century CE was one of the great ages of Jewish apocalypticism.

The Noncanonical Religious Books and Jewish Eschatological Hopes

Besides the Apocrypha and the Dead Sea Scrolls, there have survived a number of other Jewish religious writings from the last two centuries

BCE and the first two centuries CE. Preserved by various Christian communities in Syria, Ethiopia, and elsewhere, they were originally written in Hebrew or Aramaic, from which a Greek translation was made for diaspora Jews or for Christians; the Greek, in turn, was the basis for further translations into other languages. (As a result, these writings contain Christian interpolations, but in some cases their Jewish origin is confirmed by fragments found in the Qumran caves.) Most of these books are pseudepigraphical, that is, "falsely attributed" because the true authors hid their identities behind the name of biblical personages.[16] As mentioned in Chapter 3 in connection with the biblical book of Daniel, the pseudepigraphical form is an attempt to project into the distant past revelations and teachings that the writer wished to have accepted as true, the antiquity of a doctrine being then a widely acknowledged criterion of its veracity. Moreover, parts of the biblical canon were still in flux, so that the author may even have hoped that his revelations would be accepted as divine word. In most cases, it is impossible to pin down when and by whom these noncanonical works were written, nor do we know how wide a circulation they enjoyed and whether they are to be identified with any particular Jewish grouping. Nevertheless, the pseudepigraphical works, together with the Dead Sea Scrolls and those books of the Apocrypha with a Judean origin, testify to crucial ideas and beliefs fermenting in some pious circles of late Second Temple Judaism.

In content and style the noncanonical books are extremely diverse. Two dozen or more have survived, the most important being the following: The book of Jubilees, a retelling of Genesis and the first twelve chapters of Exodus in the form of a revelation imparted to Moses at Sinai by an angel; among his other interests the author of Jubilees wishes to show that certain Mosaic laws were already observed by the patriarchal figures of Genesis. Each event is located according to a series of Jubilee periods of forty-nine years (hence the title); in place of the lunar-solar calendar used by most Jews, the purely solar calendar links it with the calendar used in Qumran. Similar to Jubilees is the Genesis Apocryphon from the Dead Sea Scrolls, which also retells biblical tales, amplifying them with edifying legends and intrepretative elaboration. Also taking their point of departure from Genesis materials are the Testaments of the Twelve Patriarchs, in which Jacob's sons admonish the reader to avoid major sins that they confess to having committed.

A second type of noncanonical work are poetical prayers modeled on the Psalms. Two of the eighteen Psalms of Solomon are thought to contain references to historical personages of the first century BCE, including Pompey and the last Hasmonean kings. (The Psalms of Solomon is not truly pseudepigraphical because there is no mention of Solomon in the prayers, apart from the title of the work as a whole; some, but not

all scholars feel these poems should be attributed to the Pharisees.)
Among the Dead Sea Scrolls were found a group of thanksgiving psalms,
which contrast man's wicked nature and deceitful ways with the remnant
who have separated themselves to live by the light of God's covenant. A
third category, found only in the Qumran caves, are verse-by-verse commentaries on passages from the Prophets and the Psalms, applying the
biblical statement to the contemporary situation of the sectarians.

A fourth category of noncanonical, pseudepigraphical work is apocalypse. (It will be remembered from the discussion of Daniel that *apocalypse* is a term meaning revelation and used to designate a pseudonymous
work revealing hidden secrets of the End of Days; the subject of apocalyptic revelation is frequently eschatological, from the Greek *eschatos*,
"last" or "furthest.") The books of Enoch, 2 Esdras, and Baruch are
directly in line with the apocalyptic tradition of Daniel, containing
eschatological visions, often symbolic, about history and its aftermath.
Enoch is a long work by various authors, some parts of which may
even antedate Daniel. In the course of the book the narrator Enoch
(see Gen. 5:21–24) describes his visits to the extremities of the earth
and his ascent to the heavenly palaces. The book also includes a treatise
on astronomy, poems on the ultimate fate of the righteous and the
wicked, and one section, the so-called Similitudes (chaps. 37–71) referring to an angelic figure, the Chosen One or the Son of Man, who will
be sent by God in the last days to judge humanity. (Aramaic fragments
of Enoch, but not of the Similitudes, have been found in the Qumran
caves.) The other apocalyptic works, 2 Esdras and Baruch, were almost
certainly written or compiled at the end of the first century CE, within
thirty years after the destruction of the Temple. In 2 Esdras (4 Ezra
in some editions of the Apocrypha) the narrator is perplexed by the
calamities befalling Israel, the apparent abandonment by God of his
beloved people, and the question why so few will merit eternal life. An
angel provides Ezra with an account of the meaning of history and its
end, instructing him to write down and conceal "seventy books" that will
be consolation to the generation living just before the last days. Baruch,
purporting to be Jeremiah's scribe, deals with similar issues and assures
the reader that the divine judgment is just and that Israel must steadfastly
continue to trust God. Among the Dead Sea Scrolls an eschatological
book, usually entitled the *War of the Sons of Light Against the Sons of
Darkness*, describes the military and ritual arrangements for a forty-year
final struggle of God's people against the forces of evil throughout the
world.[17]

The eschatological questions perplexing Jews during this period were
these: How will Israel be liberated from pagan domination and the Kingdom of God realized? What is the ultimate destiny of the righteous and

The Genesis Apocryphon of the Dead Sea Scrolls. (Courtesy of the American Friends of the Hebrew University.)

wicked? When will the chaos and evil of history come to an end—and what will follow? A variety of beliefs and attitudes are represented in the noncanonical works, especially in the apocalypses, reflecting the diversity and flux of Judean Judaism at the time. No uniform doctrine predominated, but certain themes recur.

The messianic expectation, beginning to crystallize in Judaism at this time, had as its focus the deliverance of Israel from oppression under an ideal, anointed king. (The Hebrew *mashiah*, from which our English term *messiah* is derived, originated as a biblical adjective meaning anointed with holy oil.) The seventeenth and eighteenth Psalms of Solomon promise that a descendant of David will soon appear to overthrow the wicked rulers oppressing the Jews:

> *Behold, O Lord, and raise up to them their king, the son of David,*
> *At the time in which Thou seest, O God, that he may reign over*
> *   Israel Thy servant.*
> *And gird him with strength, that he may shatter unrighteous rulers,*
> *And that he may purge Jerusalem from nations that trample [her]*
> *   down to destruction. . . .*
> *And he shall have the heathen nations to serve him under his yoke . . .*
> *And he [shall be] a righteous king, taught of God, over them,*
> *And there shall be no unrighteousness in his days in their midst. . . .*
> *Blessed be they that shall be in those days,*
> *In that they shall see the good fortune of Israel which God shall*
> *   bring to pass in the gathering together of the tribes.*[18]

Taking place in history, the messianic goal involves the restoration of harmony between God and Israel and between God and humanity. The triumph of God means the end of Israel's servitude and, eventually, the vindication of the prophetic promises that the whole world will worship the one God. Unlike the Psalms of Solomon, the Testaments of the Twelve Patriarchs and certain Dead Sea Scrolls refer to two messianic figures, an anointed king of the tribe of Judah and an anointed priest of the tribe of Levi, the latter having precedence.

More complex is the doctrine of personal transcendence over death. Some of the noncanonical books adhere to an incorporeal immortality of the soul, like the Hellenistic concept described earlier. Other books develop the notion of a resurrection of the dead alluded to in Daniel 12:12. Some apocalyptic passages refer to a resurrection of the righteous only, others to a resurrection of the righteous for eternal reward and the wicked for eternal punishment. Some envision a resurrection of Israel alone, others a resurrection of all men. There are frequent but unclear references to a determinative judgment by God, such as the following apocalyptic vision in the book of Enoch:

> *And after this, in the tenth week in the seventh part,*
> *There shall be a great eternal judgment,*
> *In which He shall execute vengeance amongst the angels.*
> *And the first heaven shall depart and pass away,*
> *And a new heaven shall appear,*
> *And all the powers of the heavens shall give sevenfold light.*

And after that there will be many weeks without number forever,
And all shall be in goodness and righteousness,
And sin shall no more be mentioned forever.[19]

Elsewhere one of the authors of Enoch promises that the righteous, after being judged, will "shine as the lights of heaven" and will have "great joy as the angels of heaven" (104:2,5). In 2 Esdras, first the Messiah will come to denounce and destroy the wicked Romans and rescue the remnant of Israel; then, 400 years later, the resurrection and last judgment will befall mankind.

And the world shall be turned back to primeval silence for seven days, as it was at the first beginnings; so that no one shall be left. And after seven days the world, which is not yet awake, shall be roused, and that which is corruptible shall perish. And the earth shall give up those who are asleep in it, and the dust those who dwell silently in it; and the chambers shall give up the souls which have been committed to them. And the Most High shall be revealed upon the seat of judgment, and compassion shall pass away, and patience shall be withdrawn; but only judgment shall remain, trust shall stand, and faithfulness shall grow strong. And recompense shall follow, and the reward shall be manifested; righteous deeds shall awake, and unrighteous deeds not sleep. Then the pit of torment shall appear, and opposite it shall be the place of rest; and the furnace of hell shall be disclosed, and opposite it the paradise of delight. [2 Esdras 7:30–36.][20]

Neither messianic deliverance nor resurrection of the dead was an exclusively apocalyptic doctrine. The Pharisees accepted resurrection as a central Jewish belief; the Qumran community awaited the appearance of anointed rulers; the Zealots were messianists. What distinguished the apocalyptics was the feeling that they were living on the threshold of a cataclysmic transformation of existence: the end of history, the annihilation of suffering and evil, a new creation. 2 Esdras conveys this apocalyptic mood more powerfully than almost any other work of the time:

If you are alive, you will see, and if you live long, you will often marvel, because the age is hastening swiftly to its end. For it is not able to bring the things that have been promised to the righteous in their appointed times, because this age is full of sadness and infirmities. [2 Esdras 4:26–27.]

The apocalyptist combined radical impatience with the course of history and a fervent faith that very soon, probably in his lifetime, God will decisively act to destroy the deepest roots of idolatry and wickedness. Esdras complains that history makes no sense: "It would be better for us not to be here, than to come here and live in ungodliness, and to

suffer and not understand why" (4:12). Various answers are proposed
as to why the world is ruled by demonic and destructive powers. Enoch
refers to fallen angels, rebels against God who now rule the earth. Other
apocalyptic authors speak of the power of Belial or Satan, who will be
destroyed by God at the end of time. Avoiding reference to such mythological figures, 2 Esdras explains that Adam's sin corrupted mankind:
"For a grain of evil was sown in Adam's heart from the beginning, and
how much ungodliness it has produced until now, and will produce until
the time of threshing comes!" (4:31). Unlike the biblical prophets who
believe that God acts in history to educate and instruct, the disillusioned
apocalyptist has no hope for bettering the world and feels no responsibility for history's course. To Esdras, history has value only as the stage
on which a few souls can accumulate merit for the sake of their reward:
"That is the meaning of the contest which every man who is born on
earth shall wage, that if he is defeated he shall suffer what you have said,
but if he is victorious he shall receive what I have said" (5:57 [127]).
God has ordained that history will come to an end "when the number of
those like yourselves is completed; for he has weighed the age in the
balance, and measured the times by measure, and numbered the times by
number; and he will not move or arouse them until that measure is fulfilled" (4:35–36). Esdras assures his reader that "creation is growing old."
The confusion and panic of the present are portents of something
drastically different in the process of being born. Soon even more terrible
omens will appear: "The sun shall suddenly shine forth at night, and the
moon during the day. Blood shall drip from wood, and the stone shall
utter its voice; the peoples shall be troubled, and the stars shall fall. And
one shall reign whom those who dwell on earth do not expect" (5:4–6).
Given the immediacy of the end, the primary decision facing the individual is whether, at the judgment, he will be found in the camp of the
righteous or the ungodly. As John the Baptist preached, "Repent, for
the Kingdom of Heaven is at hand" (Matt. 3:2).

Where did this eschatological lore and apocalyptic teaching come
from? As the fragmentary commentaries on biblical verses in the Dead
Sea Scrolls show, it was an age when many searched the Scriptures for
clues as to the meaning of the present and the shape of the future. Various
sections of the Bible were seized on and elaborated: the expulsion of
Adam and Eve from paradise, the descent of the "sons of God" to the
earth (Gen. 6:1–4), the divine theophanies of Exodus and Psalms,
promises that David's dynasty would rule forever (1 Kings 9:4–5),
prophetic depictions of the Day of YHVH and the messianic age. Some
apocalyptic material was probably absorbed from Iranian dualism (history as a struggle between good and evil divine forces) and from the
Hellenistic environment (cosmic determinism, applied by apocalyptists
not to nature but to history). The bewilderment, fear, and alienation

that encouraged the rise of apocalypse crops up in the Greco-Roman world in the following centuries in even more extreme ways (such as the Gnostic tendency, treated in the next chapter). The apocalyptic doctrine of the Two Ages, this eon and the eon about to dawn, was an effort to absorb this alienation into the biblical framework in order to buttress faith in the God of Israel. Apocalypse contributed considerably to an explosive situation that produced not only Jewish revolt against Rome but also the emergence of Christianity.

The Rise of Christianity: Jesus and Paul

The uncertainties that plague our knowledge of first-century Judaism also affect our understanding of the emergence, within it, of Christianity. Despite data culled from the New Testament and from Jewish, Greek, and Roman writings, we do not have adequate materials for a biography of Jesus. Our main source for his life is the four gospels of the New Testament, probably composed in the last quarter of the century (about fifty years after Jesus's death), when his utterances and actions, recounted by disciples and their followers, had been reformulated in light of later Christian views of his messiahship.[21] The same historiographical dilemma holds for a reconstruction of the gradual process by which Judaism and Christianity separated. As a result, our picture of the rise of the new faith must inevitably rely on a considerable amount of conjecture.

With these reservations in mind, a brief summary of the more secure facts concerning Jesus would include the following: that he grew up in the village of Nazareth and spent much of his life in the Galilee where, in the later twenties of the first century CE, he gained a reputation as a healer, exorcist, and itinerant preacher proclaiming the imminent coming of God's kingdom and calling for repentance in preparation for the divine judgment; that after a brief association with John the Baptist, Jesus attracted disciples from among the unlearned, the poor, and the unrespectable strata of Galilean society, and his personal charisma and teachings may have stirred up hostility in certain Jewish circles; that around the year 30 CE Jesus was put to death in Jerusalem on the charge, probably false, of his being a revolutionary (the inscription on the cross was said to be "King of the Jews," Mark 15:26), and that afterwards, his followers believed that he had risen from the dead, appeared to them, and, before ascending to heaven, promised shortly to return to usher in the triumph and glory of the messianic age.

Compounding the difficulty in appraising Jesus's place in Jewish society of his time are the gaps in our knowledge of Jewish religious groupings and the functioning of Jewish institutions during his lifetime. With whom, exactly, did Jesus come into conflict and why? Scribes, priests, Pharisees, Roman officials? Was he lax with respect to the Jewish religious laws—or was this gospel tradition influenced by later Christian rejection of the Jewish law in its entirety? Was Jesus a reformer calling, like the biblical prophets, for a higher standard of moral intention among the Jewish people? Or did he hold a notion of a purified covenant community limited to a minority of Jews, like the Essenes or the Qumran sect? What was Jesus' conception of himself with respect to the apocalyptic expectations of his time, the atmosphere of which permeates the oldest gospels? Do the supernatural, eschatological roles to which the gospels allude, such as "prophet," "Son of Man," and "Son of God," reflect his own messianic consciousness? Or was he called Messiah by his followers only in retrospect? Why was Jesus crucified and who decided to execute him? On all these issues the historical evidence permits various interpretations, as the scholarly literature testifies in abundance. It is acknowledged, for example, that crucifixion was a Roman punishment for political crimes. Does this indicate that the Roman governor, Pontius Pilate, was primarily responsible? Or did a Jewish council condemn him on the grounds of blasphemy? Jesus' trial, if indeed it was a formal inquest, is completely at variance with Jewish legal procedures (procedures that are, however, described in written sources dating from the late second century CE), and there is no indication that other messianic figures of the first century were tried for blasphemy by Jewish courts. This particular issue is sensitive, because the charge of deicide (the Jews as "Christ killers") was used in later centuries to justify persecution and slaughter. At present, the facts concerning Jesus' crucifixion should be a matter of dispassionate historical analysis only.[22] The main issue of faith between Judaism and Christianity is whether the person and doctrines of Jesus possess unique authority as a revelation of God's will and God's nature. For Christian theologians Jesus is pre-eminent. For Jewish theologians, however sympathetic they may be to his teachings and suffering, Jesus remains only one of many spokesmen for Jewish spirituality in the course of history.

Between Jesus' death and the outbreak of the Jewish revolt against the Romans, Christianity developed from a sect within Jewry to a movement consisting primarily of non-Jews. The Acts of the Apostles in the New Testament indicates that the followers of Jesus in Jerusalem in the 30s and 40s CE continued to pray at the Temple, observe Jewish laws, and consider themselves members of the Jewish people. (Groups of Christian Jews are mentioned in historical sources down to the fourth century.) The decision to accept gentiles into the Christian fold without requiring them to become Jews was a surprising development that required special justification. A key figure in this turn of events was Paul, a diaspora Jew from Tarsus in southeast Asia Minor, the author of a

Ivory plaque from sixth or seventh-century CE Rome, depicting Paul. (Courtesy of the Metropolitan Museum of Art, gift of J. Pierpont Morgan, 1917.)

number of New Testament epistles (letters) that are a testimony to early Christian religiosity and a major influence on Western civilization.[23]

Paul describes himself as having been a faithful Jew who lived according to Pharisaic law and persecuted the followers of Jesus, until a revelatory experience brought him into the Christian camp as an apostle commissioned directly by God and by Jesus. (See Gal. 1:12–17, 1 Cor. 9:1 and 15:3–9.) The main area for Paul's activity as a Christian missionary was Asia Minor and Greece, where Jewish communities had been in existence for some time. However, Paul was not the originator of diaspora Christianity: Even before he became active among Christians in the early 40s, Jews and gentiles in such cities as Damascus and Antioch had already begun worshiping Jesus as "Lord" (*Kyrios*) and Christ (the Greek translation of the Hebrew *mashiah*, anointed). Paul apparently made use of prayers and proclamations already formulated by these groups for baptismal initiation and the Lord's Supper, the central rites of the nascent movement. But Paul drew drastic and radical conclusions from Jesus' crucifixion and resurrection—conclusions that were a major factor in furthering the spread of Christianity beyond the Jewish orbit.

Paul's thought is an original fusion of elements from Judean and Hellenistic Judaism. There is a pronounced apocalyptic streak in Paul, who believed that This Era of domination by demonic powers was coming to an end—probably in his lifetime—and that the Last Judgment was near. (1 Thes. 4:15–17, 1 Cor. 7:25–31.) However, Paul depicted the eras before and after the coming of the Christ according to a dichotomy of two states of being: the fleshly and the spiritual. The fleshly was the realm of the perishable, of death, of bondage, of the rule of sin; the spiritual was a condition of eternal life, of freedom, of right relationship with God (a relationship that Paul called justification or righteousness). (See, for example, 1 Cor., chap. 15, Rom. 8:11.) The Christ's crucifixion and resurrection represented the decisive inbreaking of the New Era. Even though the final Day of the Lord had not yet come, those who accepted the Christ already lived under the new dispensation, redeemed from the burden of evil, death, and sin. Paul by-passes philosophical argumentation to appeal directly to the confidence of salvation experienced by those who accepted the action of God in the Christ: "God was in Christ reconciling the world to himself" (2 Cor. 5:18–19). Sent forth to crucify the flesh and vanquish death, God's archetypal Son humbled himself to expiate sin, so that all could become sons of God. The Christ's dying and rising became man's dying and rising, transforming human existence into a "new creation." (See, for example, 2 Cor. 5:17, Gal. 4:4, Romans 3:25.) Central to Paul, therefore, was the contrast between "works" and "faith." In view of man's insufficiency and moral impotence, faith is a gift freely given, a sign of divine grace and love. Salvation cannot be earned through obedience to the law, for "he who through *faith* is righteous shall live" (Gal. 3:11 and Rom. 1:17, which give a distinctive Pauline twist to Hab. 2:4).

Although Paul's conception of deliverance through the Christ permeates his writings, the specific occasions of most of his epistles revolve around two immediate concerns: the need to distinguish the new life "in Christ" from licentiousness and from the belief that all things are permitted to those who have faith (see especially 1 and 2 Corinthians), and the desire to free the Christian from feeling that he should be observing the Mosaic law (Galatians and Romans). The first theme leads Paul to issue various ethical instructions, with special emphasis on love: Just as God's act in Christ was motivated by love, so love is the supreme spiritual gift—more important even than prophecy, speaking in tongues, and other signs of divine possession. (In view of the imminent passing away of This Age, Paul's sexual ethics are rather ascetic and his political views respectful of Roman authority.) The second theme, rejection of the Mosaic law, led him to argue that it was wrong to ask Christians to become circumcised and to follow the Jewish regulations governing permitted and prohibited foods.

Behind Paul's attitude toward biblical legislation was an apocalyptic history of salvation, formulated according to his Christ-centered perspective. As a result of Adam's transgression, sin and death entered the human condition. Abraham's trust in God (see Gen. 15:6) showed that faith preceded the law—the law in this case being the specific commandment of circumcision, which was only later (in Gen. 17:9–14) revealed to Abraham. The Mosaic legislation given at Sinai was a temporary divine custodianship, binding for a limited period only (Gal. 3:25). In a passage affirming the sanctity of the Scriptures, which come to fulfillment in Jesus Christ (Rom. 7:7–25), Paul argues that while the law is holy, it cannot enable one to be justified before God. The more one strives to fulfill the law, the more one becomes conscious of sin—conscious, that is, of not being able to realize God's most profound expectations on one's own, such as not to covet (the last of the Ten Commandments). Because God loves man, he has made available Christ to overcome man's inherent propensity to fail morally.

In Galatians 4:21–31, Paul offers an allegorical interpretation of Abraham's two sons, Ishmael and Isaac. Ishmael, the son of Hagar the slave, symbolizes the Old Covenant with the fleshly Israel. Isaac, the son of Sarah, symbolizes the New Covenant with the spiritual Israel. Now that Christ has come, "Not all those who are descendants of Israel belong to Israel" (Rom. 9:6). Those whom God has called through Christ, Jew and Greek alike, are the true heirs to the original promise; they are "the Israel of God" (Gal. 6:16). Upholding the authority of the Jewish Scriptures according to their "spirit" while abandoning the written code (see 2 Cor. 3:6), Paul severed Christianity from the Jewish people.

The subsequent history of New Testament literature goes beyond this chapter, but a brief discussion of some of its themes completes our account of the separation of the two religions. Not all early Christians limited themselves to the Pauline preoccupation with the crucifixion and resurrection of Christ. Traditions about the historical Jesus were carefully passed on and formed the basis of the gospels, which were written down in the last quarter of the century outside Judea. Each gospel shows a further enrichment of the Christian concept of the Christ and a further movement away from the Jewish concept of the messiah. In the Gospel of Mark, usually considered to be the oldest, Jesus is portrayed as a figure divinely appointed to establish God's rule on earth—the Son of Man, now clearly an apocalyptic title. In the Gospel of Matthew, Jesus is a lawgiver greater than Moses, instructing his audience in the principles of Christian living and demanding moral and religious perfection. The Gospel of Luke and the Acts of the Apostles (a two-volume work by the same author) begins with Jesus' birth in the reign of Herod and ends with Paul preaching in Rome. Luke-Acts has, as its overall theme, the fulfillment among the Jews of Judea of the Old Testament in the coming of Christ and the subsequent transference of the Church to the gentiles of the Greco-Roman world. In the Gospel of John, Jesus is the divine Logos, incarnate in human form, who discourses at length (rather than in brief parables) on Christ as "the way, the truth, and the life." (On the Logos, see the discussion of Philo in this chapter.) For the author of the Gospel of John, the conviction that God's kingdom is a present reality in the Christian Church overwhelms the apocalyptic orientation evident in previous New Testament writings. And for John, the opponents of Jesus are not certain groups of Jews, such as scribes and Pharisees, but the nation collectively, who, from the very start, are Christ's enemy, as though Jesus was an outsider to the Jewish people. The Letter to the Hebrews avoids the narrative framework entirely and depicts, in an allegorical fashion, Jesus as the prototypical High Priest, the perfection of a type foreshadowed in the Old Testament. In the book of Revelation, the mysterious symbolism of Jewish apocalyptic literature returns to be transferred to the Second Coming of Christ at the End of Time.

Like the Old Testament, the New Testament is not a uniform work, but retains traces of the historical process by which a religion comes to define its own identity. The legacy of Paul is criticized in the epistle of James, which warns that "a man is justified by works and not by faith alone" (James 2:24). Other epistles testify indirectly to the gradual development of a formal structure of Church leadership. With the growing stability of Christian belief and institutions comes the appearance of

heresy. A simplified interpretation of Paul, stripped of Paul's nuance and tension, is advocated by a mid-second-century figure, Marcion, who rejects the Old Testament as the work of a demonic creator deity into whose evil realm the Christ descends to show men the way to their true, transmundane destiny. (Marcion is usually grouped with the Hellenistic tendency known as Gnosticism, which will be described in Chap. 6.) Possibly in opposition to Marcion, the Church established the first canon of the New Testament and reaffirmed the sanctity of the Old Testament. By the fourth century, orthodox Christianity had begun to formulate its classical creeds using Greek philosophical terms to assert that Christ was fully human while present on earth and yet that he was a single divine substance with God the Father who created the universe. Trinitarian Christianity—that the one God was three persons: Father, Son, and Holy Spirit—moved in a direction quite different than that taken by the Judaism surviving the confusion, violence, and spiritual upheaval of the beginning of the Common Era.

Messiah or Law? The Parting of the Ways

The forces that shaped rabbinic Judaism and Christianity were diverse and complex, each tradition representing a regrouping and coalescing of the theological, social, and psychological patterns that had emerged within Jewry after the Maccabean revolt. The early Jerusalem Church seems to have been, at least indirectly, indebted to the Essenes for a celibate style of life and the sharing of property (Luke 18:29, Acts 2:44–45 and

"Judea Capta" coin of the Emperor Vaspasian, 71 CE, commemorating the Roman victory over the Jewish rebels. (Courtesy Jewish Museum, New York.)

4:32–5:2). But, like the Pharisees, the early Christians did not withdraw to the desert but remained in the cities to spread their faith. Apocalypticism was especially crucial for the rise of Christianity. Apocalyptic expectations were certainly present among Jesus's immediate circle and probably (with due respect to the difficulty of establishing the historical Jesus) in his own frame of mind. After the crucifixion, his followers' expectation that he would shortly return is likewise indebted to the hope for the imminent coming of the last judgment. Paul's writings contain a similar eschatological tension. Although he had ties with Judea, Paul was a diaspora Jew, probably an important component of his make-up. For an understanding of the crystallization of the gentile Church, therefore, a comparison of Paul and Philo is instructive.

Like Paul, Philo saw as the allegorical significance of the biblical narrative a deliverance of the individual from internal bondage. Philo had insisted on fidelity to the commandments according to their plain meaning, criticizing those Alexandrian Jews who abandoned the law for the sake of allegorical enlightenment alone. Paul, however, preached the abrogation of the law on principle. Philo was an erudite philosopher who welcomed proselytes; Paul was an enthusiastic missionary who went out to win them over. Inspired by the messianic enthusiasm prevalent among Jesus' disciples and having himself experienced release in Christ, Paul refocused Jewish monotheism around a radical deliverance, through Christ, from the repressive powers and instincts of This Eon. The result was a synthesis of certain elements of Judaism with features of the Hellenistic salvation cults. From Judaism came the idea of one God, the rejection of pagan idolatry, an ancient religious literature claiming absolute authority, a strong moral sense, the advantages of belonging to a closely knit and mutually sustaining community. From Hellenistic religion came the call to identify with a divine personage whose suffering, death, and return to life provided a sure source of salvation. To this synthesis must be added the factor represented by Jesus himself: an undoubted historical figure that had just been recently present in the Galilee and Jerusalem preaching repentance and love. For the early Christians the cult of Jesus and the atonement of sin wrought by his death and resurrection replaced and superseded the cult of the Temple and the atonement of sin wrought by the sacrificial offerings. Gradually, as Christianity took on its own identity, the explosive apocalyptic element was brought under control and the new community evolved a stable mode of living in the "already now" (the Messiah had come) and the "not yet" (he would return).

A word should be said about the timing of Christianity's appearance, when Judaism was in such flux that the religious establishment had little ability to repress various kinds of deviance. The conflict with Rome also boosted Christian morale: Destruction of the Temple seemed a convincing confirmation that God had rejected the Old Israel and caused his spirit to dwell permanently in their midst. (Perhaps the political tension between Jews and the Roman government facilitated conversion to Christianity among pagans not eager to join a people so prone to take up arms against the empire.) Although Christianity faced strong opposition from Jews and had to contend with suspicion and occasional persecution from the Roman authorities, it grew and overtook Jewry in numbers in the Hellenistic diaspora—but not in Palestine until it had the official support of the Roman government in the fourth century.

Many varieties of Judaism were wiped out by the military defeat of 70 CE, but the groundwork had been laid, through the synagogues and the Pharisaic tradition of learning, for a better defined and more stable Jewish theological and social structure after the war. A majority of Jews continued to find in Torah, not Christ, the living presence in their midst of divine love and the divine mind, a hope for salvation if they did their best to live according to God's commandments, and an effective atonement of sins through good deeds. The dry connotation of the term *law* does not express the meaning of Torah to Jews, but law, of course, was a component of Torah. An articulate defense of the Jewish law has been left by Josephus, which conveys its role as a primary source of Jewish unity and strength of character (quite in contrast to Paul's view).

Like Philo, Josephus was a cosmopolitan and sophisticated man; like Paul he was acquainted with Judean and Hellenistic Jewry. Unlike both he was not a particularly religious man and he lacks the mystical exaltation found in their writings. Regardless of his personal motives for defecting to the Romans in the course of the revolt (self-interest was quite evidently among them), his realistic appraisal of Roman power was also shared by pious Jews who rejected Zealot or apocalyptic extremism. Among his works Josephus left a defense of Judaism against pagan detractions entitled *Against Apion*.[24] Using Stoic motifs to explain the Jews' loyalty to their traditions, *Against Apion* is written with common sense, respect for what Jews felt about their law, and a stance sufficiently outside the tradition to permit a more focused perspective than did the Jewish sectarian literature of Judea.

According to Josephus, the Jewish people was unique because of its "constitution," which Josephus defined as a *theocracy* (he apparently coined the term): "a placing all sovereignty and authority in the hands of God" (*Against Apion* II, 164–65). Josephus contrasts the universalism of the Jews' "polity" with the particularism of the Greeks. The ancient Greek legislators did not pay sufficient attention to the spiritual nature of the deity, whereas the Jewish polity was founded on a clear and lofty concept of the one transcendent God. The Greek *polis* did not accept as citizens all those who wished to share its way of life, whereas Jewry was open to all who wished to accept its principles and observances.

Moses at the burning bush (Ex. 3:1–6); fresco from the third-century CE synagogue at Dura-Europas. (Courtesy of the Union of American Hebrew Congregations.)

It will be seen that [Moses] took the best of all possible measures to secure our own customs from corruption, and to throw them open ungrudgingly to any who elect to share them. To all who desire to come and live under the same laws with us, he gives a gracious welcome, holding that it is not family ties alone which constitute a relationship, but agreement in the principles of conduct. [*Against Apion* II, 210.]

The Mosaic system provided for the moral training of youth through intensive education and regulated practice, so that the common man would not be ignorant of how to live virtuously. Indeed, Moses achieved what Plato had only dreamed of establishing in his famous Republic. Although obedience to the Jewish laws was voluntary, it inculcated fortitude, bravery, and self-sacrifice:

From these laws of ours nothing has had the power to deflect us, neither fear of our masters, nor envy of the institutions esteemed by other nations. . . . To defeat in any other form we patiently submit, but when pressure is put upon us to alter our statutes, then we deliberately fight, even against tremendous odds, and hold out under reverses to the last extremity. [*Against Apion* II, 271–72.]

In his brief description of Jewish ethics, Josephus emphasizes industriousness, sobriety, mutual trust, sharing with the needy, and the value of strong family ties, which required Jewish parents to educate children in the deeds and practices of their forefathers, and obligated Jewish children to honor their parents next to God. Josephus concludes:

I would therefore boldly maintain that we have introduced to the rest of the world a very large number of very beautiful ideas. What greater beauty than inviolable piety? What higher justice than obedience to the law? What more beneficial than to be in harmony with one another, to be a prey neither to disunion in adversity, nor to arrogance and faction in prosperity; in war to despise death, in peace to devote oneself to crafts and agriculture; and to be convinced that everything in all the whole universe is under the eye and direction of God? [*Against Apion* II, 293–94.]

Not everyone admired Jewish fortitude, self-control, and mutual concern. A younger contemporary of Josephus, the Roman historian Tacitus, left the following description, written with a mixture of scorn, revulsion, and surprise that indicate, perhaps, an awareness that Judaism was subversive of pagan civilization.

Whatever their origin, these [Jewish] observances are sanctioned by their antiquity. The other practices of the Jews are sinister and revolting, and have entrenched themselves by their very wickedness. Wretches of the most abandoned kind who had no use for the religion of their fathers took to contributing dues and free-will offerings to swell the Jewish exchequer; and other reasons for their increasing wealth may be found in their stubborn loyalty and ready benevolence toward brother Jews. But the rest of the world they confront with the hatred reserved for enemies. They will not feed or intermarry with gentiles. Though a most lascivious people, the Jews avoid sexual intercourse with women of alien race. Among themselves nothing is barred. They have introduced the practice of circumcision to show that they are different from others. Proselytes to Jewry adopt the same practices, and the very first lesson they learn is to despise the gods, shed all feelings of patriotism, and consider parents, children, and brothers as readily expendable. However, the Jews see to it that their numbers increase. It is a deadly sin to kill an unwanted child, and they think that eternal life is granted to those who die in battle or execution—hence their eagerness to have children, and their contempt for death. Rather than cremate their dead, they prefer to bury them in imitation of the Egyptian fashion, and they have the same concern and beliefs about the world below. But their conception of heavenly things is quite different. The Egyptians worship a variety of animals and half-human, half-bestial forms, whereas the Jewish religion is a purely spiritual monotheism. They hold it to be impious to make idols of perishable materials in the likeness of man; for them the Most High and Eternal cannot be portrayed by human hands and will never pass away. . . .[25]

What of the yearning for personal salvation so evident in Hellenistic Jewish literature and in the noncanonical religious writings of Judea? Although Josephus does refer once to the Jewish belief in "a renewed existence and, in the revolution of the ages, the gift of a better life" (*Against Apion* II, 218), he has described the nature and appeal of Judaism without reference to mystical or apocalyptic deliverance from ordinary reality. This Judaism—a Judaism that successfully absorbed the principle of salvation but concentrated on regulating "the practical life"—was to predominate. Intense eschatological hopes were to percolate among Jews until the middle of the second century, and from time to time messianic and apocalyptic moods were to flare up in later Judaism and Christianity, but more mundane concerns formed the everyday content of both traditions.

CHAPTER 6

The Efflorescence of Rabbinic Judaism, Second to Seventh Centuries

After settlement in Canaan, the social and the political history of the Jewish people in its homeland up to the last quarter of the first century CE falls into four major divisions. The first comprises the two hundred years when Israel was a collection of tribes united by the worship of YHVH and occasionally by charismatic, intertribal leaders. The second is the five centuries of monarchy: the united kingdom of Saul, David, and Solomon, the northern Israelite kingdom until 722 BCE and the southern Judahite kingdom until 587 BCE. The third period of Jewish history, lasting four centuries from Babylonian exile to Maccabean revolt, was focused mainly on the rebuilding and maintenance of Jerusalem as a semi-autonomous temple city, headquarters of a province in a Persian or Hellenistic empire. The fourth constitutes the two and a half centuries from the establishment of an independent Hasmonean monarchy to the destruction of Jerusalem by the Romans in 70 CE. The sources permit only an incomplete, episodic treatment of the first and third periods; the second and fourth, because of information preserved in the Bible, Apocrypha, and Josephus, lend themselves to a fuller chronological narrative of reigns, wars, and other political-military developments.

For the next phase of Jewish history, from 70 CE to the rise of Islam, we again have no detailed chronicle and are left to reconstruct important turning points and changes from scattered references in Greco-Roman sources, the Church fathers, rabbinic literature, and archeological data.

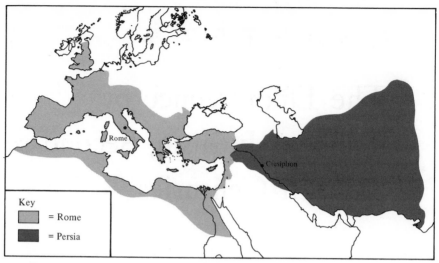

The Roman and Persian Empires at the End of the First Century CE. Persia under the Parthian dynasty to 224 CE and then under the Sassanian dynasty was the only adjacent state to withstand Roman conquest; its substantial Jewish population, therefore, remained outside the sphere of Roman control.

The classic works of rabbinic Judaism offer a wealth of information on Jewish life and ideas, but their historical recollections are anecdotal, semilegendary, and homiletic; only the most sophisticated text and form criticism will elicit from them the raw material for modern·historical synthesis.

During the five and a half centuries of late antiquity covered in this chapter, the Jews still are largely a Near Eastern people, despite the continuation of the western diaspora. Jewish merchants, craftsmen, and religious intellectuals reside in the large cities of the Mediterranean and Mesopotamia, but the majority of Jews are peasants and artisans living in smaller towns and villages. New forms of political leadership replace the Temple hierocracy and Hasmonean-Herodian aristocracy: a Jewish patriarchate under the Romans and an exilarchate under the Persians that administer Jewish affairs for their respective governments and claim the authority of Davidic descent among their own people. Although patriarch and exilarch are conciliatory to and cooperative with the Roman and Persian rulers, an undercurrent of messianism testifies to persistent yearnings for redemption. During these centuries there takes place a crucial transition from ancient to medieval world: Polytheistic paganism gives way to organized religions claiming far more exclusive truth. In the third century Persia acquires a state church based on the revived Zoroastrian tradition; in the fourth century the Roman empire adopts Christianity as its official faith, so that Jews find themselves a minority in a society where a government-backed creed directly conflicts with Judaism on important points and claims to have superseded it. Within the Jewish people the decisive transformation during these centuries is the emergence of the Pharisaic component of pre-70 CE Judaism into a leadership class that seeks to reshape Jewish identity throughout the Near East according to a system of thought and action crystallized in the rabbinic academies of Palestine and Babylonia. If Christian clergy and missionaries convert the pagans in the Roman empire and the barbarians beyond to their symbols and rites, the rabbis convert much of the Jewish people into a religious community whose ideological unity is more extensive, ramified, and comprehensive than ever before.

Historical Background, 70 CE–630 CE

The Jews in the Roman Empire

The Roman reconquest of Judea between 66 and 70 CE resulted in great physical and human destruction, the enslavement of many thousands and widespread confiscation of property, but economic reconstruction began immediately and Jews continued to constitute the largest proportion of the population of the area. (The destruction of Jerusalem did not mean the beginning of a physical exile from the holy land; the diaspora had been a significant feature of Jewry long before and a decisive migration out of Palestine occurred two to three centuries later for other reasons.) The Romans penalized the Jews with a two-drachma tax in lieu of the former half sheckel contribution to the Temple, but they did not withdraw their recognition of Judaism as a lawful religion that was exempted from emperor worship and other duties incumbent on pagans. Although apocalyptic tendencies persisted, the Sadducees and Essenes disappeared and a far-ranging spiritual revival and reorientation was launched. The outstanding figure of the postwar period was Johanan ben Zaccai, who escaped from Jerusalem during the siege and assembled, with Roman permission, those Pharisaic sages and scribes who had survived the fighting. In the town of Yavneh, near the Judean seacoast, a rabbinic blueprint for Jewish survival was articulated. Indicative of Johanan ben Zaccai's stance and characteristic of the new age is the statement attributed to him, as he and another sage contemplated the ruins of the Temple: R. Joshua mourned that the place where Israel's sins found atonement was now laid waste; R. Johanan consoled him (and his generation) with Hosea 6:6, "I desire love and not sacrifice," his proof text for the principle that loving deeds were atonement equal to that offered by the Temple.[1] Although rabbinic Judaism took as its central task the development of the legal component of Torah, it was also the fulfillment of an essential impli-

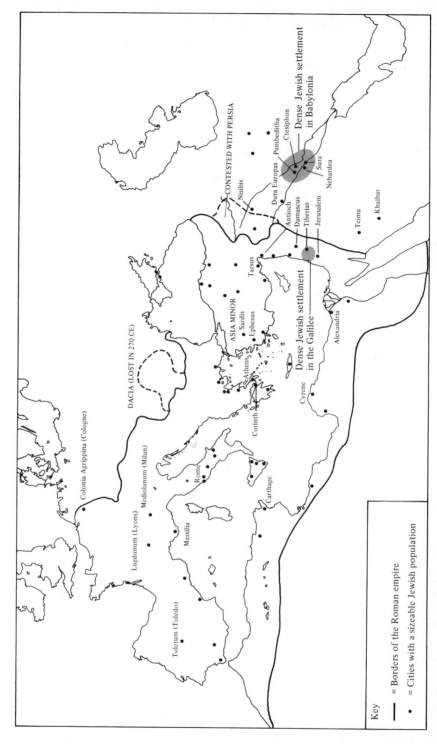

Key

— = Borders of the Roman empire

• = Cities with a sizeable Jewish population

The Diaspora from the First to the Fifth Centuries CE. Despite the decimation of the Jewish communities of Egypt, Cyprus, Crete, and Judea in the first decades of the second century CE, the Jews remained concentrated in the East: in Asia Minor, the Galilee, and Babylonia. But Jewish settlements were also found in North Africa, Greece, Macedonia, Italy, Spain, Gaul, and as far north as the Rhine and the Crimea.

Labels on map:

Dense Jewish settlement in Babylonia

CONTESTED WITH PERSIA

Pumbeditha
Ctesiphon
Dura Europas
Sura
Nehardea
Nisibis
Antioch
Damascus
Tiberias
Jerusalem
Teima
Khaibar

Tarsus

ASIA MINOR
Sardis
Ephesus
Athens

DACIA (LOST IN 270 CE)

Dense Jewish settlement in the Galilee

Alexandria

Cyrene

Corinth

Colonia Agrippina (Cologne)

Mediolanum (Milan)

Lugdunum (Lyons)

Rome

Massilia

Carthage

Toletum (Toledo)

cation of classical prophecy: that the religious life does not depend on a functioning sacrificial cult but on ethical and penitent action in the mundane world.

Under Rabban Johanan ben Zaccai, and later, toward the end of the first century, under Rabban Gamaliel II, the Sanhedrin (rabbinical assembly) at Yavneh strengthened a post-Temple, nonhierocratic Judaism. (The term *rabbi* now comes into general use for a sage recognized as such by his peers; the title *rabban* is reserved for the head [*Nasi*] of the Sanhedrin.) The sages at Yavneh summarized the teachings of the earlier schools of Hillel and Shammai, with those of the Hillelites prevailing on most legal matters. They completed the canonization of the Scriptures, gave a more precise form to the daily prayers, and transferred to synagogue and Sanhedrin some of the observances associated with the Temple, especially rituals associated with pilgrim festivals, the Passover seder, and the blowing of the *shofar* (ram's horn) on the New Year. An ordination procedure for rabbis (*semikhah*) was instituted and the Sanhedrin assumed supreme legislative and regulatory functions, such as the right to control the date of the New Year and leap months. (The Jewish calendar was still determined by empirical evidence rather than by arithmetic calculation.) Within no more than two decades it was apparent to the Romans that the rabbis had the popular support to be recognized as the official leadership of the Jewish people.[2]

The Yavneh Sanhedrin was high court, supreme legislature, and assembly of peers; the *Nasi* (an old biblical title with the vague meaning of "prince") presided but did not rule unchecked. The rabbis collectively constituted a new religious leadership class. Drawn from all levels of society, relying for their livelihood on a craft, trade, or private wealth, and serving the communities as judges and adjudicators, they individually attracted students who came to learn their oral traditions and scriptural interpretations and to see them actualize Torah in daily life. The new sages settled throughout Judea and the Galilee with their circles of disciples: R. Eliezar ben Hyrcanus, R. Elazar ben Azariah, R. Joshua ben Hananiah, and others of the generation after Johanan ben Zaccai; R. Hananiah ben Taradion, R. Tarfon, R. Ishmael ben Elisha, R. Akiva ben Joseph, and others of the following generation. During the first decades of the second century the most prominent and creative figure was R. Akiva (c. 50–135), legal systematizer, mystic, and exegete. (Akiva was the pioneer of an extremely flexible method of biblical interpretation based on the assumption that no word in Scripture was redundant, in contradistinction to R. Ishmael's school, which held that Torah uses "human language" and follows normal usage; Akiva's system made it possible to elicit infinite levels of meaning from the texts of the Bible.)

Despite the rabbinic reformation of the turn of the century, messianic agitation in Judea and the diaspora led to further Jewish revolts. In 114

Silver tetradrachm from the Bar Kokhba revolt. (Courtesy of the Jewish Museum, New York.)

the Roman Emperor Trajan launched an invasion of the east that brought him to the Persian Gulf; but uprisings among Babylonian Jews and other peoples behind the Roman lines prevented the Romans from consolidating their hold on Mesopotamia. Moreover, riots and fighting broke out in many parts of the Roman diaspora. Little documentary evidence has survived, but the fourth-century Christian writer Eusebius reports,

> In Alexandria and the rest of Egypt, and in Cyrene as well, as if inflamed by some terrible spirit of revolt [the Jews] rushed into a faction fight against their Greek fellow-citizens, raised the temperature to fever heat, and in the following summer started a full-scale war. . . . Against them the emperor sent Marcius Turbo with land and sea forces, including a contingent of cavalry. He pursued the war against them relentlessly in a long series of battles, destroying many thousands of Jews, not only those from Cyrene but others who had come from Egypt to assist Lucuas their king.[3]

(Lucuas may have been a messianic pretender among the North African Jews.) The Jewish center of Alexandria and the populous diasporas of Cyrenaica, Egypt, and Cyprus were decimated in the revolt of 114–117 CE. Forced to withdraw from Persian territory, Trajan died soon after, and his successor, Hadrian, abandoned the effort to extend the Roman frontier in that direction. The large Jewish diaspora in Babylonia, therefore, remained free from Roman domination and soon began to play an important role in Jewish social and intellectual history.

Jewish turbulence in the Roman empire continued, however, and in 133 a messianic revolt erupted in Judea, led by Simon bar Kosiba (called in some sources Bar Kokhba, "son of the star," a messianic allusion to

Num. 24:17). The Bar Kokhba revolt seems to have been triggered by Hadrian's championing of Hellenism in the area, perhaps by a ban on castration that included a provision against circumcision, and a plan to rebuild Jerusalem as a pagan city. Besides the social and economic burdens of Roman rule, the Bar Kokhba revolt was prompted by the belief that God would aid the penitent Jews to regain control of the holy land and rebuild the Temple. This time the rebels carefully prepared for the fighting by storing up arms in advance and by establishing a unified leadership, but the Roman empire was at the height of its power, and despite courageous efforts there occurred an even greater destruction than that after the Roman-Jewish war of the previous century. Specific data on the revolt of 133–135 are limited. Coins issued by Bar Kokhba's government and letters sent by him to deputies around the country have been recovered in Judean desert caves, but narrative accounts are confined to a few brief references in Roman historians and in Eusebius. According to the early third-century historian Dio Cassius, legions had to be brought from a considerable distance, fifty fortresses and more than one thousand settlements were destroyed, hundreds of thousands of Jews were killed, and Judea was left almost completely devastated. The war came to an end with the fall of Bethar, southwest of Jerusalem, in the summer of 135. Because of extensive Roman casualties, Hadrian, in his report to the Roman Senate, refrained from the usual formula that he and his troops were well.[4]

After the Bar Kokhba war there was little left of the Jewish peasantry in the south. The city of Aelia Capitolina, on the site of Jerusalem, was officially prohibited to Jews; Hadrian outlawed Judaism throughout the holy land, and the sages who supported Bar Kokhba were executed. Rabbi Akiva and other scholars tortured to death by the Romans became hallowed prototypes of the Jewish martyr in the liturgical poetry and other medieval writings on this theme.

Hadrian died in 138; early in the reign of Antoninus Pius (138–161) prohibitions on the practice and teaching of Judaism in Palestine were dropped. The Bar Kokhba defeat set the stage for a pacific and conciliatory policy of the Jewish authorities toward the Romans and for the resumption of the rapid development of rabbinic Judaism. The center of Jewish intellectual life in the Roman empire shifted to the Galilee, still densely populated by Jewish farmers and townspeople. The Sanhedrin, dominated by disciples of Akiva, reassembled at Usha (not far from modern-day Haifa). Rabban Simeon ben Gamaliel II (son of Gamaliel II) served as *Nasi;* by this time, his family claimed descent from the first-century sage Hillel. (By the end of the second century they would claim a Davidic origin.) Outstanding scholars of the generation of Usha included R. Elazar ben Shammua, R. Jose ben Halafta, R. Judah bar Illai, R. Sim-

Coin from the Bar Kokhba revolt, depicting the front of the Temple. (Courtesy of the American Numismatic Society.)

eon bar Yohai (in the Middle Ages he was to be looked on as the major personage in the mystical tradition), and R. Meir. Meir was the most distinguished scholar of his time and the compiler of a preliminary canon of laws based on those collected by his teacher, Akiva. (Meir's wife, Beruria, the daughter of a sage, was the only woman mentioned in ancient rabbinic writings for her expertise in technical matters of Jewish law.) The *Nasi* and Sanhedrin regained control over Jewish law and the calendar. (Babylonian Jewish leaders had taken tentative steps toward independence on matters of calendation, which they were persuaded to drop.) The sages at Usha began the task of systematizing the legal precedents of the previous centuries, thus preparing the ground for the comprehensive religious law refined in the next generation.

By the early third century, economic conditions in the Galilee had temporarily improved, as indicated by ruins of impressive stone synagogues built at that time. Under the Severan dynasty of emperors between 193 and 235 the Jewish establishment enjoyed amiable relations with the Roman administration. In 212, when Roman citizenship was extended to most of the inhabitants of the empire for various fiscal and legal reasons, the Jews were included. The Severans endowed the *Nasi* (called in Roman documents patriarch of the Jews) with such prerogatives as the right to collect taxes to support Jewish institutions, authority to appoint judges for the Jewish courts and to send official emissaries to the diaspora communities, and grants of large estates, which enabled the *Nasi* to maintain a considerable retinue. Simeon ben Gamaliel II's son Judah—Judah ha-Nasi in Jewish history and "Rabbi" par excellence in rabbinic literature—was a quasimonarchical personage, a scholar of great stature, and a pivotal figure in the history of rabbinic law. The major achievement of his patriarchate was the redaction of the Mishnah (from a Hebrew verb "to repeat" but here with the acquired meaning of "learning").

Drawing on and refining the collections of rulings and paradigmatic cases prepared by Rabbis Akiva, Meir, and others, the Mishnah was the intellectual crystallization of the orally transmitted teachings of scribes, Pharisees, and sages from the Second Temple period down to Judah ha-Nasi. The authority of the Mishnah was said to derive from Sinai, and to constitute, together with Scripture, "Torah" in the broad meaning given to it by the rabbis. "Moses received the Torah from Sinai and handed it down to Joshua, and Joshua to the elders, and the elders to the prophets, and the prophets to the men of the Great Assembly." In this passage of the Mishnah (Pirkei Avot 1:1) the rabbis claim a continuous chain of transmission for an oral Torah as well as the written Torah (*Torah she-be'al peh* as well as *Torah she-biktav*) from Moses to the spiritual leaders of the tribal and monarchical periods to the scribal body of the postexilic period from which they traced their own authority via the great "pairs" of Pharisees, the schools of Hillel and Shammai, and the post-70 CE Sanhedrin. (It should be noted that the priesthood is omitted, probably deliberately, from this intellectual genealogy.) Law code, textbook, and repository of traditions deemed most authoritative, the Mishnah assumed a status in rabbinic Judaism not unlike the New Testament in Christianity (although the analogy cannot be pushed too far because their respective contents differ considerably): Old Testament and New Testament are the supreme holy books of Christianity; Bible and Mishnah constitute together the matrix of subsequent rabbinic Judaism.

That the Galilean rabbinate should produce a legal canon at this time reflects not only the internal dialectic of post-70 CE Jewish intellectual history but also, perhaps, the indirect influence of a similar development taking place in Roman law: the assembling by great Latin jurists beginning with the reign of Hadrian of the classical digests that were to be important components of the Roman law codes of the late empire. The Mishnah, however, was a work of religious, not secular literature, intended for the most careful memorization and contemplation. As we shall explain later in this chapter, it was through the Mishnah that the world view of rabbinic Judaism achieved maturity, and a literary focus was created for its continued development.

Judah ha-Nasi's seat of government was first at Bet She'arim and later at Sepphoris. (Bet She'arim contains the catacomb tombs where members of the Sanhedrin were buried.) The Sanhedrin met in various Galilean cities until it and the patriarchate eventually settled in the Roman district capital of Tiberias. Gradually the roles of patriarchate and rabbinate diverged. In addition to his administrative functions, the *Nasi* remained

Colonnade in the third-century Galilean synagogue at Capernaum. (Photo by the author.)

nominal head of the Sanhedrin, but scholars established their own independent centers of learning in the Galilee and even in Judea, where they interpreted and applied the Mishnah to everyday situations, together with many old rabbinic teachings (*beraitot,* "external traditions") that had not been incorporated in the Mishnah. Great efforts were also made to link Mishnah and *beraitot* to biblical verses through a system of logical (hermeneutic) rules. This oral activity of elaboration and exegesis, and the written collections of opinions that would result a century and a half later, is called *Talmud* (another rabbinic synonym for "learning"). Of the third-century Galilean authorities especially prominent was Rabbi Johanan ben Nappaha (died c. 275), whose many decisions and ethical and religious dicta were carefully studied in Palestine and Babylonia. Among the other important Palestinian teachers of that century were his student and son-in-law R. Simeon ben Lakish (reported to have been a gladiator in his youth), R. Joshua ben Levi who established an academy in Lydda in the south, R. Abbahu of Caesarea (said to have had an especially fluent knowledge of Greek and to have engaged in debates with the Christian intellectuals of that city), and a number of Babylonian scholars who settled and taught in the land of Israel. It was a characteristic feature of rabbinic Judaism in late antiquity that there should be concurrently a number of centers of learning, coalescing around individual sages, and yet that the scholars of each generation together constituted a collective body within which debate was highly prized, differences of opinion respected, and dialectical acument honored.

By the 230s the Roman empire had entered a time of troubles. Inflation, population decline, and lack of technological advance contributed to the growing difficulty of finding resources to support the enormous military force needed to defend the empire from pressures on the barbarian frontier to the north and from the Persians in the east. The period between 235 and 285 saw a massive breakdown in effective government and bloody struggles between rival generals. Like the masses throughout the empire, the Jews suffered from the financial exactions of contending claimants for power, as well as from famine, epidemics, and the increase in banditry. The deteriorating economic situation, especially that of the small farmer, brought about an outflow of Jews from the Galilee that contributed to the Jews eventually becoming an almost completely diaspora people.

Toward the end of the third century, order was restored by the Emperor Diocletian (ruled 284–305), who promulgated reforms that gave the empire renewed stability and strength. Division into Western and Eastern administrative units was to result, by 400, in permanent separation of the Latin and the Greek-speaking halves. Under Diocletian the

Decorations on the gallery frieze of the synagogue of Capernaum: Star of David and citron motifs. (Photo by the author.)

republican façade of the early empire was replaced by a fully absolutistic monarchical system. Efforts were made to stem fiscal and economic decline through an elaborate regimentation of prices, offices, and occupations. And the evident loss of vitality on the part of classical paganism led to a need for new sources of ideological authority and spiritual unity. Diocletian had undertaken a large-scale repression of Christianity; his successor, Constantine the Great (ruled 306–337), dropped this futile effort and extended official toleration (Milan, 313) to the Christian religion.

By the beginning of the fourth century Christianity had, on its own, won a substantial minority of the urban population of the empire, especially in the east. Despite sporadic persecutions by the government, the appeal of Christian spirituality and social forms had enabled it to pull ahead of competitors; an articulate group of homiletic and theological writers maintained Christian distinctiveness yet demonstrated Christianity's ability to appropriate the culture and ideals of the Greco-Roman world. Although careful not to antagonize pagans, Constantine increasingly threw his support behind the Church. He legalized the privileges of the clergy, convened a worldwide Church council (Nicea, 325) to resolve doctrinal disputes, and soon after moved his government to the new eastern capital of Constantinople (formerly Byzantium). Just before his death, Constantine was baptized. The Christianization of the empire continued through the fourth century, with the sole interruption of the reign of the emperor Julian the Apostate (361–363), who unsuccessfully tried to infuse new life into paganism. By the early 400s, Christianity was in every sense the state religion and the last pagan rites were abolished.

At first the merger of Roman government and Christian Church did not drastically affect the legal rights of Jewish institutions, although there was a pronounced change in the state's attitude to Judaism, fed by denunciations from militant Christian preachers and monks. Close contact between Galilee and diaspora was disrupted: Prohibited from notifying the Jews outside Palestine in advance about the dates of Jewish holy days, the Patriarch Hillel II in 359 made public the mathematical rules for calculating the Jewish calendar, thus diminishing his and the Sanhedrin's authority. The first half of the fourth century saw the hasty redaction of the teachings of the later generations of rabbis in the academies of Tiberias, Caesarea, and Sepphoris; organized as extended discussions of the Mishnah, this material became the Palestinian Talmud (more traditionally, the Jerusalem Talmud, although the editing was done in the Galilee). A brief reversal in the decline of Jewis status occurred in the 360s when Julian the Apostate, who expressed favorable opinions about Judaism, offered to rebuild the Temple, but his sudden death brought to an end this flurry of pro-Jewish interest. Once Christianity became the official faith of Rome and Constantinople, Judaism was assigned a position of permanent legal inferiority. (Unlike paganism it was not out-lawed, but rights achieved under Caracalla's edict of 212 were gradually withdrawn.) Imperial laws from the first half of the fourth century prohibited, on penalty of death, conversion to Judaism and intermarriage of Jews with Christians; unlike Christians, Jews were not to possess slaves. When the Patriarch Gamaliel VI died in the 420s, the Roman government refused to approve a successor. In the early fifth century, Jews were excluded from government posts. The attitude behind these measures can be seen in Theodosius II's edict of 439:

> No Jew . . . shall obtain offices and dignities; to none shall the administration of city service be permitted; nor shall any one exercise the office of a defender (overseer) of the city. Indeed, we believe it sinful that the enemies of the heavenly majesty and of the Roman laws should become the executors of our laws—the administration of which they have slyly obtained—and that they, fortified by the authority of the acquired rank, should have the power to judge or decide as they wish against Christians, yes, frequently even over bishops of our holy religion themselves, and thus, as it were, insult our faith.[5]

This approach to the legal rights of the Jews was to predominate in most places until the end of the eighteenth century.

During the rest of the fifth century, the Christian emperors were more concerned with sectarian controversies in the Church than with the Jews, but the most energetic and successful of the later rulers, Justinian (525–565), issued a new round of discriminatory legislation that was incorporated into his legal code, so influential in later European centuries. Signaling the government's aim to further conversion of the Jews was a decree by Justinian ordering that the Greek translation be allowed in synagogue worship and that rabbinical exegesis be prohibited. The official stance of the Church, as worked out during these centuries by Pope Gregory the Great and others, rejected all illegal means to pressure Jews to convert, but encouraged preaching and other lawful forms of persuasion to this end. Judaism should be allowed to survive because the Jewish people, in its dispersed condition, was a "living testimony" to the truth of Scriptures and because the Jews would eventually recognize the messiahship of Jesus. This position, however, did not militate against the burning of synagogues and other outbursts of violence in the fifth and sixth centuries.

By then Jews were a minority in the Galilee, but still a substantial one. The influx of religious Christians and the building of churches, shrines, and monasteries throughout the holy land brought renewed prosperity to Palestine. (Some of the most beautiful mosaic floors of Galilean synagogues date from this period.) Local Jewish institutions did survive: A substitute for the Sanhedrin met in Tiberias and scholars continued to redact the rabbinical traditions. The beginnings of new directions in Jewish scholarship and literature may date from this period: a Tiberian system of vocalizing and punctuating the Hebrew Bible (the work of the Masoretes) and a liturgical poetry (*piyyutim*) deeply rooted in rabbinic materials. When the Persians invaded between 614 and 617, the Jews of Palestine rose up against the Christians and attempted to drive them out of Jerusalem. Christian reprisals followed the Persian retreat, but a new era was about to commence, because in the 630s, Egypt, Syria, and Palestine fell to Arab conquerers.

The history of most of the diaspora will be taken up in the next chapter, when we trace Jewish adjustment to the collapse of the Roman government in Spain, Gaul, Italy, and the Rhineland, and the role of the Jewish settlements in Arabia and Yemen in the rise of Islam. During the second to the sixth centuries, these areas did not produce a distinctive system of Jewish thought or a Jewish literature. The largest branch of the diaspora, however, the approximately half-million Jews living in Babylonia, maintained close contact with the Jews of Palestine and yet was sufficiently independent of their control to develop into a major seat of rabbinic learning, as we shall see in the next section.

The Jews in the Persian Empire

Babylonian Jewry had a continuous history from the deportations of Nebuchadnezzar in the sixth century BCE to the post-World War II emigration of Iraqi Jews to Israel—a period of over 2,500 years. Of the earliest centuries under the Achaemenid dynasty (Cyrus, Darius, Xerxes, and so on) and under Hellenistic kings (the Seleucids controlled Mesopotamia for two centuries) almost no information about the religious institutions of the Babylonian Jews has survived. In the mid-third century BCE the Arsacid dynasty of Parthia ousted the Seleucids from Iran; in the 120s BCE they became overlords of Mesopotamia. Urban life and international commerce (especially the silk trade between China and the Mediterranean, which passed through Persia) continued to flourish under the Parthians, who did not interfere with the autonomy of the various ethnic and religious groups in Mesopotamia, including Greeks and Jews. The Parthian rulers used Jewish contingents in their armies; in the 40s BCE, trying to extend their power westward, the Parthians supported the claims of a Hasmonean prince against Herod and the Romans. The Parthians were helped by Jewish uprisings during Trajan's invasion of 114 CE, when anti-Roman sentiment among Jews was high. By the second century CE at the latest, the Persian king had recognized as official head of the Jews an exilarch (in Aramaic, *resh galuta*, "head of the exile"), who claimed descent from kings of Judah taken in captivity by Nebuchadnezzar. The exilarch collected taxes from the Jews, appointed judges and supervised the court system, and represented his people in the Persian royal court. In endorsing the exilarch, the Parthian rulers may have wanted to offset Roman control over Jews west of Persia, for in the first few centuries CE the Jews were a force to be taken into account in Near Eastern power politics, even though they did not have a state of their own. Likewise, Roman support for the Galilean patriarchate, apart from internal considerations, may have reflected a desire to counteract the appeal of a Davidic prince residing in the Persian capital.[6]

By the middle of the second century CE rabbinic Judaism was beginning to spread eastward; some Palestinian scholars temporarily settled in Babylonia during the Bar Kokhba war and Hadrianic persecutions, and afterward Babylonian Jews came to study in the academies of the Galilee. Canonization of the Mishnah helped to further rabbinic study in the east, because it provided a central text for discussion in the schools. The exilarch encouraged the emergence of a Babylonian class of rabbis, whom he used as administrators and judges. (At first, they did not supervise synagogue rituals, which were conducted according to local precedents, nor did the exilarch give them a major role in criminal proceedings.) The long-range impact of the Babylonian rabbis, like that of the Palestinian, derived from the disciples and students who flocked to hear their interpretations of Scripture and Mishnah, to study their legal and ethical teachings, and to emulate them as models for holy living. When post-Mishnaic teachers in the holy land were laying the groundwork for the Palestinian Talmud, the same development was occurring in third-century Babylonia. Rav (Abba bar Aivu, "Rav" par excellence—rav was the synonym for rabbi in Babylonia), a student of Judah ha-Nasi, founded an influential academy at Sura in central Mesopotamia; his illustrious contemporary Samuel was the head of the academy at Nehardea. Other centers of learning appeared wherever sages of stature settled, including Mahoza adjacent to the Persian capital of Ctesiphon, and after 259, when Nehardea was razed in an invasion, the dominant school for some time at Pumbeditha. The names Sura and Pumbeditha were to be revered in rabbinic Judaism down to the present.

In 226 CE the Arsacid dynasty of Parthia was overthrown by the Sassanians, who introduced far-reaching changes in the structure of the Persian empire. The Sassanian rulers developed a more centralized bureaucratic administration and imposed greater government supervision over their heterogeneous population. Claiming to be a revival of ancient Achaemenid glory, they also promoted a revived Zoroastrianism as the state church of Persia, staffed by a priesthood (the *magi*) hierarchically organized and possessing judicial powers. Eager to spread their teachings, the Mazdean clergy exerted considerable pressure on Jews and other minorities during the reign of Ardashir (226–240), the first Sassanian king. However, after his death, Shapur I (240–271) confirmed the religious freedoms of the non-Zoroastrian communities and the status of the exilarchate. But adjustments had to be made: Jewish authorities were compelled formally to recognize the authority of Persian state law on such matters as ownership of property and taxation. This understanding was expressed in the dictum of the sage Samuel that the "law of the government is the law" (*dina de-malkhuta dina*), a principle of great importance in the history of Jewish law. In Palestine, Jewish law had not recognized the theoretical legitimacy of Roman sovereignty, although it came to accept the Roman presence on pragmatic grounds; but the diaspora situation required a clarification of this crucial point. *Dina de-malkhuta dina* qualified the applicability of Torah law as expounded by the sages by admitting that it could be superseded by non-Jewish civil law and that this supersedence was morally binding—a qualification that actually enabled Torah law to be preserved in a wide variety of sociopolitical situations through the Middle Ages and afterward. (*Dina de-malkhuta dina* does not apply to Jewish religious rituals and ceremonies, and the new political-legal arrangement still maintained considerable Jewish social and legal autonomy in the Sassanian empire.)

Sassanian Babylonia was a relatively prosperous, urbanized, lively, and challenging environment, and the intense religious atmosphere stimulated Jewish intellectual life. Iran produced several new religious groups, such as the Manichaeans, a dualistic salvation religion repressed in Persia by the end of the third century but surviving elsewhere, especially as an underground heretical tendency in Christian Europe. Orthodox and dissident forms of Christianity, a Persian literary revival, astrology, various aspects of Hellenistic and Indian thought all flourished. A large reservoir of Aramaic-speaking Jewish farmers and townspeople faithful to Scripture but in need of religious leadership provided a fertile ground for the spread of the rabbis' Torah. The sages came to be revered for their medicinal skills and occult lore, as well as for their mastery of law and ethical teachings. They and their students formed a distinctive religious estate, with recognizable forms of dress, speech, and deportment. At their height, the rabbinic academies of Babylonia were centers of Jewish living as well as of instruction for those who came to sit at the feet of the masters throughout the year or in months when agricultural work halted. The Babylonian rabbis carried on and developed further the Galilean tradition of imaginative questioning, precise disputation, and rational thinking within the overall contours of the rabbinic world view. In the first half of the fourth century, they produced, among other illustrious sages, two especially eminent figures of the fourth generation of sages in Babylonia: Abbaye and Rava. Abbaye (c. 278–338) was head of the academy at

Silver-gilt bust of a Sassanian king, probably Shapur II. (Courtesy of the Metropolitan Museum of Art, Fletcher Fund, 1965.)

Pumbeditha; Rava (c. 299–352, a contraction of "Rav Abba") taught at Mahoza, and after Abbaye's death, at Pumbeditha. The disputes between these two men over points of law, found on almost every page of the Babylonian Talmud, are models of intricate, subtle argumentation on questions resolved by the most careful analysis of earlier legal precedents.

The impact of rabbinical Judaism was also felt by the exilarch. The goal of rabbinic Judaism was to transform Jewry into that theocracy to which Josephus had earlier alluded, but a theocracy in the rabbinical sense that all Jews were to become rabbis, masters of God's Torah, living according to the will of the King of the kings of kings. (This rabbinic phrase for God was deliberate one-upmanship of the Sassanian "king of kings.") Whatever their earlier claims to direct Davidic authority, the later exilarchs also became rabbis. (Indeed, in the early sixth century, the son of an exilarch became head of the rabbinic academy of Tiberias.) With the decline of the Jewish institutions of Palestine, Babylonia became, until the early eleventh century, the single most important center of Jewish learning in the world.

Although from time to time disruptions occurred in Sassanian Persia that affected the Jews, the Christians were far more suspect and vulnerable to persecution after their faith became the state religion of Persia's main military enemy, Rome; in the fourth and fifth centuries there were prolonged periods where *magi* and their followers attacked and martyred clergy, monks, and lay Christians and destroyed churches. Only in the mid-fifth century was repression specifically directed against Jews, especially between 455 and 475, when synagogues and academies were closed, the exilarchate suspended, Torah banned, and Jewish children seized by the Zoroastrian priesthood. Social and political chaos lasted until the 530s, when another era of stability set in and Jewish institutions were reconstructed. Babylonian Jewish scholars again addressed themselves to the redaction of the materials that comprised the Babylonian Talmud. (This editorial work had already begun under the aegis of Rav Ashi [c. 335–427] at Sura and continued into the sixth century and perhaps even later as other explanatory notes were added to the text.) Babylonian Jews fought in the Persian army that occupied Syria and Palestine at the beginning of the seventh century. Not long afterward, however, the Persians were defeated by the Arab invaders even more thoroughly than the Eastern Roman emperors: In 651 the last Sassanian king was killed, and all Mesopotamia and Iran fell under the control of Islam.

Main Works of Rabbinic Literature

The legacy of the intellectual and religious life of the Palestinian and Babylonian sages is contained in a series of works that summarize, refine, and condense a vast body of orally transmitted statements culled from more than five centuries. These writings are not "literature" in the modern sense; they were not merely meant to be read but to be "learned": studied sentence by sentence and phrase by phrase, until their inner significance was fully absorbed. Rabbinic writings presuppose a thorough command of the Bible, complete familiarity with Jewish observance, and mastery of the rabbinic system of hermeneutic logic. Later they came to be surrounded by an elaborate apparatus of commentary and cross-reference, which, in itself, exemplifies the belief that Torah was an unending process of interpretation continually bringing forth new implications.

Rabbinic thought can be divided into two types: halakhah and aggadah. *Halakhah,* from a root meaning "to go," designates the correct way, the

Catacomb decorated with menorah relief at Bet She'arim in the Galilee. (Courtesy of the Consulate General of Israel.)

required action, the practical rule of ritual or civil law. Halakhah is the path on which and by which a rabbinic Jew guides his life. Like the English word *law*, halakhah can be used for a specific law ("What is the halakhah in this situation?") and for the entire system of law ("He is a master of halakhah"). The centrality of halakhah in rabbinic Judaism is such that all other matters are subsumed under the term *aggadah* (sometimes *haggadah*), from a verb meaning "to tell." Aggadah is theological speculation, general ethical teachings not yet susceptible to halakhic concretion, parables and maxims, legends and folklore. The two categories are complementary: Aggadah seeks to inspire and enlighten; halakhah seeks to apply the divine will to specific mundane circumstances.

The sages of the period between Yavneh and the completion of the Talmuds are grouped into two major divisions. From 70 CE to the death of Judah ha-Nasi in the early third century, rabbinical teachers are called *tannaim* (singular, *tanna*). From the third through the fifth centuries they are known as *amoraim* (singular, *amora*—both *tanna* and *amora* mean "teacher"). Rabbis mentioned in the Mishnah are tannaim; the names of more than 275 are known, divided usually into four generations. Rabbis cited in the talmudic expansion and interpretation of the Mishnah are amoraim; rabbinic literature mentions more than 1,250 individuals, comprising four generations of Palestinian amoraim and six generations in Babylonia. (Babylonian sages of the sixth century who added marginal notes to the text of the Talmud are known as *savoraim*.) Many of the teachings and the editorial framework of rabbinic literature are anonymous, hence the difficulties of establishing when and by whom these works were redacted, a problem we have already encountered in connection with biblical literature. There are, however, vast differences between the biblical and rabbinic writings. Whereas the Bible does not transmit stories, poems, and laws in the name of an individual, the sages saw themselves as a collectivity in which the outstanding individual was revered. The Bible is intensely interested in the meaning of historical events; the sages' Torah is a timeless, eternal blueprint of ideal truth. Whereas for the classical prophets, God speaks through the individual ("Thus says YHVH"), the rabbis presupposed for themselves a more reflective, nonverbal revelation through the working of the sages' minds in concord with the divine mind ("Rabbi so-and-so taught that . . ."). As indicated in an earlier chapter, rabbinic thought had its roots in the fusion of the biblical wisdom tradition and the revealed word of God in Pentateuch and prophecy, a fusion that occurred under the stimulus and in the presence of the rich philosophical tradition of Hellenism. The result was a form of religious rationality unique to Judaism, combining verbal revelation through the written text (the *Torah she-biktav*) and the indirect inspiration through the oral discussions of the sages (the *Torah she-be'al peh*), which together formed Torah in the full rabbinical meaning.

The Mishnah

Written in fluent Hebrew and published (i.e., made public) around 200 CE in the Galilee, the Mishnah is almost entirely a halakhic work. (A few passages of aggadah are sometimes included at the end of each section.) Mishnah is divided into six orders (*sedarim;* singular, *seder*), each comprised of a series of tractates (*massekhtot;* singular, *masseket*) on a single subject. (The tractates are divided into chapters and the chapters into individual *mishnayot,* plural of *mishnah.*) The six orders are as follows:

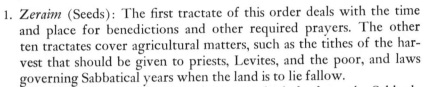

1. *Zeraim* (Seeds): The first tractate of this order deals with the time and place for benedictions and other required prayers. The other ten tractates cover agricultural matters, such as the tithes of the harvest that should be given to priests, Levites, and the poor, and laws governing Sabbatical years when the land is to lie fallow.

2. *Moed* (Set Feasts): Twelve tractates on the holy days: the Sabbath, Passover, and other festivals, the Day of Atonement and other fasts, as well as laws dealing with shekel dues for the Temple and proclamation of the New Year.

3. *Nashim* (Women): Seven tractates on matters affecting womankind and the family, such as betrothal, marriage contracts, divorce, the biblical ritual for a woman suspected of adultery. Laws of religious vows are also treated in this order.

4. *Nezikim* (Damages): Ten tractates on property rights and legal procedures, compensation for damage, ownership of found objects, proper treatment of employees, sale and purchase of land. In this order are tractates on types of Jewish courts, on legal penalties and punishments, and on matters of criminal law. A tractate of general ethical maxims (Pirkei Avot, Sayings of the Fathers) is placed in this order, as well as a tractate of laws concerning idolatry.

5. *Kodashim* (Holy Things): Eleven tractates on sacrificial offerings and other Temple concerns.

6. *Teharot* (Purifications): Twelve tractates on types of ritual uncleanliness and methods of their cancellation.

It will be noted that the Mishnah is not a commentary to the Bible; indeed, biblical citations are rare in the Mishnah, in contrast to such citations in other works of rabbinic literature. The law as developed down to the end of the second century CE has been reformulated in the Mishnah according to a set of rubrics quite different from those used to organize the legal corpora of the Pentateuch. As mentioned earlier in this chapter, the Mishnah imposed order and decisiveness on rabbinic law at a time when the patriarchate had become the central administrative authority to oversee Jewish courts and appoint judges. There is in the Mishnah a certain effort to standardize practice, and numerous tannaitic teachings are deliberately omitted. But this sociopolitical factor does not fully account for the nature of Mishnah. On many subjects Judah ha-Nasi did include dissenting opinions without taking a definite stand; moreover, the Mishnah contains extensive treatments of matters no longer actually practiced in Judaism, especially the Temple cult. (It has been suggested that the authors of the Mishnah, quite aware after the Bar Kokhba defeat that the Temple was not soon to be rebuilt, transmuted Temple law to a different plane where study of the laws served as a religious substitute for holy actions performed in the priestly ritual.) The Mishnah was, therefore, more than a law code: It was a holy book containing a finely honed selection of paradigmatic instances of Jewish action.

Conceived by its authors as an intrinsic part of the Mosaic revelation, the Mishnah was cast in a form hitherto unprecedented in Jewish literature, being neither imitative of biblical forms nor pseudepigraphical, as were the Dead Sea scrolls and the apocalyptic literature. Not only was Mishnah "Oral Torah" in the sense that some of its traditions were thought to have been delivered to Moses at Sinai, then passed on by word of mouth and not written down in the Bible, but the Mishnah presupposed that Oral Torah was an ongoing, revelatory process in which each successive generation could participate by reasoning and reflection. Earlier in this chapter we drew a certain parallel between Mishnah in rabbinic Judaism and New Testament in Christianity, inasmuch as both were considered by their respective communities of faith as the authoritative supplement to the Hebrew Scriptures. Mishnah can be viewed, like Christ in the Gospel of John, as an embodiment of Logos, the Greek conception of reason so important to Philo: Whereas in the New Testament Jesus is Logos in the flesh, in the Mishnah divine Mind takes on the character of a balanced legal language that shapes and orders the flux of reality. The formalized Mishnaic style represents a special mode of discourse that conveys patterns of enduring relationships in mundane life, serving as models of how the Torah can be discovered in and applied to the concrete. Meant to be memorized and internalized by an audience capable of acute concentration and able to make explicit the implied significance of these patterns, Mishnah demanded—and received—constant, keen, and subtle exegesis.[7]

The English translation of the Mishnah by Herbert Danby runs to 789 pages, about 70–75 per cent of the size of the usual English Old Testament. Whether the text was actually written down by Judah ha-Nasi and his associates is uncertain; through most of the talmudic period, from the third to the fifth centuries, it was probably transmitted in the academies by expert memorizers who could recite a relevant law on request.

Pharisaic and tannaitic traditions not included in the Mishnah but preserved and studied by later generations of sages are known as *beraitot* (*baraita*, singular, from a word meaning "outside," i.e., pre-200 CE statements external to the Mishnah). Sometime between 200 and 400 CE, and probably in Palestine, many *beraitot* were gathered together in a work known as the *Tosefta (Supplement)*, organized according to the Mishnah's table of contents, but of lesser authority.

The Talmud

We saw earlier that there are two Talmuds: the Jerusalem (Palestinian) Talmud, which is the product of amoraic discussions in the rabbinic academies of the Galilee, redacted just before the patriarchate was abolished in the early fifth century, and the Babylonian Talmud, which summarizes the amoraic teachings of the academies of Sassanian Persia, largely completed by 500 CE. Whereas the editing of the Jerusalem Talmud was hasty and incomplete because of pressures resulting from the Christianization of the Roman empire, the Babylonian Talmud is more polished and extensive. It is the Babylonian Talmud that has been studied most continuously and widely in subsequent Jewish history. Although diverging on certain points of law, the two Talmuds overlap, the Palestinian quoting Babylonian sages and, to an even greater extent, the Babylonian text containing many opinions of Palestinian amoraim.

Both Talmuds are elaborations of the Mishnah: Each paragraph of Mishnah is followed by a lengthy amoraic exposition, occasionally running to the size of a small book. This amplification has come to be called Gemara. (The term *Talmud* refers to the total material, Mishnah plus Gemara.) Neither Talmud contains Gemara on every Mishnah passage: The extant Jerusalem Talmud contains Gemara on 39 of the 63 Mishnah tractates, and the Babylonian treats 37 Mishnah tractates, not necessarily the same ones. The Palestinian Gemara is about one fourth the size of the Babylonian, running to about 750,000 words in comparison with the Babylonian's 2½ million. Both are multivolume works, many times the size of the Mishnah. Whereas the Mishnah is in Hebrew, the language of the Gemara is the Aramaic dialects spoken in the vicinity of the academies, with some Hebrew used from time to time.

The Gemara text consists of extremely compressed summaries of discussions and essential points. Most of the Gemara is in dialogue form: a chain of questions and answers, objections and rejoinders, refutations and counterrefutations. Each phrase of the Mishnah is carefully interpreted by the amoraim; apparent discrepancies are resolved and redundancies

Catacomb of the Jews of Rome showing burial niches. (Courtesy ENIT.)

explained. Conflicting opinions of tannaim are contrasted and reconciled, often by defining the specific circumstances to which each opinion implicitly refers. Anonymous tannaim are identified on the basis of opinions mentioned elsewhere in the Mishnah or in *beraitot;* unusual words are explained; the text of the Mishnah is occasionally corrected where it seems to have been transmitted inexactly. Hermeneutic rules determining what kind of halakhah can legitimately be deduced from a scriptural verse are used to find biblical support for Mishnaic law. From time to time, the amoraim bring into the discussion reports of cases they have adjudicated and of local customs; some novel rulings are accepted and others dismissed. The Gemara also pursues hypothetical eventualities to see whether an acceptable solution can be found or they must be left hanging as not at present resolvable. Talmudic argumentation uses such phrases as "If you do not say so, the difficulty is this" (i.e., if you deny my presentation of the case, you face the following dilemma); "If you assume this, then" (we confront the following dilemma); "You assert so-and-so, but the reverse is more reasonable," and so on. Of exceptional importance is the effort by the amoraim to articulate basic principles of law, binding the halakhah into a just, harmonious system that maintains the Oral and Written Torahs together as a self-consistent whole.

Debate can be between contemporary members of one academy or between a teacher and his most important disciples; in one generation an outstanding pair of disputants often dominates the discussion, such as Rabbi Johanan and Rabbi Simeon ben Lakish in third-century Palestine or Abbaye and Rava in fourth-century Babylonia. But the canonized Gemara creates a unity transcending its historical strata, so that participants living centuries and hundreds of miles apart seem to communicate directly to each other.

The scope of the Gemara is much greater than that of the Mishnah; it includes all that it can of tannaitic and amoraic legal teaching, augmented by stories of the religious practices, ethical viewpoints, and episodes in the lives of the sages. (A precise terminology distinguishes Mishnah from *baraita* and tannaitic from amoraic authorities.) Halakhic discussion is frequently interrupted by aggadic digressions, the text of the Mishnah becoming at times a peg on which the editors of the Gemara fastened a variety of other topics. It has been estimated that one third of the Babylonian Talmud and one sixth of the Jerusalem Talmud consist of aggadah. (The aggadah of the Babylonian Talmud contains more folklore than the Jerusalem.) In Palestine the aggadah was the basis for a separate class of rabbinic literature, the Midrash, to be described below, whereas in Babylonia this material was included by the redactors into the body of the Gemara.

The Midrash Literature

The term *midrash* (probing, searching) refers to the eliciting from biblical verses of meanings beyond the literal. Unlike Mishnah, which is law presented independent of any scriptural basis, midrash interprets a biblical text or group of texts according to their contemporary relevance.

Tombstone from the Jewish catacomb of the Via Appia in Rome, second or third century CE, reading "Aelia Alexandria set up [this stone] to Aelia Septima, her dearest mother, in grateful memory." (Courtesy of the Jewish Museum, New York.)

Collections of midrashic interpretations can be divided into two categories: halakhic midrash in which the material is mainly legal and aggadic midrash in which it is nonlegal.

The halakhic midrashim are commentaries, mainly on legal verses of the Bible, by tannaitic authorities who lived before the death of Judah ha-Nasi, although the books themselves were compiled in Palestine after the end of the fourth century. We have halakhic midrashim on the book of Exodus beginning with chapter 12 (the *Mekhilta*), on Leviticus (the *Sifra*), on Numbers and Deuteronomy (the *Sifrei*). (Perhaps there is no companion midrash volume on Genesis and the first part of Exodus because these biblical books contain almost no law.) Written in mishnaic Hebrew, the halakhic midrashim do contain aggadah when the verse being interpreted is part of the biblical narrative. At one time there existed two separate sets, one attributed to the school of Ishmael and another to the school of Akiva, founded by the great sages of the early second century; fragments of lost versions have been rediscovered in modern times from medieval midrashic anthologies.

The second category, the aggadic midrashim, derive from homilies given by the amoraim in synagogues and academies. The language is usually Aramaic and the style and content much freer than those of halakhic midrash, since the teachers sought to convey general moral and religious truths, to offer inspiration, and to give consolation in times of trouble. In the edited midrashic works, sermons are given only in summary; however, traces of the original format can sometimes be seen in the *proem*, an interpretation of a verse from another part of the Bible, used to introduce the main text.

Most of these aggadic works were edited in Palestine, but the dating of their redaction is uncertain. The final writing down may have taken place several centuries after the sages whose homilies are recorded. The almost two dozen extant midrashic collections can be divided into four periods: early midrashim (compiled between 400 and 600 CE), middle period works (assembled between 640 and 1000), late-period midrashim (dating from 1000 to 1200), and midrashic anthologies from the thirteenth century. Versions of the same homily can sometimes be found in several midrashic collections and in the Gemara of the Babylonian Talmud.

There are several large families of midrashic books, each series containing works dating from the various periods just mentioned. One family of aggadic midrashim, the Midrash Rabbah (the Great Midrash), covers the five books of the Pentateuch and the five scrolls of the *Ketuvim* (Hagiographa): Song of Songs, Ruth, Lamentations, Ecclesiastes, and Esther. Genesis Rabbah is one of the earliest aggadic midrashim; another very old collection is Leviticus Rabbah, based on sermons on the weekly Torah portion according to the triennial cycle used in Palestine. (The Pentateuch was read in the synagogues of Palestine over the course of three years, rather than the one-year cycle of Babylonia, which has subsequently become common Jewish practice.) Lamentations Rabbah is an ancient midrashic work containing legends on the destruction of the Temple. Other volumes of the Midrash Rabbah were assembled in the middle or late period.

A second family of midrashim contains sermons on the Pentateuch and prophetic readings (the *sidra* and *haftarah*) for festivals and special Sabbaths, in which the liturgy commemorates a distinctive theme in connection with a holy day close at hand. An ancient work of this type is the *Pesikta de Rav Kahana*. (The term *Pesikta* is the plural of the Aramaic word piska, "section," referring to the biblical passage read and discussed.) A third group, the Midrash Tanhuma (after Rabbi Tanhuma bar Abba, a fourth-century Palestinian amora who is frequently cited), contains homilies that open with the phrase "Let them teach us," dealing with a question of general interest to the congregation, often halakhic, before turning to the principal message. The midrashic literature as a whole testifies to a highly polished art of preaching among the ancient rabbis; it is a major source, as we shall see later, for reconstructing the underlying theology of rabbinic Judaism.[8]

Before we give several examples of the kinds of rabbinic literature just described, the following charts may help fix the basic terms in the reader's mind.

Examples of Rabbinic Literature

The following excerpts from the Babylonian Talmud will convey an impression of the general interpretative process—the mental concentration, concern for detail, incorporation of digressions, dedication to order and consistency, and different levels and textures of material included.[9] After quoting the Mishnah passage and the beginning of the Gemara in order to show the character of the original text, we shall outline and summarize the ensuing discussion. (Words omitted from the Hebrew or Aramaic original are supplied in brackets; clarifications are added in parentheses.)

From Tractate Berakhot (Blessings), the first five pages (folios 2a–4a)

Mishnah: From what time may one recite the Shema in the evening? (The Shema is the biblical proclamation of the oneness of God, repeated twice daily and comprised of Deuteronomy 6:4–9, Deuteronomy 11:13–21, and Numbers 15:37–41.) From the time that the priests enter [their houses] in

	Halakhah: "the going," the religious norm of action, the lawful way.	Aggadah: "the telling," ethics, folklore, homiletics, all nonlegal religious discussion.
Talmud: exposition of the Mishnah.	Halakhic discussion and debate in the Mishnah and Gemara.	Aggadic digressions and discussion in the Mishnah and Gemara.
Midrash: expositions of biblical verses.	Halakhic midrashim: Mekhilta, Sifra, Sifrei.	Aggadic midrashim: Midrash Rabbah, Pesikta, Tanhuma, etc.

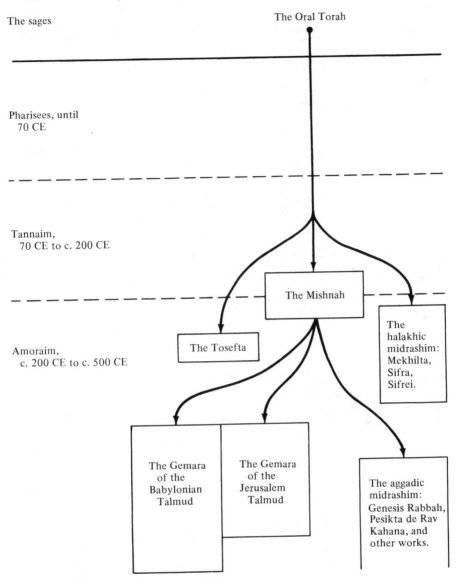

The sages   The Oral Torah

Pharisees, until
  70 CE

Tannaim,
  70 CE to c. 200 CE

The Mishnah

The Tosefta

The
halakhic
midrashim:
Mekhilta,
Sifra,
Sifrei.

Amoraim,
  c. 200 CE to c. 500 CE

The Gemara
of the
Babylonian
Talmud

The Gemara
of the
Jerusalem
Talmud

The aggadic
midrashim:
Genesis Rabbah,
Pesikta de Rav
Kahana, and
other works.

order to eat their *terumah* (the heave offering, a type of sacrifice in which they share) until the end of the first watch; these are the words of R. Eliezer. The sages say: Until midnight. R. Gamaliel says: Until the dawn comes up. Once it happened that his (R. Gamaliel's) sons came home [late] from a wedding feast and they said to him: We have not yet recited the [evening] Shema. He said to them: If the dawn has not yet come up, you are still bound to recite. And not in respect to this alone did they so decide, but wherever the sages say "Until midnight," the precept may be performed

The daughter of Pharaoh finding Moses in the bullrushes and appointing Moses' mother and sister as his nurses (Ex. 2:5–8). Fresco from the third-century synagogue of Dura-Europas in the Syrian desert. (Courtesy of the Union of American Hebrew Congregations.)

until the dawn comes up. The precept of burning the fat and the [sacrificial] pieces (in the Temple) too, may be performed till the dawn comes up. Similarly, all [the offerings] that are to be eaten within one day may lawfully be consumed till the coming up of the dawn. Why then did the sages say "Until midnight"? In order to keep a man far from transgression.

Gemara: On what does the Tanna base himself that he commences: "From what time"? Furthermore why does he deal first with the evening [Shema]? Let him begin with the morning [Shema]!—The Tanna bases himself on the Scripture, where it is written "[And thou shalt recite them] when thou liest down and when thou risest up" (Deut. 6:7), and he states [the oral law] thus: When does the time of the recital of the Shema of lying down begin? When the priests enter to eat their *terumah*. And if you like, I can answer: He learns [the precedence of the evening] from the account of the creation of the world, where it is written, "And there was evening and there was morning, one day" (Gen. 1:5). Why then does he teach in the sequel: "The morning [Shema] is preceded by two benedictions and followed by one. The evening [Shema] is preceded by two benedictions and followed by two?" Let him there, too, mention the evening [Shema] first?—The Tanna commences with the evening [Shema], and proceeds then to the morning [Shema], he expounds all the matters relating to it, and then he returns again to the matters relating to the evening [Shema].

OUTLINE AND SUMMARY

1. The Gemara poses two questions: What is the source for the commandment that the Shema has to be recited at all, and why should the Tanna discuss the timing of the evening recitation first? The answer to both is found in Deuteronomy 6:7, which mentions that one should repeat these words when lying down and rising up. From this verse we learn that we must recite the Shema twice daily; since lying down is mentioned first, the Tanna begins by discussing the evening recitation. An additional scriptural proof is provided by Genesis 1:5, where evening is mentioned before morning.

2. An objection is raised: If "evening before morning" is to be our agenda, why, in the fourth Mishnah of this chapter, does the Tanna discuss the benedictions accompanying the morning recitation before those of the evening? The answer is that he was dealing with the morning Shema at that point; hence for the sake of convenience he went on to discuss the appropriate benedictions for the morning liturgy. (Here the Gemara quoted above ends; we will now summarize several following pages to indicate how this Gemara seeks to demonstrate the consistency of other traditions on this subject and how an aggadic digression is inserted.)

3. The question is asked, why should our Mishnah link the timing of the layman's recitation of the Shema with a Temple ritual, rather than merely state that the Shema must be recited beginning with the appearance of the stars, which is the correct halakhah. The answer is that our Mishnah wishes to teach concurrently a detail concerning the *terumah*. *A propos* of the *terumah*, the Gemara discusses various conditions that render the priest ritually clean to eat this sacrificial offering, details that are verified by a *baraita* on the subject.

4. The question is then posed, whether this *baraita* correctly interprets the meaning of Leviticus 22:7 to which it alludes. A Babylonian *amora* clarifies the meaning of a key word in that verse, confirming the accuracy of the *baraita's* interpretation; a folk expression of Babylonian Jewry is cited to buttress this interpretation. The Gemara notes that the academies of Palestine were unaware of the preceding explanation, but that they had a different *baraita* at hand which satisfactorily proves that the time for reciting the evening Shema and the time when the priest was entitled to eat the *terumah* were, identically, the appearance of the stars.

5. The Gemara now cites three other *beraitot* on the same subject as our Mishnah, although diverging in significant details. (One of them is the full text of the Palestinian tradition just quoted.) These *baraitot* are carefully

analyzed for their logical compatibility with our Mishnah; there are now seven alternative definitions, in addition to that given in our Mishnah, as to the sign when the evening Shema is to be recited. The Gemara demonstrates that these are not redundancies, and that the apparently conflicting views attributed to individual scholars can be adequately resolved.

6. The Gemara now turns to the second subject of our Mishnah, the terminal point for reading the evening Shema. According to the opinion of Rabbi Eliezer, it is the end of the first watch. What hour does he have in mind? Some ancient sages divided the night into three watches, some into four. The question can be answered by an aggadah in the name of Rabbi Eliezer that begins, "Rabbi Eliezer says, 'The night has three watches . . .'"

7. The Gemara digresses to discuss the contents of this aggadah, which teaches, incidentally, that there are watches among the ministering angels in heaven, as well as among men on earth. A debate ensues concerning the three signs that R. Eliezer gives in this aggadah: Do they refer to the beginning, middle, or end of a watch? Then the Gemara quotes two related aggadot. The first also deals with heavenly watches: "R. Isaac ben Samuel says in the name of Rav, The night has three watches, and at each watch the Holy One, blessed be He, sits and roars like a lion and says, 'Woe to the children, on account of whose sins I destroyed My house and burnt My Temple and exiled them among the nations of the world.'" The second aggadah, a story about a rabbi who met the prophet Elijah in a ruin and learned several rules from him, ascribes a similar plaint to a divine voice. The Gemara discusses the dangers of going into ruins.

8. Now the Gemara cites a rabbinic tradition that the night should be divided into four watches. The mention of a psalm verse attributed to David leads to a discussion of David's piety and his concern for having sinned. The Gemara notes that sin can bring a withholding of miracles. (Here the Gemara returns to our Mishnah to take up R. Gamaliel's position on the terminal point for reciting the Shema. The full discussion of our Mishnah occupies ten more pages in the Talmud.)

From Tractate Baba Metziah (The Middle Gate), 103a–103b

Mishnah: If one leases a field from his neighbor (paying either an agreed percentage of the crops or a fixed measure of the grain in rent), where it is the usage to cut [the crops], he must cut; to uproot [them], he must uproot [them]; to plough after it (to plough after reaping and weeding so that the weeds should not grow again), he must plow after it. It is all determined by local custom. And just as they divide the grain (when the rent is a percentage of the produce), so they also share in the straw and stubble. And just as they divide the wine, so do they share in the branches [cut from the vine] and the canes [used for supporting the vines], and both supply the canes.

Gemara: It has been taught: Where it is the usage to cut [off the crops], he must not uproot; to uproot, he must not cut. And each can restrain the other [from varying the usual procedure]. "To cut he must not uproot": the one [the lessor] can say, "I want my field manured with stubble"; and the other may say, "It is too much labor [to uproot thus]." "To uproot he must not cut." The one [the lessor] can say, "I wish my field to be cleared [of stubble]"; and the other, "I need the stubble." "And each can restrain the other [from varying the usual procedure]." Why state this?—This gives the the reason. [Thus:] Why may he not uproot when the usage is to cut, and vice versa? Because each can restrain the other. "To plough after it, he must plough after it": is this not obvious?—It is necessary only for a place where weeding is not done [while the grain is standing]; and he [the lessee] went and weeded it. I might think that he can plead, "I weeded it in order to be exempt from [subsequent] ploughing." Therefore we are taught that he should have distinctly stated this [beforehand].

OUTLINE AND SUMMARY

1. The Gemara opens with a *baraita* (signaled by the phrase "it has been taught") that discusses the same matter as our Mishnah but in the negative. The Gemara spells out the conditions to which the *baraita* alludes: that the lessor might want the field fertilized with stubble or that the lessee might not be able to uproot the stubble; conversely, the lessor might want the field completely cleared, or the lessee might want to keep the stubble for his own use. Why is it necessary for the *baraita* to state explicitly that each may prevent the other from changing the prevailing custom, when this principle is implied in the opening phrase? Because each can prevent the other from departing from custom when he has a reason for so doing.

2. The Gemara now turns to the statement in our Mishnah that one must plow afterwards, if it is customary so to do. Is this not obvious? No, because in some localities weeding is not customary; if the lessee went ahead and weeded, assuming that he would not have to plow, the Tanna informs us that he has not fulfilled his legal obligation, since he should have informed the owner, when agreeing to the terms of the lease, that he would not afterwards plow. (Here the Gemara quotation ends; the following continuation shows how other details of our Mishnah are explained.)

3. Why does our Mishnah state that in "all" respects one should follow local custom? To cover the principle stated by the following *baraita:* "Where it is customary to lease the trees together with the field—they are leased. Where it is not customary to lease them—they are not leased." Is this not obvious? No, because there are some localities where it is customary for the tenant to pay one third of the produce as rent. If the owner has rented the field for a one-quarter share, he might think that he could later argue that the trees were not included in the lease. The *baraita*, therefore, informs us that the owner must stipulate this to the tenant beforehand, or the general rule that the trees are included in the lease must be enforced by the court. The converse is included in the *baraita* to cover a similar misunderstanding on the part of the tenant: Paying a higher rental than usual does not mean, contrary to custom in his region, that the trees are included.

4. The Gemara now deals with the statement in our Mishnah that as they share the grain, they also share the straw and stubble. Rav Joseph says, "In Babylonia it is the practice not to give a share of the straw to the tenant." What bearing does this statement have on the halakhah? (It should be noted

that the Mishnah was formulated in the Galilee, whereas our Gemara reflects conditions in Babylonia.) It is considered generous but not legally necessary among Babylonian Jews for the owner of the field to give the tenant a share of the straw. Rav Joseph also explains how owner and tenant in Babylonia share in the construction of fences and boundaries to protect the crops. From this information, the general principle is deduced that whatever is essential for guarding the boundary line of the field is to be provided by the landowner; additional protection is to be provided by the tenant. Rav Joseph also furnishes data on the respective duties of lessor and lessee in connection with the digging of irrigation channels. (In Sassanian Babylonia, agricultural productivity was dependent on a highly developed irrigation system.)

5. The Gemara turns to the ending of our Mishnah and explains that the canes are necessary to prop up the grape vines. Why stipulate that they share in the canes? Because they both supplied them. (This ends a complete Gemara for one Mishnah.)

From Tractate Baba Kamma (First Gate), 83b

Mishnah: One who injures a fellow man becomes liable to him for five items: for depreciation, for pain, for healing, for loss of time, and for degradation. (The rest of our Mishnah explains how these five factors are to be estimated in computing compensation for injury.)

Gemara: Why [pay compensation]? Does the Divine Law not say "Eye for eye" (Ex. 21:24)? Why not take this literally to mean [putting out] the eye [of the offender]?—Let not this enter your mind, since it has been taught: You might think that where he put out his eye, the offender's eye should be put out, or where he cut off his arm, the offender's arm should be cut off, or again where he broke his leg, the offender's leg should be broken. [Not so, for] it is laid down, "He that smiteth any man. . . . And he that smiteth a beast. . . ." (Lev. 24:17–21); just as in the case of smiting a beast compensation is to be paid, so also in the case of smiting a man compensation is to be paid (but there is to be no resort to physical retaliation). And should this [reason] not satisfy you, note that it is stated, "Moreover ye shall take no ransom for the life of a murderer, that is guilty of death" (Num. 35:31), implying that it is only for the life of a murderer that you may not take "satisfaction" (i.e., a ransom that would release him from capital punishment), whereas you may take "satisfaction" [even] for the principal limbs, though these cannot be restored.

OUTLINE AND SUMMARY

1. The Gemara asks, does not Exodus 21:24 teach that if one blinds another, he must be blinded in retaliation? Definitely not, as indicated by the *baraita* ("it has been taught" is the characteristic phrase for introducing a *baraita*), which notes that Leviticus 24 juxtaposes the case of an animal's injury to the case of a human being's. Just as compensation is to be paid for the former, so also for the latter. The *baraita* continues by offering a second biblical proof text, should the first not be satisfying: Numbers 35:31 specifies

that monetary payment does not release a murderer from capital punishment, which is held to imply that payment is to be arranged in cases where injury is inflicted even on limbs that cannot be returned to their normal condition. (Our Gemara quotation ends here.)

2. Several questions are raised in the continuation of the Gemara concerning Leviticus 24:17-21 from which the *baraita* establishes the scriptural basis for the principle that compensation is to be paid for injury in every case but willful murder. Does the *baraita* depend mainly on verse 21, "He that kills a beast shall make it good and he that kills a man shall be put to death?" The latter half of this verse refers to murder, where a form of retaliation (capital punishment) actually applies. The Gemara answers by citing verses 18-19 instead: "He that smites a beast mortally shall make it good, life for life; if a man cause disfigurement in his neighbor, as he has done so shall it be done to him." Just as he shall pay compensation for a dead animal, so shall he pay compensation for disfigurement.

3. The objection is raised that the technical term "smiting" is not mentioned in verse 19. The answer is that the *effect* of smiting (disfigurement) is clearly implied, just as the *effect* of smiting (the death of the beast) is mentioned in verse 18; hence the penalty of both offenses is payment of compensation.

4. A further objection is raised concerning the second half of verse 17, "He that kills a man shall be put to death." (Because the rabbis assume that there is no redundancy in the Torah and because they have learned elsewhere that a murderer is to be put to death, the word "kills" in this verse is taken to refer not to murder but to total disablement of a limb.) Perhaps the phrase "put to death" refers to destruction of a limb in retaliation? No, this verse also refers to monetary compensation. Why not take the verse literally? First, because it is linked with the case immediately following in verse 18, where a man who kills a beast shall "make it good" by financial payment, and second, because the phrase "as he has done, so shall it be done to him" in verse 19 has also been showed to mean financial compensation.

5. Why does the *baraita* find it necessary to state that Leviticus 24 may not provide a fully satisfying textual proof and offers, in addition, Numbers 35:31? A first proposal is that it occurred to the Tanna that someone might ask why the law of "man injuring man" should be derived from the law of "smiting a beast" and not from the law of "man killing man." The *baraita* therefore indicates that it is proper to derive the law concerning an injury to a human being from a law concerning another type of injury, and not from the law governing murder.

6. It could, however, be argued to the contrary, that cases involving harm to human beings should be linked together, rather than cases involving injuries to human beings and animals. Probably the Tanna is establishing in the latter part of the *baraita* the alternative line of reasoning that the injunction not to take ransom for the life of the murderer implies that one does take ransom for injured limbs even though these cannot be restored. How can we prove that this is the correct interpretation? Perhaps the purpose of Numbers 35:31 may not have been to exclude retaliation for loss of principal limbs, but to teach that the murderer should not be subjected to two punishments,

i.e., to payment of monetary compensation as well as to capital punishment. In answer to this proposal, the Gemara points to the phrase, "according to his crime" in Deuteronomy 25:2 (the word *crime* is in the singular), which serves as a wholly adequate basis for the legal principle that a person should not be held liable to two punishments for one offense.

7. But still, was it not possible that Numbers 35:31 merely taught that you should not take monetary compensation from a murderer and release him from capital punishment, and that it had no additional meaning? The rejoinder is that, if so, the verse would have been written, "Moreover, ye shall take no satisfaction from him who is guilty [and deserving] of death." On the contrary, the biblical verse reads "for the life of the murderer" in order to indicate that it is only for his life that you may not take ransom, whereas you may take ransom for principal limbs. But the objection is raised, if this is the meaning of Numbers 35:31, why then do I require the analogy of "smiting" in the case of a human injury and "smiting" in the case of a beast's injury, the argument earlier developed using Leviticus 24? The response to this objection is that if we only had Numbers 35:31 and not the reasoning based on Leviticus 24, we might have thought that the offender has the option of paying with the loss of his eye. The amoraim therefore conclude that the *baraita* contains both lines of reasoning to enable us to learn that, just as in the case of smiting a beast the offender is liable only for monetary compensation, so also in the case of injuring a man he is liable only for monetary compensation, and most certainly he does not have the legal right to choose mutilation instead.

The *Mekhilta* on Exodus 35:2–3 (an example of halakhic midrash)

[Exodus 35:2–3: "Six days shall work be done but on the seventh day you shall have a holy Sabbath of solemn rest to the Lord; whoever does any work on it shall be put to death; you shall kindle no fire in all your habitations on the Sabbath day."]

"You shall kindle no fire": Since it says "In plowing time and in harvest thou shalt rest" (Ex. 34:21), which means: Refrain from plowing in the harvest time, that is, that one must refrain from plowing in the sixth year for the sabbatical year, I only know that already on the sixth year one must rest from work which is done for the sabbatical year. But one might think that in like manner a person should rest on Friday from work done for the Sabbath. And the following argument might be advanced: The sabbatical year is observed in the name of God, and the Sabbath day is also observed in the name of God. Now, since you have proved that one must rest during the sixth year from work for the seventh, it follows also that one should rest on Friday from work for the Sabbath. And furthermore, by using the method *kal va-homer* [the hermeneutic rule of "light-to-heavy"], one could reason: If in the case of the sabbatical year, for the disregard of which one does not incur the penalty of extinction or of death at the hands of the human court, one must begin already on the sixth year to rest from work for the seventh, it is but logical that in the case of the Sabbath, for the disregard of which one incurs the penalty of extinction or of death at the hands of the human court [if the violation of the Sabbath is committed presumptuously and in spite of the warning of witnesses], one should already on Friday rest from work done for the Sabbath. In other words, or to be specific, one should not be permitted on Friday to light a candle, or to put away things to be kept warm, or to make a fire, for the Sabbath. Therefore Scripture says: "Ye shall kindle no fire in your dwelling-places on the Sabbath day." On the Sabbath day itself you may not kindle a fire, but you may on Friday kindle a fire for the Sabbath.

(This legal midrash establishes, contrary to a hypothetical argument based on analogy with the sabbatical year, that Scripture indeed permits a fire and warm dishes on the Sabbath if these are prepared beforehand.)

Genesis Rabbah on Genesis 1:1 (an example of aggadic midrash)

[Genesis 1:1: "In the beginning God created the heavens and the earth."]

"In the beginning God created": Six things preceded the creation of the world; some of them were actually created, while the creation of the others was already contemplated. The Torah and the Throne of Glory were created. The Torah, for it is written, "The Lord made me as the beginning of his way, prior to his works of old" (Prov. 8:22). The Throne of Glory, as it is written, "Thy throne is established of old" (Ps. 93:2). The creation of the Patriarchs was contemplated, for it is written, "I saw your fathers as the first-ripe in the fig-tree at her first season" (Hos. 9:10). [The creation of] Israel was contemplated, as it was written, "Remember thy congregation, which thou hast gotten aforetime" (Ps. 74:2). [The creation of] the Temple was contemplated, for it is written, "Thou throne of glory, on high from the beginning, the place of our sanctuary" (Jer. 17:12). The name of the Messiah was contemplated, for it is written, "His name existeth ere the sun" (Ps. 72:17). Rabbi Ahabah ben Rabbi Zeira said, Repentance too, as it is written, "Before the mountains were brought forth" (Ps. 90:2) and from that very moment "Thou turnest man to contrition and sayest: Repent, ye children of men" (Ps. 90:3). I still do not know which was first, whether the Torah preceded the Throne of Glory or the Throne of Glory preceded the Torah. Said Rabbi Abba ben Kahana: The Torah preceded the Throne of Glory, for it says, "The Lord made me as the beginning of His way, ere His works of old," which means, ere that whereof it is written, "Thy Throne is established of old." Rabbi Huna, reporting Rabbi Jeremiah in the name of Rabbi Samuel ben Isaac, said: The intention to create Israel preceded everything else. This may be illustrated thus: A king was married to a certain lady, and had no son by her. On one occasion the king was found going through the market-place and giving orders: "Take this ink, inkwell, and pen for my son," at which people remarked: "He has no son; what does he want with ink and pen? Strange indeed!" Subsequently they concluded: "The king is an astrologer, and has actually foreseen that he is destined to beget a son!" Thus, had not the Holy One, blessed be He, foreseen that after twenty-six generations Israel would receive the Torah, He would not have written therein, "Command the children of Israel" (Num.

23:2). Rabbi Banayah said: The world and the fullness thereof were created only for the sake of the Torah: "The Lord for the sake of wisdom [i.e., Torah] founded the earth" (Prov. 3:10). . . .

(This midrashic passage illustrates the theme that certain ideas of supreme importance and value were said to have been present in God's mind before he created the world, a concept that we will discuss further in the next section.)

The outlines and summaries of these few passages of Gemara attempt to illustrate a few of the stylistic features of rabbinic thought, but a fuller awareness of the intricacy and originality of the Talmud may only be gained by studying the text itself. The first selection shows how tannaitic statements were compared to insure that the Oral Torah was a consistent whole; an aggadah clarifying a sage's legal statement also conveys the compassionate but just nature of God in rabbinic Judaism. The second Gemara is an analysis of fairness in landowner–tenant obligations, based on the principle that one has the right to expect local custom will be followed unless departure from it is agreed on in advance by both parties. (This passage also indicates the importance of agriculture to Babylonian Jewry in the Sassanian period.) The third selection shows that there was no question of applying *lex talionis* literally ("eye for an eye") in Mishnaic law; the Mishnah launches directly into the kinds of

Samuel anoints David as king (1 Sam. 16:6–13), in a panel of the Dura synagogue frescos. (Courtesy of the Union of American Hebrew Congregations.)

compensation to be paid the injured party. The Gemara, which wants to tie the Written and Oral Torahs more closely together, interprets biblical citations of *lex talionis* in line with the principle of monetary compensation for injury; an unspoken assumption is that no scriptural verse is superfluous and that any apparent repetition teaches a special halakhic lesson. This discussion also establishes that the guilty person cannot choose to accept mutilation in order to escape paying financial compensation to the injured party.

The excerpt from the halakhic midrash shows that the biblical verse in question permits the comforts of a fire (and, therefore, warm food) on the Sabbath, as long as it is kindled beforehand. The aggadic midrash selection, by establishing the absolute priority of Torah, Israel, and redemption (in each case buttressed by a relevant scriptural verse interpreted in line with rabbinic exegesis), affirms their centrality in rabbinic theology as part of the meaning of creation.

Rabbinic Theology

The Near East in late antiquity was filled with many kinds of holy men: pagan magicians, ascetics, and philosopher-mystics; Christian clergy, monks, and hermits; Zoroastrian *magi*, Manichaean elect, and Jewish sages. Each had its own particular complex of roles vis-à-vis earthly society and the heavenly realm. More than any other religious leadership of the time, the rabbis were pre-eminently jurists, although, to be sure, the *magi* had legal functions and the Christian bishop had administrative ones. Inasmuch as the central focus of rabbinic thought was halakhah, the rabbis did not attempt to forge a Jewish creed; among other reasons, they were not caught up, as was Christianity, in a situation that required doctrinal precision as an accompaniment of mass conversion. Nor were they concerned with demonstrating the philosophical validity of their beliefs. Rabbinic Judaism, unlike patristic Christianity, was not inclined to clothe its doctrines in forms borrowed from Greek metaphysics so as to convince the pagan intellectual of their validity. There is no clear-cut parallel in rabbinic Judaism to the treatises of the great Neo-Platonic pagan thinker Plotinus or the important Christian theologians Origen and Clement of Alexandria and Augustine of Hippo. If theology is conceived of as a carefully formulated system directed to someone outside the immediate circle of one's faith, the rabbis did not have a theology. However, if theology is a reflection on the nature of religion and the attempt to resolve underlying dilemmas posed by a tradition's beliefs and values, then rabbinic Judaism certainly had a theology, as we shall see in the course of this section.[10]

The halakhah presupposes a theology that emerges in the aggadah in the form of epigrams, maxims, anecdotes, parables, and harmonization of biblical verses. Rabbinic theology is often marked by wit, playfulness, and willingness to make daring comparisons between the divine and the human that are qualified only by the phrase "as it were" (*kivyahol*). One modern scholar has called rabbinic theology "organic."[11] Its various concepts are so closely interrelated that each one implies several others, and, like talmudic law, together form a world view in which an isolated unit can be understood only from the perspective of the whole. Living mentally and socially in the realm of Torah, the rabbis were least concerned about reconciling their ideas with the systems of thought of other peoples than almost any class of Jewish intellectuals in history, certainly less than the medieval Jewish philosophers and probably less than the biblical authors.

Nevertheless, currents and challenges from outside filtered through. Aspects of popular Stoic and Platonic thought can be found in rabbinical teachings: the comparison of God to the soul, the belief that before birth the soul knew the entire Torah but then forgot it. The rabbis knew enough about the Epicureans, especially the Epicurean belief that the gods were of no help to a human being searching for inner peace of mind, so that *epikorus* became the rabbinic term for heretic—he who denies that there is a divine Judge and divine justice. There is surprisingly little mention of Christianity, except a few obscure references to Jesus as a magician and the insistence that, despite the spread of Scriptures, only Israel has the full Torah, written and oral (e.g., Num. R. XIV:10).

Judging from various rabbinic teachings denouncing the idea of two divine powers, a more serious concern was Gnosticism. The Gnostics—actually a number of competing salvation sects, some deriving from the Iranian tradition and others using biblical and Christian symbols—viewed the world as the work of an evil deity who sought enslavement of man's spirit in physical matter. Salvation was achieved through knowledge (*gnosis*) of the transmundane origin of the spirit, a liberating knowledge that enabled one to be reunited with the true, but generally unknown God. According to the Church father Clement, Gnostic initiates were taught "who we were and what we have become, where we are and where we were placed, whither we hasten, from what we are redeemed, what birth is, and what rebirth." Some Gnostics interpreted the creation story of Genesis as a trick by a demonic YHVH to trap man in this evil world, and they viewed the serpent of the Garden of Eden as a hero. Christianity struggled with Gnostic tendencies in its midst during the second and third centuries, and the rabbis may have engaged in such polemics also. This seems a likely interpretation of the Mishnah's warning, "Whoever gives his mind to four things, it is better for him if he had not come into the world—what is above, what is beneath, what was beforetime, and what will be hereafter" (Hag. 2:1). The biblical heritage as understood by the rabbis prevented a capitulation to the extreme other-worldliness prevalent in the religion of these centuries.

Although maintaining the Bible's faith in the value of the mundane world and of man's task in it, the rabbis transposed Scripture into something quite different from its original ancient Near Eastern context. Biblical figures are embroidered with innumerable legendary details—redressed, as it were, into men completely a part of the contemporary environment of the sages. Moses is a rabbi (*Mosheh rabbenu*, "Moses our teacher," is a favorite term); the patriarchs and David study Torah and pray according to the rabbinical liturgy. Holding firm to the divine origin of the Bible and no longer expecting to learn any important new lessons from the events of history, the rabbis found in the biblical narratives a comprehensive and fully adequate model for understanding Israel's role in This World and its relation to the World to Come. (They did not, however, transform biblical personages and events into pure metaphysical symbols or universal types, as did Hellenistic Jewish allegory and some forms of patristic Christian thought.)

To cover the complete spectrum of rabbinic views and currents extending over so many centuries is beyond the scope of this volume, but let us sketch some aspects of rabbinic theology. We shall first consider the inter-relationship of Torah and Israel in rabbinic Judaism, showing how each was redefined in a special rabbinic way.

Torah and Israel

In the excerpt from Genesis Rabbah quoted in the previous section, the enumeration of things said to precede the creation of the world included Torah and the idea of Israel. The concept of a premundane Torah, which resembles the premundane Christ in Christian theology (a Christ who was "with the Father" before the world was formed), expresses the purposiveness of creation in the thought of the rabbis. In another midrash, R. Oshaya, drawing on Proverbs 8 and related passages, asserts that Torah is the divine "working tool" for creation: In human affairs a king builds a palace with the help of an architect and the architect uses plans and diagrams; in like manner God consulted his blueprint, the Torah, as he created the world (Gen. R. I:1). Torah is not, however, a visual diagram for nature; its commandments are the moral and religious goals to be actualized in the everyday world. The heavenly Torah is an ideal pattern to be realized on earth by man. Because, after creation, Torah includes a written component (the Scripture) and an oral component (the laws and interpretations of the sages), the human mind discovers God's will by reasoning about the contents of revelation. That the rabbis participate in the articulation of Torah is epitomized in an aggadah which relates that R. Eliezer, while trying to convince other rabbis of his position on a

The allegory of the valley of dry bones (Ezek., chap. 37) from the Dura synagogue. (Courtesy of the Union of American Hebrew Congregations.)

certain halakhic matter, called on heaven to substantiate his view. Even though a carob tree miraculously moved a hundred yards from its place, the water of a canal flowed backward, the walls of the house of study bent inward, and a heavenly voice proclaimed its agreement with him, the rabbis were not budged. R. Joshua quoted Deuteronomy 30:12: "It is not in heaven," which R. Jeremiah explained as meaning in this context, "The Torah was given us from Sinai; we pay no attention to a heavenly voice. For already from Sinai the Torah said, 'By a majority you are to decide'" (Ex. 23:22 as interpreted homiletically, an almost complete reversal of its plain meaning). The aggadah ends with R. Nathan meeting Elijah the prophet in a field and asking what God did in that hour. Elijah replied, "He laughed and said, 'My children have defeated me.'" (B.T. Baba Metzia 59b.) This aggadah, like much of the midrash, has several facets, being an example of homiletic playfulness, of the authority to interpret Torah that the sages ascribed to themselves, a polemic against charismatic religion, and an indication of the rabbis' belief that God performs miracles for those he loves but that miracles do not determine halakhah. Above all, this story points to the comprehensiveness of the rabbinical conception of Torah, an endless unfolding of divine truth to be realized by human thought and action.

The midrash in Genesis Rabbah cited earlier noted also that Israel was present in the mind of God before creation. Israel has as great a priority as Torah because a people is needed to actualize Torah in the created world. This World without a nation of Torah would be meaningless. In Ruth Rabbah, R. Elazar describes the "deed of charity" that Israel did for God by accepting the Torah. God is said to remark, "If you had not accepted My Torah, I should have caused the world to revert to void and destruction" (Ruth R. *Proem*, I:1). Such statements are also made of the righteous man ("Even for the sake of one righteous man the world would have been created, and for the sake of one righteous man it will continue," B. T. Yoma 38b, Sab. 30b) and for such exemplary men as Abraham ("The world was created for the sake of Abraham," Gen. R. XII:9). Indeed, a human being who lives up to the ideal accomplishes what the angels, purely spiritual beings without any physical component, cannot achieve:

> R. Simon said: When the Holy One, blessed be He, came to create Adam, the ministering angels formed themselves into groups and parties, some of them saying, "Let him be created," while others urged, "Let him not be created." Thus it is written, "Love and Truth fought together, Righteousness and Peace combated each other" (Ps. 85:11). Love said, "Let him be created, because he will dispense acts of love"; Truth said, "Let him not be created, because he is compounded of falsehood"; Righteousness said, "Let him be created, because he will perform righteous deeds"; Peace said, "Let him not be created, because he is full of strife." What did the Lord do? He took Truth and cast it to the ground. [See Dan. 8:12.] Said the ministering angels before the Holy One, blessed be He, "Sovereign of the Universe! Why do You despise Thy seal? Let Truth arise from the earth!" Hence it is written, "Let truth spring up from the earth" (Ps. 85:12). . . . While the ministering angels were arguing with each other and disputing with each other, the Holy One, blessed be He, created [Adam]. Said He to them: "What can ye avail? Man has already been made!" [Gen. R. VIII:5.]

This midrash, an adroit dramatization of the psalm verses being interpreted, brings out the theme that Torah was destined only for man, a creature standing between heavenly beings and animals and partaking of both their natures. (We will return later to the rabbinic conception of the nature of man.)

Out of all the nations, Israel's merit was to have accepted the Torah at Sinai and pledged to hearken and obey. The Torah was given in the wilderness, in no-man's-land, for had it been given in the land of Israel, the nations of the world could have said that they had no portion in it. According to a midrash, God had previously gone to several nations, offering them the Torah in turn, but they rejected it because one or another of its commandments conflicted with their customary way of life or impugned their origins. (*Mekhilta*, II, 234–37.) Indeed, the covenant with God is

Israel's only *raison d'être:* "For had it not been for My Torah which you have accepted, I would not recognize you or look upon you more than other idol-worshippers" (Ex. R., XLVII:3).

Although Israel is obligated to obey all the revealed commandments, there were certain laws considered binding on all men "which if they had not been written, would have to be written", that is, which the human intellect unaided by revelation can perceive (see B. T. San. 56a–b and Yoma 67b). These are called by the rabbis the seven laws of Noah, an expansion of the covenant in Genesis 9. These seven universal principles are avoidance of idolatry, unchastity (incest and adultery), bloodshed, profaning the name of God, robbery, cutting off flesh from a living animal, and the establishment of courts of justice. Inclusion of idolatry and blasphemy with the other, purely ethical laws expresses the rabbis' conviction that monotheism is a necessary precondition for righteousness. Rabbinic Judaism did not limit salvation in the World to Come to those who belong to Israel, but it held that all men should believe in the oneness of God: "He who repudiates idol worship may be called a Jew" (B. T. Megillah 13a).

From the perspective of the rabbis, Israel was the only nation that has taken on the "yoke of Heaven" by honoring the unity of God. "Taking on the yoke of Heaven" is the rabbinic interpretation of the Shema—"Hear, O Israel, the Lord our God, the Lord is one"—followed in the liturgy by "taking on the yoke of the commandments," that is, accepting God's decrees in the Torah. Israel's act at Sinai is a crucial moment of cosmic history because it was, so to speak, the beginning of Torah's incarnation in the world. Exodus Rabbah XXIII:1 explains that the divine throne remained unstable when only a few, like the patriarchs, worshiped the one God. Israel stabilized God's throne when it agreed to proclaim him King on earth. (The allusion is to Ex. 15:1–18, which ends with "The Lord will reign forever and ever.")

By assuming the yoke of the commandments, Israel became a holy people. Holiness means not just abstaining from fusion with other nations and from following their ways, but imitating God's attributes through acts of mercy and through study. (God not only does merciful deeds on earth but he studies Torah in heaven, just as the rabbis study Torah in their academies, B. T. Avodah Zara 3b.) Because Israel has accepted the Torah, its actions either "sanctify God's name" or "profane God's name" on earth. Thus the everyday behavior of Jews is the most important datum of history. Making daring use of *kivyahol* ("as it were," "if it is possible to say so"), R. Azariah in the name of R. Judah ben Simeon said, "When Israel does God's will, they add to the power of God on high. When Israel does not do God's will, they, as it were, weaken the great power of God on high" (Lam. R. I:6, section 33). Indeed, nothing matters more than Israel's obedience or disobedience: " 'You are my witnesses, says the Lord, and I am God' (Isa. 43:12), that is, when you are my witnesses, I am God, and when you are not my witnesses, I am [as it were] not God" (*The Midrash on Psalms*, Ps. 123:2).

Unlike the Bible, the rabbis do not emphasize the election or chosenness of Israel: Israel exists to be the recipients of Torah. On Israel's behavior—testifying that it is indeed the people of Torah—God's "presence" in the world depends.

The Names and Attributes of God

Living in an environment where everyone believed in the reality of the divine, the rabbis felt no need to establish formal proofs for God's existence. It was enough to point out that a castle implied the existence of an owner and a ship that of a captain. They also tended to sidestep the issue of God's relation to the natural order that would preoccupy Jewish philosophy later. Asked by a pagan why a certain temple burned down and its idol was saved, R. Gamaliel responded with the question: against whom does a king wage war, the living or the dead (i.e., the idol was a dead thing). A continuation of this discussion in the *Mekhilta* (II, 245) is found in the Gemara: "Philosophers asked the [Jewish] elders in Rome, 'If your God has no desire for idolatry, why does He not abolish it?' They replied, 'If it was something of which the world has no need that was worshiped, He would abolish it; but people worship the sun, moon, stars, and planets; should He destroy the universe on account of fools! The world pursues its natural course, and as for the fools who act wrongly, they will have to render an account'" (B. T. Avodah Zara 54b). The rabbinic God was a continuation, in some ways a modification, of the biblical God, a being whose existence was an unquestioned surety and not a philosophical conclusion.

A crucial feature of the biblical concept of God is his transcendence over nature and history. Although early biblical narratives describe YHVH as personally appearing to patriarchs and others, these theophanies gave way in later narratives to angelic messengers and to the divine voice (less frequently to heavenly visions) experienced by the prophets, which became the modes of God's immanence in the world. Postbiblical Jewish thought develops new ways to express God's otherness from creation and his presence in it. The Aramaic translations (the *Targumim*) of the Bible used in the synagogue frequently employ the term *memra* ("word," i.e., word of God) in relating God's actions in order to militate against a too literal anthropomorphism and to emphasize a more refined, transcendent concept of deity. Other euphemisms were also devised as substitutes for the ancient name YHVH. The most important rabbinic designation for God's presence in the world is Shekhinah, based on the biblical expression that God dwells (*shakhen*) in the midst of his people, in the Tabernacle (*mishkan*) during the wilderness wanderings and in his House on Mount Zion. But the application of Shekhinah is enlarged to apply to God's relation to history and to all moral-religious behavior.

A midrash explains that although the Shekhinah came to earth at creation, as a result of man's sins—those of Adam, Cain, the generation of the flood, and so on— the Shekhinah withdrew to higher and higher heavens, to be brought to earth again by the patriarchs and other righteous men (Num. R. XIII:2). When Israel accepted the Torah at Sinai and carried out instructions to worship God by erecting the Tabernacle, God was again fully present:

> While the Holy One, blessed be He, was alone in His world He yearned to dwell with His creatures in the terrestrial regions but did not do so. As soon, however, as the Tabernacle was erected and the Holy One, blessed be He, caused His Shekhinah to dwell therein and the princes came to present their offerings, the Holy One, blessed be He, said, "Let it be written that on this day the world was created" (Num. R. XIII:6).

How can God who "fills heaven and earth" be said to confine his presence to a small dwelling? Various analogies are offered, such as the comparison to a cave by the seashore. When the tide rises, the cave fills with water without diminishing the sea. After the Tabernacle is filled with the radiance of the Shekhinah, the world is no less filled with God's glory (Num. R. XII: 4).

The rabbis use the concept of the Shekhinah to designate God's nearness to men in various moments of extra holiness. For example, the Shekhinah is present when men study Torah (Pirkei Avot 3:3), when they pray together (Pirkei Avot 3:9), when sages learn esoteric lore (B.T. Hag. 14b). The Shekhinah is attracted by special acts of hospitality, benevolence, and faithfulness. Judges who gave true verdicts "cause the Shekhinah to dwell in Israel" (B.T. San. 7a). Conversely, arrogance, slander, and perversion of justice "drive the Shekhinah away." There is no place, however lowly, where the Shekhinah cannot dwell. A pagan asked R. Joshua ben Karha why God spoke to Moses from a thorn-bush. The rabbi replied, "Were it a carob tree or a sycamore tree, you would have asked the same question; but to dismiss you without any reply is not right, so I will tell you why. To teach you that no place is devoid of God's presence, not even a thorn-bush" (Ex. R. II:5). The Shekhinah is a term for God with the connotation of palpable immediacy and protective love (the "radiance of the Shekhinah," the "wings of the Shekhinah"). The highest bliss of the righteous is to enjoy the radiance of the Shekhinah in the World to Come (B.T. Ber. 17a). To convert a gentile to Judaism is to bring him under the wings of the Shekhinah (*Mekhilta*, II, 186). In the diaspora, where the Jews cannot fulfill the commandments that depend on residence in the holy land, even there the Shekhinah accompanies them (*Sifrei Num.* 62b–63a).[12]

Besides Shekhinah, as many as ninety other synonyms for God were devised to express a gamut of human needs and theological nuance.[13] The most frequent are *Ribono shel olam* (Lord of the universe), *Mi-she-amar v'haya ha-olam* (He who spoke and the world was), *Avinu she-ba-shamayim* (Our Father in heaven), *Rahmana* (the Merciful One), *Gevurah* (Might), *Makom* (Place). The last two have a complex history. *Gevurah*, which referred at first to God's mighty power over nature and his power to resurrect the dead, in the later rabbinic period was used only in the phrase "*mi-pi ha-Gevurah*" (From the mouth of Power) to express God's might in giving the Torah, his greatest act in history. The history of *Makom* as a divine name has been the subject of much scholarly investigation. It seems that originally *Makom* was used in the tannaitic period as a complement to *Shamayim* (Heaven). The epithet "God of Heaven" emphasizes a certain distance and reserve between God and man, as retained in the expressions "fear of Heaven," "yoke of Heaven," and "kingdom of Heaven," whereas *Makom*, like Shekhinah, expressed the immanence of God in the world and His closeness to man. (This usage of *Makom* for God had associations with the Temple and may have been derived from the Deuteronomic phrase "the *place* where the Lord your God shall choose.") By the third century CE, when Makom had dropped out of common use, it received the opposite meaning of divine transcendence. Rather philosophically, a midrash explains that the world is contained in God, not God in the world:

> R. Hune said in R. Ammi's name: Why do we give a changed name to the Holy One, blessed be He, and call him "the Place?" Because He is the Place of the world. . . . R. Isaac said: "The eternal God is a dwelling-place" (Deut. 33:27). Now we do not know [from this verse] whether the Holy One, blessed be He, is the dwelling-place of His world or whether His world is His dwelling place. But from the text, "Lord, Thou hast been our dwelling-place" (Ps. 90:1), it follows that the Lord is the dwelling-place of His world but His world is not His dwelling-place. R. Abba b. Judan said: He is like a warrior riding a horse, his robes flowing over on both sides; the horse is subsidiary to the rider, but the rider is not subsidiary to the horse. [Gen. R. LXVIII:9.]

The term that prevailed in the early amoraic period for God, embracing both his transcendence and immanence, was "the Holy One, blessed be He" (*Ha-Kadosh barukh hu*).

Unlike Philo's Logos and the three persons (Father, Son, Holy Spirit) of the Christian Trinity, the various terms for God have no separate ontological status in rabbinic Judaism; even Shekhinah is merely a way of speaking about God when one wishes to emphasize a certain aspect of his relationship to the world. The midrash is aware that the use of various names and the ascription of different actions to divinity create a possibility of multiplicity in God (which will trouble the medieval thinkers considerably). The response of the rabbis was merely to reiterate that these names were metaphors for the same God's taking on different roles in different situations. Thus, R. Abba ben Memel explains the variety of names for God in the Bible as an expression of the variety of functions that he undertakes: "I am called according to my deeds," for example, judging, waging war against the wicked, having compassion on the world (Ex. R. III:6).

In rabbinic theology, God's two principal attributes (*middot*) are the ethical qualities of justice and mercy. There is a decided tendency to emphasize the latter over the former, without, however, identifying God solely with love. Commenting on the verse "Blow the shofar on the new moon" (Ps. 81:3), an aggadist links the newness of the moon to "making new" one's deeds, which will cause God to arise from the throne of judgment and sit on the throne of mercy, so that "the attribute of judgment shall be changed for you into the attribute of mercy" (*Pesikta de-Rav Kahana*, Piska 23:8). Whereas in Philo (and to a far greater extent among the Gnostics), the divine name YHVH was translated as Lord and identified with judgment, and the more general term Elohim translated as God and identified with mercy, the rabbis, probably in response, associated YHVH with divine compassion and mercy.[14]

The God of rabbinic Judaism was as anthropomorphic as the God of the Bible, but in different ways. He studies Torah, he dresses in a prayer shawl; he prays—to himself. (We shall quote God's prayer later in this chapter.) Qualified by "as it were," the human qualities that the rabbis identify as godly lead them to depict a fatherly deity, intimate and personal, loving without compromising his ethical rigor, a God who weeps when he must punish. In a number of midrashim God explains that when He conquers, he loses; when he is conquered, he gains. He "conquered" the wicked generation of the flood, but he lost, for he had to bring destruction on his world (*Pesikta Rabbati*, Piska 9:3). The rabbinic God will not let his angels rejoice when the waters cover the Egyptians at the Red Sea: "My childen lie drowned at the sea, and you would sing?" (B.T. Meg. 10b).

The Nature of Man

In rabbinic Judaism, man has a dual character in several respects: composed of body and soul, he is moved by an evil and a good impulse and belongs to This World and the World to Come. In comparison with the extreme dualism of Hellenistic religion and Gnosticism, these dichotomies

Aaron and the priests bring sacrificial offerings to the Tabernacle, from the Dura synagogue. (Courtesy of the Union of American Hebrew Congregations.)

are not allowed to veer toward asceticism and a determination to escape from the world.

An aggadah compares the soul's relation to the body with God's to creation: "As God fills the whole world, so the soul fills the whole body; as God sees but cannot be seen, so the soul sees but cannot be seen; as God nourishes the whole world, so the soul nourishes the whole body; as God is pure, so the soul is pure; as God dwells in the inmost part of the universe, so the soul dwells in the inmost part of the body" (B.T. Berakhot 10a). Yet soul and body are not fully separable entities. A midrashic parable compares them to two watchmen, one lame and the other blind, who steal some figs. When asked by the king what happened to his fruit, the blind man points out that he cannot see; the lame man that he cannot walk. The king merely places the lame man astride the blind man to show how they got the fruit. When body and soul appear before God in judgment, he will not listen to their separate excuses: "He brings the soul and injects it into the body, and judges both as one" (Lev. R. IV:5). Perhaps in deliberate contrast to the belief that only the soul is truly immortal, such as in Philo and Neo-Platonism, rabbinic Judaism affirmed the resurrection of the body together with the soul. Immortality was not an impersonal absorption into a universal world soul, but was individual and personal, a notion closer to the biblical conception of the unity and integrity of the living personality than to the more mystical alternative.

The instinct that inclines man to rebel against the divine commandments is called the "evil impulse" (*yetzer ha-ra*); the force that enables him to do the right is the "good impulse" (*yetzer tov*). The evil impulse causes one to gravitate toward the forbidden: to anger, gluttony, dishonesty, impatience, fornication—all of which are sins involving loss of self-control. In some aggadot the *yetzer ha-ra* is personified as a being external to the individual, an evil spirit or a Satan. Elsewhere, however, it is considered an intrinsic part of human nature as created by God, a life instinct with which everyone has to cope, even great scholars. "The greater the man, the greater his *yetzer*" (B.T. Sukkah 52a).[15]

A strong personal effort, together with God's help, enables the individual to overcome the impulse to sin. If he yields on minor matters, he may be tempted to yield on major ones, perhaps even to commit idolatry (B.T. Shabbat 105b). Recommended antidotes are deeds of loving-kindness, recitation of the Shema, and contemplation of death. Especially efficacious is study: "As long as you occupy yourselves with Torah, the *yetzer* will not rule over you" (B.T. Kiddushin 30b). But monastic isolation, sexual abstinence, and mortification of the body are not approved. Rav went so far as to say, "A man will have to give account in the judgment for every good thing which he might have enjoyed and did not" (J.T. Kiddushin IV: 12, 66d).[16] Nowhere is the *yetzer ha-ra* identified with the body and the *yetzer tov* with the soul.

The struggle against the impulse to sin must be persistent and sincere. "R. Simon compared it with a stone sticking up at a certain crossroads, a stone that men were always stumbling over. The king of the region said: Keep chipping away at the stone until the time comes for me to have it removed entirely from its place" (*Pesikta de Rav Kahana*, Piska 24:17). Man is to subjugate, not eradicate, the *yetzer*. R. Nahman ben Samuel interprets "And behold, it was very good" (Gen. 1:31) as referring to the *yetzer ha-ra*. "Can then the evil impulse be very good? That would be extraordinary! But for the evil impulse, no man would build a house, take a wife, and beget children" (Gen. R. IX:7). Life requires an element of natural passion, which must be directed toward good ends. An exegesis of the verse "And thou shalt love the Lord thy God with all thy heart" explains the phrase "with all they heart" as meaning with both the *yetzer ha-ra* and the *yetzer tov* (*Sifrei Deut.* 73a–b).[17]

Another dichotomy built into the nature of man is gender: As in all premodern societies, rabbinic Judaism sharply distinguished between the social and religious roles of the man and the woman. The halakhic principle was that "The observance of all the positive ordinances [those that require performance of an act] that depend on the time of the year is incumbent on men but not on women, and the observance of all the positive ordinances that do not depend on the time of the year is incumbent both on men and on women." With a few exceptions, "The observance of all the negative ordinances [prohibitions], whether they depend on the time of year or not, is incumbent both on men and women" ((Mishnah Kiddushin 1:7). Women are also not required to fulfil ordinances that depend on a given time of day or to study Torah. Rabbi Joshua taught that a man is to say each day: "Blessed art thou, O Lord our God . . . who has not made me a pagan . . . who has not made me a woman . . . and who has not made me a brutish man (B. T. Menahot 43b), a statement jarring to the modern reader but in its original context an expression of gratitude for being able to take on the yoke of the commandments that others cannot assume. The woman's responsibility was the home and the care of the children, and her special religious commandments were related to that domain. The intense seriousness of Torah study predisposed Jose ben Johanan to warn against "gossip with womankind" (Pirkei Avot 1:5), just as R. Simon warned against interrupting one's study to admire a beautiful tree (Pirkei Avot 3:7). Inasmuch as sexuality was considered an aspect of the *yetzer ha-ra*, women were a source of temptation, an attitude that reflects an age in which ascetic tendencies were prevalent among the religious of all traditions. However, sexuality within proper bounds and for the sake of procreation was considered necessary for the fulfilled life: "R. Tanhum stated in the name of R. Hanilai, "Any man who has no wife lives without joy, without blessing, and without goodness. . . . Concerning a man who loves his wife as himself, who honors her more than himself, who guides his sons and daughters in the right path and arranges for them to be married near the period of their puberty, Scripture says, 'And thou shalt know that thy tent is in peace' " (Job 5:24; B.T. Yevamot 62b). Apart from the halakhic matters mentioned above, man and woman have the same basic and obligatory ethical duties.

The personal religion of rabbinic Judaism, as we have seen, presupposed God's judgment of every individual on the threshold of the World to Come (*ha-olam ha-ba*). "This World (*ha-olam ha-zeh*) is like a vestibule to the World to Come. Prepare yourself in the vestibule, so that you may be admitted into the banquet hall" (Pirkei Avot 4:16). Awareness of the World to Come gives an ominous intensity to actions in This World:

Everything is given on pledge, and the net is cast over all the living. The office is open; the broker gives credit; the ledger is open; the hand writes; whosoever will borrow comes and borrows; the bailiffs go around continually every day and exact from man whether he wills or not; they have whereon to lean; the judgment is a judgment of truth. And everything is prepared for the banquet. [Pirkei Avot 3:16.]

Contemplation of the beginning and end of life should induce humility: "Know whence you came: from a fetid drop. Whither you are going: to worms and maggots. Before whom you are about to give account and reckoning: before the King of kings of kings, blessed be he" (Pirkei Avot 3:1).

One of the striking features of rabbinic Judaism is that it assimilated the concept of personal immortality without devaluing This World. The comparison of This World to a vestibule cited above is followed by an affirmation of the intrinsic importance of both Worlds. "Better is one hour of repentance and good deeds in This World then all the life of the World to Come; better is one hour of bliss of spirit in the World to Come than all the life of This World." This balanced evaluation might be considered a rabbinic answer to Ecclesiastes and the apocalyptic literature: Although the frustration and pain inevitable in life will find compensation in the bliss of the hereafter, one's eyes must be fixed, not just on the future hope, but on perfecting the workaday world. "It is not for you to finish the work, nor are you free to desist from it" (Pirkei Avot 2:19).

Rabbinic Judaism can also be contrasted to the Pauline belief that personal salvation is achieved in an instantaneous movement of faith, a transforming reception of God's grace that radically reshapes the individual's character. There is no born-again experience of salvation in rabbinic Judaism. According to R. Elazar ben Simeon, the proper attitude is to regard oneself as half-guilty and half-deserving. If he fulfills one commandment, the scale is inclined toward merit; if he commits one transgression, the scale is inclined toward guilt (B.T. Kiddushin 40b). In the words of R. Eliezer, "Repent one day before your death" (Pirkei Avot 2:10). A later rabbinic text drives home this laconic maxim: "Let him repent today lest he die tomorrow; let him repent tomorrow lest he die the day after. Thus all his days will be spent in repentance" (*Avot de Rabbi Nathan*, chap. 15). In rabbinic Judaism immortality is earned only through a continual effort of the mind and will.

Classical prophecy's notion of a human capacity "to turn" (*shuv*) was developed by the rabbis into the expression "to make repentance" (*aseh teshuvah*). To make repentance is to express contrition, confess wrongdoing, make reparation for injury, and demonstrate one's sincerity by subsequent change of conduct. Thus the Mishnah on Yom Kippur explains that fasting and prayer on this day effects atonement for sins before man and God, but that it effects atonement for sins between man and man only if one has appeased his fellow (Yoma 8:8–9). R. Judah defines the penitent man as he who, being given the same opportunity to sin again, refrains (B. T. Yoma 86b). A daring midrash juxtaposes biblical verses to emphasize the supreme efficacy of repentance, compared with other means of expiation such as retribution, punishment, and sacrifice:

> "Good and upright is the Lord, because He doth instruct sinners in the way" (Ps. 25:8). When Wisdom is asked, "The sinner—what is to be his punishment?" Wisdom answers: "Evil pursues sinners" (Prov. 13:21). When Prophecy is asked, "The sinner—what is to be his punishment?" Prophecy replies, "The soul that sinneth, it shall die" (Ezek. 18:4). When Torah is asked, "The sinner—what is to be his punishment?" Torah replies: Let him bring a guilt offering in expiation and his sin shall be forgiven him. When the Holy One is asked, "The sinner—what is to be his punishment?" the Holy One replies: In penitence let him mend his ways and his sin shall be forgiven him. [*Pesikta de Rav Kahana*, Piska 24:7.]

Everyone has the opportunity to repent. Meeting his father, Cain tells him that he repented and was pardoned of his sin. Adam replies, "Is the power of repentance as great as that? I did not know it was so" (Lev. R. X:5).

Presupposed in the rabbinic doctrine of repentance, as in the prophetic, is that man is free to choose the good and reject the evil. To be sure, there are circumstances not under an individual's control; Rava used to say that length of life, children, and sustenance depend not on merit but on luck (*mazal*, B.T. Mo'ed Katan 28a). A paradoxical dictum, affirming both providence and free will, is Akiva's "All is foreseen, yet freedom of choice is granted" (Pirkei Avot 3:15). Even if freedom in the outer world is circumscribed, however, man has the ability to overcome inner obstacles to goodness.

The respective divine and human shares in determining the outcome of moral action involve the question of how God's grace operates. In Pauline Christianity grace is a free and unmerited gift from God to regenerate and reconcile his creatures to him; God takes the initiative to set man free. In the rabbinic view, God aids man, but grace can never be completely unmerited. Sometimes the rabbis purpose that God's and man's wills act simultaneously; elsewhere they suggest that man is free initially, but the habits he chooses receive an additional boost from God. ("One is allowed to follow the road he wishes to pursue," B.T. Makkot 10b.) However qualified, a core of self-determination remains inviolate: "Everything is in the hand of Heaven except the fear of Heaven" (B. T. Berakhot 33b). Rabbinic Judaism seems to have been spared Paul's special agony that one cannot overcome by himself the burden of Adam's sin so as to will to do the good. An emphatic expression of man's freedom to combat passivity, selfishness, and procrastination is Hillel's series of maxims: "If I am not for myself, who will be for me? If I am only for myself, what am I? If not now, when?" (Pirkei Avot 1:14). The divine attribute of mercy responds to the human attribute of self-creation in repentance. The rabbis are not able to resolve the dilemma of determinism and freedom in a theoretical fashion, but, as with other polar elements of man's nature, they reject alternatives that seem to be a flight from human responsibility.

The Religious Life; Rabbinic Ethics

Rabbinic Judaism is a system of *mitzvot* (commandments), observance of which is rewarded, if not in This World, then in the World to Come. Since conformity to the mitzvot is a sign of obedience to God, one does not have the right to pick and choose. R. Elazar of Modi'in taught that if a man accepted the whole Torah with the exception of only one commandment or if he acknowldeged that all the Torah was from God with the exception of only one passage which he believed was by Moses, then he despised God's word and merited being thrust out of the World to Come (*Sifrei Num.* 33a.)[18] In the Gospel of John, Jesus says, "If you continue in my word, you are truly my disciples, and you will know the truth, and the truth will make you free" (8:32). Similarly, in rabbinic Judaism, Torah brought true freedom. R. Joshua ben Levi expounded "And the tablets were the word of God and the writing was the writing of God, graven

Entrance façade of the third-century CE synagogue at Kfar Baram in the Galilee. (Photo by the author.)

upon the tablets" (Ex. 32:16) thus: "Read not 'graven' (*harut*) but freedom (*herut*), for the free man is he who studies the Torah" (Pirkei Avot 6:2). Torah is basic necessity and sweetest nutriment, comparable to water, olive oil, wine, honey, and milk. Rabban Johanan ben Zaccai used to say, "If you have learned much Torah, ascribe no merit to yourself; for this reason you were created" (Pirkei Avot 2:8).

Rabbinic Judaism, like the Pentateuch, gives reasons for various laws, but those for which no human reason could be fathomed, especially certain cultic practices, must be accepted without challenge: "I have decreed it; you are not at liberty to criticize" (B.T. Yoma 67b). Still, the laws for which a specific rationale could not be discerned were for man's sake, not God's: "The mitzvot were given to purify man" (e.g., on the law of the red heifer in Num. 19 as interpreted in Lev. R. XX:13).

Other philosophical topics are also adumbrated in talmudic and midrashic discussion of the nature of true religiosity. Which was more important, thinking about Torah or observing Torah? R. Simeon ben Gamaliel I taught: "Learning is not the root, doing is" (Pirkei Avot 1:17), but Rabban Gamaliel son of Judah ha-Nasi used to say, "An ignorant man cannot be pious" (Pirkei Avot 2:5). An effort to resolve this dilemma is the following: "Once R. Tarfon and the elders sat in the upper chamber of the house of Nitzah in Lydda, and the question was raised, 'Is study greater or practice?' R. Tarfon said, practice was greater. R. Akiva said, study was greater. Then they all said that study was greater, for it led to practice" (B.T. Kiddushin 40b). Like Socrates in this regard, the rabbis believed that virtue depends on knowledge and should be pursued by means of dialectical discussion. But Torah was a combination of the two styles of human life as defined by Greek philosophy; it was both the "theoretical life," contemplation of eternal truths, and the "practical life," action in the mundane world.

Which was more important, observance or intention? Again the views are nuanced. Observance is a value in itself: R. Hanina's dictum was that "He who is commanded and fulfills is greater than he who fulfills though not commanded" (B.T. Kiddushin 31a). Contrary to Paul, there *is* special merit in going against the appetites and instincts. R. Eliezer taught that a man should not say he has no desire to eat pork or to have intercourse with a woman he may not marry. Instead, he should say, "Yes, I would like to do these acts, but what can I do, my Father in heaven has forbidden them" (*Sifra* 93d).[19] It is not wrong to be aware of the reward in store for obedience to the laws—although one is warned against assuming that an apparently major commandment will earn a greater reward than an apparently minor one (Pirkei Avot 2:1). The saintly ideal is to be "like servants that minister to the master without the condition of receiving a reward" (Pirkei Avot 1:3)—to fulfill the Torah "for its own sake" (*lishma*). "Man should always engage in the study of Torah and in good deeds, though it is not for their own sake, for through doing good for a selfish purpose there comes doing good for its own sake" (B.T. Pesahim 50b). He who busies himself with the Torah for its own sake "makes peace in the upper family [the angels] and the lower family [human beings] . . . he protects the whole world . . . he hastens the redemption" (B.T. Sanhedrin 99b). Similarly with prayer: One must pray regularly, but the desired attitude is *kavvanah* (intention, concentration). Despite their devotion to the life of the intellect, the rabbis were quite aware that bringing all Israel into the academy was a distant goal, and that God judges on other grounds too. In a midrash in Exodus Rabbah, the congregation of Israel is personified as saying:

> "We are poor and have not the wherewithal to bring sacrifices." God replied: "I desire words, as it says, 'Take with you words, and return unto the Lord' (Hos. 14:2) and I will pardon all your sins." The "words" here referred to are words of the Torah, as it says, "These are the words which Moses spoke unto all Israel" (Deut. 1:1). Then they said to God: "We know no Torah." "Then weep and pray unto Me and I will accept [your remorse] . . ." [Ex. R. XXVIII:4.]

Another instance in which observance is subsumed under a higher degree of piety is "going beyond the strict line of justice" (*lifnim mishurat ha-din*): doing more than what the law specifically requires, in order to act in an exceptionally merciful and charitable manner according to a standard of absolute goodness (e.g., *Mekhilta* II, 182; in B.T. Berakhot 7a God himself so acts). Characteristically, this principle could not be left outside Torah and, at times, is said to be a requirement of the law, according to Deuteronomy 6:18, "You shall do what is right and good in the sight of the Lord."[20]

Although all mitzvot were equally binding, some rabbis moved toward creating a theory of ethics by speculating on the primary commandment under which all the rest could be subsumed. In a consideration of this question, R. Simlai begins by noting that 613 mitzvot were given to Moses, 365 prohibitions corresponding to the days of the year, 248 positive laws corresponding to the parts of the human body. (These specific numbers, the exegesis of which will have a long history in Jewish thought, is probably R. Simlai's invention for homiletic purposes, to teach that each day has its temptations and each part of the body its holy function.) He continued, David reduced them to the eleven commandments found in Psalm 15. Isaiah reduced to six, as one may see in Isaiah 33:15. Micah reduced them to three: "To do justly, love mercy, and walk humbly with your God" (Mic. 6:8). Isaiah came back and reduced them to two: "Keep ye judgment and do righteousness" (Isa. 56:1). Amos reduced them to one, "Seek me and live" (Amos 5:6), or, one might say, Habbakuk reduced them to one, "The righteous shall live by his faith" (Hab. 2:4; B.T. Makkot 23b–24a).

Another attempt to show that the basis of the entire mitzvah system was contained in a single idea brings together two such teachings by Ben Azzai and R. Akiva. " 'This is the book of the descendants of Adam' (Gen. 5:1) is a great principle of the Torah," asserts Ben Azzai. R. Akiva responds, " 'Thou shalt love thy neighbor as thyself' (Lev. 19:18) is an even greater principle, for you must not say, Since I have been put to shame, let my neighbor be put to shame." R. Tanhuma harmonized the two views by citing the conclusion of Genesis 5:1: "In the likeness of God made He him" (Gen. R. XXIV:7). Because man is made in God's image, the dignity of the fellow man must be revered. According to Hillel the essence of the Torah was the Golden Rule. Asked by a pagan to teach him the Torah while the questioner stood on one foot, Hillel answered, "What is harmful to you, do not do to your fellow. That is the whole Torah; all the rest is commentary. Go and learn" (B.T. Shabbat 31a).

Another answer to the question which of the Torah's requirements were most important was to rank transgressions. An early precedent for the medieval efforts to construct a system of fundamental doctrines for Judaism was chapter 10 of Mishnah Sanhedrin, which lists the sins that exclude one from his share in the World to Come: those who say that the Torah is not from Heaven, those who deny there is a divine judgment and Judge (as noted earlier, the rabbinic definition of an atheist), those who do not believe in the resurrection of the dead. Some aggadists hold that he who treats repentance as a mere formality will not be forgiven by God (Mishnah Yoma 9:1, *Avot de Rabbi Nathan*, chap. 40). Among the other cardinal transgressions are "groundless hatred" (said to be the cause of the fall of the Second Temple in B.T. Yoma 9b) and "usury" (which rabbinic law defined as any loaning of money on interest). Lending money for profit was viewed as taking advantage of those in need, rather than extending a charitable hand. Likened to atheists, robbers, and shedders of blood, moneylenders are said not to have a share in the World to Come (Ex. R. XXXI:13). (In the later Middle Ages, Jewish ethics changed its attitude toward banking and investment, as did Western ethics as a whole.[21])

That there is a hierarchy of the commandments can also be seen in the legal principle of "regard for human life" (*pikuah nefesh*). When life is in danger, the prohibitions of working on Sabbath and eating on Yom Kippur are overridden (Mishnah Shabbat 2:5, Mishnah Yoma 8:6; B.T. Yoma 85a–b). *Pikuah nefesh* is justified biblically by "Ye shall keep my statutes and ordinances, which if a man shall do, he shall live by them" (Lev. 18:5), which the rabbis interpret as meaning that one should not die as a result of observing them. The principle of regard for human life became the basis for a number of paradigmatic discussions of ethical and religious issues. An example is the hypothetical case of two men traveling far from civilization, only one of whom has a small supply of water (B.T. Baba Metzia 62a). If both drink, both will die; if one drinks, he will survive. Ben Peturah taught that both should drink and die, rather than one be forced to cause his companion's death. R. Akiva taught that the one with the water should drink and save his life. There were, however, circumstances when saving of life was not considered the highest good. In B.T. Pesahim 25b a man tells Rava that the governor of the town has ordered him to kill so-and-so, or he will be killed instead. Rava replies, "Let him kill you, rather than you should commit murder. Why should you think your blood is redder than his?" Mishnah Terumot 8:12 postulates a situation in which a group of women are told to surrender one of them for rape, or they will all be raped. The ruling is, "Let them defile them all, but not betray to them one soul from Israel." In the last two cases, the principle is that one should not consider his own life more valuable than another's; in the case of the two men far from civilization, the principle is that one's own life is not less valuable than another's.

Self-sacrifice for the sake of a higher end becomes most urgent when the honor of the Torah is at stake and one must avoid profanation of God's name (hillul ha-Shem). The principle here is that one may transgress all commandments in order to save life, except unchastity (incest and adultery), murder, and idolatry. According to some opinions, an individual is allowed to commit an act of idolatry in private when his life is threatened by a gentile motivated by personal reasons, but in public one should suffer death, rather than bring disrepute on the Torah. There were, however, those sages who took the more stringent view: R. Dimi taught that if there was a royal decree against Torah, one must incur martyrdom (kiddush ha-Shem, sanctification of God's name) rather than transgress even a minor precept in public (B.T. San. 74a). This discussion leads us back to two issues considered already in the late biblical writings: the nature of religious faith and the relationship between human suffering and divine retribution.

Theodicy

The biblical and rabbinic term for faith, emunah, is best rendered trust, a trust that includes accepting as God's will the inexplicable perplexities of life. Resignation in the face of God's providential rule is tzidduk ha-din (justifying the divine decree). "When Aaron heard of the death of his two sons, he 'held his peace' (Lev. 10:3); he acknowledged the justice of the divine decree. With the righteous it is habitual to act thus" (Sifra 45a).[22]

Faith in God entails the belief that God dispenses not according to what the individual thinks he needs, but according to a higher standard. To be sure, God performs miracles continually, not the least of which are the arrangement of good marriages and provision of daily bread; but one should not expect a miracle in times of danger or distress. Similarly, God listens to prayer; but it is wrong to expect that one's prayer will surely be answered, since He responds when the request is in the true interests of the petitioner.

Whatever happens, God must be blessed. An interpretation of "Thou shalt love the Lord thy God with all thy heart, with all thy soul, and with all thy might" (Deut. 6:5) explains that the word "might" (*me'odekha*) means "with whatever measure (*middah*) He metes out to thee, do thou give him thanks (*modeh*) exceedingly" (Mishnah Berakhot 9:5). On hearing good tidings, one is to recite, "Blessed art thou, O Lord our God, King of the universe, who art good and dispenses good." On hearing evil tidings, one should say, "Blessed art thou, O Lord our God, King of the universe, the true judge" (B.T. Berakhot 48b).

With this faith in the omnipotent God of justice, the rabbis approached the vexatious problem of theodicy: whether there was a rational vindication of divine justice in face of the existence of evil. To be sure, some of the sting is removed by the belief that all good people will enjoy bliss in the World to Come. But why death and suffering in the first place? A discussion in the Gemara on this subject begins with R. Ammi's statement that one's sins cause his death and his sufferings. Objections are raised, and the conclusion is reached that there is indeed death and suffering without commensurate iniquity (B.T. Shabbat 55a). Another discussion, in Genesis Rabbah IX:5, views death as part of the human condition from the very beginning, a consequence of the moral freedom that man has been given. Why does death occur to the righteous as well as to the wicked? If it did not, the wicked would say that the righteous live forever because they practice Torah and good deeds and the wicked will do so too, thereby fulfilling the commandments deceitfully. A second explanation is that death befalls the righteous because they struggle with the evil inclination all their lives and, in death, they are finally at peace.

A further answer to the disproportion of pain to merit in This World is to assert that the wicked are rewarded for the little good they do, so that they may be punished without interruption in the World to Come; the good are punished for their few sins in This World, so that they may be rewarded without interruption in the World to Come (*Avot de Rabbi Nathan*, chap. 39). R. Josiah suggests that God permits some of the wicked long lives because they may repent or because some righteous sons may issue from them (Eccles. R. VII: 15, 1). According to yet another approach, God does not afflict the evil person, because he knows that the wicked lack the moral fiber to demonstrate faith in God by withstanding pain. Endurance of suffering is the means whereby the righteous purify themselves for the World to Come. This doctrine is illustrated by the following aggadah concerning two third-century rabbis:

> R. Johanan had the misfortune to suffer from gallstones for three and a half years. Once R. Hanina went to visit him. He said to him: "How do you feel?" He replied: "My sufferings are worse than I can bear." He said to him: "Don't speak so, but say 'Faithful God.'" When the pain was very great he used to say "Faithful God," and when the pain was greater than he could bear, R. Hanina used to go to him and utter an incantation which gave him relief. Subsequently R. Hanina fell ill, and R. Johanan went to see him. He said to him, "How do you feel?" He replied: "How grievous are my sufferings!" He said to him: "Surely the reward for them is also great!" He replied: "I want neither them nor their reward." He said to him: "Why do you not utter that incantation which you pronounced over me and which gave me relief?" He replied: "When I was out of trouble I could help others, but now that I am myself in trouble do I not require another to help me?" . . . R. Johanan said: "When a potter tests his furnace, he does not test it with cracked jars, because a single blow would break them, but he tests it with sound jars, which can withstand many knocks. So the Holy One, blessed be He, does not try the wicked; whom does He try? The righteous, as it says, 'The Lord tries the righteous.'" [Ps. 11:5; Song of Songs R. II:16, 2.]

It is a common teaching that "there is no man in the world to whom suffering does not come" (e.g., Gen. R. XCII:1). Some are "sufferings of

The binding of Isaac (Gen., chap. 22), part of the mosaic floor of the Bet Alpha synagogue, sixth-century Galilee. (The Photographic Archive of the Jewish Theological Seminary of America, New York, Frank J. Darmstaedter.)

reproof," which should lead a man to examine how he has sinned. Others are "sufferings of love" (*yisurin shel ahavah*), afflictions totally out of proportion to one's misdeeds. "Everyone in whom God delights, he crushes with sufferings" (Rava's interpretation of Isa. 53:10, B.T. Berakhot 5a). Not signs of divine displeasure or warnings that one has ignored some important mitzvah, these "love pangs" are instead virtually compliments that God pays to those he loves; the concept of "chastisements of love" therefore emphasizes not the cause but the response to suffering. Job is the prototype for the innocent sufferer, but in the rabbis' eyes, Job is less than ideal, for he complained too much.

> Behold, when suffering befell Job, had he overcome his resentment and not raised a cry against the measure of justice, he would have risen to great and praiseworthy eminence. As R. Hanina bar Papa said: Had he not raised a cry, even as now we say in the [daily prayers] "God of Abraham, God of Isaac, and God of Jacob," we would also be saying "and God of Job."
> [*Pesikta Rabbati*, Piska 47:3.]

While sympathizing with Job's pain, some of the aggadists contrast him with the unprotesting, more secure faith symbolized by the biblical patriarchs.

Among the "chastisements of love" are suffering and deaths that come as a result of keeping the mitzvot, most starkly in times of martyrdom like the Hadrianic persecutions.

> "Of them that Love me and keep my commandments" [Ex. 20:6] . . . R. Nathan says: "Of them that love Me and keep my commandments" refers to those who dwell in the land of Israel and risk their lives for the sake of the commandments. "Why are you being led out to be decapitated?" "Because I circumcised my son to be part of Israel." "Why are you being led out to be burned?" "Because I read the Torah." "Why are you being led out to be crucified?" "Because I ate unleavened bread." "Why are you getting a hundred lashes?" "Because I performed the ceremony of the *lulav*." It says: "Those with which I was wounded in the house of my friends" (Zech. 13:6); these wounds caused me to be beloved of My Father in heaven. [Mekhilta, II, 247.]

The most remembered exemplar of rabbinic martyrdom was R. Akiva; aggadot emphasize the joy with which he accepted death in the form it came to him. While being tortured, the hour came for saying the Shema. Seeing Akiva smile, the Roman officer asked him, "Old man, are you a sorcerer, or do you mock at your sufferings, that you smile in the midst of your pain?" Akiva replied that all his life he wondered if he would be able to fulfill the words, "Thou shalt love the Lord thy God with all thy heart and with all thy soul and with all thy might," for he did not know if he could love him with all his soul. "Now that I am giving my life, and the hour for saying the Shema has come, and my resolution remains firm, should I not laugh?" "So speaking his soul departed" (J.T. Ber. IX:7, 14b[23]).

The following aggadah, illustrating the principle that the whole Torah, written and oral, was given to Moses, treats Akiva's martyrdom in a manner akin to the climax of the book of Job:

> Rav Judah said in the name of Rav, When Moses ascended on high he found the Holy One, blessed be He, engaged in affixing crowns to the letters of the Torah [the small strokes on the Hebrew letters]. Said Moses, "Lord of the Universe, [Why are these crowns necessary]?" He answered, "There will arise a man at the end of many generations, Akiva b. Joseph by name, who will expound for each letter heaps and heaps of rulings." "Lord of the Universe," said Moses, "permit me to see him." He replied, "Turn around." Moses went and sat down behind eight rows [of Akiva's students while Akiva and they discoursed on the laws]. Not being able to follow their arguments he was ill at ease, but when they came to a certain subject and the disciples said to the master "Whence do you know it?" and the latter replied "It is a law given unto Moses at Sinai," he was comforted. Thereupon he returned to the Holy One, blessed be He, and said, "Lord of the Universe, Thou hast such a man and Thou givest the Torah by me?" He replied, "Be silent, for such is my decree." Then said Moses, "Lord of the Universe, thou hast shown me his Torah, show me his reward." "Turn around," said He; and Moses turned around and saw them weighing out his flesh at the market-stalls. "Lord of the Universe," cried Moses, "such Torah, and such a reward!" He replied, "Be silent, for such is my decree." [B. T. Menahot 29b.]

The aggadist is dealing here with the instance of that individual who truly does God's will for its own sake. Such a person is described in R. Joshua ben Levi's dictum: "He who joyfully bears the chastisements that befall him brings salvation to the world" (B.T. Ta'anit 8a). There are many variations on the theme that the death of the righteous atones for the sins of others and, so to speak, vindicates God's faith in man. The idea that the world was created for the sake of the righteous and because of them it endures, is linked to such verses as "The righteous man is the foundation of the world" (Prov. 10:25), giving rise to the view, expressed by Abbaye, that in every generation the world must contain no less than thirty-six (in some versions, thirty) just men (B.T. Yoma 38b, Kiddushin 72b).

The following midrash on Daniel 3 develops the theme of the man who voluntarily witnesses to God, despite imminent sufferings:

Nebuchadnezzar set up an image and selected three from every nation to bow down to it, and three from Israel. Now the three from Israel, who were Hananiah, Mishael, and Azariah, made up their minds not to worship the idol. They went to Daniel and said to him: "Our master Daniel, Nebuchadnezzar has set up an idol and has selected us from all Israel. What do you tell us to do? Shall we bow down to it or not?" He replied: "Here is the prophet within reach; go and consult him." They then went to Ezekiel, and put to him the same question as to Daniel: "Shall we bow down to it or not?" He replied: "I long ago was told by my teacher Isaiah, 'Hide thyself for a little moment, until the indignation be past' " (Isa. 26:20). They said to him: "Do you desire then that people should say that *all* nations bow down to this idol?" He said to them: "What then do you say?" They replied: "We want to insult it, by being there and not bowing down, so that people should say, 'All nations bow down to this image except Israel.' " He said to them: "If that is your idea, wait till I consult the Almighty"; and so it is written, "Certain of the elders of Israel came to inquire of the Lord, and sat before me" (Ezek. 20:1). Who are they? Hananiah, Mishael, and Azariah. He said before the Holy One, blessed be He: "Sovereign of the Universe, Hananiah, Mishael, and Azariah seek to give their lives for the sanctification of Thy name. Wilt Thou stand by them or no?" He replied: "I will not stand by them"; and so it is written, "Son of man, speak unto the elders of Israel, and say unto them . . . Are ye come to inquire of Me?" (Ezek. 20:3). Since ye have caused Me to lay waste My house and to burn My Temple and to send My sons into exile among the nations, and after all that ye come to seek Me. As I live . . . I will not be inquired of by you." Thereupon Ezekiel began to weep and lament and wail, saying, "Alas for the enemies of Israel!" [A euphemism for "alas for Israel"] . . . When he returned to them, they said to him: "What did the Holy One, blessed be He, say to you?" He replied: "He will not stand by you." They replied: "Whether He stands by us or does not stand by us, we will sacrifice our lives for the sanctification of God's name." . . . [Song of Songs R. VII:8, 1.]

In this midrash as in rabbinic thought generally, evil and suffering are not treated as a philosophical problem, but a moral one.[24] A further extension of Job and of Second Isaiah, the idea that the just testify to the reality of God's truth is also implied in statements cited earlier that the world was created for the sake of the righteous and that when Israel witnesses to God, then (as it were) God is truly God. The belief that there are such men is an intrinsic part of rabbinic optimism, as of biblical. Faith in the triumph of God's justice, despite evidence to the contrary, is the opening theme of the rabbinic doxology, the *Kaddish* (sanctification), recited at frequent intervals during study and worship:

> Glorified and sanctified be God's great name throughout the world He has created according to His will. May he establish His kingdom in your

lifetime and during your days, and within the life of the entire house of Israel, speedily and soon; and say Amen.

Redemption and Eschatology

Under the concept of the World to Come are subsumed two theological topics: the fulfillment of the messianic visions of history and an existence beyond history in which justice is meted out to everyone. The first is the "Days of the Messiah" (*yemot ha-mashiah*), when Israel will again be redeemed—this time permanently—from oppressive foreign rulers, when it will live in the holy land on intimate terms with God, when throughout the world right and truth will prevail. In a prayer (the *Alenu*, now part of every Jewish worship service) composed by a third-century Babylonian sage, the universal dimension of the messianic expectation is expressed:

> We therefore hope in thee, O Lord our God, that we may speedily behold the glory of thy might, when thou wilt remove the abominations from the earth, and the idols will be utterly cut off, when the world will be perfected under the kingdom of the Almighty, and all children of flesh will call upon thy name, when thou wilt turn unto thyself all the wicked of the earth. Let all the inhabitants of the world perceive and know that unto thee every knee must bow, every tongue must swear. Before thee, O Lord our God, let them bow and fall; and unto thy glorious name let them give honor; let them all accept the yoke of thy kingdom, and reign over them speedily and for ever and ever. For the kingdom is thine, and to all eternity thou wilt reign in glory; as it is written in thy Torah, "The Lord shall reign for ever and ever" (Ex. 15:18), and as it is said, "And the Lord shall be king over all the earth; in that day the Lord shall be one and his name one" (Zech. 14:9).[25]

Sometime after the Days of the Messiah will come a second stage, the "Future Time" (*atid la-vo*) when, after being judged, the righteous enter Paradise (*gan Eden*, the "garden of Eden") and the wicked are consigned to *Gehinnom* (the netherworld, hell). Some rabbis teach that the individual is judged immediately after his death; others, that he sleeps in his grave until the resurrection of all.

As on other subjects, there was a variety of rabbinic opinions on these matters and, perhaps, a certain reluctance to dwell overly on them. (Speculation on ultimate questions does not take up much space in rabbinic literature.) That there would indeed be an end to the exile, an ingathering of the Jewish people, a messianic age, a restoration of harmony between God and man, a righteous judgment by the Judge, a postresurrection existence, were all considered essential items of Jewish faith, but as concrete future expectations these beliefs posed the danger of igniting the explosive potential of messianism and apocalypticism, the appeal of which the sages sought to restrain. But then they themselves were not entirely immune to that appeal.

The Bar Kokhba revolt is our main instance during this period of the longing for messianic redemption. R. Johanan b. Torta was said to have told Akiva, who recognized Bar Kokhba as messianic prince, "Grass will grow in your cheeks and the son of David will still not have come" (Lam. R. II:2, sec. 4). Some sages dwelled on the agonies and suffering that would precede the coming of the Messiah (the "birthpangs," "footprints," or "travails" of the Messiah, see Mishnah Sota 9:15 and B.T. San. 97a–98a) to warn that one was better off not being too close to that time. (The very same warnings could encourage one to believe, in periods of terrible distress, that the Messiah was close at hand.) Perhaps in order to caution not to expect too much of the messianic age, the third-century Babylonian amora Samuel taught, "There is no difference between This World and the Days of the Messiah except [that in the latter there will be no] bondage of foreign powers, as it says, 'For the poor shall never cease out of the land'" (Deut. 15:11). However, in that same Gemara (B.T. Berakhot 34b) the contemporary Palestinian amora, R. Johanan, affirms a utopian End of Days on earth when there will be no war, disease, or poverty: "All the prophets prophesied only for the Days of the Messiah, but for the World to Come applies the verse, "Eye hath not seen, O God, besides thee, what He will do for him that waiteth for Him'" (Isa. 64:3).

Only a few passages in the talmudic and midrashic literature touch on the role and person of the Messiah. We find no trace in rabbinic writings of the Essene belief in a priestly Messiah and a royal Messiah, but mention is made of a "Messiah ben Joseph" who will appear first and be slain (perhaps originally an allusion to Bar Kokhba), followed by a "Messiah ben David" who would rule victoriously. There was also a notion, probably an offshoot of the teaching that the sufferings of the righteous atone for the sins of mankind, that the Messiah was already present on earth, covered with wounds and sores, among the beggars of Rome. The following ironic aggadah illustrates an important rabbinic teaching concerning the messianic age: that its advent is conditional on human repentance.

R. Joshua b. Levi met Elijah standing by the entrance of R. Simeon b. Yohai's tomb. He asked him: "Have I a portion in the World to Come?" He replied, "If this Master [i.e., God] desires it." R. Joshua b. Levi . . . then asked him, "When will the Messiah come?"—"Go and ask him himself," was his reply. "Where is he sitting?"—"At the entrance [to Rome]." "And by what sign may I recognize him?"—"He is sitting among the poor lepers: all of them untie [their bandages] all at once, and rebandage them again, whereas he unties and rebandages each separately, thinking, should I be wanted, I must not be delayed." So he went to him and greeted him, saying, "Peace upon thee, Master and Teacher." "Peace upon thee, O son of Levi," he replied. "When wilt thou come, Master?" asked he. "Today," was his answer. On his returning to Elijah, the latter enquired, "What did he say to thee?"—"Peace upon thee, O son of Levi," he answered. Thereupon [Elijah] observed, "He thereby assured thee and thy father of the World to Come." "He spoke falsely to me," he rejoined, "stating that he would come today, but has not." [Elijah] answered him, "This is what he said to thee, 'Today, if ye will hearken to [God's] voice'" (Ps. 85:7). [B.T. San. 98a.]

The Babylonian Gemara from which this aggadah is cited (San. 97b–99a) is the principal collection of material relating to messianic matters in the Talmud, and contains a number of apocalyptic traditions about the sequence of signs and wonders that is to appear before the end of history. The perennial fascination with such matters was accompanied by an awareness of the dangers involved. R. Jonathan taught, "Blasted be the bones of those who calculate the end. For they would say, since the predetermined time has arrived, and yet he has not come, he will never come" (San. 97b). The dominant tendency resulting from the emphasis on man's freedom of choice that the rabbis carried over from classical prophecy, is that the Messiah's coming depended on human merit. R. Eliezer asserted, "If Israel repent, they will be redeemed; if not, they will not be redeemed." Similarly, we find such statements as, "If Israel were to keep two Sabbaths according to the laws, they would be redeemed immediately" (B.T. Shabbat 118b) and "All the predestined moments [for redemption] have passed and the matter [now] depends only on repentance and good deeds" (B.T. San. 97b). One sage who wanted to balance this and a view emphasizing the divine initiative in bringing the Messiah, offered the following compromise: When the time is ripe, "The Holy One, blessed be he, will set up a king over them, whose decrees shall be as cruel as Haman's, whereby Israel shall engage in repentance and he will thus bring them back to the right path." God will intervene to force Israel to become worthy. The supreme ideological goal of the rabbis was to prepare all Israel for this redemption, not through political means in the narrow sense, but through Torah in the broad sense.

Rabbinic teachings on other eschatological matters are even more guarded and fragmentary. According to Rava, a man led in for judgment is interrogated thus: Was he honest, did he fulfill the duty of procreation, did he study Torah regularly and search carefully for wisdom, did he continue to hope for the messianic salvation of his people—or, at the least, was his life infused by proper fear of God? (B.T. Shabbat 31a). One must face God with awe, humility, and apprehension: All one's deeds will be weighed in the balance. But God will be compassionate.

The Talmud ascribes the following prayer to God himself: "May it be my will that my mercy may suppress my anger, that my mercy will prevail over my [other] attributes, so that I may deal with my children according to the attribute of mercy, and, on their behalf, stop short of the limit of strict justice" (lifnim mishurat ha-din, B.T. Berakhot 7a). According to Mishnah Sanhedrin 10:1, "All Israel has a share in the World to Come," some Jewish sinners being excluded and the righteous gentiles being included. (In Tosefta San XIII:2, R. Joshua holds that there are gentiles who merit paradise, a position that becomes the norm in Jewish theology.)

Resurrection will take place in the land of Israel. (According to one sage, underground channels will be formed so that the bodies of Jews buried in the diaspora can reach the holy land, J.T. Ket. XII:3, 35b[26].) People will be revivified fully clothed and only later will be cured of their physical defects, so that it cannot be said that God did not restore to life exactly the same ones he put to death. The thoroughly righteous will go immediately to Paradise and the thoroughly wicked to Gehinnom. What of the "intermediate?" According to an aggadah, the School of Shammai taught that they will be sent to Gehinnom to be punished and will then rise to Paradise; the School of Hillel taught that God will incline the scales toward mercy and at once inscribe them for eternal life (B.T. Rosh Hashanah 16b-17a). Almost no one is assigned to the fires of Gehinnom forever (only those who had completely repudiated their loyalty to the faith of Israel, according to one view). Most of the wicked are punished for twelve months and then annihilated (B.T. Rosh Hashanah 19a). One midrash taught that the inhabitants of Gehinnom are relieved of suffering on the Sabbath (Gen. R. 11:5). Another opinion is that there is no real Gehinnom because sinners will be immediately destroyed on Judgment Day by unshielded radiation of the sun or by a fire breaking out in their bodies (Gen. R. VI:6).[27]

In rabbinic Judaism, Paradise is known by the same name as the earthly Eden where Adam and Eve first lived. It is said to be a "topsy-turvy" world where the lower class enjoys higher status than the upper class and where martyrs have a special place of honor (B.T. Baba Batra 10b, Pesahim 50a). Talmudic folklore describes the wondrous banquet to be held from the meat of the Leviathan and from wine preserved since the six days of creation (B.T. Baba Batra 74a-75a and Berakhot 34b). But it was a favorite saying of Rav's: "Not like This World is the World to Come. In the World to Come there is neither eating nor drinking, no procreation of children nor business transactions, no envy or hatred or rivalry. The righteous sit enthroned, their crowns on their heads, and enjoy the radiance of the Shekhinah" (B.T. Berakhot 17a). In the perpetual Sabbath of that spiritual existence, everyone will enjoy the highest pleasure imaginable to the rabbis: to study the mysteries of Torah with God himself (B.T. Hagigah 14a).

Rabbinic Judaism in Its Classical Age and Afterward

To grasp classical rabbinic Judaism in the correct historical context, it should be seen as contemporary with patristic Christianity—the thought and beliefs of the great theologians, preachers, and bishops of the second to the sixth centuries—and as a response to the social and spiritual needs to which these Christian figures also were responding. Although Jewish and Christian presentations of their faith took different forms (and form determined content to a great extent), the underlying problems faced by the two groups of religious intellectuals were similar: the nature of sin and atonement, God's presence in the world and the saintly man's transcendence of the world, the relation of biblical promise to messianic fulfillment. In an age of anxiety and chaos, both faiths found answers through

Mosaic floor of the sixth-century synagogue of Bet Alpha in the Galilee: the signs of the Zodiac with Hebrew inscriptions. (Courtesy of the Consulate General of Israel.)

symbols offering comfort and hope: the Torah that existed before creation and entered the world at Sinai; the Christ that existed before the world and suffered for its sins at Calvary. Both thought they were the "Israel of God," the earthly witness to the divine plan for history. And both offered the tangible benefits of belonging to a people that, in a time of little social and emotional security, encouraged its members to help others and to act charitably and ethically.

There were, to be sure, fundamental and irreconcilable differences. The creedal controversies that split Christendom in the fourth and fifth centuries—were God the Father and God the Son of like substances or the same substance; did Christ have two natures, divine and human, or only one?—reflected social and intellectual needs that Judaism did not face, the absence of which permitted rabbinic theology freedom from the necessity of dogmatic formulation. The prayerbook (*siddur*) remained the only Jewish creed. But the rabbis did not have to cope with the conversion of whole nations; they could devote themselves to making Jews and a dwindling number of proselytes into the people of Torah, avoiding a bifurcation that arose in Christianity between those who wanted to live a fully religious life (and became clergy or monks) and a laity from whom a much less rigorous religiosity was expected. Out of the same biblical and Hellenistic matrix, Judaism and Christianity diverged: the one to a religion of sacraments and priestly atonement, the other to a religion of law and atonement through mitzvot; the one to a religion that emphasized sinful man's need for a mediator, the other to a religion that emphasized man's ability to effect repentance and satisfy God directly.

With respect to rabbinical Judaism in its original historical context another line of inquiry can be posed as well: How characteristic are the Talmuds and the Midrashim of what Jews actually believed and practiced at that time? Archeologists and literary scholars have produced evidence that there were aspects of Judaism not readily apparent in rabbinic literature. Excavations in the Syrian desert uncovered a third-century synagogue in the Roman-Persian border town of Dura-Europas, the walls of which were covered with frescos illustrating biblical stories and religious themes, a seeming contradiction to the second commandment forbidding graven images. Mosaic floors of Galilean synagogues in late antiquity contain astrological signs and human forms. Perhaps the rabbis interpreted the second commandment of the Decalogue so as to permit such depictions; perhaps these synagogue decorations reflect currents of Jewish religiosity other than rabbinic. The religious significance of these frescos and mosaics has been the subject of much scholarly speculation. Also pertinent has been the discovery in Mesopotamia by archeologists of a number of bowls designed for magical purposes and containing Aramaic incantations involving demons and Jewish divine names. The Talmud itself indicates that Jewish masses and rabbis alike believed in such evil and good spirits and held that a knowledge of the secret names of God was, quite literally, a source of creative power.

There is yet another kind of evidence that talmudic masters had teachings alluded to only elliptically in our texts: "The Work of Creation" (*ma'aseh bereshit*) and "The Work of the Chariot" (*ma'aseh merkavah*). The first involved cosmological lore on such topics as the spiritual light that constituted the first stage of the divine creative process, and the idea that God created previous worlds which he destroyed until he found this one to be suitable for his purposes. The latter were visions, evoked by the opening chapters of Ezekiel and experienced by some of the greatest rabbis, of an ascent to the heavenly world. A group of documents called the *hekhalot* (palaces) literature describe such trips to the realm above, during which one encountered angelic gate-keepers and other beings guarding the heavenly Throne. (We will return to this literature when we discuss medieval Jewish mysticism.) The "popular" religion of the Jews, therefore, presupposed a cosmos containing demons and angels, magical powers and occult sciences, and offering the possibility of journeys to and from God's palace—features that coexisted with rabbinic condemnation of magic, with rigorous legal dispute, with teachings about the sanctification of the Name on earth, and with aggadot of a rather philosophical character.[28]

These other dimensions of Jewish folk religion survived into the Middle Ages and the early modern period, when rabbinic Judaism prevailed among the people, except for a few outlying and isolated districts of the diaspora and in certain sectarian movements. It was talmudic Judaism that became the cement that held the Jewish people together and furnished the main *raison d'être* for its survival. Talmudic Judaism became the unifying popular religion through the way of life it inculcated; and the canonized Babylonian Talmud produced other Talmuds in other lands by way of interpretation and commentary. Living in a world dominated by monotheistic faiths that, unlike Judaism, enjoyed the benefits (and suffered the consequences) of being state religions, Jews needed their own law on internal matters affecting ties with each other and with God. On another level, rabbinic Judaism provided the intellectual momentum and ideological integrity that enabled Jewish identity to remain relevant. And more: the Talmud humanized the Judaism of the Bible. As one scholar has written,

> In studying the Written Torah the student was confronted with the word of God directly, and he felt overwhelmed by the Divine Majesty. . . . To the word of God there can be only one reply: "We will do and obey." In the Oral Torah the student met his fellow man, true enough, men of sublime attainment, but nonetheless men, human beings. There, he frequently found himself drawn into the disputations of the various talmudic schools

and authorities. The Talmud with its varying interpretations and legalistic analyses introduced the student into the innermost recesses of the Oral Torah and made him a participant in the process of its creation.[29]

If it is an overstatement that all Jews in the Middle Ages studied Talmud and its ever-growing body of ancillary texts, in certain diasporas, as we shall see in subsequent chapters, this ideal was approximated for a sizable proportion of the middle and upper classes. In those communities, the world of Mishnah, Gemara, and Midrash—their style of thinking and their contents—became a major component of Jewish consciousness. And these were among the most important disaporas for Jewish survival.

In other times and places, however, during the Middle Ages and early modern periods, circumstances were to be conducive to renewed encounter with Hellenism. Unlike Hellenistic Judaism, it would not be a biblical Judaism face to face with a Hellenistic philosophy still concretely embedded in its pagan matrix, but rabbinic Judaism facing a depaganized

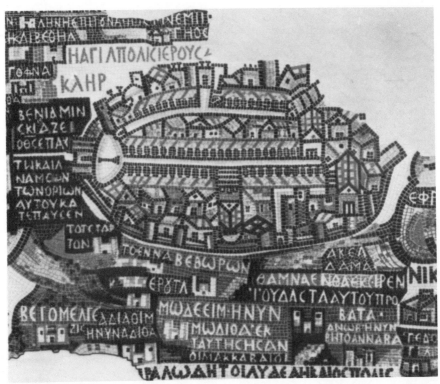

Jerusalem as depicted on the sixth-century Madaba map, showing walls, gates, main public buildings, churches, and the Western (Wailing) Wall at upper right.

Greek philosophy already brought much closer to radical monotheism. Many rabbinical statements about God's attributes, divine providence and human freedom, the reasons for the mitzvot, and the nature of the messianic age would be reinterpreted in a rationalistic light to show that natural science and revealed religion could coexist in harmony. Other elements of the aggadah would be fused with Greek metaphysics to produce a speculative mystical tradition (the *Kabbalah*), drawing on the doctrine of God's names and on the role of man in actualizing deity in the world and in bringing divine judgment and divine mercy into balance. The sociopolitical setting of these later developments will be the subject of the next chapter.

PART THREE

The Middle Ages and Early Modern Times

CHART 3A. MEDIEVAL PERIOD, 600–1200

General History	The Jews Under Islam	The Jews Under Christendom
600		
		614. Jews return to Jerusalem during Persian invasion of Palestine; Byzantine reoccupation in 629 is followed by Christian reprisals.
622. The Hegira: Muhammad's flight from Mecca to Medina.		
632. Death of Muhammad.		
630s–640s. Arab conquest of Syria, Palestine, Egypt, and Persia.	c. 618–670. Bustanai, the first exilarch of the Arab period.	612. Beginning of repeated issuance of anti-Jewish legislation and persecutions in Visigothic Spain, culminating in outlawing of Judaism in 694.
661. Consolidation of the Ummayad dynasty of caliphs, which ruled the Arab empire to 750.		
700		
711–715. Muslim conquest of Spain.		
733. Battle of Tours; defeat of Muslim invasion of France by Charles Martel.	c. 740. First conversions to Judaism among Khazars on the Volga River.	
750. Abbasid dynasty of caliphs. (The Abbasids lose political power after 940 but last to 1258.)	Mid-8th century. Jewish messianic movements in the Middle East.	
756. Independent Ummayad caliphate of Cordova in Spain.	762–767. Anan ben David's break with the Rabbanites; beginnings of the Karaite tradition.	
786–809. Harun al-Rashid, Abbasid caliph.		
780–800. Western North Africa breaks away from Abbasid rule.	c. 757–761. Yehudah, gaon of Sura.	
		797. Charlemagne sends Isaac the Jew as an emissary to Harun al-Rashid.
800. Charlemagne, king of the Franks, crowned Roman emperor in the west by the Pope. (Charlemagne ruled 768–814.)		

General History	The Jews Under Islam	The Jews Under Christendom
800		
814–840. Reign of Louis the Pious, son of Charlemagne.	c. 825. Authority of the exilarch over the geonim begins to decline.	Early 9th century. Jewish traders given favorable privileges as "merchants of the palace" by Louis the Pious.
843. Treaty of Verdun, dividing the Frankish empire into three parts between the heirs of Louis the Pious.		
813–833. Al-Mamun, Abbasid caliph; cultivation of natural sciences, theology, and philosophy at Baghdad.	830–860. Benjamin of Nahawend; considerable growth of Karaism.	
9th–10th centuries. Raids, migrations, invasions by Northmen (Vikings).		
899. First appearance of Magyar raiders in central Europe.		
900		
911. Rollo the Viking granted a fief by the Frankish king in what was later Normandy.	882–941. Saadia, gaon of Sura and Jewish philosopher.	
962. Otto I the Great, ruler of Germany, crowned Roman emperor in the West by the Pope. (Otto I ruled 936–973.)	10th–11th centuries. Karaite academy in Jerusalem. 915–970. Hisdai ibn Shaprut, government administrator and patron of Jewish learning at Cordova.	
969. The Fatimid dynasty of caliphs in Tunisia conquers Egypt. (The Fatimids rule Egypt to 1171.)	968–1006. Sherira ben Hanina serves as gaon of Pumbeditha; author (c. 987) of a letter narrating how the Mishnah, Talmud, and other rabbinic works were compiled.	c. 960–1028. Gershom ben Judah of Mainz, one of the first great Ashkenazic talmudists.
987. Hugh Capet crowned king of France; end of the Carolingian dynasty and beginning of the Capetian.		
989. Conversion of Prince Vladimir of Kiev to Greek Orthodox Christianity.		

General History	The Jews Under Islam	The Jews Under Christendom
1000		
980–1037. Avicenna, Muslim physician, scientist, and philosopher.	1008. Jews of Egypt persecuted by al-Hakim.	
1066. Norman conquest of England.	993–1056. Samuel ibn Nagrela, vizier and Jewish poet, scholar, and patron at Granada.	
1077. Penance of the emperor Henry IV before Pope Gregory VII (Hildebrand) at Canossa, part of the struggle between Holy Roman empire and papacy.	1004–1038. Hai ben Sherira, last important gaon in the East.	1040–1105. Rashi (Rabbi Solomon ben Isaac) of Troyes, biblical and talmudic commentator.
	c. 1020–1057. Solomon ibn Gabirol, poet and first important Jewish philosopher in Spain.	
1085. The king of Castile captures the Toledo from the Muslims, leading the Muslims to invite the Berber sect and dynasty of the Almoravides into Spain.	c. 1055–1135. Moses ibn Ezra, Hebrew poet and literary critic.	1066. Jews settle in England.
		1096. Massacre of Rhineland Jews by crusaders.
1095. Pope Urban II calls for the first crusade to reconquer Palestine from the Seljuk Turks.	1075–1141. Judah Halevy, physician, poet, and philosopher.	
1033–1109. Anselm of Canterbury; beginning of growth of Western scholasticism.	1089–1164. Abraham ibn Ezra, poet, astronomer, physician, biblical commentator.	
1100		
1079–1142. Peter Abélard, French scholastic theologian.	c. 1110–1180. Abraham ibn Daud, philosopher and historian.	c. 1100–1171. Jacob ben Meir Tam, one of the first of the tosafists.
1126–1198. Averroës, Muslim physician, philosopher, commentator on Aristotle.		c. 1125–1198. Abraham ben David of Posquières, a talmudist of southern France.
1145–1150. The Almohades, a Berber dynasty, invade and conquer Muslim Spain.	1135–1204. Moses Maimonides, physician, legist, and philosopher.	c. 1160–1235. Isaac the Blind, son of Abraham ben David of Posquières and early kabbalist.
1147–1149. The Second Crusade.		
1187. Saladin captures Jerusalem from the Christians.	1146. Beginning of persecution of Jews in Muslim Spain by the Almohades.	

General History	The Jews Under Islam	The Jews Under Christendom
		c. 1150–1217. Judah he-Hasid of Regensberg, an Ashkenazic pietist.
1189–1192. The Third Crusade.		1144. Ritual murder charge at Norwich.
1152–1190. Reign of Frederick I Barbarossa, Holy Roman emperor.		1171. Blood libel at Blois, the first in France.
1154–1189. Reign of Henry II Plantagenet in England.		1182–1198. Expulsion of Jews from the royal domain in France by Philip II Augustus (ruled 1180–1223).
1189–1199. Richard I, Coeur de Lion, king of England.		1190. Massacre of Jews at York.

General History	Jews in Spain, Portugal, Italy, Southern France	Jews in England, Northern France, Germany, East Europe
1200		
1198–1216. Pontificate of Innocent III. 1200–1225. Establishment of the Franciscan and Dominican Orders. 1208. Beginning of crusade against the Albegensian heresy in southern France. 1212. Battle of Los Navas de Toloso leaves most of Spain in Christian hands. 1215. Fourth Lateran Council. 1225–1270. Thomas Aquinas, Christian scholastic philosopher. 1226–1270. Reign of Louis IX (St. Louis) in France. 1249. Mamluk regime in Egypt (until 1517). 1258. Mongols capture Baghdad and put an end to the caliphate there. 1272–1307. Reign of Edward I of England. 1265–1321. Dante Aligheri, Italian poet and author of the Divine Comedy.	1194–1270. Moses ben Nahman (Nahmanides), Spanish talmudist, biblical commentator, mystic. 1235–1310. Solomon ibn Adret, rabbi of Barcelona and talmudic scholar. 1263. Disputation of Barcelona. c. 1286. Completion of the Zohar by Moses de Leon. c. 1261–1328. Immanuel of Rome, Hebrew poet.	1215–1293. Meir ben Baruch of Rothenburg, talmudic authority and last of the great tosafists. 1240. Disputation of Paris, leading to the burning of the Talmud in 1242. 1244. Charter of Frederick II, Duke of Austria. 1255. Ritual murder charge at Lincoln. 1264. Charter of Prince Boleslav the Pious of Poland. 1288. Blood libel of Troyes. 1290. Expulsion of Jews from England. 1298–1299. Rindfleisch persecutions in Germany.
1300		
1304–1373. Francesco Petrarca (Petrarch), Italian poet and humanist, one of the first great writers of the Italian Renaissance. 1347–1349. The Black Death. 1304–1378. The popes at Avignon in France (the Babylonian Captivity of the Church).	c. 1270–1340. Jacob ben Asher, rabbinic codifier, author of *Arba'ah Turim*. 1288–1344. Levi ben Gershom (Gersonides), scientist and philosopher. c. 1340–1414. Hasdai Crescas, philosopher and communal leader.	1306. Philip IV the Fair orders the expulsion of Jews from France. 1315. Jews recalled to France. 1320–1321. Pastoureaux (Shepherds) massacres in France. 1336–1339. Armleder massacres in Germany.

General History	Jews in Spain, Portugal, Italy, Southern France	Jews in England, Northern France, Germany, East Europe
1356. The Golden Bull defines the electoral system of the Holy Roman empire.	1391. Massacres and conversions in Castile and Aragon.	1348–1349. Black Death massacres, mainly in central Europe and France.
1378–1417. Rival popes at Avignon and Rome (the Great Schism).		1334, 1364, 1367. Casimir the Great, king of Poland, confirms and extends the charter of 1264.
1325–1345. Rise of the Ottoman Turks in Asia Minor.		1394. Final expulsion from France.
1400		
1414–1417. Council of Constance ends the Church schism.	c. 1360–1444. Joseph Albo, theologian and preacher.	1421. Persecution of Jews in Austria.
1453. Ottomans capture Constantinople; end of the Byzantine empire.	1413–1414. Disputation of Tortosa.	1424. Expulsion from Cologne.
		1439. Expulsion from Augsburg.
1456. The Gutenberg Bible, first European book printed with movable type.	1449. Anti-Converso riots in Toledo.	1452–1453. The Franciscan preacher John of Capistrano campaigns against Jews and instigates expulsions.
	1473. Blood libel of Trent.	
1461–1483. Reign of Louis XI of France.	1473–1474. Massacre of Conversos in Cordova.	
1463–1494. Giovanni Pico della Mirandola, Italian philosopher and humanist.		1453. Casimir IV of Poland ratifies the charter of Casimir the Great.
1479. Marriage of Ferdinand of Aragon and Isabella of Castille; unification of kingdom of Spain.		1450–1500. Expulsion of Jews from many cities and districts of Germany.
1480. Establishment of the Spanish Inquisition.		1462. Establishment of the Frankfort ghetto.
1491. Fall of Muslim Granada to Ferdinand and Isabella.		
1492. Columbus discovers America.	1492. Jews expelled from Spain.	
	1497. Jews coerced into baptism or expelled from Portugal.	

CHAPTER 7

Medieval Jewry to 1500

At the beginning of the seventh century, the Jews were preponderantly a diaspora people—a web of communities scattered from Spain to Persia and from central Europe to the Sahara. Despite the loss of its homeland, Jewry maintained a common identity and social interconnectedness: Judaism was the religion of one people and the Jews were a people of one religion, a socioreligious unity resulting primarily from the traditional Jewish self-conception but also from more limited historical factors. The biblical portrait of the people's unbroken continuity from patriarchal times had not prevented the emergence within Judaism of the idea and practice of proselytism, but proselytes were absorbed into the Jewish people as individuals: Even though Jews had occasionally converted other small nations, this happened rarely and without major consequences for the overall unity of Jewry. In the Middle Ages regional and other Jewish subcultures were to be formed; with the exception of one major rupture over the authority of talmudic law, internal differences were never to result in the formation of separate Jewish peoples. Earlier unifying institutions, such as Davidic kingship and the Temple, were conserved in the liturgy and as subjects for religious study. Above all, messianic hope for eventual ingathering and restoration served as an overarching bond between all the branches of the Jewish people. Had Judaism become the official religion of several populous, sovereign states, the momentum of political and military events might have produced

323

Thirteenth-century synagogue in Toledo, Spain, converted into the church of St. Maria la Blanca in 1411. (Courtesy of the Zionist Archives, New York.)

schisms, making Judaism multinational in the usual sense. Because this did not occur, minority status was the common destiny of Jews everywhere and another link between them. Although medieval Jews were one monotheistic people among others, social and religious boundaries around the Jews remained sharply etched, unaffected by the conversion of individuals or by the occasional forced incorporation of Jewish communities into the ruling Christian or Muslim faiths.

In contrast, Christianity's historical destiny was to become the religion of many peoples who preserved their previous identities after conversion. Some of the early Christian nations in Europe were eventually to lose their linguistic and other peculiarities over the course of time, but national differences between Christians and various distinctive ethnic forms of Christianity survived in many regions. In the East, after the Arab conquests, the separate Christian traditions came to resemble Judaism as religions of minority peoples. Despite major controversies between branches of Christianity on matters of creed, ritual, and authority, the distinctiveness of Christendom compared with Jewry was reinforced by crucial elements of Christian faith, such as Incarnation, Trinity, and Virgin Birth, which, together with the unifying symbols and forms of Judaism, maintained as self-evident the difference between being a Christian and being a Jew.

The formation of the medieval context of Jewish history was completed with the rise of Islamic monotheism. Central beliefs of Islam, like those of rabbinic Judaism and Christianity, are derived from the biblical matrix. For the Arabic-speaking pagan population of the Arabian peninsula, Islam created a new religious nation of those who "submitted to God" (the meaning of the word *Islam*). Not all the early Arab tribes were polytheist; some were Jewish and some Christian. The presence of Judaism is evident in the early stages of the new faith in various details of Islamic doctrine and practice. With Judaism and Christianity for models of a mature monotheistic religious system, Islam's development toward its own identity was rapid. The Hebrew Scriptures had taken more than one thousand years to achieve final form; the New Testament contains writings produced in less than a century, spanning the time when Christianity was a Jewish sect until it had its own separate institutions and self-definition vis-à-vis the Jews. The contents of the Islamic Scriptures, the Koran, were completed after Muhammad's prophetic career of three decades, and were redacted soon after his death. Despite the influence of Judaism and Christianity, Islam took its stance outside these faith communities, claiming to have superseded them with revelations from the one God that reiterated and corrected the messages of former prophets and apostles to other nations. With the appearance and spread of Islam, the overall tripartite division of the family tree stemming from biblical monotheism was complete.

The Jews Under Islam in the Middle Ages

Judaism and the Origins of Islam

Muhammad was born in the city of Mecca, in the northwest of Arabia, between 570 and 580. Many of the Arab tribes were still nomadic; others had not too long before settled in urban centers like Mecca where, as merchants, they participated in the caravan trade between the Orient and the Mediterranean. (Before announcing himself as a prophet, Muhammad was a caravan merchant.) The Arabs of the Arabian peninsula in his time, except for tribes converted to Judaism or Christianity, were polytheists; Mecca contained a pagan shrine, the Kaaba, of great antiquity and holiness. Muhammad in his earliest prophetic messages denounced paganism from the standpoint of ethical monotheism. Claiming that his prophecies came from the one and only God (Allah, in Arabic), he warned the Meccans that that Lord of Creation will judge each person according to his deeds in that final day

> When the sky is rent asunder; when the stars scatter and the oceans roll together; when the graves are hurled about; each soul shall know what it has done and what it has failed to do. [Sura 82:1–5.[1]]

فاذا زدا لعصير نصفه فهذا الشراب موافق لوجع الحلق والجنب والربين

والاسترواللين ولمن به لغم غليظ فى حلقه يصفى اللون وكثر النوم

وليبس له غايله موافق للنانه والكلام ع ع ع ع

Physician preparing a cough medicine, from a thirteenth-century Iraqi manuscript.
(Courtesy of the Metropolitan Museum of Art, Rogers Fund, 1913.) Many of the
outstanding Jewish philosophers of the Middle Ages were physicians.

For the righteous there would be bliss in Paradise; for the wrongdoers,
eternal torment in Hell. Already in the first phase of his preaching, with
only a handful of followers, Muhammad aligned himself with the Judeo-
Christian conception of history, asserting that biblical figures like Noah,
Abraham, and Moses had been sent by God to warn mankind to give up
its idols. Peoples that had rejected the prophets were eventually destroyed, except for Jews and Christians, who had preserved the revelations given them from God's heavenly book in the Torah and the Gospel.
The Arabs now had their opportunity to hearken to the message of God's
Book, which they were receiving in their own language through Muhammad. The sole miracle on which Muhammad based his authority was the
content and style of his prophecies, which he insisted could have come
only from Allah.

Rejected by most of the Meccans, Muhammad left Mecca in 622 to
settle in the town of Yathrib, about 280 miles to the north. The exodus
from Mecca to Yathrib (Yathrib was subsequently known as Medina,
the City of the Prophet) marks the first year of the Muslim calendar,
because from then on Muhammad was the leader of a theocratic commonwealth. In addition to those who came with him and the pagan Arabs
of Medina, Muhammad soon won the allegiance of many Bedouin tribes

of the peninsula. After several skirmishes against the Meccans, Muhammad and his supporters were able to re-enter Mecca in triumph in 630. By 632, when Muhammad died, the shrine of Mecca had been purified of pagan deities to become the chief holy place of the new religion, and the Arab armies were on the verge of their great campaigns beyond the confines of Arabia.

As mentioned already, Jews and Christians influenced Muhammad's message, although the exact nature of this indebtedness and whether it came from mainstream or from sectarian forms of Judaism and Christianity are controversial questions among modern scholars. (It is also possible that Jewish and Christian elements in Muhammad's earliest preaching may have reached him indirectly through other Arabic monotheists of the sixth century.) The presence of Judaism in the Arabian peninsula during Muhammad's time (and long before) is a matter of historical record. In the early 500s, the king of the Himyar tribe, which had controlled Yemen (the extreme southwest corner of the peninsula) since the beginning of the Common Era, had converted to Judaism.[2] But the Judaized dynasty of the Himyarites soon fell to an army of Christian Abyssinians, who in turn were driven out by Persian troops later in the century. In the northern part of Arabia a number of localities had been populated largely by Arabic-speaking Jews for centuries. One of the famous sixth-century pre-Islamic Arabic poets, Samuel ibn Adiya, was a Jew. Yathrib itself had been founded by Jewish date-growers.

Muhammad at first had expected the Jewish tribes of Medina to accept him as a true prophet. In anticipation he instructed his followers to face Jerusalem in prayer and to observe the fast of Yom Kippur. His demand was rebuffed, however, probably on the grounds that no one could supersede Moses and the Torah. This rebuff led him to castigate the Jews as enemies of God, of his angels, and of his messenger; they had always been disobedient; they were damned for their mischief and stubbornness.

To Moses We [i.e., God] gave the Scriptures and after him We sent other apostles. We gave Jesus the son of Mary veritable signs and strengthened him with the Holy Spirit. Will you then scorn each apostle whose message does not suit your fancies, charging some with imposture and slaying others? They [the Jews] say: "Our hearts are sealed." But Allah has cursed them for their unbelief. They have but little faith. And now that a Book confirming their Scriptures has been revealed to them by Allah, they deny it, although they know it to be the truth and have long prayed for help against the unbelievers. May Allah's curse be upon the infidels! To deny Allah's own revelation, grudging that He should reveal His bounty to whom He chooses from His servants! They have incurred Allah's most inexorable wrath. When it is said to them: "Believe in what Allah has revealed," they reply: "We believe in what was revealed to *us*." But they deny what has since been revealed, although it is the truth, corroborating their own scriptures. [Sura 2:87–91.]

According to Muhammad's Medinan prophecies, the Jews (and Christians) have twisted the words of Allah, and their Scriptures contain lies.[3] Actually, Muhammad's versions of a number of biblical stories (he refers to Adam, Noah, Abraham, Moses, Samuel, Saul, and David, but not to the classical prophets) diverge considerably from the biblical text. In part this is so because he acquired his knowledge of the Bible orally from Jewish preachers, as indicated by his use of details from the midrash, and in part because he may have confused certain matters related to him. For instance, in the Koran, Haman is depicted as Pharaoh's prime minister during the exodus of the Israelites from Egypt and is asked by Pharaoh to erect the Tower of Babel (Sura 28:38).

Muhammad's position was that the Koran proves the Torah and the Gospel, and corrects them, and that only *his* revelation was God's Book in its perfect form. Islam is superior to Judaism and Christianity, not because it is a new religion, but because it is the restoration of the original form of monotheism—the religion of Abraham, the first Muslim. (*Muslim* means "a man who submits to God.") Muhammad is the "Seal of the Prophets" (Sura 33:20), the last, culminating, and decisive apostle of Allah.[4] Thus Muhammad's confrontation with the Jews in Medina left an ambiguous historical legacy; for Muslims, Judaism was indeed a legitimate religion, but the Jews were a blind and dangerous people who refused the more complete truth offered them by Islam. Muhammad quickly withdrew his concessions to Jewish ritual. The fast of Yom Kippur was dropped, replaced by the duty to abstain from eating during the daytime hours of the month of Ramadan; and the direction of prayer was changed from Jerusalem to Mecca.[5]

By 626 two Jewish tribes had been expelled from Yathrib and the third was exterminated, the men being put to death and the women and children enslaved. In 628 the Muslims conquered the Jewish oasis of Khaybar to the north; there the Jews were permitted to remain, on the condition that they give half their produce as tribute to the Muslims. Gradually the Muslim principle evolved that as a "People of the Book" the Jews had the right to practice their own traditions, but that Islam would inevitably triumph in history. (The special legal status formulated for Jews and Christians by the rulers of Islam will be discussed in the next section.)

In origin and structure Islam bears many similarities to Judaism. In both Judaism and Islam salvation is attained through obedience to divine commandments revealed by a supreme prophet, rather than, as in Christianity, through the atoning death of the Messiah. Both Islam and Judaism pride themselves on being religions of uncompromising monotheism that reject the Christian doctrines of Trinity and Incarnation.[6] Unlike the sacramental system and the priesthood of traditional Christianity, Judaism and Islam emphasize a religious jurisprudence interpreted by scholars and judges. Like Judaism, Islam originated among one people; like Christianity but much more rapidly, Islam became the state religion of a vast empire. Eventually the Muslim religion was adopted by other peoples, some of whom (Persians, Turks) retained their sociocultural distinctiveness from the Arabs. Philosophical and mystical streams frequently crossed the boundaries between the three religious faiths in the Middle Ages, but these boundaries themselves remained primary in the geography of religious identity.

In the Middle Ages, Jews were a monotheistic people in an environment that had assimilated much of the biblical tradition, but in which the ruling religions were in sharp disagreement with Judaism and each other on authoritative particulars. With Christians and Muslims, Jews shared the belief that there was only one God who created heaven and earth, who guided history, who inspired such spiritual heroes as Abraham, Moses, and David—a God who revealed a single correct path by which salvation and eternal life could be attained. But who was the decisive prophet? Who was the true Messiah? Which language and community was the most holy? Which law was the correct path to which man must cleave? The answers constituted issues between the three faiths on which no compromise was possible. In juxtaposition and confrontation with Christianity and Islam, the contours of being Jewish were firmly established for a thousand years and more.

Impact of the Arab Conquests on the Jews

By 644 Syria, Palestine, Egypt, Iraq, and Persia had been occupied by Muslim troops. The eastern frontier of the Byzantine empire had been pushed back to Asia Minor; the Persian state had been destroyed. By the 660s the Ummayad dynasty of caliphs (*caliph* means "successor"—successor to Muhammad as the leader of the faithful) had consolidated their control of the Muslim empire from their capital at Damascus. Muslim armies continued to campaign at the extremities of the realm. Between 711 and 715, a mixed army of Arabs and Muslim Berbers (the Berbers were a native people of western North Africa) crossed the Straits of Gibraltar to conquer the Iberian peninsula, bringing Muslim rule to continental Europe. The first century of the Arab empire also was marked by social and religious conflicts over who had the right to rule the Islamic state. In 750 persistent unrest resulted in the overthrow of the Ummayads and the establishment of the Abbasid dynasty of caliphs, who removed the capital to Baghdad. During the following century, when the Abbasid caliphate was at its zenith, the Muslim postscriptural oral tradi-

The Dome of the Rock in Jerusalem, Muslim shrine built on the site of the Jerusalem Temple in the late seventh century. (Courtesy of the Consulate General of Israel.)

tion crystallized, Muslim jurisprudence and theology flourished, and a brilliant revival of ancient science and philosophy was under way.

At first the Arab conquerors, a minority of the vast population that came under their control, did not encourage widespread conversion to Islam. (Non-Arab Muslims had a distinctly inferior status until 750.) For practical and ideological reasons they had to work out arrangements on an ad hoc basis with the Jewish and Christian communities, recognized by Islam as Peoples of the Book, which meant, as mentioned earlier, that Islam acknowledged that they possessed Scriptures with some claim to divine inspiration. Although the conquests had been accompanied by acts of personal enslavement, confiscation of booty, and exaction of heavy tribute, the *dhimmi* (the technical term in Muslim law for "dependent" peoples, i.e., Jews and Christians) were guaranteed religious toleration, judicial autonomy, exemption from military service, and security of life and property. In turn, the *dhimmi* had to acknowledge the unquestioned political supremacy of the Islamic state. Various outward signs of *dhimmi* subordination were gradually incorporated into what came to be called the Pact of Omar. (Some scholars feel that the concept of the Pact of Omar and many of its provisions date from about 800.) According to the Pact of Omar, Jews and Christians were not permitted to make converts, build new churches or synagogues, or make a public display of their rituals (church bells, processions); they were not to live in houses higher than those of Muslims, carry weapons, or ride horses (only donkeys). They were supposed to wear distinctive clothing. On the whole, these restrictions were not enforced in the early Muslim centuries, except by an occasional pious and fanatic ruler. Even the prohibition against *dhimmi* exerting political authority over Muslims was sometimes ignored, and talented Jews and Christians were brought into the state administration. *Dhimmi* paid a yearly poll tax, graded according to wealth, and *dhimmi* farmers were obligated to pay a land tax consisting of a large portion of their produce. But in those centuries when the economy of the Islamic realm flourished (until the thirteenth century in most areas), the *dhimmi* were not economically segregated; they were able to participate fully in the burgeoning industry and commerce of the vast territories controlled by Islam.

Readjustment of Jewish life under these conditions was painful but successful. Although the economic and social transformation of Jewry in the first two centuries of Muslim rule cannot be traced in detail, it seems that a major turning point in Jewish history occurred during that time: The Jews became almost completely urban. Confiscatory land taxes made it almost impossible for *dhimmi* to remain farmers and peasants, but creation of new cities and revival of old ones provided attractive new sources of livelihood. Military camps established by the Arab armies (such as Basra and Kufa in Iraq, Fostat-Cairo in Egypt, Kairouan in present-day

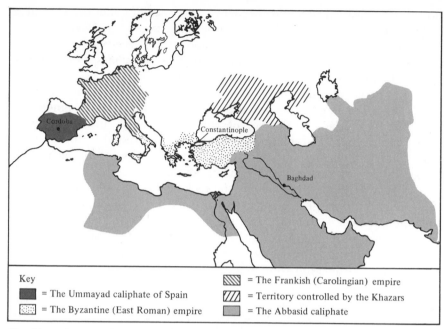

Key
■ = The Ummayad caliphate of Spain
▦ = The Byzantine (East Roman) empire
▧ = The Frankish (Carolingian) empire
▨ = Territory controlled by the Khazars
▨ = The Abbasid caliphate

The Major Powers about 800 CE. The majority of Jews lived in the Abassid realm, but considerable numbers were to be found in the Byzantine empire and in Muslim Spain. Jewish settlements were expanding in northwest Europe beginning in the reign of Charlemagne. By the ninth century the Khazar royal family had converted to Judaism.

Tunisia) and the new capital of the Abbasid empire (Baghdad) became prosperous commercial and administrative centers. Trade was stimulated by the merger into one realm of former Byzantine and Sassanian provinces stretching from the Atlantic to India. Demand for all kinds of artisan skills enabled the Jewish masses to earn enough to pay the poll tax. Jews were employed in dozens of crafts in the Muslim cities, such as tanning, dyeing, weaving, silk manufacture, and metal work. The Jewish upper classes were able to participate in the large-scale interregional trade, using letters of credit, establishing networks of local agents and representatives, and helping to develop other sophisticated early capitalist techniques. In the early tenth century in Baghdad, and soon after in Egypt, many Jewish merchants—not only the very rich—deposited money with Jewish banking firms who made loans to the state. Although large numbers of impoverished Jews lived on communal charity even during the most prosperous times, the Jewish middle class in medieval Islam acquired a size and importance unprecedented in earlier Jewish history.

That such a vast area was brought into one political and economic framework also facilitated the migration of Jews from places of their most compact settlement in Babylonia to outlying regions, where they rein-vigorated distant branches of the diaspora and created new centers of Jewish life. Enterprising groups of Jews even went outside the Muslim empire to conduct trade and establish settlements. (The Jewish traders in early medieval Christian Europe will be described later in this chapter.) In the early eighth century Jewish merchants or missionaries converted to Judaism the kings of a Turkish people on the Volga, the Khazars.[7] Of particular importance was the gradual migration of Jews westward from Iraq and Persia to Syria and Palestine, to Egypt and North Africa, and to Spain. Even though there was a movement back to the east at certain times between the tenth and twelfth centuries, the overall geographical redistribution of Jews was such that, by the thirteenth century, the ma-jority of Jews, for the first time in history, lived in Europe rather than in the Middle East.[8]

Yet another consequence of the Arab conquests was one of the most dramatic linguistic transformations in history. Almost all the conquered peoples in the Middle East abandoned Aramaic and Greek for Arabic—which did not necessarily entail leaving their traditional religions, since Arabic was not only the vehicle for the religious literature of Islam but also for a secular culture that incorporated many elements of the science and philosophy of ancient times. Adopting Arabic as a spoken language brought Jews into contact with forms of expression and cultural attitudes that fostered a new phase of Jewish intellectual creativity. Indeed, the Arabs' pride in their language stimulated a Hebrew revival as well, a revival based on scientific investigations into Hebrew grammar and phi-lology.

Of the older religious traditions of the areas conquered by the Muslims, Judaism adapted most successfully to the Islamic regime and to the politi-cal, economic, and cultural changes that resulted. The Zoroastrians lost most of their adherents and dwindled to a small minority in eastern Per-sia and India. Orthodox Christianity, which earlier had been the state religion of the Byzantine-ruled territories, suffered great loss of status. Other branches of Christianity in Egypt and Syria preferred Arab rule to repression by Byzantine emperors. Christianity survived in the East, but large numbers of Christians converted to Islam. For Jews in the for-mer Byzantine provinces, the Arab conquests brought relief from the persecution they had experienced in late antiquity—and a significant change in their position. Instead of being the only non-Christian religion, theoretically tolerated but usually oppressed, they now had a defined legal standing as second-class but protected subjects of the state, along-side Christians. Some Jews did convert to Islam, but in the long run Judaism seems to have retained the loyalty of a larger proportion of its adherents than the other minority religions. For the Jews, being a minor-ity was not new: The political status of Jews under Islam resembled the

Jewry of Sassanian Persia before the Muslim conquest, when the rabbis had adapted talmudic law to persistent diaspora conditions. The Muslim conquests unified the Jewish world even more than it had been under Roman rule, inasmuch as Iraq and Persia were brought together into the same empire with the Mediterranean provinces. And it was the ancient Jewish institutions of Sassanian Babylonia that became the recognized leadership of the Jewish diaspora in the first few centuries of Islamic rule.

Central Jewish Institutions in the Ummayad and Abbasid Caliphates

Owing to the paucity of Jewish sources and limited mention of Jews in Muslim writings, information on Jewish history in the first two centuries of the Islamic empire is meager. When the Arabs conquered Babylonia, they confirmed the authority of the exilarch, who had ruled the Jews of Babylonia since the first century CE at least. During the period when the political might of the caliphs was at its height, the exilarch was the single most powerful official of Jewry; honored by Jews and Arabs as a descendant of King David, the exilarch represented the Jews in the caliphal court, supervised the dispensation of justice and charitable support among his people, and collected the poll tax for the Muslim government. By the early Abbasid period, the exilarch had to share power with

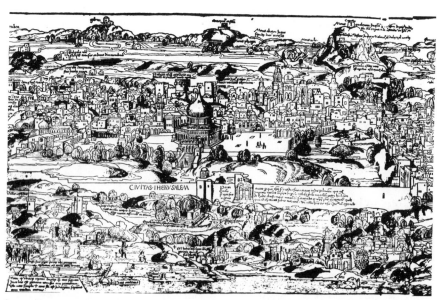

Jerusalem according to a fifteenth-century pilgrims' map of the holy land. (Courtesy of the Rare Book Division of the New York Public Library, Astor, Lenox, and Tilden Foundations.)

the heads of the great rabbinical academies of Babylonia. (The Jews continued to use the term Babylonia even after the Arabic name for the area, Iraq, was generally accepted.) The enhanced power of the scholars was perhaps influenced by a parallel development in Islam: the emergence of a class of jurists responsible for creating a systematic and logical groundwork for Islamic law. Jewry had for many centuries possessed such a class of legal experts in the rabbis, and during the early Islamic period the authority of the two rabbinical academies (*yeshivot*) of Babylonia, Sura and Pumbeditha, won increasing recognition from the Jewish diaspora and from the Muslim state as sources of authoritative guidance for Judaism.

In the eighth century, exilarch and academy heads cooperated in establishing the Babylonian halakhah as binding law throughout the diaspora, especially in those areas, such as Syria and Egypt, that had previously taken their direction from the rabbinic Sanhedrin in the Galilee. In the view of Pirkoi ben Baboi, a Babylonian scholar of the late eighth century, the rulings of the Palestinian Talmud not in accordance with the Babylonian had been formulated under the pressure of Christian persecution, and hence were invalid. The Palestinian rabbinate revived in the ninth century, but never regained pre-eminence. An attempt in the early tenth century by Palestinian rabbis to reassume control of the calendar, which would have enabled them to determine leap years, festivals, and fasts, was soundly defeated by the Babylonian leadership. The triumph of the Babylonian halakhah as the authoritative rabbinic law was to be an important factor making for a more uniform style of Jewish life and for the cohesion of the Jewish legal tradition throughout the Middle Ages and into modern times.

In the eighth century the exilarch was still clearly supreme over the academies and appointed their heads at will. Soon afterward the heads of the academies became more independent, claiming the right to nominate the exilarch. (His appointment had to be confirmed by the caliph.) Taxes from certain districts in Iraq and Persia were now sent directly to the academies rather than to the exilarch, and in these areas the academy heads had the exclusive right to appoint judges. This three-way division of power and revenue did not always function harmoniously; instances of discord between exilarchs and academy heads and of rivalry between the two academies are mentioned in the few historical sources surviving from that time. Gradually the authority of the exilarch declined relative to the academies, and by the tenth century the yeshivot had moved from their original locations in Sura and Pumbeditha to Baghdad, where their leadership had direct access to Jewish bankers influential in the government. By the eleventh century the exilarch had become an honorific position, and the Pumbeditha-Baghdad yeshivah (it retained its original name after moving to the capital) had gained pre-eminence over the Sura-

Baghdad yeshivah, reversing the relationship between the two academies in the earlier Muslim period. By the end of that century, however, a new network of yeshivot of a different kind, to be discussed shortly, had arisen in the West, so that the Baghdad rabbinate lost its primacy in world Jewry.

In their heyday, the rabbinic academies of Iraq were institutions of great prestige throughout the diaspora, and students came from all over to study there. But like the yeshivot in talmudic times, the yeshivot of Sura and Pumbeditha during the caliphate were much more than institutions for the training of young rabbis: They were institutes of advanced study and discussion among scholars, and they were judicial bodies whose rulings were a form of legislation—legislation through the interpretation of talmudic precedents. The scholars of the yeshivot did not hesitate to adjust certain aspects of Jewish law to the new economic situation of the Jews. Furthermore, as previously mentioned, the academies exerted direct control over many Jewish communities: They invested local and territorial leaders with their offices, and they collected revenues from the local communities in order to maintain a large salaried staff at the mother yeshivah.

From the seventh century on, the president of the academy, known as the gaon (excellency), was a powerful figure in whose name all the legal rulings of the yeshivah were issued. (The title *gaon* was a shortened form of the Hebrew phrase *rosh yeshivat geon Ya'akov*, "head of the academy which is the pride of Jacob," the last phrase being based on Ps. 47:4.) During the months of Adar and Elul in the spring and fall (the *kallah* months, as they were called) the gaon delivered lectures on the law to large groups of scholars and laymen who traveled to the yeshivah to study. At this time he announced his binding opinions on halakhic inquiries addressed to him from throughout the diaspora. Extant rabbinic literature of this period consists of many such *responsa* (answers to questions on rabbinic law) and a few incompletely preserved law codes. Some of these responsa are lengthy treatises, which contain almost our only information on certain aspects of the history of Judaism at this time, such as the responsa by the geonim Amram and Saadiah on the correct order of prayers, our earliest written prayer books; and Sherirah Gaon's letter on the chain of rabbinic authority, the main source for the history of the rabbinical institutions during the first millennium. The geonic literature (so-called because the responsa were issued in the name of the gaon) forms an important link between the legal thought of the talmudic period and the later authorities.

Just as an exilarchic dynasty supplied political leadership to Jewry, the geonim were, with few exceptions, drawn from a half dozen venerable Babylonian families who provided the uppermost echelon of rabbinic leadership. During the height of the influence and prestige of the geonic yeshivot, a small group in Iraq virtually monopolized a fixed system of rabbinic precedence and honor designated by special seats and titles in the collegium of scholars. The rabbinic academies of Iraq from the seventh through the eleventh centuries were far more hierarchical in their structure and exclusive in their membership than Jewish intellectual institutions in earlier or in later times. As we shall soon see, this closed, tightly knit religious establishment provoked considerable opposition among Jews to the authority of talmudic law.

The Babylonian leadership, at its most harmonious and dignified, is portrayed in the following (abbreviated) description of the installation of an exilarch, from an old chronicle.

> On Thursday they assembled in the synagogue, blessed the exilarch, and placed their hands on him. They blew the horn, that all the people, small and great, might hear. When the people heard the proclamation, every member of the community sent him a present, according to his power and means. All the heads of the community sent him magnificent clothes and beautiful ornaments, vessels of silver and vessels of gold, each man according to his ability. . . . When he arose on Sabbath morning to go to the synagogue, many of the prominent men of the community met him to go with him to the synagogue. At the synagogue a wooden pulpit had been prepared for him on the previous day. . . . They spread over it magnificent coverings of silk, blue, purple, and scarlet, so that it was entirely covered, and nothing was seen of it. Under the pulpit there entered distinguished youths, with melodious and harmonious voices, who were well-versed in the prayers and all that appertains thereto. . . . When all the people were seated, the exilarch came out from the place where he was concealed. Seeing him come out, all the people stood up, until he sat on the pulpit which had been made for him. Then the head of the academy of Sura came out after him, and after exchanging courtesies with the exilarch, sat down on the pulpit. Then the head of the academy of Pumbeditha came out, and he, too, made a bow, and sat down at his left. . . . Then the exilarch would begin to expound matters pertaining to the biblical portion of that day, or would give permission to the head of the academy of Sura to deliver the exposition, and the head of the academy of Sura would give permission to the head of the academy of Pumbeditha. They would thus show deference to one another, until the head of the academy of Sura began to expound. . . . He expounded with awe, closing his eyes, and wrapping himself up in his *tallith*, so that his forehead was covered. While he was expounding, there was not in the congregation one that opened his mouth or chirped or uttered a sound. If he became aware that anyone spoke, he would open his eyes, and fear and terror would fall upon the congregation. . . .[9]

Messianism and Karaism

Widespread sectarian conflict within Islamic society during the early Middle Ages had its equivalent in Jewish society too. That the social and

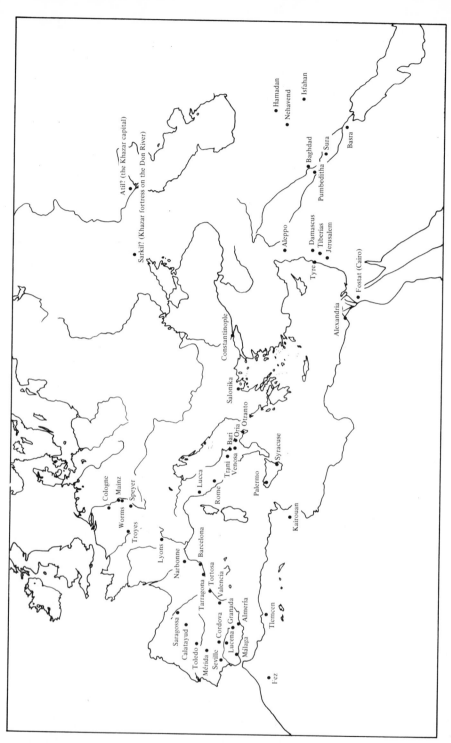

Important Jewish Centers Between the Seventh and the Early Eleventh Centuries. During this period there was a movement of Jewish population from the Middle East to the West, especially to Muslim Spain. The earliest centers of Ashkenazic Jewry in northern France and western Germany were well-established homes of Jewish learning by the eleventh century.

cultural dislocation of the time produced upheaval among the Jews of the Middle East is evident in the many Jewish sects mentioned in the historical sources. (The Hellenistic and Roman periods, which also brought about a major transformation in Jewish life, had likewise been times of conflict between different Jewish groups.) Unfortunately, information about these matters is limited. Several brief Arabic and Jewish descriptions refer to messianic movements among Persian Jews in the mid-eighth century, involving armed uprisings against the Muslim authorities. Although the practices and ideology of the groups headed by Abu Isa of Isfahan (probably 745–755) and his disciple Yudghan (756–765) cannot be determined in detail, it is known that they advocated ascetic practices, additional daily prayer services, and the recognition as legitimate of certain prophets to the gentile nations (especially Muhammad), and presumably they desired to bring an immediate end to the Jewish exile. These revolts were quickly suppressed, but a more enduring threat —this time, not to the Muslim state but to the Jewish establishment— appeared later in the eighth century and eventuated in a separate, anti-rabbinic form of Judaism: Karaism (from the Hebrew word *mikrah*, "Scriptures").

According to later sources, the first in the line of Karaite sectarians was Anan ben David, who founded a group known as the Ananites sometime in the 760s.[10] Anan's conception of Jewish observance is extremely pietistic and severe. He considered rabbinical practices that emphasize the joy of the Sabbath and the festivals to be contrary to the mourning that should mark Jewish life in exile. Anan did not allow lights or fire in Jewish households during the Sabbath, which were permitted by rabbinic law as long as they were kindled beforehand. He promulgated a seventy-day fast resembling the Muslim Ramadan, extended the prohibited degrees of marriage far beyond the rabbinic definition of incestuous relations, and declared that consulting physicians showed lack of religious faith. Additional matters in which Anan and later Karaites criticized excessive rabbinic leniency were *kashrut* (dietary laws) and regulations concerning ritual impurity. The Karaites also returned to a calendar based on direct observation of the new moon. Underlying these details was the Karaite rejection of the Talmud and their insistence that Jewish law should adhere as literally as possible to the Bible. (In their legal writings the Karaites reasoned by analogy from biblical verses, one of the methods also used by the Muslim jurists.)

After Anan, the next early figure of the Karaite tradition was Benjamin of Nahawend in Persia (second quarter of the ninth century), who wrote several law books in Hebrew. (Anan had used Aramaic and later Karaites used Arabic.) Benjamin was the first to use the term *Karaites* to designate followers of the Bible only, in contrast to the term *Rabbanites*, designating those who adhered to the rabbinic tradition. Benjamin seems to have taught that Jews should decide individually which practices were implied by the biblical legislation.[11] Personal freedom of interpretation became a fundamental Karaite principle: A Karaite scholar from the end of the tenth century cited as a dictum of Anan: "Search thoroughly in the Scriptures and do not rely on my opinion."

By the early tenth century, a wide range of different Jewish groups could be found in Palestine, Iraq, and Persia, all of whom rejected rabbinic law and devised their own regulations in its stead. The metamorphosis of this deviant fringe into a coherent movement was helped by the establishment of a Karaite academy in Jerusalem. Daniel al-Kumisi, a Persian Karaite of the late ninth century, seems to have been the first to call on Karaites to settle in Jerusalem in order to pray constantly that Israel's sins be forgiven and to appeal to God for redemption. Karaite "mourners for Zion" (*avelei Zion*) deprived themselves of wine, meat, and other luxuries. One of the epistles of a Jerusalem Karaite, who traveled around the diaspora to win Jewish converts to the movement, conveys the rhetorical passion of the Karaite demand for repentance and the bitterness of their attacks on the Rabbanites:

> This is the practice of Karaite Israelites who have sought God's pleasure and secluded themselves from the desires of this world. They have given up eating meat and drinking wine and have clung to the Lord's Law and have stood in assiduous watch before the doors of His Temple. Because of the greatness of their grief and the depth of their sighing, they have lost their strength to stand up against all stumbling blocks, and the skin of their bodies has become wrinkled with premature senility. Yet notwithstanding all this, they forsook not their goal, nor did they relinquish their hope; rather they continue to read the Law and interpret it, acting as both teachers and pupils, turning many persons away from evildoing, and saying, "O all ye who are athirst, come ye to the water!" . . . May God fulfill regarding them His promise to turn the ashes covering heads of Zion's mourners into an ornament of splendor. . . .
>
> In God's mighty Name have I come to awaken the hearts of His people of Israel; to turn them back to the Law of the Lord; to arouse their conscience and their thoughts to the fear of their God; to make them dread the Day of Judgment, which is coming with terror and wrath, and the day of the Lord's vengeance upon those who forsake His Law; and to warn them not to rely upon ordinances contrived by men and learned by rote [i.e., the rabbinic law]. . . . How can I fail to do so, when my bowels cry out within my belly and my kidneys are consumed within my bosom with pity for my brethren and for the children of my people? Many of them have been forced to put a great distance between themselves and the Lord and to walk in a way which is not good, because of their leaders [the rabbis] who oppress them remorselessly. . . . Whosoever does not give according to their demand, they wage holy war against him; they subjugate and tyrannize him by means of bans and excommunications and by recourse to

the gentile officials. They punish the poor by forcing them to borrow at a high rate of interest and to make payment to them. Part of what they thus take from the poor they present to the gentile officials, so that they may strengthen their hold over the people. They vaunt their holiness and purity and demand that the people bring them all kinds of sweetmeats and wine, exacted as payment of fines, so that they may eat and drink. . . .[12]

In the tenth and eleventh centuries, the Jerusalem Karaites included some of the most distinguished literary figures of eastern Jewry. Karaite scholars in Jerusalem composed handbooks of law, wrote commentaries on the Bible, furthered the growth of Hebrew philology, and engaged in theological and philosophical speculation. Some Karaites were among the first Jews to use the rationalist approach being developed at the time by Muslim thinkers.[13]

The main characteristics of Karaism in the first centuries of its history are asceticism, yearning for an end to exile, rejection of rabbinic authority, individualistic biblical interpretation, and growing interest in rationalistic criticism of rabbinic Judaism and rationalistic defense of the Jewish faith. We do not know how extensive their following was among the Jewish masses, but the emergence of the Karaite intellectual was an understandable consequence of the exilarchic-geonic system.[14] Many of the Karaite leaders drew on the example of the prophetic literature of the Bible to attack what they saw as hypocrisy and compromise. The Jewish commandments meant for them self-denial and separation from the gentile world. Though opposed to rabbinic authority, they did not evolve a nonlegal form of Judaism; though acknowledging the right of individual interpretation, they did not advocate leniency. Frustrated by the closed character of the Babylonian yeshivot and imbued with calling the people to return to God, the Karaites were willing to strike out on their own and defy the growing power of the established Jewish leadership. (The Muslim rulers permitted the Karaites to secede and live by their own practices.) Attacking the rabbis meant attacking the Talmud itself, the source of rabbinic authority. One Karaite author of the tenth century (Jacob al-Kirkisani, to whom we are indebted for most of our information about Jewish sects of the early Muslim period) compiled a history of the movement in which he links Karaism to the Sadducees of the Second Temple, who, he claims, wanted to restore the Judaism of biblical times against the usurpation of the Pharisaic sages. The Karaites thought of themselves as adherents of the only authentic form of Judaism; they were, in the biblical phrase, the "remnant of Israel."

Apparently, the Karaite intellectuals capitalized on a resistance to the growing uniformity of practice being achieved in rabbinic Judaism at that time and to feelings of resentment against the wealth and comfort enjoyed by the Jewish elite. They were also an early sign of an important long-range development: the broadening of the Jewish scholar class to include men not tied to the personal direction and patronage of the dominant group in Babylonia. (The vast enlargement of the leadership of Judaism will be described in the next section.)

By the tenth century, the Karaites had successfully established their own network of synagogues in the Middle East. (Apart from one small group that appeared in Spain, the Karaites never gained a following in Western Europe.) Polemics against the Karaites became frequent among writers loyal to the Talmud. As the social composition of the movement changed, Karaism lost much of its earlier severity; Karaites in Egypt and elsewhere became prosperous merchants. (It is not unusual for small, ascetic religious groups to attain economic success.) The ascetic features of Karaite ritual were modified accordingly (for instance, the prohibition on Sabbath lamps was gradually dropped) and the concept of a postbiblical tradition, called by them *sevel ha-yerushah*, the "burden of the heritage," was accepted. After the destruction of the Jerusalem community during the First Crusade, the center of Karaite literary activity moved to the Byzantine empire; from there Karaites founded settlements in the Crimea and in medieval Poland and Lithuania. The Karaite community in Egypt also continued to maintain itself.[15] Relations between Karaites and Rabbanites varied in the following centuries; sometimes ties were close and there was intermarriage between them, although at other periods one or the other side emphasized the gulf between their respective ways of life. After the eleventh century, however, Karaism did not have a large base of support, and it has survived down to the present as a small minority in a larger minority, the Jewish people.

The Revival of the Western Diaspora; the Jews of Muslim Spain

Already in the eighth century, the unified Muslim empire began to break apart. When the Abbasid caliphs overthrew the Ummayads in 750, Muslim-ruled Spain remained independent under the single surviving descendant of the Ummayads. Even during the century when the Abbasids were at the height of their prestige and power, they were losing control of outlying territories: Morocco (780s), Tunisia (around 800), large areas of Persia (820s), Egypt (860s). After 850 the Abbasids began to find themselves virtual captives of their Turkish troops, a process that reduced the office of caliph to a façade behind which Turkish generals held the real power. In 909 the Fatimids, a Shiite dynasty, took over control of North Africa; in 969 the Fatimids conquered Egypt and Palestine.[16] By the end of the tenth century, the Islamic realm was divided into a number of smaller states, frequently at war with each other; nevertheless, there was an active exchange of goods and ideas through the

Synagogue of Samuel Halevy in Toledo, now called El Transito, built in 1366. (Courtesy of the Spanish Government Tourist Office.)

whole area and beyond to India and China. As mentioned earlier, this far-flung mercantile network was open to Christians and Jews between the ninth and the twelfth centuries. A growing middle class of Jewish traders, small manufacturers, bankers, physicians, and scholars provided a stimulating social setting for new tendencies that were arising in Jewish intellectual culture.

With the breakup of the political unity of Islam there occurred a decentralization of rabbinic Judaism as well. The geonic yeshivot of Iraq faded to local significance. In many areas new yeshivot were established, in which the text of the Talmud was studied and analyzed together with the responsa and other halakhic sources. (For the first time in the tenth century copies of the Talmud were becoming available outside the Babylonian yeshivot.) The formation of new yeshivot meant that Jewish law became a cooperative endeavor of jurists whose personal standing was based on their individual reputation for learning and intellectual acumen, rather than on their position as heads of the academies of Sura or Pumbeditha. The Jewish scholar class was now drawn from an enlarged social and geographical base. And the interests of the Mediterranean Jewish intellectual were broadening to include natural science, philosophy, philology, and poetry. The expansion of the horizons of Jewish learning in these areas began in Iraq, but it had its greatest impact in the diaspora to the west.

The first region outside Iraq where the local rabbinate began to assert itself was Palestine. Despite the persecution of Jews in the Christian Roman empire in the fifth and sixth centuries, there remained a rabbinic academy in the city of Tiberias when the Muslims conquered the Galilee. Tiberias was also the main center of the Masoretes, scholars who established the standard tradition (*Masorah*) of vocalizing and punctuating the Hebrew text of the Bible.[17] By the ninth century the rabbinical academy of Tiberias moved south to Ramleh, then the administrative center of Palestine, and from Ramleh to Jerusalem. Although unable to regain its ascendancy over the Babylonian institutions, the Jerusalem rabbinical academy was supported by the Jews of Egypt, Yemen, and Syria during the period when the Fatimid dynasty ruled Egypt and Palestine. It declined only when the security of Jewish life in the holy land was undermined by the disasters of the eleventh century brought about by Turkish and Christian invasions.

Egyptian Jewry was also restored to an intellectual and economic vitality it had not enjoyed for almost a thousand years. Born and brought up in Egypt was the outstanding rabbinic and philosophical figure of the tenth century, Saadiah ben Joseph al-Fayyumi. (His career and ideas will be described in the next chapter.) Saadiah was an energetic opponent of Karaism and a loyal defender of the Babylonian yeshivot over the Palestinian; he became the first gaon of a Babylonian yeshivah brought from the outside, rather than appointed from the local families who dominated these institutions. Except for one period of persecution, Jewish life thrived in Egypt under the Fatimids. By the end of the tenth century a rabbinic yeshivah had been founded in Fostat (old Cairo); in Fostat, in Alexandria, and in other Egyptian towns additional synagogues had been established by Jewish immigrants from Palestine and Babylonia, as well as by Karaites.[18]

By the tenth century the city of Kairouan (in modern Tunisia) had become an important home for Jewish learning and economic activity. During the great age of Kairouan Jewry, academies were established by important talmudists, and prosperous Jewish merchant families supported Jewish scientists and philosophers. In what is now Morocco, the city of Fez became a center of Jewish scholarship. In Fez resided one of the most influential talmudists of the West, Isaac Alfasi (1013–1103), whose digest of talmudic law became a classic of early post-geonic rabbinical scholarship. Alfasi left Fez in 1088 to settle in Muslim Spain, symptomatic of the migration of the Jewish intellectual elite to what was to become the most brilliant center of Jewish culture in the Muslim Middle Ages.

There had already been a sizable Jewish community in the Iberian peninsula during the late Roman empire. In the seventh century, however, when the Germanic Visigoths ruled Spain, some of the Visigothic kings and the Catholic hierarchy carried out a brutal though intermittent persecution of Jews. The situation of the Spanish Jews was greatly improved after the area was conquered by an Arab-Berber army between 711 and 715. In the next three hundred years Spanish Jewry was augmented by immigrants from the Middle East and North Africa, so that it became the most populous Jewish settlement outside of Babylonia. (In medieval Hebrew, Spain was known as *Sepharad* [from Obad. 1:20], and the Spanish Jews as *Sephardim*.) Jews not only spread throughout Muslim Spain, but began to settle in the small Christian kingdoms of northern Spain. The Jews in Spain, as elsewhere in Islam, were active in most branches of trade and industry, but the Spanish Jews retained for a long time a position as landowners and farmers as well.

Muslim authorities in Spain ruled a heterogeneous population, which included Berbers, Arabs, and Christians; the Jews were considered a useful and especially loyal sector of the population. The greatest Ummayad caliphs of Spain, Abd al-Rahman III (912–961) and Hakam II (961–972), employed Hisdai ibn Shaprut (915–c. 970) as court physician, administrator of the department of customs, and diplomat. Hisdai ibn Shaprut was also the official head of the Jewish community and a generous patron of Jewish writers and scholars. The capital of the Ummayad caliphate, Cordova, became a thriving and sophisticated center of Muslim and Jewish civilizations, one of the great urban centers of the Western world at that time. An important yeshivah was established there, and Hebrew grammarians and poets were attracted to Cordova, where they set the stage for what has been called the Golden Age of medieval Jewish literature.

In the early eleventh century, however, the Ummayad caliphate in Spain began to fall apart, recapitulating on a smaller scale what had earlier happened to the Abbasid realm. In its place arose many small Muslim principalities, often at war with each other. A number of these "petty kings" also employed Jewish courtiers in their administrations. The most famous of this generation was Samuel ibn Nagrela of Granada (c. 993–1056), hailed (especially by the poets and writers he financially supported) as dignified, cultivated, and courageous—the epitome of the Sephardic ideal of a harmonious synthesis of secular and religious pursuits. Samuel ha-Nagid (he was the first to be known by the Hebrew title *nagid*, "prince," which was soon to be widely used by the leaders of the regional Jewries of the Muslim world) knew mathematics and philosophy, possessed a fluent literary style in Arabic and Hebrew, and was an energetic and adroit statesman. For thirty years he served as vizier (prime minister) of Granada and led its armies on the battlefield. He composed distinguished Hebrew poetry, some in commemoration of his military victories, and wrote an introduction to the Talmud. He was only one, though the most versatile, of many courtiers, writers, and scholars who resided in Seville, Saragossa, Cordova, Toledo, Calatayud, and other Spanish cities. The town of Lucena, not far from Cordova in the rich agricultural district of Andalus (Muslim Spain is sometimes referred to as Andalusia), became famed for its talmudic academy, where the elderly Isaac Alfasi from Morocco trained a group of disciples who were among the most eminent Spanish halakhists. By the mid-eleventh century, therefore, Sephardic Jewry had come out of its cultural isolation and intellectual dependence on the East to produce a broad stratum of men who emulated the model of Samuel ibn Nagrela, combining an appreciation of general culture, natural science, and literary elegance with refined taste in secular and religious poetry, fidelity to rabbinic Judaism, and lively interest in Jewish theology and philosophy.

In 1086 the security of Jewish life in Muslim Spain was shaken when the Almoravides, fanatics from North Africa, were invited to Spain to lead a counteroffensive against the Christian kingdoms of the north. (The Christians had just captured the important city of Toledo in the central part of the country.) The Almoravide ruler purged the Jews from the state administration and extorted a heavy fine from the Jews of Lucena for daring to remain Jewish in the face of certain Muslim predictions. But soon a favorable state of affairs was restored. The next generation produced other outstanding Sephardic poets, philosophers, biblical commentators, theologians, and talmudic scholars. The first part

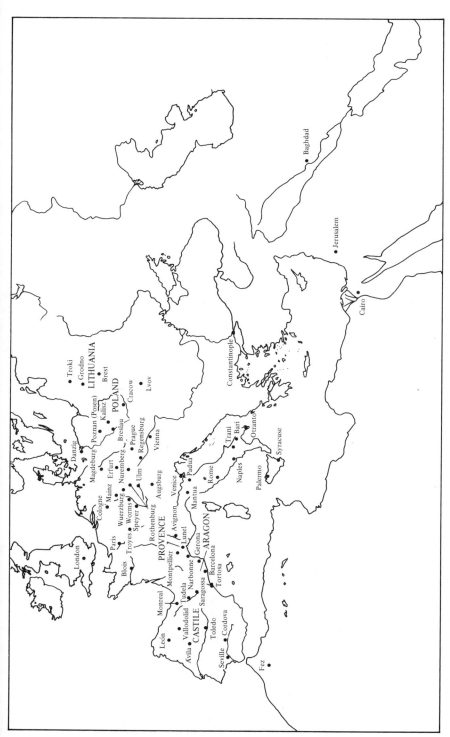

Important Jewish Centers from the Eleventh to the Mid-Fifteenth Centuries. During this period the majority of Jews lived in Europe. The Jewish population of northern Spain, southern France, and northern Italy expanded; the Jewish population of southern Italy, North Africa, and the Middle East declined. Jews were expelled from England in 1290, from France in 1394, from Spain in 1492, and from Portugal in 1497. In the fourteenth and fifteenth centuries, Ashkenazic Jews moved eastward to Poland-Lithuania in increasing numbers.

of the twelfth century was the climax of the Golden Age of Andalusian Jewry.[19]

In 1146 this remarkable epoch came to an end. Threat of Christian conquest once again brought into Spain zealous Muslim troops from North Africa, this time the Almohades, a Berber dynasty of Morocco. In their realm the Almohades launched one of the most uncompromising persecutions of Christians and Jews in the history of medieval Islam. Synagogues and academies were closed, and Jews were forcibly converted to Islam. Some continued to practice Judaism secretly; others fled to the Middle East; large numbers migrated to Christian Spain where they were welcomed as valuable settlers. When the Almohades were pushed out of Spain about a half century later, the balance of power had swung decisively to the Christian side. After a victory at Los Navas de Toloso (1212), the Christian kingdoms were in control of the greater part of the former Muslim territories in Spain, leaving only Granada in the hands of a Muslim dynasty. The continuation of Spanish Jewish history takes place under Christendom.

Jewish Life in Muslim Lands in the Late Middle Ages

Eventually every Jewry under Muslim rule found itself facing difficult and inhospitable circumstances in the twelfth or thirteenth centuries. The Muslim states became military despotisms. The Italian cities of Pisa, Genoa, and Venice took over most of the Mediterranean trade, leading to the decline of the international mercantile class in Muslim lands. Religious minorities were increasingly subject to the full pressure of the degrading provisions of the Pact of Omar. To be sure, there were a few exceptions: When the Almohades were finally overthrown in western North Africa, the Jewish communities were able to come out in the open. Although the bulk of Jews there were impoverished, some prosperous North African Jewish merchant families participated in the Saharan gold trade and maintained close economic ties with the kingdom of Aragon in Spain. In the mid-twelfth century during the Almohade persecutions, Sephardic Jews settled in Egypt, the most eminent being the greatest medieval Jewish philosopher, Moses Maimonides, and the generally good situation of the Egyptian Jews lasted another century. Jewish life in Palestine diminished during the crusades, but small communities did survive, augmented by a steady stream of Jewish pilgrims to the holy land. Iraqi Jewry maintained traces of its former glory even after the death of the last important gaon, Hai bar Sherira, in 1038. But the destructive Mongol invasions of the Middle East around 1258 were a devastating blow to the region as a whole, even though the Mongol armies were stopped in Palestine in 1260. Egypt, Syria, and Palestine fell under the control of the Mamelukes, a Turkish military caste in-

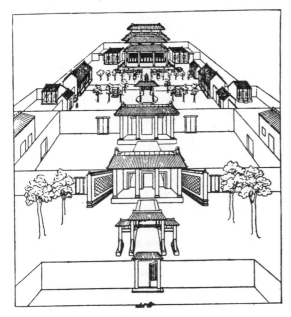

The synagogue of Kaifeng, China, a community founded in the ninth or tenth century, from a drawing by an eighteenth-century Jesuit missionary.

tolerant of Christians and Jews. Jewish life continued in Egypt, Yemen, Persia, and elsewhere; and pockets of Jews survived in the Caucasus, central Asia, India, and China—but the opportunities for sustained intellectual growth were limited.[20] Only in the sixteenth century was eastern Jewry to re-emerge, taking a leading part in the history of Jewish thought again.

A Chinese Jew, from the **Illustrated London News,** 1851.

The Jews in Medieval Christian Europe

Mediterranean Jewries Under Christian Rule

The heartland of the Byzantine empire did not fall to the Arabs in the seventh century, nor did the Muslim armies in Spain succeed in conquering France and Italy. The Jewries of these lands remained under Christian rule throughout the Middle Ages. For the Jews in the cities of the Byzantine empire (Asia Minor, Greece, southern Italy), occasional periods of persecution and forced conversion alternated with periods of relative prosperity and security. (An example of the latter was the first part of the eleventh century, when the Byzantine empire had some military successes.) On the whole, the Byzantine Jews in Greece and Asia Minor did not live under conditions conducive to exceptional Jewish intellectual creativity, and they did not produce scholars and philosophers who exerted an impact on Jewish thought elsewhere in the Middle Ages.

The situation in southern Italy and Sicily was different. There, the Jews of such cities as Bari, Otranto, Oria, Venosa, and Brindisi maintained close economic ties with Arab lands and were an important channel for the transplantation of Jewish learning to Christian Europe farther north, including elements of old Palestinian Jewish culture that had been submerged by that of the Babylonian Jews. Hebrew books were composed in southern Italy from the ninth century on,[21] rabbinic writings flourished, and Jews were active in the cosmopolitan scientific and philosophical circles that made this region important in European intellectual history under Byzantine, Norman, German, and French rulers through the thirteenth century. The Jewry of Rome, which has had a continuous history from the first century BCE down to the present, also became a center of rabbinic studies in the eleventh century.[22] In the Middle Ages, only a small number of Jews lived in northern Italy until about 1300, but southern France (the area known as Provence, which included Languedoc and northern Catalonia) contained old Jewish settlements that were to play an important role in Jewish cultural life after the decline of Muslim Spain.

It was common for an area of the Jewish diaspora of the Middle Ages to have its own liturgical rite and sometimes its own distinct Jewish dialect of the local language. The best known of these regional Jewries were Spain (the Sephardim), southern France (Provençal Jews), Italy (the Italyani), Greece (the Romaniyots), North Africa and the Middle East (Arabic-speaking Jews sometimes called Musta'rabim), Iran (Judeo-Persian and, in the eastern Caucasus, Judeo-Tat). North of the Alps a new branch of Jewish culture was forming in the late eighth century—one that was to develop unique features and have far-ranging influence in Jewish history: the Ashkenazic Jewry of Germany and northern France.

The Rise of Ashkenazic Jewry

The development of Ashkenazic Jewry took place in the special circumstances of early medieval Christendom in Western Europe. (The place name *Ashkenaz*, applied by the Jews in the Middle Ages to northern France and western Germany, is from Gen. 10:3.) After the Germanic invasions that brought an end to the Western Roman empire, city life dwindled almost to a vanishing point and central government was ineffectual. The devolution of political power into the hands of local lords was reversed, for a time, by a powerful monarchy brought into being by the early Carolingian rulers of France—especially by Charlemagne (742–814), who revived the imperial Roman title in the West and amassed a considerable empire extending into central Europe. But a half century after Charlemagne's death, the Carolingian realm broke up into three kingdoms, which in turn were further fragmented, so that early Ashkenazic Jews were faced with a society almost completely agrarian and increasingly feudal.

Jewish merchants in northern France and the Rhineland in the Carolingian period were economic pioneers, treated well because of their trading connections with the Mediterranean and the East. A testimonial to their far-flung activities has been preserved in the descriptions by

Representation of Charlemagne, from a manuscript of the Song of Roland. During his reign Jewish merchants began to play an important role in the economy of northern Europe.

tenth-century Arab geographers of Jewish merchant groups called Radanites. (The etymology of the word is obscure.) From their headquarters in France the Radanites crossed sparsely settled eastern Europe, passing through the steppes of what would later be Russia, in order to reach the Middle East (an alternate route was across the Mediterranean and North Africa), and from there visited India and China. Perhaps one of these enterprising businessmen was a certain Isaac the Jew, sent by Charlemagne with a deputation to the Abbasid caliph. (Several years later Isaac brought back an elephant as a gift from the caliph to Charlemagne.) Charlemagne's son, Louis the Pious (778–840), placed the economic endeavors and property of the Jewish traders under royal protection, ignoring the criticism of Agobard, bishop of Lyons, who wrote several attacks on the Jews. In the tenth and eleventh centuries Jewish merchants were on excellent terms with kings and barons in northern France and Germany. Although the share of the Ashkenazic Jews in international trade declined toward the end of this period, their activities in regional and local trade continued. Jewish communities soon appeared in many growing urban centers, such as the county of Champagne (Troyes and other cities) and along the Rhine River (Mainz, Worms, Speyer, Cologne). In 1084 the bishop of Speyer issued the following proclamation:

> In the name of the holy and indivisible Trinity, when I, Rüdiger, also called Huozmann, Bishop of Speyer, changed the town of Speyer into a city, I thought that I would add to the honor of our place by bringing in Jews. Accordingly, I located them outside of the community and habitation of the other citizens, and that they might not readily be disturbed by the insolence of the populace, I surrounded them with a wall. Their place of habitation I had acquired in a just manner, the hill partly with money, partly by exchange; the valley I had received from [some] heirs as a gift. That place, I say, I gave over to them on the condition that they would pay three pounds and a half of the money of Speyer annually for the use of the [monastery] brothers. Within their dwelling place and outside thereof, up to the harbor of the ships, and in the harbor itself, I granted them full permission to change gold and silver, to buy and sell anything they pleased, and that same permission I gave them throughout the state. In addition, I gave them out of the property of the church a burial place with hereditary rights. I also granted the following rights: If any stranger Jew lodge with them (temporarily), he shall be free from tax. Further, just as the city governor adjudicates between the citizens, so the head synagogue officer is to decide every case that may arise between Jews or against them. But if, by chance, he cannot decide, the case shall be brought before the bishop and his chamberlains. Night watches, guards, fortifications, they shall provide only for their own district, the guards, indeed, in common with the servants. Nurses and servants they shall be permitted to have from among us. Slaughtered meat which, according to their law, they are not permitted to eat,

they can sell to Christians, and Christians may buy it. Finally, as the crowning mark of kindness, I have given them laws better than the Jewish people has in any city of the German empire.

Lest any of my successors diminish this favor and privilege, or force them to pay greater tribute, on the plea that they acquired their favorable status unjustly, and did not receive it from a bishop, I have left this document as a testimony of the above-mentioned favors. And that the remembrance of this matter may last through the centuries, I have corroborated it under my hand and seal, as may be seen below.[23]

The early Ashkenazic Jewish communities were small and homogeneous. Jewish craftsmen and artisans, a widespread segment of Mediterranean Jewry, did not emigrate to northern Europe; moreover, once the system of Christian artisan guilds was established, Jews were effectively barred from these occupations. Besides trade, another occupation held by Jews was the growing of grapes and making of wine (a necessity for Jewish ritual); Jewish ownership of vineyards was common in France. The Ashkenazic Jews were not trained in the military skills of the feudal nobility; however, they carried arms and knew how to use them in defense. The Jews of each town constituted an independent, self-governing, sociolegal entity. (The term *kahal* or *kehillah*, which designates the community as a whole, is also used for the elected board that ran the affairs of the community.) Unlike the Jewries of Muslim lands, the Ashkenazic *kehillot* had no professional bureaucracy and no equivalent of an exilarch or *nagid* appointed or confirmed by the government to serve as their official leader: Each Ashkenazic kahal established its own special regulations (*takkanot*) and jealously guarded its prerogatives—even against Jews of nearby cities. The judicial court of each kahal retained the rights accorded the ancient Sanhedrin and the high courts of the exilarchs and geonate in Babylonia; the local kahal courts enforced their jurisdiction and rulings through the threat of excommunication (*herem*), which would, if carried out, effectively deprive the Jew of social intercourse with his coreligionists. The kahal system of Jewish self-government was the Ashkenazic adaptation to the decentralized power structure of feudal society.

Among the early Ashkenazim, biblical and talmudic studies were pursued with exceptional intensity. Flourishing centers of rabbinic scholarship appear in the tenth century in the Rhineland cities of Mainz and Worms, and soon afterwards in northern France at Troyes and Sens. At first, Ashkenazic scholarship was confined mainly to oral discussion. The most famous of the early teachers was Rabbenu Gershom of Mainz "the Light of the Exile"; among his *takkanot* and legal opinions that have survived in the responsa literature is the responsum definitively prohibiting polygamy among Ashkenazic Jews.

"Rashi Chapel" of the synagogue of Worms; a photograph taken before its destruction by the Nazis. (Photographic Archive of the Jewish Theological Seminary of America, New York, Frank J. Darmstaedter.)

Solomon ben Isaac of Troyes (1040–1105), known by his acronym as Rashi, was the first major literary figure of Ashkenazic Jewry—and one of the greatest. His commentaries on the Bible and Talmud became fundamental texts of Ashkenazic Jewish education. Although drawing on the midrashic literature, Rashi's exegesis of the Bible emphasizes his understanding of the plain meaning of the Scriptures, an effective presentation of the Jewish view of the Bible against the medieval Christian emphasis on allegory. (Later, some of Rashi's biblical interpretations were used by medieval Christian exegetes.) Rashi's Talmud commentary is a masterpiece of conciseness and clarity, opening up the extremely condensed talmudic text to the average Jewish youth attending one of the schools that had been established in most Ashkenazic communities.

In the next generations after Rashi, the analysis of talmudic law by the Ashkenazic Jews reached a height of intellectual subtlety and independence. Advanced talmudic scholars in northern France and in Germany (some were members of Rashi's family) introduced new deductive methods and critical insights into their analysis of talmudic argumentation and halakhah. The work of these men, the tosafists (from *Tosafot*, "additions," i.e., additional comments and elaborations on the Talmud), virtually constituted a new Franco-German Talmud created out of the text of the Babylonian Talmud. Ashkenazic Jews also composed religious poetry modeled on the *piyyutim* (liturgical poems, with elaborate allusions to the midrash) of fifth- and sixth-century Palestine.

The Ashkenazic ideal, with its emphasis on talmudic learning for every man, is quite in contrast with the Sephardic admiration for universal culture, the study of science and philosophy, and the writing of secular as well as religious Hebrew poetry patterned on Arabic literary forms. The difference between the two Jewries reflects their different environments: Muslim Spain at the height of its cultural splendor and feudal Europe just on the verge of intellectual renaissance. Indeed, the two Jewries had little contact at this time.

The First Crusade and Its Aftermath; The Negative Image of the Jew in Medieval Christendom

Although even during their period of greatest security, Ashkenazic Jews faced occasional difficulties from fanatic churchmen and brutal lords, mob violence against them erupted only at the end of the eleventh century. In November 1095, Pope Urban II proclaimed the First Crusade at Clermont in southeastern France and triggered a widespread exultation, especially among the knights of northern France, for the salvation and booty that would be the reward of those who participated in reconquering the holy land from the Turks. Even before the official Christian armies assembled, gangs of would-be crusaders set out through the Rhineland, attacking such unbelievers as were to be found there. In the late spring and summer of 1096, the Jewries of one city after another were besieged, pillaged, and slaughtered, unless they would consent to baptism. (That baptism could save their lives is an indication that they were perceived as religious enemies and not as aliens.) Where local bishops acted quickly and effectively (e.g., in Speyer) the Jews survived. In some places, even though the Jews defended themselves, crusaders and locals exterminated most of the Jewish community (Worms, Mainz). The supercharged religious atmosphere had its parallel among the Ashkenazic Jews, many of whom were eager to die as martyrs for the sake of God (an act called *kiddush ha-Shem*, sanctification of the divine name), rather than save their lives and property by conversion. (Out of this emotional crucible came an Ashkenazic pietism that will be described in Chapter 9.)

The massacres of 1096, though they revealed the vulnerability of Jews in the Christian environment, did not result in a change in the propitious Jewish legal status. The violence had not been instigated by the authorities and was not condoned by the emperor (Henry IV). Jews who had converted to Christianity under duress were permitted to return to Judaism. In 1103 the emperor took the step of extending to Jews

the protections accorded to the clergy. Attacks on them were answerable
to the emperor, although this meant that Jews, like priests, did not have
the right to carry weapons, and that they became even more dependent
on the good graces of individual rulers.

In the twelfth and thirteenth centuries, there occurred an important
shift in the economic activities of the Ashkenazic Jews—into moneylending. The move into moneylending by many of the Jews of Germany,
northern France, and England (the settlement of French Jews in England
occurs in the wake of the Norman conquest of 1066) was a result of the
growing monopoly of Christian merchant guilds, which forced Jews out
of trade, and also a result of the great demand for loans accompanying
the rise of a money economy in Western Europe. Jews were never the
only moneylenders in Europe; there were groups of Christians in this
occupation too, such as the Lombards (as the northern Christians called
the Italian bankers), the Cahorsins from southern France, and the clerical
order of the Templars. But the Jews had the advantage of standing outside
the legal jurisdiction and control of the Church at a time when the
Church was opposed to the making of profits on loans.[24] There was
great competition for loans from Jews, one of the few groups that had
liquid assets, amassed when they were merchants. The efforts of the
Church to abolish usury could not touch the Jews as long as they were
supported by the barons and the kings. Indeed, the secular rulers became
silent partners in the business of moneylending, taking their share of the
profits in the form of various regular taxes and extraordinary exactions.

Thirteenth-century Altneuschul in Prague, oldest extant synagogue building in Europe after World War II. (Courtesy of Zionist Archives, New York.)

Nevertheless, moneylending did not increase the popularity of the Jews in Europe, especially among those who could not pay back the loans with accumulated interest, and it made them more vulnerable in the long run.

Economic motives can be detected in the persecution of Jews in the later Middle Ages, but there was always the religious factor: For some Christians the mere physical presence of Judaism posed a subtle but dangerous threat to the spiritual health of society. The anti-Judaism of Christian Europe, which became more evident in the twelfth and thirteenth centuries, functioned on two levels: popular superstition and official Church doctrine. On the popular level was the stereotype of the Jew as a deliberate disbeliever with demonic qualities. First appearing in the English town of Norwich in 1144 was the accusation that the Jews murdered Christian children at Passover to use their blood for making matzah. This "blood libel" crops up repeatedly in European history, down to the twentieth century. Important early blood libels occurred in the French city of Blois in 1171 and in the English city of Lincoln in 1255. Echoes of the legend of Hugh of Lincoln are found more than a century later in Chaucer's *Canterbury Tales*. In "The Prioress's Tale" Chaucer depicts the Jews as being infuriated by a young Christian, who wanders through their quarter singing a Christian hymn:

> *The Serpent, our first foe, who has his nest*
> *Of hornets in Jews' hearts, puffed up and said,*
> *"O Hebrew people, is it for the best*
> *That a mere boy, just as he likes, should tread*
> *Your street, and bring contempt upon your head,*
> *And sing to such a purpose, for a cause*
> *That is against the reverence of your laws?"* . . .
> *From this time on the cursed Jews conspired*
> *This innocent boy out of the world to chase.*
> *A murderer for their purposes they hired*
> *Who in an alley had a secret place,*
> *And as he went by at his childish pace,*
> *This Jew seized on him, and held him fast, and slit*
> *His neck, and threw his body in a pit.*
> *Into a privy they threw the boy, I say,*
> *A place in which these Jews purged their entrails.*
> *O cursed people, unchanged since Herod's day,*
> *What think you that your foul design avails?*

When, through a miracle, the supposed crime is revealed,

> *The magistrate at once put every Jew*
> *To death with torment and with shamefulness.*[25]

In most cases the rumor of the murder by Jews of a Christian child was accompanied by the expropriation of Jewish property, the rumor often being spread by those who wanted the property. Another important element of the anti-Jewish folklore of Christian Europe that appeared about the same time was the accusation that the Jews conspired to steal and pierce the wafer of the Host in order to torture the body of Jesus.[26]

The blood libel and host desecration myths never received backing from the popes, who from time to time were persuaded to deny publicly the veracity of these charges. The official anti-Jewish ideology was concerned with the discrepancy between the Jews' prosperity and the lowly status it was felt they should occupy. The most important pope to take a stand critical of Jewish moneylending was Innocent III (pope between 1198 and 1216). In a letter to the King of France in 1205 he wrote:

> Though it does not displease God, but is even acceptable to Him, that the Jewish Dispersion should live and serve under Catholic kings and Christian princes until such times as their remnant shall be saved, . . . nevertheless, such [princes] are exceedingly offensive to the sight of the Divine Majesty who prefer the sons of the crucifiers, against whom to this day the blood cries to the Father's ears, to the heirs of the Crucified Christ. . . . . Know

Pope Innocent III, one of the most powerful popes of the Middle Ages and major proponent of restrictions on Jewish status. From a later engraving.

then that the news has reached us to the effect that in the French kingdom the Jews have become so insolent that by means of their vicious usury, through which they extort not only usury but even usury on usury, they appropriate ecclesiastical goods and Christian possessions. Thus seems to be fulfilled among the Christians that which the prophet bewailed in the case of Jews, saying "Our heritage has been turned over to strangers, our houses to outsiders." Moreover, although it was enacted in the Lateran Council that Jews are not permitted to have Christian servants in their homes either under pretext of rearing their children, nor for domestic service, nor for any other reasons whatever, but that those who presume to live with them shall be excommunicate, yet they do not hesitate to have Christian servants and nurses, with whom, at times, they work such abominations as are more fitting that you should punish than proper that we should specify.

Moreover, although the same Council decided to admit Christian evidence against Jews in law-suits that arise between the two, since they use Jewish witnesses against Christians, and although it decreed that whoever preferred the Jews to the Christians in this matter should be anathematized, yet they have to this day been given the preference in the French realm to such an extent that Christian witnesses are not believed against them, while they are admitted to testimony against Christians. Thus, if the Christians to whom they have loaned money on usury, bring Christian witnesses about the facts in the case, [the Jews] are given more credence because of the document which the indiscreet debtor had left with them through negligence or carelessness, than are the Christians through the witnesses produced. . . .[27]

Church property was falling into Jewish hands as collateral for defaulted loans, and the Church was losing its tithes. All this was, in Innocent III's view, contrary to Christianity's conception of the proper place of the Jewish people. The doctrine that Innocent III set out to enforce was that Jews have a right to survive, but only in perpetual servitude:

The Lord made Cain a wanderer and a fugitive over the earth, but set a mark upon him, . . . lest any finding him should slay him. Thus the Jews, against whom the blood of Jesus Christ calls out, although they ought not to be killed, lest the Christian people forget the Divine Law, yet as wanderers ought they to remain upon the earth, until their countenance be filled with shame and they seek the name of Jesus Christ, the Lord. That is why blasphemers of the Christian name ought not to be aided by Christian princes to oppress the servants of the Lord, but ought rather be forced into the servitude of which they made themselves deserving when they raised sacrilegious hands against Him Who had come to confer true liberty upon them, thus calling down His blood upon themselves and upon their children.[28]

Innocent III's Jewish policy was also related to his efforts to establish his authority over the secular rulers of Europe and to extirpate Christian heresy, especially in southern France. (On the crusade he proclaimed against the Christian Albigensians of southern France, see Chap. 8.) The Fourth Lateran Council, convened by him in 1215, attempting to enforce discipline on Christendom, reaffirmed and strengthened the Church's regulations concerning the Jews, some of which went back to Roman law and to the epistles of Pope Gregory I (590–604). Not only should Jews not employ Christian servants and should Jewish usury be combated, but Jews should be distinguished by a special badge or dress from the Christians. (This measure was borrowed from the Islamic Pact of Omar; the need for a special badge acknowledges that the Jews could not at that time be distinguished by their dress or appearance from Christians.) These regulations were not immediately enforced in most Christian lands, but in the long run they contributed to the decline in Jewish status.

Also in the early thirteenth century, as part of the campaign against heresy, two new preaching orders of the Church were established, the Dominicans and the Franciscans. The Dominicans were especially active against the Jews. In 1240 they participated in a public disputation with Jews in Paris, ordered by the king of France and supported by the pope, which resulted in a decision to burn the Talmud, its being considered the main cause of the Jews' refusal to accept Christian truth and a work that contained slanders of the Christian religion. (The ensuing massive destruction of talmudic manuscripts dealt a serious blow to Jewish scholarship in France.) Soon afterwards, another disputation was arranged by Dominican friars in Barcelona (1263) where they attempted to prove the opposite: that rabbinic lore actually supported the Christian conception of the Messiah. Political conditions in Spain at that time were not favorable to degrading the Jews and the Dominican efforts did not result in a general persecution. The practical consequences of the negative image of the Jews and Judaism throughout Christian Europe depended on local conditions.

Expulsions and Massacres

In 1182 Philip Augustus, king of France, expelled all Jews from the royal domains (then confined to the areas around Paris), confiscated their property, and declared Christian debts to Jews canceled, except for a fifth to be paid to the royal treasury. In 1198 the Jews were recalled, and an additional royal tax imposed on their activities. In the following century French Jews were increasingly considered property of the king rather than free men.

In the thirteenth century the English kings compensated for the deficits in the royal treasury by continually increasing taxes on the Jews. When Italian banking firms began supplying the king with adequate funds at the end of the century, the first mass expulsion of Jews from

Jewish moneylender and German peasant, from a sixteenth-century woodcut.

a whole country was feasible. In 1290 all Jews were ordered to leave England, their dwellings and capital reverting to the king. Most went to France.

By this time the situation of French Jewry was ominous. Louis IX (Saint Louis, who reigned 1226–1270) had conducted a campaign against usury, liberating his subjects from part of their debts to their Jewish creditors. Toward the end of the century Philip IV (the Fair, reigned 1285–1314), who had brought vast additional territories under royal control, lent his support to several events designed to strengthen popular animosity against Jews: a ritual murder trial at Troyes in 1288, a host desecration trial at Paris in 1290. In 1306 an edict of expulsion was issued, the French treasury taking over all debts owed the Jews.[29]

The situation in Germany was more complex. Throughout most of the thirteenth century Jews continued to establish new communities and remained a valuable source of imperial revenue. In Bohemia, Austria, Hungary, and other areas of East Central Europe they received charters protecting their lives, property, and freedom of movement. (The Austrian charter of 1244 was a model for those issued elsewhere.) Only at the end of the century did outbursts of violence against the Jews become frequent there. The most eminent rabbi of the time, Meir of Rothenberg (c. 1215–1293, the last of the tosafists) was taken prisoner in 1286 while seeking to make a pilgrimage to the holy land. Outraged by an attempt to impose a special tax signifying that the Jews were the emperor's property, Meir refused to allow himself to be ransomed and died in prison. In 1298 plundering gangs marched from province to province in Germany, wiping out about 140 Jewish communities. After several decades of quiet, another wave of massacres broke out in 1336. In 1348–1349, during the Black Death (the bubonic plague, which some modern scholars hold may have killed more than a third of the population of Europe), it was widely believed that the Jews had poisoned the wells of Europe with a mixture of animal and human parts, and dough from the sacred Host. The butchery of Jews was unprecedented in its geographical extent and number of victims. Beginning in southern France in September 1348, the slaughter of Jews spread to Switzerland and western Germany. Temporarily dying down from March to July 1348, the persecutions flared up again in Belgium, northern Germany, and Bavaria

Woodcut showing Jews being burned alive during the Black Death persecutions of 1348–1349.

until late in 1349. The main instigators were often flagellants, wandering bands of religious fanatics who marched from place to place whipping and beating each other to atone for the sins of Christendom. Some outbursts can be attributed to local rulers who arranged in advance for a division of the Jewish property in anticipation of the massacres. The Ashkenazic Jews tried to defend themselves at times, but where they realized that this was impossible, they almost always preferred martyrdom to apostasy.[30]

The surviving Jews were never expelled from Germany in the Middle Ages, as they were in the West, because there was no central German authority that could have expelled them. In the fourteenth century the

German woodcut from 1493 of the Simon of Trent blood libel; Jews wear the circular badge required of them at the time.

Holy Roman emperor was becoming progressively weaker, and Germany was fragmented into dozens of principalities and independent cities. Jews who remained were always able to find some place to reside, despite continual expulsions throughout the latter half of the fourteenth and in the fifteenth centuries. Many localities expelled the Jews and then recalled them for a limited period of time, confining Jewish residence to a special district of the town. (Later the term *ghetto* is applied to these Jewish quarters.) The Jews were legally serfs of the royal exchequer (*servi camerae nostri*), that is, the property of the emperor or whatever agency to which the emperor ceded the right to control and tax them. German Jews continued to engage in moneylending (but only for small sums, the Italian and south German firms having taken over the major part of the banking business); Jews also engaged in petty trade in agricultural products and in used clothes. The greatest talmudic scholars moved to Poland or to Spain, so the thirteenth to fifteenth centuries were also a period of intellectual impoverishment for German Jews.

The expulsions and massacres of the Jews in the late Middle Ages were a symptom of Jewish vulnerability in an age of social breakdown, recurrent plague, protracted feudal wars, and economic stagnation. A brief description of these events as they affected Jewish history probably obscures the good relations that individual Jews had with non-Jews who considered them trustworthy businessmen. But the negative stereotype of the Jew, deeply rooted in European civilization, had its own momentum, remaining in the people's minds and folklore even when the Jews no longer lived there, and infecting countries where the Jews were still considered valuable subjects. The history of the Jews in Christian Spain was an epitome of this latter tendency, with features unique to Sephardic Jewry.

The Jews in Christian Spain

As a result of the reconquest of most of the Iberian peninsula, the Christian kingdoms of Spain (Castile, Aragon, Portugal) contained large numbers of Muslims and Jews. For almost two centuries the three religions lived side by side under Christian kings. Jewish life in Christian Spain reflected a mixture of features characteristic of the Jews in Muslim lands and in Christian feudal countries. Like most of the Jewries around the Mediterranean, the Sephardim had a wide range of occupations: shopkeepers, artisans (e.g., in textiles, metal work, leather goods), physicians, and only a small number of moneylenders. Spanish Jewry was far more numerous than the Ashkenazic Jews of any single country. (There were at least 200,000 Jews in Castile, Aragon, and Portugal.) It had a much broader range of social classes, ranging from poor and lower-middle-class Jews to a small but influential stratum of courtiers who participated

A fifteenth-century depiction of a host desecration accusation in Passau, ending with the torture and execution of Jews.

in the state administration as royal councilors and financial experts. In the thirteenth century, almost every Spanish king had several Jewish favorites, a policy dropped in fourteenth-century Aragon but continued in Castile. Because a Jew could not aspire to political power on his own, he was considered a particularly dependable royal adviser. Nevertheless, the rise and fall from favor of the Court Jews, as a result of changing whims and policies of a king, were frequently abrupt and dramatic. The Jewish courtiers' reputed inclination to luxurious living and irreligious behavior was often attacked by Jewish preachers.

The legal status of the Spanish Jewish communities was much closer to that of the kehillot of northern Europe than to the legal status of the Jewries under medieval Islam. The separate communities were each given charters (*fueros*), guaranteeing the economic rights of the members and the community's freedom to live according to custom and talmudic law. The *aljamas* (the term used for the Sephardic communities) were much larger in population than the northern kahals; they were virtually Spanish Jewish cities alongside and within the Christian cities, with their own bureaucracy, social services, educational institutions, and system of courts. During the thirteenth century there were many disputes within the aljamas over the representation on communal boards of the different classes of Jews, similar to the social conflict that often took place in the European cities of the Middle Ages. The relation of the Jewish courtiers to the aljamas was a particularly bitter issue.

The intellectual life of the Sephardic Jews was also a mixture of conflicting tendencies. As in Muslim Spain, a significant number of Spanish Jews studied the natural sciences, mathematics, and philosophy and made important contributions to geography, astronomy, and medicine. The thirteenth century was an age of intense cultural creativity, marked by the spread of a new form of speculative theology among Spanish Jews—the mystical tradition known as the Kabbalah. The presence of Ashkenazic Judaism was also felt in the thirteenth century: The greatest rabbis of the time, Moses ben Nahman (Nahmanides) and Solomon ibn Adret, both of Barcelona, were thoroughly acquainted with the tosafists of northern Europe and used their ideas in halakhic matters. In 1303 Asher ben Yehiel, a student of Meir of Rothenberg, fled from Germany to Spain, where he became a rabbi in Toledo. His son, Jacob ben Asher (c. 1270–1340), compiled one of the most influential codes of Jewish law, the *Arba'ah Turim* (*Four Rows*), summarizing the laws still practicable in the diaspora concerning Jewish rituals and ceremonies, family and civil matters, and religious prohibitions.

The thirteenth century in the north was a period when hatred and violence toward Jews were on the rise. (Asher ben Yehiel had come to Spain because it promised refuge from persecution.) On the whole, effective action by the kings of Castile and Aragon prevented the large-scale massacres of Jews that took place elsewhere during the Black Death. In the final stages of reconquering the Iberian peninsula from the Muslims, Spanish kings even gave large tracts of land to Jews to repopulate and develop. Only toward the end of the fourteenth century did the situation of the Spanish Jews noticeably deteriorate.

In the 1360s, the victor in a long military struggle for the throne of Castile (Henry of Trastamara) used anti-Jewish slogans to win support, although afterwards he continued the old policy of having Jewish advisers. Further political instability and weakness set the stage for widespread anti-Jewish violence in 1391. Encouraged by Jew-haters in the Church, mobs slaughtered Jewish communities in one city after another throughout Castile and Aragon. The massacres of 1391 were a symptom of a wave of social unrest in which Jews were the first and chief victims. When the rioters began to turn on Christians and their property as well, the authorities reimposed order as quickly as possible. The year 1391 was a turning point in the history of Spanish Jewry, for two reasons. First, tens of thousands of Jews, especially among the upper classes, converted to Christianity to save their lives and possessions. Second, the

Jews in court taking the special Jewish oath, from an early sixteenth-century engraving.

Spanish rulers, for the first time, introduced legislation degrading the Jews (the Castilian laws of 1412, which sought to isolate Jews socially and economically from Christians). The new policy was underlined by a public disputation (1413–1414) in the town of Tortosa, where Jewish leaders were forced to debate their doctrine of the Messiah. (The prosecution was led by a converted Jew, and the proceedings were given the

Scenes from the Spanish Inquisition: seizure of suspects, forms of torture, the condemned being led away to punishment.

blessing of one of the men competing for recognition as pope.) Another wave of conversion to Christianity resulted from pressure applied during the Tortosa dispute, so that when the quarter century of anti-Jewish pressure (1391–1415) finally subsided, there was a large population of former Jews in Spain (called "New Christians" or *Conversos*), perhaps equal in number to Jews who had refused to apostasize. The presence of these two groups, Conversos and Jews, shaped the course of Jewish history in Spain during the fifteenth century.

At first the Conversos found that their situation had been improved by baptism. Barriers against their participation in many aspects of Spanish life disappeared, and new opportunities opened up in city government, the state administration, and the Church. (Several Conversos and children of Conversos became important bishops and church officials who, in order to emphasize the sincerity of their Christian faith, were among the most outspoken enemies of Judaism in fifteenth-century Spain.) The Spanish nobility and even the royal family of Aragon eagerly sought to marry their offspring to children of wealthy Conversos. While the Conversos were seemingly being absorbed into Spanish society, the Jews were attempting to reconstruct their communities and educational institutions. *Aljamas* were re-established in some places (though not in the great centers, such as Toledo and Barcelona, where Jewish life had been totally destroyed), and new Jewish settlements were founded in many small towns of northern Castile.

In the mid-fifteenth century, a new wave of hostility surfaced. At first, popular hatred was directed mainly against Conversos conspicuous as tax collectors. (The first anti-Converso riot was in Toledo in 1449; in the succeeding decades these attacks became more common, culminating in an especially violent outburst in Cordova in 1473.) Attacks on the New Christians were rationalized by the accusation that they were Jews in disguise and practiced Jewish ceremonies secretly. The term *Marrano*, "swine," applied to the Conversos by their enemies, enters Jewish history at this time. Eventually *Marrano* loses its connotation of loathing and becomes a badge of honor among Jews.[31]

In 1469 Isabella, Queen of Castile, married Ferdinand, heir to the throne of Aragon; ten years later the two realms were joined into one Spanish kingdom. In 1480, Ferdinand and Isabella established the Spanish Inquisition to investigate the charges circulating against the Conversos. An inquisition was a religious court to root out heresy; although the Spanish Inquisition was officially under the jurisdiction of the pope, for all practical purposes it was controlled by the monarchy. In the first twenty years of a history that lasted almost three and a half centuries, the Spanish Inquisition claimed to have discovered several thousand secret Jews among the New Christians; their property was confiscated and they were condemned to various penances. Those who refused to repent were turned over to the secular authorities to be burned at the stake. In the late 1480s inquisitors using threats of torture extracted confessions concerning a blood libel (the case of the "infant of La Guardia"—although no corpse was ever discovered), which set the stage for the expulsion of Spanish Jewry. After Ferdinand and Isabella conquered Granada in 1492 (the last Muslim territory on the Iberian peninsula), they issued

Ferdinand and Isabella, the Spanish monarchs who expelled the Jews in 1492.

an edict making Judaism illegal in Spain. Supporters of this measure argued that the Conversos had to be quarantined against Judaism. Some Jews converted in order to avoid having to leave, but an estimated 100,000–150,000 Jews departed from Spain in the summer of 1492. Many went to Portugal, where despite royal promises, they were coerced into baptism five years later (1497). Others went to North Africa, Italy, and Ottoman Turkey.

By 1500 the greatest medieval European centers of Judaism had either been destroyed (England, France, Spain, Portugal) or much diminished (Germany). In Eastern Europe and in the eastern Mediterranean, however, Judaism was about to find new strength.

CHAPTER **8**

Medieval Jewish Theology and Philosophy

The Rise of Jewish Philosophy in the Middle Ages

Philosophy is the critical and methodical inquiry into the most general facts, causes, and principles of reality.[1] Philosophy relies on the power of logical consistency and intellectual discrimination, rather than on the authority of a received tradition or the immediate certainty of intuition. Nevertheless, philosophers inherit a body of beliefs about the universe and human life from the culture in which they are reared, from their inherited religious traditions, and from the previous stages of philosophical inquiry. And the philosophical issues and controversies of an age are shaped not only by the independent judgment of the philosopher himself, but by the general climate of opinion as well. Philosophy in the Middle Ages had a conception of its proper field of study that was at once broader and narrower than that of modern philosophy. Philosophical learning sought to integrate all the natural and moral sciences into one comprehensive system. (The word *science* originally included all knowledge acquired through disciplined study.) At the same time, medieval philosophy was called, in the Christian phrase, the handmaiden of theology, and theology in turn was called the queen of the sciences. (Theology refers to the rational clarification of religious beliefs and to a systematic presentation of the faith of a given religious tradition.) In the Middle Ages, philosophers touched on theological matters, and theologians on

Fifteenth-century German depiction of a disputation between Christians, on the left, and Jewish scholars in conical hats, on the right.

scientific ones. In the Islamic world, as we shall see, theology and philosophy do correspond to two distinct traditions: *Kalam*, a rational clarification of the authoritative revelation, and *Falasifa*, the exposition of the philosophical classics of ancient Greece. To some extent the difference between the two was carried over into medieval Jewish thought.

Jewish philosophy has been defined as "the thinking and rethinking of the fundamental ideas involved in Judaism and the attempt to see them fundamentally, that is, in coherent relation one with another so that they form one intelligible whole."[2] A religion like Judaism offers answers to such questions as the origin of the universe, the destiny of man, and the nature of right action—questions that philosophy also has posed. Philosophy demands that these ideas be treated with a concern for meticulous proof, for precise definition of concepts, for coherent processes of deduction—in short, according to the requirements of reason. Although the conception of reason differs from period to period, it has always involved the conviction that man's mind can trace out the logical implications of a combination of facts and suppositions, however they may have first come into human consciousness. Jewish philosophy is a gradual sifting and elucidation of those Jewish beliefs most amenable to rational interpretation. New points are raised, old difficulties removed, and the implications and significance of Judaism defined with greater clarity. But there is no final and perfect Jewish philosophy, because Judaism can be interpreted in the light of a variety of general systems; there are almost as many philosophies of Judaism as there are general philosophies.

Medieval Jewish philosophical literature first emerged when Judaism sought other intellectual tools besides a direct appeal to received tradition and talmudic hermeneutics to justify and strengthen loyalty to the Jewish religion among questioning members of the expanded Jewish middle class in the Islamic world—a middle class that was actively participating in general trade and commerce, and that, because it spoke Arabic, was absorbing the cultural riches, especially from ancient Greece, increasingly available in Arabic. A significant body of Jews were now becoming knowledgeable in sophisticated scientific and philosophical concepts and very much aware of the intellectual ferment going on outside Judaism. The beginnings of medieval Jewish philosophy reflect the heated religious controversy and discussion in ninth-century Iraq, during the height of the Abbasid caliphate, when rabbinical Judaism was challenged from several directions. First, some of the Karaites had taken an interest in philosophical concepts and had gone beyond attacking talmudic law to criticize anthropomorphic views of God in talmudic and midrashic literature. Not only did the Rabbanites have to defend the legitimacy of the rabbinic tradition against Karaism, but they had to show that these anthropomorphic expressions did not detract from the rationality of their concept of God. Second, Muslims asserted that Muhammad's revelation in the Koran had superseded Judaism. The question of which was the true revelation involved the reliability of all historical traditions: What criteria could be used to evaluate a revelation? For example, was it rational to conceive of God as having changed his mind by issuing different commands at different times or having abrogated one law by revealing another? Third, Zoroastrians and Manichaeans attacked the monotheistic faith that Judaism, Christianity, and Islam shared, pointing to the existence of evil as a disproof of a God who was both omnipotent and infinitely just. These dualists, who believed in both good and evil divine forces, criticized the biblical concept of God as contrary to reason and as ethically deficient. Fourth, there was the challenge to religion of the Greek scientific and philosophical world view, which explained the origin and structure of the universe without recourse to a supernatural, personal, creative God who guided history and revealed his word to prophets. In this view, why should it not be possible to rely exclusively on the human intellect to attain the truth, rather than acknowledge as true a prophetic revelation that took the form of specific laws and doctrines concerning the redemption and salvation of select individuals or peoples?

Several of the first Jewish philosophers were strongly influenced by the Muslim theology of the high caliphate: the Kalam. (The term *Kalam* comes from an Arabic word meaning "discussing"—i.e., discussing religious beliefs using rational criteria.) Among the various Kalam schools of the eighth to eleventh centuries, Jewish writers borrowed most from the Mutazilites. The Mutazilites believed that logically consistent belief was crucial in religious matters, that there was nothing in the Koran repugnant to human reason, and that the philosophical arguments and terminology of Greek philosophy could resolve difficulties arising from perplexing scriptural expressions concerning the nature of God and his relation to man. Particularly relevant to Judaism were two central theological concerns of the Mutazilites: the vindication of God's unity and his justice. Against the dualists the Mutazilites defended the existence of only one God. Equally important to them was the principle that no resemblance whatsoever existed between God and his creatures. Accordingly, all expressions that described God as though he resembled a human being were to be understood metaphorically, not literally, a position that raised the philosophical question: In what sense can attributes be ascribed to God at all? Although the Mutazilites acknowledged that God possesses life, power, and wisdom, they insisted that these attributes were not superadded to God's essence nor did they introduce multiplicity into his unity. How certain characteristics could be attributed to God in a logically coherent way, so as not to undermine the simplicity of his essence or imply that there is more than one eternal principle, remained a central theme of Jewish theology throughout the medieval period.

The Mutazilites' defense of God's justice entailed a rejection of the idea of predestination. Against the belief that God creates all human actions, even evil actions, the Mutazilites argued that if man is divinely rewarded or punished according to his deeds, it must be true that he has free will. It would be unjust of God to condemn or recompense man for something that man could not help doing. Reconciliation of human free will with divine omnipotence and omniscience also became a central concern of Jewish thought in the medieval period.

The Mutazilite Kalam was used by the Karaite philosophers in eleventh-century Jerusalem and by the rabbinic leadership in the Middle East and North Africa, including several of the most prominent geonim. We will describe the most outstanding Jewish theological work written in this tradition by Saadiah ben Joseph, the illustrious gaon of the yeshivah of Sura.

Saadiah Gaon

Saadiah ben Joseph (882–942) was born and educated in Egypt, but had a meteoric and turbulent career in Syria and Iraq. A champion of the rabbis against the Karaites and of the Babylonian institutions against the Palestinian, he was the first outsider to be appointed gaon of one of the prestigious yeshivot of Iraq—whereupon he became embroiled in a bitter power struggle with the exilarch that led to mutual excommunications and a disruption of the Babylonian leadership until just before Saadiah's death. Saadiah was a prolific author who made pioneering contributions to such fields as Hebrew philology, Jewish liturgy, and halakhah; he polemicized against the Karaites (and his rabbinical enemies); he translated most of the Bible into Arabic and commented on many of its books; and he produced the first major medieval Jewish theological treatise: the *Book of Beliefs and Opinions*.

The intense intellectual ferment of ninth and tenth-century Iraq stimulated and shaped Saadiah's treatise. Whereas previous rabbinic literature only briefly mentions pagan, Christian, or Jewish heretical opinions, Saadiah explicitly sets out to refute a wide variety of views held by Christians, Zoroastrians, and Muslims on the origins of the cosmos, the nature of the soul, and other theological topics. Inasmuch as defense of Jewish beliefs entails an appeal to reasonable arguments that all intelligent men should be able to accept, he prefaces his book with an introduction on the sources of truth and error, adapted from the Kalam. The three roots of human knowledge are sense experience, intuition of self-evident truths, and logical inference. A fourth, based on the first three, is "reliable tradition." Reliable tradition is a mainstay of all civilization and an indispensable aid to the reasoning process applied to religious matters. Why is reliable religious tradition, given man by God through prophetic revelation, necessary? Because speculation requires time and persistence. Doubt and bewilderment occur to the thinker, who may lack the ability or patience to finish his investigation adequately. Reliable tradition provides guidance and protection from the uncertainties of thought. And reliable tradition makes the truth available to everyone, including the vast majority who do not have the opportunity or training to philosophize. According to Saadiah, revealed religion has nothing to fear from philosophical inquiry. Its validity is not undermined by correct speculation, and its authority can only be enhanced by rational arguments. Like other medieval thinkers, Saadiah is not concerned with religion in general but with the truth of his religion: Only the Torah had a divine origin, being revealed by God to the prophets and passed on in its written and oral forms. (The principle that the Mosaic revelation was given

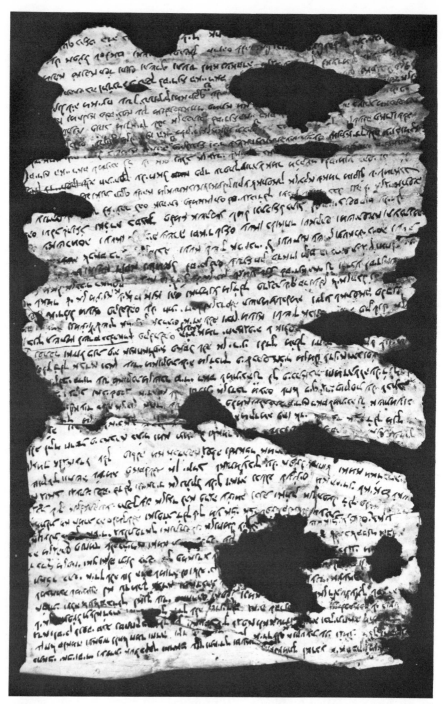

Parchment fragment from the Cairo Genizah, a storeroom of medieval documents in Hebrew script. (The Photographic Archive of the Jewish Theological Seminary of America, New York, Frank J. Darmstaedter.)

publicly in the presence of all of Israel, and not merely privately to a solitary prophet, was frequently used in defense of the Torah in the Middle Ages.) Even though he seeks to buttress the authority of the Jewish revelation, Saadiah's enthusiastic acceptance of the compatibility of reason and religion establishes the basis for the whole philosophical enterprise in medieval Judaism.

The main body of his treatise deals with the following topics: the existence and attributes of God; the rationale for the divine commandments and prohibitions; man's freedom to choose good and evil; the nature and destiny of the soul; messianic and eschatological expectations; human existence in the World to Come; the most satisfactory human life in This World.

Saadiah's strategy for demonstrating the Jewish doctrine of God is taken from the Mutazilite Kalam: We can prove that God exists because reason leads us to conclude that the cosmos had a starting point in time. The force that maintains everything is finite, which indicates the world has a beginning and an end in time; everything is composed of two or more elements, which indicates that the universe and its contents were skillfully put together at a point in time; all substances are bearers of "accidents"[3] that originate in time, which indicates that the whole cosmos must have originated in time. And time itself is only rational if one assumes a beginning, because from infinite past to the present cannot be traversed. Other arguments are brought to support his contentions that the universe could not have made itself, that it has a single, incorporeal[4] creator external to it, and that this being (God) created the universe out of nothing (the technical phrase being *creatio ex nihilo*).

The question of God's attributes arises in connection with God's unity. How can we assert that God necessarily possesses the attributes of life, power, and wisdom if God is a simple unity? Like the Mutazilites, Saadiah argues that if these three qualities are considered as separate from God's essence, a philosopher opens himself to the charge that God is a composite being, which Judaism rejects. His solution is that these attributes are implications of God as Creator and are thus identical with his essence: Only deficiencies of human language make it necessary to describe God with three different words. Like the Mutazilites, Saadiah insists that all biblical phrases describing God in human terms must be taken as metaphorical. If God is incorporeal, how is it that the prophets were able to envision God and hear his voice? The prophets saw a special Divine Glory and heard a special sound miraculously created for them by God, in order to verify that it was indeed a divine inspiration that they were experiencing.

Saadiah then turns to God's relation to the universe. Why did he create it? In order that his wisdom be manifested in its harmonious order, and so that his creatures could achieve happiness. Why did God not endow man with a blissful life, without imposing on him commandments and prohibitions? Because he who obtains reward as a result of his actions enjoys far greater satisfaction than he who receives happiness through divine grace only. The moral importance of having to work for one's salvation is a recurrent theme in Saadiah's philosophy.

The laws of the Torah are divided by Saadiah into two categories: those that can be discovered by reason, and those that are known only through revelation. Rational laws, such as the commands to express gratitude to the Creator and to refrain from harming other people, are included in the Torah not only for pedagogic purposes, but because abstract rational principles must be supplemented by specific details. Thus revelation enables man to have a code of law without waiting the lengthy time it would have taken to do this entirely through his own efforts. Revelational laws, such as the prohibition to eat certain foods and abstain from sexual intercourse at certain times, known only through authentic tradition and not through reason, also have a rational purpose in that they serve to promote the happiness that comes from obedience to God. In this context Saadiah explains the relation between miracles and reason:

> The reason for our belief in Moses lies not in wonders or miracles only, but the reason for our belief in him and all the other prophets lies in the fact that they admonished us in the first place to do what was right, and only after we heard the prophet's message and found it was right did we ask him to produce miracles in support of it. If he performed them we believed in him, but if we hear his call and at the onset found it to be wrong, we do not ask for miracles, for no miracle can prove the [rationally] impossible.[5]

Miracles strengthen faith, but faith does not rest on miracles.

Saadiah then proceeds to a defense of man's freedom of will: It would be a fatal contradiction if God were conceived as giving man commandments and prohibitions were He to have predetermined that man was compelled to act in a certain way. Like the Mutazilites, Saadiah insists that men are responsible for their actions; otherwise God's rewarding and punishing these actions would be unjust. The problem of reconciling man's freedom with God's foreknowledge was resolved by Saadiah with the principle that God knows in advance the outcome of man's deliberation, but that God's knowledge does not cause or determine the outcome of human free choice, because God's knowledge is totally different from man's.

In discussing Jewish beliefs on the afterlife Saadiah asks why it is that suffering befalls the pious and that good happens to the evil in this world. He summarizes the traditional solutions: The pious suffer as an immediate punishment for their small number of transgressions (the reverse being true of the wicked); the sufferings of the pious are a purification and a test, which God knows that they can endure; for some, suffering leads to a bliss that is all the greater because it is a reward rather than a gift. Because there is admittedly more suffering than happiness in life, the affirmation of divine justice requires that the soul be immortal so that misery and pain in this world can be compensated by bliss in the hereafter. According to Saadiah, the soul is a pure, luminous substance that can act only through the body. The body as such is not impure: God will resurrect the body together with the soul, so the whole person can enjoy the World to Come. (Saadiah argues: if one believes that it is reasonable that God created the world *ex nihilo*, then there should be no difficulty in believing that God can re-create the bodies of the dead.) The final phases of human existence will come to pass in two stages. First, the messianic age will be initiated by resurrection of the pious of Israel, who will be permitted to share in a restoration of the Jewish monarchy. There will be an end to poverty, oppression, and war. Then, when God will have finished calling into being the total number of humanity he has decided in his wisdom to create, the "world of reward" will be established. The dead of all nations will be resurrected and judged. Recompense in the world of reward will take place by means of the radiance of the divine light, a subtle essence created by God to illuminate the righteous with joy and to burn the wrongdoers in punishment.

Seen as a whole, Saadiah's treatise goes beyond a defense of Judaism to become the first systematic rabbinic theology in which central doctrines of Judaism are clarified and described, appropriate biblical and rabbinic quotations cited, and rational argument used to refine traditional formulations. Saadiah's commitment to rationalism is that of the Mutazilite Kalam: Although he is confident that reason cannot but confirm revelation, the results of reason are kept under control so as not to threaten any major element of religious belief. Saadiah's faith in the power of the mind to solve all intellectual perplexities is that of the theologian, rather than the philosopher. Reason is allowed to criticize religion only in a limited way. For instance, we must interpret the anthropomorphic descriptions of God in the Scripture as metaphors, so that we can affirm without qualification the essential principle of God's incorporeality. But reason does not allow us to question the principle that there is an absolute law of justice that governs the world and by which all suffering is explained. Inasmuch as Saadiah does not recognize that there may be metaphysical problems not fully resolvable by man, that reason may have its limits, and that fundamental religious doctrines may require radical reformulation, he can be called a dogmatic rationalist—dogmatic in his faith in reason as applied to religion.[6] The criticism that reason has certain inherent limitations will arise when medieval Jewish thought comes to grip more profoundly with the Greek philosophical systems.

From Mutazilite Theology to Aristotelian Philosophy

The Kalam played little role in influencing Jewish thought after the eleventh century. In Islam the Mutazilites were superseded by another, more orthodox, school of theology (the Asharyites), who employed reasoned arguments to arrive at a position more in accord with an unquestioning traditionalism; for example, they emphasized the omnipotence of God to the point of virtually denying man's freedom of choice. (Muslim science eventually declined as a result.) One of the most widely discussed (and rejected) elements of the Asharyite Kalam among Jewish thinkers was their principle that everything happens, at all times and places, because it is God's will. The Asharyites postulated that physical existence is composed of "atoms" of time and space, each directly created by God. This position saves religious faith at the price of denying that the universe possesses an orderly structure of causes and effects. For the Asharyites, there was no need to justify miracles as occasional interferences by God in the regularity of natural law: Everything that happens is a miracle. Such a stance undermines the very basis for construct-

The ancient Greek thinker, Aristotle, a major philosophical influence in the Middle Ages, in a twelfth-century sculpture on the cathedral of Chartres.

ing a philosophy of religion, which attempts to bring the truths of religion into line with reason.

More useful to Jewish philosophy was Neo-Platonism, a highly religious interpretation of Plato's philosophy developed by pagan philosophers in late antiquity, and used, with certain changes, by Christian and Muslim mystics. (Philo, the Jewish philosopher of the first century CE, played a role in the formation of the Neo-Platonic system but his writings were apparently not known to medieval Jewish philosophers.) Neo-Platonism is a monistic view of the world which posits as the absolute cause of everything a pure spiritual principle, the One, the acme of perfection, that "emanates" from itself lower levels of spiritual existence, like light from the sun or like water from an everflowing spring. At the other end of the Neo-Platonic chain of being is the material world of change and decay. (Pure matter has no real existence in itself: It is only the absence of spirit.) Neo-Platonism is not only a philosophical system, but a doctrine of salvation. Man's soul, derived from the universal soul, can reascend to the upper, supernal world of the spirit by means of intellectual and ethical purification. A few medieval Jewish philosophers are usually classified as Neo-Platonists, though they modified this system of philosophy to allow for the creative will of God. (Neo-Platonism conceives of emanation as a necessary, not a voluntary emergence of the world from God.) Neo-Platonism was particularly important in Jewish mysticism and the Kabbalah, which we will examine in the next chapter.

For medieval Jewish philosophy, the most influential system of Greco-Arabic thought was Aristotelianism ("Greco-Arabic" because the Jewish thinkers were acquainted with Aristotle, the great Greek thinker of the fourth century BCE, through the writings of Muslim commentators and interpreters such as al-Farabi, Avicenna, and Averroes). "Aristotelianism" —the general tendency construed in the medieval world as the philosophy of Aristotle—was of decisive importance for Muslims, Jews, and Christians because it provided the philosophical structure for the natural sciences of the Middle Ages.[7] All those thinkers who were scientists and physicians studied the known corpus of Aristotle's writings on logic, physics, astronomy, biology, psychology, ethics, and metaphysics. (Metaphysics is the study of the nature of being as such, and of cause as such: the science of the fundamental processes underlying all nature in their most abstract form. As we shall see, this entailed discussions of the nature of a final and most basic absolute: God.) Aristotelianism moves from observations of processes in the natural world to metaphysics, whereas Neo-Platonism had dismissed the independent reality of physical nature in its exclusive concern for the spirit.

A brief description of the Aristotelian world picture is necessary in order to understand medieval Jewish philosophy. The earth is the center of the cosmos, the outermost boundary of the universe being the sphere

of the fixed stars. Between the earth and the farthest heaven are intermediary spheres, one for each planet. These spheres are made of a very
fine substance, unlike the four basic elements (fire, air, water, earth)
of which everything below the moon is composed. The celestial region
above the moon is not subject to growth and decay; its motion is circular,
the most perfect kind of motion, and it is governed by incorporeal souls,
known as Intelligences. Things in the sublunar or terrestrial regions are
composed of two or more of the four elements mentioned above and can
be divided into minerals, plants, animals, rational beings. All beings in
the terrestrial world are subject to growth and decay, and are composed
of "matter" and "form." Form is what makes an entity representative
of its species. The Aristotelian concept of matter is quite different from
the modern; in Aristotelianism matter does not exist by itself, but is the
underlying substratum for the forms of being. "Potentiality" and "actuality" are another pair of key terms, paralleling matter and form. The
potentiality of an object is due to its matter; its essence is due to its form.
Each species has its own characteristic form, toward which an individual
plant or animal develops as its potentiality is actualized. A thing with
no matter at all would be fully actualized form, not liable to any change.
(Only the celestial Intelligences and God consist of pure form.)

Metaphysics is concerned with the causes of motion and the actualization of form as such. In Aristotelianism, nothing that is in a state of potentiality can make itself actual; everything requires an external agent
to actualize its potential. As we shall see later in more detail, because there
cannot be an infinite chain of causes, there must be one final and ultimate
cause, a Prime Mover that is unmoved and yet causes motion and change
in other things. This First Cause is not first in time, but first in the total
sequence of causes. Its priority is that of logical necessity: It is the
ultimate explanation for the whole sequence of causes operating in the
cosmos. (That a rational mind cannot accept an infinite regress of causes
is a fundamental principle of Aristotle's philosophy.) Since the First
Cause is form only, devoid of matter and potentiality, its nature is pure
thought: God is the being who thinks the highest, unvarying thought—
God is "thought thinking thought."

Man, the highest being on earth, is distinguished from other animal
species by possessing an intellect. The purpose of human life is to actualize
this rational faculty. As a human being matures, the capacity for reason
gradually develops from a potential into an actual state. Man's soul is the
actualization of the form of the body (the body has the position of matter
in relation to the soul), but the soul is more than this, because intellect
is characteristic of the celestial beings and God. Intellect is deathless and
eternal. A force outside the individual human being, called the Active
Intellect (often identified with the lowest of the celestial Intelligences),

causes the potential intellect in man to develop and mature. Man's immortality is directly tied to the Active Intellect inhering in the cosmos.

From this brief sketch it will be apparent that there are some aspects of Neo-Platonism and Aristotelianism that were supportive of religion, and others that posed severe problems. Both philosophies appeared to confirm monotheism by postulating a supreme incorporeal principle (the Prime Mover in Aristotelianism, the divine One in Neo-Platonism). Both conceive of the soul as an entity that can exist independently of the body, thus appearing to confirm the religious concept of immortality. (In Aristotelian thought, the intellective faculty, though not the other faculties of the soul, does not perish with the body.) Both philosophies are compatible with the idea that the human spirit can be illuminated by God, which provides a basis for the concept of revelation. Finally, both are strongly ethical: In Neo-Platonism man is taught to free himself from the chains of matter and return to his spiritual home; in Aristotelianism man is encouraged to discipline his passions in order to perfect his mind. Both approaches can be used in arguing for the rationality of religious ethics.

Perhaps the greatest dilemma facing religious philosophers was that in both Greek philosophical systems God is not a creative will, but an impersonal principle. God was not the force that brought the world into being from nothing, but the ultimate, changeless cause of multiplicity and the starting point of the finite chain of causation in the world. Neither Aristotelianism nor Neo-Platonism had a conception of the creation of the universe in time, because form and matter in Aristotelianism and spirit in Neo-Platonism were infinite with respect to time. Furthermore, the Neo-Platonic idea of emanation and the Aristotelian concept of causation are necessary, regular, automatic processes, not voluntary ones. If God could not be conceived of as possessing a will, this weakened considerably the effort to construct a philosophy of religion faithful to the main features of the Jewish, Muslim, and Christian conception of God. Likewise, the effort to make the religious view of the divine nature philosophically respectable by eliminating anthropomorphic descriptions of God could be carried to the extreme where the idea of God is deprived of its personal relevance to most human beings. It was one thing to deny that God had a body, but quite another to deny that God was just and loving, which are also anthropomorphic traits.

There are other difficulties as well in reconciling rational philosophy and religious faith. Greek philosophy provided a basis for immortality, but an immortality acquired through the intellect and not moral action. Philosophy provided a basis for prophecy, but as a natural process and not a mission. These and other issues indicate that tensions and even contradictions existed between the doctrines of philosophy and religion that could not be ignored. The search to delineate and resolve these issues forms the heart of medieval Jewish philosophy from the twelfth century on.

The Rise of Jewish Philosophy in Muslim Spain; The Philosophy of Judah Halevy

In the Mediterranean West, beginning in the eleventh century, there appeared a series of Jewish writers trained in Greco-Arabic philosophy who each made substantial contributions to the development of medieval Jewish philosophy. The first Spanish Jewish philosopher, Solomon ibn Gabriol (c. 1020–c. 1057), produced a work in the Neo-Platonic tradition, the *Fountain of Life*, which was, however, not written with specific reference to Judaism, and had much greater impact on later Christian theology than on Jewish thought. Gabriol was one of the major Hebrew poets of the Middle Ages, and his long religious poem, the *Kingly Crown* (*Keter Malkhut*), uses some Neo-Platonic images in its depiction of God and the soul. Another distinguished writer with philosophical interests was Bahya ibn Pakuda (late eleventh century), the author of a much revered ethical treatise, *Duties of the Heart* (*Hovot ha-Levavot*), drawing on the Kalam, Neo-Platonism, and the writings of the Muslim mystics, in addition to Jewish sources. Bahya extols a hierarchy of inward values, the duties of the heart, in contrast to the duties of the limbs, which are overt religious actions. Sincerity, humility, repentance, self-examination, abstinence are steps culminating in a pure love of God that is the ultimate attainment of the religious man. A third figure of importance was Abraham ibn Daud (c. 1110–1180), best known for his historical treatise *The Book of Tradition* (*Sefer ha-Kabbalah*) in defense of the rabbinic tradition. Ibn Daud's philosophical writing, *The Exalted Faith* (*Emunah Ramah*), was the first Jewish work fully in the medieval Aristotelian framework. In this book, Ibn Daud offered an original defense of man's free will that qualified God's omniscience by arguing that God does not know what is objectively contingent, that is, that God cannot know, in advance, the as yet undecided outcome of man's decision.

A fourth eminent Jewish philosopher of Muslim Spain must be described in much greater detail, because he questioned the very basis of a rationalistic formulation of Jewish belief. Judah Halevy (probable dates, 1075–1141) left a theological defense of the Jewish religion in determined opposition to Aristotelian philosophy. Born in central or northern Spain of a wealthy and learned family, Halevy went south to study in the great

וְנִסְפְּחָה נַחֲלָתָן עַל נַחֲלַת הַמַּטֶּה אֲשֶׁר תִּהְיֶינָה לָהֶם וּמִגֹּרַל נַחֲלָתֵנוּ יִגָּרֵעַ אַסְתִּים יֵרַע נַחֲלָתֵן: וַיְצַו
מֹשֶׁה אֶת בְּנֵי יִשְׂרָאֵל עַל פִּי יְהוָה לֵאמֹר כֵּן מַטֵּה בְנֵי יוֹסֵף דֹּבְרִים: זֶה הַדָּבָר אֲשֶׁר
יִצַּו יְהוָה לִבְנוֹת צְלָפְחָד לֵאמֹר לַטּוֹב בְּעֵינֵיהֶן תִּהְיֶינָה לְנָשִׁים אַךְ לְמִשְׁפַּחַת מַטֵּה
אֲבִיהֶן תִּהְיֶינָה לְנָשִׁים: וְלֹא תִסֹּב נַחֲלָה לִבְנֵי יִשְׂרָאֵל מִמַּטֶּה אֶל מַטֶּה כִּי אִישׁ בְּנַחֲלַת
מַטֵּה אֲבֹתָיו יִדְבְּקוּ בְּנֵי יִשְׂרָאֵל: וְכָל בַּת יֹרֶשֶׁת נַחֲלָה מִמַּטּוֹת בְּנֵי יִשְׂרָאֵל לְאֶחָד
מִמִּשְׁפַּחַת מַטֵּה אָבִיהָ תִּהְיֶה לְאִשָּׁה לְמַעַן יִירְשׁוּ בְּנֵי יִשְׂרָאֵל אִישׁ נַחֲלַת אֲבֹתָיו: וְלֹא
תִסֹּב נַחֲלָה מִמַּטֶּה לְמַטֶּה אַחֵר כִּי אִישׁ בְּנַחֲלָתוֹ יִדְבְּקוּ מַטּוֹת בְּנֵי יִשְׂרָאֵל: כַּאֲשֶׁר צִוָּה
יְהוָה אֶת מֹשֶׁה כֵּן עָשׂוּ בְּנוֹת צְלָפְחָד: וַתִּהְיֶינָה מַחְלָה תִרְצָה וְחָגְלָה וּמִלְכָּה וְנֹעָה
בְּנוֹת צְלָפְחָד לִבְנֵי דֹדֵיהֶן לְנָשִׁים: מִמִּשְׁפְּחֹת בְּנֵי מְנַשֶּׁה בֶן יוֹסֵף הָיוּ לְנָשִׁים וַתְּהִי
נַחֲלָתָן עַל מַטֵּה מִשְׁפַּחַת אֲבִיהֶן: אֵלֶּה הַמִּצְוֹת וְהַמִּשְׁפָּטִים אֲשֶׁר צִוָּה יְהוָה בְּיַד
מֹשֶׁה אֶל בְּנֵי יִשְׂרָאֵל בְּעַרְבֹת מוֹאָב עַל יַרְדֵּן יְרֵחוֹ:

חֲזַק

סַךְ פְּסוּקֵי דְּסֵפֶר
וַיְדַבֵּר אֵלֶּה
וּבָאתֶם שָׁמָּם
וּשְׁמֹנֶה סִימָנֵי אֶלֶף
רֹפְחֹ וְדָבֵיד מַטֶּה
יֹתֵרֹת וְסֹרֵךְ עֶשְׂרִי
וּשְׁלֹשׁ שַׁבַּע עָשָׂר הָרֵא
בִּיהֶם יוֹם וּשְׁלֹשָׁה יָמִים
הַבֵּן:

Jew reading a Torah scroll, an illumination from a fourteenth-century Pentateuch.
(Courtesy of the British Library.)

centers of Jewish learning in Granada (while still young he acquired a reputation as a poet of outstanding talent), and later resided in various Spanish cities where he earned his living as a physician. He died while on a pilgrimage to the holy land. (According to legend he was killed in Jerusalem, but evidence indicates that he probably died in Egypt.)

Halevy's poetry is among the greatest in medieval Hebrew literature. He wrote poems on all the standard secular and religious themes: the pleasures of wine and friendship, the passion of love, the beauty of nature, the exalted meaning of the holy days—and he created a special genre, songs of yearning for Zion, which are important for an understanding of Halevy's distinctive perception of Judaism's relation to philosophy.

The immediate historical background to Halevy's love for Zion was the First Crusade and the Almoravid conquest of Muslim Spain. At both ends of the Mediterranean, Muslim and Christian armies struggled for dominion. Earlier than any other major thinker, Halevy sensed the implications of this clash for Spanish Jewry. Jews had felt at home in Andalusia, perhaps more than anywhere else in the Middle Ages, but Halevy apparently sensed that the heightening of religious fanaticism would soon doom the Jewish communities of Muslim Spain. The feeling of not being at home in this world, prevalent in much medieval spirituality —a yearning for a higher, purer form of perfection and inner peace—took the specific Jewish form, in Halevy's poetry, of meditating on the physical desolation and spiritual grandeur of the holy land. In his lyrics, the beauty and luxury of Spain were depicted as unreal, in contrast to the one place where the people of Israel can fulfill its special destiny, where the Jewish nation first realized it was God's people, where patriarchs and prophets received the divine revelation, where the Temple offerings represented man's most intimate communion with God. Halevy contrasts the current situation of the Jews with the emptiness of life in exile under alien rulers:

> *My heart is in the East, and I am in the depths of the West.*
> *My food has no taste. How can it be sweet?*
> *How can I fulfill my pledges and my vows,*
> *When Zion is in the power of Edom, and I in the fetters of Arabia?*
> *It will be nothing for me to leave all the goodness of Spain.*
> *So rich will it be to see the dust of the ruined sanctuary.*[8]

The poet becomes a spokesman for the return of the people to the holy land, which will restore them to their rightful place in history. He addresses Zion:

> *I am a jackal mourning your affliction, and when I dream*
> *Of the return of your captives I am a lyre accompanying your songs.*
>
> *. . .*
>
> *Happy is he who hopes to come and see*
> *Your light rise, and your dawns break over him,*
> *To see the happiness of your chosen ones, and to exult*
> *In your joy, as you live youth's first vigor once more.*[9]

In Halevy's thought, the uniqueness of Israel's election points to those particular qualities of Jewish faith that cannot be understood by the intellect alone. That Judaism stood above reason was the basis of his theology.

Halevy's treatise, *The Book of Argument and Proof in Defense of the Despised Faith*, is generally known as the *Book of the Khazars* (*Sefer ha-Kuzari*), because of its dramatic form: a dialogue between a king of the Khazar people and a Jewish sage who defends Judaism against its detractors and competitors.[10] This setting allows Halevy to present his views as though they were being delivered before a non-Jew uncommitted to any monotheistic religion, who is willing to approach Judaism sympathetically and objectively. (Eventually the king converts to Judaism.) The book opens with the statement that the Khazar king dreams that an angel tells him that his intention is pleasing to the Creator, but not his ways of acting. As a result, the king invites to his court representatives of Aristotelian philosophy, Christianity, and Islam. The philosopher describes God as the source of all forms of being, the Cause of Causes whose rational nature cannot involve desire, and who is above any specific intention. The highest goal for man is to attain true knowledge of the universe, through which one acquires purity of soul and, eventually, union with the divine mind. The Khazar king explains that his dream had condemned not his thinking, but his actions (he has been zealous in performing the rites of the pagan Khazar religion), and sends the philosopher away. He then interviews the Christian and the Muslim, who both indicate that their religions derive from Judaism and that the validity of their faith is ultimately based on God's revelation to Israel. Reluctantly (because of Jewry's low status in the world), the king invites a Jewish scholar to appear before him. The Jew opens the defense of his religion by affirming

I believe in the God of Abraham, Isaac, and Israel [Jacob], who led the children of Israel out of Egypt with signs and miracles, who fed them in the desert and gave them the land, after having made them traverse the sea and the Jordan in a miraculous way, who sent Moses with his law and subsequently thousands of prophets, who confirmed his law by promises to the observant and threats to the disobedient. Our belief is comprised in the Torah—a very large domain.[11]

Except for a few remarks about Christianity and the Karaites, the main position that Halevy opposed in the *Kuzari* was Aristotelian philosophy, which he considered the greatest internal danger to Jewish faith in his day. Halevy's argument stems from the conviction that biblical revelation—not philosophy—provides the proper guidance to life in

Torah scroll case, copper inlaid with silver, from sixteenth-century Damascus. (Courtesy the Jewish Museum, New York.)

communion with God. To be sure, reason is useful for religion inasmuch as it indicates that an understanding of the world leads to the idea of a single divine cause. Halevy acknowledges also that the intellect alone is reliable to deal with logic and mathematics. But Aristotelian metaphysics is not really scientific, as it claims. Its arguments and conclusions on ultimate matters are shallow, uncertain, and defective. The philosophers' God is an entity unconcerned with man, who pays no attention to worship and prayer, and who exerts no providential direction over history. In contrast, the Torah is based not on a mere theory about God, but on concrete historical encounter with Him. The God of Judaism is a personal God concerned about men, in nearness to whom men feel their greatest happiness, and away from whom, their greatest misery. According to the philosophers the highest human attainment is knowledge of the pure forms of being. According to Torah the highest life is the suprarational experience of God in prophecy. In Halevy's view, prophecy is not an actualization of the intellective faculty: It is a divine gift that has instructed Israel in those sacred deeds that produce effects on the soul that no rational theory can explain.

According to Halevy, the prophetic faculty is possessed only by a minority. After Adam, who was created with this aptitude, one man in each generation possessed it. Prophetic ability was passed from Abraham to Isaac to Jacob, and from Jacob to the people of Israel, the only people in history among whom prophecy flourished. Thus Halevy adds an additional level to the usual medieval hierarchy of terrestrial beings: As inorganic beings are distinguished from organic beings, organic beings from animals, and animals from men, Halevy posits that men in general, who have a potential to reason, are to be distinguished from prophets, who have a potential to receive divine revelation. (Halevy's idea of prophecy is, perhaps, an analogy drawn from his own experience as a poet: The capacity to write great poetry is more like an inborn talent than like a craft that can be taught and learned.) Possession of the prophetic talent does not automatically insure that one will be a prophet. Just as a superior vine must be planted in choice soil and cultivated with special skill before it will provide grapes that make excellent wine, so prophecy flourishes solely in a special land (the land of Israel) and needs special means of cultivation (the Hebrew language and the ceremonial law of the Bible). Only under these conditions do prophets hear the divine word and see celestial visions. Since Israel has come to live completely in exile, away from its sacred land and deprived of its sacred Temple, no true prophets have appeared. Only when Israel is redeemed, will it actualize its special gift.[12] There is a certain paradox here in Halevy's theory: Although critical of philosophy, he offers in rebuttal a theory that explains the distinctiveness of Israel and of biblical prophecy in naturalistic, even biological terms. Similar to Neo-Platonism, Halevy's theology is based on the idea of an emanation that pours out from God to elicit the special potential of each lower level of reality, under suitable conditions.

Halevy's conception of the significance of biblical law is almost the obverse of Saadiah's. Whereas Saadiah had defended its rationality, Halevy emphasizes those features that are not explicable. Unaided human reason can attain to a conception of personal and social ethics, but revelational laws are unique because they are suprarational. They concern ritual actions, the efficacy of which our intellects cannot understand, and they bring about spiritual effects that transcend reason. Halevy extends this principle to include the ritual of the synagogue. Even in exile the ceremonial law enables the Jew to live a life similar in kind, but different in degree, from prophecy: a life of piety, humility, and service to God. Unlike Jewish writers influenced by Neo-Platonism, such as Bahya, however, Halevy does not depict Jewish law as inculcating asceticism. Bodily desires should be controlled, but the goal of the religious life is that joy which is a foretaste of bliss in the World to Come.

Although Halevy criticizes a rationalistic concept of God, prophecy, and ritual, he is not opposed to scientific knowledge as long as it is confined to its proper sphere. (He was a trained and experienced physician.) He is convinced that natural science originated among Jews and that the rabbinic sages cultivated scientific subjects relevant to their religious concerns. Judaism does not oppose the study of nature, nor does the Torah contradict what human reason has truly demonstrated. Indeed, if philosophers had proved without doubt that matter existed eternally, Jewish exegetes would have no alternative but to interpret the biblical creation story accordingly.[13] Halevy has, however, certain objections to the physics of his time, for example, to the assumption that everything in the terrestrial world is composed of only four primary elements, earth, air, fire, and water. This, as well as the Aristotelians' complicated explanation of how the heavenly spheres emanated from the First Cause, seem to Halevy to be only conjecture and riddled with contradictions.

Halevy's position is a rational antirationalism, a criticism of the defects of philosophical thought when applied to matters of religious concern. Halevy defends the uniqueness of Israel's revelation, its history, and its ideal of piety. Judaism is not explained by the intellect. Torah is suprarational in essence. As the Khazar king remarks after listening to the arguments of the Jewish sage, "I see how far the God of Abraham is different from that of Aristotle." A poet of great sensitivity, Halevy defends the particularity and concreteness of Judaism. He was not, however, able to stem the growing appeal of Aristotelian thought to Spanish Jewish intellectuals. The challenge of Aristotelianism in the century after Halevy was to produce a far more subtle synthesis of Judaism and philosophy than that which Halevy had sought to discredit.

Moses Maimonides

Moses Maimonides (Moses ben Maimon, usually referred to in Jewish writings by his acronym Rambam) was the greatest figure in the intellectual history of medieval Jewry, both for the quality of his thought and for the influence he exerted for centuries afterwards. Maimonides (1135–1204) was born in Cordova, Spain, where his ancestors had for generations been judges and scholars. In 1148 the great age of Jewry in Andalusia came to an abrupt end: Cordova fell to the Almohades, who persecuted the religious minorities far more severely than had the Almoravides who so troubled Halevy in the previous century. Maimonides and his family were forced to wander through Spain and North Africa, hiding their Judaism. (Both father and son later wrote letters expressing great sympathy for Jews forced to live under these circumstances.) After five years in Fez, the capital of the Almohade state, the family left in 1160 for the eastern Mediterranean. After a visit to the holy land, they settled in Cairo, the capital of Egypt, where Maimonides spent the rest of his life. Maimonides continued to work on his writings, but when his beloved brother, a merchant in precious stones, was drowned on a voyage to India, he turned to medicine for his livelihood. By 1185 Maimonides had been appointed one of the court physicians to the Muslim ruler of Egypt; he was a leader of the Jewish community of Cairo, and his reputation had spread throughout most of the diaspora. (Unlike Saadiah, he occupied no official position among the Jews.) After his death, on December 13, 1204, public mourning was proclaimed by Jews in many lands. He was buried in the Galilee in the city of Tiberias, where his grave is still a place of Jewish pilgrimage.

Maimonides' learning and achievements were all the more remarkable because of the chaotic circumstances in which he was educated and the trying conditions in which his halakhic and philosophic works were written, but he had one advantage over Saadiah, in that he lived after two and a half centuries of further progress in the recovery and interpretation of the Aristotelian system. As we saw earlier, Jewish thinkers had become deeply involved in Aristotelianism only after a series of great Muslim philosophers had already launched the enterprise of reconciling revealed religion with the philosophies of ancient Greece. Twelfth-century Muslim Spain, where Maimonides' intellectual roots lay, had become a great center of scientifically oriented metaphysics. (By then the Muslim theologians of the East had turned away from philosophy to the conservative Asharyite Kalam or to mysticism.) Maimonides, who did not think very highly of his Jewish philosophical predecessors, relied directly on the great Muslim expositors of Aristotle such as al-Farabi and Avicenna. The

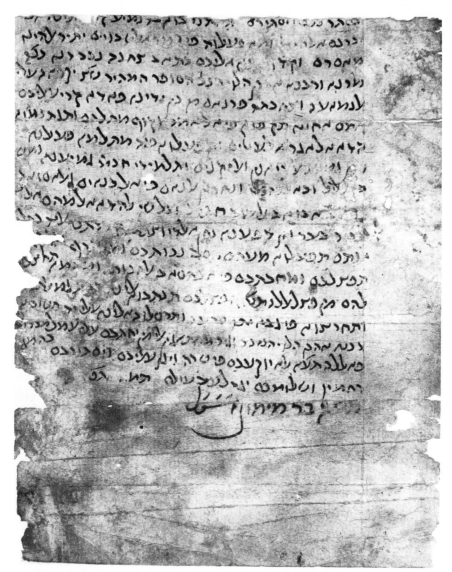

Letter written in 1173 by Maimonides and signed by him, appealing to North African Jews for funds to redeem Jewish captives. (The Photographic Archive of the Jewish Theological Seminary of America, New York, Frank J. Darmstaedter.)

roots of Maimonides' halakhic work also lay in Spain, where careful systematization had been applied to the study of the texts of talmudic law. Just as Judah Halevy's writing was an exemplification of the high poetic standards of Andalusian Jewry, Maimonides' rationalism reflected the rigorous scientific concerns of that Jewish culture.

In everything he wrote, Maimonides strove to demonstrate that philosophy and religion point to the same truth. On the one hand, nothing in Judaism could contradict reason; on the other hand, Greco-Arabic philosophy had not yet come to grips fully with issues posed by Jewish monotheism. Maimonides did not permit himself an easy apologetics. Traditional Jewish statements or popular beliefs not consistent with his view of Judaism must be expunged. For example, God could not be thought of as having a body in any sense, astrology was nonsense, blind trust was not in itself especially meritorious. Religious faith required not just outward consent, but a conviction that the truths of faith have been rationally demonstrated to the fullest extent possible. His reconciliation of Judaism and philosophy was not a mechanical bringing together of the two, using any philosophical argument at hand that seemed to substantiate Jewish doctrine. (Saadiah can be accused of this.) The challenge of Aristotelianism requires a philosophical purification of Judaism: The Torah is not to be understood literally where doing so would not be compatible with conclusions clearly demonstrated by reason. This also means that Aristotelianism must be revised to take into consideration certain ideas about ultimate reality and human action derived from ethical monotheism (ideas that Aristotle did not include in his own system because of biases and limitations inherent in ancient Greek paganism).

Maimonides' thought is, therefore, shaped by a conviction that Judaism is logically and intellectually consistent. His halakhic works organize the details of Jewish practice into a unified whole, which makes explicit the fundamentals of legal methodology and the philosophical underpinnings of Jewish law. Conversely, his philosophical writings have the aim of clarifying the rational status of religious belief and of the legislation in the Torah.

Maimonides' principal religious writings are a commentary to the Mishnah, a code of Jewish law, and *The Guide for the Perplexed*.[14] He began writing his Mishnah commentary at the age of twenty-three, finishing it about ten years later. It includes the halakhic decision for each paragraph of the Mishnah, as well as analytic introductions discussing the theoretical and doctrinal foundations of the material found in each tractate. His introduction to tractate Sanhedrin is especially well known, because of its list of the thirteen principles of faith that Maimonides considered essential for a Jew: that God exists; that he is one, incorporeal, and eternal; that idolatry (the worship of any being besides God) is absolutely prohibited; that there are true prophets, among whom Moses is unique; that both the oral and written Torah are divine and immutable; that God is omniscient; that he rewards and punishes; that the Messiah will surely come and the dead be resurrected. Maimonides' code, the *Mishneh Torah*, was completed about 1178; it contains an all-inclusive digest of the halakhah up to his time, including such ancient laws as the Temple sacrificial offerings, as well as rules still operative in the diaspora. He reorganized all this material into fourteen books, according to topics arranged by himself. The most striking innovation was to introduce the code with a summary of the basic metaphysical and ethical postulates of Judaism (Book One, *Sefer ha-Madda, The Book of Knowledge*). The *Mishneh Torah* is written in Hebrew, (unlike Maimonides' other works, which were written in Arabic) to make it easily understood by Jewish judges everywhere. Although immediately hailed as a masterpiece, the *Mishneh Torah* quickly attracted sharp criticism on several grounds. In it Maimonides had resolved all conflicting interpretations, giving only his unilateral, undocumented decision. And Maimonides hinted that the *Mishneh Torah* rendered superfluous the need to study the Talmud directly. His inclusion of philosophical matters also provoked sharp criticism. It became an influential step in the further development of Jewish law, but not the ultimate, authoritative summation that Maimonides may have intended.

The Guide for the Perplexed, composed between 1185 and 1190, was deliberately written not to be understandable to a reader untrained in philosophy. In the introduction Maimonides indicates that he has intended the *Guide* only for those whose study of logic, mathematics, natural science, and metaphysics have led them to be troubled about seeming contradictions between this knowledge and the Torah. He states that certain passages of the prophets, in apparent conflict with Aristotelian philosophy, were actually parables with an esoteric meaning for the few. (Maimonides does not, however, confine himself to biblical exegesis, but deals with most of the major issues of religious philosophy.) In his introduction he also warns that he has taken great care with the language and structure of the *Guide* in order deliberately to obscure his true position—that he has even occasionally contradicted himself. He wrote in this manner probably so as not to undermine the religious faith of those Jews unequipped to follow subtle philosophical reasoning and for whom he would create perplexities rather than resolve them.[15]

Even though Maimonides had not constructed the *Guide* as a textbook for beginners in religious philosophy, there is a clear progression of ideas through it. Part One opens with an explanation of anthropomorphic terms in the Bible that might be thought to imply the corporeality of God; Maimonides treats each such term as an allegory for a concept in Aristotelian physics or metaphysics. This allegorical glossary of biblical descriptions of God leads him to discuss the vexed question of God's attributes. After giving his solution to this issue, Part One concludes with a sharp criticism of Asharyite atomism and its definition of God's omnipotence, which deny the regularity and orderliness of nature. (Maimonides considers this a weak defense of religion.) Part Two begins with a summary of Aristotelian principles deemed useful in establishing God's existence, unity, and incorporeality. After presenting the formal proofs, Maimonides turns to the issue of creation *ex nihilo*, which he considers the most urgent subject in the philosophy of religion. Having rejected the Mutazilites' approach, which made knowledge that God exists dependent on arguments that the world began in time, Maimonides insists that God's existence was best established through Aristotelian philosophy. Because Aristotle assumed the eternity of the world, Maimonides therefore endeavors to establish the rational plausibility of the idea of creation. Creation *ex nihilo*, which is contrary to the Aristotelian understanding of natural law, leads him to discuss the question of whether miracles are possible. Part Two concludes with a discussion of revelation, a specific type of miracle that must also be shown to be philosophically sound. To do this, Maimonides must differentiate between prophetic inspiration and philosophical intellection.

Part Three, the final section of the *Guide*, opens with a metaphysical interpretation of Ezekiel's vision of the divine chariot. Maimonides then turns to philosophical aspects of divine providence, God's knowledge, and the existence of evil. After defending the rationality of the Torah's com-

Depiction of the creation of the universe according to Genesis 1:2–3. On the right, the spirit of God moving over the face of the deep; on the left, the separation of light and darkness. From the Sarajevo Haggadah (fifteenth-century Spain). (Courtesy of the Union of American Hebrew Congregations.)

mandments, he concludes with a description of the inner religious life of the ideal type of man.

Maimonides was convinced that Aristotelian philosophy provided a scientific proof for the existence of God. Aristotle had demonstrated that all change in the world had its ultimate cause in a Prime Mover, an incorporeal being whose nature was self-thinking thought. The Neo-Platonists had taught that the world is derived from the One, a primary divine unity beyond knowledge. The Muslim Aristotelians had combined the two concepts, identifying Aristotle's Prime Mover with the Neo-Platonic ideal of the One from which all multiplicity emanates. Maimonides uses the arguments for the existence of God devised by the Muslim Aristotelians and the concept of divine attributes expounded by the Neo-Platonists. Maimonides gives several variations on the argument for a First Cause, such as we described earlier, that an infinite regress of causes is logically impossible, so that there must exist an Uncaused Cause, or Unmoved Mover. He also added a fourth argument: that the accidental and contingent character of all things must have its source in an entity that possesses necessary existence. God is a Being that cannot *not* exist.[16]

This conception of the First Cause had to be reconciled with the religious idea of God. How can God's attributes be brought in harmony with the principle that God's unity must exclude all plurality, even conceptual plurality, as especially demanded by the Neo-Platonic element in Maimonides' thought? Saadiah had asserted that the three crucial positive attributes of God (divine life, knowledge, and power) were part of His essence in a manner that human language cannot express. Maimonides goes much further: He asserts that no positive attributes can be predicated of God's essence and that negative attributes alone are compatible with God's absolute unity. This famous doctrine has a long history in earlier thought, but Maimonides gave it his own twist by insisting that negative attributes do provide real knowledge of God. We know an object with increasing precision if we can reject an increasing number of alternative descriptions. Each negative attribute excludes from God's essence some shortcoming or imperfection. For example, when we say God is immaterial we mean he has no body, thereby distinguishing God from the whole corporeal world. When we say he is eternal, we mean he has no cause. When we say he is omniscient, we exclude from God all ignorance. When we say he possesses existence, we deny his nonexistence (i.e., we affirm that the essence of God contains within itself in an eminent way that which we usually call existence).

Besides negative attributes, however, there is another class of attributes Maimonides also considers philosophically legitimate. These are the attributes of action—descriptions of the effects of God's essence on the universe. For example, when we speak of God's love or anger we refer to some effect of the First Cause in the world. If God is said to be merciful, this does not involve attributing an emotion to him (the Aristotelian Unmoved Mover is impassive); it means that God does good to his creatures even when they are not deserving of it. In one passage Maimonides compares God to a ship captain:

> What then should be the state of our intellects when they aspire to apprehend Him who is without matter and is simple to the utmost degree of simplicity, Him whose existence is necessary, Him who has no cause and to whom no notion attaches that is superadded to His essence, which is perfect—the meaning of its perfection being, as we have made clear, that all deficiencies are negated with respect to it—we who only apprehend the fact that He is? There is accordingly an existent whom none of the existent things that He has brought into existence resembles, and who has nothing in common with them in any respect; in reference to whom there is no multiplicity or incapacity to bring into existence things other than He; whose relation to the world is that of a captain to his ship. Even this is not the true relation and a correct likeness, for this likeness has been used in order to lead the mind toward the view that He, may He be exalted, governs the existent things, the meaning of this being that He procures their existence and watches over their order as it ought to be watched over.[17]

It will be noted how careful Maimonides is to apologize for such a figure of speech. It is only an analogy, but all we predicate of God is by the way of analogy.

The question of God's attributes leads to the question of God as creator. As we pointed out earlier, Maimonides had relied on the Aristotelian arguments for God's existence. But for Aristotle matter and form were eternal, so that a moment of creation was rationally impossible. On this question Plato is closer to the biblical tradition: Although the Platonic cosmology assumes that matter is eternal, it does depict a moment when God imposes a determinate structure on it. (Maimonides, like Judah Halevy, acknowledged that this concept of Plato's could be read into the biblical creation story, if no better solution were forthcoming.) In the Aristotelian system the universe, with all its species, is eternal, though finite in space and finite also in the chain of causes reaching back to the eternal First Cause. Maimonides' strategy was to admit that the creation of the universe cannot be conclusively proven and that the eternity of the universe cannot be conclusively disproven. But creation *ex nihilo* can be shown to be logically and even empirically plausible.

Maimonides accomplished this goal through two searching criticisms of Aristotelianism. First, he argues that, even if Aristotle's philosophy is the best possible explanation for the order of nature (which Maimonides believed), it is not valid to extrapolate from the conditions that exist in the cosmos to the coming-into-being of the cosmos itself. To be sure, nothing can come into being *in* the universe unless there is already form and matter. But the principle that denies the possibility of creation *ex nihilo* in the universe, does not apply to the universe as a whole. The origins of the entire system are not similar to the origin of things within it. Maimonides gives the example that the conditions of life of the embryo are very different from those of the adult; knowing the latter only, we could not deduce the former by logic alone. Maimonides goes so far as to admit that God has probably made an eternal cosmos—that the Bible teaches the future indestructibility of the world—but for him this does not contradict the principle of its having been created in the past.

Maimonides' second line of argument for creation points to certain astronomical data militating against the view that the world is the result of a necessary and automatic emanation of the Prime Mover. The heavenly spheres do not exhibit the simple arrangement that they would possess if the world proceeded from God eternally. If the Aristotelian philosophy were true without qualification, it should be possible to apprehend by logic alone why the composition of the heavens was just so and not otherwise. But no such logical consistency in nature can be found. Maimonides holds, therefore, that there are individual and unique aspects of the natural order that make plausible a belief that God, at creation, arranged the phenomena in a manner not deducible by reason, though understandable by it. The world is an interconnected whole, bound together by certain laws, which in their totality depend on an initial voluntary act of God, an act unlike any other event in the history of the cosmos.

Why is the principle of creation so important? According to Maimonides, the fundamental issue is not merely whether or not the world had a temporal beginning. The plausibility of creation is important because it indicates that God possesses a power analogous to free and spontaneous creative activity. This underlying idea, not a literal interpretation of the first chapter of Genesis, is what Maimonides wishes to save.

> Know that our shunning the affirmation of the eternity of the world is not due to a text figuring in the Torah according to which the world has been produced in time. For the texts indicating that the world has been produced in time are not more numerous than those indicating that the deity is a body. Nor are the gates of figurative [i.e., allegorical] interpretation shut in our faces or impossible of access to us regarding the subject of the creation of the world in time. For we could interpret them as figurative, as we have done when denying His corporeality. Perhaps this would even be much easier to do: We should be very well able to give a figurative interpretation of those texts and to affirm as true the eternity of the world, just as we have given a figurative interpretation of those texts and have denied that He, may He be exalted, is a body. . . . The belief in eternity the way Aristotle sees

Israelites crossing safely through the Sea of Reeds, while Egyptian soldiers drown (Ex. 14). Pharoah appears at right. From the Sarajevo Haggadah. (Courtesy of the Union of American Hebrew Congregations.)

it—that is, the belief according to which the world exists in virtue of necessity, that no nature changes at all, and that the customary course of events cannot be modified with regard to anything—destroys the Law in its principle, necessarily gives the lie to every miracle, and reduces to inanity all the hopes and threats that the Law has held out. . . . Know that with a belief in the creation of the world in time, all the miracles become possible and the Law becomes possible, and all questions that may be asked on this subject, vanish. Thus it might be said: Why did God give prophetic revelation to this one and not to that? Why did God give this Law to this particular nation, and why did He not legislate to the others? Why did He legislate at this particular time, and why did He not legislate before it or after? Why did He impose these commandments and these prohibitions? Why did He privilege the prophet with the miracles mentioned in relation to him and not with some others? . . . If this were said, the answer to all these questions would be that it would be said: He wanted it this way; or His wisdom required it this way.[18]

Maimonides does not merely aim to justify a traditional religious doctrine, but to overcome limits inherent in the Aristotelian concept of God's relation to the world, so as to make room for individuality and uniqueness in nature and history. And he wants to show that this view-point, which is at the heart of Judaism, is acceptable to reason.

In referring to miracles Maimonides does not imply that God's super-natural activity consists in a continual, arbitrary suspension of the regular processes of nature. He makes very cautious and sparing use of miracles, explaining many of the biblical depictions of them as poetical descriptions of natural events, or allegorical prophetic visions. He feels, however, that religious metaphysics must allow for the possibility of miracles, in the sense that God, when he created the world, implanted in the cosmos the ground for events completely out of the ordinary that realize his pur-poses in the world.

Next to creation, the most important miraculous process is prophecy. Some medieval thinkers offered completely naturalistic explanations of prophecy, identifying it with the thought of someone who has fully acti-vated his reason. In this Aristotelian interpretation, prophecy, like reason itself, comes about as an effect exerted on the potential intellect of human beings by the Active Intellect, the celestial Intelligence that governs the world beneath the moon. A naïve view of prophecy was that God picks out any one he wants to send as his messenger, regardless of intellectual qualifications. Maimonides rejected both approaches: Prophets were men of moral and mental perfection, but first, the effect of the Active Intellect extended not just to the mind of the prophet but to his imagination. (Mai-monides disinguishes between the philosopher, who uses only his intel-lect; the ordinary statesman, who uses only his imagination; and the prophet, who uses both.) This explains why prophets presented the truth not in the form of technical philosophy, but in the form of metaphors and symbols. Second, God withholds prophetic inspiration from all but those he chooses, so that God's will remains the crucial factor in deter-mining who is a prophet. Third, all prophets teach speculative truth and admonish the people to observe the Divine Law. However, only Moses, the supreme prophet, is a legislator. He differs from all other prophets in that they prophesied by means of dreams and visions, intermittently, and in a state of ecstasy; Moses prophesied continually, in a normal state, with clear thoughts, and he revealed a perfect law. The content of Moses' prophecy, the divine legislation, is the single greatest miracle of history.

According to Maimonides, the divine legislation has been revealed by God in a manner suitable to the intellectual levels and needs both of the masses and the elite. Maimonides follows his Muslim predecessors in viewing the prophetic lawgiver according to Plato's conception of the philosopher as creator of the ideal state. The Mosaic law regulates the political relations between men, furthers their external well-being, and establishes the basis for a just society. But it also is concerned with man's spiritual well-being and the perfection of his soul. The law brings peace and harmony between human beings, making possible the actualization of the intellect; the law also instructs man in controlling his instincts, making possible the internal freedom that is a prerequisite for the acquisition of knowledge. The most difficult portion of the divine legislation to explain rationally is the biblical ceremonial law, as Saadiah admitted and Halevy stressed. Maimonides hazards several explanations for biblical rituals. Drawing on information about paganism culled from Arabic books, he proposes that the purpose behind certain commandments was to prevent Israel from engaging in pagan practices that would lead to even further concessions to polytheistic thinking and to idolatry. (According to Maimonides, idolatry—the worship of created things rather than the Creator—is a heinous sin because it perverts the mind.) The sacrificial system, Maimonides daringly suggests, was a concession to the popular mentality in ancient times. Because people could not conceive of worship without sacrificial offerings, the Torah instructs them to present such offerings only to the incorporeal God.

> As at that time the way of life generally accepted and customary in the whole world and the universal service upon which we were brought up consisted in offering various species of living beings in the temples in which images were set up, in worshipping the latter, and in burning incense before them—the pious ones and the ascetics being at that time, as we have explained, the people who were devoted to the service of the temples consecrated to the stars—: His wisdom, may He be exalted, and His gracious ruse, which is manifest in regard to all His creatures, did not require that He give us a Law prescribing the rejection, abandonment, and abolition of all these kinds of worship. For one could not then conceive the acceptance of [such a Law], considering the nature of man, which always likes that to which it is accustomed. At that time this would have been similar to the appearance of a prophet in these times who, calling upon the people to worship God, would say: "God has given you a Law forbidding you to pray to Him, to fast, to call upon Him for help in misfortune. Your worship should consist solely in meditation without any works at all."[19]

Maimonides was not interested here in historical analysis as such, which he thought a waste of time, but wanted to show that even those laws that have no obvious purpose exhibit divine wisdom and are intended by God to educate the human mind to grasp the truth.

Discussion of the divine legislation forms the climax of Book Three of the *Guide*. Earlier in that section Maimonides explores certain equally fundamental issues of religious faith bearing on man's place in the universe: the existence of evil, the purpose of creation, the nature of providence. Maimonides strenuously denies that evil exists as an independent force in the world. Aspects of reality that seem to be evil, are frequently man's fault. Social evils, man's inhumanity to man, can be corrected by good government and well-ordered human relations, one of the goals of the divine legislation. Personal evils often result from man's indulgence in vices that weaken his health and interfere with his becoming a fully rational being (such as excessive drinking, eating, and sexual activity). A third source of apparent evil, not the result of human failings, is a by-product of physical nature. Man is affected by earthquakes, disease, and death because he is a natural being, with a body as well as a soul. For Maimonides, then, evil is a privation, the absence of good. Complaints that there is more evil than good in the world (a view that Maimonides opposes) are the result of a self-centered, anthropomorphic perspective on man's place in the cosmos. In this connection, Maimonides rejects the idea that man can know the final purpose of God's creation. Even Saadiah's dictum that God created the universe so that His creatures can achieve happiness is unsatisfactory. All attempts to define the ultimate purpose of reality lead to an infinite regress, because, for any single answer, one can ask what further purpose it serves. The only solution is that God created the universe according to His will and His wisdom. Every species is an end in itself and existence is a good in itself.

The Aristotelian concept of the Active Intellect, so important for his explanation of prophecy, helped Maimonides define divine providence. Aristotelian philosophers acknowledged a general providence extending to species, not to individuals. Maimonides conceives of a particular providence extending to human individuals. (He does not go so far as Saadiah, who extended particular providence to animals as well.) For Maimonides, divine providence is proportionate to the extent to which the individual has activated his intellect: God protects the innocent by warning him of danger, warnings which come through the contact of the human mind with the Active Intellect. In his chapter on Job, Maimonides suggests that the true happiness of man lies in the bliss of communion with God, which raises man above all outward sufferings he may have to endure.

In the concluding chapters of the *Guide*, Maimonides summarizes his ideal of human perfection, synthesizing the Aristotelian conviction that reason is man's supreme goal with the Jewish emphasis on the ethical life. He illustrates his position with a parable: The levels of human intellectual development are symbolized by the location of various groups of people around the palace of a great king. Some are outside the walls of the city; these are "human beings who have no doctrinal belief, neither one based on speculation nor one that accepts the authority of tradition." Some are within the city, with their backs to the palace; these have "adopted incorrect opinions either because of some great error that befell them in the course of their speculation or because of their following the traditional authority of one who had fallen into error." Others seek to enter the ruler's palace but cannot perceive the way in; they are the naïve Jewish

Moses presents the tablets of the law to the Israelites at Mount Sinai; God's presence is indicated by a pillar of fire. From the Sarajevo Haggadah. (Courtesy of the Union of American Hebrew Congregations.)

adherents of the law. Learned Jews who "believe true opinions on the basis of traditional authority," but do not engage in philosophical speculation, are described as walking around the outside of the palace. Inside are those who have "plunged into speculation concerning the fundamental principles of religion" (i.e., inside are those men for whom Maimonides wrote the *Guide*). Only he who has achieved the highest possible level of intellectual communion with God is with the ruler, near his throne. This is the person "who has achieved demonstration, to the extent that that is possible, of everything that may be demonstrated; and who has ascertained in divine matters, to the extent that that is possible, everything that may be ascertained; and who has come close to certainty in those matters in which one can only come close to it."

Is intellectual communion, then, the goal of religion? Not quite. Maimonides qualifies his position by indicating that the perfected person goes beyond contemplation of God to an even higher state. The key passage is his interpretation of Jeremiah 9:23–24 where the prophet proclaims:

> Let not the wise man glory in his wisdom, neither let the mighty man glory in his might, let not the rich man glory in his riches; but let him that glorieth glory in this, that he understandeth and knoweth Me, that I am the Lord who exercises mercy, justice, and righteousness in the earth, for in these things I delight, saith the Lord.

Maimonides interprets this passage from Jeremiah as teaching that the individual must raise himself above dependence on everything transitory. Wealth and possessions can disappear overnight. Physical strength and bodily perfection vanish with sickness, old age, and death. Even ethical behavior is dependent on the presence of others. Just as God is totally self-sufficient, so the individual must aspire to self-sufficiency. There is, however, one intellectual and ethical mode of living that does not rely on anything but oneself. The supreme knowledge—the understanding of God within the limits possible for man—includes the knowledge of God's attributes of action and is, therefore, a knowledge that leads one to imitate God. The full purpose of the verses cited from Jeremiah is to be expounded in the following manner:

> It is clear that the perfection of man that may truly be glorified in is the one acquired by him who has achieved, in a measure corresponding to his capacity, apprehension of Him, may He be exalted, and who knows His providence extending over His creatures as manifested in the act of bringing them into being and in their governance as it is. The way of life of such an individual, after he has achieved this apprehension, will always have in view "mercy, justice, and righteousness," through assimilation to His actions, may He be exalted, just as we have explained several times in this treatise.[20]

Just as the prophet describes God as merciful, just, and righteous "in the earth," that is, with respect to earthly matters, so the perfected individual models himself on these ethical actions of God, behaving in a merciful, just, and righteous manner always.

In this conclusion, the tension between Aristotelian intellectualism and Jewish moral values is to some extent resolved. Not completely. Intellectual knowledge remains a precondition for the immortality of the soul. Maimonides strongly affirms the primacy of reason: The Maimonidean conception of faith meant that one had to achieve as complete a proof of the central beliefs of Judaism as the human mind can attain. Some of Maimonides' statements in this regard verge on agnosticism, such as when he says that God's essence is hidden from man, and that even the philosopher knows only *that* God is, not *what* he is. But this is not truly agnosticism, because a negative knowledge that comes from denying imperfections to God implies there is an analogy, one knows not what, between God's wisdom and will and human wisdom and will. Man can grasp, through the study of nature, some of the ways in which God guides the world. The fundamental beliefs of Judaism, such as creation *ex nihilo*, are plausible. Miracles occur, though fewer than many religious people suppose. There is individual providence, though it is a spiritual contact between God and certain men, not a personal and physical supervision of everything that happens to everybody.

Maimonides' rationalism has passion and subtlety—it is a precisely balanced, critical rationalism unlike Saadiah's enthusiastic and more naïve faith in reason and unlike Judah Halevy, who used philosophy to reject philosophy. Maimonides tried to make peace between Judaism and philosophy by enlarging the love of talmudic learning to include natural science and metaphysics, and by making correct philosophical doctrine a criterion of being a Jew. For the talmudic teaching that study of the law is for the sake of doing mitzvot he found an equivalent in his system: Activating the mind is for the sake of that imitation of God which is the meaning of holiness. It would seem that it was this idea that Maimonides himself tried to carry out through the intellectual and personal leadership he sought to provide for the Jews of his time.

We shall see in the next section that specific elements in Maimonides' system came under severe attack by Jews who did not accept Aristotelianism. And there were Jewish Aristotelians after Maimonides who did not see the need for his concessions to religious faith. Nevertheless, the historical impact of Maimonides is not limited to his medieval Jewish followers and detractors. Medieval Christian scholasticism learned much from him. (The great theologians Albertus Magnus and Thomas Aquinas cite the *Guide* frequently.) His goal of reconciling religion and science, and the open-ended and suggestive richness of his thought, acted as a stimulus to important modern Jewish thinkers from Spinoza in the seventeenth century through Hermann Cohen in the early twentieth century, and to others down to the present, who found in Maimonides an inspiration that transcends the specifically medieval context of his thought.

Post-Maimonidean Philosophy; Gersonides and Crescas

Maimonides was venerated in the East, but his intellectual heirs appeared in the West. In northern Spain, Italy, and especially in Provence (southern France), the Maimonidean synthesis of secular and religious learning was adopted by energetic and articulate Jews (physicians, astronomers, mathematicians, poets, preachers, and communal leaders) from the thirteenth into the fifteenth centuries. Even those who rejected philosophy had to take heed of it, because rationalist ideas were being made available in a popularized as well as a technical form in these regions of the diaspora. Whereas previously, medieval Jewish philosophy was written in Arabic and was the reaction of individual Jews to Muslim philosophical works, in the post-Maimonidean era there was a continual interchange of views in Hebrew, representing a conscious effort to make philosophical rationalism an integral part of Judaism.

A key factor was translation. By the early thirteenth century, most of the classic works of Jewish theology had been made available in Hebrew by Jews living in Provence. The ibn Tibbon family was especially prominent in this regard: Judah ibn Tibbon, who moved from Muslim Spain to Provence in the mid-twelfth century, translated into Hebrew such works as Bahya's *Duties of the Heart* (1161), Halevy's *Kuzari* (1167), and Saadiah's *Book of Beliefs and Opinions* (1186). His son, Samuel, translated Maimonides' *Guide for the Perplexed* in 1204. Basic works by Aristotle and Plato were rendered in Hebrew, as well as writings of the great Muslim commentators on Aristotle. Especially influential was the interpretation of Aristotle by ibn Roshd, usually known in Europe as Averroes. A Spanish Muslim, Averroes was a contemporary of Maimonides and much admired by him—a thinker who had an impact in his own right on the later phases of Jewish philosophy, leading some Jewish (and Christian) rationalists to a more extreme form of Aristotelianism than that of Maimonides. Successful translation required a new Hebrew scientific and philosophical terminology, which in turn made it easier to write new works in Hebrew. A growing body of scientific and philosophical writings, including important commentaries to the *Guide*, were produced by Jews in Spain, Provence, and Italy from the thirteenth century on. These Jewish translators and writers also became an important bridge in the transmission of this learning from the Muslim world to Christian Europe, helping made Maimonides, Averroes, and many others available in Latin.

Among those who admired Maimonides the halakhist, however, were some who were alarmed by the spread of the Maimonidean ideal of a

The "wise son" from the First Cincinnati Haggadah, fifteenth-century Germany. (Courtesy of the Hebrew Union College-Jewish Institute of Religion, Cincinnati.)

Judaism based on science and metaphysics. Even before his death Maimonides was accused of hiding his disbelief in the resurrection of the dead, of viewing prophecy, providence, and immortality as being determined by intellectual achievement, of asserting that knowledge of God's existence rested solely on Aristotelian principles, of proclaiming that one was not a Jew if, in any sense, he believed in God's corporeality. Maimonidean Aristotelianism was reputed to undermine talmudic study and to distort the meaning of the Scriptures, and he was said to have shown greater deference to Aristotle than to the biblical text or to rabbinic tradition.

There were two periods of open confrontation between the anti-Maimonideans and the Maimonideans. In 1230 some of the most zealous opponents of Maimonidean influence attempted to forbid the study of the *Guide* and of the philosophical sections of the *Mishneh Torah*. The clash of opinions and personalities soon widened to include more moderate critics of Maimonides, such as the great halakhist and biblical commentator Nahmanides. The spate of excommunications and counter-excommunications came abruptly to an end in 1232, when Dominican inquisitors in France had many copies of Maimonides' writings burned. Because both sides were appalled, overt polemics subsided for a while. But Maimonideanism and resistance to it continued to flourish. In 1300 the controversy broke out again. This time, a new generation of anti-Maimonideans issued a ban (largely ignored) prohibiting Jews from studying Greek philosophy and science before the age of 25. The conflict died down again in 1306, when large numbers of Jews were expelled from France.

Opposition to medieval Jewish rationalism cannot be reduced to a single motive, because several historical factors other than theology entered into the picture. In the first part of the thirteenth century, southern France was the scene of a destructive crusade, launched by Pope Innocent III with the help of the barons of northern France, against Christian heretics known as the Albigensians. The Inquisition set up by the Church to enforce orthodox belief was not averse to interfering in Jewish affairs, as previously noted. The relative security of Provençal Jews was shaken by the campaign against religious dissidence, and a fear of ideas dangerous to orthodoxy spilled over into Judaism, spurring on the more extreme anti-Maimonideans. Toward the end of the century, prominent Ashkenazic scholars fleeing German persecutions settled in Christian Spain, where they reinforced those who held that rabbinic learning was endangered by the rationalists' preference for scientific and philosophical pursuits. Dislike of Maimonideanism was also fueled by feelings of resentment against wealthy and prominent Court Jews of Spain who found rationalism congenial and traditional piety inconvenient; they were accused by their Jewish critics of neglecting the commandments and of lacking solidarity with the rest of the Jewish people. Moreover, the intellectual vitality of thirteenth-century Jewish culture was not confined to rationalists and traditionalists. A small but growing number of yeshivah students and Jewish scholars, discovering that they could not find an answer to their spiritual needs in Aristotelianism or in Talmud study alone, were attracted to another form of metaphysical speculation and allegorical Bible interpretation: the Kabbalah, which will be described in the next chapter.

Apart from those who remained faithful to Maimonides' own synthesis, Jewish philosophy after Maimonides moved in two antithetical directions. The first, at its height in the early fourteenth century, looking on some of Maimonides' conclusions as unconvincing compromises with pure scientific truth, pushed toward a more consistent and forthright Aristotelianism. The second, which climaxed in the early fifteenth century, used philosophical arguments to attack the very scientific system that Maimonides felt had given him secure knowledge about the natural world.

Levi ben Gerson (1288–1344, known as Gersonides) was the most original Jewish philosopher in the Aristotelian mode after Maimonides. A native of Provence, a keen and subtle reasoner with many-sided interests, Gersonides wrote on mathematics and astronomy (he invented several important astronomical instruments); he composed a supercommentary to Averroes' commentaries on Aristotle, a philosophical and ethical commentary to the Bible, and talmudic responsa. His philosophical treatise,

A rabbi preaching in a German synagogue, from a seventeenth-century woodcut.

Milhamot Adonai (*The Wars of the Lord*), deals with the immortality of
the soul, the nature of prophecy, God's omniscience, divine providence,
the influence on the terrestrial world of the celestial spheres, the problems
of creation *ex nihilo* and of miracles. Unlike Saadiah, Halevy, and Maimonides, Gersonides wrote in a style also characteristic of medieval
Christian scholastic philosophers: The positions held by the main Aristotelian authorities on the issue in question are exhaustively surveyed and
criticized; then his own solution is propounded. Gersonides was an original thinker who did not hesitate to disagree with Maimonides and
Averroes. Although a brief description does not do justice to his analyti-
cal acuteness, it does indicate the general direction of his thinking in contrast to that of his predecessors.

In Gersonides' philosophy God is far more remote from the specific
events of the world and from human individuals than in the philosophy
of Maimonides, although Gersonides, like Maimonides, felt his conclusions were completely in harmony with biblical teaching. (He has even
been characterized as approaching the deism of the eighteenth-century
Enlightenment; for example, the sole proof for God's existence, according to Gersonides, is the perfection and design evident in the natural
order.) Even where Gersonides took a stand that seems to resemble that
of Maimonides, his views were expressed in a more frank and forthright
manner. Immortality is intellectual: Only the rational mind of the individual survives death. People fall under the care and protection of divine
providence to the extent to which they have acquired knowledge of universal principles. Prophecy is a rational faculty in communion with the
universal intellect. Disagreeing with Maimonides, Gersonides insists that
a special act of divine will is not necessary for one to become a prophet.
Gersonides was an ardent astrologer, a system of prediction that Maimonides detested. He insisted, however, that astral determinism was not
absolute; as a result of prophetic warning, human beings can exert their
free will to change a future that had been previously indicated in the
stars.

In the Aristotelian tradition, Gersonides viewed God as the First Cause
of existence and the supreme thought. In contrast to Maimonides, Gersonides argues that it is not necessary to restrict our concept of God to
the predication of negative attributes: Positive attributes do not threaten
God's unity. We simply affirm that certain qualities, like knowledge, are
primary with respect to God and *derivative* with respect to man. For
example, Maimonides had insisted that God's knowledge bears no resemblance to man's knowledge; Gersonides affirmed that they were both
forms of the same knowledge, though vastly different in degree. God has
knowledge in the highest possible sense; human knowledge is like God's,
but in a diminished way. God's knowledge, however (and here again
Gersonides is a much more consistent Aristotelian than Maimonides), is

knowledge only of the universal cosmic laws that regulate reality. Specific details and persons are not known to God. For Gersonides, this did not constitute a divine imperfection: Even for God true knowledge was essentially knowledge of the universal principles and forms of being.

Gersonides' God is rather remote from the terrestrial world. The pure Intelligences are in direct control of their respective spheres in the heavens, and the lowest of them, the Active Intelligence, is the ruler of terrestrial existence and the immediate goal of man's reason. Therefore, Gersonides' conception of miracles tends to eliminate their supernatural character. He accepts the biblical account of miraculous events, but defines miracles as an exceptional kind of law, one which determines events of extreme rarity and occasionally supersedes the ordinary processes of nature. And Gersonides disagrees with Maimonides' conception of creation. Accepting the doctrine that God created the universe in time, he affirms that creation is indeed a unique event in the history of the cosmos. But it is philosophically impossible to assert that matter came into being at creation. This does not mean that matter existed before creation, nor does the eternity of matter limit God in any way. It is simply not reasonable to speak of the creation of matter in any sense. Thus Gersonides proposes what Maimonides and even Halevy had admitted as a philosophical alternative they preferred to avoid: that the biblical concept of creation should be interpreted not as creation *ex nihilo* but as the imposition on an eternal, inert, undetermined matter of the forms of being.

Gersonides' views show, in contrast, how far Maimonides had been able to remain faithful to key aspects of the Jewish tradition. Gersonides is much closer to (though more sophisticated than) the stereotyped Aristotelian that Halevy had attacked. Gersonides' Judaism went as far as possible toward a rigorously scientific conception of the universe within the context of the Aristotelianism of his day, and he felt he had harmonized religion and reason more adequately than had been done before. But the philosophical approach that Gersonides represented soon fell into disrepute because of historical pressures on Western Jewry. Massacres and expulsions in France, the 1391 pogroms, and the wave of conversions in Spain created a climate of opinion among Jewish thinkers in which Gersonides was looked on as verging on heresy. The final stage of medieval Jewish philosophy was a sharp attack on crucial elements in the philosophy of Aristotle.

The last great figure of Jewish philosophy in Spain was Hasdai Crescas (c. 1340–c. 1412). A member of an influential Barcelona family, Crescas was a merchant and communal leader in close contact with the royal court of Aragon. After the riots of 1391, when massacre and conversion wiped out the Jewry of Barcelona (his son was killed in the pogrom), Crescas settled in Saragossa, the capital of Aragon, where he served as

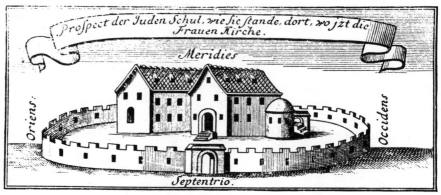

The old Jewish synagogue at Nuremberg according to an eighteenth-century drawing.

rabbi and attempted to revive the decimated Jewish communities of the kingdom. His last years were devoted to writing a philosophical treatise, *Or Adonai* (*The Light of the Lord*), completed in 1410. The overall objective of this work was the clarification of the central dogmas of Judaism. (Maimonides' brief description of the thirteen principles of Jewish faith was considered by Crescas inadequate.) Crescas distinguishes certain categories of Jewish beliefs according to their relation to the Torah: first, the logical presuppositions of the Torah (the existence and nature of God); then, the fundamental principles of the Torah (God's knowledge of existing things, divine providence and omnipotence, prophecy, free will, the purpose of the law and of human life); finally, the logical consequences of belief in the Torah (creation, immortality, resurrection, the eternity of the Torah, the superiority of Moses to all other prophets, belief in the coming of the Messiah). Crescas' treatise is organized according to these categories, each one forming the subject of a separate section.

The most original aspect of Crescas' work, however, is not his summary of Jewish doctrines but his criticism of Aristotelianism. Crescas was led to do this in order to invalidate certain conclusions of Maimonides, Gersonides, and others, but his approach is historically significant also because he foreshadows the scientific revolution about to transform European thought in the sixteenth and seventeenth centuries. First, he rejects completely Aristotle's concept of space. For Aristotle it was logically untenable to conceive of a space not occupied by a body: There could be no true vacuum. Crescas maintains that space was merely the container of things, and that a vacuum was possible. This means that, whereas Aristotle and the medievals conceived of a closed, finite universe, Crescas (and the moderns) preferred an open, infinite universe. Second, Crescas pointed toward a new concept of matter: Matter is not, as the Aristotelians maintained, the potentiality for being, a substratum that can never exist apart from form. For Crescas matter is a primary, corporeal entity capable of actual existence by itself. Third, Crescas criticized the Aristotelian rejection of infinite numbers, by holding that although an infinite number may not exist, an infinite series of numbers may. If an infinite series is possible, then the causal chain can also be infinite, thereby rendering invalid the Aristotelian proof for the existence of the Prime Mover. As a result, Crescas recognizes only one of the now-traditional philosophical arguments for God's existence: Regardless of whether the number of causes is necessarily finite (as the Aristotelians claimed) or infinite (as Crescas seems to suggest), there must be one cause that is not in itself an effect, and this is God. It is noteworthy in this regard that although Crescas is very much concerned with defending Jewish faith, he does not accord the concept of creation *ex nihilo* primary importance as a ground for affirming the divine origin of the Torah. Instead, creation is classified as a secondary belief derived from the Torah. In his philosophy, Crescas comes close to conceiving of God's creative power as a continuous activity, not as a unique event in time.

A second area in which Crescas attacks the Aristotelians is the belief that the intellect is the essence of man's nature and God's. Crescas insisted that goodness, not thought, was the basis of God's being and of all other divine attributes. The continual creative act of God is a perpetual overflowing of his goodness. Similarly, Crescas insists that the immortal part of the soul is not the mind. The soul is a spiritual substance capable of separation from the body and existing forever, regardless of whether or not the individual has attained theoretical knowledge. Human and divine bliss come not from the intellect but from feeling. Human joy does not consist in the mere possession of knowledge but in the love of God, which leads to eternal happiness and to communion with him. God's joy is manifest in his outpouring of an infinite love for his creatures, a sharp swing away from the Aristotelian idea that it diminishes God's dignity to think of him as subject to emotion. Crescas' disengagement from Aristotelianism allows him to restore a warmth and spontaneity to the philosophical idea of God lacking in the austere and logical Aristotelian concept of God as the highest thought.

On one issue, however, Crescas takes a position surprisingly at variance with the usual interpretation of the Jewish tradition. From Saadiah on, Jewish philosophers had sought to devise formulas reconciling human self-determination with divine omnipotence and omniscience. As he did with the concepts of space, matter, and number, Crescas redefines the issue in a more modern way. He turns away from the traditional defense of free will to offer an analysis of the causal factors in human willing. According to Crescas, as every action is caused, the causes that enter into

Discussion at a Passover seder, from the late fourteenth-century Darmstadt Haggadah. (Courtesy of the Hessische Landes- und Hochschulbibliothek.)

human choice fully determine what it will decide at any point. To be sure, he insists that religion is a crucial factor: The expectation of reward or punishment is a means for strengthening the resolve to do good; ethical ideals and the commandments of the Torah guide one in doing the right; the very exertion of effort is a force that helps determine the outcome. Nevertheless, Crescas insists that every act arises from specific causes such that if the causes had not been present then the act would not take place. Given the causes, the result is inevitable—which is true determinism. He argues that this is not fatalism, because fatalism is the belief that something will occur regardless of specific circumstances. Crescas' psychological determinism is not the result of a scientific concern only, but stems from his conception that God cannot but will the good and that the religious person's actions should be motivated solely by love for God. Ironically, Crescas's views here, which are related to his attack on Aristotelianism, lead him to a position close to that characteristic of the Aristotelianism that Maimonides had made such great efforts to overcome: a world system that all but eliminates freedom as a metaphysical reality.

In the fifteenth century, after Crescas, pure philosophical thinking loses its appeal to Jewish intellectuals in Spain. There were still ardent admirers of Maimonides, but Halevy's dictum that the God of Abraham was not the God of Aristotle was increasingly cited with sympathy. The conditions that had permitted Jews to act as cultural intermediaries in Europe were gone. The atmosphere that encouraged the disinterested cultivation of the sciences and metaphysics among Jews was undermined by a Christian onslaught that made the inner defense of Judaism primary. The many conversions after 1391 among members of the Spanish Jewish upper classes also contributed to discrediting philosophy among those who remained faithful to Judaism: A number of fifteenth-century writers attacked "the philosophizers" for having shown the weakness of their loyalty to Torah under the threat of martyrdom. As a response to conversionist pressures being applied by Christian clergy and former Jews, Jewish thinkers turned for a while to the problem of defining essential doctrines—somewhat as Saadiah had done but without his enthusiastic faith in reason. The best-known work of this kind, which defended the supernatural character of Judaism, was Joseph Albo's *Sefer ha-Ikkarim* (*Book of Principles*). Albo (probable dates, 1360–1444) had participated in the dispute of Tortosa with the Christian authorities and mentions that he was a student of Crescas. For him the three fundamentals of the Divine Law were the existence of God, revelation, and reward and punishment. From these are derived various secondary principles that he upholds against Christian dogmas. Although Albo's work remained popular with Jews, this mode of theological analysis lost ground after the Spanish and Portuguese expulsions of the last decade of the fifteenth century. Rationalist philosophy did not completely come to an end among Jews, however; the texts and ideas were cultivated by some in Italy, Holland, and Poland during the sixteenth and seventeenth centuries. But the impulse to create a philosophical Judaism was only to re-emerge as a major concern of Western Jewish thought at the end of the 1700s.

What had Jewish rationalism accomplished in the five centuries between Saadiah and Crescas? An exploration of the compatibility of Judaism with a philosophical science and metaphysics: the meeting on an equal level, as it is sometimes called, of ancient Jerusalem and Athens. Unaided human reason had not been the origin of the ideas of Judaism, but could be used as a test for their validity. Prophetic writings and later texts of Judaism were analyzed from a rational perspective; some ideas were easily defended, others only with great effort. Jewish beliefs having to do with God's relation to the natural order and to history (creation, miracles), God's relation to the Jewish people (revelation, redemption), and God's relation to the individual (providence, immortality) were often redefined in order to save them from the charge that they were not rational. The challenge could not have been ignored, because Jewish philosophers were forced to conceive of their religious faith from a more general perspective, as a result of the scientific and philosophical world view that they shared with Muslim and Christian thinkers. The confrontation between Judaism and philosophy was, however, more than a weighing of Jewish ideas in the balance of reason, as defined by a certain system of philosophy. The interaction was more complex, because philosophy was also being reshaped as a result of its encounter with Judaism, directly in Jewish philosophy and indirectly in Muslim and Christian philosophies that contain a strong Jewish component. Limitations inherent in ancient Greek philosophy became more apparent under the impact of the ideas of creation *ex nihilo*, the goodness of God, the transcendent meaning of history, and ethical freedom. New philosophies would emerge in modern times that absorbed this impact, ushering in yet another phase in the interaction of religion and reason in general, and of Judaism and philosophy in particular.[21] In the meantime, during the sixteenth through the eighteenth centuries, Jewish intellectual history shifted away from philosophical analysis to Kabbalah, the other speculative system of medieval Judaism.

CHAPTER 9

Medieval Jewish Mysticism and Kabbalah

Early Phases of Jewish Mysticism

Mysticism is a direct and immediate communion of the soul with the divine. Mystics claim that their knowledge and experience of ultimate reality are attainable through a different kind of insight from that of ordinary sense perception and rational thought, a supraintellectual insight that comes only after a strenuous course of personal preparation. Many of the basic terms connected with mysticism are derived from ancient Greece; a mystic originally was one initiated into a secret Greek religious cult or mystery religion. (The word *mystic* was derived from a Greek verb meaning to keep one's lips closed.) All the major religions, Eastern and Western, have given rise to some form of mysticism in which the person ascends to a state where pain and anxiety vanish, where rapture is attained, where the self and ultimate reality are in unmediated contact or even union. Each religious tradition grasps this illumination in its own symbols, contributing its own structure of expectations and values to the mystical intuition. When Jewish mystics also experienced a falling away of the mundane world, revealing an omnipresent spiritual reality, they did so in terms derived from the Jewish religious tradition.

It is characteristic of Jewish mysticism that Jewish mystics maintained a great reverence for tradition and conceived of themselves as being transmitters of a secret tradition of their own. (The Hebrew word *kab-*

Detail of an illumination for a Hebrew liturgical poem in the Darmstadt Haggadah; at left is a man in a state of mystical rapture. (Courtesy of the Hessische Landes- und Hochschulbibliothek.)

balah, "tradition," was used in a general sense long before it acquired a mystical connotation.) There were actually several Jewish mystical traditions, representing different historical influences and experiences, in loose relation to each other.

The great twentieth-century scholar of Jewish mysticism, Gershom Scholem, has proposed that mysticism arises in formal religion only after an abyss has opened between man and God—between the finite and the infinite.[1] The mystic seeks to cross this gap in his spiritual journey. The earliest Jewish mystical texts depict a quest through vast cosmic spaces so as to draw near to God's ineffable majesty. They describe the ascent of the mystic to heaven and his visions of the divine palaces, culminating in a personal experience of the divine presence. This type of literary material, known as the *ma'aseh merkavah* (the Workings of the [Divine] Chariot, from the first chapter of Ezekiel) or the *hekhalot* (palaces) literature, is extant in brief texts and fragments dating from talmudic times. The person sits in solitude for a long time without eating and drinking and recites prayers and incantations without ceasing, until gradually overwhelmed by ecstasy. Eventually he feels that he is passing through the seven palaces of the firmament. He sees that each palace is filled with hosts of angels whose secret names and functions he learns. He confronts the various doorkeepers, crosses bridges spanning the rivers of fire that flow down from the Divine Throne, and finally envisions the Holy One in the form of a supernal (heavenly) man, surrounded by a brilliant radiance. Material alluding to the dimensions of this celestial figure (*shiur Komah* traditions, "the measure of the Body") enumerate fantastically large measurements of the head and limbs. (The *shiur Komah* material seems to have been derived from a mystical exegesis of chap. 5 of the Song of Songs.) Although it seems that these measurements were symbolic and not intended to be taken literally, *shiur Komah* writings were severely attacked by the Karaites and by Maimonides as a false tradition ascribing a physical body to God.

Hekhalot mysticism places its emphasis on the sublimity of God, the awesome and magnificent King. The central theme of the literature, however, is not a doctrine of God, but the soul's preparation for the journey to a blinding vision of God. The *hekhalot* literature is connected with the apocalyptic tendency going back to the Second Temple period, when anonymous Jewish prophets claimed ascents to heaven, where they received visions concerning the End of Time.

A second type of Jewish mysticism, completely different from the Workings of the Chariot and perhaps also going back to the talmudic period, was known as *ma'aseh bereshit* (the Workings of Creation). The most important text of this kind was the small book known as the *Sefer Yetzirah* (The Book of Creation), a laconic and enigmatic work on cosmology and cosmography. The book asserts that God created the world by means of the 32 "secret paths of wisdom," which consist of 10 basic numbers and 22 basic letters. The numbers are called *sefirot* (singular, *sefirah*), which becomes a key term of the esoteric Jewish tradition. In the *Sefer Yetzirah* the 10 sefirotic numbers designate ten basic principles of reality; the "spirit of the living God," the physical elements (air, water, fire), and the six "extremities of space" (north, south, east, west, up, down). The 22 letters of the Hebrew alphabet are the source of all entities in the world, in time, and in the human body. The letters are divided into different groups, which in their intricate interconnections give rise to the seasons of the year, the planets, the days of the week, the signs of the zodiac, the months, the orifices and limbs of the body, even God's secret names. The assumption behind these permutations seems to be a belief in the creative, even magical power of letters alluded to in several places of the Talmud (e.g., B.T. Sanhedrin 55a, 65b). The text of the *Sefer Yetzirah*, extant in several versions, is thought to be influenced by some non-Jewish philosophy of late antiquity, such as Neo-Pythagoreanism. The only explicit Jewish reference comes at the very end, when it is said that Abraham was the first to comprehend the great truths that the book contains. The *Sefer Yetzirah* was expounded in many different ways, philosophical and mystical, in the Middle Ages. Saadiah wrote a commentary to it; Halevy refers to it in the *Kuzari*. But it was the medieval Jewish mystics who carried to the greatest extreme the *Sefer Yetzirah*'s idea of the creative power of the letters of the Torah.

Hasidei Ashkenaz, the Pietists of Medieval Germany

The mystical texts described in the previous section were brought to southern Italy in the early Middle Ages, from where they were carried to the Rhineland by Jewish settlers perhaps during the ninth century. The phase of Jewish mysticism known as *Hasidut Ashkenaz*, "Ashkenazic pietism," crystallized in the second part of the twelfth century and had its main period of creativity in the first part of the thirteenth century. (*Hasid*, as we have already seen, means "pious," a biblical word used throughout Jewish history for especially devout people.) The *Hasidei Ashkenaz* drew on the *hekhalot* literature and the *Sefer Yetzirah*, on a nonphilosophical rendering of Saadiah's *Book of Beliefs and Opinions*, and on writings of a Neo-Platonic character by various Spanish and Italian Jews. Though a number of men participated in this group, the core

Sixteenth-century German woodcut of the **kapparot** ceremony in which the sins of man are symbolically transferred to a fowl on the day before Yom Kippur.

was formed by several generations of the Kalonymus family, notably Samuel ben Kalonymus the hasid (the pious) of Speyer (second half of the twelfth century), his son Judah ben Samuel the hasid (c. 1150–1217) of Regensburg, and Judah's relative and pupil Eleazar ben Judah of Worms (1165–1230). Eleazar was the author of books dealing with the group's mystical doctrines, such as the *Sodei Razaya* (*Secret of Secrets*), which includes an exegesis of the *Sefer Yetzirah* and the mysteries of the Chariot.

The mystical teachings of the Ashkenazic pietists of the twelfth and thirteenth centuries were not an explicit, synthesized system, but rather a rich, amorphous combination of attitudes and ideas. Their pietism had the following characteristics: First, an emphasis on the passionate and selfless love of God, described in terms of the love of man and woman. The supreme manifestation of this love is martyrdom (*kiddush ha-Shem*), a major theme in the writings of the Hasidei Ashkenaz, who were said to be among the "first of the martyrs" during the crusade period. Love of God saturates the senses and leads to a joy so overwhelming that no room remains in the soul for sin to enter. Second, a powerful sense of the omnipresence of God. God fills and embraces everything, permeates all worlds; the human mind cannot grasp the infinite God, with whom nothing can be compared. Third, a conception of various intermediary powers between God and the created world, especially God's created Glory (*Kavod*). (According to the pietists, the exalted, brilliant, and fiery appearance of His Glory was the object of prophetic and of mystical vision.) Fourth, a fascination with holy names of God and with combinations of Hebrew letters, ideas taken from the incantations of the *hekhalot* literature and from the *Sefer Yetzirah*. Man can discover these mystical secrets through permutations of the Hebrew alphabet, such as the activities of *gematria* (where individual letters and words are reduced to their numerical value) and *notarikon* (in which the letters of a word are considered initial letters of other words). Fifth, an obsession with demons and the spirits of the dead, absorbed from medieval German culture or retained from the Hellenistic and other ancient origins of this material. (The literature of the Hasidei Ashkenaz contain lore on incantations in which holy names are used for protection against the injuries inflicted by evil spirits and ghosts.) Sixth, an exacting attention to prayer. The Jewish prayers were likened to the sacrificial offerings of the biblical Temple, and the perfection of this service required intense concentration on the words and even letters of each prayer. Meticulous concern for ritual, however, did not prevent the pietists from teaching that the prayers of simple people, even when not in Hebrew or in the established form, were effective as long as the heart was directed totally to God.

The most original aspect of the Hasidei Ashkenaz and the main focus of their teachings was their concept of the *hasid*, "the pious one," who lives by the highest moral and religious standard. Our main source for their ideal of the hasid is the *Sefer Hasidim* (the *Book of the Pious*), one of the most important medieval Jewish ethical works from the Ashkenazic milieu. The *Sefer Hasidim*, which contains many legends about Judah the hasid, is not particularly mystical in content and does not contain the group's esoteric thought, but it represents that side of the movement most influential in later Jewish history.

The hasid was not primarily a master of the talmudic text; he represents a move away from the form of rabbinical intellectuality epitomized in Ashkenazic culture by the tosafists, the Talmud commentators of twelfth and thirteenth-century northern France and Germany. The hasid was supposed to live by the highest altruistic ideal, acting in all matters beyond the measure of strict justice: The pietists refer to a "Heavenly Law" more exacting in its ethical demands even than the law of Torah. (This was not a rejection or even a criticism of the Torah, but an aspiration to go beyond its stipulations to an absolute standard of goodness.) The hasid, for example, was to avoid any possibility of shaming or embarrassing his fellow man. The hasid was to strive for a state of spiritual equanimity and serenity such that he became oblivious to any insult and accepted as the decree of God any disaster that befell him. (The preoccupation with bearing insults without being psychologically affected by them was a realistic concern in thirteenth-century Germany, when the humiliating of Jews was not infrequent.) The hasid was opposed to physical pleasure as an end in itself. Although not against sexual relations for propagation, the teachings of the Hasidei Ashkenaz were quite ascetic, leading to a renunciation of worldly things that reached its culmination in the idea of mortifying the flesh as an atonement for sins. The pietists believed that divine retribution could be forestalled by self-imposed chastisements, which, in their intensity, should correspond to the punishment awaiting the sinner in *Gehinnom* (Hell). Penances ranged from brief fasts to prolonged exile, in which the penitent voluntarily left home and family and wandered abroad for a specified time. Even if he had not committed a serious sin, the altruistic hasid viewed these penances as atonements for the sins of the Jewish people as a whole. The ultimate self-sacrifice was martyrdom, witnessing to the truth of the Jewish religion, which the Hasidei Ashkenaz had ample opportunity to practice.

The devotion of the Hasidei Ashkenaz was intensified by the same general spiritual atmosphere that produced the Franciscan movement in Christianity. (Francis of Assisi was a contemporary of Judah the hasid.) It also seems probable that the Jewish pietists borrowed from penitential tracts of popular Christian mysticism, as well as from German folklore about life beyond the grave. But this led to no blurring of the line separating Jews and Christians in medieval northern Europe: The Hasidei Ashkenaz conducted their own psychological counter-crusade against

וְאַחַר כָּךְ יִקְרָא הַמִּצְוָה הַשְּׁלִישִׁית הַתְּחַתּוֹנָה, יַבְעֶנָה
לִשְׁנַיִם וִיתֵּן עֲלֵיהָ לְאֶטּוֹגָא וְיֹאכַל בְּיַחַד בְּלֹא בְּרָכָה
אֶלָּא כָּךְ אָמַר כֵּן עָשָׂה הִלֵּל בִּזְמַן שֶׁבֵּית הַמִּקְדָּשׁ
קַדָּם הָיָה בּוֹרֵךְ מַצָּה וּמָרוֹר בְּיַחַד וְיֹאכַל   כְּמַה שֶׁנֶּ׳
מַצּוֹת עַל מְרוֹרִים יֹאכְלֻהוּ

A Passover seder, from the Prague Haggadah of 1526, one of the first printed Haggadot with illustrations.

Christianity, seeking to uphold the truth of their religion against their persecutors and to isolate the Jews from too much contact with Christianity. The ideal of inner fortitude in the face of the worst adversity remained a strong element of Ashkenazic Judaism, even after the theoretical concepts of the movement, such as the created Glory (*Kavod*) of God, were submerged by the far more intricate mystical theology of the Jews in Provence and Spain.

The Kabbalah

The Kabbalah has been defined as a form of theosophy—a teaching about the hidden nature of divinity.[2] Although usually considered a phase of Jewish mysticism, the purely mystical element in the Kabbalah is only part, albeit a central part, of a vast and complex mental world, which includes a speculative metaphysics, a theory of human nature, distinctive rituals, and considerable folklore. The Kabbalah contains imaginative and often paradoxical conceptions of God, the human soul, evil, and the religious life of the Jew—teachings not derived by the individual kabbalist from logical analysis and observation, but drawn from his imagination and intuition interacting with the Jewish tradition. (Some kabbalists allude to having had divine revelations or instruction from the prophet Elijah.)

As with earlier forms of Jewish mysticism, autobiography plays little part in kabbalistic writings; with a few exceptions, kabbalists did not write down and circulate the personal experience that lay at the root of their teachings. Much kabbalistic literature is a cross between philosophic and talmudic thought. The Kabbalah's elaborate system of symbols, pointing to invisible realities, are usually presented in the form of complicated and intricate exegesis of biblical and rabbinic statements, exegesis that claims to bring out hidden levels of Torah. (The term *mystery* occurs repeatedly in the Kabbalah for profound secrets that can never be fully explained.) The kabbalistic system has its own inner dynamism. The secret tradition is like an onion: After one level has been brought to light, contradictions lead the kabbalist to uncover another meaning underneath, so that secrets and mysteries without end are discovered, explored, and experienced. The history of the Kabbalah, like that of Judaism itself, is one of constant reinterpretation.

The Rise of the Kabbalah

The basic ideas of the Kabbalah first appear in Provence toward the end of the twelfth century in a book called the *Bahir (Brightness)*. An obscure and anonymous work, the *Bahir* is modeled on the midrash and contains concepts that had been earlier brought from the Middle East. (The exact historical connections have not yet been discovered.) The *Bahir*'s most novel feature is a reinterpretation of the term *sefirot*, which had been used in the *Sefer Yetzirah* for the primordial numbers out of which certain features of reality were created; in the *Bahir* and throughout the subsequent kabbalistic tradition the sefirot are attributes of God himself: distinct forces or powers within God. The *Bahir* refers to the ten sefirot as vessels, crowns, or words, which form an internal structure of the Godhead. That the divine realm should be conceived as a structured organism, not a simple unity, is one of the most daring features of the kabbalistic tradition, as will shortly be explained in more detail. The Kabbalah acknowledges that God is a unity, but posits a knowable inner configuration of deity, in place of the absolute simplicity insisted on by Jewish philosophers.

The author of the *Bahir* is not known, but there is information on other kabbalists of Provence around 1200, the most influential of which was Isaac the Blind (c. 1160–1235), son of the talmudist Abraham ben David of Posquières. (Abraham ben David, one of the first critics of Maimonides, was himself connected to the early kabbalists.) Although Isaac knew the *Bahir* and uses its concept of the sefirot, he was also strongly influenced by Neo-Platonism. In his extant writings, Isaac conceives of the sefirot as themselves emanations of a hidden and infinite level found deeper within the Divine Being. (This absolutely unknowable root of the sefirot is called by the kabbalists the *Ayn Sof*, the "Infinite," the "Endless.") According to Isaac, out of the Ayn Sof comes the first supernal quality, called the Divine Thought (*Mahshavah*). From the Divine Thought emanate the rest of the sefirot. The separated beings in the world below are considered materializations of the sefirot on lower levels of reality. The aim of the mystic experience is to reascend the ladder of emanation in order to unite with the Divine Thought. After Isaac the Blind, Neo-Platonism continued to influence kabbalists, but the kabbalists modified Neo-Platonism in line with their own proclivities. Thus, for example, emanation of the sefirot is considered a process taking place within God himself; the sefirot are not steps between the One and the world, as in many Neo-Platonic philosophies. There is no blurring of the boundary between God and the world in the Kabbalah, as there was in pagan Neo-Platonism.

From Provence the Kabbalah spread to northern Spain. In the thirteenth century an influential circle of kabbalists lived in the town of Gerona, north of Barcelona; one of the most important of this group was Azriel, a student of Isaac the Blind. (Azriel's writings include an explanation of the sefirot and a mystical interpretation of the liturgy and of the aggadah.) The Gerona kabbalists were also acquainted with Neo-Platonism, including the philosophical treatise of the Jewish Neo-Platonic philosopher, Solomon ibn Gabirol. Azriel's most important divergence from the teaching of Isaac the Blind was to replace the Divine Thought as the first emanation of the Ayn Sof with the Divine Will, making volition rather than intellection the first manifestation of God's being.

The most famous figure associated with the Gerona kabbalists was Nahmanides, one of the chief rabbinical authorities of Catalonian Jewry and a participant in the Maimonidean controversy of the early 1230s. (Nahmanides gave qualified support to the anti-Maimonideans.) Nahmanides did not write any purely kabbalistic treatise, but his commentary to the Torah alludes frequently to kabbalistic ideas. His influence contributed to the growing awareness of the Kabbalah outside the small groups in which it had first emerged—although for several more centuries Kabbalah still remained an esoteric tradition for an intellectual elite. While the Gerona mystics were developing and spreading their ideas, elsewhere in thirteenth-century Spain there appeared a variety of other kabbalistic approaches, ranging from some quite close to philosophy to others that concentrated on using the permutations of letters in the bibli-

Amulet for a woman in childbirth, from sixteenth- or seventeenth-century Persia. (Courtesy of the Jewish Museum, New York.)

cal text (*gematria*) as a way to achieve ecstatic trances (e.g., the writings of Abraham Abulafia).

A turning point in the history of the Kabbalah was the publication toward the end of the thirteenth century of the Zohar (the Book of Splendor). Since the nineteenth century, there has been considerable controversy over the antiquity of this work, but it has been determined that the bulk of the Zohar was composed by a Castilian kabbalist, Moses de Leon, in the 1280s. (Some additional sections were written by an anonymous kabbalist of the following generation.) Like the earlier *Bahir*, the Zohar was a medieval pseudepigraphon. (As we saw in a previous chapter, pseudepigrapha are works ascribed to a figure living long before the actual author, a literary device that goes back to ancient times.) Moses de Leon created a second-century CE setting for the Zohar, centering around Rabbi Simeon bar Yohai and his associates in the Galilee after the Bar Kokhba revolt. (Simeon bar Yohai is an important figure in the talmudic literature, although not identified there as a mystic.) The Zohar is a mystical midrash. In an elevated and rhetorical style, selected verses of the Torah are given an ethical or a mystical interpretation according to Moses de Leon's understanding of the Kabbalah. The language used is Aramaic, rather than Hebrew (Moses de Leon also wrote kabbalistic works in Hebrew under his own name); the general style of the Zohar resembles that of the Spanish Jewish sermon of the period. Other works of the same period by contemporaries of de Leon give a more methodical exposition of the kabbalistic system, but lack the grandeur and mysteriousness that have made the Zohar the classical text of the Kabbalah down to the present. Within a century after its appearance, even though many kabbalistic commentaries to the Bible and other treatises had been written, the Zohar was acknowledged as possessing an authority in kabbalistic teaching equivalent to that of the Talmud in rabbinic law.

The Kabbalistic Concept of Divinity: The Ayn Sof and the Sefirot

As previously mentioned, the most striking departure of the Kabbalah from other forms of Jewish theology is an organismic concept of God, who is described as having a complex and dynamic inner structure. The kabbalists accepted and incorporated the philosophers' principle that

Heart-shaped silver amulet typical of Jews of North Africa and the Middle East, containing the first letters of a Hebrew prayer.

God's essence is unknowable to man, but they combined this with a system of positive attributes drawn from earlier Jewish writings and from their own mystical intuition. According to the Kabbalah, the "root of roots" in God is the Ayn Sof, the infinite, limitless, impersonal First Cause, which cannot be grasped by human thought. Not mentioned in the Bible, the Ayn Sof is said by the kabbalists to be inferred from the process of divine self-revelation. Out of the hidden depths, latent powers and lights of the Ayn Sof break forth—the sefirot. The sefirot are revealed divinity, in their unity constituting the personal God of religion to which prayer and meditation are directed. Thus in one of the Zohar's descriptions of creation, the sefirot are likened to the colors of the upper portion of a flame:

> "In the beginning" [Gen. 1:1]—when the will of the King began to take effect, he engraved signs into the heavenly sphere [that surrounded him]. Within the most hidden recess a dark flame issued from the mystery of the Ayn Sof, the Infinite, like a fog forming in the unformed—enclosed in the ring of that sphere, neither white nor black, neither red nor green, of no color whatever. Only after this flame began to assume size and dimension, did it produce radiant colors. From the innermost center of the flame sprang forth a well out of which colors issued and spread upon everything beneath, hidden in the mysterious hiddenness of Ayn Sof.[3]

The sefirot are degrees or stages issuing forth from the absolute mystery of the Ayn Sof; they are not intermediary forces between God and the material world, as in Neo-Platonism. An intricate symbolism is attached to each sefirah and to the sefirotic system as a whole. The most common names of the ten sefirot are

1. *Keter Elyon,* the Supreme Crown. (The Zohar refers to this sefirah as *Ratzon,* "Divine Will".)
2. *Hokhmah* (Wisdom), the primordial, undifferentiated divine thought.
3. *Binah* (Understanding); in contrast to *Hokhmah, Binah* is the principle of intellect that makes distinctions.
4. *Gedullah* (Greatness), sometimes called *Hesed* (God's Overflowing Love).
5. *Gevurah* (Power), often called *Din* (Rigorous Judgment).
6. *Tiferet* (Beauty), often called *Rahamim* (Compassion).
7. *Netzah* (Endurance).
8. *Hod* (Majesty).
9. *Yesod* (Foundation), sometimes called *Zaddik* (Righteous One).
10. *Malkhut* (Kingdom), often called by the traditional term *Shekhinah* (Divine Presence) and considered the divine archetype of *Knesset Yisrael* (the Community of Israel).

The meaning of each sefirah in relation to the whole is the subject of inexhaustible and loving kabbalistic meditation.

There is a formal structure to the relationship between the sefirot, which are usually divided into groups of three. *Keter, Hokhmah,* and *Binah,* the first triad, form the intellectual level within the divine organism: will, thought, intellect. The names for the lower seven are taken from 1 Chronicles 29:11 and do not convey the precise symbolic significance of each. *Gedulah, Gevurah,* and *Tiferet* form a second triad, a psychic or moral level in divinity. *Netzah, Hod,* and *Yesod* constitute (in those kabbalistic treatises most influenced by Neo-Platonism) the archetypes for certain forces in nature. The tenth sefirah, *Malkhut,* has an elaborate symbolism of its own. It is the Queen, the specifically female

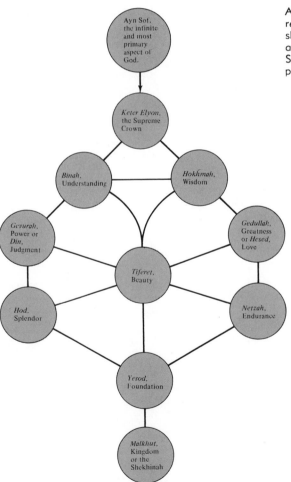

A common kabbalistic representation of the relationships between the infinite aspect of deity (the Ayn Sof) and the revealed aspects (the sephirot).

sefirah; it is also the divine counterpart of the people of Israel. The tenth sefirah is the channel between the divine and the lower, nondivine worlds.

So complex was the lore that grew up about the sefirot that no single diagram can convey the entire system. In some kabbalistic diagrams the sefirot are arranged in concentric circles, like the spheres in the Aristotelian concept of the heavens surrounding the earth. The sefirot are at times described as a cosmic tree whose roots reach back to the Ayn Sof and whose trunk and branches extend downward in the direction of the lower worlds. The most common metaphor is that the sefirot constitute the form of a heavenly man (the kabbalistic term is *Adam Kadmon,* the "Archetypal" or "Primordial Man"): The first three sefirot are his head, the second three his arms and chest, the third group his legs and genitals, and the tenth sefirah the harmony of the whole figure. They are also divided vertically: In the left column are the female sefirot; the right, the male sefirot. (Thus the feminine element was associated with Rigorous Judgment on the left side, whereas the masculine was the manifestation of Pure Mercy on the right side.) The middle column, the mediating sefirot, brings the extremes into correct balance. The sixth sefirah, *Tiferet,* links justice and love, keeping those moral qualities in harmony. A different name for God was associated with each sefirah. The seven lower sefirot were considered the timeless prototypes of the six days of creation and the first Sabbath of creation, as well as prototypes for the various dimensions of space. The possibilities for linking the sefirot with biblical symbols were virtually endless.

The sefirot were not static in relation to each other; through them pulsated divine grace or "abundance" (*shefa*). This energy flowed through the system like a river emerging out of its source (the Ayn Sof), breaking apart into separate channels (the sefirot), reuniting in the lowest sefirah to flow into the sea. In the words of the Zohar,

> One, is the source of the sea. A current comes forth from it making a revolution which is *yod.* [*Yod* is the first letter of God's most holy name.] The source is one, and the current makes two. Then is formed the vast basin known as the sea, which is like a channel dug into the earth, and it is filled by the waters issuing from the source; and this sea is the third thing. This vast basin is divided up into seven channels, resembling that number of long tubes, and the waters go from the sea into the seven channels. Together, the source, the current, the sea, and the seven channels make the number ten. If the Creator who made these tubes should choose to break them, then would the waters return to their source, and only broken vessels would remain, dry, without water.[4]

The kabbalists alternated between conceiving the sefirot as the very substance of God, their separateness being, as it were, an optical illusion, and explaining the sefirot as vessels (as in the above quotation), tools, or instruments of God and separate containers of His essence. In other metaphors the sefirot were "the flame linked to a burning coal" and "a candle flickering in the midst of ten mirrors" set one within the other and each a different color. The kabbalists realized that maintaining a coherent monotheism with such a conception was difficult, but they turned this dilemma into yet another divine mystery: the secret of unity (*sod ha-yihud*). A prayer ascribed in the Zohar to Elijah emphasizes the unity of Ayn Sof and sefirot:

> Elijah began to praise God saying: Lord of the universe! You are One but are not numbered. You are Higher than the highest. You are the mystery above all mysteries. No thought can grasp You at all. It is You who produced the ten perfections which we call the ten sefirot. With them You guide the secret worlds which have not been revealed and the worlds which have been revealed, and in them You conceal Yourself from human beings. But it is You who binds them together and unites them. Since You are in them, whoever separates any one of these ten from the others it is as if he had made a division in You.[5]

The dynamism of the sefirot was also expressed by the mystery of coupling (*sod ha-zivug*), a sexual metaphor describing the relation between the sixth and tenth sefirot. The secret of unity and the secret of coupling are closely connected to humanity's role in the cosmos, as we shall see.

Since the sefirot are a system of emanation, the kabbalists had to face the question of how this process could be reconciled with the idea of creation *ex nihilo*, which involves an abrupt leap from nonbeing to being. Several answers were given. First, the moment of creation was the point at which the sefirot emerged from the Ayn Sof. By a play on words, the Ayn Sof (the Infinite) was called the Ayin (the Nothingness) with respect to the first sefirah; thus the divine self-manifestation in the sefirot became, quite literally, the self-creation of the revealed God out of divine Nothingness. In this interpretation, creation *ex nihilo* is rooted in a free movement by the Ayn Sof who emerges from concealment to manifestation—an ultimate mystery, which cannot be explained. (Because it is God's decision to reveal himself thus, it was important to place Divine Will before Divine Thought in the sefirot.) Here creation is depicted as the emergence within God of the positive divine attributes of traditional religious faith. A second interpretation of creation, however, moved the creative leap down to the gap separating the bottom sefirah from the lower worlds of created beings. In this view, creation is not a process occurring within God. The sefirot are God's substance, not vessels created by him, so that creation *ex nihilo* is the formation of creatures whose separate being is distinct from God's essence. The kabbalists had as much trouble with the concept of creation *ex nihilo* as the philosophers did. To the extent to which the Kabbalah emphasized the process of emanation rather than that of creation, that is, continuity rather than discontinuity in the cosmic process, the Kabbalah veered in the direction of pantheism: that God is all. This was counteracted by an opposing tendency, in line with traditional Jewish theology, to affirm the separateness of God, world, and man. Tension between monism and pluralism appears in other topics of kabbalistic thought as well.[6]

The Origin of Evil; The Lower Worlds

The kabbalists were much more inclined than the philosophers to accept the belief that evil was a dynamic power in its own right. To be sure, there were some early kabbalists who, like the philosophers, conceived of evil as the absence of good, not an objective reality but an indication that the influx of divine good had been cut off from human beings. For most of the kabbalists, however, evil was the *sitra ahra* (the "other side"), antithetical to the divine abundance and grace. Some kabbalists even speak of a hierarchy of "emanations of the left," countersefirot, dark, unclean powers in opposition to the forces of holiness and goodness.

> At the beginning of the night, when darkness falls, all the evil spirits and powers scatter abroad and roam about the world, and the "other side" sets forth and inquires the way to the King from all the holy sides. As soon as

A hare hunt, from the First Cincinnati Haggadah, fifteenth-century Germany. (Courtesy of the Hebrew Union College-Jewish Institute of Religion, Cincinnati.)

the "other side" is roused to this activity here below, all human beings experience a foretaste of death in the midst of their sleep. As soon as the impure power separates itself from the realm above and descends to begin its rule here below, three groups of angels are formed who praise the Holy One in three night watches, one following another, as the Companions have pointed out. But whilst these sing hymns of praise to the Holy One, the "other side," as we have said, roams about here below, even into the uttermost parts of the earth. Until the "other side" has thus departed from the upper sphere, the angels of light cannot unite themselves with their Lord. This is a mystery comprehensible only to the wise. The angels above and the Israelites below both press upon the "other side" to oust it. . . .[7]

The evil forces are engaged in a fierce struggle against the powers of holiness and the Shekhinah for domination of the world. (The Kabbalah contributed much to Jewish demonology, such as the concept of Samael, the kabbalistic equivalent of Satan, and his mate Lilith.)

How did the evil powers come into being? Evil is often traced by the Kabbalah to the superabundant growth of the sefirah of Rigorous Judgment (*Din*), when it is separated from the sefirah of Pure Love (*Hesed*) which balances it. Evil continually receives fresh strength from man's sinful deeds. In a kabbalistic interpretation of the story of Adam in the Garden of Eden, Adam's eating of the Tree of Knowledge of Good and Evil is treated as an allegory for the first appearance of evil. Adam separated the Tree of Knowledge from its fruits (this is called the "mystery of the cutting of the shoots"), which activates the potential evil contained within the Tree by creating division in the divine unity. "For whoever takes of it (the Tree) causes separation and associates himself with the lower hordes which are attached to it."[8] The channels between the upper and lower worlds are disturbed, the lowest sefirah (*Malkhut*) is separated from the others (leading to the kabbalistic interpretation of the exile of the Shekhinah), and the unity between the Creator and his creation is damaged. Other great sins mentioned in the Bible are often interpreted in a like manner, whereas the good deeds of biblical heroes are paradigms for setting this flaw aright.

Nevertheless, the kabbalists were monotheists and insisted that evil was only a secondary existence, infinitely less real than God. In the Zohar evil is compared to the bark (*kelippah*) of the tree of emanation, an important term in later kabbalistic speculation. Evil is a husk or shell in which lower levels of existence were wrapped, as the divine light spread out, thickened, and coarsened.

King Solomon, when he "penetrated into the depths of the nut garden" (as it is written, "I descended into the nut garden," Song of Songs 1:11), took a nut-shell (*kelippah*) and drew an analogy from its layers to these spirits which inspire sensual desires in human beings, as it is written, "and the delights of the sons of men [are from] male and female demons" (Eccles. 2:8). This verse also indicates that the pleasures in which men indulge in the time of sleep give birth to multitudes of demons. The Holy One, blessed be He, found it necessary to create all these things in the world to ensure its permanence, so that there should be, as it were, a brain with many membranes encircling it. The whole world is constructed on this principle, upper and lower, from the first mystic point up to the furthest removed of all the stages. They are all coverings one to another, brain within brain and spirit within spirit, so that one is a shell to another.[9]

From this perspective, evil is a by-product of processes in divinity, comparable to the dross remaining after gold has been refined, or to the dregs left over when good wine is separated out. Using an old aggadah that God created and destroyed worlds prior to this cosmos, evil was depicted as the refuse or waste left behind by earlier worlds. The Kabbalah never identified evil with physical matter as such. (Generally speaking, the nature of matter was not an issue for the kabbalists, who were uninterested in natural science.) As evil was a branching off from the divine emanation, the kabbalists believe that there was a spark of holiness even in the "other side," and that man's mission was to extract the good and to restore holiness to its rightful place in the scheme of being.

The kabbalistic cosmos was composed of spiritual entities, ordered into levels and degrees. A Neo-Platonic ladder of spiritual being was common to much medieval thought, and the kabbalists had their own version of this principle. Bringing together earlier Jewish mystical traditions and their own insights, the Kabbalah usually depicted a hierarchy of four distinct worlds:

1. The realm of *atzilut* (emanation), the divine world of the ten sefirot that formed the *Adam Kadmon*. This was the most important subject of kabbalistic speculation.
2. The realm of *beriyah* (creation), occupied by the Throne of Glory and the seven heavenly palaces. The imagery of the *beriyah* world was drawn from the old *hekhalot* literature, which had been eclipsed for a while when the kabbalists were first developing the concepts of the Ayn Sof and sefirot; later there was a resurgence of interest in and visions of the *ma'aseh merkavah* (the Divine Chariot).
3. The realm of *yetzirah* (formation), where most of the angels dwelled. (The kabbalists added to Jewish angelology, as to demonology.)
4. The realm of *asiyah* (making), the spiritual archetype of the world of the material cosmos, the heavens, and the earthly world perceived by human senses.

(Like the names of the seven lower sefirot, the names of the three lower worlds are based on biblical verses, in this case Isa. 43:7, and do not in themselves convey the kabbalistic meaning of the concept.)

Each of the three lower worlds reflects the pattern of the sefirot. The seven sefirot, which are the seven timeless days of creation in the uppermost world, give rise to the seven days of the week in the lower worlds. The fourth world, *asiyah*, the realm where man's soul seeks to achieve perfection, is full of forces that symbolize the sefirot: the rainbow, the dawn, the trees, the blades of grass, the raging and calming of the seas

Hanukkah menorah with birds and Moorish style arches.

—all of which are bound to the upper spheres. For example, the Zohar teaches

> It is written: "Thou rules the proud swelling of the sea; when the waves thereof arise, thou stillest them" (Ps. 89:10). When the stormy waves of the sea mount on high, and beneath them yawn the chasms of the deep, the Holy One, blessed be He, sends down a thread from the "right side" which in some mysterious way restrains the mounting waves and calms the rage of the sea. How is it that when Jonah was cast into the sea, and had been swallowed by a fish, his soul did not at once leave his body? The reason is that the Holy One, blessed be He, has dominion over the swelling of the sea, which is a certain thread from the "left" that causes the sea to heave, and rises with it. And if not for the thread of the "right side" it would never be removed, for as soon as this thread descends into the sea, and is fairly grasped by it, then the waves of the sea are stirred up, and begin to roar for prey until the Holy One, blessed be He, thrusts them back to their own place. . . .[10]

There is an ambivalence in the kabbalistic attitude toward the realm of *asiyah*, which is, on the one hand, the last link and final garment of the divine chain of being, and, on the other hand, the place where the *sitra ahra* at times seems to prevail. The gloomy picture of the world of *asiyah* as a battle ground of the forces of good against demons is a reflection of a pervasive terror of ghosts and fear of evil spirits ever seeking to enlarge their dominion. (We saw that the Hasidei Ashkenaz also absorbed this attitude from their environment.) But this anxiety also echoes the increasing insecurity of the later Middle Ages, full of violence and hatred against the Jews. This contradictory attitude to the mundane world is paralleled by the kabbalistic attitude toward evil. The monotheistic, even monistic tendency of the Kabbalah led it to depict all reality as a harmonious system in which the divine light dwells throughout. But elsewhere a dualistic tendency emphasizes the positive reality of evil and the need to struggle against it. No complete resolution of this tension is found in the Kabbalah.

The Soul

The kabbalists went much further than earlier Jewish thinkers in depicting the body as merely the outward cloak for the spark of divinity that is the soul. The soul's home, before and after its temporary residence in the body, is the higher worlds. The biblical saying that man was created in the image of God means, to the kabbalists, that man was created on the model of the sefirot; man can understand these aspects of divinity because he himself is a microcosm of the spiritual blueprint for all existence. To man alone, of all created beings, has been given free will. Adam used his freedom to commit the sin that first brought about separation between the Creator and his creation, but human volition, as we shall see, can bridge the abyss and repair the disharmony.

The moments of birth and death are the subject of much kabbalistic lore. All souls that will ever live are stored up in one of the heavenly palaces in the world of *beriyah*. When the time is ripe, they are taught divine secrets, which they forget when they enter the world of *asiyah*. (This is a direct parallel, apparently a borrowing, of Plato's doctrine of recollection: that all knowledge is a remembering of ideas that the soul understood before it entered the body.) According to the Kabbalah, the soul protests when it has to leave the heavenly world, but God commands it to depart, so that it can undergo a process of self-perfection that cannot be undertaken in the upper worlds. (The deeper kabbalistic secret, as we shall shortly see, is that the soul can bring about, in the lower world, the restoration of harmony on high.)

Some kabbalistic statements treat the body virtually as the handiwork of the *sitra ahra;* others describe the body as neither good nor bad in itself but capable of being made holy through human actions. A third view treats the functions of the body, especially sexuality, as sacraments mirroring processes that take place in the upper world. Speculation on sexuality is an important kabbalistic theme: for example, each soul is originally a composite of male and female; only in descent are souls separated into masculine or feminine. Marriage and sexual relations are the restoration of a complementarity that was sundered by birth.

> It behooves a man to be "male and female," always [together with his wife as one unified pair], so that his faith may remain stable, and in order that the Divine Presence may never leave him. You will ask: How [is it] with the man who makes a journey, and, away from his wife, ceases to be "male and female"? . . . Remark this. The whole time of his traveling a man should heed well his actions, lest the holy union [with the Shekhinah, the female element in divinity] break off, and he be left imperfect, deprived of the union with the female. If it was needful when he and his wife were together, how much greater the need when the heavenly mate is with him? And the more so, indeed, since this heavenly union acts as his constant guard on his journey, until his return home. Moreover, it is his duty, once back home, to give his wife pleasure, inasmuch as she it was who obtained for him the heavenly union.[11]

Drawing on elements in the medieval Platonic and Aristotelian traditions, the kabbalists taught that the soul was composed of several faculties, each one designated by a Hebrew word for soul or spirit. The lowest, *nefesh*, is the source of vitalistic, animal force in the person. The next, *ruah*, is occasionally identified with the moral qualities. The highest, *neshamah*, is aroused in man when he occupies himself with Torah and

Eighteenth-century Middle Eastern silver spice container, for use in the Havdalah ceremony at the end of the Sabbath. (Courtesy of the Jewish Museum, New York.)

commandments, which give him the ability to apprehend God mystically and to glimpse cosmic secrets. *Neshamah* is an acquired soul, which only the holy attain. Each of the three souls has its root in a different sefirah: *Nefesh* is related to the tenth sefirah, *Malkhut; ruah* to the sixth sefirah, *Tiferet; neshamah* to the third, *Binah*. The three souls reflect the idea that human nature is a microcosm of higher forces, and that one can understand important elements of divine existence by understanding one-self. In the Zohar the human soul is second only to the sefirot as a subject for mystical learning:

> The "soul" [*nefesh*] stands in intimate relation to the body, nourishing and upholding it; it is below, the first stirring. Having acquired due worth, it becomes the throne for the "spirit" [*ruah*] to rest upon, as it is written, "until the spirit be poured upon us from on high" [Isa. 32:15]. And when these two, soul and spirit, have duly readied themselves, they are worthy to receive the "super-soul" [*neshamah*], resting in turn upon the throne of the spirit [*ruah*]. The super-soul stands preeminent, and not to be perceived. There is throne upon throne, and for the highest a throne.
>
> The study of these grades of the soul yields an understanding of the higher wisdom; and it is in such fashion that wisdom alone affords the linking together of a number of mysteries. It is *nefesh*, the lowest stirring, to which the body adheres; just as in a candle flame, the obscure light at the bottom adheres close to the wick, without which it cannot be. When fully kindled, it becomes a throne for the white light above it, and when these two come into their full glow, the white light becomes a throne for a light not wholly discernible, an unknowable essence reposing on the white light, and so in all there comes to be a perfect light.
>
> It is the same with the man that arrives at perfection and is named "holy," as the verse says, "for the holy that are in the earth" [Ps. 16:3]. It is likewise in the upper world. Thus, when Abram entered the land, God appeared before him, and Abram received *nefesh* and there erected an altar to the like grade [of divinity]. Then he "journeyed toward the South" [Gen. 12:9], and received *ruah*. He attained at last to the summit of cleaving to God through *neshamah*, and thereupon he "built an altar to the Lord," whereby is meant the ineffable grade which is that of *neshamah*. Then seeing that he must put himself to the test, and pass through the grades, he journeyed into Egypt. There he resisted being seduced by the demonic essences, and when he had proved himself, he returned to his abode; and, actually, he "went up out of Egypt" [Gen. 13:1], his faith was strong and reassured, and he attained to the highest grade of faith. From that time, Abram knew the higher wisdom, and cleaved to God, and of the world he became the right hand.[12]

In death the soul is separated from the body in preparation for its return to the higher worlds. The righteous long for this moment and die joyfully because they are to be freed from the pains of the lowest world and dressed in a pure spiritual garb in which they can uninterruptedly envision the angels and the sefirot. The soul's liberation from the body and its judgment by God are treated in much detail in certain kabbalistic books. The idea of reincarnation, that certain souls take on a body several times, is already mentioned in the earliest work of the Kabbalah, the *Bahir*. In the Kabbalah before the Spanish expulsion, the idea of reincarnation or transmigration (*gilgul*) is limited to those who have committed sins so serious that they must be reborn in new bodies in order to make atonement for them. (In later times it becomes a general law for almost all souls, who, through being born again, are given additional opportunities to fulfill commandments that they had not been able to carry out previously.) When all souls will have finally entered the world of *asiyah*, the Messiah will come.

Although self-perfection is one purpose of the soul's descent into the world of *asiyah*, the most important role of the soul there is to help in the cosmic process of *tikkun* (repair) by means of which disharmony among the sefirot is corrected. This disharmony, the cutting off of the sefirah *Malkhut* from the other sefirot through Adam's sin, was one of the greatest sources of evil in the world, and it was through this flaw that the *sitra ahra* achieved a dominion that will not be completely abolished until the final redemption. This concept of the corruption of the world undoubtedly entered the Kabbalah through the influence of the Christian doctrine of Adam's Fall. But there is no Christian equivalent of the kabbalistic idea that sin disrupts even the higher worlds and that man has a unique role to play in restoring creation to its original grandeur. Not even the angels can bring about *tikkun*. Man's soul originates on a plane higher than the angels. Although capable of plunging to greater depths of depravity, the soul can rise above the angelic realm through religious action. The idea of *tikkun* is the most daring conception in the Kabbalah. While there is some analogy in the earlier aggadah to the view that God depends on man to witness for him in the world and that man is God's partner, in the Kabbalah it is the restoration of perfect harmony in the very inner life of God that depends on human volition. Although this notion might seem to verge on magic, in *tikkun* man does not force his will on the upper worlds: He helps them achieve their perfection.

Then "there went up a mist from the earth" to make up for the lack, by "watering the whole face of the ground" [Gen. 2:6]; and the mist rising is the yearning of the female for the male. Yet another interpretation says that we take the word "not" from the first verse [see Gen. 2:5] to use in the second with "mist," and this means that God failed to send rain because a mist had not gone up, for from below must come the impulse to move the power above. Thus, to form the cloud, vapor ascends first from the earth. And likewise, the smoke of the sacrifice ascends, creating harmony above, and the uniting of all, and so the celestial sphere has completion in it.

Oil painting of the Passover seder by Dieric Bouts (Flemish, about 1415–1475).
(Courtesy of the Religious News Service.)

It is from below that the movement starts, and thereafter is all perfected. If the Community of Israel failed to initiate the impulse, the One above would also not move to go to her, and it is thus the yearning from below which brings about the completion above.[13]

The Inner Life of the Kabbalist: The Concepts of Tikkun, Kavvanah, Devekut

The Kabbalah strikingly reinterpreted and transformed certain key concepts connected with the individual's religious life. The term *tikkun* (repair) is used in rabbinic literature and the traditional prayers with reference to improving the social order (*tikkun ha-olam*, repairing the world). In the Kabbalah it is broadened to cover a whole range of mystical actions. There is the tikkun of an individual's soul, self-purification through curbing one's desire for wordly things and sensual pleasures for their own sake—a self-purification that overcomes the separation of the soul from its divine source. Other deeds of tikkun (*tikkunim*) activate the forces of physical nature to praise God and sustain the world. There are *tikkunim* that involve the kabbalistic *sod ha-zivug* (mystery of coupling), the heavenly counterpart to sexual intercourse, bringing together the tenth sefirah, the *Shekhinah*, with its mate the sixth sefirah, *Tiferet*. (Incidentally, the Kabbalah does not use the imagery of the love of husband and wife to symbolize the soul's yearning for God, as is often done in Christian mysticism and among the Hasidei Ashkenaz; in the Kabbalah the soul's relation to God is compared more frequently to the love of a daughter to a father, the sexual metaphor being used primarily for forces within the divine realm.)

Tikkun is accomplished by carrying out the divine commandments, so that the kabbalistic interpretation of the reasons for the commandments differs completely from that given by Jewish philosophy. Philosophers who wanted to demonstrate the rationality of the mitzvot interpreted the commandments as means for acquiring rational beliefs and as guides for leading an ethical life. The kabbalists, however, viewed the commandments as vessels for establishing contact with the divine and for tipping the balance of mercy against judgment in the cosmos. As the Zohar reiterates: Stirring up holiness below results in stirring up divine grace above.

Like the talmudic sages and the philosophers, the kabbalists placed great emphasis on one's inner attitude when carrying out the mitzvot. But here again they reshaped the traditional conception of intention in line with their mystic activism. For the kabbalists, intention (*kavvanah*) was a concentration of thought and will on the mystical significance of the action performed; kabbalistic prayer was often accompanied by special meditations that focused on the kabbalistic meaning of the traditional words. Kavvanah in prayer meant that the body as well as the soul was caught up in the enthusiasm of the mystical act. Kavvanah was an indispensable accompaniment of the mystery of unification (*sod ha-yihud*, the secret of unifying), which drew divine abundance down to the lowest world and which tied the sefirot to each other and to their source, the Ayn Sof. The kabbalists agreed with the philosophers that meditation was the most important aspect of prayer, but against the philosophers they insisted that prayer had to be uttered aloud properly in order to achieve its cosmic effect.

So prayer is made up of both action and speech, and when the action is faulty, speech does not find a spot to rest in; such prayer is not prayer, and the man offering it is defective in the upper world and the lower. The main thing is to perform the act and to give utterance to words in co-ordination with it; this is perfect prayer. . . . Both upper and lower worlds are blessed through the man who performs his prayer in a union of action and word, and thus effects a unification. . . . This service must be performed by the man with full devotion of heart, and then the Holy One, blessed be He, will take pity on him and forgive his sins. Happy is the man who knows how to persuade, as it were, and how to offer worship to his Master with devotion of will and heart.[14]

Each traditional prayer had its special significance in bringing about a certain tikkun if carried out properly, that is, with the right intention. The kabbalists worked out their own elaborate symbolism of the Jewish ritual; they embellished traditional rituals with new meanings (especially the Sabbath and the festivals), and even created new rituals (something the philosophers never did).

Through prayer with kavvanah the kabbalist aimed to achieve *devekut*, "cleaving" to God. (The term *devekut* is based on the biblical expression in Deuteronomy 13:5 and elsewhere: "You shall cleave unto Him.") Step by step the soul reaches up to where the human will is almost effaced by the divine will. Devekut is the state of mind when one is constantly in the presence of God—even while engaged in worldly matters. (At the end of the *Guide for the Perplexed*, Maimonides describes the supreme intellectual perfection of man in similar terms.) There is some dispute among modern Jewish scholars as to whether the kabbalistic concept of devekut was the same total absorption in God that is found in Christian or Muslim mysticism, or whether there remained some distance between the Creator and the creature even when one had ascended through the upper worlds and reached the ultimate state of mystic rapture. If the latter is the case, it would indicate the preservation of human individuality even in the ecstasy of cleaving to the Divine —an instance in which the Jewish tradition applied a brake to the more common kind of unitive mystical experience. Descriptions of devekut in the Zohar, however, come very close to abolishing the gap between man and God:

Happy is the portion of whoever can penetrate into the mysteries of his Master and become absorbed into Him, as it were. Eespecially does a man achieve this when he offers up his prayer to his Master in intense devotion, his will then becoming as the flame inseparable from the coal, and his mind concentrated on the unity of the lower firmaments, to unify them by means of a lower name, then on the unity of the higher firmaments, and finally on the absorption of them all into the most high firmament. Whilst a man's mouth and lips are moving, his heart and will must soar to the height of heights, so as to acknowledge the unity of the whole in virtue of the mystery of mysteries in which all ideas, all wills, and all thoughts, find their goal, to wit, the mystery of the Ayn Sof.[15]

Embroidered curtain for the synagogue ark, showing the tablets of the law and Jerusalem, from seventeenth-century Italy. (Courtesy of the Jewish Museum, New York.)

The Kabbalah in Historical Perspective

As indicated in the previous chapter, the spread of the Kabbalah in the thirteenth century was one manifestation of the antagonisms developing in the Jewish communitities of Provence and Spain during that time. Accusations leveled against worldly Jewish courtiers, that philosophy provided them with excuses for not observing the commandments, for lax moral behavior, for a contemptuous attitude to certain Jewish beliefs as irrational and superstitious, crop up in kabbalistic writings too. While kabbalists were not the only or even the main critics of philosophy, some kabbalists did participate in the attack on those who saw in "Greek" scientific learning the prerequisite for spiritual achievement (and hence immortality) and the key to the true interpretation of Judaism.[16]

Although the Kabbalah was the most original aspect of the growing antiphilosophical trend, the Kabbalah was a positive religious revival in its own right, a resurgence of a pious, devout, and passionate commitment to traditional Judaism. Yet even before 1200 the Kabbalah had shown certain novel features and inner tensions that accompanied it through most of its history. From its very onset, the Kabbalah contained a strong element of mythological thinking, especially in its depiction of God as an organic process affected by, as well as having an effect on, the mundane world. (This tendency to mythologize Jewish theology is quite extraordinary in view of the prolonged struggle against myth in classical Jewish thought.) Some modern scholars, especially Gershom Scholem, the most eminent twentieth-century historian of the Kabbalah, find in this mythological aspect of the Kabbalah strong affinities with, and even signs of a historical connection to Gnosticism, a religious tendency of the first centuries CE. We saw earlier that Gnosticism is the general term for the beliefs of a variety of religious sects that offered their followers an esoteric knowledge (*gnosis*) of the secrets of cosmology and salvation. Elements in the Kabbalah that resemble Gnosticism include the idea that the unknowable God gave rise to a series of partial expressions of his perfection, hypostatized into quasi-separate beings (*aeons*) with abstract names, constituting a hierarchy in the divine realm (the *pleroma* or plenitude); that man's soul is a stranger in the physical world and that his life in the flesh is only a brief moment between his descent from above and his re-ascent to pure spiritual existence; and that human salvation can be a means to the salvation of the deity itself. In addition to this tendency toward myth, the Kabbalah also showed the influence of Neo-Platonism's depiction of reality as gradations of a monistic spiritual Absolute. In the Neo-Platonic wing of kabbalistic thinking, for example, the Gnostic conception of evil as independent demonic forces in control of the lower worlds is played down, and evil is explained as a by-product of the emanation of the spiritual realm from the Ayn Sof.

Important as were Gnosticism and Neo-Platonism in the Kabbalah, there were certain aspects of the Jewish tradition that intervened to militate against dissolving the unity of God and the unity of the human personality, so that the Kabbalah was a complex interweaving of several attitudes and influences.

The distinctiveness of the Kabbalah becomes clearest when it is contrasted to medieval Jewish philosophy. Unlike Judaism before the Middle Ages, Kabbalah and philosophy both viewed metaphysical doctrine as central to Judaism. They were both highly intellectual definitions of Judaism of concern mainly to those whose education prepared them for abstruse speculation. But the kabbalistic approach was the antithesis of the Maimonideans' concern for defining the limits of human knowledge in order to affirm only those religious ideas consistent with scientific and logical thought. The kabbalists were not challenged by the need to reconcile Judaism with science and Aristotelian metaphysics, and did not direct themselves to a defense of Judaism's rationality. Therefore, on the issue of anthropomorphic depictions of God, the kabbalists took a position opposite to the philosophical doctrine that God's essence could not be described by positive attributes. The most anthropomorphic depictions of God in the Bible and the aggadah became the very basis

Solomon on his throne. Seventeenth-century Italian embroidery. (Photographic Archive of the Jewish Theological Seminary of America, New York, Frank J. Darmstaedter.)

of kabbalistic speculation: They were considered valid because the structure of man's being itself was a microcosm representing in miniature the macrocosmic structure of ultimate reality. Thus the kabbalistic interpretation of the biblical statement that man was created in the image of God meant for them that will, emotion, gender, sexuality—as well as thought—were forces within divinity, even though, to be sure, there was a mysterious, undetermined level of God (the Ayn Sof) beyond these forces, forever inaccessible to man. Therefore, the ancient *shiur Komah* material describing the dimensions of God as though he were a supernal man, vehemently rejected by most philosophers, was an important element in kabbalistic imagery. On the whole, the kabbalists were not concerned with contradictions, an abhorrence of which is the basis of rationalism. As mentioned earlier, apparent contradictions, far from being a source of discomfort, were only a spur to further kabbalistic speculation: A contradiction was actually a paradox, giving rise to the exploration of deeper levels of the mystery of reality.

The difference between Kabbalah and philosophy can be seen also in their respective concepts of the allegorical meaning of Scripture. Among the Maimonideans, many biblical expressions were regarded as metaphors for rational principles: The Torah was a vehicle for metaphysical and ethical truths consonant with reason. The kabbalists also interpreted the Bible allegorically, but with a different conception of a symbol. For them the Bible contained hints of hidden and inexpressible mysteries—signs pointing to structures and forces of a deeper spiritual order. In the Kabbalah, words of Torah are garments of a higher life form that can be perceived in flashes of supraintellectual insight. Drawing on earlier esoteric speculation, the kabbalists believed that even the letters of the biblical words were clues for the unraveling of divine secrets; Torah was a series of God's holy names, even one enormous holy name, to be deciphered by the mystic as a source of vast power in the universe.

For the kabbalist, his esoteric tradition was Israel's most ancient learning, a learning that went back to the beginning of time, temporarily forgotten but now restored and renewed. This claim, substantiated by the apparent rediscovery of the Zohar, made philosophy appear as a recent novelty and a turning away from authentic Judaism. Thus, kabbalists were found among those who claimed to defend traditional Judaism against the supposed corrosive and heretical effects of philosophy, even though the Kabbalah's departures from earlier Judaism were far more daring than the redefinitions of Jewish belief undertaken by the philosophers (God an organism, God needing man's help in unifying His own being, reincarnation, and so on).

In the Spanish period the Kabbalah remained an esoteric tradition for small groups of educated Jews, but it retained important links with the nonintellectual religion of the masses and developed doctrines with the potential for consolation in times of great trouble. Although its intellectuality was a source of prestige, challenging the prestige of philosophy as a sophisticated interpretation of Jewish belief, the Kabbalah was capable of being popularized (we shall see this in a later period)—perhaps more easily popularized than medieval philosophy. Kabbalah was able to justify certain beliefs that did not easily find a place in the philosophical world view. In the Kabbalah the Ayn Sof was beyond the grasp of man's mind, but the traditional depiction of God as loving and just was literally true (although a truth that implied an awesome task for the Jew). Evil and disharmony, even demons and the terrors of the night, had to be overcome by unleashing the forces of holiness in ritual and prayer. Despite their negative feelings about physical existence, for the kabbalists sexuality was a symbol of a relation existing on the higher spiritual levels of the cosmos. Even more than the philosophical concept of immortality, the kabbalistic view of the soul abolished death by portraying the person's life on earth as only a transitory existence in order to accomplish a certain mission before returning to his spiritual home. And above all, Israel's observance of the halakhah was an act of supreme importance to the health of the universe. Most Jews had been condemned to political passivity, but the kabbalists taught that Jews were active protagonists in the only important cosmic drama of tikkun. Victims of hatred and persecution on earth, they were God's main champions on high.

The Kabbalah was, therefore, both a symptom and a response to an age in which the limited openness of Western society to Jewry was shrinking. The Kabbalah was a withdrawal, for the purposes of reinvigoration, into Judaism alone. Whereas Jewish philosophers had necessarily pointed to common features between their and other monotheistic faiths, the kabbalists emphasized the vast difference between the role of the Jewish people in the spiritual destiny of the universe and that of other religious communities. Thus, the Kabbalah justified the agonies suffered by Jews who remained committed to their faith and reaffirmed the unique destiny of Israel among the nations.

CHART 4. EARLY MODERN PERIOD (1500–1780)

General History	Jews in Western and Central Europe, the Mediterranean lands, and the Middle East	Jews in Eastern Europe
1500		
1520–1566. Reign of Suleiman the Magnificent; zenith of the Ottoman empire.	1502. Publication of the *Dialoghi di Amore* by Judah Abravanel.	
1517. Martin Luther's 95 Theses mark the beginning of the Protestant Reformation.	c. 1511–1578. Azariah dei Rossi, greatest Jewish scholar during the Italian Renaissance.	
1534. Ignatius of Loyola founds the Jesuit order.	1510–1520. The Christian humanist J. Reuchlin defends Hebrew learning against the apostate J. Pfefferkorn.	
1546–1555. Lutheran-Catholic wars in Germany.		
1545–1563. The Council of Trent: Roman Catholic reform and response to the Protestant Reformation.	1536. The Inquisition permanently introduced in Portugal.	1551. Charter of Sigismund Augustus, giving the Polish Jewish communal leadership broad powers.
1543. Publication of Copernicus's *On the Revolutions of the Celestial Spheres*.	1553. Burning of the Talmud in Italy.	1580. Earliest surviving ordinances of the Council of the Four Lands.
	1554. Church censorship of Hebrew books established.	
1564. Death of Michelangelo and birth of Shakespeare.	1555. Pope Paul IV orders the Jews of Rome into a ghetto.	
1562–1598. Religious wars in France.	1553. Gracia and Joseph Nasi arrive in Constantinople.	16th and first half of 17th centuries. Rapid development of talmudic scholarship in Poland, including such eminent authorities as Solomon Luria (1510–1573), Moses Isserles (1530–1572), Samuel Edels (1555–1631), Joel Sirkes (1561–1640).
1568. Beginning of the revolt of the Netherlands from Spain.	1567. Publication of Joseph Caro's code of Jewish law, the *Shulhan Arukh*.	
1588. Defeat of the Spanish Armada.	1569–1572. The kabbalist Isaac Luria resides at Safed.	
	1590. Marranos begin to arrive in Amsterdam.	
1600		
1603. Death of Queen Elizabeth I of England.	1612. Sephardic community at Hamburg.	
1618–1648. 30 Years' War.	1614. Temporary expulsion of the Jews from Frankfort-on-Main.	
1620. Pilgrims land at Plymouth.		

General History	Jews in Western and Central Europe, the Mediterranean lands, and the Middle East	Jews in Eastern Europe
1606–1669. Rembrandt van Rijn, Dutch painter and etcher. 1637. Publication of the *Discourse on Method* by René Descartes, marking a new era in philosophy disregarding scholastic methodology. 1642–1648. English Civil War. 1649–1660. England a Commonwealth under Oliver Cromwell (died 1658). 1660. Restoration of the Stuart monarchy in England (Charles II). 1688. The Glorious Revolution places William and Mary on the throne of England. 1643–1715. Louis XIV, king of France. 1682–1725. Peter I the Great, Tsar of Russia. 1687. Publication of Isaac Newton's *Principia Mathematica* (*Mathematical Principles of Natural Philosophy*). 1690. Publication of John Locke's *Essay Concerning Human Understanding* and *Two Treatises on Civil Government*. Locke is a major influence on the Enlightenment of the 18th century. 1646–1716. Gottfried Wilhelm Leibnitz, German philosopher and mathematician.	1604–1657. Manasseh ben Israel, Jewish writer and scholar in Amsterdam. 1632–1677. Baruch Spinoza, Dutch philosopher. 1654. Jews arrive at the Dutch colony of New Amsterdam. 1656. Jews begin to resettle openly in England. 1665–1666. Shabbatai Zevi (1626–1676) acclaimed Jewish messiah in Turkey. 1648–1678. Alsace and Lorraine, with a population of Ashkenazic Jews, annexed by France. 1650s. Rise of Court Jews in the German states. 1670. Jews expelled from Vienna; some readmitted. 1671. Some Jews admitted to Prussia.	1648–1649. Cossack uprising under Bogdan Chmielnitski in the Polish Ukraine, with widespread massacres of Jews. 1655–1667. Russian and Swedish invasions of Poland lead to further massacres of Polish Jews.

Chart 4. (con't)

General History	Jews in Western and Central Europe, the Meditteranean lands, and the Middle East	Jews in Eastern Europe
1700		
1715–1774. Louis XV, king of France.	1723. Residence of Sephardic Jews in Bordeaux legalized.	1720–1791. Elijah, the Gaon of Vilna, tal-mudist and kabbalist.
1740–1786. Frederick II the Great of Prussia.	1745–1748. Tempor-ary banishment of Jews from Prague.	1726–1791. Jacob Frank, founder of the Frankist sect in the Shabbatean tradition.
1740–1780. Maria Theresa, empress and Hapsburg ruler; from 1765 she rules jointly with her son Joseph II.	1750. Frederick the Great's restrictive charter for the Jews of Prussia.	
1762–1796. Catherine II the Great of Russia.	1707–1746. Moses Hayyim Luzzatto of Padua, Hebrew poet, kabbalist, writer of ethical treatises.	1700–1760. Israel ben Eliezer (the Besht) and the rise of Hasidism.
18th century. Spread of the Enlightenment, including such eminent writers as Montesquieu (1689–1755), Voltaire (1694–1778), David Hume (1711–1776), Denis Diderot (1713–1784), Adam Smith (1723–1790), G. E. Lessing (1729–1781), Edward Gibbon (1737–1794), J. J. Rousseau (1712–1778).	1727–1786. Moses Mendelssohn, writer of the Ger-man Enlightenment and major figure in the rise of the Jew-ish Enlightenment (the Haskalah).	1710–1776. Dov Baer of Mezeritch, disciple of the Besht and major figure in the spread of Hasidism,
1772. First partition of Poland between Russia, Prussia, and Austria.		1764. Council of the Four Lands abolished by the Polish govern-ment.
1776. American Declaration of Inde-pendence.		1768. Most serious at-tack on Jews in the Polish Ukraine by armed bands of Haidamacks (the Uman massacre).
		1772. First denuncia-tions of the Hasidic movement by its Jewish opponents in Vilna and elsewhere.

C H A P T E R 1 0

Jews and Judaism in the Early Modern Period (Sixteenth to Mid-Eighteenth Centuries)

The period known as "early modern" in Western Europe was, for most Jews, a continuation of the Middle Ages. In the two areas where the majority of Jews lived, the dominant cultural pattern derived from the medieval Jewish West, the Jewry of Poland-Lithuania being an extension of the German Ashkenazim, and the Jewry of Ottoman Turkey being strongly influenced by the Sephardim of Spain and Portugal. Through the eighteenth century and even later, most branches of the Jewish people retained their medieval status as autonomous communities living according to their own law and customs, a distinct segment of the urban middle classes of Christian and Islamic societies. Medieval forms of thought still predominated: Jewish theology was mainly confined to the Kabbalah, which entered a new creative phase, manifesting itself sometimes as a unifying force, sometimes as a disruptive one. There were significant developments in halakhah as well. Jewish law, in its Sephardic and Ashkenazic modes, achieved a standard form that it was to hold for many years afterward. Renaissance humanism, the Protestant Reformation, and the scientific revolution in the West did not affect the world view of most Jews. In contrast to the great innovative ages of the Jewish past (the Hellenistic era, the early Islamic period), the early modern period in Jewish history was predominantly a time of intellectual and spiritual isolation; the sixteenth century was generally a period of recovery (of course each area of the diaspora was different), but social and political

AVTO DE LA FE CELEBRADO EN LIMA A 23. DE ENERO DE 1639.

AL TRIBVNAL DEL SANTO OFICIO de la Inquificion, de los Reynos del Perù, Chile, Paraguay, y Tucuman.

POR EL LICENCIADO DON Fernando de Montefinos, Presbitero, natural de Offuna.

CON LICENCIA DEL ILVSTRISSIMO feñor Inquifidor General, y feñores del Confejo de fu Mageftad, de la Santa, y General Inquificion.

En Madrid, En la Imprenta del Reyno, año de 1640.

Title page of a description of an **auto da fé**, in which the Inquisition turned Marranos over to the secular authorities to be burned at the stake; Lima, Peru, 1639.

conditions from the mid-seventeenth into the eighteenth centuries were among the most burdensome and miserable of Jewish history. Yet signs can be detected of major changes in the circumstances of Jews who became part of the expanding capitalist economy of Europe. The age, therefore, opens with a move of the Jewish population eastward, and it closes with the beginnings of a shift westward toward new geographical and new mental horizons.

The Jews in Ottoman Turkey

The Revival of Jewish Life in the Eastern Mediterranean

In the fourteenth century the Ottoman Turks ruled a small state in Asia Minor, one of several established by Muslim warriors who had been fighting the Byzantines for three hundred years. Gradually, the Ottomans absorbed the other Turkish principalities and extended their rule in southeastern Europe and the Middle East. By the mid-fifteenth century they had conquered large areas of the Balkans and Greece. (In 1453 Constantinople was captured, putting an end to the Byzantine empire.) In 1516–1517 they seized Syria, Palestine, and Egypt; in 1526 they occupied most of Hungary; in the 1530s, Iraq. By the 1550s they controlled Arabia, most of North Africa, and many islands in the eastern Mediterranean. The Ottoman state was Muslim in religion, Turkish in language, ruled by a military caste quite willing to leave most economic activities to the religious minorities (Greek Orthodox, Armenians, Jews), whose taxes were an important source of government revenue. The Ottoman attitude contrasts favorably with the frequent persecutions of Jews in Persia during the same time.[1]

The vast Ottoman empire included many Jewish communities that had been there from ancient times: Greek-speaking (Romaniyot) Jews in the former Byzantine territories and Arabic-speaking (Musta'rab) Jews in the Middle East and North Africa. In the late fifteenth century some Ashkenazic Jews arrived, attracted by the security and economic opportunities the Ottoman state offered. After the expulsion from Spain in 1492, large numbers of Sephardic refugees came to the Ottoman realm. A Jewish tradition reports that Sultan Bayazid II remarked, upon hearing that King Ferdinand of Spain had expelled the Jews, "How can you consider [him] a wise ruler, when he has impoverished his own land and enriched ours?" The Sephardic Jews brought with them their trading connections with Western Europe, valuable techniques for the manufacture of cloth, weapons, and gunpowder, and medical expertise. Sephardic physicians, such as Joseph Hamon and his sons, became prominent in the Ottoman court in Istanbul (formerly Constantinople).

Throughout the sixteenth century the Sephardic population of the Ottoman realm was augmented by Marranos fleeing the Inquisition in Spain and Portugal. (The Inquisition was introduced in Portugal in 1536.) The height of Jewish participation in the Ottoman court came with Gracia Mendes Nasi and Joseph Nasi. From a prominent Converso family, Dona Gracia (1510–1569) was born in Portugal, where her husband and brother-in-law headed a prosperous banking house. After her husband's death she settled first in Antwerp, then in Italy where she reverted to Judaism. In 1553 she moved to Istanbul and became a leader of the Jewish community, subsidizing scholars, establishing yeshivot, and continuing to direct her business undertakings in Europe. Her nephew Joseph Nasi (c. 1524–1579) joined her in Istanbul, where he too reconverted to Judaism. Because of his intimate knowledge of European affairs, the information he received from his agents, his contacts with Christian royalty, and his commercial ties with Western Europe and with the Jews of Poland, two sultans relied on him for advice. Among his projects,

Joseph Nasi sought to attract Jewish refugees to Tiberias in Palestine in order to build up a center of textile production and a seat of Jewish learning there. At the zenith of his career, the sultan granted him the title of duke along with authority over a group of islands in the Aegean. In 1569 he persuaded the Turkish government to declare war on Venice in order to conquer Cyprus, but after the Turkish defeat by the Spaniards and Venetians at the naval battle of Lepanto (1571), Joseph Nasi's influence declined. By the end of the century Greeks had become the main advisers to the sultan, bringing to an end any significant Jewish political rule in the Ottoman court.

As a result of favorable conditions in the sixteenth-century Turkish empire, thriving Jewish communities existed in the Balkans (e.g., Adrianople), in Greece (more than half of the population of Salonika was Jewish), in Istanbul (said to have 50,000 Jews at that time), as well as in Cairo, Damascus, Aleppo, Izmir, and other cities. The Jewish population in Jerusalem increased manyfold. Although Joseph Nasi's plans for Tiberias did not materialize, nearby Safed became an influential intellectual center. In the larger cities, alongside the other Jewish groups, Sephardim from different localities in Spain and Portugal established congregations. In Salonika and Istanbul there were over thirty Jewish synagogues, each administering the Jewish affairs of its own members. Only occasionally did they join together to take care of common matters (unlike the local communal structure of earlier Spanish and Ashkenazic Jewry). Eventually the separation of the Jewish groups began to disappear and the Sephardic tradition prevailed. Sephardic Jews of Turkey maintained many of their old customs, their prayer book, their folk music, and their language (the Spanish vernacular used by the Sephardic Jews came to be known as *Ladino*) down to the twentieth century.

Talmudic Law in Ottoman Turkey: Joseph Caro

In intellectual as well as economic affairs, the Sephardim were a stimulant to the Jewry of the Ottoman realm. A number of outstanding rabbis established yeshivot in Salonika, Istanbul, Cairo, and elsewhere, and a large body of responsa was published adjusting Jewish law to conditions in the East. The most illustrious figure in this new burst of rabbinical scholarship was Joseph ben Ephraim Caro (1488–1575).

Born in Spain, Caro was taken by his family to Portugal in 1492; after the forced conversions of 1497, they fled to the Balkans. In the early 1520s Caro began to write a vast work that sought to summarize all the Jewish laws in use at the time. Caro's magnum opus, entitled *Bet Yosef* (the *House of Joseph*), was a detailed commentary to Jacob ben Asher's fourteenth-century code, the *Arba'ah Turim*. Caro was quite aware that Sephardic practice often conflicted with that of other Jewish

Leaf from a sixteenth-century manuscript relating the history of the Ottoman Turks.
(Courtesy of the Metropolitan Museum of Art, Bequest of George D. Pratt, 1935.)

groups in Turkey, undermining the unity of Jewish law, and that the rise of printing had resulted in the circulation of individual legal treatises that contradicted each other, creating further confusion. The *Arba'ah Turim* and the *Bet Yosef* together provided a summary of all the talmudic sources and important post-talmudic opinions up to Caro's day on every halakhic issue of practical relevance. In Caro's decision as to the correct ruling, he followed the majority among the three earlier authorities he considered most eminent: Alfasi, Maimonides, and Asher ben Yehiel. Where this did not suffice, he decided according to the majority of other rabbinic authorities. (This method, rather than his determining each rule independently on the basic of talmudic teaching and logical analysis, was a practical necessity, given the magnitude of his task, but it was criticized by some rabbis.)

Caro's vast knowledge and thoroughness made the *Bet Yosef* a landmark of Jewish legal literature, but it did not fully solve the problem of unifying and standardizing Jewish practice. Therefore, after completing his commentary, Caro compiled a much briefer digest, giving only the binding rulings (*pesakim*), so that students and judges could have a clear, decisive guide to the halakhah. This book, the *Shulhan Arukh* (*Prepared Table*), became the definitive code of traditional Jewish law, the last and most authoritative comprehensive summation of Jewish practice down to the present. It appeared first in 1564, was reprinted several

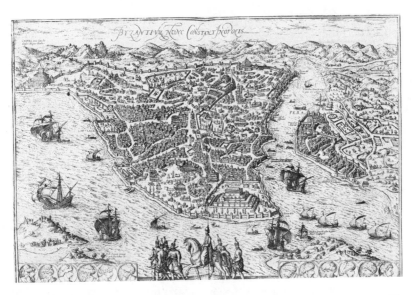

Sixteenth-century map of Constantinople, after its conquest by the Ottomans. (Courtesy of the Rare Book Division of the New York Public Library, Astor, Lenox, and Tilden Foundations.)

times, and was soon disseminated throughout the diaspora. (Incidentally, the speed with which the *Shulhan Arukh* became available to Jewish scholars reflects the way in which printing furthered the spread of traditional Jewish learning at the time.) The drawback of Caro's *Shulhan Arukh* was that it expressed contemporary Sephardic views, but it was eventually to be adapted for use by Ashkenazic Jewry (as we shall see).

The *Shulhan Arukh* is an austere and functional code, eliminating all exhortation and theological interpretation for the sake of conciseness. Although Caro's code deals only with law and does not reveal anything of his inner religious life, his other writings indicate that Caro himself was a fervent mystic. Throughout most of his life he kept a diary of the messages that a heavenly mentor (a *maggid* or "herald") spoke through his mouth. (A number of rabbis of his time claimed these special revelations.) Caro's *maggid* gave him kabbalistic interpretations and personal advice, encouraged him to be modest, gentle, and patient, exhorted him to pray with devotion and to follow ascetic practices. It praised or criticized his legal decisions and promised that his desire to die a martyr's death for God's sake would be fulfilled (which did not happen). Caro's *maggid* also encouraged him to settle in the holy land. About 1535, while still working on the *Bet Yosef*, Caro moved to Safed, which was becoming the most remarkable spiritual center of Eastern Jewry at that time.

The Jews of Sixteenth-Century Safed

Between 1500 and 1600, the hillside town of Safed in the upper Galilee grew from a handful of Jewish families to a community of over 10,000 Jews. Safed had close economic ties with nearby Damascus, and became a center for the manufacture of cloth. Talmudic yeshivot were founded, and many small groups engaged in the study of the Kabbalah. Through them Safed was the center of a spiritual revival taking place among Jews of the Middle East, a revival permeated with yearnings for the messianic age.

Messianism was especially prevalent among Sephardic Jews after the Spanish and Portuguese expulsions. Earlier in the Middle Ages the Sephardim had produced several transient messianic figures, but the dispersion of the Sephardim from the Iberian peninsula had intensified their consciousness of exile, which in turn stimulated renewed eschatological hopes. In the 1520s David Reubeni, a mysterious adventurer claiming to have been sent from a distant Jewish kingdom of lost biblical tribes, visited Italy and Portugal, where he created a stir among the Marranos. Especially affected in Lisbon was a young man who circumcised himself and took the name Solomon Molcho. Molcho went to Salonika to study Kabbalah (Joseph Caro met him there and was impressed

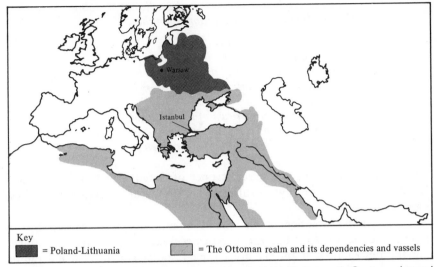

The Ottoman and Polish-Lithuanian Realms in the Mid-Seventeenth Century. Around 1648 both states were still at their maximum geographical extent and contained the bulk of the Jewish population of the world at that time.

by him); he then visited Italy where he briefly attracted the friendly attention of Pope Clement VIII. Eventually Molcho announced that the messianic kingdom would come in 1540 and was burned at the stake by command of the Emperor Charles V in 1532.

Messianic longings can be seen in many of the writings of the Safed scholars and poets, where it was an underlying theme but not an overt, activist movement. One of the most popular religious hymns composed in sixteenth-century Safed reflects this atmosphere. The poem *Lekha Dodi* ("Come, My Beloved"), now sung in the synagogue on Friday eve, personifies the Sabbath as Israel's divine bride, the Shekhinah. Using biblical, talmudic, and midrashic allusions, the poet (Solomon Halevy Alkabetz, a close friend of Joseph Caro) bids the royal city of Jerusalem to arise from its ruins and become a fitting home for the Sabbath queen and the Davidic king:

> *Come, my beloved, to meet the bride;*
> *Let us welcome the presence of the Sabbath.*
>
> . . .
>
> *Come, let us go to meet the Sabbath, for it is a*
> *well-spring of blessing;*
> *From the beginning, from of old it was ordained,*
> *Last in production, first in thought.*
>
> *O sanctuary of our King, O regal city, arise, go forth*
> *from thy overthrow;*

Long enough hast thou dwelt in the valley of weeping;
Verily He will have compassion upon thee.

Shake thyself from the dust, arise;
Put on the garments of thy glory, O my people!
Through the son of Jesse, the Bethlehemite [David],
  draw Thou nigh unto my soul, redeem it.
      . . .
Come in peace, thou crown of thy husband,
With rejoicing and with cheerfulness,
In the midst of the faithful of the chosen people.[2]

Similarly, the work of the greatest poet of Safed, Israel Najara, is suffused by memories of Jewish suffering and hopeful expectations of messianic redemption.

The religious practice of the Safed community was marked by an intense asceticism. At midnight, mystics recited a special liturgy mourning the destruction of the Temple; they fasted frequently, made public confessions of sins, dressed in sackcloth and ashes, and prayed at the reputed graves of ancient sages, such as Simeon bar Yohai, the hero of the Zohar, at nearby Meron. An eminent Jewish scholar once observed,

> The impression that Safed of the sixteenth century leaves in us is that of a revival camp in permanence, constituted of penitents gathered from all parts of the world. . . . Life practically meant for them an opportunity to worship, only occasionally interrupted by such minor considerations as the providing of a livelihood for their family and the procuring of the necessary taxes for the government.[3]

The greatest kabbalistic author of Safed, a student of Joseph Caro's and the brother-in-law of the author of *Lekha Dodi*, was Moses Cordovero (1522–1570). At the age of twenty Cordovero heard a heavenly voice which commanded him to devote his life to making known the mysteries of the Torah. His prolific writings are the most methodical and logical summary made of the Spanish Kabbalah of the Middle Ages, to which he added his own intricate and complex speculations about the dialectical nature of divine emanation. Cordovero was the most philosophical among Jewish mystics. But the subsequent impact of Safed mysticism came not from him, but from another, far more original personality, who produced a striking reorientation of the Kabbalah away from philosophy and toward mythical thought: Isaac Luria.

The Lurianic Kabbalah

Isaac Luria (1534–1572), known since the end of the sixteenth century as *Ha-Ari Ha-Kadosh*, "the Holy Lion," an acronym of "the divine

Interior of the Ari Synagogue, named after the kabbalist Isaac Luria, at Safed in the Galilee. (Courtesy of the Zionist Archives, New York.)

(or the Ashkenazi) Rabbi Isaac," was born in Jerusalem of an Ashkenazic father and a Sephardic mother. His father having died when he was a child, Luria's mother took him to Egypt, where he was brought up in the home of a wealthy uncle. Luria studied Talmud and briefly tried his hand at business but soon gave these up to immerse himself in the Kabbalah. Later tradition (most of what is known about his short life was recorded in the seventeenth century, when he had become a legendary figure) recounts that he withdrew for seven years to a life of seclusion on an island in the Nile, where he meditated on the Zohar and practiced asceticism. In 1569 he settled in Safed with his family, studied with

Cordovero, and gathered around him a group of disciples on whom he made a profound impression. After living in Safed only two or three years, he died of the plague at the age of 38.

Luria was an imaginative rather than a systematic thinker, a mystic who added a whole new layer to kabbalistic imagery and symbolism by means of interpretations of the Zohar that he and his disciples announced as revelations from Elijah. Only a few unimportant writings by him have survived, and those do not contain his novel ideas. The Lurianic Kabbalah was transmitted by his students and by kabbalists who gained access to their notes, so that several versions of his teachings circulated after his death.[4] Despite certain discrepancies between the various accounts of his thought, the most important feature of his approach is clearly a heightened emphasis on redemption, reflecting the messianic undercurrent of sixteenth-century Safed spirituality.

The Kabbalah of the Zohar had been primarily concerned with the mysteries of creation. The Lurianic Kabbalah, although it focuses on the end rather than the beginning of the cosmos, also provides an explanation of the creation of the world—a theory of creation far more complex and paradoxical than the undirectional emanation by which the earlier kabbalists described the emergence of the sefirot from the Ayn Sof. In the Lurianic theosophy, the first movement of creation was not an outpouring but a contraction: The Ayn Sof at first withdrew from a central point in order that a spiritual vacuum could come into being. (The term in the Lurianic Kabbalah for this contraction of the Ayn Sof is *tzimtzum;* the vacuum left is the spiritual archetype at creation for physical space.) *Tzimtzum* was a retreat of the Ayn Sof (the infinite root of God's nature) into itself, freeing a region in which the cosmic drama could be enacted and where real entities separate from the Ayn Sof could exist in their own right.

After *tzimtzum*, the Ayn Sof sent out a ray of light into the vacuum, which gave rise to the spiritual figure of *Adam Kadmon*, the Primordial Man. (Whereas in the earlier Kabbalah *Adam Kadmon* was a symbol for the overall structure of the sefirot, in the Lurianic system it appeared prior to the sefirot.) From the ears, nostrils, and mouth of the *Adam Kadmon* emerged rays of divine light. The light that burst forth from the eyes took the forms of sparks or points that were to be caught in bowls or vessels also made of light. According to the Lurianic system, at a crucial moment, while they were being filled, the vessels collapsed. Most of the scattered sparks of light reascended to their source, but some (usually given as 288) adhered to fragments of the shattered vessels. The shards of the broken vessels became husks (*kelippot*), evil forces that surrounded and trapped the remaining sparks. The shattering of the vessels (*shevirat ha-kelim*) was a cosmic mishap resulting in the imprisonment of divine sparks in husks of evil.[5]

The decorative carvings of the ark of the Ari Synagogue, Safed. (Courtesy of the Consulate General of Israel.)

Immediately after the vessels shattered, the process of restoration (tikkun) began, and the universe gradually returned to the original design of the Creator. The divine plan is manifested in the formation of spiritual structures called *partzufim* (faces, configurations).[6] The doctrine of the *partzufim* is the Lurianic interpretation of the emanation of the sefirot in earlier Kabbalah, but in a highly anthropomorphized manner constituting a new Kabbalistic mythology. There are five divine *partzufim: Arikh Anpin* (the Long-Suffering One), identified with the first sefirah; *Abba* and *Imma* (Father and Mother), identified with the second and third sefirot; *Ze'eir Anpin* (the Impatient One), identified with the next six sefirot; and *Nukba de-Ze'eir* (the female of *Ze'eir*), the tenth sefirah. Luria's *partzufim* have been described as "power centers" through which the creative dynamism of the Godhead is able to take on definite form and functions. The main self-manifestation of the Ayn Sof takes place through *Ze'eir Anpin*, born from the union of *Abba* and *Imma*, who matures to couple with his mate, the Shekhinah, effecting a harmonious balance of justice and compassion in the divine. The Lurianic expositions of the secrets of the *partzufim* contain bewildering and even inconsistent detail, but the essential idea is that they constitute God's giving birth to himself as the living deity of religion, a process by which the Ayn Sof evolves his own fully developed personality. In the Lurianic Kabbalah the lower worlds are a complex ladder of spiritual existences, each containing the *partzufim* and the sefirot, each separated by a curtain that filters out some of the divine light radiating from above. The lowest world is the realm to which human souls—and the *kelippot*—have descended.

In the Lurianic system, when the human Adam of the Bible was created, the process of tikkun (repair) had almost reached completion on the divine level, most of the sparks having been reintegrated in their source. Adam had only to administer the final acts of tikkun, which had deliberately been left for man to accomplish. But through Adam's sin the cosmic mishap is re-enacted on a lower level. Adam's failure to obey God interrupts his communion with the divine and repeats in the human world the havoc wrought by the breaking of the vessels in the highest realm. The supernal soul of Adam was shattered. As created, Adam had contained all human soul-families and soul-clusters. Now the individual souls were cut off from their roots and dispersed through the cosmos to enter material bodies. Restoration of a soul to its source is a long process that can take many lifetimes. The Lurianic Kabbalah made the idea of reincarnation or metempsychosis (*gilgul*) central: A soul is fated to be reborn again and again, until it finally succeeds in achieving perfection.[7] Souls are reborn in human bodies, in animals, in plants, in stones. The whole earth is full of souls in captivity. Only the souls of the saintly can escape the fate of rebirth and only the saintly can help others to escape. The especially pious are said to have the power to see into a person's heart, to know which biblical personage he has been in a previous existence, to discern the supernal root of an individual's soul, and to give him a special tikkun, a penance that will enable him to purify himself and reascend to his root.

The basic metaphor of the Lurianic Kabbalah is exile. Even God experiences exile, a scattering of sparks that must be restored to the divine unity. By carrying out the divine commandments with proper mystical intention and concentration, Israel becomes God's partner in redeeming the divine light dispersed among the nations of the world. By liberating the few fragments of holiness left in captivity, the Jews aid in the messianic restoration. Having projected onto the universe the tragedy of dispersion of which the Spanish Jews were doubly aware, the hopeful message of the Lurianic Kabbalah was that the process of tikkun was almost complete.

Shabbatai Zevi

In the 1630s the Lurianic Kabbalah had made considerable headway where Sephardic Jews and Marranos resided. Between 1648 and 1655, as we shall see later, there occurred one of the worst massacres in Jewish history in the Ukraine and Poland. The Inquisitions in Spain and Portugal were still active in rooting out any traces of Judaism they could find, and the Counter Reformation in Italy and elsewhere in Europe was blatantly hostile to Jews. In 1665–1666 much of the Jewish people was caught up in a frenzied turmoil centering around a self-proclaimed messianic king, Shabbatai Zevi. This millenarian fervor was an emotional revolt against the humiliation and vulnerability which pressed against the Jews in the best of times, and even more so under current conditions. The messianic exhilaration was a dreamlike episode that passed, but it left a persistent underground, which surfaced from time to time in parts of Jewry during the next century and revealed the dissident potential of some of the kabbalistic ideas.

Shabbatai Zevi was born in Izmir (Smyrna) in 1626, possibly on the ninth of Av, the Jewish midsummer fast commemorating the destruction of the Temple. His father was an agent of Dutch and English trading companies; his brothers were well-to-do merchants. Having received a traditional rabbinic education, as an adolescent Shabbatai embarked on the study of the Zohar and engaged in ascetic practices. He was said to have shown wide swings of emotion from euphoria to depression, but in his more stable periods he impressed people with his dignified bearing and beautiful singing voice.[8] As a young man in Izmir he contracted two unconsummated marriages, both ending in divorce. Already then he may have had a notion of himself as the Messiah: Several bizarre and deliberate violations of Jewish law led to his expulsion from Izmir in the early

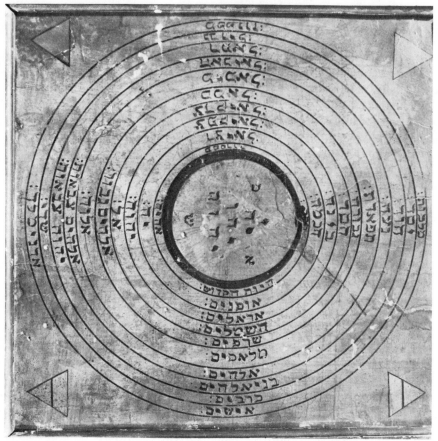

Kabbalistic plaque, wood painted with oil, showing the names of God, the sefirot, and the names of the angels. (Courtesy of the Jewish Museum, New York.)

1650s. During the next decade Shabbatai visited various cities of Greece, spent a few months in Istanbul, returned briefly to Izmir, spent a year in Jerusalem, and went to Cairo. (His stays in Salonika and Istanbul were also marked by peculiar violations of the law, such as his composing a benediction to God "who permits the forbidden," substituting *matir issurin* for the traditional *matir asurim* of the benediction "Blessed be Thou . . . who frees the captives.") In Cairo, Shabbatai Zevi was part of a kabbalistic circle that included the head of Egyptian Jewry. In April 1665 he went to Gaza where he met Nathan, who was to become his chief prophet. It was the twenty-year-old Nathan, born and brought up in Jerusalem, who finally convinced Shabbatai that he was indeed the Messiah. On May 31 the Messiah's presence was announced in Gaza, triggering immense excitement in the synagogue. In letters to the diaspora that called for repentance and demanded faith in Shabbatai Zevi, Nathan claimed that the moment had arrived when no holy sparks were left under the dominion of the *kelippot*, the powers of evil. He promised that in a short time Shabbatai would peacefully take the crown from the Ottoman sultan, bring back the lost biblical tribes, and be victorious in the final tribulations that would be the birth pangs of redemption. Special mystical prayers were composed for the extended fasts proclaimed as preparations for the great events to follow. Nathan warned that even the most righteous would be punished with divine afflictions if they doubted the good news.

Meanwhile, Shabbatai appeared briefly in Jerusalem where he won some support, but was rejected by prominent rabbis who, however, maintained a discreet silence. Making his way north, he stayed briefly in Aleppo; after he left, a wave of prophesying seized the community. He reached Izmir just before Rosh Hashanah and in December he entered the synagogue during Hanukkah wearing royal apparel. The community was soon polarized between believers and those that Shabbatai's supporters called infidels (*kofrim*), among whom were some local rabbis. Breaking into the Portuguese synagogue on the Sabbath (the headquarters of his opponents), Shabbatai proclaimed himself the Anointed of the God of Jacob, denounced the disbelievers, and distributed kingdoms to his associates. Mass hysteria followed: People from all walks of life and of all ages, including children, fell into trances and reported visions of him on a royal throne, crowned as king of Israel. Shabbatai then set out for Istanbul, but when he arrived (February 1666), he was arrested by the order of the grand vizier and put in prison. Because the sultan and the vizier were involved in a war with Venice, Shabbatai was transferred in April to the fortress of Gallipoli on the European side of the Dardanelles, where important state prisoners were detained. In the next few months, through appropriate bribes, the prison was converted into Shabbatai's court. Pilgrims came from all over, joining in messianic rituals and in acts of penance and mortification. The news spread rapidly through many parts of the Jewish world. Doubters were forced to keep silent; hymns were written in his honor; new festivals were announced, climaxed by the transformation of the fast of the ninth of Av into a celebration of Shabbatai's birth. In his writings of that summer Nathan, who had remained in Gaza, explained that the alternation of the Messiah's mood from excited illumination to passive withdrawal was symptomatic of the struggle of his soul with demonic powers in which, at certain times, Shabbatai was held prisoner by the *kelippot* and, at others, prevailed over them.

In early September a Polish kabbalist, Nehemiah ha-Kohen, spent three days in conversation with Shabbatai at Gallipoli and rejected his claims.

Afterwards Nehemiah probably denounced Shabbatai to the Turks for fomenting sedition, but the authorities may have already been alarmed. Taken to Adrianople, where the sultan was staying, the following day (September 16) Shabbatai was brought before the court and given the choice of conversion to Islam or death. He agreed to apostasize, was awarded a Turkish name, an honorary title, and a government pension. The shock of his converting brought the messianic commotion to an end.

But some who had been caught up in the experience refused to give up their faith. Biblical, talmudic, midrashic, and kabbalistic statements were cited as prophecies of his conversion. For example, the book of Esther was read as a Shabbatean allegory: Just as Esther appeared to forsake her religion in order to become queen of Persia so that eventually she could save her people, Shabbatai Zevi appeared to hide his Judaism so that he could redeem the last dregs of evil and reveal himself in complete triumph. Nathan explained that Shabbatai's messianic task was to take on the shame of being called a traitor to his people for esoteric reasons. Nathan added a further complexity to the Lurianic doctrine of *tzimtzum:* that there were two kinds of divine light, a creative light and another light opposed to the existence of anything besides the Ayn Sof. While the creative light erected the structures of creation in the vacuum left after *tzimtzum*, the other light became the power of the evil *kelippot*. Beneath the universe described in the Lurianic doctrine, Nathan posited a region, "the deep of the great abyss," where the soul of the Messiah had been struggling against the dominion of the *kelippot* from the beginning of time. The Messiah's aim was to open up this realm to the penetration of the creative light and bring tikkun to all *kelippot*. In order to accomplish this, the Messiah's soul, unlike other souls, need not obey the laws of the Torah. The Messiah is left completely to his own devices ("strange actions" that no other Jew would do) in his final redemptive undertaking. Like a spy in the enemy camp, therefore, Shabbatai Zevi descended into the abyss to liberate sparks that he alone could reach and thus conquer evil completely.

Shortly after Shabbatai Zevi's conversion, Nathan managed to visit him in the Balkans, and then went to Rome where Nathan performed secret rituals designed to hasten the fall of the papacy, returning to the Balkans where he spent the rest of his life. Shabbatai remained in Adrianople and Istanbul leading a double life, appearing to be a Muslim but also observing Jewish ceremonies. In 1672 the Turks lost patience with their supposed convert and deported him to Dulcigno in Albania. Some of his supporters continued to visit him there, and he revealed to them a kabbalistic mystery of his own devising: that the Ayn Sof exerted no providential care at all over creation. Only the God of Israel who came into being after *tzimtzum* was the true God of religious faith. Just before he died, Shabbatai formulated this notion into a kabbalistic trinity

Contemporary engraving of the messianic pretender, Shabbatai Zevi.

composed of the Ancient Holy One, the God of Israel, and the She-khinah. Shabbatai Zevi died in Dulcigno on Yom Kippur, 1676. Nathan claimed that Shabbatai's death was a self-concealment and that he had actually ascended to the supernal world. (Nathan died in 1680.)

A number of small Shabbatean groups survived, especially in Salonika, Izmir, and Istanbul. Although Nathan and other Shabbateans refrained from teaching that one should emulate their Messiah and publicly violate the laws of the Torah, a group in Salonika, led by the family of Shabbatai Zevi's last wife, apostasized in 1683. They formed a sect known as the Doenmeh, professing Islam in public, but adhering to their own form of religion in secret. They married among themselves and in time developed subsects, some of which were extremely antinomian, deliberately flouting the sexual laws of Judaism and affirming the divinity of Shabbatai Zevi and their leader, Baruchiah Russo.[9] There were also several secret Shabbatean circles in Italy which did not deviate from halakhic practice, and various Shabbatean missionaries who propagated their beliefs in Eastern Europe during the late seventeenth and early eighteenth centuries. A widespread heresy-hunting campaign was conducted against such men by rabbis of Germany and Poland.

The best-known Shabbatean group in Europe formed around a Polish Jew known as Jacob Frank (1726–1791), who spent several years in Turkey where he had close relations with the Doenmeh. Returning to Poland, Frank presented himself as the spiritual heir and reincarnation of Shabbatai Zevi and preached his own version of the extremist Shabbatean principle that the nullification of the Torah was its true fulfillment (the holiness of sin, as it is sometimes rendered). Persecuted by the rabbis for their orgiastic rites, Frank and his followers (there were several hundred) converted to Catholicism between 1756 and 1760. The conversion was encouraged by certain Polish Catholic clerics, until they discovered that Frank intended that his sect would continue to maintain its separateness and loyalty to him under a Christian guise. As a result Frank spent thirteen years in prison. Released in 1772 he established a headquarters for his sect in Moravia and later in Germany.

Frank's ideology was opportunistic and anarchistic: He proclaimed that he was the representative of the second person of the Shabbatean trinity, and taught that true believers could pass through all religions and assume their outward appearance, annihilating them from within in order to break their dominion in the world. Frank claimed to reveal a new road to the unbridled flow of true life, not tied to any constricting law—only to his (Frank's) will. For many Frankists the sect was apparently a liberation, not the nihilistic kind that Frank advocated but an emotional liberation from the burden of being Jewish. Families in Warsaw and Prague, some of whom were outwardly observant and eminently respectable Jews and others Christians, continued to maintain their Frankist ties and marry among themselves through the first half of the nineteenth century.[10]

How does Shabbateanism fit into Jewish intellectual history? The Lurianic Kabbalah contributed to the atmosphere surrounding his messianic career, but quite apart from Shabbateanism, the Lurianic tradition continued within the mainstream of Judaism, becoming an important element in eighteenth-century Polish Hasidism, which will be described later in this chapter. Luria's teaching that the shattered elements of the cosmos were about to be restored to harmony heightened the messianic tension of the 1660s, and Shabbatai Zevi's associates used Lurianic motifs, such as the ingathering of the sparks, to justify his behavior. But there are crucial differences between the two tendencies. The Lurianic Kabbalah, like the earlier Spanish Kabbalah, offered a justification for the greatest possible devotion to the halakhah, whereas Shabbatai Zevi and some of his followers had an ambivalent, even hostile, attitude to the law, combining traditional ascetic penances with daring and deliberate violations of Jewish norms. In the Lurianic system the coming of the Messiah was only an outward sign of a redemptive process, invisible but real, taking place underneath the surface of events. Through living a religious life all Jews participate in the gradual process of bringing about the unification of the highest realm. For the Shabbateans, not the Jewish people but the person of the Messiah was crucial: The believer was he who had faith in the efficacy of Shabbatai Zevi's mystic acts. In addition to Lurianic ideas, Marrano experiences may have contributed to the Shabbatean concept of the Messiah. To be sure, there were Sephardim and former Marranos among Shabbatai Zevi's greatest opponents after 1666, but tensions and polemics that Jews in Spain had faced in their relations with the Christian Church had made the idea of the Messiah an exceptionally sensitive issue to them—an issue that was even more critical for the secret Jews, the Marranos. Was the Christian claim correct that Jesus was the Messiah, or was the Jewish counterclaim valid that the Messiah had not yet come but would finally appear to redeem the Jewish people? The paradoxical idea of the Messiah who took on the guise of another religion that he did not believe in poignantly reflects one aspect of Marrano existence.[11]

The Shabbatean outburst was a messianic episode that reached Jews almost everywhere in the diaspora, unlike earlier occasions which evaporated before they had more than local or regional impact. The speed with which the announcement spread through the diaspora is a testimony to the lively communication between Jewish communities at that time, especially among the Sephardim and Marranos whose correspondence and trade connections kept Jews in the Middle East in close touch with Italy, Holland, and northern Germany. The arrival of rumors concerning the Messiah in areas far from Izmir and Istanbul created a mood of excitement and release. Some Jews announced with pride and dignity that they were no longer in bondage because their king had come. Gershom Scholem suggests that some found in this momentary inner liberation a psychological transformation too precious to give up, which explains why they remained loyal to Shabbatai even after his apostasy. The political expectations aroused by the news of the Messiah's advent were, however, totally unrealistic. Even Shabbatai's regal actions have a fantastic quality that does not reflect any practical appraisal of the political situation of the Jews at that time or any realistic notion of how to improve it. He and his followers were acting out a drama of redemption of their own devising, though they may also have been gratifying quite real desires for power over others.

For many Jews who welcomed the great news in 1665–1666 and who knew nothing of Lurianic Kabbalah and of Marranism, Shabbatai Zevi briefly seemed to be a fulfillment of ancient apocalyptic beliefs that had survived in talmudic and midrashic literature and in medieval apocalyptic tracts. God had set in motion the long-awaited restoration of David's kingdom, the end of Israel's centuries of persecution and exile. Messianic hopes, long dormant in Judaism though enshrined in the daily prayers, exploded when the emotional climate, the political conditions, and the specific personalities came together in the right combination. (Christianity and Islam also had this potential; indeed, mid-seventeenth-century Puritan England was a hotbed of expectations of the millennium.) But the messianic longing that surfaced in 1665–1666 was essentially medieval, spiritual, passive. When the brief flareup subsided, the regular rhythm of Jewish life recommenced.

It seems that the Shabbatean movement and the divisive residue it left after 1666 exhausted the religious creativity of Jewry in the Ottoman realm. There was no overall communal structure in which a permanent revitalization of Eastern Jewry could take place, only occasional court favorites who pleaded the cause of the Jews in the Turkish capital. The autocratic Ottoman empire entered a period of standstill and decline as army revolts and widespread corruption undermined the state. Degrading aspects of the old Islamic *dhimmi* legislation were again imposed. In these conditions it was difficult enough for the Ottoman Jews to keep their communities intact on a local level. Only in the nineteenth century did the eastern Sephardim noticeably revive.

The Jews in Poland and Lithuania

The Establishment of Polish Jewry

In the medieval period, Jews migrated to Poland from the Crimea and the Russian steppes, from the Middle East (the Karaites who settled in Lithuania), and from Spain (small groups of Sephardim arrived after 1492), but the largest and dominant component in Polish Jewry was Ashkenazic. Personal names, institutional structure, early economic roles all indicate this—as well as the Yiddish language, based on medieval German with the addition of Hebrew words and phrases and some Slavic expressions, which became the Jewish vernacular in Eastern Europe. There were Jews in Poland in the eleventh and twelfth centuries, but the period of group immigration began in the second half of the thirteenth century, when in order to develop urban life after the destructive Mongol invasions of the 1240s, Polish rulers encouraged the settlement of German burghers and Jews. In 1264 Boleslav the Pious, prince of Kalisz, issued a charter to the Jews (modeled after similar charters issued around that time by the rulers of Austria, Bohemia, and Hungary), promising Jews as much legal protection as possible in conditions that were still

CRACOVIA.

Panorama of the city of Cracow, Polish capital until 1609; the Jewish community of the adjacent suburb of Kazimierz was one of the most important in Poland.

quite primitive and precarious. In 1334, 1364, and 1367, King Casimir III (the Great) widened the earlier charter to cover the whole kingdom of Poland. In 1388–1389 the Grand Duke of Lithuania granted broad rights to Jews in his domain. In 1453 Casimir IV Jagiello renewed and ratified Casimir III's charter. Thus a series of Polish and Lithuanian rulers welcomed Jews as useful and desirable subjects, just as the rulers of Western Europe had done five hundred years before.

Soon after they settled in Poland, most Jews took advantage of new economic opportunities to drop moneylending and become fiscal agents, collectors of taxes, managers of the estates of Polish noblemen, merchants, and craftsmen. Jews leased lands from the nobility and kings, supervised the farming of crops, the harvesting of timber, the manufacture of flour and spirits, and the exporting of agricultural products. They considered that their situation was, on the whole, quite favorable. Even in times of peace and security, Polish Jews were not unaffected by the Church's efforts to impose the segregationist measures of the Fourth Lateran Council, nor were they untouched by the outbursts of anti-Jewish violence that swept through Europe from time to time, such as during the Black Death. Christian burghers in the Polish cities and some of the Polish nobility resented Jewish competition. There were periodic blood libels and host desecration episodes (there was even a short expulsion of the Jews from Lithuania between 1495 and 1503), but these negative pressures were exceptions in a generally propitious environment.

In 1500 Polish Jewry was already a substantial group of at least 10,000 to 15,000. Between 1500 and 1648 the Jewish population increased to 150,000 or more, making it the largest Jewish community in the diaspora. (The rate of growth continued such that by 1900 a majority of the Jews in the world were descendants of Polish Jewry.) During the sixteenth century Jews moved from western Poland to the east and south. Economic competition and anti-Jewish feeling in the older cities of Poland (some of which won the right to banish Jews) was offset by the opening up of large tracts of land owned by the Polish nobility in the southeast. During the sixteenth and seventeenth centuries the political power of the Polish nobility (the *szlachta*) increased at the expense of royal authority; officially Poland was a republic, ruled by a king elected by the *szlachta*. And the *szlachta* controlled the Polish diet (*sejm*), which, unlike many other European parliaments of the time, was a significant and powerful institution. The upper stratum of the *szlachta*, the magnates, owned huge properties in the Ukraine, where they were the absolute rulers of the peasants (really serfs) on their lands.[12] The magnates were eager to develop these territories, and they found the Jews useful in this regard. Jews leased estates from the nobles and collected taxes, fees, tolls, and produce from the serfs. Some noblemen founded private cities where Jews were welcome, laying the basis for the large zone of Eastern Europe where much of the middle class was Jewish, a situation that persisted through the nineteenth century. (The small urban centers where a majority of the inhabitants were Jews are known in Jewish history as *shtetlech*, "little towns" [*shtetl*, singular]). Even in the older Polish cities that had excluded Jews, houses owned by the Polish nobility did not fall under the control of the city government, and Jews could reside in them in order to conduct business for themselves and their lords. Thus, although the Jews fell increasingly under the control of the Polish nobility, conditions, on the whole, were considered to be satisfactory within the limits of a medieval pattern of Jewish-Christian relations in the sixteenth and into the seventeenth centuries.

The Polish Jewish Community and the Rabbinate

Polish Jewry adapted the Ashkenazic system of communal self-government to Jewish comunities far more diversified than the *kehillot* of the Middle Ages, and much larger. Each local kehillah elected a committee of trustees that apportioned and collected taxes from its members for the Polish government and insured that basic educational needs and other requirements of Jewish life were adequately maintained. Each community also had a number of special associations (such as the *hevra kad-*

Synagogue at Gabin, one of the many elaborate wooden synagogues of Poland.

disha, the "burial society"), and there were Jewish crafts guilds of various kinds, so that the average level of participation in Jewish public affairs was quite high. Each kehillah had the right to determine who, besides descendants of old members, would be admitted to official membership. In addition to the threat of excommunication, the community maintained discipline by the implied warning that it would not defend a Jew who got into trouble with the non-Jewish authorities if his actions did not reflect creditably on the Jewish people.

In the bigger cities, the kehillot had a staff of paid officials, including a rabbi. From the late fourteenth century, the Ashkenazic rabbinate had become a paid profession limited to those found qualified by other rabbis, and formally authorized by them to teach and issue rulings in Jewish law. The Polish rabbi was elected to serve as the expert in talmudic law, usually for three-year periods, by the kehillah board; in the larger cities the rabbi would often be also the head of the yeshivah, the talmudic academy for Jewish youth above the age of thirteen. The core of the advanced curriculum of Polish Jewish youth was talmudic and rabbinic texts. Excerpts from a seventeenth-century chronicle convey the Ashkenazic educational ideal:

Each community maintained young men and provided for them a weekly allowance of money that they might study with the head of the academy. And for each young man they also maintained two boys to study under his guidance, so that he would orally discuss the Gemara, the commentaries of Rashi, and the Tosafot, which he had learned, and thus he would gain experience in the subtlety of talmudic argumentation. The boys were provided with food from the community benevolent fund or from the public kitchen. If the community consisted of fifty householders it supported not less than thirty young men and boys. One young man and two boys would be assigned to one householder. . . .

There was scarcely a house in all the kingdom of Poland where its members did not occupy themselves with the study of the Torah. Either the head of the family was himself a scholar, or else his son, or his son-in-law studied, or one of the young men eating at his table. . . .

The program of study in the kingdom of Poland was as follows: The term of study consisted of the period which required the young men and the boys to study with the head of the academy in the academy. In the summer it extended from the first day of the month of Iyar (April) till the fifteenth day of the month of Av (July), and in the winter, from the first day of the month of Heshvan (October), till the fifteenth day of the month of Shevat (January). After the fifteenth of Shevat or the fifteenth of Av, the young men and the boys were free to study wherever they preferred. From the first day of Iyar till the Feast of Weeks (in June) and in the winter from the first day of Heshvan till Hanukkah (in December) all the students of the academy studied Gemara, the commentaries of Rashi, and the Tosafot, with great diligence. . . .

In each community great honor was accorded to the head of the academy. His words were heard by rich and poor alike. None questioned his authority. Without him no one raised his hand or foot, and as he commanded so it came to be. In his hand he carried a stick and a lash, to smite and to flog, to punish and chastise transgressors, to institute ordinances, to establish safeguards, and to declare the forbidden. Nevertheless everyone loved the head of the academy. . . .[13]

Beginning in the late fifteenth century, Polish Jewry produced an outstanding series of commentators on talmudic law, whose mastery of the rabbinic texts and ability to apply them to practical matters made Poland one of the greatest centers of the rabbinic halakhah in Jewish history. In the yeshivah, talmudic disputation became almost an end in itself; the method of *pilpul* (literally, "pepper") or *hilluk* (subtle differentiation and reconciliation of rabbinical opinions) was so widespread that some of the greatest talmudists in Poland sharply criticized the practice for losing a firm connection to reality. The method of *hilluk*, rooted in the earlier Ashkenazic textual exegesis of Talmud (that of the tosafists of medieval France and Germany and their successors), made possible a creative participation in rabbinic religious intellectuality, a tearing down and building up of subtle argumentation that kept the halakhic tradition alive and flourishing in East Europe.

In Polish rabbinical scholarship there was no direct borrowing of

Renaissance ideas and attitudes, as among Italian Jews of the time, but there were indirect influences from Renaissance humanism: careful attention to textual criticism in order to determine the precise reading of ancient texts and to correct errors that had crept in during many generations of copying, an erudite concern for gathering up and summarizing the legal interpretations of former Ashkenazic and Sephardic halakhists, pride in individual authorship facilitated by the printing press that made rabbinic works available to a large readership in the yeshivot. A major issue among the scholars was the value of Joseph Caro's *Shulhan Arukh*. Some were not pleased that this code should be used as a main text for study in the academy and as a guide for the average rabbi, preferring that the adjudication of cases be based on a thorough analysis of the original talmudic sources and the opinions of all the most recent authorities. Certain outstanding men embarked on their own analysis of the entirety of rabbinic law. Eventually the *Shulhan Arukh* was accepted because it was surrounded by notes and commentaries added by Polish scholars of the sixteenth and seventeenth centuries—and because the age of self-confident mastery of talmudic learning in Poland came to an end for a while later in the seventeenth century.[14]

Talmudic law was a matter of practical as well as theoretical interest because the leadership was faced with the opportunity—and necessity—of administering a large part of the functions of government for Polish Jewry. The weakness of the central Polish government required delegation of autonomy to groups such as the Jews. Polish Jews evolved their own equivalent of the regional and national parliaments of the Polish nobility, a series of supra-kehillah federations that coordinated Jewish affairs from the mid-sixteenth century to the mid-eighteenth. In the Middle Ages representatives from several Ashkenazic communities had met together occasionally to resolve conflicts between them, deal with special crises, and head off threats posed by notorious anti-Jewish agitators. In Poland-Lithuania an additional level was added to earlier regional synods of kehillot: a national body, the Council of the Four Lands (*Vaad Arba'ah Aratzot*), composed of the most eminent rabbinical and lay leaders of the time.[15] The Council of the Four Lands usually met twice a year during important fairs; it allocated to the provincial synods of kehillot the tax burden assigned to Jewry as a whole; it selected and financed the Jewish representatives (*shtadlanim*, "intercessors") to the Polish court, who negotiated the taxes with the Polish government and defended Jewish interests through persuasion and through the bribes that were often necessary to insure the physical protection of the Jews. The Council of the Four Lands issued ordinances (*takkanot*) for Polish Jewry in matters of education, public morals, and qualifications for the rabbinate. The strong institutional structure of Polish-Lithuanian Jewry was a vital fac-

A seventeenth-century Jewish tombstone in the Prague cemetery.

tor in the smooth functioning of Jewish affairs in times of relative security—and in coping with unexpected disasters that could have destroyed the social fabric of Polish Jewry in periods of political chaos.[16]

The Chmielnicki Massacres and the Deluge (1648–1667)

Although mid-seventeenth-century Poland was one of the largest and most prestigious states in Europe, internal stresses and external threats led to two decades of almost uninterrupted war, a period that is called in Polish history the Deluge. While its own central government was becoming weaker and the power of the nobility stronger, Poland found itself surrounded by a strong Sweden, an expansionist Russia, and other dangerous enemies. In 1648 the Cossacks of the Ukraine, allied with the Crimean Tatars and supported by the peasants, revolted. The leader of the rebellion was Bogdan Chmielnicki, a partly Polonized Cossack chief, who took advantage of social and economic tensions in the Ukraine to turn the insurrection into a political struggle with international repercussions.[17] The Ukrainian situation was explosive because of the complex ethnic and religious make-up of the population: The peasants were Ukrainian in language and Greek Orthodox in religion; the landlords were Roman Catholic Polish nobility; the administrators of the estates and much of the city population were Jewish. In May and June 1648 Cossacks and their supporters marched from one city to another, slaughtering Jews, Poles, Catholic clergy, and Uniates (Greek Orthodox who had accepted the authority of the pope and become affiliated with the Roman Catholic Church). One of the Jewish chronicles of the time describes the havoc and brutality that resulted:

Many communities beyond the Dnieper and close to the battlefield, such as Pereyaslaw, Baryszowka, Piratyn, and Boryspole, Lubin, and Lachowce and their neighbors, who were unable to escape, perished for the sanctification of [God's] Name. These persons died cruel and bitter deaths. Some were skinned alive and their flesh was thrown to the dogs; some had their hands and limbs chopped off, and their bodies thrown on the highway only to be trampled by wagons and crushed by horses; some had wounds inflicted on them, and were thrown on the street to die a slow death; they writhed in their blood until they breathed their last; others were buried alive. The enemy slaughtered infants in the laps of their mothers. They were sliced into pieces like fish. They slashed the bellies of pregnant women, removed their infants and tossed them in their faces. . . . Some children were pierced by spears, roasted on the fire, and then brought to their mothers to be eaten. Many times they used the bodies of Jewish children as improvised bridges upon which they later crossed. . . . Many were taken by the Tartars into captivity. Women and virgins were ravished. . . . Similar atrocities were perpetrated in all the settlements through which they passed. Also against the Polish people, these cruelties were perpetrated, especially against the priests and bishops. . . . Scrolls of the Law were torn to pieces, and turned into boots and shoes for their feet. . . . Some were used for kindling purposes, and others to stuff the barrels of their guns. The ears ring at the hearing of this.[18]

As the Cossacks advanced, the Polish king died, adding to the confusion. His successor, John Casimir, tried to negotiate with Chmielnicki, who demanded an independent Ukraine under Cossack rule. After several more years of fighting and massacre, Chmielnicki, deserted by his former Tatar allies, turned to the Russians, who invaded northeastern Poland and the Ukraine. In 1655 the Swedes invaded western Poland. By the end of that year almost all of Poland was occupied by Cossacks, Russians, and Swedes. In the following year, however, a Polish partisan movement emerged, and soon the reorganized Polish army began to turn back the Swedish troops, the Cossacks, and other invaders. The Deluge came to an end finally in 1667 when Poland and Russia signed the Treaty of Andrusovo, ceding the eastern Ukraine and the Smolensk region to Russia, retaining the western Ukraine as part of Poland.

During the fighting Jews were slaughtered by almost everyone. The Cossacks and Ukrainian peasants looked on them as agents of the Polish nobility they were trying to eliminate. The Russians, who would not permit any Jews to settle in their lands, assisted the Cossacks in wiping out the Jews in any territory that fell under their control. Even the Polish partisans (but not the Polish army) killed Jews on the pretext that they were allied with the Swedes. The Jewish martyrological literature of the time—dirges, memorial prayers, chronicles—memorialized the massacre of communities such as Nemirov, Tulczyn, Ostrog, Narol, where Jews willingly died for their religion, in accordance with the traditional ideal of *kiddush ha-Shem,* revered in Ashkenazic pietism. (There were also instances in which Jews took part in the defense of besieged cities, sometimes only to be betrayed by the Polish population.) Epidemics and famine increased the death toll. It is thought that at least a quarter of the Jewish population of Poland died during this period. (Estimates range from 40,000 to 100,000.) Many Jews fled to Germany and Holland. Thousands were ransomed from the Tatars in the slave markets of Istanbul. The Jewish population of the world probably fell to a low of about one million as a result.

The catastrophe of 1648 ranks with the First Crusade, the Black Death, and the Spanish attacks of 1391 in Jewish history for its devastation. Despite the magnitude of the disaster, however, the Council of the Four Lands undertook measures to save as many Jews as possible, and many communities were re-established afterwards, even in the Polish Ukraine. But the economic prosperity and security that made the high degree of Polish rabbinic culture possible remained shattered for decades.

Polish Jewry in the Eighteenth Century: The Vilna Gaon

In the last decades of the seventeenth century, the Polish state had some military successes (the Polish king John Sobieski helped turn back the Turkish siege of Vienna in 1683), but the decline of the Polish political structure continued. The parliament was paralyzed by the veto power of each individual member, and the *szlachta* fell prey to manipulation by foreign powers. Under these conditions Jewish life in Poland became exceedingly insecure.

Poverty was widespread. The population growth of Polish Jewry commenced again; by the end of the eighteenth century the Jews of Eastern Europe had increased three- or four-fold. In a declining economy, earning a living was increasingly difficult. By the middle of the eighteenth century as much as one third of Polish Jewry were scattered over the countryside in small groups, as few as two or three Jewish families in a village. Furthermore, Polish Jewry had to contend with a continual series of blood libels. (Some of the most infamous were Sandomir in 1698, Posen in 1736, Zaslav in 1747.) In the 1730s and 1740s Cossack detachments known as *Haidemaks* raided the Ukraine, robbing and killing Jews,

Engraving depicting the temporary expulsion of the Jews from Frankfort after the anti-Jewish riots of 1614.

a series of incursions that climaxed in the large-scale massacre of Jews in the city of Uman in 1768. A huge financial burden fell on the kehillot, which had to borrow from the Polish nobility and from the Church in order to cover expenses incurred for the protection of Jews. Internal tension within the kehillot also surfaced; complaints were widespread that the Jewish institutions were controlled by an oligarchy of wealthy families who exploited their connections with the Polish ruling class to monopolize positions of authority and to place most of the tax burden on the poor. Artisan and craftsmen guilds protested that they were excluded from running communal affairs. The kehillot and the councils lost a great deal of their moral prestige.

An exception to the overall pattern of decline in Eastern Europe was Lithuania. Owing to its proximity to Prussia and trade connections with the West and with Russia, the Jews of Vilna and several other Lithuanian towns maintained a certain prosperity in the eighteenth century. Vilna became an important focus of Jewish intellectual life from the mideighteenth century until the twentieth century. (Vilna came to be called the Jerusalem of Lithuania—a lively center not only of traditional rabbinic scholarship, but of the nineteenth-century Jewish Enlightenment and Jewish social radicalism as well.) The key figure in the rise of Vilna to prominence as a home of talmudic learning was Elijah ben Solomon Zalman, known as the Vilna Gaon. (Unlike the early Islamic period, in Europe *Gaon* was now used as a purely honorific term for a rabbinic genius.)

The Vilna Gaon (1720–1797) was a man of prodigious learning, whose scholarly diligence and iron will acquired legendary dimensions. Never occupying an official position in the Vilna community, he was given a stipend by the kehillah in order that he might devote all his time to study. He also lectured on rabbinic topics to a circle of disciples through whom he exerted a profound influence on Lithuanian Judaism, espousing a rigorous intellectuality that came to characterize what was colloquially known as Litvak Jewry.

Memorial Book of Frankfort Jewry, containing the names of martyrs and other important members of the community for whom memorial prayers were recited. Such books are an important source for the history of Central European Jewry in early modern times.

The Vilna Gaon's approach represents a revitalization of the Polish rabbinical tradition of the sixteenth and seventeenth centuries and the development of its method in a somewhat more modern direction. He left an enormous body of writings, mostly in manuscript: He wrote commentaries to the Bible, the Mishnah, the Babylonian and Jerusalem Talmuds, the midrash literature, the *Sefer Yetzirah*, the *Zohar*, the *Shulhan Arukh*. But his most important influence was his approach, rather than the details of his teaching. Like some of the earlier giants of rabbinic scholarship in Poland, he rejected elaborate argumentation (the technique of *hilluk* that was so popular in the yeshivot) and espoused an exact, meticulous interpretation of the common-sense meaning of the text. His concern to understand the sequential and logical meaning of rabbinical dispute extended even to criticizing the scholars of the talmudic age when he felt they had not interpreted adequately the foundations of rabbinic law in the Mishnah. His interests also led him to investigate many branches of secular learning, such as algebra, geometry, astronomy, geography, Hebrew grammar, and chronology, in order to elucidate talmudic discussions; and he encouraged his disciples to translate European works on these subjects into Hebrew. (His knowledge of mathematics and science was derived from medieval books, however, and he was unaware of and unaffected by the revolutionary implications of modern astronomy and Newtonian physics, so that his world view was quite removed from that of the Jewish Enlightenment beginning to appear during his lifetime in Prussia.) He disliked Maimonidean philosophy, but he had a considerable interest in the Kabbalah, which he sought to bring into harmony with talmudic teachings.

The Gaon was revered in Vilna almost as a saint. His ascetic temperament and his belief that perpetual learning was the means to communion with God led him to reject as a perversion of Jewish values the religious revivalism beginning to sweep large segments of Polish Jewry in the south during the later part of his life. The Vilna Gaon became the symbol of those who condemned the emotional excesses of the new Hasidic movement, which subordinated talmudic study to inward, mystical experience and which threatened to split Polish Jewry into two hostile camps.

Hasidism

In the second half of the eighteenth century, the autonomous authority of the Jewish communal structure was considerably weakened as a result of developments without and within Polish Jewry. In 1764 the Polish government abolished the Council of the Four Lands and the Lithuanian Jewish council, undertaking to collect taxes from the Jews directly. Meanwhile the Polish state was in dire straits. In 1772 Russia, Austria, and

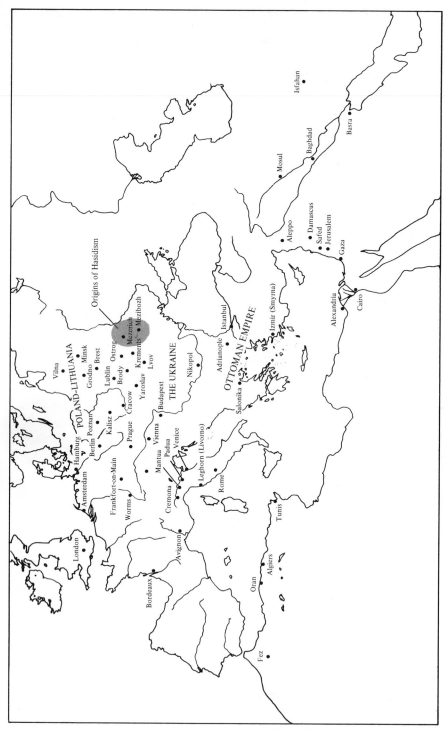

Important Jewish Centers from 1500 to 1780. In the early modern era, Sephardic Jews resettled in Italy, North Africa, the Balkans, Asia Minor, and Palestine. The Jewry of Poland-Lithuania expanded toward the southeast (the Ukraine, then under Polish rule) and continued to grow in numbers, despite the terrible massacres of 1648–67. Portuguese and Spanish Marranos founded settlements in the North Atlantic ports soon augmented by Ashkenazic Jews. Court Jews in various German states and cities founded new communities in Central Europe.

Map labels:

Isfahan

Baghdad
Basra
Mosul

Aleppo
Damascus
Safed
Jerusalem
Gaza

Alexandria
Cairo

Origins of Hasidism
Mezerich
Medzibozh

POLAND-LITHUANIA
Vilna
Minsk
Grodno
Brest
Lublin
Ostrog
Brody
Kremenets
Lvov
Yaroslav
Cracow
Budapest
THE UKRAINE
Nikopol
Istanbul
Adrianople
Izmir (Smyrna)
OTTOMAN EMPIRE
Salonika

Hamburg
Berlin
Poznan
Kalisz
Prague
Vienna
Padua
Venice
Mantua
Leghorn (Livorno)
Amsterdam
Frankfort-on-Main
Worms
Cremona
Rome
London
Avignon
Bordeaux
Tunis
Oran
Algiers
Fez

Prussia agreed that they would each annex a large slice of Polish territory (the first partition of Poland). Despite an era of Polish reform, a second partition was carried out in 1793; after a revolutionary outburst of Polish nationalism, the final partition of 1795 led to the total extinction of Poland.

The kehillah system survived the partitions, but its power was diminished and it had to contend with Hasidism, a major internal rebellion that won the enthusiastic loyalty of a large segment of the Jewish masses. The new pietism drew on the Kabbalah to create an ideology espousing a reinterpretation of the concept of the rabbi as the spiritual guide of the masses. In Hasidism, for the first and only time, the Kabbalah provided the ideological basis for a broad and permanent movement of great vitality and diversity. The Kabbalah lost most of its esoteric character and was reshaped to emphasize its psychological and social rather than its speculative character.[19]

Hasidism first appeared in the villages of the Polish Ukraine, especially the province of Podolia, where the Shabbatean Frankists had won notoriety for their heretical beliefs and orgiastic practices. Podolia in the first part of the eighteenth century had also become the home of nonconformist Christian sects that had split off from the Russian Orthodox Church. Like these other groups, the early hasidim were known for their ecstatic worship and their willingness to sanction deviations from established religious norms. According to the Hasidic tradition, the seminal figure of the movement was a folk healer and itinerant wonder-worker named Israel ben Eleazer, known as the Baal Shem Tov (1700–1760, usually abbreviated the Besht). The term *Baal Shem*, "Master of the (divine) Name," refers to a man who wrote amulets against diseases and evil spirits; there were several Jews known by this title in the seventeenth and eighteenth centuries, before the Besht became the Baal Shem par excellence in Jewish history. Like Isaac Luria, the Besht left no writings of importance, except for a few letters. His oral teachings began to appear in print twenty years after his death, in the 1780s, and stories circulating about him were published in 1814. The *Shivhei ha-Besht (Praises of the Baal Shem Tov)* contains tales and legends about the Besht and his disciples and is our main source for biographical information about him. Dating from a time when the movement had already evolved considerably from its original form, it has to be used with caution as a historical source.

According to the *Shivhei ha -Besht*, Israel ben Eleazer was born of poor parents in a small town in southern Poland, left an orphan in childhood, and as a young man eked out a meager living in a variety of menial capacities, such as a *heder* (elementary school) assistant. In his twenties he was said to have gone with his wife to the forests of the Carpathian Mountains, where he meditated on the Kabbalah and did physical labor. In the mid-1730s he gave up his seclusion and made his headquarters the town of Medzibozh in Podolia, where he became known for curing physical and mental illnesses, expelling demons, working miracles, perceiving the secrets of people's souls, and teaching how to reach mystical exhaltation. In the *Shivei ha-Besht* he is portrayed as a man without extensive talmudic expertise but learned in the Kabbalah. By the 1740s he had attracted a considerable body of followers, including wandering preachers (*maggidim*), ritual slaughterers, and other lower-echelon Jewish functionaries, as well as well-educated rabbis who came to him for spiritual advice and help. The stories relate that their lives were transformed by his influence.

After his death in 1760, leadership of the nascent movement passed to the *Maggid* (preacher) Dov Baer (1710–1772), who settled in the town of Mezeritch in Volhynia, closer to central Poland. Under the aegis of Dov Baer, proponents of the new pietism began to settle in a large number of communities of southern Poland, the Ukraine, and Lithuania, where they won thousands of adherents. By 1772, hasidim had attracted the open hostility of the kehillah authorities in several places, especially Vilna, causing an edict of excommunication to be issued against them. The hasidim were accused of holding the study of Torah in contempt, being permissive in their observance of the commandments, behaving like madmen in their rituals, praying with the Lurianic rather than the Ashkenazic prayerbook, and using excessively sharp knives in their kosher slaughtering of meat. (These accusations actually indicate that they did not depart from the halakhah.) The Vilna Jewish community was being torn by social conflict, and the attack on the hasidim may have been used by the kehillah oligarchy to discredit its critics. But there is no doubt that the hasidim posed a challenge to the official Jewish leadership. In the 1780s and 1790s hostility between the hasidim and their enemies (who came to be called *mitnagdim*, "opponents") was bitter. When Jacob Joseph of Polonnoye, one of the Besht's closest disciples but not himself involved in actively spreading Hasidism, published the first book that quoted the Besht extensively and that attacked the indifference of the established rabbinate to the needs of the masses, another storm was aroused. His work was apparently burned in several localities, and another excommunication was issued in 1781 by the mitnagdim, who ordered Jews to cut off all contact with the hasidim. At the end of the eighteenth century, the Vilna mitnagdim denounced the hasidim to the Russian government, and several Hasidic leaders were briefly imprisoned.

In the long run neither side prevailed. The Russian and Austrian governments extended recognition to the Hasidic movement, which was, by then, deeply entrenched in the Jewish communities. But the hasidim did not succeed in capturing the loyalty of a majority of Jews outside southern Poland and the Ukraine. (They did achieve a foothold in Lithuania and central Poland.) Hasidim became split into a number of groups, each

The synagogue of the Besht in the Ukrainian town of Miedziboz. (Courtesy of the Zionist Archives, New York.)

owing allegiance to a local leader. By the first quarter of the nineteenth century, Hasidism had crystalized its typical pattern of organization by dynasties (great Hasidic figures passed on their personal authority to their children), and the movement lost its earlier provocative *élan*. Soon some of the mitnagdim, especially in Lithuania, began to address themselves to some of the charges made against them by the hasidim and others, and introduced ethical instruction (*musar*) into the yeshivot. With the appearance of modern rationalistic ideologies among Jews in the nineteenth century, the hasidim drew closer to the mitnagdim as separate branches of the traditionalist wing of East European Jewry.

Hasidism is not easily summarized, owing to the limited historical evidence for the early stage of the movement and the great diversity of views that developed among Hasidic leaders as the movement spread. But it seems that the Besht was responsible for initiating a change in Jewish mystical pietism—a change in emphasis rather than in ideas—with far-reaching consequences. Before the Besht, Ashkenazic pietists tended to engage in regular, often prolonged penances to achieve self-perfection, an aspect of the medieval tradition of Ashkenazic pietism reinforced by the Lurianic Kabbalah. Especially in the period after the Chmielnicki massacres, there was a pervasive feeling of sinfulness and fear of evil spirits and demons. Solomon Maimon, a Polish Jew who moved to Berlin where he became a philosopher and wrote an autobiography, gave several examples of extreme self-mortification that he had seen in his youth:

Two or three instances, of which I was myself an eyewitness, will be sufficient to show what I mean. A Jewish scholar, well known on account of his piety, Simon of Lubtsch, had undergone the severest exercises of penance. He had aready carried out the *teshuvat ha-kana*—the penance of *kana*—which consists in fasting daily and avoiding for supper anything that comes from a living being (flesh, milk, honey, etc.). He had also practised *galut*, that is, a continuous wandering, in which the penitent is not allowed to remain two days in the same place; and, in addition, he had worn a hair shirt next to his skin. But he felt that he would not be doing enough for the satisfaction of his conscience unless he further observed the *teshuvat ha-mishkal*—the penance of weighing—which requires a particular form of penance proportionate to every sin. But as he found by calculation, that the number of his sins was too great to be atoned for in this way, he took it into his head to starve himself to death. After he had spent some time in the process, he came in his wanderings to the place where my father lived, and, without anybody in the house knowing, went into the barn, where he fell upon the ground in utter exhaustion. My father came by chance into the barn, and found the man, whom he had long known, lying half-dead on the ground, with a Zohar (the principal book of the kabbalists) in his hand. He brought him at once all sorts of refreshments, but the man refused them. My father came several times, and repeated his urgent request that Simon would take something; but it was of no avail. My father had to attend to something in the house, whereupon Simon, to escape from his attention gathered all his strength, raised himself, went out of the barn, and eventually out of the village. When my father came back into the barn again, and found the man no longer there, he ran after him, and found him lying dead not far from the village. The affair became known among the Jews, and Simon was looked on as a saint.

Jossel of Klezk proposed nothing less than to hasten the advent of the Messiah. To this end he performed strict penance, fasted, rolled himself in the snow, undertook nightwatches and similar severities. By all sorts of such operations he believed that he was able to accomplish the overthrow of a legion of evil spirits, who kept guard on the Messiah, and placed obstacles to his coming. . . .[20]

In opposition to this ascetic tendency, the Besht and his group minimized preoccupation with guilt and demonic forces, rejected excessive penances, and denounced melancholy as a state of mind that created a barrier between man and God. They accepted the Lurianic world picture, but concentrated on the omnipresence of God, rather than on the catastrophic shattering of the divine sparks and their imprisonment in husks of evil. As the sparks filled the world, "there is no place where God is not" (*let atar panui minei*, a kabbalistic phrase that the hasidim frequently quoted). Some Hasidic masters interpreted the Lurianic notion of *tzimtzum* as only an apparent withdrawal of God from the world: The divine light was everywhere, if one could perceive the true spiritual reality behind the veil. Jacob Joseph of Polonnoye quotes the Besht, "As I heard from my teacher: 'In every one of man's troubles, physical and spiritual, if he takes to heart that even in that trouble God himself is there, the garment is removed and the trouble is cancelled. . . .' "[21] A main characteristic of Hasidism was complete trust in God's goodness and providence—a faith that is realized in the total cleaving (*devekut*) of the soul to God in worship, but also in man's other activities.

In some Hasidic formulations, such as that of Dov Baer of Mezeritch, the highest aim of *devekut* in prayer was the annihilation of individual selfhood (*bittul ha-yesh*, the negation of [mere] existence) and the ascent of the soul (*aliyat ha-neshamah*) to the divine light. Joy, humility, gratitude, spontaneity are hallmarks of Hasidic worship. Solomon Maimon, quite critical of the Hasidic way of life, nevertheless gives a rather sympathetic account of their religious intensity during prayer:

> Their worship consisted in a voluntary elevation above the body, that is, in abstracting their thoughts from all things except God, even from the individual self, and in union with God. By this means a kind of self denial arose among them which led them to ascribe, not to themselves, but to God alone, all the actions undertaken in this state. Their worship therefore consisted in speculative adoration, for which they held no special time or formula to be necessary, but they left each one to determine it according to the degree of his knowledge. Still they chose for it most commonly the hours set apart for the public worship of God. In their public worship they endeavored to attain that elevation above the body which has been described; they became so absorbed in the idea of the divine perfection, that they lost the idea of everything else, even of their own body, which became in this state wholly devoid of feeling.
>
> Such abstraction, however, was a very difficult matter; and accordingly, whenever they emerged from this state through new suggestions taking possession of their minds, they labored, by all sorts of mechanical operations, such as movements and cries, to bring themselves back into the state once more, and to keep themselves in it without interruption during the whole time of their worship. It was amusing to observe how they often interrupted their prayers by all sorts of extraordinary tones and comical gestures, which were meant as threats and reproaches against their adversary, the Evil Spirit, who tried to disturb their devotion; and how by this means they wore themselves out to such an extent that, on finishing their prayers, they usually fell down in complete exhaustion.[22]

The greatest stumbling blocks to the attainment of the total mental concentration in prayer were distracting thoughts. One of the most im-

Ornate brass menorah from eighteenth-century Poland, with birds, lions, and the façade of a building.

portant Hasidic innovations was the teaching that "strange thoughts" (*mahshavot zarot*) and sinful impulses do not have to be completely repressed, but contain a divine spark, which can be released as a step toward reaching God. Jacob Joseph of Polonnoye wrote

> Behold, I received from my teacher: When evil causes good, it becomes a footstool for the good and everything is completely good—which is almost the nullification of the *kelippot,* as in the [messianic] future. Also there are deep matters here for the subject of strange thoughts.[23]

> I heard from my teacher: If some nullification of Torah or prayer happens to the complete man, he must understand that even here it is God's hand who thrusts him away in order to draw him closer, the secret meaning of "His left hand is under my head and his right hand embraces me" (Songs of Songs 2:6).[24]

Thus Hasidism shifted the center of gravity in the Kabbalah from metaphysical speculation to mystical psychology, from a theory about the origin and repair of the cosmos to a method for attaining inner bliss.

According to Beshtian Hasidism, *devekut* was also attainable in eating, drinking, sexual relations, business affairs—even in smoking tobacco. That material needs and bodily impulses contain possibilities for making the profane holy, gave rise to the Hasidic principle of *avodah ba-gashmiyut,* "worship through the physical." A physical act became religious if in performing it, one intended to cleave mentally to God (a favorite Hasidic interpretation of the biblical statement, "In all your ways, know Him" [Prov. 3:6]). *Devekut* could be achieved by everyone in his daily life and according to his capacities; it was accessible in some manner to every Jew, not just to an intellectual or spiritual elite.

Early Hasidism, in some ways, resembled Shabbateanism: in its doctrine of the enjoyment of physical pleasure, in its permissive attitude toward the halakhah (one could wait for the right mood to pray, rather than adhere rigidly to the usual fixed times), and in its concept of the sublimation of evil. But the differences between Hasidism and Shabbateanism were drastic, and account for Hasidism and not Shabbateanism winning the loyalty of the Jewish masses and of some scholars. The modest and moderate Hasidic form of ecstasy was quite within the bounds of the normative tradition, unlike the orgiastic excesses of the extreme Shabbateans. The joy of carrying out the commandments was an old Jewish principle, to which Hasidism merely gave physical outlet: Hasidic worship became known for its revivalistic fervor, its use of singing and dancing, even skipping and whirling—behavior that appeared bizarre to the mitnagdim but was not per se heretical. Although Hasidism adhered to the traditional messianic expectation and had certain messianic secrets of its own, it was the antithesis of the Shabbatean revolt against the Jewish exile. The main concern of Hasidism was individual redemption, here and now. By denying the reality of evil and building a strong inner world dedicated to cheerful devotion to God, Hasidism actually fostered an optimistic acceptance of the situation in which the Jews found themselves during a particularly chaotic age.

A second major element in early Hasidic ideology was a new doctrine of religious leadership, stemming from its criticism of the isolation of the scholars from the everyday life of the ordinary Jew, and of the alienation of the masses from the kehillah oligarchy. The hasidim emphasized the responsibility of all Jews to each other and rejected excessive chastisement of the religious failings of the Jews as unfair and self-defeating. But Hasidism was not itself a movement of the uneducated: Many of the early Hasidic leaders were learned Jews in revolt against the frustrating monopoly, by a small group of powerful families, of the main rabbinical positions in Poland and Lithuania. (The new emphasis on *devekut* did involve a demotion of the importance of talmudic study, inasmuch as cleaving to God laid claim to the greater part of one's time; but eventually the pendulum swung back toward disciplined learning among certain Hasidic groups.) The alternative conception of leadership that Hasidism offered was based on the Lurianic idea of the spiritually superior individual who attains an especially high level of *devekut*. In Hasidism this ideal became institutionalized in the *zaddik* (the completely righteous man). The zaddik is an individual of extraordinary spiritual gifts whose *devekut* is nevertheless dependent on the congregation that gathers around him. His special task is to raise the souls of his followers toward the divine light, which means that he must at times step down from his own spiritual level to that of the common people. (This Hasidic concept of *yeridah letzorekh aliyah,* "descent for the sake of ascent," is perhaps a Hasidic reinterpretation of the Shabbatean Messiah's role in the cosmos.) The zaddik's duties include pleading to God for the people, involving himself in their daily cares and anxieties, counseling them, strengthening their faith. Thus the relation between the Hasidic zaddik and his hasidim is much more intimate and personal than that of the professional kehillah rabbi: The zaddik was the "rebbe" (a more affectionate Yiddish term) rather than the "rov" (the more dignified scholarly title).

The concept of the zaddik was, however, quite authoritarian. For the ordinary hasid, faith in God meant faith in the miraculous powers of the individual zaddik who was his intercessor and protector in the higher worlds. Hasidic interpretation of the biblical statement that "The righteous man is the foundation of the world" (Prov. 10:25) was that the zaddik acted as the channel through which divine grace flows down and the ladder by which the individual's soul rises up. *Devekut* meant cleaving to the zaddik—in order to cleave to God. Never before in rabbinic Judaism did unquestioning loyalty to the person of the religious leader

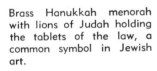

Brass Hanukkah menorah with lions of Judah holding the tablets of the law, a common symbol in Jewish art.

become, to such an extent, such a prerequisite for salvation. (This idea was more often the hallmark of movements viewed by Judaism as sectarian, such as early Christianity and Shabbateanism.) Reverence for the teacher was a duty of a Jewish student, but the hasidim carried their awe for their masters much further, to include everything the zaddik said or did. A Hasidic saying relates, "I did not go to the Maggid of Mezeritch to learn Torah from him, but to watch him tie his bootlaces." The zaddik was virtually the saint whose advice, prayers, and most incidental or bewildering actions were latent with mysterious significance. Not merely his teaching but his character was the living incarnation of Torah.

Hasidic literature consisted, therefore, in two kinds of writings: summaries of the master's biblical and kabbalistic interpretations, often set down in writing by a disciple, and stories of the master's miraculous deeds and profound sayings. Recounting the tales of the zaddik was an act of worship and homage on the part of the followers and an important form of propaganda for the movement.

Although Hasidism encouraged a psychological dependence of the hasid on the zaddik, it also fostered a striking degree of individualism among the zaddikim themselves. In the third generation of the movement (the last quarter of the eighteenth century), a remarkably diverse series of rebbes came to the fore, each of whom had his own approach to Hasidic doctrine and practice. Zusya of Hanipol was known for his innocence and humility, the Hasidic "fool of God." His brother, Elimelekh of Lyzhansk, in Galicia, theorized about the ideal hasid and the ideal zaddik and the relation between them, teaching that the hasidim were obligated to support the zaddik as a token of the bounty they received through him. Shneur Zalman of Liady applied Litvak (Lithuanian) intellectuality to Hasidic theology; Levi Yitzhak of Berdichev, the "lover of Israel" (*ohev Yisrael*), defended the Jews vis-à-vis heaven in an almost Jobian fashion. The Besht's grandson, Nahman of Bratzlav, master storyteller and critic of the other zaddikim of his day, had a quasi-messianic self-conception that did not permit his followers to select another zaddik after his death. And there were many others.

Each zaddik won his own following, developed his own particular customs, doctrines, and even melodies for worship. Hasidism's primary units were the brotherhoods that gathered, especially during holiday seasons of pilgrimage, at the courts of the various zaddikim. Thus the hasidim created a network of social ties outside the kehillah system, although in the smaller towns of southern Poland they virtually took over the kehillot. The greatest strength of Hasidism was among the village and shtetl Jews, the innkeepers, leaseholders, rural merchants, and so on. In the Ukraine and in Polish Galicia the zaddik attained an almost regal splendor amid the simple devotion of his followers. Hasidism also spread to many of the larger cities, where it remained a distinct subgroup, with its own prayer houses (*shtiblekh*) and other institutions. In Lithuania, Lubavich or Habad Hasidism emphasized a distinctive fusion of kabbalistic speculation and rabbinical learning. In central Poland, Hasidism put great emphasis on perfecting the individual's faith and on the personal duty of talmudic study.

From time to time in the nineteenth and twentieth centuries the religious vitality of Hasidism flared up again to lead a counterattack against modern secularism among Jews. (In post-World War II United States and Israel certain Hasidic groups have been active in proselytizing for a return to a traditional observance of the commandments.) And Hasidism had a career in modern Jewish literature and thought, separate from the movement itself. The Hasidic tale, despised at first by Jewish modernists for its medieval superstition, in the late nineteenth century was rediscovered as a genuine expression of Jewish folk culture. In recent decades the dicta of the zaddikim on the nature of faith and authentic human existence have been probed for their profound philosophical and theological insights.

The Western Diaspora in the Early Modern Period

Italy

The Jewish communities of southern Italy and Rome, among the oldest in Europe, had been a cultural bridge between the Middle East and Ashkenazic Jewry in the early Middle Ages. Contacts with Spain and Provence brought Maimonidean philosophy and other aspects of Se-

Procession on the Piazza di San Marco, Venice (sixteenth-century woodcut, after Titian). (Courtesy of the Metropolitan Museum of Art, Whittelsey Fund, 1949.)

phardic civilization to Naples, Rome, and other Italian cities. In the fourteenth century the ancient Jewish communities in the south declined because of persecution and forced conversion, but Jews were invited to the northern cities to provide small loans for the lower and middle classes. (The Italian bankers were not interested in this business.) Special charters, *condottas*, were drawn up between these municipalities and Jewish moneylenders, extending the latter certain privileges for a specified period of time. Gradually Jews arrived from southern France, Germany, Spain, and Portugal. In the sixteenth century Marranos settled in Italy, where they returned to Judaism even in the papal territories. In addition to loan banking and pawnbroking, Italian Jews turned to trade and crafts, and there were a considerable number of Jewish physicians, some employed by Renaissance dukes and popes. By the early 1500s, Jewish communities, not large but thriving, were found in such cities as Ferrara, Mantua, Venice, Padua, Florence, and of course Rome.

The Italian Jews of the Renaissance were comfortably Italian in language and culture. Renaissance Jewish bankers adopted the style of the Italian upper classes and cultivated a taste for art, literature, and affluent living. Some Jewish scholars had close personal contact with Italian humanists and taught them the Hebrew language. The famed Florentine philosopher Pico della Mirandola was fascinated by the Kabbalah; he had several kabbalistic treatises translated into Latin by Jews, and made use of the concept of the sefirot in his writings as a key to the metaphysical structure of the universe and man. Pico and other Christian humanists felt that the Zohar contained ancient occult knowledge that confirmed the truth of Christianity, and dabbled in what is called the Christian Kabbalah. Judah Abravanel (known in Renaissance literature as Leone Ebreo), the son of an eminent Sephardic Court Jew who left Spain in 1492, wrote a work on cosmic love in the Neo-Platonic tradition (the *Dialoghi d'amore*) that was widely admired by Italian humanists.[25] The Renaissance study of the literary classics of ancient Greece and Rome found echoes among the Jews: Jewish preachers wove quotations from Greek and Latin literature into their sermons, and Jewish biblical exegetes applied classic rhetoric to the study of Scripture. Italy became the greatest early center of Hebrew printing. Jewish composers (e.g., Solomone Rossi of Mantua) wrote music for the synagogue in the Renaissance style, and a Jewish theater was established by Leone de' Sommo, also of Mantua, that produced Hebrew dramas. In 1564 a proposal was even circulated for the establishment in Mantua of a Jewish college that would combine Jewish religious training with general humanistic learning. There were, however, no major Jewish sculptors or painters in Italy during the Renaissance, nor did Italian poetry, enchanted by images of ancient paganism, exert an influence on Jewish writers. Italian Jewry produced no giants of philosophy or theology, but did have a number of religious thinkers who carried on the medieval rationalist tradition after it had ended in Spain or who criticized Maimonidean rationalism in the spirit of Judah Halevy.

The Jewish creativity of the Renaissance period did not coalesce into a Jewish Renaissance. But certain writers introduced ideas that were to come to fruition later—tentative signs of a new historical awareness that made it possible for a few Jewish scholars to recognize as medieval certain features of the Jewish tradition that were generally thought to be of extreme antiquity.[26] The most original of these investigators into the Jewish past was Azariah dei Rossi (c. 1511–1578), from an ancient and distinguished Mantuan family, who late in life published a work entitled *Meor Einayim* (*Light to the Eyes*), containing the results of his research in Jewish literature. Dei Rossi was the first Jew to rediscover Hellenistic Jewish writings (Philo, Josephus, the Letter of Aristeas), and to bring to bear on the historical evaluation of talmudic legends non-Jewish sources of late antiquity. Dei Rossi was a man of enormous erudition in Latin as well as Hebrew literature, and cited in his work not only the classical authors of ancient Greece and Rome, but the New Testament, Augustine, Aquinas, Dante, Petrarch, and many other Christian writers of Roman times, the Middle Ages, and the Renaissance. Although an observant Jew whose world view was essentially medieval, he avoided the traditional rabbinic concern for reconciling all contradictions in Jewish texts. Acknowledging that many talmudic legends contained moral lessons but not historical facts, he sought to link events and personages in Jewish history with those in general history according to a careful weighing of the evidence (which led him to conclude that the Jewish calendar dating the years from creation was devised in late talmudic times). His research into chronology and his critical examination of primary sources pointed toward modern methods of Jewish historiography. Dei Rossi's book provoked considerable outrage among rabbis in Italy, central Europe, and the Middle East (Joseph Caro being incensed by it) and a ban was issued against reading it without special permission. Only in the nineteenth century did the pioneering efforts of Dei Rossi win belated recognition among Jewish historians.

Despite good personal relations between Renaissance princes and humanists and some Jews, the Renaissance remained deeply attached to the traditional Christian image of the Jew as deliberate disbeliever. Blood libels still led to expulsions. (A particularly bad period occurred after 1475, when a Franciscan monk stirred up a charge of ritual murder in the city of Trent that had considerable repercussions in Italy and elsewhere.) The political fragmentation of Italy enabled Jewish victims of persecution to seek refuge in other cities when a storm of hatred was directed

Heretics and Marranos being sentenced by the Inquisition in an **auto da fé.**

against them, but in the second half of the sixteenth century the situation of the Jews worsened considerably in most parts of Italy.

It was the Counter Reformation Church, determined to turn back the tide of heresy, that launched a campaign that barred Jews from the intellectual life of Italy. In 1553 there were burnings of the Talmud sponsored by the papacy, leading to the imposition of a Church censorship on all Jewish writings. In 1555 Pope Paul IV, who was quite hostile to the Jews, issued a bull (*Cum nimus absurdum*) that reiterated the segregationist measures of the Fourth Lateran Council. Immediately afterwards he forced the Roman Jews into an unhealthy and overcrowded ghetto and barred them from most economic opportunities except the most marginal. (Prior to this time the Jews of Rome had for centuries enjoyed exceptionally good relations with the papal government.)[27] Marranos who reverted to Judaism were burned at the stake in the papal territories, and all Jews were soon expelled from these Church-ruled areas, except Rome and the port of Ancona. (Jews were also allowed to remain in the papal possessions around Avignon in France.) In the large sections of Italy ruled by Spain, Jews were also driven out.

The Counter Reformation nipped in the bud the Jewish culture of the Renaissance. Italian Jews retired to the disciplined, circumscribed world of the halakhah and the consoling spirituality of the Kabbalah. Most Ital-

ian Jews of the seventeenth and eighteenth centuries found themselves living in medieval conditions, when other Jewries to the north were beginning to break out of them.[28]

Germany

The Protestant Reformation had important long-run consequences for Jewish history. The breakup of Christian unity eventually generated a policy of practical religious toleration for dissident Christians in some lands, a policy that was extended to Judaism. And Protestantism, especially Dutch Calvinism and English Puritanism, was more receptive to the ideas and symbols of the Old Testament, making possible a changed perspective of the Jews and a greater respect for them.

In the short run, however, the rise and spread of Protestantism in the sixteenth and the first half of the seventeenth centuries did not bring about an improvement in the status of the Jews in Germany (although fewer Jews were slaughtered while Christians were killing each other).[29] Martin Luther, for example, had at first some charitable words to say about the Jews, because their rejection of the papacy was quite understandable to him. Later, when Luther realized that the Jews were not going to adhere to his reformed church, he issued one of the most vituperative denunciations ever of Jewish perfidy, drawing extensively on the satanic image of the Jew in medieval German folklore.

The social situation of the Jews in sixteenth-century Germany was precarious and marginal: The early modern period in Germany was the age of the ghetto par excellence. Jews had been expelled from most German cities; they lived in villages, sometimes on land owned by petty German rulers adjacent to places that had excluded them. They were harassed and subjected to an onerous burden of degrading laws and economic restrictions. Only Frankfort, Worms, Vienna, and Prague had important Jewish communities, and even there they were subject to periodic oppression and expulsion. However, in the middle of the seventeenth century, after the Thirty Years' War, a new class of German Jews emerged, exempted from living in the ghetto for reasons of economic and political expediency. (Germany was, of course, at that time only a geographical term for the area occupied by several hundred principalities, free cities, and other small or medium-sized states.) Many of the central European princes wanted to emulate the absolutism of Louis XIV in France and increase the power and prosperity of their realms. This

Martin Luther and other German Protestant leaders. At first somewhat friendly to the Jews, in later years Luther was outraged by continued Jewish refusal to convert to Protestant Christianity. Oil painting c. 1530 by Lucas Cranach the Younger. (Courtesy of the Toledo Museum of Art.)

attempt often entailed a difficult struggle against the entrenched privileges of the medieval estates, guilds, and burghers. A new stratum of Court Jews (*Hofjuden*, which became a recognized title) appeared as a consequence, consisting of men able to offer valuable economic services to German princes, both Protestant and Catholic, because of their abilities and connections. The German Court Jew, was, in part, a recapitulation of the medieval Spanish pattern, in which certain elite Jewish families developed close financial and personal relations with the Christian rulers. The *Hofjuden*, however, were a modern development: They were able to make a place for themselves in the expanding capitalist economy of Western Europe and use, to the advantage of their rulers, their commercial relationships with Jewish businessmen in the North Atlantic ports, in Poland-Lithuania, and in the Mediterranean. They served as military contractors, provisioning armies with gunpowder, grain, timber, and horses; they arranged for loans and the extension of credit; they managed the mint; they provided the court with such commodities as precious stones and fine clothing; they helped found new industries within the framework of mercantilist policies. In turn, they received the status of "extraordinary" and "protected" subjects freed from the humiliating forms of discrimination that fell on most German Jews.[30]

Because the *Hofjuden* had the opportunity to settle in areas that had been off limits to Jews for many years, and to bring with them their families and a retinue of agents and employees, they were able to establish new communities that were to play an important role later in German Jewish history, for example, Hanover (1650), Mannheim (1660), Berlin (1671), Dresden (1700). Although *Hofjuden* were not under the jurisdiction of the rabbinic courts, they were occasionally appointed as chief elders of the Jews by their rulers, and they acted as spokesmen and defenders (*shtadlanim*) of the Jewish communities. Unlike most German Jews, Court Jews and their families were usually contemporary in dress, speech, and manners and increasingly aware of general European literature and ideas. In the second half of the eighteenth century the new German Jewish milieu of protected Jews and their protegés provided the setting for the rise of a Jewish Enlightenment—the first important phase in the interaction of Ashkenazic Judaism and modern thought.

Marrano Merchants and the New North Atlantic Communities

Throughout the seventeenth century there was a continual exodus of Marranos from the Iberian peninsula, where the Inquisition was still in operation. In Spain, descendants of Jews were excluded from many secular and religious organizations on the ground that their Jewish blood made

Jewish businessmen of the Upper Rhine, from a seventeenth-century engraving.

them dangerous to Christian society. (This principle, called *limpieza de sangre* [purity of blood], first advanced in the fifteenth century by the Old Christian enemies of the Conversos, became an obsession in Spain in the sixteenth and seventeenth centuries and was used to exclude anyone who could not devise a convincing Christian genealogy from membership in guilds, colleges, military and religious orders, and the Church hierarchy.) The Inquisition in Spain and Portugal continued to uncover Judaizers and other heretics and to sentence them publicly in spectacles called *autos da fé*, until well into the eighteenth century. Some were turned over to the government to be burned at the stake. In the course of two and a half centuries over 30,000 Marranos, crypto-Muslims, Protestants, and others were executed in this way.

But the Marranos were also considered by certain European states as very useful residents. Even after the Counter Reformation had turned against the Jews, the rulers of Venice and Leghorn, aware of Jewish trade connections, refused to allow the Inquisition to interfere with Marranos who came there and returned to Judaism. Especially important was the appearance of new Jewish communities, founded by Marranos fleeing Spain and Portugal, in the ports of northern Europe. In the 1590s, soon after the northern provinces of the Netherlands had won *de facto* independence from Catholic Spain, Portuguese Marranos arrived. In the early 1600s the Amsterdam city government consented to the establishment of several Jewish congregations and a Jewish academy. By the mid-seventeenth century the Sephardim of Amsterdam played an important role in what was then the greatest center of world trade and finance. In the wake of the Marranos, Ashkenazic Jews came to Amsterdam and established their own synagogues, gradually winning a place for themselves in the dynamic economy of Holland: By the end of the century, Amsterdam Jewry approached 10,000—the largest Jewish community in Western Europe. Jews were active in the Dutch East and West India companies; they helped organize the Amsterdam stock exchange; they engaged in international trade in sugar, tobacco, and diamonds; they developed insurance companies, manufacturing, printing, and banking. Although not formally recognized as Dutch citizens, the Jews of Holland enjoyed religious freedom, protection of life and property, and diplomatic support in foreign countries. They were the most distinctively modern of all Jews of the time—in dress, speech, the high level of their secular culture, and synagogue decorum. And being alert entrepreneurs, they kept up their connections with Spain and Portugal.

In 1612 a community of Portuguese Marrano merchants was established in Hamburg, also a thriving port. Public Jewish worship there was officially recognized in 1650. During the period of Oliver Cromwell's rule in England, a Jewish community was founded in London. (Legal residence of declared Jews was formally acknowledged there in 1664 during the reign of Charles II.) London Jewry grew in size and importance as London overtook Amsterdam as the dominant commercial center of the world at the end of the century. In these Protestant countries it was often an advantage to be a Jew, rather than a Catholic who was apt to be closely identified with a Spanish government that was the enemy of Holland and England. Portuguese New Christians also settled in the port of Bordeaux and other places in southern France, but only in the early eighteenth century was it no longer necessary to maintain the fiction that they were Christians. (Until then it was an open secret that they were Jews.) Like the other new Sephardic communities, the Marranos of Bordeaux laid the basis for other Jewish immigrants: Jews from the papal territory of Avignon soon arrived to establish their own congregation. Sephardic merchants were the first Jews to settle in the New World, briefly in Brazil (between 1630 and 1654 when Holland had temporarily conquered the Portuguese colony), thereafter in New Amsterdam (1654) as well as Newport, Rhode Island (in the eighteenth century were added Savannah, Charleston, Philadelphia), and in the English, Dutch, and French colonies of the Caribbean (Barbados, Martinque, Curaçao, Jamaica, Surinam).

Of all the new European Jewish communities, Amsterdam became the most lively center of Jewish literature, where Jewish writers published a variety of Hebrew and Spanish works of drama, theology, and Kabbalah.[31] Although the Amsterdam community was traditional in religious belief and practice, the first signs appeared there of the disturbing impact of modern science and philosophy on thinkers raised as Jews. (Baruch

Spinoza will be discussed in a later chapter.) The new Sephardic settlements in Holland, England, and elsewhere were only a minuscule proportion of world Jewry in the seventeenth and eighteenth centuries, but they were forerunners of modern Jewish history in several respects. They participated in far-ranging and pioneering enterprises in the most dynamic, expanding economies of the world. They had greater political security and a greater degree of social acceptance as individuals than any other branch of the Jewish diaspora. Although they did not have rights equal to those of Christians, their corporate status as Jews was less circumscribed, less loaded with special restrictions and burdens, than that of any other Jewry. Together with the Court Jews of Germany, the Jewish communities of the North Atlantic were already well on the way to modernity, with its new opportunities and with its new dilemmas.

PART FOUR

The Modern Period

CHART 5. MODERN PERIOD (1775–1880)

General History	The Jews in Western and Central Europe and America	The Jews in Eastern Europe and the Middle East
1775		
1778. Deaths of Rousseau and Voltaire.	1779. Lessing's *Nathan the Wise*.	1780. Publication of Jacob Joseph of Polonnoye's *Toldot Yaakov Yosef*, the first work of Hasidic literature.
	1781. W. Ch. Dohm's "Concerning the Amelioration of the Civil Status of the Jews."	
	1782. Joseph II of Austria issues an Edict of Toleration.	1781. Second wave of excommunications by the Mitnagdim against the Hasidim.
	1783. Publication of Moses Mendelssohn's *Jerusalem*. Founding of *Me'asef* and beginnings of the Berlin Haskalah.	
1789. Implementation of the United States Constitution; beginning of the French Revolution.	1791. Emancipation of all Jews of France.	1791. Jewish merchants barred from central Russia, but allowed to settle in Odessa.
1793–1797. First coalition against France.		1791. Publication of Shneur Zalman of Lyady's *Tanya*, a major work of the Lubavitcher stream of Hasidism.
1793. Second partition of Poland; 1795. Third and final partition of Poland.		
	1796. Emancipation of the Jews in the Batavian (Dutch) Republic.	1794. Berek Joselewicz, Jewish colonel in the Polish armed forces during the Kosciuszko rising of 1794.
1799. Napoleon Bonaparte comes to power in France as First Consul.	1797–1799. Temporary emancipation in areas of Italy by the French Revolutionary army.	
1800		
1804. Napoleon crowned emperor of the French.	1807. Napoleonic Sanhedrin at Paris.	1804. Tsar Alexander I's Jewish Statute regularizing the Pale of Settlement.
	1808. Napoleon's "Infamous Decree" (lapsed in 1818). Emancipation in Westphalia.	
1812. Napoleon's invasion of Russia.	1812. Partial emancipation in Prussia.	
1813. Battle of Leipzig, major defeat of Napoleon.		1814. First publication of the *Shivhei ha-Besht*, the collection of tales in praise of the Baal Shem Tov.

General History	The Jews in Western and Central Europe and America	The Jews in Eastern Europe and the Middle East
1814–1815. Congress of Vienna. 1814–1830. Bourbon Restoration in France.	1815. The Congress of Vienna permits the withdrawal of emancipation in the German states. 1818. Hamburg Reform temple. 1819. Anti-Jewish riots in Germany. Formation of the *Verein für Kultur und Wissenschaft des Judentums.* 1820s. Spread of Haskalah to Austrian Galicia.	1824. Russian attempts to implement the plan to deport Jews from the villages.
1825 ——————		
1829. Emancipation of Catholics in England. 1830. July Revolution in France.	1830s. Beginnings of sizable German-Jewish immigration to the United States. 1831. Judaism put on legal par with other religions in France. 1832. Full rights for Jews of Canada. Publication of Zunz's *Sermons of the Jews.* 1836. Publication of S. R. Hirsch's *Nineteen Letters of Ben Uziel.* 1844–1846. Reform synods in Germany.	1827. Tsar Nicholas I orders Jewish youth inducted into the army and enrolled as cantonists. 1835. Revised Russian code of laws pertaining to the Jews, with additional residence restrictions. 1840. Damascus blood libel. 1840s. First pamphlets and books of Judah Alkalai, rabbi of Semlin (now in Yugoslavia), advocating return to Zion. 1840s. The Haskalah spreads to Russia, especially in the southwest and in Vilna. 1844. Government schools established for the Jews and autonomy of the kahals abolished in Russia.

Chart 5. (con't)

General History	The Jews in Western and Central Europe and America	The Jews in Eastern Europe and the Middle East
	1847. Start of parliamentary dispute in England over seating of Lionel de Rothschild.	
1848. Revolutions in France and in Central Europe.	1848. Frankfort Constitution endorses full rights for German Jews.	
1848–1849. Abortive Frankfort Constitution for Germany.		
1850 ——————		
1852. Napoleon III becomes French emperor.		
1853–1856. The Crimean War.	1853–1878. Publication of Graetz's *History of the Jews*.	1853. Publication of Mapu's *Ahavat Zion*, the first Hebrew novel.
	1854. Breslau Seminary opened.	1856. Cantonist legislation in Russia abrogated.
	1858. Rothschild permitted to take seat in Parliament.	
1859. Independence of Rumania.	1860. *Alliance Israélite Universelle* founded.	1859. Beginning of limited easing of restrictions on the Jews living outside the Pale of Settlement in Russia: merchants of the first guild (1859), Jews with university degrees (1861), Jewish craftsmen (1865), discharged soldiers (1867), medical personnel and holders of other diplomas (1879).
1861. Emancipation of the serfs in Russia and beginning of the era of reforms under Alexander II.	1862. Publication of Moses Hess's *Rome and Jerusalem* and Zvi Kalischer's *Derishat Zion*, two early Zionist treatises.	
1861. Unification of Italy except for Rome (which was absorbed in 1870).		
1861–1865. Civil War in the United States.		
		1864. Jews admitted to the Russian legal profession.
	1866. Emancipation of Swiss Jews.	
1867. Austrian empire becomes dual monarchy of Austria-Hungary.	1867. Final emancipation of the Jews of Austria-Hungary.	
1870–1871. Franco-Prussian War.	1870. Abolition of the ghetto of Rome and final emancipation in Italy.	1870. Mikveh Israel agricultural school established in Palestine by the Alliance Israélite Universelle.
1871. Final unification of Germany.	1870. Algerian Jews granted French citizenship.	1871–1872. Attacks on the Jews in Rumania.

General History	The Jews in Western and Central Europe and America	The Jews in Eastern Europe and the Middle East
	1871. New German constitution gives Jews full rights.	
	1872. Reform rabbinic seminary and center for scholarly study of Judaism founded in Berlin (the *Hochschule*).	
1873. German financial crisis and economic depression.	1873. Orthodox seminary founded in Berlin.	
	1873. German law passed allowing the Neo-Orthodox to seceed from the general Jewish community.	
	1870s. First use of term *anti-Semitism*.	
	1873. Union of American Hebrew Congregations founded in the United States for Reform synagogues.	1874. New military service law with educational exemptions spurs the flow of Jews into Russian schools.
	1875. Hebrew Union College (Reform rabbinic seminary) opened in Cincinnati, Ohio.	
1875 ——————————————————————————————————————		
1877–1878. Russo-Turkish War.		1876. First Yiddish theater, in Rumania.
1878. Congress of Berlin.		1878. Jewish farming community of Petah Tikvah in Palestine.

CHAPTER 11

The European State and the Jews, 1770–1880

Because Judaism is a tradition of ideas and values and Jewish people-hood is a social and communal bond, a Jewish presence is found both in intellectual history and in politics and society. Jewish history in its widest sense embraces the ideational and the social and their interplay, against the background of a larger environment which affects Jewish existence and is sometimes affected by it. In the modern world both levels of Jewish history undergo striking transformation. A brief review at this point will introduce some of the specific changes to be described in the remaining chapters of this book.

In the ancient world, the Jews had been the first nation with a religion developing around the oneness of God. In the last centuries before the Common Era, the broader potential of the uniquely monotheistic culture of ancient Israel was made actual through a number of innovative developments, including canonization of the Scriptures, the spread of the synagogue, formalization of Jewish proselytism, the ascendency of the sages, and the crystallization of rabbinic law. As a result, Jewish identity was able to perpetuate itself wherever diaspora communities were established, and Judaism survived almost total exile from its homeland. Medieval rabbinic Judaism preserved continuity with the past, yet maintained a sufficient degree of flexibility to adjust to changing conditions in the present. Where propitious, some Jewish intellectuals explored the rationality of prophetic revelation and rabbinic teaching according to canons of thought

Dress of Nuremberg Jews of the mid-eighteenth century, from a contemporary engraving.

derived from Greek and medieval philosophy. Other exegetes and mystic visionaries developed, out of Jewish materials and contemporary general models, new forms of pietistic and speculative religiosity, especially in the Kabbalah.

In late antiquity, when Judaism was undergoing the reformation just described, elements of the Judaic heritage had been taking root outside the social boundaries of the Jewish people. First Christianity and then Islam absorbed biblical and later Jewish patterns into their own distinctive spiritual structures. Between the fourth and seventh centuries CE these monotheistic religious became the ruling ideologies of European and Middle Eastern states. Now the Jews were one monotheistic people among others. Unbridgeable differences remained, not as to whether there was one God or many, but in matters of theological emphasis, religious symbolism, and sacred authority. As a minority everywhere, Jewry was also different from most other nations in that it was deprived of a government, except for the circumscribed role of autonomous communal and legal institutions. In the medieval period, Jews gravitated to those social niches where survival of Jewish religious identity was most feasible; these niches shaped a Jewish economic profile, different in different lands, but always more specialized than that of the general population. This divergent and conspicuous profile, with its inherent potential for competition and conflict, combined with anti-Jewish dogmas and stereotypes incorporated into the Christian and Muslim traditions at their gestation, made the Jews particularly vulnerable to persecution. But medieval social boundaries made for the preservation of Judaism as well. Not only did an unambiguous distinction remain between being Jewish or Christian or Muslim, but religion, politics, and personal life were so interfused that Judaism was perceived as a seamless garment—an identity cut from a whole cloth woven of tradition, intellection, and social ties. Only in exceptional circumstances, such as that of the Marranos of the Iberian peninsula, was there confusion as to who and what was a Jew.

There are many factors involved in the different context of Jewish life in the modern period—economic, political, psychological, intellectual— but one of the most unsettling was the changed definition of "nation." The modern nation-state offered Jews an opportunity for fraternal belonging to the citizenry of the lands where they lived, just as the modern economy offered them the opportunity to move into a wider range of occupations and professions. But modern developments also threatened Jewry with disintegration and dissolution, while Jewish distinctiveness and stereotyping made them vulnerable to new forms of discrimination and mass hatred.

The sense in which the Jewish bond is still national in the modern secular and politicized meaning of the term is only one of the issues facing Jewish thought in its modern phase. The concept of religion also undergoes some striking modifications under the impact of philosophies and

An engraving depicting Frankfort Jews on their way to pay respects to a visiting archduke, 1716.

ideologies critical of revealed truth. For all its secularization, the modern period is an age of religious vitality within the historical traditions. And new insights are gained into the theological and philosophical underpinnings of religious faith and into the historical evolution of religion. Absorbed by thinkers working within the symbols and norms of Judaism, modernity produces a far greater consciousness of the complex ramifications of being Jewish in the world, of the relationship between belief, history, and observance in Judaism, and of the rational and non-rational components of Jewish faith. There appears a broadening spectrum of Jewish ideologies, philosophies, and organizations seeking to define what is meant by Jewish normalization, equality, survival, and redemption. Because of the surprises of history, the amplification of this modern Jewish self-awareness is a slow, involved process with several partial reversals of direction. The full scope of what is to be discovered is hardly yet in sight.

Jewish Legal Status in Eighteenth-Century Europe

The legal structure of eighteenth-century Europe before the French Revolution remained more medieval than modern in its unequal distribution of rights and duties among the general population. Even though sweeping changes had taken place in the early modern period in most Western countries, society and law still deferred to a hierarchy of inherited prerogatives and honors. Most European monarchs claimed absolute sovereignty by divine right. The nobility usually enjoyed exemption from direct taxation, special rights to high government offices, and personal access to the ruler. Every European country had its established Church, which had privileges denied other faiths. Native merchants of economically advanced countries tolerated some competition from newcomers, for it added to the total wealth in circulation, but in the more backward nations merchant privileges were carefully guarded from infringement by outsiders. Artisan guilds were closed, monopolistic corporations. The higher one's status, the more one's position was protected from encroachment. The further down in the social system, the more one's station in life entailed legal disabilities and obligations to one's betters. In France the peasantry still owed the landowning nobility feudal dues and fees; in Central and Eastern Europe the serfs were virtually chattel, living under the jurisdiction of their lords and obligated to work most of the time on their estates. The Jews were, therefore, only one of various segments of the population whose status was determined by the freedoms they were denied and the opportunities from which they were barred.

There were about 2.25 million Jews in the world around 1770, of whom 1¾ million lived in Christian Europe.[1] The social position of the Jews

A Frankfort Jewish peddler of kitchen-ware, eighteenth century.

varied enormously from area to area. In England and Holland they were least burdened by economic restrictions, an acknowledgment of the contribution to the expansion of trade made by Jewish merchants who settled there in the seventeenth century. The Dutch and English governments did not intervene in the private lives of the Jews or supervise their religious affairs. The Jews of England (about 15,000 toward the end of the eighteenth century) and Holland (about 35,000) were restricted mainly in those matters that affected everyone not in communion with the established Church (theoretical limitations on owning real estate, becoming naturalized citizens, and eligibility to public office). At the other end of Europe, for quite different reasons, Jews also had considerable freedom. In Poland the 1.2 million Jews were a sizable part of the middle class in a largely agrarian society with a weak central government; there was open to them a wide range of economic options, including the export trade, many crafts, leasing of noble estates, and village innkeeping. Polish Jewry was left to run its own communal affairs with little interference from the authorities. The partitions of Poland between 1772 and 1795, which brought Polish Jews under Russian, Austrian, or Prussian control, did not at first drastically change their way of life.

In comparison to the Jews of the West and the East, the Jewish communities of Central Europe (about 420,000)[2] were subject to a constricting and complicated body of laws, some of which were the heritage of the later Middle Ages when Jews had been locked into a marginal social position, others of which were formulated by the more centralized state of early modern times. The absolute monarch of the eighteenth century sought to tighten his control of the population in order to enhance the prestige of his state relative to other countries, to strengthen the effectiveness of the civil administration and the army, to increase the wealth of society and the economic resources available to the government. Previously autonomous social groups like the Jews were therefore subject to increasing regulation and supervision. The attitude of most eighteenth-century rulers in Central Europe was that the Jews must be prevented from causing harm to Christians, which would result if Jews could compete too freely with them, but that there were certain Jews who could be granted special privileges because of their usefulness. If the state did not bar all settlement by Jews, it limited their residence to ghettos, specific Jewish streets, or even particular Jewish houses. A quota was imposed on the total number of tolerated Jewish families in a country (the Familiants laws). Tolerated Jews paid special protection taxes. Heavy marriage fees were extracted from those allowed by the government to wed. When Jewish travelers passed through a city or a principality in the course of their business, they had to pay the same body toll (*Leibzoll*) collected on livestock being moved from place to place. When Jews testified in the general courts, they had to swear by a special oath (*more Judaico*), worded to emphasize their "untrustworthy" nature. To protect Christianity, Jews were required to sew distinctive signs on their cloaks or wear hats of a special shape, and were prohibited from employing Christian domestic servants or from appearing in the streets during Christian religious processions.

The treatment of those Jews deemed "useful" can be seen in the Jewish charter issued by Frederick II (the Great) of Prussia in 1750. All Jews were divided into four groups: "generally privileged," "regularly protected," "specially protected," and "tolerated." The first were the few who, for extraordinary reasons, were favored with full residence and economic rights. The "regularly protected" Jews could transmit their rights of domicile and occupation only to their oldest son. (An exception was made for a second-born son wealthy enough to establish a new factory.) "Specially protected" was a personal status that no child could inherit; an outstanding Jewish writer might be placed in this category. "Tolerated" Jews were everyone else, including all children of the more privileged groups who could not inherit their father's status; Jews in this category were not allowed to marry and could live in Prussia only as long as they were employed by a licensed Jew. The business opportunities of all Jews were carefully defined by Frederick: No Jew could engage in a manual trade where a Christian guild held a recognized monopoly. Commodities that a Jewish merchant could or could not buy and sell were specified in detail. Although taxes were allocated to the Jewish community as a body, its autonomy was severely curtailed: Legal jurisdiction of rabbis was limited to marriage, inheritance, and other family matters, and a dissatisfied Jew could appeal from the rabbinical to the general court for a new verdict. The right of Jews to practice their religion was affirmed, but the government banned prayers it considered insulting to the Christian faith. The declared aim of Frederick's charter was to promote the well-being of all the inhabitants of the country in a spirit of justice and fairness. Jews were considered Prussian subjects and brought under the paternalistic direction of the government, but they were viewed with contempt and distrust as semialiens who could be expelled if they did not bring benefits to Prussia which no other, Christian, group was able to provide.

In the 1770s and 1780s signs appeared of a change in attitude toward the Jews in Central Europe, a change that led several daring writers to criticize religious intolerance as contrary to the ideals of enlightenment and reason. One of the most eloquent of these defenders of the Jews was the German historian and diplomat Wilhelm Christian Dohm. In 1781 Dohm published an essay entitled "Concerning the Amelioration of the Civil Status of the Jews" in which he argued that the Jews were not a danger to society and that they would become patriotic citizens if the more blatant discriminations were eliminated. Qualities that people objected to in the Jews did not result from their religion as such, Dohm explained, but from the oppressive conditions under which they had been forced by Christianity to live for centuries, conditions that had taught them to be distrustful of Christians and concerned for their own economic interests rather than those of the state. Dohm (like many other advocates of improvement in the treatment of the Jews) was not totally free of the common stereotype of the Jew and of condescending attitudes, but he defended the sobriety and integrity of Jewry against the usual justifications for the restrictive legislation: People who envy Jews ascribe to fraud what is actually only a consequence of Jewish industriousness; fidelity to Judaism is not just a stubborn rejection of the self-evident truth of Christianity but an admirable adherence to the divine law as Judaism understands it. Dohm also has warm words for Jewish family solidarity and for Jewish willingness to help their poor. He concludes that a wise and benevolent government will abolish those measures that prevent Jews from having close personal contact with Christians and that make it difficult for them to acquire secular knowledge. It will open all occupations to Jews and make available educational opportunities that would allow future Jewish generations to better themselves and enter other than commercial professions. Dohm's approach marked the beginning of a historical perspective on the Jewish situation, buttressed as it was by contemporary evidence that dissident religious groups enriched America, England, and Holland, where they were allowed to participate freely in the economy.

By no means all the illustrious writers and philosophers of the eighteenth century overcame their prejudices and advocated that Jews should be treated as human beings and not as outcasts. But the idea of "improving" and "reforming" the Jews by tearing down the legal walls segregating them from general society did attract attention among the enlightened public and government officials in Central Europe. The Holy Roman Emperor Joseph II (1741–1790) was the most committed of all absolutist rulers to the introduction of sweeping reforms in the Hapsburg territories of Austria, Hungary, Bohemia, and Moravia. Along with measures designed to limit the privileges of the nobility, improve the condition of the peasants, break down regional separatism, and reduce the

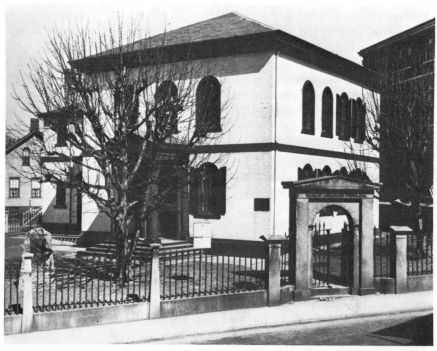

The Touro Synagogue of Newport, Rhode Island, dedicated in 1763, the oldest extant synagogue building in North America. (Courtesy of the Zionist Archives, New York.)

power of the Catholic clergy in his realm, Joseph II also broadened the rights of non-Catholics. In 1781 he abolished the Jewish badge and the *Leibzoll*. The following year he issued a *Toleranzpatent* (an edict of toleration) for the Jews of Vienna and Austria, granting them more freedom in trade and industry and eliminating domicile restrictions and ghettos. Tolerated Jews (still, however, subject to a strict quota and special taxes) could live outside a ghetto, learn any craft and trade, employ Christian servants. Also dropped were regulations requiring Jewish married men to wear a beard, prohibiting Jews from leaving their homes before noon on Sundays and Christian holidays, and barring them from places of public amusement. Jews were encouraged to send their children to public schools or to set up German-language schools of their own. Inasmuch as Jews were supposed to show themselves worthy of better treatment by adhering to the general culture, the Austrian government also required that Jewish business records no longer be kept in Hebrew or Yiddish. In 1784 the judicial autonomy of the Jewish community was abolished, and in 1787 Jews were inducted for the first time into the Hapsburg army.[3]

Joseph II's measures, tentative and cautious steps in the direction of extending Jewish rights, were widely noted and discussed. However, like his other rationalistic reforms, the *Toleranzpatent* met with considerable opposition from groups who saw Joseph's policy as endangering their carefully guarded privileges. As long as hierarchical social ranking and legal compartmentalization survived, improvements in the legal rights of some were a threat to the special status of others. Truly revolutionary change in the Jewish condition would come only with revolutionary change in the political foundations of the European state, one that would wipe out those traditional monopolies and inherited birthrights that Europe had for so long taken for granted.

The French Revolution and the Napoleonic Era

Not only in Germany but also in France during the 1770s and 1780s was the "improvement" and "fusion" of the Jews a matter of public interest. France had two distinct Jewries at that time, one resembling the Jews of Holland and England, the other similar to the Jews of Central Europe. The Sephardim (who numbered about 3,500 in Bordeaux and Bayonne in the southwest) lived in relative comfort and security as highly respected international merchants. Some had moved to Paris, forming the nucleus of a semilegal Jewish community there. The Jews of the papal territory of Avignon in southern France had benefited from the privileges of the Sephardim, but not the Ashkenazic Jews of Alsace and parts of Lorraine. The 30,000 Jews of these northeastern French provinces were, like the

Jews of Germany, confined mainly to petty trade and moneylending; they spoke Yiddish, retained their autonomous communal structure, and were burdened with the traditional restrictions of Central European Jewry. (Dohm's pamphlet, mentioned in the previous section, was actually written on the request of the prominent Alsatian Jewish army contractor and philanthropist, Herz Cerfbeer, who was trying to persuade the government to eliminate some of the worst Jewish disabilities.) The French monarchy showed the same contradictory attitude as the German rulers, wanting to integrate the Jews and to discriminate against them at the same time. In 1784, as a concession, the body toll was canceled but the same edict imposed further restrictions on the economic activities of poorer Jews in preparation for expelling them, and it required all Ashkenazic Jews to obtain royal approval before they could marry. Within a few years this piecemeal, restrictive approach to Jewish legal rights in France was rendered obsolete.

In 1789 the political scene in France was transformed. Louis XVI had called representatives of the three estates (the clergy, the nobility, and the rest of the population) to Versailles to resolve the financial difficulties of the monarchy. The third estate, joined by some members of the first two, proclaimed itself a National Assembly and set out to reform the whole French legal system. Uprisings in Paris and in the countryside quickly undermined the regime's ability to resist. In August 1789 the Assembly issued a Declaration of the Rights of Man and the Citizen, which established that "all men are born, and remain, free and equal in rights" and that "no person shall be molested for his opinions, even such as are religious, provided that the manifestation of those opinions does not disturb the public order established by the law." Drawing on the political ideologies of the French Enlightenment and the American Revolution, French revolutionaries were to press for full equality before the law for all citizens and complete freedom of worship. Already in December 1789 the question was raised as to what this meant for the Jews. In January 1790 the Sephardim of southwest France and the Jews from papal Avignon (now annexed to France) were granted full citizenship rights. The question of the Ashkenazic Jews, however, was tabled. Only in September 1791, after the National Assembly had completed a new constitution and was about to adjourn, was the legal status of the Jews as such fully confronted. Opponents of Jewish equality argued that the nature of Jewish religion prevented the Jews from being active citizens. Some Alsatians insisted that the Jews should be denied equal rights because they exploited the peasants. (The medieval image of the Jew was still quite powerful there.) Even defenders of the Jews agreed that they should be equalized as individuals, not as an autonomous corporate group. The view finally prevailed that the completion of the revolution, which had abolished the privileges of the nobles, the special obligations of the peasants, and the immunities of the clergy, also demanded that Jews be liberated from their former legal bondage. On September 27–28 the following resolution was adopted:

> The National Assembly, considering that the conditions requisite to be a French citizen, and to become an active citizen, are fixed by the constitution, and that every man who, being duly qualified, takes the civic oath, and engages to fulfil all the duties prescribed by the constitution, has a right to all the advantages it insures—
> Annuls all adjournments, restrictions, and exceptions, contained in the preceding decrees, affecting individuals of the Jewish persuasion, who shall take the civic oath, which shall be considered as a renunciation of all privileges granted in their favor.[4]

The final phrase indicated that any legal exemptions granted the Jews as a nation, rather than a religious group, were no longer in force. A logical consequence of the revolution was the principle that Judaism was to be treated exactly like Christianity by the state, but the articulation of this idea was still in the future.[5]

Throughout the 1790s the French Jews were affected by the general upheaval like everyone else. Jews served in the National Guard and as contractors to the Revolutionary Army. During the most turbulent part of the revolution, the years of the Cult of Reason and the Reign of Terror when traditional religion was proscribed and suspected antirevolutionaries were guillotined, synagogues, churches, and religious property were confiscated. Meanwhile, the French armies, enlarged by enthusiastic recruits, carried the ideology of the Revolution abroad. In 1795 a revolution, helped by the French army, took place in Holland. The Jews of the new Batavian (Dutch) republic were granted full citizenship rights (September 9, 1796). They were required to renounce all special rights as a corporate body, a requirement which some Jewish leaders opposed. When the French army conquered northern Italy, the ghettos of Padua and Rome were abolished (1797), with the exception of a brief period when the French forces were driven out and the ghettos reimposed; Jewish equality was maintained as long as the French armies remained. When the Rhineland was occupied, a similar Jewish liberation took place there.

In 1799 a *coup d'état* brought Napoleon to power as First Counsul of France; five years later he proclaimed himself emperor of the French. The Napoleonic regime was a far more efficient and centralized royal absolutism than that of the eighteenth century. The new code of civil law of 1804 consolidated the post-feudal concept of private property, guaranteed the right of all men to pursue any branch of manufacture and trade, and affirmed the formal equality of all the nation's citizens. A series

Napoleon Bonaparte (1769–1821), emperor of the French, who was seen as a supporter of civil equality for the Jews abroad while reversing it in France.

of brilliant military victories almost gave France hegemony over the European continent, and, as a result, the status of many Jews in Central Europe was affected. After 1806 several German principalities were united in the French satellite kingdom of Westphalia and Jews were put on a footing of equality there. Frankfort, now in the French sphere of influence, gave its Jews equal rights in 1811 (only after they paid a large

sum of money to the city government). The kingdom of Prussia, defeated by Napoleon in 1806–1807, undertook a program of major reforms
that included an edict (1812) affirming the citizenship of its Jews and
giving them most rights, except appointment to judicial and administrative offices. (Other German states, however, regardless of whether or
not they were under French control, did not change their Jewish policy
significantly.)

The Napoleonic period, for all its ostensible progress toward equality,
showed evidence of the continued vulnerability of the Jews in the new
political order. In 1806 tensions between Jews and peasants in Alsace
were brought to Napoleon's attention. Alsatian Jews had continued
in their old economic role as peddlers, small traders, and moneylenders
even after 1791, and inevitably the peasants could not repay some of
the loans, feeding traditional hostility against the Jews. In May 1806
Napoleon suspended for a year all debts owed Jews in eastern France,
taking a stance as the champion of the peasantry against "Jewish" usury.
(He did nothing about "Christian" usury in the area.) In raising the
question of the Jews at this time, Napoleon had several other aims. He had
just completed the reorganization of the Catholic and Protestant Churches
in France, bringing them under the control of the state, and he was interested in regulating Jewish affairs in a similar manner. Napoleon was
becoming deeply involved in Eastern European affairs (he had just
reconstituted the core of the Polish state as the Duchy of Warsaw) and
was mindful of enhancing his reputation among East European Jews as
protector and regenerator of the Jewish people. In July 1806 he convened
an "Assembly of Jewish Notables" from France and Italy to define the
position of Judaism vis-à-vis the state and to establish a new set of Jewish
institutions. The Assembly was presented with a series of questions, such
as these, by government commissioners: Did Jewish marriage and divorce
procedures conflict with French law? Were Jews permitted to marry
Christians? (Napoleon wanted to encourage intermarriage.) Did Jews
consider Frenchman their brothers and France their country? What was
the Jewish view on usury?

Overt disagreement with the emperor of the French being out of the
question, the replies of the Assembly were cautious and tactful. (Jews
had been fighting and dying for the Revolution and for Napoleon for
some time, and aspersions on their patriotism were unsettling.) The notables endeavored to make clear that Jewish religious law was unquestion-
ably compatible with French civil law. They affirmed that Jewish marriage
and divorce had no validity unless preceded by a civil act; that mixed
marriage was binding according to civil law, but could not be religiously
sanctified (they pointed out that Catholic priests did not conduct such
ceremonies); that Jews regarded France as their fatherland and French-
men as their brothers. Usury and other "discreditable occupations" were

Depiction of a formal session of the Paris Sanhedrin, an assembly of rabbis and laymen that met in February and March 1807 at the request of Napoleon.

condemned. Although Napoleon could not make the notables sanction
voluntary assimilation, he had put them on the defensive and had cast suspicions on the place of Jews in French society. In February 1807 Napoleon called together a "Grand Sanhedrin" of rabbis and laymen to
confirm the responses of the notables as Jewish doctrines. The Sanhedrin
pledged its undying loyalty to the emperor and declared as no longer
binding any aspect of the Jewish tradition that conflicted with the political requirements of citizenship.

Napoleon concluded his interest in the Jews with two edicts in March
1808. The first set up a system of district consistories (boards of rabbis
and laymen) to oversee Jewish affairs under the supervision of a central
consistory in Paris. Besides maintaining synagogues and other religious
institutions, the consistories were to enforce the conscription laws, encourage certain changes in Jewish occupations ordered by the government, and act as Jewish policemen. (Unlike the salaries of clergy of the
Christian denominations, the salaries of the rabbis were not paid by the
state.) The second decree suspended, reduced, or postponed all debts
owed to Jews. (The Sephardic Jews were exempted.) Jewish trade and
residence rights were also restricted and regulated. Jewish army conscripts
could not hire substitutes, a procedure allowed everyone else. These discriminatory regulations were promulgated for a period of ten years, sub-

ject to renewal if the emperor was not pleased with Jewish progress by that time.

The edict singling the Jews out for special treatment and limiting their rights was known in French Jewish history as the *décret infâme*, the "infamous decree." The *décret infâme* illustrates a dilemma that would recur elsewhere in the nineteenth century: On the one hand, the Napoleonic government wanted to compel the Jews to amalgamate with general society and normalize themselves by eliminating any elements of their social or religious makeup that made them conspicuously different from Christians; on the other hand, the Jews were still useful as a scapegoat because they enabled the government to demonstrate that it was on the side of the peasants rather than the Jews, without having to solve the economic plight of the peasants as such. Moreover, Napoleon's treatment of the Jewish question indicated that acceptance of the Jews was not only a matter of legal proclamation. Where the old negative image of the Jew persisted, the acceptance of the Jewish people and the Jewish religion as legitimate constituents of Western civilization was not to be easily achieved.

The Progress of Jewish Emancipation in Central Europe, 1815–1871

After Napoleon had retreated from his disastrous invasion of Russia in 1812, he was defeated by the Russians, Prussians, and Austrians at the battle of Leipzig (October 1813), forced to abdicate (April 1814), and after an effort to recover his throne, defeated for the last time by the British and Prussians at Waterloo (June 1815). Between September 1814 and June 1815 the Congress of Vienna set out to stabilize as much as possible, the balance of power in Europe. France was returned to the Bourbon dynasty, the German states (now reduced from over 300 to 39) were organized in a defensive alliance (the Germanic Confederation) in place of the defunct Holy Roman Empire, and the map of Europe was redrawn to reward the victors and restore the principle of dynastic legitimacy. Some Jewish communities of Germany sent delegates to Vienna to seek confirmation of Jewish rights acquired under French rule. The diplomats finally agreed on a resolution that instructed the Germanic Confederation to consider effecting an amelioration in the civil status of the Jews: "Until then, however, the rights of the adherents of this creed already granted to them by the individual Confederated States shall be maintained." By specifying the rights granted *by* the states rather than *in* the states, German governments were easily able to disown the equality bestowed on the Jews by the French, so that many earlier limitations on Jewish residence and occupation were retained or even reimposed.

German cartoon mocking Napoleon's emancipation of the Jews in the Rhineland.

Post-1815 Europe was a period of political conservatism. Fearful of the disruptive ideas and forces stirred up by the French Revolution, legitimist rulers considered subversive such notions as constitutional government, freedom of the individual and the press, and a national, rather than a dynastic state. What soon came to be called Jewish "emancipation" (the attainment of equal rights before the law) was likewise attributed to the revolutionary threat to a sacrosanct social order. After 1815 the dominant intellectual atmosphere in Germany was also not conducive to Jewish rights. In place of the Enlightenment's emphasis on universal human nature and rational criticism of medieval institutions, the wars against the French had stirred up a patriotic idealization of the German folk spirit, a revival of conservative Christian sentiments, and a Romantic enthrallment with tradition and the organic society. A barrage of pamphlets by German academic figures argued that the Jews were "Asiatic aliens," and that they could not take part in German-Christian culture without converting to Christianity. The emergence of some German Jewish financiers, especially the Rothschilds, was also the cause of much hostility. In 1819 there were attacks on the Jews in many German cities and in the countryside (the Hep Hep riots, from the rallying cry of the rioters), which were used by the governments to postpone emancipation to the distant future.

Only after 1830 did political liberalism take root in Central Europe and the struggle for Jewish equality find significant support among non-Jews.

German Jews began to make their voices heard in the literary movement known as Young Germany through the essayist Ludwig Boerne and the poet Heinrich Heine. (Both had converted to Christianity for admittedly practical reasons, but defended the humanity of the Jews in their writings.) The most important Jewish spokesman for emancipation was Gabriel Riesser, who insisted in his articles and pamphlets that requiring conversion to Christianity as the means to attaining legal rights hardly showed respect for the sincerity of Christian as well as of Jewish religious conscience. Rejecting the widespread notion that a national element in Judaism prevented Jews from being good Germans, Riesser insisted that Jews were not a separate nation, and that Judaism did not prevent the Jews from loving Germany as their fatherland. (The attempt to demonstrate that Judaism was a religion and not a nationality was an important concern in the Jewish Reform movement of the time, as we shall see in a later chapter.) In the 1840s philosophical radicalism and socialism also found forceful voices (Ludwig Feuerbach, Karl Marx). Many of them were not sympathetic to the idea of Jewish emancipation as such, but did contribute to the intellectual ferment about to undermine the foundations of the post-Napoleonic restoration.

The arrangements made by the Congress of Vienna had already been shaken by the 1830 revolution in France, which brought a more liberal

Heinrich Heine (1797–1856), German Jewish poet and essayist, who formally converted to Christianity, yet regained a positive assessment of Jewish faith toward the end of his life.

Karl Marx (1818–1883). At the age of six converted by his father to Protestantism, Marx identified Judaism with the bourgeois capitalism he despised.

monarchy into power.[6] Another revolution in Paris in 1848 reverberated throughout Central Europe. Insurrections broke out in Prussia, Austria, Hungary, Italy, and Bohemia. Many European monarchs were pressured to grant constitutions guaranteeing freedom of speech, assembly, and religion. (Jews were active in the vanguard of the revolts in Berlin and Vienna.) A National Assembly was convened in Frankfort to write a constitution for Germany as a whole. There were several Jewish delegates; Gabriel Riesser was elected a vice-president. In December the Assembly issued a bill of rights for the German people, which specified the enjoyment of civil or political rights by adherents of all religious confessions and which stipulated that no religion was to benefit from any state prerogatives denied the others. In 1849, however, when the revolutionary upheaval had been suppressed, the Prussian king rejected the crown of a united Germany from the Frankfort Assembly, which would have meant his accepting the revolutionary principle of the sovereignty of the people. The victory of political liberalism in central Europe was averted—a fateful development for future German history. (The failure of the revolutions of 1848–1849 demonstrated not only that monarchy and aristocracy were still powerful forces, but that the German liberals could not accept the aspirations of national independence by the Poles and Czechs in territories they considered part of historic Germany.)

Although Jewish rights were again restricted after 1850, the tide had turned. The 1850s and 1860s were decades of economic and industrial expansion in Germany. The liberals were still an important political force (several of the most important leaders of the German Liberal Party were Jews), and they worked for the equality of all citizens before the law as an essential feature of a strong, prosperous and stable political order. Conservative forces were also pressing for a united Germany. Under the direction of Otto von Bismarck, the Prussian chief minister, a series of quick wars against Denmark and Austria led to the formation of a North German Confederation under Prussian domination. In 1869 the Parliament of the North German Confederation decreed complete Jewish emancipation to all its constituent states, including those that previously had refused to accept the idea. The south German states had also extended Jewish rights in the early 1860s. When all of Germany outside Austria was brought into the newly proclaimed German Reich (Empire) under the Hohenzollern dynasty after the Prussian victory over France in 1871, Jewish emancipation throughout Germany was consolidated, and all remaining restrictions on Jewish residence, marriage, choice of professions, acquisition of real estate, and right to vote were eliminated. Although political democracy did not triumph (the newly established German Reich had a parliament but not a government responsible to it), the principle of legal equality did.

– Elsewhere in Central Europe, Jewish emancipation was gradually accepted. During the Austrian revolution of 1848 freedom of religious conscience was included in the new constitution, and despite restoration of Hapsburg authority under the Emperor Francis Joseph I, the principle of religious equality was not dropped. There was considerable opposition to the Jews by the Hungarian rebels in 1848, but when Jewish support was needed, their rights were affirmed. After the Hungarian uprising was suppressed and Hapsburg rule reimposed in 1850, Francis Joseph adopted the same benevolent attitude toward the Jews in Hungary that he had shown in Austria. As a result of military defeats by the Italians and the Prussians, the Hapsburg realm was reorganized in 1867 as the dual state of Austria-Hungary, and the constitutions of both parts affirmed the rights of the Jews. (In 1867 Jewish equality before the law was also and for the first time extended to the Austrian province of Galicia.) A similar development took place in Italy. In 1848 Jewish equality had been proclaimed in most Italian states, but a period of reaction followed. Italy was finally united between 1859 and 1866, under the auspices of the king of

Jew and clergyman discuss the admission of Jews to the House of Commons during the debate on full Jewish emancipation in England; a contemporary satirical lithograph.

Sardinia-Piedmont, who became king of Italy, and this unification brought about the complete emancipation of the Jews. (When Rome was annexed to Italy in 1870, the ghetto was finally abolished there.) The last country in Central Europe to hold out was Switzerland, which had only a miniscule Jewish population. Pressure by foreign powers to end discrimination against their own Jewish nationals finally resulted in the elimination of restrictions on Jewish residence in 1866. (Full emancipation was included in the new Swiss constitution of 1874.)

It took a little over a half a century before European society had changed sufficiently for Jewish emancipation to be accepted as reasonable and benign by all the governments of Western and Central Europe. The abolition of legal and political distinctions between citizens of different religions was no longer considered dangerous to the established order. Toward the end of the emancipation process, the monarchs of Germany, Austria-Hungary, and Italy even imposed Jewish rights on those territories under their control that had resisted doing so on their own. To be sure, social discrimination did not end; Jews remained excluded in Central Europe from various departments of the government, which remained the informal prerogative of the aristocracy. Warnings of the supposed Jewish threat to Christian civilization continued to be heard. But now it was widely accepted in Central Europe that the gradual disappearance of anti-Jewish prejudice was inevitable.[7]

The Jews of Russia, 1772–1880

As a result of the partitions of Poland between 1772 and 1795, and the decision by the Congress of Vienna to award the Napoleonic Duchy of Warsaw to Tsar Alexander I, most of Polish Jewry found itself under Russian rule.[8] As a result, its history in the nineteenth century was quite different from that of the Jews of Central Europe.

The political and social development of Russia was much slower than that of Germany and Austria (to say nothing of France and England). While forces of change were being felt in other dynastic states in the first half of the nineteenth century, Russia retained almost intact the pre-modern order of legally separated social classes, aristocratic privileges, an enserfed peasantry, a state Church under direct government control, and the other prerogatives and disabilities of the old regimes in Europe and some peculiar to Russia. The government set up a national judiciary that eliminated separate courts for each social class, only after the peasants were emancipated in 1861. Other modernizing reforms were subsequently introduced (they will be discussed later in this section), but the tsars remained determined to hold on to their autocratic authority and to prevent any constitutional limitation on their powers. Yet, although Russia lagged behind the evolution of Western society in many respects, it was a major European power. Russia had been a factor in European diplomacy since the beginning of the seventeenth century; its army had played a crucial role in defeating Napoleon; it had acquired an enormous empire in Siberia, the Caucasus, the Ukrainian steppes, and the eastern Baltic. And

Russia possessed a small but distinguished stratum of intellectuals in close touch with the most advanced ideas of European thought. The cultural contrast between the extremes of Russian society was enormous: In the nineteenth century, therefore, Russia was partly within and partly without the mainstream of Western civilization.

After the Polish partitions, Russian Jews continued to occupy their traditional economic niches in that part of Russia where they lived. In many towns and villages (*shtetlech*), they formed a majority of the population, engaging in various trades and crafts. In the countryside they continued their old role as leasers of estates, mills, forests, distilleries, and inns. Increasingly in the course of the nineteenth century, village Jews migrated to bigger towns and cities, where they became a large segment of the poor working classes. Unlike the emancipated Western Jews, Russian Jewry retained its ethnic distinctiveness and its intensely traditional religious culture. Whereas western Ashkenazim increasingly came to speak French, German, or Hungarian, most Russian Jews continued to speak Yiddish as their native language. Modernity made inroads, though. A segment of Russian Jews was influenced by the rationalist, reforming ideals of the Jewish version of the Enlightenment (the Haskalah, which first appeared among the Jews of late eighteenth-century Prussia and which will be described in a later chapter). In Warsaw a small group of Jews spoke Polish and identified themselves with Polish national aspirations. The number of Russian-speaking Jews also grew after the 1860s.

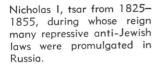

Nicholas I, tsar from 1825–1855, during whose reign many repressive anti-Jewish laws were promulgated in Russia.

Modern forms of Jewish journalism and literature began to appear in Hebrew, Yiddish, and Russian. By the last decades of the nineteenth century, East European Jewry also exhibited some of the cultural cleavage between traditional and modern patterns of life found in Russian society as a whole.

The policies of the Russian state toward the Jews resembled and were often modeled on the treatment of the Jews by the absolutistic rulers of Prussia and Austria before the French Revolution: an inconsistent mixture of attempts to "reform" them and to compel them to merge with the Christian population, and measures that singled out the Jews for special discrimination. As a result of the brutality of the government's methods, edicts supposedly designed to facilitate the integration of Jews often provoked considerable Jewish suspicion and hostility. Nevertheless, despite the limitations under which the Jews lived, there were certain advantages to the Jewish situation in Russia—advantages having nothing to do with the attitudes of the government and which maintained Jewish identity. There were no major wars fought in areas where Jews resided between 1812 and 1914 that might have decimated them and destroyed the social fabric of Jewish society (there were famines though). Being subject to a single imperial power facilitated contact among Russian Jews. The inefficiency of the Russian administration and the prevalence of bribery sometimes mitigated the severity of the government's harshest edicts. Finally, the cohesiveness of Russian Jewish society and the difficulty that the Russian state faced in deciding how to integrate the Jews was also a consequence of the size of the Jewish population. Russian Jews numbered 1,600,000 around 1825 (3 per cent of the total population of the Russian empire but almost 12 per cent in the areas where Jews lived); by 1850 there were about 2.35 million Jews in Russia, about 4 million in 1880, and they continued to increase rapidly in the following decades. In Russia there were indeed Jewish masses.

For a while after 1772 the Russian ruler, Catherine the Great, expressed a certain friendliness toward the new Jewish subjects she had suddenly acquired. (Prior to this, Jews had not been allowed to settle in tsarist Russia.) Soon a concern for prohibiting Jews from infringing on monopolies of other groups came into play: In 1791, as a result of requests by Christian merchants of Moscow that they should be protected from Jewish competition, Jewish merchants were barred from settling in central Russia. An exception was made in the former Tatar territory of the southern Ukraine, which had been taken over by Russia from the Ottoman empire in the 1770s. This region, "New Russia," was opened to Jews and other minorities in order to populate the area and develop its economy; its main city, Odessa, quickly became an important center of Jewish life. In the mid-nineties, Jews were also allowed into other limited

East European **sofer** (scribe), preparing a Torah scroll. (Courtesy Women's American ORT.)

areas, such as Kiev. Soon the Russian government began to solicit an interminable series of special reports and memoranda on how to "prevent the Jews from harming the peasants." Because the government relied on the nobility as the main support of the state, it preferred to blame the miserable plight of the peasants on Jewish middlemen, rather than on the serf laws. After various consultations, a Jewish statute was issued in 1804 by Alexander I (reigned 1801–1825), which codified the Jewish status in Russia. (There were various later revisions and additions.) The code of 1804 defined those territories of western Russia in which Jews were permitted to reside legally, an area that came to be known as the Pale of Settlement. Another measure prohibited the Jews from leasing the land of nobles and from operating taverns, and ordered their complete expulsion from the villages. (The expelled Jews, most of whom were very poor, were supposed to farm or establish factories.) Sudden eviction from the countryside was, however, postponed to 1808, when the government became apprehensive of the impact on the Russian Jews of the news about Napoleon's Sanhedrin. It soon became clear that this expulsion was an impossible undertaking; the Jews were still a necessary element of the rural economy, and the government was not prepared to resettle the dispossessed Jews on the land. (Eventually a Jewish farming population was established—about 20,000 by mid-century—in southern Russia, but agricultural settlement was clearly not viable for most of

Russia's Jews.) Eviction from the villages were deferred again as a result of Napoleon's military campaign in Russia in 1812. The government was pleased and somewhat surprised that the Jews remained a loyal element of the population during the French invasion.

In the post-Napoleonic era Alexander tried a new policy to promote Jewish fusion in 1817 by establishing a Society of Israelite Christians, which extended financial and legal concessions to baptized Jews. (Few Jews were attracted to Christianity this way.) Deportations from the villages were begun again in 1824. The following year Alexander died. His successor, Nicholas I (ruled 1825–1855), was immediately faced by an insurrection among some of the young nobles infected with Western concepts of a constitutional order (the Decembrist revolt), and this insurrection strengthened his determination to seal Russia off from any infection by progressive ideas. At a time when most European monarchs were fearful of liberalism, Nicholas I's regime stood out as the most reactionary absolutism in Europe. His attitude to the Jews was correspondingly severe. In 1827 an edict was issued to induct young Jews into the Russian army. Army service had also been introduced in the eighteenth century by such rulers as Joseph II of Austria only after economic restrictions on the Jews had been somewhat eased; one of Nicholas's main intentions was to use the army to increase the number of Jewish converts to Christianity without having to liberalize the laws on the Jews. Russian soldiers served for twenty-five-year periods, usually from age 18. Many recruits, however, were taken at the age of 12 for six additional years of training in the military (cantonist) schools set up for the children of Russian soldiers. Responsibility for filling the government's quota was placed on the Jewish communal authorities, who in turn often shifted the burden onto the Jewish poor, an action which provoked much antagonism. At times kidnapers were paid to find fugitive children for the army quota. In military barracks and cantonist schools, every effort was made to compel the draftees to submit to baptism. Nicholas I also continued the policy of deporting Jews from the villages of certain areas; in 1827 the Jews were expelled from the city of Kiev and in 1830 from the surrounding province. Much hardship resulted, but economic and administrative difficulties prevented the plan from being extended throughout the Pale. In 1835 the government issued a revised code of laws concerning the Jews, which included a prohibition on Jews living within a certain distance (50 versts) of the western border of Russia, in order to prevent them from smuggling. Again, for practical reasons, this expulsion from the frontier was never fully carried out.

In 1841 the government decided to reform Jewish education so as to reduce Jewish "self-isolation." A young German Jewish educator, Max Lilienthal, was invited to establish a network of reformed Jewish schools

East European Jews teaching a child to read. (Courtesy of Women's American ORT.)

in the Pale that would replace the traditional Jewish educational institutions. (The school that Lilienthal had set up in Riga, along with similar modern Jewish schools in Odessa and Kishinev, were the first successful efforts by Russian Jews to emulate Western educational methods and curricula.) Lilienthal sought to convince prominent rabbis and community leaders that by supporting the new school system they could show the tsar that the Jews deserved better legal treatment. A few years later, however, Lilienthal hastily left Russia when he discovered that the government, which opposed the spread of enlightened ideas among the Russian population as a whole, was willing to support the Enlightenment movement among Jews on the grounds that it would undermine the Talmud. (The Talmud was considered the main cause of the "demoralization" of the Jews, i.e., their refusal to convert to Christianity in larger numbers.) The new Jewish schools, staffed mainly by Christians, were established in 1844, but attracted only a small student enrollment, and the government dropped its plans to abolish traditional Jewish schools. This episode contributed to discrediting the followers of the Jewish Enlightenment in Russia, whose efforts to modernize the Jews were seen by many as only furthering the government's interests.

In 1844 the tsar abolished the kehillot and put the Jews directly under the supervision of the police and the general municipal authorities, but like other government measures, this one had little effect. The administrative functions of the kehillot could not be carried out by the Russian bureaucracy, so a substitute Jewish authority was necessary for recruiting cantonists and students for the state-supported schools, and for collecting the special Jewish taxes. Voluntary Jewish societies continued to handle religious and communal needs. A few years later (1850–1851) the government tried to prohibit traditional Jewish dress, *peyot* (uncut locks of men's hair in front of the ears) and the ritual shaving of women's hair at marriage. In 1851 a major plan was announced to categorize all the Jews in the country into various groups according to their economic value to the state. "Useful" Jews were craftsmen, farmers, and wealthy merchants; "unproductive" were the remaining Jews (the vast majority), who were to be subject to further legal pressures and a higher recruitment quota for the army. The conscription laws were indeed tightened, but before the assortment regulation could be enforced, Russia found itself at war.

The Crimean War (1853–1856) was a turning point in Russian history. In order to prevent the Russians from dominating the Balkans and Palestine, then under Ottoman rule, the British and French landed an army in the Crimea and besieged the Russian naval base of Sevastopol. (Eventually the Russians backed down and adhered to a general European settlement of the various disputes in question.) The weak Russian showing in the war demonstrated that Russian military power had drastically declined since the Napoleonic era relative to the Western powers. Catching up economically and industrially meant introducing some of the reforms that Nicholas I feared would undermine the traditional autocracy. Nicholas died during the war, and his successor, Alexander II (ruled 1855–1881), seized the opportunity to initiate changes.

In 1861 the tsar emancipated the serfs. (Although a decisive step in Russian history, the emancipation of the serfs did not solve the problem of peasant backwardness; the arrangements for payment for their allotments of land and the power given the peasant communes inhibited the rapid development of a prosperous stratum of independent farmers and kept the agrarian question one of the major social issues in Russia for many more decades.) In 1864 a modernized judiciary and a system of local self-government were established; in 1870 municipal government was reformed; in 1874 universal military service replaced the taking of soldiers mainly from the poor. Some concessions were made to the Jews as well. Forced recruitment of Jewish cantonists was dropped at the beginning of Alexander's reign. Then the government permitted certain favored groups of Jews to reside outside the Pale of Settlement: substantial merchants (1859), university graduates (1861), certified artisans (1865), discharged soldiers (1867), all holders of diplomas, including medical personnel such as dentists, pharmacists, and midwives (1879).

Formal portrait of a Russian Jewish family, late nineteenth century.

The permission granted to some of these groups was so circumscribed that it had little impact, but enough were affected so that permanent Jewish communities appeared for the first time in such cities as St. Petersburg and Moscow. District councils and the legal profession were opened to a limited number of Jews. The government-sponsored Jewish schools began to attract more Jewish children: The Army Law of 1874, which granted deferments to students and reduced time of service for graduates, persuaded many parents of the advantages of secular education for their children. In the 1860s and 1870s a noticeable group of Russian-speaking Jews with a modern secular education began to make their presence felt, so much so that some Russian writers warned that this would lead to a Jewish take-over of Russian economic and professional life. Although restrictions had been only partly eased, the feeling was widespread among many Jews that the Russian government had taken the first steps toward emancipation.

Emancipation and the Transformation of Jewish Life

Jewish emancipation was a logical consequence of the principle that a nation should have a uniform system of law for all its citizens, a system that abolished the special statutory rights and disabilities of time-honored feudal estates and other separate social enclaves. Although the drive for universal human rights was a political struggle, it had economic causes and consequences. Freedom to innovate in the production and distribution of goods, legal guarantees for the security of capital investment, a government that did not arbitrarily interfere with the economic laws that governed the market place—in short, the ideology of laisser-faire capitalism—constituted a powerful component of the liberal attack on the old regime. An increasing number of businessmen and political thinkers in the late eighteenth and the nineteenth centuries agreed that a concept of property rights not defined or limited by the inherited status of various classes was the most efficient and rational means for the growth of wealth. As a result, closer integration of such groups as the Jews in the larger society was a necessary by-product of the new social order.

Destruction of time-honored monopolistic patterns opened up a new range of economic options for the Jews, at the same time destroying the means by which the Jews had survived during the previous period. The growth of the middle class, the increased tempo of business activity, the development of new industries, all occurred whether Jews were present or absent. But where Jews were present in a capitalist economy they were able to step into certain economic roles—indeed, they had to, in order to find new livelihoods to replace the old ones that were disappearing. And since equal rights took many years to be written into law, Jews were affected by the changing economy before their political emancipation was complete.

As a result of changes in Europe between 1770 and 1880, Jews became far more diverse in their occupations and professions. This had been expected by eighteenth-century advocates of abolishing the restrictions on the Jews, who anticipated a gradual Jewish redistribution through the

Baron Lionel de Rothschild being admitted to Parliament, the first Jew to take a seat in the House of Commons. **The Illustrated London News,** July 28, 1858.

economy. Jews did become farmers in Eastern Europe (which many defenders of emancipation wished), but only to a limited extent, because they were more attuned to urban occupations. Even more important, Europe had a surplus and not a shortage of agricultural labor (peasants in increasing numbers left the land to find employment in the factories of the bigger cities) so that the expansion of business, industry, and the professions offered the greatest outlet for Jewish skills. In the nineteenth century, descendants of German Court Jews played a prominent role in merchant banking in such financial centers as Frankfort, Hamburg, London, Paris, Berlin, Vienna, and St. Petersburg. The most famous were the Rothschilds, originally of Frankfort, who established branches in Vienna, Paris, and London, where they floated government loans on a large scale. Among Jewish banking families, however, the Rothschilds were most unusual because they did not assimilate into the European nobility but remained active as philanthropists in Jewish affairs. Although Jewish bankers played a role in railroad construction on the European continent, they were few compared to the large proportion of Jews who turned to wholesale and retail trade of all kinds, especially consumer goods, or who entered new industries where the possibility for personal initiative was great. In Russia, in the second half of the nineteenth century, Jewish capitalists were active in sugar refining, textile and tobacco manufacture, timber and grain export, railroading and shipping. In Germany and Austria, Jews were prominent in journalism, as publishers and as reporters. Once barriers were eliminated in the medical and legal professions, these areas attracted many Jews. (Government service, which included most universities, was still largely barred to Jews in most European countries.)

As a result, the pattern of Jewish migration of the preceding era was reversed. Whereas Jews had earlier moved from the more developed regions where they were no longer wanted, to less developed areas where they were welcome, in the nineteenth century they left backward districts and villages to settle in localities where the economy was expanding. In Germany, they moved from the former Polish territories in the east to the Rhineland and to such cities as Leipzig, Cologne, Frankfort, especially Berlin; in France, from Alsace to Paris; in Austria, from Moravia and Galicia to Vienna; in Hungary, to Budapest; in Russia, from White Russia to the cities of the Ukraine, including Odessa; in Poland, to Warsaw. By 1880, over 200,000 Central European Jews had come to America, and a mass migration of Eastern European Jews to the United States was just beginning.

The economic situation of many Jews in Western and Central Europe improved in the prosperous decades of the 1850s and 1860s, making them substantially a middle-class group. For the bulk of Russian Jews, conditions worsened. Especially after the emancipation of the serfs, Jews were squeezed out of their old roles in the villages and smaller towns. Impoverishment became endemic. In the cities of the Russian Pale of Settlement most Jews were employed (where they could find a job) in small workshops, as porters, as domestic servants, and in other kinds of unskilled manual labor. The emergence of a large East European Jewish

Friends toasting Benjamin Disraeli, Prime Minister of Great Britain. **The Illustrated London News,** August 3, 1878. Although raised a Christian, Disraeli always proudly acknowledged his Jewish descent.

proletariat was to become an important factor in Jewish history by the end of the nineteenth century.

Social change so drastic and far-reaching could not but affect, on several levels, the psychology of being Jewish. Emancipation meant the destruction of the old corporate status of Jewry, the end of the quasi-political functions of the kehillot, a consequent weakening of the Jewish community's power to enforce religious discipline and to provide that inner security that comes from knowing where one stands in relation to the outside world. The result of emancipation was to make Jewish identity a private commitment rather than a legal status, leaving it a complex mix of destiny and choice. Having made the transition to a modern style of life, some Jews found that they could not cope with the persistent discrimination and the still widespread negative image of the Jew that prevented them from being completely accepted in Christian society. To them Judaism seemed obsolete, and baptism was (in Heinrich Heine's phrase) the entrance ticket to European civilization. Conversion was particularly noticeable in Berlin during and after the Napoleonic era, but it occurred everywhere, even in Russia, where it was required for advancement in various professions such as academic scholarship and where it brought tangible rewards. The vast majority of Jews rejected this path to assimilation and remained loyal to Judaism and to the Jewish people. But what did Jewish identity signify now that Germany or England or France was the fatherland of the Jews who dwelled there? One of the most important conceptual changes brought about by the new state was a narrowing of the meaning of *nation* to a culturally homogeneous, self-governing entity. On the one hand, the *political nation* was no longer just the nobility but included all the citizens of the land; on the other hand, the many different social groups that had been previously called *nations* could no longer be designated by that term without creating considerable confusion. If Jews were a religious denomination only, what about those aspects of traditional Judaism that did not easily fit into the contemporary Christian understanding of religion?

As being modern seemed to require adapting to the culture of one's new fatherland (acculturation)—although not assimilation (cutting off one's social ties to other Jews)—how much of time-honored Jewish custom and observance was still meaningful? Almost all German Jews gave up the Yiddish language without any regrets. All agreed that Jews should readily demonstrate their patriotism by serving in the German army and fighting the French (including French Jews) in a war between the two countries. But were the kosher food laws, which created a certain social distance between Jews and non-Jews, still relevant? Should Jewish worship be

Sir Moses Montefiore (1784–1885), businessman and philanthropist. Deeply concerned about the Jews of the East, Montefiore was the most eminent English Jew of the nineteenth century. (Courtesy of the Zionist Archives, New York.)

Westernized so as to appear less exotic and "oriental" to the contemporary Christian and the acculturated Jew? Did the belief in the messianic ingathering of the Jewish people retain its validity? On all these and other issues German Jews, in particular, came to disagree among themselves. The more differentiated Jewish life, the more diverse the range of views on the essence of Jewishness, first in Germany, and then in Eastern Europe, which were the two areas of the greatest ideological ferment in nineteenth-century Jewry.

Furthermore, having acquired a modern higher education, Jews concerned with the continued vitality of Judaism as a religious faith found themselves faced with new intellectual challenges that could not be ignored. What were the implications of the ongoing scientific revolution to the Jewish conception of God, the world, the nature of man? Modern philosophical thought had to be considered if Judaism was to remain intellectually respectable. A new historical awareness that appeared in the late eighteenth century, and especially in the nineteenth, raised the question of how the concept of progress and the understanding of the origins of Judaism were to affect Jewish theology. The next two chapters will deal with some of the most articulate Jewish responses to the changing political and mental climate in Europe before 1880.

Julius Meyer, Jewish Indian trader of the 1870s, poses among his customers.

CHAPTER 12

First Encounters with Modern Thought, from Spinoza to Krochmal

Seventeenth-Century Science and Spinoza's Break with Judaism

Baruch Spinoza was a major figure in European intellectual history and one of the most brilliant minds of seventeenth-century Jewry. His philosophical system indicates in a stark manner the dilemmas that the scientific revolution of early modern Europe was to pose for religious faith. A brief description of these issues is necessary not only as background to Spinoza himself, but as an introduction to modern Jewish religious thought—indeed to modern religious thought as a whole.

The new science that took shape beginning in the mid-sixteenth century (historians frequently point to the publication of Copernicus's *Concerning the Revolution of the Celestial Spheres* in 1543 as the beginning and to Newton's *Mathematical Principles of Natural Philosophy* in 1687 as a climax of the scientific revolution) broke with certain fundamental assumptions of the Aristotelian science of the Middle Ages. The medievals conceived of the cosmos as a finite, closed, and hierarchical whole, ranging from the heavy and imperfect earth in the center to the higher, more spiritual perfection of the heavenly spheres and stars, and culminating in a Prime Mover, the divine cause of all contingent existence and ultimate goal of human contemplation. The new astronomy and physics placed the earth in orbit around the sun, rejected the Aristotelian belief that there was a fundamental difference between the composition

547

Etching by Rembrandt of Dutch Jews in the synagogue.

and motion of the terrestrial and celestial worlds, eliminated from the purview of science any concern for intelligible essences and final causes, and shifted the emphasis from the cause of motion as such to the cause of *changes* of motion. The result was an elegant, austere new picture of the natural universe, far more successful than medieval science in accounting for the behavior of heavenly bodies and inanimate objects on earth. The motion of all bodies was now described in terms of simple mathematical ratios between measurable and impersonal factors such as distance, time, and mass. The resulting conception of a machinelike universe, infinite in space and homogeneous in composition, ruled by invariable and uniform mathematical laws, eliminated many points of contact on which medieval philosophers had grounded the teachings of religion. In short, the new science undercut the medieval reconciliation of reason and faith. A gulf loomed between man's understanding of physical reality and the realm of religious belief.

To be sure, the new science was the coming to fruition of certain earlier ideas, such as the Greek philosophers' belief in the intelligibility of reality, ancient Israel's struggle against the deification of natural forces, and the fruitful medieval interplay between the biblical concept of creation and the Greek notion of the unity of the cosmos. But seventeenth-century science fostered a feeling of liberation from the authority of the past that was especially threatening to established religion. An increasing number of Western intellectuals rejected the supremacy of ancient learning, criticized as sterile the methods of scholastic reasoning, and confidently assumed that future investigation would bring vast increments in knowledge. The older rationalism had remained within the context of tradition and relied on the classic authors for guidance; the new rationalism was driven by a desire to construct original theories, not just rehash previous ones. A reverential attitude toward the past was the hallmark of revealed religion: The truth had been set forth with finality centuries before and subsequent insights must be brought into harmony with the Scriptures through exegesis and allegorical interpretation, no matter how far-fetched. Clash between the religious authorities and the scientists was inevitable. The former felt they had to protect truth against intellectually prideful men, but for the scientists this pride was nothing other than humility before a method of inquiry that questioned old beliefs, corrected old errors, and discovered new facts. The confident assumption that human reason could grasp the laws of nature (including the laws of human nature), inevitably required a far-ranging and fundamental rethinking of the essence of religion.

For Jewry the first symptoms of the challenge of the new scientific world view appeared in seventeenth-century Amsterdam. The Spanish and Portuguese Marranos, fleeing the Inquisition, had settled in Holland to return to traditional Judaism. But there appeared a few among them who were led by the new concept of nature to reject the oral tradition of Judaism and to doubt the cogency of supernatural religion. Uriel Acosta (c. 1590–1640) repudiated the principle of personal immortality and denied the authority of the rabbis. Excommunicated, he returned to the community, but persisting in his views, he was excommunicated again, repented a second time, and, after a humiliating public recantation, committed suicide. Toward the end of his life Acosta decided that the Pentateuch was probably not divine in origin "for it contained many things contrary to natural law; and God, the creator of nature, cannot possibly have contradicted himself, which would have been the case had he given to men a rule of obedience contrary to that first law."[1] That Jewish community leaders reacted so strongly to heterodoxy in their midst was analogous to the nervousness and outrage with which Christianity greeted similar threats to orthodox faith. In the 1630s Roman Catholic authorities in Italy had severely condemned Galileo for advocating the Copernican astronomy over the Aristotelian. Even in Holland, which had the most liberal intellectual climate in Europe, too blatant criticism of the tenets of revealed religion were not condoned. An outstanding philosopher like René Descartes, living in Holland at the time, was very cautious about circulating views that appeared to threaten established religious doctrine. The Jewish authorities had an additional motive: fear that views such as Acosta's would reflect unfavorably on the Jews as a whole and endanger their tolerated status. And, finally, many Marranos had suffered greatly in order to be able to reaffirm Judaism, and were appalled at heresy in their midst. For these reasons Spinoza too was forced out of the Jewish community when his views on religion became known.

Baruch Spinoza (1632–1677, who is sometimes called by the Latin equivalent Benedict) was born in Amsterdam of a former Marrano family active in the Jewish community. Spinoza studied Hebrew, Bible, talmudic literature, and the medieval Jewish philosophers in the Jewish communal school. After leaving school, the study of Latin opened up for him the natural sciences and contemporary philosophy, especially that of Descartes. In July 1656, shortly after his father's death (Spinoza was twenty-three years old), he was questioned by the Jewish leadership about certain unorthodox beliefs he had apparently espoused. They reputedly offered Spinoza a stipend if he would remain publicly silent and conform to Jewish practice. When he refused, he was excommunicated and the Dutch authorities were formally notified that he had been expelled from the Jewish community. During the remaining years of his short life Spinoza resided in various towns of Holland, supporting himself by grinding and polishing optical lenses. Some of his friends belonged to a Protestant sect similar to the Quakers (he did not, however,

The Sephardic (Portuguese) synagogue in Amsterdam, eighteenth century.

become a Christian) and around him gathered a circle of philosophically minded colleagues, including physicians and several prominent Dutch political figures. He declined a professorship at the University of Heidelberg. (Like other important philosophers of the seventeenth century, he remained outside the academic world.) In 1670 Spinoza published his *Tractatus Theologico-Politicus* (*Theological-Political Treatise*) on freedom of thought in relation to religion and the state, a work that met with a storm of protest from Christian theologians; for reasons we shall see later, this work was a major factor in earning him a reputation, lasting for over a century, as an atheist. Spinoza died in the Hague, of consumption, at the age of 45. Even those who vehemently rejected his philosophy, admired his serene personality and his simple, austere life devoted to rational inquiry.

In the *Theological-Political Treatise* Spinoza rejects the synthesis of reason and revelation that had been the goal of medieval theology, especially that of Maimonides, whose work Spinoza knew quite well. (He also was well acquainted with the writings of Gersonides and Crescas.) In order to justify freedom of thought on all theoretical and scientific matters, Spinoza set out to shatter the belief that the Bible should be reconciled with philosophy. In so doing he takes a critical stance toward the Bible that makes him one of the forerunners of modern biblical study.

In the first part of the *Treatise* Spinoza argues that prophecy is a product of an extremely vivid imagination, unassociated with reason, as Spinoza understands reason. The prophets were nonphilosophical men possessing moral insight, but not theoretical truth. On matters of scientific knowledge, the biblical prophets—including Moses—held conflicting opinions, according to Spinoza, and were often ignorant of the natural causes of the events to which they alluded. Rejecting the view of Maimonides that the Bible was addressed to the masses and the intellectuals, each on their own level, Spinoza conceives of the Bible as popular thought only. God is presented as a lawgiver in concession to the mentality of the multitude. The biblical law was merely the legislation of the ancient Israelite state to assure its political stability: The ceremonies and ritual it prescribes (indeed all religious ceremonies and rituals) are not divine law in the true sense. To be sure, Maimonides had speculated on the practical and educational utility of the biblical commandments, but Spinoza uses this principle as a point of departure to conclude that the biblical laws were suited only to the social life of the Jews in ancient times. Postbiblical Judaism has no rational validity. (He admits only that the law could serve as the basis of a re-established Jewish state.) Spinoza's blanket dismissal of diaspora Judaism and of the religious significance of Jewish survival since biblical times betrays more than a little venom, perhaps a residue of bitterness from his conflict with the Jewish leadership in Amsterdam. In contrast, he adopts a benign, diplomatic attitude toward Christianity, the theoretical validity of which he equally rejects.

He is similarly forthright on the question of miracles. God's nature and existence cannot be known from miracles but only from the fixed, immutable order of nature and from clear, distinct, self-evident ideas. Maimonides and the medievals agreed that faith in God's existence must be based on rational argument, but they retained a suprarational element in their world view, in that creation, revelation, and some miracles transcend the usual order of nature. For Spinoza, nothing can happen contrary to natural law. The Bible attributes events, not to their proximate, scientific causes, but to God alone, because the biblical narrative is composed in a style intended to move the uneducated man to devotion.

In effect Spinoza treats the Bible as one would any work of ancient literature. He repeatedly insists that the proper method of understanding Scripture is in its own terms. Because, for the medievals the Bible contains theoretical as well as moral truth, the allegorical method had to be used to bring certain key passages into harmony with the findings of reason. In rejecting this method, Spinoza singles out for special criticism Maimonides' assertion that if philosophy had proven that the world was eternal, he would have explained the creation story of Genesis in harmony with this doctrine. Spinoza insists that the biblical books must be interpreted only according to the intentions of their authors. This leads him to examine who wrote the books of the Bible, why were they written, and how they entered the canon. Noting various duplications and contradictions in the text of the Pentateuch (which, of course, he refuses to reconcile), Spinoza concludes that the Torah as a whole was not written by Moses, though writings of Moses may have been included in it. The historical books were compilations assembled many generations after the events related. Spinoza suggests that it was Ezra who probably collected earlier writings and, without harmonizing their discrepancies, joined them together. (Spinoza's approach to biblical literature is a remarkable anticipation of nineteenth-century biblical scholarship.)

What, then, is the valid function of religion? The essence of religion, Spinoza insists, is a life of right conduct. "Philosophy has no end in view save truth; faith, as we have abundantly proved, looks for nothing but obedience and piety." Most men are not philosophically enlightened, and therefore have to rely on the consolations that the Bible brings: "All are able to obey, whereas they are but very few, compared with the aggregate of humanity, who can acquire the habit of virtue under the unaided guidance of reason." It follows that philosophers and scientists must not be constrained in their freedom to speculate by religious doctrines.

Faith, therefore, allows the greatest latitude in philosophical speculation, allowing us without blame to think what we like about anything, and only condemning, as heretics and schismatics, those who teach opinions which tend to produce obstinacy, hatred, strife, and anger, while, on the other hand, only considering as faithful those who persuade us, as far as their reason and faculties will permit, to follow justice and charity.[2]

What should be the attitude of the state to religion and philosophy? The full title of Spinoza's book indicates his answer: *A Theological-Political Treatise containing certain discussions wherein it is shown that freedom to philosophize not only may, without prejudice to piety and the public peace, be conceded, but may not be withheld without danger to piety and public peace.* The clergy must not have the power to interfere with a ruler's exercise of sovereignty. (For over a century before Spinoza wrote his treatise, European states had been torn by religious civil war, and the policies of the Inquisition constituted another case in point.) Religious toleration is justified as long as the actions of religious men are peaceful and law-abiding:

The safest way for the state is to lay down the rule that religion is comprised solely in the exercise of charity and justice, and that the rights of rulers in sacred, no less than in secular matters, should merely have to do with actions—but that every man should think what he likes and say what he thinks.[3]

It is a usurpation of the social contract and a violation of an essential and natural right of man, Spinoza concludes, for the sovereign to seek to control the beliefs of his subjects on speculative matters.

Despite his heterodoxy, Spinoza's own metaphysical system, as presented in his other writings, especially the *Ethics,* has its own distinctive religiosity based on his desire to describe the best way to live. (The *Ethics* and the fragment *On the Improvement of the Understanding* were published posthumously in 1677.)

After experience had taught me that all the usual surroundings of social life are in vain and futile . . . I finally resolved to inquire whether there . . . might be anything of which the discovery and attainment would enable me to enjoy continuous, supreme and unending happiness.[4]

In answering this question, Spinoza develops one of the most impressive pantheistic systems in Western philosophy. He starts with the proposition that there exists only one infinite, unlimited, self-caused Substance, which is God-or-Nature (*Deus sive natura*)—God and nature

Portrait of Baruch Spinoza by Samuel van Hoogstraeten, painted during Spinoza's lifetime. (The Jewish Museum, New York.)

being two aspects of the ultimate unity of existence. Substance possesses a theoretical infinity of attributes, only two of which are apprehended by man: extension (matter) and thought (mind).[5] God-or-nature can also be viewed as a whole made up of finite, individual entities. All the particular ideas and bodies of the world are defined by Spinoza as "modes" of the one Substance. God exists in all things as their universal essence; they exist in God as subsidiary modifications.

Spinoza's metaphysics is the ground for his conception of the three grades of human knowledge. The first and lowest form is dependent on sense perception, consisting of ideas joined together by mere association. Such insights are of great practical value, but are "inadequate" because they do not entail an understanding of the reason and causes of things. The second grade is systematic knowledge, exemplified by mathematical thinking in which propositions are deduced from axioms and postulates in a coherent and consistent manner. According to seventeenth-century science, the laws of physics have this character. Spinoza's *Ethics* uses as its model the rigidly demonstrative exposition of Euclid's geometry to arrange elementary truths of consciousness into a rigorously deductive system. The third and highest form of knowledge is intuitive reason: the grasp of the interconnection of the whole. Because it is based on scientific and logical thinking, intuitive knowledge is not mystical in the usual sense. He who has reached this level apprehends the parts of reality as a single, concrete unity "under the aspect of eternity" (*sub specie aeternitatis*), and he thus reaches the state of blessedness for which the true philosopher strives.

The man who has arrived at intuitive reason has overcome the limited passions of life with the one emotion that is true freedom from human bondage: an active love of God through knowledge (*amor dei intellectualis*).

> The wise man . . . is scarcely at all disturbed in spirit, but being conscious of himself, and of God, and of things, by a certain eternal necessity, . . . always possesses true acquiescence of his spirit. If the way which I have pointed out as leading to this result seems exceedingly hard, it may nevertheless be discovered. Needs must it be hard, since it is so seldom found. How would it be possible, if salvation were ready to our hand, and could without great labor be found, that it should be by almost all men neglected? But all things excellent are as difficult as they are rare.[6]

How does Spinoza's metaphysics compare with Judaism—with, for instance, Maimonides' Judaism? Maimonides had sought to eliminate anthropomorphic and anthropocentric elements from Judaism, including even the belief that there was a single, final purpose to creation. Spinoza not only rejects all teleology, but that God is transcendent, purposive, and creative. God does not exist separate from the world. For Spinoza, God is totally immanent as the uniformity of law and the sum of all laws: God is the very principle of law and its exemplification in nature and thought. Whereas Maimonides had rejected the corporeality of God, Spinoza rejects, in effect, God's incorporeality, since, under the attribute of extension, he views God as the material component of reality and the totality of bodies in the physical universe. Therefore there is no room

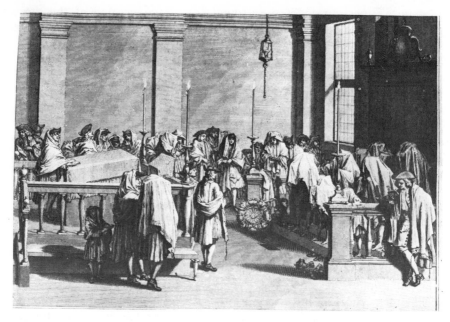

Interior of the Sephardic synagogue of the Hague, one of a series of etchings depicting Jewish rites by the Protestant artist Bernard Picart (1673–1733). The figures
at right, covered with prayer shawls, are delivering the priestly benediction.

in Spinoza's God-or-nature for creation or even for freedom in the sense
of choice between alternatives. Only what actually exists can exist.
Spinoza's philosophy is thoroughly deterministic.

> But in eternity there is no such thing as when, before, or after; hence it
> follows solely from the perfection of God, that God never can decree, or
> never could have decreed, anything but what is; that God did not exist be-
> fore his decrees and would not exist without them.[7]

The whole is free only in the sense that it is self-caused, although in the
narrow sense a man who knows and loves God and recognizes that he
is made of God is also free—free from useless anxieties and inner disturbances. Submission to the logical and necessary interconnection of
reality produces mental peace, a liberation from the triviality of everyday life, an attachment to that which alone is eternal. Spinoza finds happiness in the intellectual joy of pure science, in the blessedness of virtue
for its own sake, in a serene worship of God that verges on resignation.

Seen from the vantage point of a later, more secular age, Spinoza
managed to retain in his philosophy more than he may have intended of
traditional piety and reverence. A century after his death, when his
system was appreciated more objectively and when the background had

changed to permit its inherent religious quality to stand out, Spinoza was to be called a "God-intoxicated man." And in much later modern thought, Spinoza begins to find Jewish admirers who seek to recapture him for Judaism.

The Eighteenth-Century Enlightenment and Moses Mendelssohn's Defense of Judaism

The principles of rational autonomy and scientific inquiry propounded by Galileo, Descartes, Spinoza, and others in the seventeenth century were applied in the following century to the critique of all traditional social institutions and received opinions. The eighteenth-century Enlightenment has been defined as a "loose, informal, wholly unorganized coalition of cultural critics, religious skeptics, and political reformers" who advocated a cosmopolitan and humanitarian program, above all, who advocated the extension of human freedom—intellectual, economic, political, creative freedom—to further the perfecting of moral, rational men.[8] France and England were the principal centers of the Enlightenment, but representatives of the movement were also found throughout Europe and in North America. The German wing of the Enlightenment (the *Aufklärung*) affected the Ashkenazic Jews most directly. The *Aufklärer* were not as radical in their political views, as aggressively secular, and as immersed in the natural sciences as some of the French and English *philosophes*. The German Enlightenment retained an interest in the religious implications of classical metaphysics and was marked by a concern for the philosophy of art, two subjects prominent in the writings of the most illustrious Jewish *Aufklärer:* Moses Mendelssohn (1729–1786).

Born in Dessau in central Germany, the son of a poor Torah scribe, Mendelssohn received a traditional Jewish education but, indicative of the awakening of philosophical interests in Ashkenazic Jewry, an education that included Maimonides' *Guide for the Perplexed*. When his teacher was appointed rabbi of Berlin, the fourteen-year-old Mendelssohn followed in order to continue studying with him. There, in addition to German and Hebrew, he acquired a knowledge of French, Italian, English, Latin, and Greek. In the mid-1750s young Mendelssohn developed a close and lifelong friendship with Gotthold Ephraim Lessing (1729–1781), the celebrated dramatist, literary critic, and outstanding exponent of enlightened toleration in Germany. Even before he had met Mendelssohn, Lessing had written a short play portraying a Jew of exceptional nobility. (More characteristic of the Germany of his time was the response of his critics that such a Jew was impossible.) For Lessing and other liberal Germans, Mendelssohn was the realization of the Enlightenment ideal that non-Christian peoples could also produce men of innate refinement, profound knowledge, and cosmopolitan rationality. With Lessing's encouragement, Mendelssohn began to publish, in fluent and elegant German, a series of aesthetic and philosophical essays. At the height of his literary fame he was called the "Jewish Socrates," praised for his literary style, the breadth and clarity of his intellect, his delightful conversation, and his modest character. In 1779, Lessing wrote one of his most famous plays, *Nathan the Wise*, in which the Jewish hero, modeled on Mendelssohn, appears as a spokesman for brotherhood and love of humanity. In the Enlightenment spirit, Nathan exclaims to the crusader knight: "Are Jew and Christian sooner Jew and Christian than man? How good, if I have found in you one more who is content to bear the name of man!"[9]

Among Mendelssohn's general works, his most original contribution lay in the theory of art, but his writings on religious topics have the most bearing on his attitude to Judaism. Mendelssohn's philosophical position was drawn from Gottfried Wilhelm Leibnitz (the third of the great European rationalists after Descartes and Spinoza) and from Christian Wolff, who rendered Leibnitz's ideas accessible to the educated public. Leibnitz and Wolff, unlike Spinoza, were sympathetic to revealed religion. Mendelssohn's conception of God, the subject of his *Morgenstunden* (*Morning Hours*, 1785), drew on Wolff's formulation

A contemporary portrait of Moses Mendelssohn, father of the Haskalah.

of the traditional ontological argument for God's existence: The concept of a most perfect Being necessarily includes its reality. Mendelssohn's God is not the impersonal First Cause of the eighteenth-century deists; he argues that the world results from a creative act through which the divine will seeks to realize the highest good; because God is the most perfect Being, the divine will must be directed toward producing the highest moral perfection. Faith in God's wisdom, righteousness, mercy, and above all, faith in God's goodness are Mendelssohn's most fundamental religious convictions.

Unlike deists who denied all possibility of miracles and historical revelation, and who accepted only a religion of natural reason, Mendelssohn and the wing of the Enlightenment he followed, accepted the veracity of miracles and revelation, with the proviso that belief in God was prior to and independent of any supernatural evidence and that revelation cannot contradict the findings of reason. But like the deists, he believed that, apart from any supernatural inspiration, reason could discover the reality of God, divine providence, and the immortality of the soul; indeed, without these doctrines, life would be devoid of value. Mendelssohn's widely acclaimed *Phaedo* (1767), a reworking of Plato's treatise of the same name, deals with the question of personal immortality. Drawing on the Leibnitz–Wolff metaphysics, Mendelssohn argues that the universe contains an infinite number of elemental and imperishable spiritual components. The soul imposes a unifying pattern on the body, but death does not mean the soul's annihilation. Does the soul possess consciousness after death? Mendelssohn argues that God's wisdom and goodness would not allow the soul's natural, constant drive for self-perfection to relapse into nonexistence: The soul must eternally continue to pursue the good, the beautiful, and the true. Although Mendelssohn believed in God's providential retribution in this world and that it is a means for purging the individual for the future world, he rejected eternal punishment. Immortality of the soul is a consequence of God's justice because in the future world the soul will find a true happiness that it failed to attain in the body. Mendelssohn's views on religion preserve some of the basic elements of traditional Judaism in the guise of a natural theology that reflects Leibnitz's famous dictum that this is the best of all possible worlds.

At the height of his career in German literature Mendelssohn was publicly challenged by a Christian apologist to explain how a man of such noble and enlightened views could remain faithful to the "backward" Jewish religion.[10] Beginning in 1769 Mendelssohn was forced, against his earlier inclinations, to defend Judaism in print and also to assume an active role in Jewish affairs. In 1783, three years before his death, he published his most important Jewish writing: *Jerusalem, or On Religious*

Power and Judaism. The immediate occasion of the book was a critic's attack on Mendelssohn's statement, in one of his essays, that the power of religious excommunication should be abolished. His antagonist remarked, "Clearly, ecclesiastical law armed with coercive power has always been one of the cornerstones of the Jewish religion."[11] The aim of the first part of *Jerusalem* was to demonstrate that no religious institution has the right to use coercion. Like Spinoza's *Tractatus*, Mendelssohn's *Jerusalem* defends freedom of conscience. The state alone has the authority to employ force for the sake of the common good of all citizens. The Church's task is to convince men of their duties to God and fellow men solely through persuasion. As the only criterion that should determine a man's beliefs is his conviction of their rational truth, the right to decide what principles one holds on religious questions is inalienable and cannot be delegated to an external authority. Indeed, the threat of excommunication causes mental suffering only to the sincere, not to the hypocrite. Mendelssohn's conviction that religion should be based only on persuasion leads him even to argue that the Church should possess no property and that the religious teacher should receive no financial payment, except as a compensation for his time. The first part of *Jerusalem* also indirectly defends the idea of Jewish emancipation, by insisting that "neither church nor state has the right to impose any restraint upon man's principles and convictions, or to make his status, rights, or claims contingent upon these principles and convictions." He qualifies this freedom only inasmuch as the state has the right to prohibit atheism as a danger to society.[12]

At the beginning of the second part of *Jerusalem*, Mendelssohn turns to the question whether the Mosaic law does sanction religious coercion, which has led Christians to argue that their religion represents freedom from "burdensome Jewish ceremonies" and hence that Christianity is inherently more liberal and rational. Mendelssohn's response is that Christianity coerces the mind through its dogmas, whereas Judaism permits freedom of thought.

> I believe that Judaism knows nothing of a *revealed religion* in the sense in which Christians define this term [that is, the term *religion*]. The Israelites possess a *divine legislation*—laws, commandments, statutes, rules of conduct, instruction in God's will and in what they are to do to attain temporal and eternal salvation. Moses, in a miraculous and supernatural way, revealed to them these laws and commandments, but not dogmas, propositions concerning salvation, or self-evident principles of reason. These the Lord reveals to us as well as to all other men at all times through nature and events, but never through the spoken or written word.[13]

Mendelssohn's distinction between the self-evident principles of rational religion and the positive requirements of Judaism is rooted in his

A prosperous family celebrates the Passover seder, from an early eighteenth-century Haggadah. (Courtesy of the Hebrew Union College-Jewish Institute of Religion, Cincinnati.)

conception of three kinds of truth: logically necessary truths (principles of pure mathematics and logic); contingent truths (laws of nature as determined by observation); temporal truths that occur only once in history (knowledge of which comes from a reliable narrator).

> Whenever God intends man to understand a certain truth, His wisdom provides man with the means most suited to this purpose. If it is a necessary truth, God provides man with whatever degree of reason he requires for its understanding. If a natural law is to be disclosed to man, God's wisdom will provide him with the necessary capacity for observation; and if a historical truth is to be preserved for posterity, God's wisdom authenticates its historicity by establishing the narrator's credibility beyond any doubt.[14]

All men have an innate power to discover that there is a God, a divine providence, and a future life. To make these truths dependent on a supernatural revelation would be to assume that God was not omnipotent or good enough to give human beings the capacity to arrive at these beliefs rationally and through them to attain salvation. It follows that Judaism, unlike Christianity, does not claim exclusively to possess the doctrines that constitute the natural religion of all mankind. Israel's unique heritage is a specially revealed ceremonial law valid only for them, the special path for their salvation.

Mendelssohn argues that the biblical account is most consistent with his interpretation of the purpose of the Mosaic revelation.

> The voice that was heard at Sinai on that great day did not proclaim, "I am the Eternal, your God, the necessary autonomous Being, omnipotent and omniscient, who rewards men in a future life according to their deeds." This is the universal religion of mankind, not Judaism, and this kind of universal religion—without which man can become neither virtuous nor happy —was not and, in fact, could not have been revealed at Sinai. For who could have needed the sound of thunder and the blast of trumpets to become convinced of the validity of these eternal verities?[15]

No, the Jews heard at Sinai the historical truth that "I am the Lord your God who brought you out of the land of Egypt," a proclamation introducing laws binding only on the Jews.

To be sure, Mendelssohn does not view the law as an end in itself. Regulating action, the ceremonial precepts of the Bible have a certain noncoercive relation to theoretical truth. The law stimulates reflection and contemplation, thus linking daily conduct to religious and moral insight and protecting Israel from the tendency to relapse into idolatry. Even though the ability to grasp the pure truths of reason is universal, some civilizations depicted these verities in visible images. Originally intended as symbols but taken for realities, these images later became objects of superstitious worship. Because biblical religion relied on deeds and practices, not on tangible symbols for God, Judaism did not succumb to paganism.

> And now I am finally at the point at which I can elucidate my hypothesis about the purpose of the ceremonial law in Judaism. Our people's patriarchs —Abraham, Isaac, and Jacob—had remained faithful to the Eternal and tried to preserve pure religious concepts free of all idolatry, for their families and descendants. And now these descendants were chosen by Providence to be a nation of priests, that is, a nation which, through its constitution and institutions, through its laws and conduct, and throughout all changes of life and fortune, was to call wholesome and unadulterated ideas of God and His attributes continuously to the attention of the rest of mankind. It was a nation which, through its mere existence, as it were, would unceasingly teach, proclaim, preach, and strive to preserve these ideas among the nations.[16]

Mendelssohn can now give his complete answer to the question of coercion in Judaism: The Mosaic law, as interpreted by the Jewish oral tradition, does not bestow power upon the authorities to punish unbelief and heterodoxy. To be sure, when the Mosaic constitution was the actual law of an Israelite state, certain deeds were punished as crimes against the sovereign. But not false doctrines. After the destruction of the Israelite commonwealth, "Our religion, as religion, knows no punishment, no penalty save the one that the repentant sinner voluntarily imposes upon himself."[17] At present all laws connected with the Temple, the priesthood, and land ownership in ancient Palestine have lapsed. Remaining in effect are personal religious duties, which must be strictly observed until such time as God might arrange an unquestionable public manifestation that would introduce new rituals to link all men. Because Jews (in his opinion, even baptized Jews) cannot absolve themselves from the divine legislation given all Israel, Mendelssohn insists that the Jews must be integrated into civil society in such a way that their right to observe the ceremonial law is not infringed. "If we can only be united with you Christians on the condition that we deviate from the law which we still consider binding, we sincerely regret the necessity of declaring that we renounce our claim to civil equality."[18] And to the Jews Mendelssohn remarks:

> Adopt the mores and constitution of the country in which you find yourself, but be steadfast in upholding the religion of your fathers, too. Bear both burdens as well as you can. True, on the one hand, people make it difficult for you to bear the burden of civil life because of the religion to which you remain faithful; and, on the other hand, the climate of our time makes the observance of your religious laws in some respects more burdensome than it need be. Persevere nevertheless; stand fast in the place which

Providence has assigned to you; and submit to everything which may happen, as you were told to do by your Lawgiver long ago.

Indeed, I cannot see how those who were born into the household of Jacob can in good conscience exempt themselves from the observance of the law. We are permitted to reflect on the law, to search for its meaning, and occasionally, where the Lawgiver himself provides no reason [for a particular law], to surmise that it must perhaps be understood in terms of a particular time, place, and set of circumstances. Therefore, the law can perhaps also be changed according to the requirements of a particular time, place, and set of circumstances, but only if and when it pleases the supreme Lawgiver to let us recognize His will—to make it known to us just as openly, publicly, and beyond any possibility of doubt and uncertainty, as He did when He gave us the law itself. As long as this has not happened, as long as we can show no such authentic dispensation from the law, no sophistry of ours can free us from the strict obedience we owe to it. Reverence for God must draw a line between speculation and observance, beyond which no conscientious person may go.[19]

Jerusalem concludes with a defense of the individuality of historical religions. Mendelssohn rejects the proposal that all religions should be merged into one universal creed, for such a creed would only impose additional restrictions on man's freedom to think. Indeed, the very multiplicity of religions has a religious significance: "Brothers, if you care for true godliness, let us not pretend that conformity exists where diversity is obviously the plan and goal of Providence."[20] Respect should be granted to all peoples to worship according to the light of natural reason and the practice of their ancestors.

Mendelssohn's definition of Judaism is actually close to Spinoza's: The Jewish religion is the particular law of the Jewish people, not a distinctive system of beliefs or a unique view of the world. But unlike Spinoza, Mendelssohn was comfortably at home both in philosophical circles and in the Jewish community. Mendelssohn experienced no conflict with the leadership of the Berlin community—a sign that Jewish openness to modern thought was increasing there—and he shows no agonizing inner struggle between his two principal loyalties. Whereas Spinoza held that the law had lost its validity with the end of the biblical state, Mendelssohn firmly believed that it was still binding, and that Jewish survival was spiritually meaningful. Although Mendelssohn admired Spinoza as a person and even contributed to a more positive assessment of his philosophical importance, he thoroughly rejected Spinoza's pantheism. For Mendelssohn, God is transcendent as well as immanent; he is a commanding and benevolent God, not merely an impersonal matrix of natural law and logical order.

After Lessing's death in 1781, Mendelssohn became embroiled in a

Depiction of a Jewish wedding on a glazed stoneware plate made in Staffordshire and decorated in Delft, 1769. (The Jewish Museum, New York.)

dispute connected with Spinoza's pantheism that attracted much attention among German philosophers.[21] An opponent of the Enlightenment, F. H. Jacobi, had announced that Lessing confided to him a leaning toward Spinoza's system that Lessing had hidden from Mendelssohn. Mendelssohn sought to refute this story as a canard against the memory of his lifelong friend. Regardless of the veracity or lack of it in Jacobi's report, Lessing had quite clearly moved away from the Enlightenment view of reason in his late works. In *The Education of Mankind*, he had proposed that human reason was dynamic and evolving: The spirit of man matured in the course of history, so that the Old Testament was but a stage of human childhood and the New Testament a somewhat later step in the progressive advance of humanity toward higher truth. In *Jerusalem*,

Mendelssohn had rejected this position, arguing that there was no progress in the sense that the human race as a collective steadily moves ahead in history toward some grander manhood. Progress applies only to the individual's journey to self-perfection. Everyone goes through that segment of his existence which he spends on earth faced with the same challenge to be ethical. Nations may pass through cycles in which they refine their primitive notions but "the extent and intensity of their morality remains essentially unchanged through the diversity of these successive epochs."[22] Mendelssohn's admitted lack of interest in history was a result of the assumption that the methods and findings of reason were everywhere and always the same. But the concept of reason was itself to change, as advanced German intellectuals began to consider a greater sense of historical development (beginning with the Romantic reaction to the Enlightenment) and to question the inherent limits of human reason (in the philosophy of Immanuel Kant to be discussed in a later chapter). This left Mendelssohn's philosophy outdated soon after he died.

On other levels, too, Mendelssohn's legacy was ineffectual. His exemplary reputation in Christian circles did not inhibit the continued strength and even growth of anti-Jewish feeling in Germany in the early nineteenth century. Although many of Mendelssohn's ideas about Judaism were to recur in a more developed manner in later thinkers, his reconciliation of philosophical theism and Jewish traditionalism did not satisfy either religious liberals or conservatives. Many German Jews after Mendelssohn's time were not as comfortable with the old forms of Jewish observance as he, or else they found his rationalism lacking in profundity. But the man Mendelssohn as a symbol, the first eminent Jewish figure to make the transition from the ghetto to modernity without breaking away from the Jewish people, was to inspire several generations of young Jews looking for new moorings. Mendelssohn's greatest impact was to foster a Jewish Enlightenment, the *Haskalah*, just getting underway at the end of his life.

The Haskalah and the Problem of Catching Up

In the 1770s Moses Mendelssohn had taken the initiative in various attempts to ward off threatened expulsions and additional discriminatory decrees and to hasten Jewish acculturation. It was Mendelssohn who convinced Christian von Dohm to write his classic essay on bettering the legal status of the Jews, an essay that was occasioned by the problems of the Alsatian Jews in France. Mendelssohn translated the Pentateuch into German to encourage Jews to abandon Yiddish, a language that he detested as a debased form of German. The Mendelssohnian Pentateuch was accompanied by a Hebrew commentary (the *Biur*), pointing out the literary and moral beauty of the Bible. Friends and associates who helped Mendelssohn with the *Biur* and other literary activities became the nucleus of the first stage of Haskalah.

Strictly speaking, the Haskalah is a phase of Hebrew literature in which Jewish writers broke away from traditional patterns to borrow the forms of secular European literature. At certain times in the Middle Ages and in the Renaissance, Jewish writers composed a wide variety of works in prose and poetry outside the areas of halakhah, theology, and commentary. Some historians date modern Hebrew literature from certain seventeenth and early eighteenth-century writers in Italy and Holland who used such genres as the allegorical drama.[23] But the Haskalah was more than just a change in literary fashion; it was also an ideology. From Mendelssohn's time to the 1880s, most of the *maskilim* ("enlighteners"; singular, *maskil*) felt that Jews needed to modernize their style of life and to absorb the new learning current outside the periphery of traditional Judaism. Like the writers of the European-wide Enlightenment of the eighteenth century, the maskilim were a loose group of social critics who called for an end to medievalism, praised the value of science, and advocated various measures of social melioration. Above all, the maskilim preached the reform of Jewish education, especially the curtailment of the traditional Ashkenazic concentration on talmudic studies. The ideal Haskalah curriculum made room for religious instruction (especially in ethics), but emphasized secular knowledge, modern languages, and practical training in productive labor—all of which were felt to be indispensable if the Jews were to be accepted in society. The maskilim were active in setting up new Jewish schools and wrote textbooks in Hebrew for Jewish students educated according to their program. The Haskalah goal was a Jew who would embody a synthesis of Judaism and general culture and who would live up to the standards of common sense, tolerance, and reasonableness as espoused by universalistic humanitarianism.

The maskilim who were disciples of Mendelssohn form the first period of the Haskalah, when its main center was in Prussia. Many of them contributed to the commentary to the Mendelssohn Pentateuch and wrote for the first modern Jewish literary magazine, *Ha-Me'assef* (*The Gatherer*). *Ha-Me'assef* was started in Koenigsburg in 1783, and transferred to Berlin in the late eighties. (From 1790 to 1811 it appeared only irregularly.) The writers of this journal rejected rabbinic Hebrew and sought to return to the classic style of the Bible, embellishing their writing with the elegant but artificial decoration that to them symbolized literary refinement. *Ha-Me'assef* published poetry (in praise of wisdom, nature, and notable personages), fables, biblical exegesis, studies on Hebrew linguistics, essays on Jewish history, and news about the Jewish people. Most

Title page of the first issue of **Ha-Me'assef,** the first important periodical of the Jewish Enlightenment. (Courtesy of the Leo Baeck Institute, New York.)

of the authors were conservative in their religious views, but there were a few who inclined to deism. By the second decade of the nineteenth century, Germany was no longer a center of the Haskalah: Because German Jewish thought increasingly tended to employ the German language, the demand there for a modern Hebrew periodical disappeared.

By the 1820s the center of the Haskalah was in the Austrian empire: Bohemia, northern Italy, and especially Galicia. The most important organ of the new phase was the journal *Bikkurei ha-Ittim* (*First Fruits of the Times*), published annually in Vienna between 1821 and 1832. In addition to poetry and fine literature, *Bikkurei ha-Ittim* included philological studies, biography, and satire of those aspects of traditional Jewish life (especially Hasidism) that the maskilim opposed. By the 1830s there appeared the first Hebrew journal devoted solely to modern Jewish scholarship, in which the growing number of Jewish historians in Germany and Eastern Europe announced their findings (*Kerem Hemed* [*Vineyard of Delight*], published in Vienna, Prague, and Berlin between 1833 and 1856).

From Germany and Galicia, the Haskalah was carried into Russia. Although there were already signs of an indigenous Russian Jewish modernization movement in late eighteenth-century Lithuania (the Vilna Gaon and his circle, described in Chap. 10), by the 1840s the Haskalah had found its main home in Russia, where it entered its third and final phase. In Lithuania, European fiction and textbooks were translated into Hebrew, the first Hebrew novel was published (1854), and several significant Hebrew poets added a quality of personal lyricism previously missing in Haskalah verse. During the reign of the more liberal Tsar Alexander II, modern Hebrew weeklies appeared, and the Society for the Promotion of Culture among the Jews of Russia was established (1863). During the 1860s and 1870s a number of Hebrew writers who had rejected the decorative style of the earlier maskilim turned to literary and social criticism. By the end of a hundred years of development, therefore, the Haskalah had introduced into Hebrew literature not only the ideas of the eighteenth-century Enlightenment, but almost every other European intellectual movement since then, including romanticism, philosophical idealism, positivism, and utopian socialism.

In the dense and compact Jewries of Galicia and Russia the maskil became a recognized type and the Haskalah a social as well as a literary force. Maskilim were often isolated from the Jewish masses, distrusted because they were willing to rely on the support of the Austrian and Russian governments to carry out their educational and other reforms. Like many reformers, the maskilim were convinced that their program alone represented progress and advancement for the Jews, and that its adoption would convince the government that the Jews were worthy of emancipation. Even when respectful of talmudic Judaism, maskilim were usually convinced that they stood for light and knowledge against the "darkness" and "obscurantism" prevalent in the old Jewish way of life. Most of them despised Yiddish as a barbaric jargon and berated the hasidim for their fanaticism and superstition. The more extremist maskilim (like their anticlerical French predecessors in the eighteenth century) criticized the rigidity of the traditional rabbinate and preached the liberation of "life" from the burdensomeness of religion.

In the perspective of comparative history, the Haskalah was a ideology typical of incipient modernization, because something like the Haskalah usually emerges when an ethnic group or nationality has begun to be affected by economic and social developments that erode its hallowed way of life and that produce an intelligentsia imbued with the manners, aspirations, and knowledge of the advanced nations. This new leadership come to see themselves, first and foremost, as cosmopolitan "human beings"; as a result they perceive their own people to be behind the times and in desperate need of catching up. Bothered by the outside world's image of them, these ideologists publish writings that often have a self-abnegating tone, critical of the dominance of the ancient sacred values among their people. (Once modernization is well under way, however, later generations seek nostalgically to recover the uniqueness of their own identity and are far more critical of the defects of the West.)

The Haskalah was, therefore, a transitional ideology. The maskilim were recruited from men reared in traditional Judaism, seeking to break out but not to assimilate. Seldom did their children follow them in devoting their lives primarily to Hebrew literature. The Haskalah flourished when there were some signs of modern capitalism (a number of maskilim were either well-to-do merchants or supported by them), when the concept of political equality, but not its actuality, was in the air, when a Jewish public receptive to new ideas and information could be reached through Hebrew books and journals. Many of the changes ardently desired by the Haskalah were realized by large segments of East European Jewry in the last quarter of the nineteenth century, a development that made Haskalah ideology appear anemic and negative. But during its heyday, the Haskalah contributed considerably to the emergence of a fully modern Hebrew literature, and to the painful, but inevitable, preparation of Jewish identity to come to grips with modern secularism in that part of the world.

Beyond the Eighteenth-Century Enlightenment: Luzzatto and Krochmal

Even in its heyday the more simplistic and doctrinaire Haskalah rationalists were criticized by certain Jewish thinkers, themselves mas-

Brass Hanukkah menorah with fish decoration; the inscription reads "On the miracles, on the deliverance, on the mighty deeds."

kilim, who were searching for a broader and more profound definition of Judaism's uniqueness. We will briefly examine two scholarly and dedicated men who exemplify contrasting streams of early nineteenth-century Jewish thought. Both Samuel David Luzzatto (1800–1865) and Nahman Krochmal (1785–1840) lived in the Austrian empire, Luzzatto in northern Italy and Krochmal in eastern Galicia. Luzzatto, often known by his acronym as Shadal, was born in Trieste, the son of a poor but learned woodworker devoted to the Kabbalah. He received a thorough Jewish education and attended one of the newly established modern Jewish schools set up after Joseph II's Edict of Toleration, where he learned modern and classical languages, geography, and natural sciences. Although Luzzatto rejected the Kabbalah revered by his father, he never wavered in his devotion to the Jewish faith, to the Hebrew language, and to the study of Jewish literature. In his twenties he eked out a meager living as a tutor, writing erudite essays for the Haskalah yearly *Bikkurei ha-Ittim;* in 1829 he was appointed to the faculty of the newly established rabbinical college in Padua, where he taught for the rest of his life. Even though dogged by misfortunes (penury and the early death of loved ones), Luzzatto was a prodigious scholar, publishing studies in the Bible and its ancient translations, the prayer book, medieval Jewish poetry, and Hebrew grammar; he translated the Bible into Italian, wrote a Hebrew commentary to many biblical books, composed textbooks on Jewish theology and an autobiography in Italian. His passion for the recovery of the treasures of Judaism led him to spend his meager resources to buy rare Hebrew manuscripts, which he generously shared with Jewish scholars throughout Europe; many of his personal letters to them, published in three volumes, are virtually scholarly treatises in themselves. Even those colleagues who disagreed with his theological views spoke admiringly of his integrity, his sincerity, and his devotion to Jewish research.

Whereas the Jews among whom Luzzatto lived were rather well integrated into Italian culture, Krochmal (also known by his acronym Ranak, Rav Nahman Krochmal) lived at the other extremity of the Austrian empire, where East European traditionalism and Hasidism were still strong. Krochmal was born in Brody, an important trade center between Central Europe and Russia; his father was a successful merchant who had met Moses Mendelssohn and the German maskilim on business trips to Berlin. Like Luzzatto, Krochmal received a traditional training in rabbinical Judaism. He also educated himself in general literature, mastering ancient and modern languages, and studying the German philosophers of the late eighteenth and early nineteenth centuries: Kant, Fichte, Schelling, and Hegel. Married at the age of fourteen (quite usual in the traditional Ashkenazic milieu), he lived for a number of years at the home of his father-in-law at Zolkiew, near Lemberg (Lvov), where he developed close friendships with many of the men that were to be leaders of the Galician Haskalah during the 1820s and 1830s. When his in-laws died in 1814 he became a merchant—not a very successful one. After his wife's death twelve years later, his remaining life was passed in poverty, sickness, and loneliness. Although Krochmal published only a few Hebrew essays in his lifetime, his reputation had spread so that he was even offered a rabbinical post in Berlin; he refused, preferring to work as a bookkeeper in Zolkiew. The last two years of his life were spent at his daughter's house in the Galician city of Tarnopol, where he tried to complete his philosophical and historical researches. After his death his papers were sent to the eminent German Jewish scholar, Leopold Zunz, who published them in 1851 under the Maimonidean title *Morei Nevukhei ha-Zeman* (*A Guide for the Perplexed of Our Time*).

Both Luzzatto and Krochmal were deeply learned Jews, at home in the Jewish tradition and devoid of ambivalence about their ties to their people, or about Judaism's status as a religion of truth. But the kind of truth that Judaism represented to each was quite different. Krochmal was attracted to systematic philosophy as the key to Judaism's continued significance; like Maimonides before him (the comparison with Maimonides indicated by the title of his magnum opus is apt), he sought to affirm the essential harmony between Jewish faith and the ultimate principles behind natural science. Luzzatto rejected the compatibility of Judaism with rational metaphysics, and like his own spiritual hero,

Judah Halevy, insisted on the uniqueness of the Jewish way of life, in opposition to a theoretical and speculative approach to reality.

Luzzatto begins, like Mendelssohn, with the view that the Bible does not teach metaphysical doctrines. The basis of natural religion—faith in a transcendent, benevolent, and creative God—was discovered by Abraham and the other biblical patriarchs through their own efforts. A divine commandment cannot elicit faith; it can only regulate human action. Unlike Mendelssohn, however, Luzzatto rejected all efforts to establish the truth of natural religion by metaphysical argument. Influenced by Jean Jacques Rousseau and the Romantics, Luzzatto believed that the religious impulse was an affair of the heart, rather than of the understanding, of faith rather than knowledge, of the feeling rather than the mind. Arguing that innate, self-evident ideas and philosophical reasoning were not the grounds on which our notions of ultimate truth are constructed, Luzzatto drew on the empiricist philosophy of the eighteenth-century French writer Etienne Condillac, who had sought to reduce all complex ideas to an origin in sensation. As all human knowledge is derived from experience, the certainty of human knowledge rests on intuitive conviction, not formal proof. Therefore, a priori reason should not be given precedence over revelation, especially over the Mosaic revelation, which was witnessed by all the Israelites at Mount Sinai and hence is based on reliable evidence. Israel accepted the commandments at Sinai because it had faith in God. The purpose of the commandments was not to impart wisdom and knowledge, but to lead the people to righteousness. Ethical conduct, not rational belief, is the essence of true religion.

Drawing again on one strand of Enlightenment thought, Luzzatto acknowledges that human motives are determined by the passions, not the intellect. Indeed, biblical laws can be grouped according to the psychological factors used to encourage the perfection of virtue and the maintenance of Judaism. In his treatise *The Foundations of the Torah*, Luzzatto analyzes three principal emotions to which the biblical legislator appeals. First and foremost, the capacity to feel compassion: Many laws rely for their motive on sensitivity to the sufferings of others and seek to strengthen this feeling. (Vehemently rejecting Spinoza's philosophy, Luzzatto points out that Spinoza disparaged "womanish pity" as an irrational attitude.) Compassion alone, however, does not enable man to subdue all his selfish instincts. A second appeal used by the Torah is the hope of reward and the fear of punishment. Many Jewish sages had considered obedience because of reward and punishment inferior to obedience for its own sake, but to Luzzatto man's desire to have pleasure and avoid pain is a realistic means of habituating him to act morally. The third incentive is the feeling of *noblesse oblige* inherent in the conception of Israel's election: that God has chosen the Jews to be his people. A normal human yearning for honor, esteem, and prestige sustains the Jewish people in its pursuit of the highest ideals. Some important precepts, such as the dietary laws, he suggests, are intended to separate Israel from societies not rooted in divine ethics. Trained in the pursuit of the strictest virtue, Israel is to be a living example for other peoples to admire and therefore to emulate.

That Israel's existence has intrinsic and universal worth leads Luzzatto to formulate, in the sharpest possible manner, the antithesis between Judaism and the other great intellectual tradition of antiquity, which he designates Atticism (the heritage of Athens). The dichotomy between what are often called Hebraism and Hellenism is frequently used by Christian and Jewish writers in the nineteenth century, but Luzzatto formulates the difference so as to criticize certain tendencies within Judaism that he feels are inimical to preserving its special character. (Maimonides, certain other medieval Jewish intellectuals, Spinoza, and modern Jewish rationalists are considered by him as following an Attic rather than a Judaic approach to truth, in contrast to such men as Judah Halevy and Rashi.) The goal of Judaism is to foster righteousness, goodness, purity, sympathy; the goals of Atticism are artistic beauty and scientific and metaphysical truth. Atticism therefore stresses outer harmony over inner sanctity, theoretical speculation over moral practice, the mind over the heart. Judaism is essentially static and immutable, because morality does not change; Atticism is dynamic and progressive, ceaselessly striving for novelty and innovation. The Greek tradition is rationalist, the Jewish supernatural. The roots of Jewish creativity,

Samuel David Luzzatto, Italian Jewish scholar and writer. (Courtesy of the Jewish Division, the New York Public Library, Astor, Lenox, and Tilden Foundations.)

the source of the original and unique values that shaped Jewish history, transcend human reason. Therefore, Israel's survival depends on rejecting the autonomy of reason, which, Luzzatto believes, necessarily brings into Judaism an external criterion that undermines the ethical imperative, denies the historical singularity of the Jewish people, and destroys the uniqueness of its religion.

Krochmal emphatically rejects Luzzatto's attitude that Judaism has nothing to do with philosophy. Like Maimonides, Krochmal conceives of religion as presenting in imaginative language the same metaphysical content that philosophy describes in abstract concepts. Krochmal's metaphysics draws on certain tendencies in the German philosophical idealism of the end of the eighteenth century and the first part of the nineteenth, a brief description of which is necessary at this point.

Against the seventeenth and eighteenth-century mechanistic conception of nature, the German philosophers (especially Schelling, whose influence on Krochmal was considerable) reaffirmed the teleological principle of purposiveness, especially in the organism, in which the whole is more than the sum of its parts. Nature itself is conceived as an organic unity, a superorganism, through which *Geist* (a concept difficult to render into English, but referring to the realm of the spirit, mind, and the intellect) manifests increasingly higher levels of expression. Finite things exist in their own right, but are produced by an all-comprehensive infinite reality—the Absolute—which expresses itself as a dynamic movement toward self-consciousness in and through mind's self-reflection. Philosophical analysis seeks to reproduce the unfolding of the Absolute in nature and in mind, using as its model the logical relationship of antecedent to consequence. As a result of their emphasis on the internal unity of all aspects of existence, the German idealists came to think highly of Spinoza, although they added a temporal dimension to their concept of the Absolute lacking in Spinoza. And through their role in Krochmal's thought, elements of Spinoza's philosophy returned to Jewish thought.[24]

For Krochmal, the sense data of human experience are ordered in a network of categories and causal laws through which the human mind comes to perceive reality as one coherent system. Abstract concepts grasped by thought are actually the dynamic sources of the natural objects of empirical existence, constituting a supersensual reality that has its root in an ultimate principle, which Krochmal calls the Absolute Spirit. The Absolute Spirit is present in Krochmal's system on two levels: as the force generating the specific laws from which, in turn, the finite particulars of the world are derived, and as the ultimate subject and unity within which everything dwells. The Absolute Spirit generates the finite world out of itself through a nontemporal, continuous, and spontaneous act of self-limitation. (Krochmal drew a parallel between his view and the kabbalistic concept of the creation of the world out of God through a voluntary act of divine self-confinement.) The Absolute Spirit is the logical source for the world's intelligibility and the most general substance in which everything is grounded.

The religions of mankind, according to Krochmal, are to be understood in light of this metaphysics. The essence of all religion is a belief in spiritual powers; the difference between religions is the degree to which they worship the most general spiritual principle as such. The gods of paganism are each symbols of an aspect of the suprasensuous reality governing existence. In biblical religion, however, faith was not directed toward a particular spiritual power, but toward the cause of causes, the Absolute Spirit. Even though biblical prophecy grasped the Absolute Spirit through imaginative representation and feeling, rather than through pure conceptual understanding, the connection in Israelite prophecy between the human spirit and the divine was the clearest and the most comprehensive found among all ancient peoples.

As we have seen, for Krochmal metaphysical concepts grasped by the mind are dynamic forces that produce the objects of the world. Similarly, the spiritual powers symbolized by the religious cult of each people constitute the causal principle that sustains its cultural potential. Drawing on the eighteenth-century philosophers Vico and Herder, Krochmal avers that every nation has its own form of spirituality, which is the source of its sense of unity and its power to create a distinct heritage. Each national culture is an integrated whole: The creativity of the members of a national group in such fields as law, ethics, science, art, are marked by certain common features. Therefore, each nation has a unique historical mission—a spiritual aptitude—exemplified by the character of its deities. The religious values of a people establish and shape the "spiritual treasure" it creates during its history.

A nation is a spiritual organism, but every organism passes through a life cycle of birth, growth, maturity, decline, death. Certain sociological and psychological factors determine the rise and fall of a national group. For instance, the nation's material successes during its period of greatest vitality often lead to an unbridled pursuit of wealth, power, pleasure, and novelty—forms of individual self-indulgence that eventually undermine the integrity of the national religion and the confidence of the culture to sustain itself, resulting in degeneration and disintegration. When a nation dies, however, its outstanding characteristics are taken up and developed further by other peoples, so that human civilization as a whole shows an overall pattern of progressive growth.

There is, according to Krochmal, one people whose spiritual essence is different from that of all others and whose history is therefore different. The God of Judaism from the very beginning was not a symbol of a particular spiritual truth but of the Absolute Spirit as such. The

Immanuel Kant (1724–1804) and Georg Wilhelm Friedrich Hegel (1770–1831), German philosophers who were major influences on Jewish thought in the nineteenth and into the twentieth centuries.

principle of divine unity is the source of Israel's national character and historical essence: Without monotheism there would be no Israel. Because the Jewish people is a social organism, it passes through the usual cyclical process. The biblical period from the patriarchs to the conquest of Canaan was its period of "growth"; the settlement of Israel in the promised land until the death of King Solomon was its period of "maturity"; the history of the divided kingdoms until the destruction of Judah in 587 BCE was its age of "decline." But because its religion was rooted directly in the Absolute, Israel possessed the ability to regenerate itself. As Judaism is absolute monotheism, Israel is the "eternal people." A second period of growth, characterized by a greater understanding of the Absolute Spirit and a more reflective faith (seen in postexilic biblical writings on questions such as theodicy), occurs from the Babylonian exile to the conquests of Alexander the Great. A second period of maturity lasts until the death of the Hasmonean Queen Salome Alexandra, followed by another decline ending with the Bar Kokhba revolt (135 CE). In the early Middle Ages a third rebirth occurs, marked by further self-awareness through philosophy and Kabbalah. Krochmal may have envisioned a fourth cycle of Jewish history commencing in the seventeenth century.[25]

Krochmal's achievement was a presentation of Judaism consisting of two interrelated elements: metaphysics and philosophy of history. The Jewish idea of God was philosophically rational, and the inner development of Judaism was a gradual clarification of the idea implicit in the biblical depiction of God, the significance of which became increasingly explicit in the course of the historical destiny of the Jewish people. Thus the philosophical meaning of Jewish existence could be recognized only through the comprehensive history of the people and its spirit, together forming an indissoluble unity revelatory of the Absolute, which is the ultimate cause of all reality.

To return again to Spinoza: Spinoza had concluded that modern metaphysics rendered Judaism obsolete, its concept of God and its law invalid, its ethics scientifically and logically inadequate. This attitude, to the extent to which it accompanied the development of modern civilization, made imperative a defense of the rationality of Judaism. Mendelssohn, Luzzatto, and Krochmal were deeply religious men for whom the truth of Judaism was a central conviction. Each was able to find a philosophical approach that reassured him of the value of Jewish faith. Mendelssohn took from the Leibnitz–Wolff metaphysics the ideas with which he formulated those basic doctrines of natural religion that were, for him, the theoretical content of Judaism. Unlike Christianity, Judaism required one to believe only what the religion of universal reason affirmed. For Krochmal, certain elements of absolute idealism, combined with Maimonides and other medievals, provided a foundation for a philosophy of Jewish history in which the concept of God achieved full self-manifestation. Luzzatto, who did not accept the rationalistic interpretation current among the maskilim of his day, also argued that Judaism was reasonable: Although the source of Judaism is God's will alone, this will has intelligible goals. Luzzatto, of course, stands out in his rejection of the autonomous human reason as the main source of truth and of the ethical life.

Perhaps paradoxically, the identification of Judaism with the religion of reason raises the question of Judaism's uniqueness. What was the value of those particular elements of Judaism that stand outside the obviously rational? For Mendelssohn and Luzzatto, the commandments were the pattern for a way of life separate from the other peoples of the world, maintaining the Jews as a community with a destiny apart from other nations and a special role among them. The religion of reason, together with the revealed law, made up the permanent and unchanging core of Judaism, loyalty to which defined the task of Israel as a guide to humankind. Only Krochmal made the very process of Jewish history central, but even for him it was a process that made explicit only what was implicit in biblical Israel at the beginning. The more radical approach that Spinoza had taken, viewing the Bible itself as the product of historical development, was to become a major concern of Jewish religious thought only later in the nineteenth century.

All three men were responding to a feeling of crisis resulting from the great social changes to which the Jewish people in Western and Central Europe were being subjected. The old legal and communal structure that held the Jews together was disintegrating. Mendelssohn, at the beginning of the new age, felt that the Jews had to prepare themselves to enter the mainstream of European thought, while remaining faithful to the ceremonial observance of their ancestors. Krochmal, who saw himself standing between the traditionalists and the hasidim, on the one hand, and those who seemed about to reject all spiritual values, on the other hand, attempted a reformulation of the basis of Judaism that would provide the self-knowledge that modern Jewry required, a reformulation like that which Maimonides had accomplished six and a half centuries earlier. For Luzzatto a philosophical reconstruction of Judaism would only hasten the erosion of its distinctive character, which he feared was already under way.

All these concerns—the rationality of Jewish belief, the uniqueness of Israel, the impact of a historical perspective, the need for rejuvenation and reformulation—were the issues at stake in the ideological controversies that surfaced in mid-nineteenth-century German Jewry, producing the three modern forms of Judaism that came to be known as Reform, the Positive-Historical School, and Neo-Orthodoxy.

CHAPTER 1 3

The Question of Jewish Religious Reform in Nineteenth-Century Germany

Reform According to the Enlightenment

Enlightenment attitudes, so important in Hebrew literature of the Haskalah period, also produced during the second decade of the nineteenth century the first efforts to modernize Jewish worship. This early phase of the Reform movement sought to bring the externals of Judaism into closer harmony with contemporary European standards of decorum, solemnity, and reverence, in order to improve the image of the Jews in the eyes of enlightened Christians. Reform Judaism was also an attempt to stem the conversion to Christianity by Jews estranged from the traditional ritual and frustrated by legal and social discrimination against them and their children.

One of the most active and energetic of the early Reformers was Israel Jacobson (1768–1828), financier, philanthropist, and Jewish communal leader. Jacobson combined a strong emotional attachment to Judaism with the rationalistic humanitarianism of the Enlightenment. The French Revolution led him to believe that sweeping changes for the better were about to take place in the status of the German Jews, and that a suitable Jewish response was necessary. In 1801 Jacobson founded, at his own expense, a Jewish vocational school in the small town of Seesen in central Germany. (Modernized schools were gradually being opened in the larger Jewish communities of Central Europe.) When

Israel Jacobson, an early Jewish Reformer. (Courtesy of the Jewish Division, the New York Public Library. Astor, Lenox, and Tilden Foundations.)

much of western and central Germany fell under the domination of Napoleon, Jacobson became influential at the court of Napoleon's brother Jerome, ruler of the newly established and short-lived kingdom of Westphalia. As president of the Westphalia Jewish consistory, modeled on that set up for the Jews of France by Napoleon, Jacobson tried to impose on the synagogues under his jurisdiction changes in the direction of greater simplicity and dignity of worship. In 1810, adjacent to his school in Seesen, Jacobson built the first Reform temple. It was dedicated with great pomp in the presence of prominent Christian officials and clergymen, and Jacobson felt that his temple heralded a new era of brotherly understanding between religions.

After Napoleon's empire collapsed and the old regimes were restored in 1815, Jacobson moved to Berlin where he opened a private temple first in his home and then in the larger home of a wealthy banker and communal elder. In 1823 Jewish traditionalists convinced the conservative Prussian government to close down the Berlin temple. In 1818, however, a temple was opened in Hamburg, spurred by Eduard Kley, a preacher of the Berlin Reform group, who had become head of the new Hamburg Jewish school. Like Jacobson and other early advocates of reform, the members of the Hamburg temple were businessmen without rabbinic ordination, although a few did possess some Jewish learning. Worship in the Hamburg temple followed the pattern set in Seesen and Berlin: The sermon and many of the prayers were in German; choral singing was accompanied by an organ. In 1819 the Hamburg temple took the additional step of issuing a new prayer book, which eliminated repetitions, dropped the medieval liturgical poems (*piyyutim*), and reworded some of the traditional prayers felt to be inconsistent with loyalty to universal reason and the German fatherland, such as those referring to a national redemption of the Jewish people in the messianic age. Sharp polemics ensued. The rabbis of Hamburg, supported by eminent rabbinic authorities elsewhere, denounced the new prayer book as a violation of halakhah. The defenders of the temple marshaled citations indicating that the Talmud did permit prayer in the vernacular.

The primary intention of the early reformers was to establish that Judaism was a fully modern religion and one of the acceptable denominations of Germany. The Jewish style of worship was, therefore, to be brought into harmony with the contemporary aesthetic values. In the traditional Ashkenazic synagogue worshipers responded on their own and in a highly individual way to the prayer leader; the service was entirely in Hebrew and chanted according to old musical modes. Musical instruments were not allowed in Sabbath and holy day worship. This religious atmosphere, with its spontaneity and informality, seemed undignified and oriental to those acculturated Jews who instigated the reforms. Gradually, some of the modifications that they introduced were adopted in varying degrees by Western Jewry: greater decorum in the synagogue, more unison prayer, a regular choir, hymns and musical responses in the modern style—and especially the weekly sermon emphasizing the moral and rational teachings of religion. However, use of the organ, drastic shortening of the service, and reformulation of prayers that might be construed as putting Jewish patriotism to Germany in doubt remained confined only to the few completely Reform congregations, such as the Hamburg temple. The early Reformers were not very revolutionary. Their basic convictions—that philosophical rationalism and ethical duties were the heart of religion, that ritual was only a means to moral edification, that the cultural style of the Jews needed to be brought up to date—these were solidly rooted in the optimistic faith of the eighteenth-century Enlightenment.

Viewed from the perspective of avant-garde German writers and thinkers in the first two decades of the nineteenth century, the cosmopolitan rationalism of the Enlightenment was out of date. Influential figures of the German Romantic movement had attacked Enlightenment rationalism as shallow, unhistorical, and anemic, in contrast to the power of the creative imagination to grasp the inner depths and organic wholeness of personality, nature, and culture. Moreover, in a period of reaction against the French Revolution and against French cultural models, the conservative and nationalistic aspects of German Romanticism reinforced disdain and even hostility to Judaism. No mere external reform of Judaism according to Enlightenment standards could win respect for Judaism as a living faith in the eyes of Christians and Jews subscribing to the values of Romanticism. The Romantic approach to religion, which grounded faith on feeling and subjective experience, stimulated spiritual longings in some members of Berlin Jewry that were not answered by a religion of reason. Particularly susceptible were several cultivated Jewish women who had come into close personal contact with the new wave of German writers and theologians, had absorbed their point of view, and had converted quite sincerely to Protestantism or even to Roman Catholicism. Two of Mendelssohn's daughters, Dorothea and Henriette, followed this pattern, as did Henriette Herz and Rahel Varnhagen, whose literary salons in Berlin were important meeting grounds for German intellectuals at the height of the Romantic movement. The paradox of German Jewish conversion to Christianity in the early nineteenth century was that the men were usually deists or agnostics who viewed all religion as reducible to universal principles of morality, so for them Christianity was a matter of form and convenience rather than faith. The small group of women converts yearned for rapturous faith, sublime devotion, and mystical bliss, finding in Christianity a personal religiosity that their Enlightenment upbringing and Romantic emotions did not enable them to perceive in either traditional or reformed Jewish worship.

Romantic concern for the past, together with post-Enlightenment philosophy, however, eventually had a more constructive impact on Jewish thought in Germany. The first tentative signs had already appeared in 1819, when a small group of young men with university educations formed a Society for the Culture and Academic Study of Judaism (*Verein für Kultur und Wissenschaft des Judentums*). *Wissenschaft*, careful and systematic scholarship in the humanities and history, a respect for facts, meticulous research, and the scientific methodology, was the new positive ideal replacing the eighteenth-century concern for "eternal verities." Avoiding both veneration of the past and rejection of it, *Wissenschaft* was to be the means to that reliable knowledge that would guide the development of the social organism in a healthy spiritual direction. Members of the *Verein*, searching for their own identity as Jews and believing that an objective portrayal would win for Judaism the respect due it in the history of civilization, proposed that the Jewish past be investigated with the methods of *Wissenschaft* in order to determine the inner nature and essential characteristics of Jewish consciousness. The new direction was not fully clear even in the minds of the principal figures of the *Verein*, most of whom were interested in philosophy and literature, rather than historical scholarship. In 1824 the association disintegrated, several of its members (the Romantic poet Heinrich Heine and the historian of law Eduard Gans) converting to Christianity for the sake of their future careers. The *Verein*'s most important activity was a short-

Watercolor depicting the consecration of the synagogue of Cleve in the Rhineland, c. 1820. (Courtesy of the Leo Baeck Institute, New York.)

lived periodical devoted to Jewish historical scholarship, the first of several such journals that were to make nineteenth-century Germany a major center of modern Jewish *Wissenschaft*. The editor, Leopold Zunz, was to become one of the greatest Jewish researchers. Despite its limited impact, the legacy of the *Verein* pointed to two crucial assumptions of the next phase of Jewish intellectual life in Germany: first, that Judaism could recover its true character by being raised to the level of rigorous *Wissenschaft;* second, that Judaism was the unfolding of a fundamental religious principle placing its imprint on every form and aspect of the Jewish spirit. The conviction that Judaism could be understood as an organic unity developing out of an essential and comprehensive idea was very much the impact of the philosopher Hegel, then at the height of his influence in Germany. With the revival of Jewish religious thought in the 1830s, the Hegelian approach inspired several quite different interpretations of Judaism.

The Neo-Orthodoxy of Samson Raphael Hirsch

By the beginning of the nineteenth century the term *Orthodox* had come into general use for those who maintained, contrary to the Reformers, that the entire written and oral Torah, as interpreted by the continuous chain of rabbinic authorities since ancient times, was divinely revealed and immutable. In particular, for the Orthodox, the Shulhan Arukh—the sixteenth-century code of religious law compiled by Joseph Caro—together with its commentaries and the later decisions of duly qualified rabbis, constituted a fixed and binding standard for proper Jewish practice. (Because of the centrality of religious action in rabbinic Judaism, some scholars suggest that the term *orthopraxy*, correct practice, would be more descriptive than *orthodoxy*, correct doctrine.) Throughout the first half of the nineteenth century the bulk of German Jews and their rabbis remained traditionally observant, in contrast to the rather small Reform stratum described in the previous section. The first German rabbi to become an eloquent champion of modern Orthodoxy against Reform was Samson Raphael Hirsch.

Hirsch was born in Hamburg in 1808, of an enlightened but traditionally observant family. Hirsch's ancestors had lived in that part of Germany for ten generations; a grandfather and an uncle were admirers of Moses Mendelssohn. Hirsch's father, a businessman, rejected the Hamburg temple, but was sympathetic to the moderate Haskalah, especially to the value of a modern secular education. Samson Raphael Hirsch was sent to a German grammar school, a classical high school (*gymnasium*), and the University of Bonn. During the one year he spent in Bonn, Hirsch came into close and friendly contact with Abraham Geiger, a future leader of Reform Judaism; Hirsch and Geiger organized a Jewish oratorical society, perhaps with their future careers in the rabbinate in mind. In 1830, at the age of twenty-two, Hirsch became chief rabbi (*landesrabbiner*, a government-supported position) of the Duchy of Oldenburg. In 1836 he published *The Nineteen Letters on Judaism*, a book that had considerable impact on young German Jews in search of religious faith. The following year appeared *Horeb: A Philosophy of Jewish Laws and Observances*, the first part of a comprehensive theology of Judaism and its duties, which he never completed. After occupying several rabbinic positions in northwest Germany and then in Moravia in the Austrian empire, in 1851 Hirsch settled permanently in Frankfort-on-Main as the spiritual leader of a group opposed to the influence of Reform Judaism in that large and important Jewish center. In addition to his Orthodox congregation, Hirsch established a modern Orthodox Jewish school, founded and edited a monthly in which he published articles on Jewish education and current issues, and wrote commentaries to the Pentateuch and the Psalms. Hirsch was far from being a traditional rabbi of the old type: He was not a great talmudic scholar; he wrote his works in fluent and impeccable German; he admired the classic German writers, especially the poet and dramatist Friedrich Schiller. (Schiller represented, for many nineteenth-century Jews, the spokesman par excellence for that stream of noble and humanitarian idealism in German culture with which they identified.) Hirsch introduced certain aesthetic changes in the synagogues under his direction, such as the German sermon and choral singing. Hirsch's Neo-Orthodoxy, as it is often called, is epitomized by the Hebrew phrase, *Torah im derekh eretz* (Pirkei Avot 2:2, "Excellent is the study of Torah together with a practical livelihood"), used by maskilim even before Hirsch to describe a harmonious synthesis of fidelity to Jewish religious practice and openness to secular Europeon civilization. A Jew could combine exact and faithful adherence to the divine commandments with a modern style of life. Hirsch also coined the term *Israel-man* (*Jissroel-Mensch*) to describe the person who is fully a Jew and also a cultured individual. Hirsch was, therefore, a fine example of Mendelssohn's combination of universalism and strict Jewish piety. By the time he died in 1888 his point of view had been embodied in a small but clearly defined and tightly organized segment of German Jewry.

The *Nineteen Letters on Judaism,* which made Hirsch's reputation, is a defense of an observant Jewish life written in the form of essays by a young rabbi to a friend who questions the value of being a Jew. At the onset the latter skeptically voices the typical criticisms of Judaism during the early nineteenth century: "While the rest of mankind climbed to the summit of culture, prosperity, and wealth, the Jewish people remained poor in everything that makes human beings great and noble, and that beautifies and dignifies our lives."[1] Moreover, Judaism hinders the full attainment of personal happiness and perfection; the Jewish law isolates Jews from their neighbors, arousing suspicion and hostility; the study of Judaic lore crams the mind with petty subtleties and insignificant trifles.

Hirsch's spokesman responds, "Is it so sure that happiness and perfection constitute the goal and objective of man's existence?" Before this question can be answered, one should learn what the Torah actually teaches about the destiny of mankind and the purpose of human life. According to Hirsch, Torah proclaims that the universe is a harmonious, interdependent system, in which everything was created with a special divine intent. "One glorious chain of love, of giving and receiving, unites all living things." Man alone, however, has the vocation of serving God of his own free will and choice, which means that he must learn, at times painfully, to obey God's moral will. According to Hirsch, the biblical narrative informs us that early men fell into idolatry, conceiving of nature as controlled by many gods rather than forming an all-embracing unity; men also erred in considering wealth and pleasure as ends in themselves rather than as means to a higher goal. It was necessary, therefore, that a single people be created that, through its special way of life, declares that there is only one creative cause of existence and that the only true happiness is the active service of God.

Samson Raphael Hirsch as a young man. Hirsch became the leader of Neo-Orthodoxy in Germany. (Courtesy of the Leo Baeck Institute, New York.)

This mission required for its execution a nation, poor in everything upon which the rest of mankind reared the edifice of its greatness and power, externally subordinate to the nations armed with proud self-sufficiency, but fortified inwardly by direct reliance upon God, so that, by the suppression of every enemy force, God might reveal Himself directly as the sole Creator, Judge, and Master of nature and history.[2]

Ancient Israel received from God the gifts of land and statehood solely in order to be able to carry out the Torah. Later, Israel was exiled from the holy land to enable it to perfect itself and to fulfill its mission by remaining faithful to God and the Torah, despite suffering and agony. Hirsch's portrait of Israel's role in history concludes with quotations from the servant poems of the prophet Isaiah in order to inspire in his readers the task of becoming "a mutely eloquent example and teacher of universal love." He exclaims, "If only we were, or would become, that which we should be, if only our lives were a perfect reflection of our Law—what a mighty force we would constitute for steering mankind to the final goal of all human education!"[3]

Because the heart of Hirsch's Orthodox position is the careful observance of the divine commandments, the *Nineteen Letters* contains an enumeration of the various categories into which, he believes, Israel's duties can be grouped. They are these: (1) commandments that teach fundamental ideas about God, the world, the mission of mankind, and the mission of Israel; (2) laws of social justice; (3) other laws concerned with justice toward animate and inanimate objects, including ecological matters; (4) commandments of love to all living things; (5) festivals and other ceremonies that teach essential truths through "symbolic words and acts"; (6) laws concerning worship, that is, turning aside from ordinary daily activities to purify and ennoble the individual's character. According to Hirsch, the divinely given rules of Jewish conduct do not repress the normal desire for physical pleasure and material prosperity, but subordinate them to the goal of a religious life. Economic disadvantages of abstaining from work on the Sabbath and the holy days, limits on full social intercourse with non-Jews resulting from the prohibition against eating nonkosher food, the requirement not to intermarry with Christians—these are a small price to pay for the preservation of the Jews as God's witnesses to the messianic ideal of universal human brotherhood.

The Hegelian aspect of Hirsch's theology was the idea of a self-cognition of Judaism out of its own roots through understanding the symbolic and ethical significance of the commandments. (Hirsch devotes considerable attention in *Horeb* and his later writings to allegorical interpretations of each element of Jewish law.) According to him, just as natural science looks for theories to explain the empirically given data, the true science of Judaism must approach God's revealed ordinances as primary facts constituting an interconnected system in which every detail has its special function. Torah is an organic unity, the meaning of which unfolds out of its inner principles. Hirsch rejects Maimonidean Aristotelianism of the Middle Ages and the Reformers of his day for bringing to bear on Judaism an external perspective. He also criticizes Moses Mendelssohn for not having explicated Judaism out of its own essential spiritual content. The worst error of the Reformers, however, is to diminish Judaism's duties for the sake of the convenience and the comfort of modern Jews, rather than to elevate Jewry to a Judaism "newly comprehended by the spirit and fulfilled by utmost energy."[4] What was needed was the reform of the Jews, not of Judaism.

As for emancipation, Hirsch greets it as a rectification of old wrongs and a valid means for normalizing Jewish economic life. Emancipation is a condition to which Jewry must adjust, but it should not be the primary goal. According to Hirsch, the changes in Judaism required by full citizenship in Germany are peripheral ones, because Jews are united only by the purely spiritual bond of obedience to the divine law "until that great day shall arrive when the Almighty shall see fit in His inscrutable wisdom to unite again his scattered servants in one land, and the Torah shall be the guiding principle of a state, a model of the meaning of Divine Revelation and the mission of humanity."[5] In effect, Hirsch rules out any practical Jewish initiative to bring about this messianic goal, and reiterates in his own way the Reformers' insistence that the Jewish religion does not interfere with a Jewish citizen's patriotic fulfillment of all political duties to his country. Hirsch also resembled some of the extreme Reformers in that he advocated, in the later years of his life, that his followers secede from the overall German Jewish community. Hirsch denied the religious legitimacy of Jewish communal organizations dominated by adherents of non-Orthodox positions. (As a result, in part, of Hirsch's efforts, the German government passed in 1876 a law permitting this form of separatism.)

A succinct epitome of Hirsch's definition of Judaism was given by the historian Heinrich Graetz in the mid-1840s: "Judaism is a thoroughly systematic program for cultivating an obedient disposition, a submissive subordination to the absolute will of God, its ultimate good being the inculcation of religious feeling."[6] For all Hirsch's self-assurance and eloquence, his Neo-Orthodoxy was, however, unacceptable to most acculturated Jews of his time, who not only aspired to a greater degree of social integration with non-Jews than full Orthodox observance permitted, but rejected Hirsch's fundamentalism. Despite his modern style, Hirsch had a thoroughly uncritical view of the biblical narrative, falling back on the traditional argument that the revelation of the Torah at Sinai cannot be doubted, because it took place in a public event witnessed by more than two million people. For him Torah was to be accepted (or rejected) on an all-or-nothing basis.

> The whole question is simply this. Is the statement "And God spoke to Moses saying," with which all the laws of the Jewish Bible commence, true or not true? Do we really and truly believe that God, the Omnipotent and Holy, spoke thus to Moses? Do we speak the truth when in front of our brethren we lay our hand on the scroll containing these words and say that God has given us this Torah, that His Torah, the Torah of truth and with it of eternal life, is planted in our midst? If this is to be no mere lip-service, no mere rhetorical flourish, then we must keep and carry out this Torah without omission and without carping, in all circumstances and at all times. . . .[7]

Torah is outside history; it is not a changing and therefore a changeable object of historical development. But those who took seriously the principle of historical evolution, which meant that Judaism, like every other aspect of human civilization, had undergone an evolutionary process, concluded that more drastic theoretical reformulation of Judaism was required.

Reform According to *Wissenschaft*

In the late 1830s, soon after Samson Raphael Hirsch published *The Nineteen Letters on Judaism,* and contrary to his hopes, the impetus for religious reform was renewed in German Jewry. Various political and cultural factors were responsible. Germany was now experiencing an upsurge of political liberalism critical of the conservative post-Napoleonic regimes, and, as a result, the struggle for Jewish emancipation picked up momentum. Jewish champions of emancipation, such as Gabriel Riesser, insisted that, Jews by religion only, they should receive equal rights as sons of the German fatherland. Furthermore, not only did political theorizing grow more radical in Germany during the 1830s and 1840s, but left-wing students of Hegel questioned the fundamentals of traditional Christianity, such as the historicity of Jesus (David Friedrich Strauss), and analyzed religion as a projection of human needs (Ludwig Feuerbach). In this stimulating and challenging atmosphere a new generation of German rabbis, who had attended secular universities and were aware of current philosophical and historical issues, called for an extensive re-

Leopold Zunz, outstanding figure in the scholarly study of the Jewish past. (Courtesy of the Jewish Division, the New York Public Library, Astor, Lenox, and Tilden Foundations.)

appraisal of Judaism. For this undertaking it was of great importance that the scholarly side of the Haskalah and of the *Wissenschaft des Judentums* —the scientific study of Jewish history and religious literature—had now begun to produce solid achievements, some of which had contemporary implications. One of the most noteworthy was Leopold Zunz's *The Sermons of the Jews (Die gottesdienstlichen Vorträge der Juden,* 1832) in which the midrashic literature was for the first time presented in its historical context. Primarily a work of pure scholarship, Zunz's book also showed that the weekly synagogue sermon in the vernacular was an ancient Jewish form, not a recent imitation of Christianity. In short, political and intellectual forces led a growing number of German Jews to become convinced that further reform of Jewish practice and a fundamental rethinking of Jewish theology were both necessary and advisable.

The first skirmish of the new era of reform was the controversy that accompanied the appointment of the young Abraham Geiger as second rabbi of Breslau in 1838. Opposing Geiger's fitness for the post, the head rabbi of the city, Solomon Tiktin, charged that Geiger had criticized Orthodoxy and called for religious reforms in his journal for Jewish theology. In 1842, still refusing to cooperate with Geiger, Tiktin issued a pamphlet insisting on the unquestioned validity of the laws of the *Shulhan Arukh* and the inviolable authority of the rabbinic tradition; Geiger's supporters countered with a work entitled *Rabbinic Responses on the Compatibility of Free Investigation with the Exercise of Rabbinic Functions.* While the dispute in Breslau still raged, the Hamburg temple published a revised edition of its prayer book that had eliminated many of the supplications for the messianic ingathering of Israel to Zion and had replaced the traditional idea of bodily resurrection with the immortality of the soul. The Orthodox rabbi of Hamburg denounced the work and prohibited its use. Almost all the notable German rabbis took sides on the issues raised by the Geiger-Tiktin affair and by the Hamburg Reform prayer book.

Soon a more radical note was sounded when lay groups in Frankfort (1842) and Berlin (1845) issued calls for sweeping changes in Judaism. A Frankfort Reform society proclaimed "the possibility of unlimited development in the Mosaic religion" and emphatically rejected the authority of the Talmud. The Berlin Reform association (*Reformgemeinde*) demanded a prayer service almost entirely in German and abolition of such customs as praying with covered heads and blowing the shofar on the New Year, considered by them obsolete and oriental. The Berliners proclaimed that

Our inner faith, the religion of our hearts, is no longer in harmony with the external forms of Judaism. We want a positive religion; we want Judaism. . . . We hold fast to the conviction that Judaism's teaching of God is eternally true; we hold fast to the promise that this teaching will some day become the possession of all mankind. But we want to understand the sacred Scriptures according to the divine spirit, not according to the letter. We can no longer pray honestly for a messianic kingdom on earth which shall bring us back to the homeland of our forefathers, pretending that we would return to it from a strange land—the very fatherland to which we are tied with all the bonds of love! We can no longer recognize a code as an unchangeable law-book which maintains with unbending insistence that Judaism's task is expressed by forms which originated in a time which is forever past and which will never return. . . . Thus, placed between the graves of our fathers and the cradles of our children, we are stirred by the trumpet sound of our time. It calls us to be the last of a great inheritance in its old form, and at the same time, the first who, with unswerving courage and bound together as brothers in word and deed, shall lay the cornerstone of a new edifice for us and for the generations to come.[8]

These agitations led to proposals that a rabbinic conference be convened to establish a consensus for orderly change. In June 1844 the first such synod met at Brunswick; the twenty-five rabbis who attended discussed the desirability of formulating a Jewish creed, of easing Jewish Sabbath and dietary laws, and of reforming the liturgy. In response, over a hundred Orthodox rabbis circulated a protest that no Jewish leaders had the right to abrogate any traditional law of Judaism. Nevertheless, a second and larger conference opened in July 1845 in Frankfort-on-Main. The first question was the place of Hebrew in Jewish worship. Although the majority voted that Hebrew should be retained, Rabbi Zacharias Frankel of Dresden withdrew after stating that Hebrew was "absolutely essential," not just "advisable." (The crucial role of Frankel in crystallizing a third division of German Jewry between the Reformers and the Orthodox will be discussed later in the chapter.) The Frankfort conference agreed that the messianic idea should be mentioned prominently in a revised prayer book, but that petitions for the return to Palestine and the restoration of a Jewish state be omitted.[9]

In July 1846 a third synod, meeting in Breslau, attracted only rabbis committed to the Reform movement. The main topic of debate was the talmudic prohibition on Sabbath work. The sanctity of the Sabbath as a day of recreation and spiritual elevation was reaffirmed, as were the traditional prohibitions against regular business and professional activities unless life was threatened or the welfare of the state was endangered. But the assembled rabbis declared as no longer binding the talmudic concept of the *eruv* (the stipulated boundaries for permissible walking and carrying of objects on the Sabbath). The custom of adding in the diaspora one more day to each holiday, instituted when the calendar was still based on lunar observation, was proclaimed to be of no further value.[10] A planned fourth conference was not held because of the revolution of 1848.

The rabbinical synods of the 1840s did not institute major reforms for all German Jewry, nor did they create a broadly based new religious denomination. Although a few temples in Berlin, Hamburg, and elsewhere were identified with the theology that came to be known as classical Reform, most European Reform rabbis saw themselves not as members of a separatist group but as part of the totality of German Jews, and conceived of reform as a process that would take place gradually within the established Jewish communal structure. The most important figure among the German rabbinate who advocated "reform from within" was Abraham Geiger. An outstanding example of the new type of rabbi educated in a secular university and yet thoroughly at home in Jewish texts, Geiger combined a lifelong commitment to Jewish *Wissenschaft* with an active rabbinic career of preaching, pastoral care, and other synagogue activities. It was his conviction that *Wissenschaft* would enable Judaism to reshape its theology on a scientific, not an arbitrary basis. After an initial period of radicalism, Geiger became determined that irrevocable schisms should be avoided within Jewry, and that reform should take place through persuasion rather than secession.

Born in Frankfort-on-Main in 1810 of an old and traditionalist Frankfort family, during his youth Geiger received a strong grounding in Jewish, classical, and German literature. In 1829 he began to study at the University of Heidelberg, soon moving on to Bonn where he learned Arabic and prepared his first major scholarly research, *What Did Muhammad Take from Judaism?* (his doctoral dissertation, published in 1833). (As mentioned earlier, Geiger was friendly in Bonn with Samson Raphael Hirsch, although later the two were antagonists.) In 1832 Geiger became rabbi of the small town of Wiesbaden, near Frankfort, where he edited and published *Die Wissenschaftliche Zeitschrift für Jüdische Theologie* (*The Scientific Journal for Jewish Theology*), containing essays by himself and other scholars on Jewish history and on the reform of Judaism. Geiger's appointment as rabbi in Breslau (1838) led to the prolonged and heated controversy described earlier, a landmark in the polarization between the Reform and Orthodox camps. In addition to his communal activities during more than two decades in Breslau, Geiger lay the groundwork for the establishment of a Jewish rabbinical seminary there, and published many studies on such diverse topics as the Mishnah, medieval Jewish biblical commentators, Judah Halevy and other Hebrew poets, and the Bible. He considered as his magnum opus a book on the ancient text and translations of the Bible in which he argued that postbiblical movements in Judaism shaped the canonized version of the Hebrew

Scriptures in conformity with their special ideas. Geiger played a leading part in the Reform rabbinical conferences of the 1840s. In 1860 he became rabbi of his birthplace, Frankfort-on-Main; in 1870 he was invited to Berlin as one of the communal rabbis. He was finally able to realize in Berlin a lifelong aspiration to teach in an institute of higher Jewish learning, the new Reform *Hochschule für die Wissenschaft des Judentums* (Academy for the Scientific Study of Judaism), where he was a member of the faculty for the last two years of his life. He died in October 1874.

Although Geiger did not write a systematic theology of Judaism, his studies of Jewish intellectual history embody a definite point of view on the nature of religion and the essence of Judaism.[11] Geiger was well read in the German idealist philosophy of his day and familiar with the critique of religious origins proposed by radical Christian scholars; his approach is a determined and self-assured program to reformulate Judaism so it would achieve theological clarity according to the "scientific spirit of the time." Geiger considered Hirsch's Neo-Orthodoxy merely a return of old forms when innovations were urgently needed. But like the Romantics, Geiger viewed the eighteenth-century Enlightenment as superficial, negative, and lacking in spiritual nourishment. Religion was rooted in the self's awareness of its finitude and its yearning for the Infinite. Religion is more than rational philosophy: "It is an inborn longing of a whole man who thinks, feels, and wants to act morally and rightly."[12] In a letter written in 1836 Geiger defined his personal conception of Judaism as "a faith founded on the trust in One who guides the universe and on the task imposed upon us to practice justice and mercy, a faith that becomes manifest in acts that fulfill this demand, and that is clothed in uplifting ritual forms designed to awaken such sentiments."[13] Most important was a religion's conception of man's nature. Echoing the common

Abraham Geiger, historian and Reform rabbi.

nineteenth-century theme of Hebraism versus Hellenism, Geiger (like Samuel David Luzzatto earlier) notes that ancient Greek civilization, for all its universal value, was pervaded by the idea of a mysterious, unconquerable fate to which human beings and even gods must submit, whereas the Hebrew Bible saw as man's divine nature a constant "inner striving for higher purity." Ancient Judaism was based on the consciousness that man must struggle against sensuality in order to attain the good—"a struggle which ennobles and elevates man, [and] which through repentance can lead him to worthy victory."[14]

For Geiger, the spiritual core of Judaism, which in ancient times reached a climax in the ideas of the great prophets, must be distinguished from the shell, external forms shaped as a result of outside influences and then cast off in the course of historical evolution. Thus, for example, animal sacrifices and the Aaronide priesthood were conspicuous elements of biblical Judaism, but their disappearance did not impair the survival of the Jewish religion. Similarly, Geiger held that the form of nationhood, necessary and valid at one stage of Jewish history, was no longer required at a later stage. That Judaism was able to break through the "barrier of nationality" was first evident in antiquity when gentiles converted to Judaism by declaring themselves in agreement with its tenets. According to Geiger, if the religion of a people can continue to exist when "the fetters which national life had put upon it have been broken—if it continues to live when those who are its standard bearers no longer exist as a political unit—then this religion has passed a great trial on the way to demonstrating its reliability and its truth."[15] Not birth but conviction makes one Jewish.

Geiger divides Jewish history into four periods. The first was "the age of revelation." Harking back to a theme that appeared in the philosophy of Judah Halevy, Geiger argues that "the genius of revelation was latent in the whole people and found concentration and expression in individuals."[16] The content of revelation was the "idea of Judaism," a universal, humanitarian, spiritual concept capable of infinite progressive development. During the second age of Jewish history, "the age of tradition," biblical material was constantly being reinterpreted and molded for life, ensuring that the "idea" would always be fresh and vital. The third period, "the age of legalism" after the completion of the Babylonian Talmud, was a summing up of tradition necessary to guard and preserve Judaism. The fourth period, "the era of critical study," is marked by a liberation from the fetters of legalism through critical reason and historical research. Although the chain of halakhah has been broken, this does not sever Judaism's bond with the past, but revitalizes the tradition in order to "cause the stream of history to flow forth once again."[17] Geiger's insistence that Jewish history is the history of the religion and not of the people stemmed from a conviction that the central problem of contemporary Judaism was to restore the flexibility and creativity inherent in Judaism from the start. There may be aspects of traditional Judaism that should be rejected, but these do not touch the living, still vital core of the religion; they are but "medieval abnormalities" resulting from artificial restraints and insurmountable barriers imposed on Judaism long ago by Christian societies. Rather than consider these abnormalities as features of the innermost nature of Judaism, one must, on the contrary, admire how Judaism, under the worst conditions, preserved its integrity, always sought the light, and, in the modern period, was gradually achieving its purification.[18]

Earlier brutality against the Jews was the result, Geiger felt, of the Christian belief that Judaism had been superseded by the Church and had no right to consider itself a living religion. Geiger's polemic against Christianity, however, involved more than a protest against prejudice and persecution. The modern Jewish mission derived precisely from Judaism's not having incorporated into itself the equivalent of those doctrines that the Church had added to its Judaic heritage. According to Geiger, Christianity had compromised the original purity of the religious idea by diluting the Jewish conception of an infinite, perfect, and completely spiritual God with the pagan notion that the deity could appear in a visible, bodily form. The Christian concept of original sin had compromised the scriptural conviction that man is given the power of moral improvement and self-determination. Unlike Christianity, the validity of Judaism does not rest on the personal character of a single individual, not even Moses. Judaism never "exchanged its merciful God for the God of that love which, to satisfy its anger, requires a grand, sufficiently vicarious sacrifice."[19] Unlike Christianity, Judaism did not describe the earthly life as a vale of tears in contrast to the bliss of the afterlife. Nor did Judaism devise fixed and rigid dogmas that shackled the free speculation of philosophers and scientists. For Geiger, therefore, Judaism was the ideal form of religious consciousness and the prototype of the religion of modern humanity in a liberal age.

Only in an age of *Wissenschaft* and emancipation could the truth of Judaism find its proper form. A knowledge of the past based on solid research would eliminate what was obsolete—Jewish concepts and observances that had had vital functions in earlier times but were now no longer necessary. Geiger could view with equanimity the eventual disappearance of such fundamental Jewish practices as circumcision and the dietary laws, because he insisted that the law did not constitute the core of Judaism in the way that faith in Jesus and the Trinity were at the heart of Christianity. And Geiger possessed an overwhelming, almost messianic identification with a liberal Germany. As German citizens of the Jewish faith, his coreligionists must demand that Judaism be recognized as an essential component of the German heritage, alongside Catholicism and Protestantism. Indeed, Geiger rejected the more radical Jewish Reformers because he thought they were capitulating to Christianity; thus he criticized their willingness to substitute Sunday for Saturday as the principal day of worship, despite the practicality of this change, because it implied the right of Christianity to set the pattern in German social and religious life. Geiger's liberalism sought to blend radicalism in theory with moderation in practice, a commitment to the Jewish vocation in history with an optimistic faith in progress. "For to speak plainly, the modern is not Christian and the Christian is not modern. . . . Modern culture leans in religion upon Jewish monotheism and in sciences and arts on Hellenism, while it either ignores or rejects the specifically Christian."[20] The inherent power of ideas would triumph. Just as the spirit of Judaism had ensured the survival of the Jews in the past, even in terrible times, this spirit would ensure the continued viability of a Judaism that had removed the gulf between the actual conditions of life and the purified teachings of a religious tradition of universal import.

As mentioned earlier, there were a few groups within German Jewry of the mid-nineteenth century which wanted to put the Reformers' principles into immediate practice, boldly and consistently, even at the price of separating themselves from the overall community. The most important ideologist of this second kind of reform was Samuel Holdheim (1806–1860). Holdheim grew up in an extremely traditional home in Prussian Poland and achieved a youthful reputation as a talmudic prodigy.

Samuel Holdheim, leader of the extreme Reformers in Germany. (Courtesy of the Jewish Division, the New York Public Library, Astor, Lenox, and Tilden Foundations.)

After attending university he became the rabbi of various German communities. Radicalized by Geiger and others in the late 1830s, Holdheim published a series of pamphlets and books attacking the continued validity of talmudic law and the surviving legal functions of the rabbinate. After 1846 he served as rabbi of the Reform temple of Berlin, one of the principal centers of classical Reform in Europe.

Holdheim insisted that turning to the Talmud as a source of guidance for contemporary needs was irrelevant. The Talmud was only one stage in the development of Judaism. "The Talmud speaks with the ideology of its own time, and for that time it was right. I speak for the higher ideology of my own time, and for this age I am right."[21] The essence of tradition was not conservation but innovation, "the principle of eternal youth, the principle of continuity, constant development and growth out of the primitive germs which God himself placed in Scripture."[22] In some ways his position was utterly antithetical to Samson Raphael Hirsch's: Holdheim felt that projecting a symbolic and allegorical meaning into old rituals, as Hirsch did, was useless because "We have left behind us the symbolic age. A religious truth is significant for us not because we symbolize by it some ceremony, but because we grasp it intellectually and it becomes a very part of our nature."[23] To be sure, the "ceremonial law" (in which Holdheim included the dietary prohibitions, the ritual of circumcision, the sacrificial cult of the biblical Temple, and so on) had been valuable when Jewish social isolation served to preserve the idea of monotheism. But the Jews are now a religious community without political aims of its own; therefore, all rituals alluding to a specifically Jewish nationality are obsolete and should be immediately abolished. The permanent and universal essence of Judaism was that God the Creator is absolutely different from the world, that God possesses unity, personality, and holiness, and that the messianic age, toward which Jews should work, will be marked by universal justice and brotherly love, as the biblical prophets envisioned. Holdheim was impatient to see Judaism fully modernized into a religious rationalism even more extreme than eighteenth-century Enlightenment religion at its most daring. He was one of the most determined believers in irreversible historical progress engendered by the age of emancipation.

Three German Jewish Philosophers

The impact of German philosophy, evident indirectly on Samson Raphael Hirsch and Abraham Geiger, led three other Jewish thinkers of the mid-nineteenth century to construct systematic philosophies of Judaism. Two were Reform rabbis, one was a nonaffiliated layman. Solomon Formstecher (1808–1889) and Samuel Hirsch (1815–1889), the rabbis, early in their careers used metaphysical idealism to defend the rational truth of Judaism. Solomon Ludwig Steinheim (1789–1866), a practicing physician who composed poetry and wrote on a wide range of subjects including natural science, history, and religion, opposed the view that Judaism was primarily the religion of philosophical reason. The approaches of the three differed considerably, but as we shall see, their conception of the essence of Judaism was remarkably similar, conveying, in a more abstract form, the approach to Judaism's place in the history of religion dominating German Jewish thought in their day.

Solomon Formstecher's principal work was *The Religion of the Spirit (Die Religion des Geistes)*, written in 1841 when he was thirty-three. Formstecher's metaphysics was greatly indebted to the philosopher Schelling. According to Formstecher, ultimate reality is the divine world soul, a cosmic unity manifesting itself in nature and in *Geist*. (*Geist*, as mentioned earlier in connection with Krochmal, is a concept of German idealist philosophy referring to the realm of spirit, mind, consciousness.) Like the idealists and Krochmal, Formstecher conceives of nature as an organic hierarchy of events and forces that attains self-consciousness in *Geist*. As knowledge of nature, *Geist* takes the form of physics; as knowledge of the activity by which nature is understood, *Geist* takes the form of logic; as knowledge of the ideal to be realized by natural objects, *Geist* takes the form of aesthetics. *Geist* becomes aware of the realm of nature, therefore, through physics, logic and aesthetics. It achieves direct awareness of the uniquely human existence through ethical ideals. As the highest form of consciousness on earth, man can know the divine world soul in these various manifestations of *Geist*, but Formstecher warns that this knowledge is only symbolic and does not describe God's essence completely or with full objectivity: Despite his use of German philosophical idealism he insists that the divine world soul in itself remains a mystery beyond human attainment.

Based on his metaphysics, Formstecher distinguishes between two types of religion: "the religion of nature" and "the religion of *Geist*," each with a different concept of God. The religion of nature consists of the various pagan cults, all of which deify natural forces. Paganism culminates in a "physical monotheism": nature considered as a single divine being. Physical monotheism is a pantheistic depiction of the world and everything in it as a necessary emanation of the divine; thus paganism instructs man to return to his origin in God, that is, actually to *become* God. The religion of *Geist*, on the other hand, identifies God not only with nature but especially with the ethical ideal; it elevates man above nature and gives him the task of becoming *like* God through choosing and achieving the good.

According to Formstecher, Judaism was the first religion of *Geist*, but even in Judaism there has been an evolutionary process at work. The biblical prophets conceived of truth as a revelation entering from without. Gradually *Geist* became aware of itself as the bearer of truth. Therefore Judaism moved from prophetic inspiration to canonized Scriptures and eventually to the modern notion of a fully autonomous reason. In the early phases of its history, universal truth contained in Judaism was maintained by the protective shell of a national state; later, by a theocracy of religious law. However, now that the oppression and political inferiority of the Jews are ending, the universal mission of Judaism—the messianic ideal of the prophets—can emerge in its purity. To be sure, Islam and Christianity contain elements of the religion of *Geist*, but not to the extent that Judaism does. Christianity was forced to assimilate pagan ideas and pagan cultic practices, especially in its folk religion. Only when Christianity fully overcomes the paganism within it (Formstecher thought that Protestantism had taken an important step in this direction) would it converge with Judaism. Until then, Judaism must maintain its separate existence and continue to reform itself. Eventually a universal ethical religion of *Geist* would become the faith of all men.

Samuel Hirsch's *The Religious Philosophy of the Jews (Die Religionsphilosophie der Juden)*, published in 1842 when he was twenty-seven, draws on Hegel rather than Schelling. Samuel Hirsch follows Hegel's conception that man becomes aware of his freedom by seeing himself as a distinct self, over and against the world. But he departs from Hegel in one area crucial to Hirsch's defense of Judaism. According to Hegel, man's primary, abstract freedom leads eventually to actual, concrete freedom when he discovers that he is a finite being rooted in nature and yet destined for reason. For Hegel, this is the philosophical meaning of man's awareness of sin—sin being overcome only when this dialectically necessary contradiction is resolved by rational self-determination. For Hirsch, however, sin is a moral state, not an intellectual one. Sin is inherent in man's ability to choose between alternatives and is overcome only in ethical action. Therefore, the essential content of religion, according to Hirsch, is not the eventual self-realization of God, but the present actualizing of man's moral freedom. Received as a divine gift, freedom entails the continual task of subordinating natural sensuality to ethical duty.

Like Formstecher, Samuel Hirsch distinguishes between two types of religion. The first is "passive religion," in which man renounces his freedom and believes that he is dominated by his sensual nature—thus elevating nature to the status of an all-powerful divine force. Passive religion is found in all forms of paganism. Unlike Formstecher, Hirsch insists that paganism is not even partially valid, because in the course of history pagan consciousness comes ultimately to realize its own emptiness. Only in "active religion" does man rise to the level of self-chosen freedom, realizing that this is what God desires. Judaism possessed the insight of active reli-

Jewess of Algeria and servant, engraving from Delacroix (1833).

gion at its beginning, with Abraham. The miracles and prophecies of the Bible were historically necessary in order to uproot a residue of paganism from the Jewish people as a whole. (Hirsch argues for the reality of miracles because God's intervention in the natural order expresses the divine sovereignty over nature and God's will that man be free.) Eventually the need for most miracles ceased; the only permanent miracle in the postbiblical history of the Jews is the survival of the people itself.

Hirsch, therefore, rejects Hegel's view that Judaism was a partial truth that has been superseded by the religious consciousness of Protestant Christianity (that is, Protestant Christianity as absorbed and transformed into Hegel's philosophy). In Judaism there is no evolution of religious truth as such. Development consists in the ethical education of the Jews. The aim of this education is, first, that all Jews embody in their lives "intensive religiosity" by choosing virtue rather than sin; second, that the Jewish people bring mankind closer to the truth by acting as God's suffering servant, demonstrating through its survival the impotence of evil. In contrast, Christianity is the embodiment of "extensive religiosity," the mission of bringing true religious consciousness to the pagans. According to Hirsch, Jesus and the writers of the New Testament gospels were solidly rooted in Judaism; it was Paul who brought about a partial relapse of Christianity into paganism. This happened when Paul insisted that man is under the domination of sin until he receives redemption through the vicarious atonement of the incarnate son of God. Although Pauline Christianity was necessary historically, only when Christianity finally drops the idea of man's absolute depravity (original sin) and when it gives up the belief that a mediator is required between God and man, will Christianity finally become identical with pure active religion as found in Judaism. Even so, in the messianic age Judaism will retain its special identity through symbols and forms of worship that express its special historical mission.

Solomon Ludwig Steinheim's contribution to Jewish theology was *Revelation According to the Doctrine of the Synagogue (Die Offenbarung nach dem Lehrbegriffe der Synagogue*, Vol. 1, 1835; Vol. 2, 1856; Vol. 3, 1863; Vol. 4, 1865). As mentioned earlier, Steinheim, largely ignored in his day, stood out among Jewish religious writers of nineteenth-century Germany by insisting that Judaism should not be confused with philosophical speculation. Not only did he criticize Formstecher and Samuel Hirsch for over-reliance on Schelling and Hegel, but he repeatedly denounced Moses Mendelssohn for asserting that natural religion was the source of theoretical truth and that biblical revelation was a code of laws. Steinheim was not an advocate either of Orthodoxy or Reform; indeed, he was not personally observant at all, and his position cannot be classified according to the different ideological tendencies in German Jewry.

For Steinheim, the knowledge that man acquired through the self-revealing God of the Bible consisted not of laws but of beliefs whose truth was contrary to the natural assumptions of ancient thinkers ignorant of the content of revelation, as well as of modern thinkers who chose to reject biblical teaching. Steinheim had great respect for Kant's critical philosophy, especially Kant's view that theoretical reason could not know the thing-in-itself. (A discussion of Kant's position will be found in Chapter 16.) From this, Steinheim concluded that reason will never be able to construct on a priori grounds the concrete reality known to ordinary experience and to scientific observation. Just as sense perception and natural science provide man with an empirical knowledge that speculation cannot derive from pure thinking, revelation makes available suprarational insights that are validated by man's awareness that he is a free, morally responsible agent. The content of revelation cannot be obtained from reason, but it can be subsequently verified by reason.

More than any other Jewish philosopher of his time, Steinheim returns to the central Maimonidean principle that the crucial issue of religious philosophy is whether God is a freely creative being. For Steinheim here lies the difference between "natural religion" and "revealed religion." Natural religion (religion without recourse to revelation) is based on the assumption that everything has a cause and on the belief that "nothing can come from nothing" (*ex nihilo nihil fit*). Natural religion collapses because these two ideas are not compatible. Thus, natural religion is led to define God as First Cause. But if everything has a cause, then matter too has a cause; hence "something can come from nothing," and creation *is* possible. On the other hand, if "nothing can come from nothing," there is no need to explain the existence of material reality at all, and hence no need for God, even as First Cause. Steinheim insists that the only way out of this apparent paradox is the revealed biblical doctrine of *creatio ex nihilo*—the creation of the universe by the spontaneous will of a living God. Belief in a creative God qualifies a thoroughly deterministic concept of nature and makes room for the moral freedom of man. Only revealed religion provides a solid ground for the freedom to which man's intuitive ethical consciousness attests.

According to Steinheim, in ancient times the mission of the Jews was to refute natural religion and in modern times to avoid capitulating to the ever-changing fashions of philosophical rationalism. Like the other Jewish theologians, Steinheim viewed Christianity as a mixture of biblical truth and pagan error. But unlike Formstecher and Samuel Hirsch, he did not believe that Protestantism was eliminating the pagan elements in Christianity and that its teachings would soon coincide with those of Judaism.

These three thinkers illustrate an important reversal of emphasis that had taken place since the great age of Maimonidean philosophy in the Middle Ages. Maimonides and his disciples had seen as their main task the reconciliation of Judaism with Greek philosophy, mainly Aristotelianism. Although the medievals were quite aware that there were distinctive Jewish doctrines to be defended, one of their major concerns was to

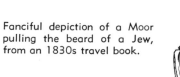
Fanciful depiction of a Moor pulling the beard of a Jew, from an 1830s travel book.

show Judaism's essential compatibility with a rational conception of the universe. Convinced that Judaism did not contradict science, the three nineteenth-century German Jewish philosophers and their contemporaries, including S. R. Hirsch and Geiger, placed at the center of their systems a radical opposition between pagan philosophy and the biblical doctrines of God's transcendence over nature and man's freedom to choose between good and evil. The intense moral seriousness and the idea of human responsibility in ethical monotheism could not have been derived from a paganism that deified various natural forces or nature as a whole and that tended to conceive of reality as a necessarily determined process. Idealist philosophy was useful to Jewish theology because its various systems subsumed nature under spirit. But even where nineteenth-century Jewish thinkers made use of the idealist metaphysics of Schelling and Hegel, men such as Formstecher and Samuel Hirsch relied ultimately on the ethical argument for the truth of religion. They were particularly appreciative of the Kantian approach, which viewed the "practical reason" that manifests itself in human moral choice as offering a firmer basis for religion than could be found in the old metaphysical arguments employed by the "theoretical reason."

The more immediate task of the Jewish theologians was to defend their religion against the position that it was superseded by Christianity—especially that Judaism stood for a narrow, particularistic legalism whereas Christianity was a religion of higher freedom and more comprehensive universalism. They replied, first, by citing the ethical imperatives of Judaism, and second, by insisting that Judaism had a theological content that was more rational than that of Christianity, in that it was less dogmatic. Stripped of accidental features conditioned by temporary historical circumstances, Judaism was the source and standard of pure ethical monotheism. To be sure, Christianity had a great task in history, but it was Judaism's special mission to remain faithful to what must become the religion of a fully rational humanity in the future.

Philosophical idealism also reinforced the Jewish theologians' conviction that the significance of Jewish history lay in the ideas of Judaism, and that the survival of the Jewish people was for the sake of these ideas. But after the mid-century point, philosophical idealism lost its primacy in the German intellectual milieu, and naturalistic and materialistic ideologies came to the fore. Even in Jewish religious thought, more attention was paid to the concrete aspect of Jewish identity and to the people as a concrete historical force. Evidence of this shift can be seen in the third of the important tendencies that emerged in Judaism during the height of the decade of reform, Positive-Historical Judaism.

The Positive-Historical School and the Historiography of Heinrich Graetz

After the Neo-Orthodox and Reform positions had crystallized at the two extremes of the ideological spectrum of German Jewry, a third viewpoint formed around Rabbi Zacharias Frankel (1801–1875). It will be recalled that Frankel, the rabbi of Dresden, withdrew from the second rabbinic conference (Frankfort, 1845), protesting the refusal of the gathering to insist that Hebrew was the essential language of Jewish prayer. In the course of the debate Frankel declared that he stood for "positive-historical Judaism." Although the Reform rabbis applauded the phrase, Positive-Historical Judaism came to apply to the non-Orthodox opponents of Reform in the Central European rabbinate. (In Germany later this position was also known as Liberal, in contrast to Reform; in America it became the ideological basis of Conservative Judaism.)

Slightly older than either Geiger or Hirsch, Frankel was more closely identified with the Jewry of Eastern Europe than with that of western Germany, where Geiger and Hirsch had been brought up. Born in Prague, he attended the University of Budapest and was the first rabbi in Bohemia with a secular education. Frankel became an important exemplar of *Wissenschaft des Judentums* through his historical investigation of talmudic law. He was not opposed to moderate ritual changes such as the elimination from the prayer service of long and recondite medieval liturgical poems or the use of a boy's choir. But in his shortlived journal of the mid-1840s Frankel sharply criticized the Reformers for bartering Judaism in exchange for emancipation with their too-hasty changes. In his view they showed insufficient respect for the countless sacrifices of earlier Jewish generations and for the loyalty of most Jews of the present day to the sacred traditions of the people. Appealing to "the spirit of historical Judaism," Frankel spoke for a segment of Jewry in which traditional piety and observance remained deeply rooted, unlike those acculturated Jews whose vanishing loyalty to Judaism so bothered the

Reformers. For the average Jew, custom and tradition meant more than pure theology. For Frankel the will of the people as a whole, as embodied in the mainstream of the Jewish heritage, was an indirect form of divine revelation, supplementing and carrying on the direct revelation of Sinai.

In 1854 Frankel became the head of the newly established Jewish Theological Seminary (*Jüdisch-Theologisches Seminar*) of Breslau, which soon became the most influential modern institute of rabbinic training in Europe. Although Geiger had originally conceived the idea of the seminary, won over the Breslau businessman who provided the funds, and therefore felt entitled to the presidency, Frankel opposed even his appointment to the faculty. The seminary was not to be identified with the Reformers—but neither was it to be Orthodox. Samson Raphael Hirsch insisted that Frankel define as the seminary's official position that God's revelation to Moses was inviolable and that the Jewish tradition had not undergone development in the course of history. But Frankel was committed to free historical inquiry; in his book on the Mishnah (1859) he did not allude to a supernatural origin of the rabbinic law. Challenged, he responded to Hirsch that he was far from denying the antiquity and worth of the rabbinic tradition, but research had not yet determined which aspects of the halakhah were Mosaic in origin. Hirsch pronounced Frankel and the seminary heretical. (In 1873 a modern Orthodox rabbinic academy was established in Berlin, completing the split.) Frankel's middle-of-the-road position increasingly prevailed in the Jewish communities of Germany through the growing number of Breslau seminary graduates serving as rabbis and recognized as outstanding scholars. By the end of the nineteenth century, the Reform and Neo-Orthodox were small minorities within German Jewry.

The year the Breslau seminary opened, Frankel appointed to the faculty Heinrich Graetz (1817–1891), a young scholar who had just published the first volume of the most influential synthesis of Jewish history written in the nineteenth century. Graetz was born in a village in the eastern (formerly Polish) part of Prussia, the son of a poor butcher. As a youth he studied in a yeshivah under a rabbi completely opposed to modern secular learning, but on his own Graetz mastered Latin and French and avidly read history and modern literature. A crisis of religious faith was resolved in 1836 by Hirsch's *Nineteen Letters on Judaism*. Graetz wrote Hirsch, then rabbi in Moravia, to express his admiration; Hirsch invited Graetz to live with him as his student and assistant. In 1840 Graetz briefly returned home, took a position as a tutor in a nearby town, and in 1842 was admitted to the University of Breslau. In 1845 he received his doctorate for a study of Gnosticism and Judaism. Failing through lack of oratorical skill to find a rabbinic position, for several years Graetz taught in various Jewish schools and published scholarly

Heinrich Graetz, historian and spokesman for Positive-Historical Judaism.

essays on Jewish history, until Frankel appointed him to the faculty of
the Breslau seminary.

In the middle 1840s Graetz had come to side openly with Frankel's
position, rejecting both the Reformers and his former mentor, Hirsch.
Geiger's approach, he wrote, was "empty deism"; Geiger lacked respect
for traditional Jewish practices and for the Talmud. Holdheim he disliked even more: Later he wrote of him, "Since Paul of Tarsus, Judaism
has not known such an enemy in its midst."[24] But Graetz was committed
to *Wissenschaft des Judentums* as the modern way of understanding
Judaism. Unlike Hirsch, for Graetz Judaism was not simply a matter of
literal obedience to God's word. Nor was he willing to accept the
supreme authority of the *Shulhan Arukh* as the binding and unchangeable
code of Jewish law.

Graetz's conception of the meaning of Judaism was already laid out
in an essay, "The Construction of Jewish History," written in 1846 when
he was 29. His aim was to show that the essence of Judaism was not only
the "idea" in its theoretical form, but also those aspects of Jewish existence
that the Reform party had considered as only temporary means for the
genesis and protection of the idea. In effect Graetz synthesizes the two
versions of the Hegelian idea of inner unfolding used by Neo-Orthodoxy
and by *Wissenschaft*. Like Hirsch, Graetz believed that all aspects of
Judaism should be understood "out of the inner nature of the substance"
—as a consistent unfolding of a unique system. Like Geiger, Graetz felt
that this was not merely a logical process, but a temporal, historical one
that emerged as Judaism coped with challenges posed by the different
conditions it encountered in the course of time. The result is what he
calls "a conceptual construction of Jewish history," which endeavors
to show how the laws and doctrines of Judaism, immanent in the original

concept, gradually manifest themselves in history, like a tree emerging from the seed.

Graetz begins by asserting that all attempts made by philosophers to reduce Judaism to a single abstract definition have failed because "the totality of Judaism is discernible only in its history."[25] The root of Judaism is a principle even more fundamental than monotheism: that God is "extramundane" and is not to be identified with nature in any way. Thus Judaism first appeared in total opposition to paganism. Paganism presupposed that nature is an omnipotent and immanent system of forces; pagan gods, even in their most highly developed forms, remain idealized nature, subject to the irresistible power of necessity and fate. Agreeing with Solomon Ludwig Steinheim (Graetz was one of the few nineteenth-century Jewish thinkers to appreciate him), he argues that only the biblical conception of a spiritual God who brings nature into being from nothingness by a free creative act constitutes the alternative to paganism that provides a firm basis for ethical freedom and the moral sanctification of human life. Up to this point Graetz has presented a widely accepted conception of the uniqueness of ancient Judaism, but he then proceeds to develop his own principle that Jewish history constitutes a test of the genuineness and truth of the root idea of Judaism. Judaism is not just an abstraction: "It must work itself out of the monotonous, dormant state of the ideal into the changing, turbulent world of reality," disproving paganism and opposing its harmful moral effects not just academically but in "the active world of experience."[26]

In each of the three major periods into which Graetz divides Jewish history, a different dimension of Judaism achieves prominence in confrontation with its antithesis. The first cycle begins with the entrance of the Israelite tribes into Canaan and ends with the destruction of the first Temple in 587 BCE. This phase is dominated by the political factor, Judaism then being a constitution for a society. Biblical Judaism is concerned with the earthly happiness of the people; it is not a religion for the individual but for the community. Even though biblical history is dominated by political concerns, however, in the course of the struggle against paganism a purely religious aspect breaks through and becomes more developed and purified. The second cycle of the history of the Jewish people in its homeland begins after the Babylonian exile and lasts until the destruction of the Temple in 70 CE. Now the religious element eclipses the social-political, with the result that at the end of the period "Judaism ceased to be the constitution for a state and became a religion in the usual sense of the word."[27] The crucial factor in the second period was the struggle against Greek paganism culminating in the emergence of the Pharisees, who introduced into Judaism the dogmas of resurrection and supernatural blessedness in the World to Come. Even though a discontinuity seems to exist between the first and second cycles, biblical and postbiblical Judaism remained "an indivisible unity" each containing both political and religious aspects. Thus, when the actual state disappeared, the idea of a Jewish commonwealth retained its vitality as the messianic goal and provided the exiled people with the consoling hope of political-religious rebirth.

The third cycle, "the diaspora period," was dominated, according to Graetz, by Judaism's search to attain intellectual self-perception and to transform "the facts of Judaism into rational truths."[28] Diaspora existence made this possible because Judaism was to be found wherever a new truth surfaced or a new form was devised to present an old truth. Hence Judaism "could discover through comparison and contrast the full depths of its content and the loftiness of its own tendency."[29] At the same time there had to be a force within Judaism that prevented total fragmentation and destructive outside influence. This was the talmudic system, the Jews' portable homeland, a system of social barriers preventing too intimate a union with a world that still retained strong elements of paganism. Talmudic law, "a logical consequence from the premise of Judaism's basic idea," also had the positive function of strengthening the distinctive style of Jewish life by incorporating neutral acts and practices compatible with the spirit of Judaism. Safeguarded in this way during the diaspora period, Judaism came increasingly to understand itself. First, the philosophical aggadah, which had absorbed much from Platonism, speculated freely on the allegorical and later the mystical meanings of biblical precepts and laws. Then, the medieval Jewish philosophers penetrated more deeply into the nature of Judaism, seeking to discover the metaphysical principles by which Judaism could justify itself rationally. Finally, since Mendelssohn, Judaism has extended its self-awareness to the inner significance of Jewish behavior and practice. Thanks to modern philosophy in general

> men now discover eternal truths not only in the ideas of the spirit but also in the far higher realm of the actions of the spirit, not only in the formalism of logic, in the abstractions of metaphysics and the externalism of nature, but especially in the concrete forms of art, science, religion, in the composite of all these factors, in the formation of the state, and particularly in the developments of history. Thus Judaism must merely appropriate this point of view, and its philosophical justification will be a simple matter.[30]

Graetz concludes his essay: "It seems that the task of Judaism's God-idea is to found a religious state which is conscious of its activity, purpose, and connection with the world."[31] Although he looked forward as eagerly

---

(Overleaf) Composite photograph, made in the 1870s, showing leaders of the Reform movement and other illustrious Jews. (Courtesy of the Jewish Division, the New York Public Library, Astor, Lenox, and Tilden Foundations.)

BERÜHMTE

Eigenthum Js. Wiesen - Kettwig (Preussen)

ISRAEL

as any of his German Jewish contemporaries to the complete emancipation of the Jews, he was not willing to give up the concrete, particular, messianic goal of Jewish history.

The themes of Graetz's youthful essay recur in his eleven-volume *History of the Jews* (*Die Geschichte der Juden*), published between 1853 and 1876, a work whose impact was the result of his erudition, the vivacity of his literary style, and his pride in Judaism. A vast panorama of the destiny of the people unfolds before the reader, which Graetz finds supremely instructive. Not only in the pre-Christian era, but even in the diaspora period did the Jewish people continue to manifest youthful vigor, remaining true to itself despite numerous transformations. Its external history in the diaspora was a "*Leidensgeschichte*, a history of suffering to a degree and over a length of time such as no other people has experienced." Its internal history in the diaspora was a "*Literaturgeschichte*, a literary history of religious knowledge, which yet remains open to all the currents of science, absorbing and assimilating them. Inquiring and wandering, thinking and enduring, studying and suffering—these fill the long stretch of this era."[32] Yet never did the Jews become a church or a religious association in the usual sense. "Though scattered over the civilized portions of the earth and attached to the lands of their hosts, the members of the Jewish race did not cease to feel themselves a single people in their religious conviction, historical memory, customs, and hopes."[33] The Jews were a living folk (*ein lebendiger Volksstamm*), acting out, under providential guidance, their role as the "messianic people." They were a messianic people because they showed themselves willing to sacrifice everything, even life itself, for the sake of their mission as the exponents of a special religious and moral conception. The survival and recovery of the Jewish people, despite repeated destructions and the agony of martyrdom, constituted a perpetual miracle.

Whereas Geiger had viewed the "national form" as a means only for the gestation of the idea of Judaism, for Graetz the spiritual nationhood of the Jews was not extraneous, but an intrinsic value and essential constituent of Judaism. World history needed not only the idea of Judaism, but the presence of the physically powerless but spiritually unconquerable Jewish nation. The nub of Graetz's disagreement with the Reformers was that they wanted, he believed, to transform Judaism into a religion in the usual sense. But Judaism was not just theory alone; it was theory transformed into practice. Judaism had universal significance because it was a national religion. Graetz was unwilling, therefore, to settle for a definition of Judaism that would sunder the unity of the people and diminish its distinctiveness. However, he was equally committed to emancipation. Although Graetz felt personal sympathy for some of the more explicitly nationalistic conceptions of the Jewish future advanced during the later years of his life (Moses Hess and the Hibbat Zion, which will be discussed in Chapter 15), he shied away from a Jewish political nationalism. In part this was the result of his having become embroiled in a bitter controversy with the German historian Heinrich von Treitschke, a supporter of extreme German nationalism and of anti-Semitism, who in 1879–1880 attacked Graetz's *History of the Jews* as evidence that the Jews could never be integrated into the German nation. But Graetz's last work indicated also a growing concern for the indifference to the Jewish religion among the Jewish upper classes in Western Europe. Both factors led Graetz to reiterate in his essays of the 1880s the same justification for Judaism's right and duty to survive as had the Reformers. To be sure, he admits that Judaism had an elaborate ritual, which "unfortunately, owing to the tragic course of history, developed into a fungoid growth which overlays the ideals," but stripped of these excesses, the religious laws of Judaism enabled the people to resist paganism and maintain a chaste, moderate, and disciplined way of life. By now "the outward appearance of Judaism has assumed a more attractive form, and the uncultivated Polish [Jewish] customs have been nearly banished from the public ceremonial."[34] The Jewish mission is far from over. The ethical values of Judaism—sanctity of life, justice for the poor, sexual self-restraint—were especially valuable in an age of rampant materialism, social decadence, and class tension. Above all, the Jewish people must survive because of its role as the defenders of true monotheism; Judaism was "the sole stronghold of free thought in the religious sphere" and the chief opponent of idolatry in its ancient and modern guises. In his final writings, Graetz showed that he remained deeply rooted in the philosophical idealism that shaped Jewish religious thought in Germany throughout the nineteenth century.

The Development of Modern Jewish Thought Before 1880: A Summary of the Main Phases and Tendencies

At the beginning of the seventeenth century the overwhelming majority of Jews lived according to an all-encompassing Jewish tradition based on Torah, halakhah, and custom. (The most dynamic aspect of Jewish religious culture was the Kabbalah, so that the socio-religious upheavals within Jewry, such as those of Shabbatai Zevi in the 1660s and Hasidism a century later, used many mystical doctrines and concepts in their ideologies.) Rabbinic learning retained its vitality; in early seventeenth-century Poland and later in late eighteenth and nineteenth-century Lithuania, the yeshivot, headed by scholars famed for their mastery of talmudic learning and only indirectly aware of modern thought, attracted large numbers of students and reinforced a high level of traditional Jewish piety and intellectualism.

New issues raised in advanced European science and philosophy at first profoundly affected only a small number of Jews in seventeenth-century Holland, where it tended to dissolve their bonds to Judaism. Baruch Spinoza, a great philosopher in his own right, undermined the medieval synthesis of biblical revelation and rational metaphysics, denied that religion had any claim to theoretical truth, and acknowledged its value merely as moral inspiration for the masses. In the eighteenth century, however, new formulations were forthcoming, which reconciled religious belief with Newtonian physics and natural reason. The Enlightenment finally took hold of certain segments of German Jewry in the second half of the eighteenth century. Moses Mendelssohn was the first to formulate a positive defense of Judaism out of an awareness of the challenges of contemporary European thought. Like many Jewish writers after him, Mendelssohn was convinced that universal reason was more in harmony with Judaism than with the dogmas of Christianity such as the Incarnation, the Trinity, and original sin. The legal tradition of Judaism was explained as a divine revelation to preserve Jewry as a holy people.

The Mendelssohnian approach, as it was developed by enlightened Jews in Central and Eastern Europe, proved to contain a liberal side and a conservative side. On the one hand, Mendelssohn called for major cultural changes to bring Jewish life up to contemporary European standards; on the other hand, he expected a strict adherence to the sacred ceremonial practices of Judaism. Among East European Jewish writers and educators the reforming aspect of the Mendelssohnian Haskalah spurred the development of Hebrew literature and social criticism through the first three quarters of the nineteenth century. In Germany it stimulated initial efforts to modernize the style and content of Jewish worship in the 1810s. The beginnings of Jewish religious Reform, in turn, produced a counterreaction in Samson Raphael Hirsch's Neo-Orthodoxy. Following the conservative side of the Mendelssohnian legacy, Hirsch insisted that a modern European education and style of life, valuable as they were, should not sway Jews from the faith that God had revealed a body of commandments that could raise them to a level of exemplary holiness and with which they had no right to tamper for the sake of convenience.

Meanwhile, however, the general intellectual climate had shifted, making the Enlightenment appear old-fashioned and inadequate. Hirsch had also been influenced by the new scale of values inculcated by the Romantic movement, which had quite different effects on other German Jews. Romanticism furthered the methodical study of the Jewish past (*Wissen-*

Sanctuary of the Central Synagogue, New York, built in 1872 and characteristic of the Moorish style popular in nineteenth-century synagogue architecture in the West. (Courtesy of the Synagogue Art and Architectural Library of the Union of American Hebrew Congregations.)

schaft des Judentums). Historical scholarship soon became the most challenging academic discipline for religion because it undermined the conception of a fixed and unchanging religious system. History was also crucial for post-Enlightenment idealist philosophy, in which the eighteenth-century concept of a static reason gave way to a notion of a dynamic, productive reason unfolding in the course of time toward the full self-consciousness of the world spirit. Intellectual defense of Judaism was now forced to contend with this world-historical perspective. The impact of early nineteenth-century thinking was felt in quite different ways by the maskilim Krochmal and Luzzatto. Krochmal emphasized that the Absolute Spirit of idealist philosophy was the philosophical meaning of the God of Judaism. Luzzatto, who rejected the attempt to show that Judaism was identical with reason, insisted on a radical contrast between the moral character of Jewish faith and the rationalistic, Hellenic philosophical stream in Western civilization. Actually, a synthesis of Krochmal's and Luzzatto's approaches was used by many German Jewish theologians in the nineteenth century: The essence of Judaism was philosophically rational and universally valid precisely because it was grounded to the greatest possible extent on the principle of man's freedom and on his ethical aspirations. Even when they were closest to the German idealists, however, none of the Jewish theologians accepted the principle that the truth was to be found only at the end of the entire historical process. They all believed that the prophetic revelation in the Bible grasped the transcendence of God and of the moral law at the beginning of Jewish history and that later Jewish thinkers clarified and provided a more systematic understanding of the essence of the tradition.

As influential as was the general intellectual setting, the political context of nineteenth-century Jewish thought was also of decisive importance. Judaism was being explained in terms of modern philosophy and theology in an era when an important segment of the Jewish people was adjusting to the new demands and opportunities of the nation-state. More than any other Western Jewry, German Jewry was forced to respond to a long-drawn-out and irregular process of political emancipation and social integration. Although constituting only a small per cent of the Jews in the world, it was the largest Jewish community yet affected by modernization. Whereas French, English, and Dutch Jewries had been re-established after a long hiatus when Jews had not lived there, German Jewry lived in a land where medieval anti-Jewish stereotypes and prejudices were still part of the living culture and where modern nationalists tended to affirm that Jews were aliens, even though they had lived in Germany since ancient times. Among a certain stratum of German Jews acculturation, but not the disappearance of frustrating legal and social barriers, proceeded quite rapidly. University-educated German Jews, finding it impossible to acquire academic positions, entered the German rabbinate during the 1830s and 1840s imbued with modern modes of thought. Sensitive to the abandonment of traditional Jewish observance among their most acculturated congregants, eager to defend Judaism's place in German religious life, they inevitably disagreed over what should be done to clarify the nature of Jewish identity.

Three crucial issues divided the German Jewish religious leadership. First, to what extent did Judaism itself need modernization? While Samson Raphael Hirsch's call for a return to Orthodox observance had won some support, it did not answer the needs and wishes of many German Jews. The Reform party sought to save the most acculturated segment of German Jewry for Judaism—they were especially worried about losing the young generation—by eliminating what they felt were outdated ritual laws and unnecessary expressions of Jewish nationhood. According to the Reformers, while the protective shell of halakhah had preserved Judaism in medieval times, the kernel of the Jewish faith, if clearly understood, would suffice to ensure Jewish survival. However, by the 1850s it was clear that the majority of German Jews who remained loyal to Judaism rejected drastic reforms, although some modifications of Jewish worship were accepted in the direction of greater decorum, intelligibility, and external beauty.

Second, the three polarized tendencies, institutionalized as Neo-Orthodoxy, Reform, and Positive-Historical Judaism, disagreed on revelation. For the Neo-Orthodox, Torah was a timeless, immutable, changeless pattern for the ideal human life. Reform and Positive-Historical rabbis adhered to a conception of revelation that related Torah at least in some way to the historical process. The Reformers tended to interpret Judaism as a progressive revelation rooted in biblical prophecy but attaining a fully adequate presentation only in the modern definition of the essence of that revelation. For the Positive-Historical stream, revelation came directly from God at Sinai and indirectly from that part of the rabbinic tradition eventually absorbed into the religious life of the Jewish people. A third area of disagreement was over the nature of Jewish peoplehood. Both the Neo-Orthodox and the Reformers presented Judaism as a religious confession only. For the Orthodox, a Jewish state would be established only in the messianic age by direct supernatural intervention. Classical Reform reinterpreted the diaspora, not as an exile, but as a providential opportunity to teach ethical monotheism to mankind. For the Positive-Historical group, however, adjustment to emancipation must not be allowed to disrupt the spiritual unity of the Jewish nation or destroy the religious primacy of Jewish peoplehood.

Despite their disagreements, the leaders of all three forms of Judaism in Germany felt that a rejuvenation of the Jewish religion was about to take place. The people of Israel had a unique mission in history, pointing to the messianic age. In their writings, Jewish religious thinkers were optimistic about the future—the future of Judaism and the future of humanity. To be sure, there were dangers: Jew-hatred still existed, and many Jews did not understand the significance of their own faith. But conditions in Europe were improving; emancipation was an irreversible process; the Jews and their religion were gradually being accepted by enlightened Europeans. As we shall see in the next chapter, events in the 1870s and 1880s were to shake that optimistic faith in inevitable progress and in the forthcoming satisfactory integration of Jews and Judaism in modern civilization.

CHART 6. MODERN PERIOD (1880–PRESENT)

General History	The Jews in Western and Central Europe and America	The Jews in Eastern Europe	Zionism, Middle East
1881. Assassination of Tsar Alexander II.	1879–1881. Spread of new anti-Semitic movement in Germany.	1881–1882. Wave of pogroms in Russia.	1881. Beginnings of the first aliyah; Biluist students from Russia arrive in Palestine.
1882. The British occupy Egypt.	1881. Beginning of mass East European Jewish migration to the United States.	1882. May Laws restricting Jewish residence rights.	1882. Publication of Pinsker's *Autoemancipation.*
1880–1914. Height of Western imperialism in Africa, the Pacific, China.		1884. Kattowicz Conference of the Lovers of Zion.	1880s–1890s. Establishment of new Jewish farming villages in Palestine: Rishon le-Zion (1882), Gederah (1884), Rehovot and Haderah (1890), and others.
	1886. Publication of Drumont's anti-Semitic *La france Juive.*	1887. Restrictive quotas on Jewish enrollment in general Russian schools and universities.	
		1891. Expulsion of Jews from Moscow. Baron de Hirsch's plan to settle thousands of Russian Jews in Argentina.	1889. First essays of Ahad Ha-Am.
	1893. Anti-Semitic parties gain 250,000 votes in German election.		
	1894–1899. The Dreyfus Affair in France.		
	1895. Karl Lueger, using anti-Semitic slogans, elected mayor of Vienna.		1896. Publication of Herzl's *Judenstaat.*
1898. Spanish-American War.		1897. October. Founding of the Jewish Labor Bund at Vilna.	1897. August. First Zionist Congress at Basle.
1899–1902. Boer War.	1899. H. S. Chamberlain's anti-Semitic treatise *Foundations of the Nineteenth Century.*		
1900			
1904. Russo-Japanese War.	1902. Jewish Theological Seminary of America in New York reorganized with Solomon Schechter as president.	1903. April. The Kishinev pogrom.	1903. Sixth Zionist Congress; the Uganda controversy.
1905. Revolution in Russia; Tsar Nicholas II forced to grant a parliament.		1905. *The Protocols of the Elders of Zion* appears in print.	

General History	The Jews in Western and Central Europe and America	The Jews in Eastern Europe	Zionism, Middle East
			1904–1914. Second aliyah to the land of Israel.
	1906. Founding of the American Jewish Committee.	1905–1907. Wave of pogroms in Russia involving the Black Hundreds.	
1908. Young Turk revolution in the Ottoman empire.	1906–1907. Peak years of Jewish immigration to the United States.		1909. City of Tel Aviv founded.
1911. Libya under Italian rule; Tunisia under French control.	1913. Establishment of the Anti-Defamation League of the B'nai B'rith.	1911–1913. Beiliss blood libel case.	1910. Establishment of Deganyah, the first kibbutz.
1912. Morocco divided between French and Spanish.			
1914. August. Outbreak of World War I.			
1917. March. Russian revolution overthrows Nicholas II.		1917. March 16. Emancipation of the Jews of Russia.	1917. British army occupies Palestine.
1917. April. United States enters World War I.			1917. Nov. 2. Balfour Declaration.
1917. November. Communist revolution in Russia.			
1918. March. Communist regime signs Brest-Litovsk treaty with Germany.		1918. Establishment of the *Yevseksiia* (Jewish Sections of the Communist Party). (Abolished in 1930.)	
1918. Nov. 11. End of World War I.		1918–1920. Wave of 2000 pogroms in the Ukraine during the Civil War. Jewish communal institutions abolished in Russia.	
1919. Peace treaties of Versailles.	1919. *Comité des Délégations Juives* at the Versailles peace conference.		
1918–1920. Civil War in Russia.	1919. Publication of H. Cohen's *Religion of Reason Out of the Sources of Judaism.*	1920s. Third aliyah.	

Chart 6. (con't)

General History	The Jews in Western and Central Europe and America	The Jews in Eastern Europe	Zionism, Middle East
1922–1923. Enormous inflation in Germany. 1924. Death of Lenin.	1921. Publication of Rosenzweig's *Star of Redemption.* 1923. Publication of Buber's *I and Thou.* 1921, 1924. Restrictive immigration legislation in the United States.		1921. Arab riots. 1922. League of Nations gives final approval to the British mandate in Palestine and to the Jewish National Home.
1925			1925. Opening of the Hebrew University in Jerusalem.
1928. First Five Year Plan in U.S.S.R. 1929. Oct. New York stock market crash; beginning of world economic crisis. 1933. Jan. 30. Nazi party comes to power in Germany. 1934–1938. Stalin uses show trials, executions, slave labor camps in a massive campaign of purges in the U.S.S.R. 1936–1939. Spanish Civil War, leading, with German and Italian aid, to Franco dictatorship. 1938. Sept. Munich crisis; western capitulation to Hitler's demands on Czechoslovakia. 1939. Sept. 1. German invasion of Poland begins World War II.	1933. April. New civil service law begins the elimination of Jews in Germany from most professions. 1935. Sept. Nuremberg Laws establish a racial definition of German citizenship, reduce Jews to status of German subjects. 1938. Nov. 9–10. *Kristallnacht,* Nazi destruction of synagogues and attacks on Jews in Germany. 1939. Organization of the United Jewish Appeal in the United States.	1928. Birobidjan project to settle Soviet Jews in an area of eastern Siberia. 1932. Height of the Yiddish school system in U.S.S.R. Late 1930s. Many Jewish intellectuals and Jewish members of the Communist old guard liquidated during the Stalinist repressions. 1937. Anti-Jewish discriminatory measures introduced in Polish universities. 1937–1939. Anti-Jewish legislation and other anti-Semitic measures by pro-Nazi governments in Rumania and Hungary.	1929. Arab riots in Jerusalem and some other cities of Palestine. 1930. British impose restrictions on Jewish immigration to Palestine. 1933. Growth in German-Jewish aliyah. 1935. Separate congress of Zionist Revisionists (Jabotinsky's party) held in Vienna. 1936. Arab strike in Palestine, followed by terrorist attacks on the yishuv. 1937. Peel Commission recommends partition of Palestine between Jews and Arabs.

General History	The Jews in Western and Central Europe and America	The Jews in Eastern Europe	Zionism, Middle East
			1939. McDonald White Paper strictly curtails Jewish immigration to Palestine.
1941. June 22. German invasion of the U.S.S.R.	1940. Nazis set up Jewish "ghettos" in Eastern European cities.		
	1941–1942. German *Einsatzgruppen* murder 1–2 million Jews in occupied U.S.S.R.		1941. Riots and attacks on Jews in Iraq.
1941. Dec. 7. Japanese attack on Pearl Harbor brings U.S. into World War II.			
	1942. Jan. 20. Wansee Conference in Berlin to arrange for transport of Jews from Nazi satellite countries to death camps.		1941. Formation of the Palmah, permanently mobilized striking force of the Haganah, the underground military organization of the yishuv.
1942. Oct.–Nov. Battle of El Alamein; beginning of German retreat in North Africa.	1942–1944. The six extermination camps— Chelmno, Auschwitz, Belzec, Sobibor, Majdanek, Treblinka—in full operation for the gassing of Jews and other "undesirables" in the Nazi Reich.		
1943. Jan. Battle of Stalingrad; beginning of German retreat in U.S.S.R.	1943. April–May. Warsaw ghetto uprising.		
	1943. Oct. Danish resistance smuggles Jews of Denmark to Sweden.		
1944. June 6. Normandy invasion.	1944. Nov. Gassing of Jews stopped at the last functioning extermination camp, Auschwitz.		1944. Jewish Brigade Group organized in the British army, fought in Italy.
1945. May 9. End of World War II in Europe.			1945–1947. Jewish-British tensions in Palestine; British efforts to stop illegal immigration and repress the Haganah and the Jewish terrorist groups.
1945. Aug. 6, 9. Atomic bombs dropped on Japan.	1947 Population of Jews in Displaced Persons camps in Germany, Austria, Italy swells to c. 220,000. (By 1950 most had been resettled.)	1946. Kielce pogrom in Poland.	
1945. Sept. 2. End of World War II in the Pacific.		1948–1952. "Black Years" of Soviet Jewry; suppression of Jewish culture and leadership.	
1945–1948. Communist regimes established in East European countries.			
			1947. Nov. 29. General Assembly of the United Nations votes in favor of the partition of Palestine.

Chart 6. (con't)

General History	The Jews in Western and Central Europe and America	The Jews in Eastern Europe	Zionism, Middle East
			1948. May 14. British evacuate Palestine and Arab armies invade; Declaration of Independence of the State of Israel.
			1949. Jan. Ceasefire brings an end to Arab-Jewish fighting (the Israel War of Independence).
			1949. Beginning of mass migration of Jews from Displaced Persons camps in Europe and from Arab and other countries to Israel.
1950			
1950-1953. Korean War.	1953. West Germany signs reparations agreement with Israel.	1952. Slansky show trial in Prague, marked by anti-Zionist and anti-Semitic propaganda. Secret execution of eminent Yiddish writers in the U.S.S.R.	
1953. Mar. 5. Death of Stalin.			
1954-1962. French-Algerian War.	1954-1968. French communities augmented by immigration of Jews from North Africa, especially Algeria.		
1956. Complete independence of Morocco and Tunisia; Suez Canal crisis; Soviet military occupation of Hungary to put down uprising.	1954. Tercentenary of the Jews in the United States.	1953. Arrest of prominent Soviet Jewish physicians, accused of planning murder of government officials (the "Doctors' Plot").	1956. Oct.-Nov. Sinai campaign.
1957. First unmanned space satellite, by U.S.S.R.			
1958. Charles DeGaulle takes power in France.			1961. Eichmann trial.

General History	The Jews in Western and Central Europe and America	The Jews in Eastern Europe	Zionism, Middle East
1963. Nov. 22. Assassination of President John F. Kennedy. 1964–1968. Height of the Vietnam War. 1965. New U.S. immigration law abolishes quotas of national origin.	1965. Formal diplomatic relations established between West Germany and Israel.		1966. S. Y. Agnon and Nelly Sachs awarded the Nobel Prize for literature.
1968. Soviet military intervention in Czechoslovakia. 1969. American astronauts walk on the moon. 1970. Death of Gamal Abdel Nasser, president of Egypt. 1973. Oct. Beginning of Arab oil embargo and quadrupling of oil prices. 1974. Aug. Resignation of President Richard Nixon.	1972. Merger of United Jewish Appeal and Federation of Jewish Philanthropies in the United States; first woman rabbi (Reform) ordained in the United States.	1968. After Six-Day War, intense anti-Zionist campaigns in U.S.S.R. and Poland. Anti-Semitism in Poland results in emigration of most remaining Polish Jews. 1970s. Upsurge of clandestine Jewish activity in the U.S.S.R. and of Russian Jewish emigration to Israel and the West.	1967. June. Six-Day War. 1969–1970. Egypt launches a war of attrition along the Suez Canal. 1973. Oct. Yom Kippur War. 1973. Dec. Death of David Ben Gurion. 1977. Israel Labor Party ousted from office; Menahem Begin becomes Prime Minister of Israel. 1977. Nov. President Anwar Sadat of Egypt visits Israel.
	1978. Isaac Bashevis Singer awarded Nobel Prize for literature.		1978. Sept. Meetings between Begin, Sadat, and President Carter of the United States at Camp David to plan for Israel–Egypt peace settlement.

Chart 6. (con't)

General History	The Jews in Western and Central Europe and America	The Jews in Eastern Europe	Zionism, Middle East
1979. Jan.–Feb. Chinese leader Deng Xiaoping visits United States, indicative of a major reversal of Communist Chinese policies. Revolution in Iran and overthrow of the Shah.			1978. Dec. Death of Golda Meir. 1979. March. Signing of Israel–Egypt peace agreement.

CHAPTER 14

The Onslaught of Modernity: Jewish History from 1880 to the Present

Up to the last quarter of the nineteenth century the majority of Jews were still living in premodern conditions. Since then, the whole complex process of modernization, the ultimate end of which is not yet in sight, has decisively transformed the old Jewish moorings—indeed the economic, social, and political structures of all countries on the globe. New technologies, new forms of industrial organization, new modes of transport, communication, agriculture, and warfare, the growth of urbanization, the spread of scientific knowledge and secular education, have left no aspect of human existence untouched. Revolutionary upheavals, world wars, the remaking of the world map, have called for vast adjustments on the part of each new generation: novel psychological and social configurations unprecedented in their extent and tempo.

Modernization affected Jews on several levels and in antithetical ways. Old Jewries have been virtually destroyed by migration, physical extermination, and government repression. Few Jews in the 1970s resided where their ancestors did in the 1870s. Traditional Jewish occupational roles and communal institutions have disintegrated and new ones have opened up. Jewish integration into general society has led to far greater assimilation than ever before, but unanticipated opportunities for Jewish renewal have surfaced—opportunities for preserving Jewish social cohesion and maintaining a distinct Jewish self-awareness.

Finally, even though Jews have become far more like their neighbors

Jewish pioneers of the 1880s in Palestine, the Biluim, eating dinner in the fields. (Courtesy of the Zionist Archives, New York.)

in dress, language, and attitudes during the past century, traditional anti-Jewish stereotypes, also modernized, have kept the Jew an object of dislike among the confused and uprooted. The great issue of recent Jewish history has therefore been Jewish survival in the face of the inescapable pressures of ever-changing circumstances and of widespread fear and hatred.

1880–1914: Mass Politics and the Crisis of Liberalism

Modern Anti-Semitism

Prior to 1880, the enlightened and the liberal believed that anti-Jewish feeling would gradually disappear under the impact of rational and scientific thought. Instead there occurred in the last decades of the century a large-scale resurgence of open hostility to the Jews. Symptomatic of the new respectability of Judeophobia was the invention of the term *anti-Semitism* to indicate that it was not religious intolerance that motivated one's dislike of Jews but alleged Jewish economic and cultural "preponderance" and certain supposedly inherent and repugnant characteristics of the Jewish people. Although earlier persecution of Marranos had had racist overtones, modern anti-Semitism went much further in secularizing Jew-hatred and in making physical descent rather than religion the primary grounds for discrimination. Nineteenth and twentieth-century anti-Semitism differed from most older forms of anti-Jewish feeling in that it was a postemancipation backlash against Jewish success upon entering the mainstream of European society, and in that the acculturated rather than the traditional Jew was the main focus of fear.

The term *anti-Semitism* was probably coined in the late 1870s by Wilhelm Marr, a German journalist who achieved notoriety for a widely read pamphlet, "The Victory of Judaism over Germandom, Considered from a Non-Religious Point of View." Marr insisted that Jews have "corrupted all standards, have banned all idealism from society, dominate commerce, push themselves ever more into state services, rule the theater, form a social and political phalanx. . . ."[1] He depicts contemporary German history as a fateful struggle between Semitic aliens (the Jews) and native Teutonic stock, a struggle that the Jews were winning, with disastrous consequences for civilization. No compromise is desirable or even possible.

The new anti-Semitism first appeared in Central Europe after a major stock market collapse in 1873, followed by persistent economic difficulties and cultural malaise. In these circumstances political liberalism, identified with laissez-faire capitalism, was put on the defensive. Liberalism, with its ideal of equality before the law and minimum government interference in the private lives of citizens, had swept away old privileges and opened the economy to competitive enterprise. Inasmuch as Jews had benefited from these changes, some antiliberal political movements found it useful to proclaim liberalism a mask for Jewish domination. Ironically, certain political achievements of liberalism—establishment of parliaments and extension of the franchise—provided the very channels for an attack on the inadequacies and weaknesses of liberalism from the left and from the right. Some conservative politicians found that anti-Semitism was an expedient tactic to win over those who blamed the parvenu Jew for their own loss of social status. Thus Adolf Stöcker, court chaplain of the German emperor, was the first to use anti-Semitism as a level for gaining a political following. In 1878 he organized a Christian Social party to compete with the Social Democrats for the votes of the proletariat; winning little support among the workers, he quickly discovered that sweeping charges against Jewish "arrogance," Jewish "control" of the press, and Jewish "finance capitalism" attracted attention among artisans, small shopkeepers, clerks, officials, and professionals who resented the economic mobility of the Jews and the need to compete with them. Stöcker's charges were supported by German nationalists who insisted that Jews must assimilate completely to a monolithic German Christian culture before they would be accepted as Germans.[2] There were still other German nationalists, not at all concerned with a Christian component in German national identity, whose anti-Semitism was more radical. Eugen Dühring, a chief spokesman for secular anti-Semitism,

Alfred Dreyfus in 1906, after his exoneration as a German spy. To the anti-Semites, Dreyfus had been a symbol of Jewish perfidy; to the French liberals he was a symbol of a gross miscarriage of justice.

proposed in 1881 that the "Jewish type" posed not only a cultural threat to the German folk but above all a biological danger—a danger all the more malevolent and insidious when members of the Jewish race, converted to Christianity, gained entree into circles hitherto closed to them. In 1881 the anti-Semites collected 225,000 signatures for a petition asking that the government stop all Jewish immigration and that various exclusionary measures against Jews be promulgated. The following year the first of a series of international anti-Semitic congresses was held. By the mid-1880s the "Jewish question" had become a recognized political issue throughout continental Europe.

The greatest electoral successes of political anti-Semitism in pre-World War I Germany came in 1893, when small anti-Semitic parties elected 16 deputies to the Reichstag on the basis of a quarter of a million votes (2.9 per cent of the total cast). In Austria demagogic anti-Semitism was taken up in the 1880s by Georg von Schönerer, who became the main spokesman for the incorporation of all ethnic Germans into one Germanic state, even though this meant the dismemberment of the Hapsburg empire. In the early 1890s anti-Semitism was used by an opportunistic former democrat, Karl Lueger, to build the first political party in Europe to attain power on the issue of "Jewish influence." Lueger's success in tapping the antiliberal and anti-Jewish sentiment of the Catholic lower middle classes in Vienna led to his election as mayor in 1895, and the reluctant Hapsburg government allowed him to take office in 1897.

In France anti-Semitism in the 1880s became a weapon of monarchist and clerical groups hostile to the political tradition associated with the French Revolution of 1789 and opposed to the Third Republic established in 1870. French anti-Semitic agitation reached a height in the Dreyfus affair. Alfred Dreyfus, the only Jew on the General Staff of the French army, was convicted of treason in late 1894 on the basis of what later turned out to be forged evidence. The question of Dreyfus' guilt or innocence polarized French public opinion between 1897 and 1899. On the one side were the anti-Dreyfusards, convinced that he was a symptom of a vast masonic and Jewish plot to undermine France and besmirch the honor of the military. On the other side were the Dreyfusards, who viewed the Dreyfus court martial as a grave miscarriage of justice endangering French democracy. Dreyfus' eventual vindication, in stages between 1899 and 1906, led to a strengthening of the Republic's authority and to a further separation of state and church, but a persistent right-wing anti-Semitism survived in French politics. In the first decade of the twentieth century militant anti-Semitism seemed to have subsided in Western and Central Europe, but anti-Semitic opinions had taken root among conservative nationalists and students almost everywhere.

Far more devastating in its immediate impact was the overt manipulation of Jew-hatred by the Russian government after 1880. Whereas in Western and Central Europe anti-Semitism was not officially sanctioned by the governments during this period, in Eastern Europe it became part of governmental policy, used to maintain and even extend regulations discriminating against the Jews and to deflect onto them popular dissatisfaction, especially among the peasants. Soon after the assassination of Tsar Alexander II in 1881 by revolutionaries, a two-year wave of pogroms commenced in the southern Ukraine, spreading to over 150 localities. Typically, the police and the army stood aside for several days while rioters looted and destroyed Jewish property. Government officials justified the pogroms as an outburst of peasant anger against Jewish exploitation. In 1882 the Russian Minister of the Interior issued a new set of rules (the "May Laws") curtailing Jewish residence in the villages of the Pale and otherwise reversing the moderately liberal Jewish policy of the previous era. The epidemic of pogroms died down in 1884, but in the later 1880s the government imposed restrictive quotas on the number of Jews admitted to various professions and to Russian schools and universities. Administrative harassment of Jews also increased, such as

PSST...!

Images par

FORAIN
CARAN D'ACHE

PARAISSANT LE SAMEDI

Nº 25
23 Juillet 1898.

Le NUMERO : 10 centimes.
Abonnements : France, 6 fr. ; Etranger, 8 fr.

BUREAUX
10, rue Garancière, Paris.

Allégorie

L'Affaire Dreyfus.

One of numerous anti-Semitic cartoons of the 1890s, unmasking the Jew as an alien force and a threat to national integrity. In this cartoon from the Dreyfus affair, behind the liberal lurks the Jew, and behind the Jew the German military. (Courtesy of the Leo Baeck Institute, New York.)

the expulsion by the police of over 20,000 Jews from Moscow in 1891–1892.

In April 1903 a bloody pogrom in Kishinev in southern Russia marked the beginning of another wave of anti-Jewish violence fostered by a government attempting to cope with a much larger revolutionary surge. Out of imperialistic ambition but also to distract the populace from internal problems, Russia entered a disastrous war against Japan in 1904. When the Russian forces were defeated, charges were widely circulated that the Jews had secretly helped the enemy. 1905 in Russia was a year of political turmoil, strikes, and mass demonstrations: In October the tsar was forced to issue a manifesto guaranteeing basic civil liberties and promising a parliament (the Duma). Immediately afterwards, armed street gangs (the Black Hundreds), with clandestine government backing, attacked Jews in dozens of towns and cities. The pogroms again ceased in 1907, when the autocracy re-established its control over the country and was able to limit the Duma's powers; however, a new right-wing political party (the Union of the Russian People) continued the barrage of anti-Semitic propaganda. In 1911 Mendel Beilis, a Kievan Jew, was brought to trial by the government on a charge of ritual murder. The Beilis affair rallied Russian liberal opinion, and Beilis was exonerated by the jury in 1913. But deep-seated suspicions of Jewish evil-doing and treason remained rooted in various segments of Russian society and were to surface again in a few years.

The general upswing of anti-Semitism after 1880 took a wide variety of forms: ritual murder charges, riots, boycotts, exclusionary quotas, pamphlets, newspaper attacks, even academic treatises. Modern anti-Semitism appealed to the fears and self-interest of all classes of society. For some politicians anti-Semitism was merely a calculated tactic to win votes. For other respectable conservatives it was a protest against the corrosion of Christian values by modern commercialism. For rabid anti-Semites and their followers, however, it was a form of political paranoia and a desperate grasp at a new identity through the frantic self-assertion that comes from hatred.

The most important novel feature of extreme anti-Semitism was racism, which offered a pseudoscientific explanation for the danger posed by the Jewish presence. Borrowing from such fields as biology and stockbreeding, the racial theory was at first not especially directed against the Jews; however, by dividing humanity into a fixed number of subspecies with supposedly invariant physical and psychological characteristics, racist theory provided an important support for ideological anti-Semitism. The concepts of "Semitic" and "Aryan" were originally used by philologists for families of languages and then taken over by some nineteenth-century anthropologists to designate clusters of cultural traits. From such loose speculation, anti-Semitic ideologists asserted that the "Semitic mentality" was egotistic, materialistic, skillful in trading and finance, deficient in physical courage, and lacking the ability to be culturally creative; in contrast, the "Aryan mentality" was life-affirming, heroic, and possessed of a vivid poetic imagination. Frequently anti-Semitic writers castigated Christianity because of its "Jewish" charity and love toward the weak, extolling in their place the virtues of ancient Germanic paganism and military vigor.

Racism was one of the many forms of Social Darwinism that became widely prevalent in the later nineteenth century. Charles Darwin's theory of natural selection, especially the cliche of the "survival of the fittest," was adapted by almost every school of thought—including even liberalism, socialism, and some modern Jewish ideologies—to justify the prediction that its values would eventually triumph. Social Darwinism lay behind the formula of the "white man's burden" as a justification for Western imperialism in Asia and Africa. Analogously, racial anti-Semitism has been called a form of imperialism directed against the largest and most conspicuous minority within Europe. Indeed, the Jews were an ideal scapegoat. The very antiquity of Jew-hatred, dating from Hellenistic and Roman times and so evident in medieval folklore, could be used to legitimize the feeling that there was always something uncanny and distasteful about the Jews. In an age of intense and chauvinistic nationalism, the fact that Jews lived throughout the world gave credence to suspicions that they constituted a sinister international force with secret purposes and aims. That Judaism involved both peoplehood and religion was especially subject to misinterpretation. The desire of Jews to preserve their tradition could be labeled "clannish separatism." The belief that Jews were elected by God for a special role could be twisted into a supposed Jewish sense of superiority. Anti-Semites culled ancient Jewish literature for expressions of distrust and hostility to outsiders to prove that Jews were actually taught to hate gentiles. In the hands of such widely read and seemingly erudite writers as Houston Stewart Chamberlain, author of the lengthy anti-Semitic classic *The Foundations of the Nineteenth Century* (published in 1899), the antiquity and the geographical and social mobility of the Jewish people are evidence that a confrontation between the inherently superior Aryans and the parasitic, oriental Semites is the central theme of history.

Out of Russia came one further element: the belief that revolutionary socialism, as well as liberalism and capitalism, was merely a façade for the Jewish will to power. In an effort to discredit the struggle for civil rights and social justice, in the mid-1890s an agent of the tsarist secret police, using an almost forgotten French political satire against Napoleon III, forged the notorious *Protocols of the Elders of Zion*, purported minutes of a hidden Jewish world government. In this tract, the Jewish

Jewish street in Opatow, Poland, known in Yiddish as Apta. In the impoverished shtetlech of Eastern Europe, the Jews frequently formed a substantial minority, sometimes more than half of the population until World War II. (Courtesy of the Jewish Daily Forward Association.)

elders supposedly review their increasing hold over the European economy, their control of the press, and their manipulation of all political parties opposed to the tsarist regime and other autocratic governments. A wide range of social and political developments, from alcoholism to freedom of speech, are explained as cynically utilized techniques to ensure confusion of the gentiles, so that they will eventually fall under total Jewish domination. Circulated in print by a Russian Orthodox priest in 1905, the *Protocols* were not accepted as authentic on a large scale until after World War I, when they began to play an important role in anti-Semitic propaganda, cementing together the contradictory collage of anti-Jewish accusations into a potent ideological weapon. The impact of extremist, fanatic anti-Semitism, even when not swallowed whole, was effective in isolating the Jews: Reinforcing the feeling that Jewry was an alien force, anti-Semitism increased Jewish vulnerability in the turbulent and harsh arena of twentieth-century mass politics and dulled the edge of sympathy when Jews were to be openly persecuted.

The Rise of Zionism and Jewish Socialism

After 1880 a new Jewish leadership emerged to deal with the special problems of the Jewish people, including the poverty of most East European Jews, the physical violence and psychological stress produced by anti-Semitism, and the need to construct social forms to cope with mass politics. A combination of factors fostered the rise of Zionism and Jewish socialism in East Europe rather than elsewhere. First, the ethnic distinctiveness of the Jews was most pronounced in this part of the world. As a result of the slow pace of social change in Eastern Europe, Ashkenazic folk culture, traditional religiosity, and the Yiddish language were still entrenched among the Jewish masses in the last quarter of the century. Second, the demography and economics of the Jews in Eastern Europe reinforced their cohesion and at the same time intensified the urgency of their plight. Despite a large migration abroad, by 1897 there were over 5 million Russian Jews, increasingly concentrated in the larger cities of the Pale. The Jewish role as middlemen between peasants and towns had disintegrated after the emancipation of the serfs in 1861; the "May Laws" had speeded up their urbanization; a high Jewish birth rate further exacerbated the difficulties of finding new sources of livelihood. Although some East European Jews were able to maintain a middle-class position and a few became important capitalists, the vast majority were poorly paid day laborers in small workshops owned by Jews. Many were destitute, relying on communal charity. Third, the policies of the Russian government inadvertently stimulated an effective resistance. Although the tsarist regime was capable of brutal acts, and although it tried to repress the spread of "dangerous" ideas through censorship and other means, it was an autocracy, not a totalitarianism. Within the government there were proponents of moderation and tolerance as well as reactionaries and anti-Semites. Sufficient freedom of Jewish action remained, despite governmental restrictions, for new modes of self-organization to take shape. The spread of Haskalah and modern education had created a core of secular, free-thinking Russian Jewish intellectuals eager to break away from the now inadequate model of Jewish modernization laid down earlier in the century in Germany. The modern Russian Jewish intelligentsia in a few decades produced a wide range of semilegal and illegal movements, parties, and organizations, all emphasizing just that element of Jewish life which had seemed to threaten the emancipation of the Western Jews—that the Jews could be considered a "nation."

The formation of the Zionist movement was triggered by the emotional shock of the pogroms of 1881–1882.[3] The hostility of the tsarist government to the victims, coupled with the indifference of the liberal and radical intelligentsia to Jewish suffering, made it clear that Jewish emancipation and social acceptance were not a likely prospect. When East European Jewish emigration increased manyfold, the Jewish press debated whether it should be directed to America or to Palestine. Most of the emigrants opted for the United States, but the idea of re-establishing the land of Israel as the center of Jewish life took hold among many maskilim and Russified Jews. During the pogrom years a new network of *Hibbat Zion* societies appeared in the Pale ("Love of Zion" societies, the members being known as *Hovevei Zion*, "Lovers of Zion"). One group, the *Bilu* association of Kharkov, composed of Jewish university students who had experienced a "return to their people" during the riots, set off for Palestine to become farmers.[4] Of the Russian Jewish intellectuals pondering the Jewish future in light of the pogroms, one of the most articulate was Leon Pinsker, an eminent Jewish physician who had been an advocate of enlightenment and Russification. In the summer of 1882 Pinsker published a widely read pamphlet, *Autoemancipation*, in which he argued that the only solution for eternal and incurable Jew-hatred was a program of self-emancipation leading to the creation of a separate Jewish homeland somewhere. (More will be said about Pinsker's ideology in the next chapter.) The Love of Zion movement in the 1880s and 1890s had a profound impact on Hebrew literature and Jewish consciousness. When nationalist movements were appearing among all East European and Balkan peoples and when the Russian government turned to Russian nationalism for support, Hibbat Zion represented the reaffirmation of a national identity by Jews caught in the crossfire of competing loyalties and searching for an honorable and effective independent stance.

By the mid-nineties the idea of Jewish nationalism had spread to Central Europe, especially among East European Jewish students attending the University of Berlin and other universities of Germany, Austria, France, and Switzerland. The crucial figure for the next phase of Jewish nationalism was Theodor Herzl. Born in Budapest and educated at the University of Vienna, Herzl was a successful journalist and playwright, the epitome of the acculturated and almost assimilated Central European Jew. Although quite aware of Viennese anti-Semitism, Herzl was converted to Zionism as a result of the anti-Jewish agitation accompanying the Dreyfus affair. (At the time Herzl was the Paris correspondent of an important liberal Viennese daily, the *Neue Freie Presse*.) In 1896 Herzl published *The Jewish State: An Attempt at a Modern Solution to the Jewish Question*. (Herzl's position will be described in Chapter 15.) Although he had arrived at his proposal for a Jewish homeland independently of the Hovevei Zion, he quickly made contacts with them and with a few like-minded Western Jews. A decisive and commanding figure, Herzl called into being the first Zionist Congress (Basle, August 29, 1897). The result of the deliberations was a platform calling for a Jewish national home in Palestine recognized by international law. Although it did not have the support of the majority of the Jewish people, the world Zionist organization created in 1897 became a permanent body with a core of dedicated leaders, an enthusiastic membership, branches in Europe and America, a Jewish national fund to purchase land in Palestine, a variety

Theodor Herzl en route to Palestine in 1898 to meet Kaiser Wilhelm II in an effort to win his support for Zionism. (Courtesy of the Zionist Archives, New York.)

of newspapers, journals, cultural and other activities—all embodying the will that the Jews reconstitute themselves a political nation for the first time in 2,000 years.

In its early decades, tensions within the Zionist movement reflected the difficulties to be faced in transforming the Jews into a "normal" nation. What were to be the priorities of Jewish nationalism? Herzl saw as the first order of business the acquisition of a legal charter permitting mass Jewish settlement in Palestine. Critics who pointed to Herzl's lack of success in winning diplomatic support for a charter, said that the primary task was to promote modern Hebraic culture and raise the Jewish awareness of the people. (Herzl's knowledge of Hebrew and of Jewish literature was minimal.) In turn the secular tone of "cultural Zionism" raised fears among the Orthodox that it would undermine Jewish religious faith. In 1902 the Orthodox Zionists formed the *Mizrahi* movement to combine Herzl's "political Zionism" with a traditional religious identity. A second troublesome issue arose in 1903 at the Sixth Zionist Congress, when Herzl submitted for discussion a possible offer of land in East Africa by the British colonial administration. The Uganda project was decisively rejected by the East European Zionists, who were convinced that Palestine was the only possible Jewish homeland. Herzl backed down, but a number of leading Zionists seceded in 1905 to found a Jewish Territorial Organization, which attempted to find another location for Jewish colonization—without success. Zionism was irrevocably wedded to Palestine, which, though underpopulated, posed the ominous question of long range relations with the Arabs.

A third dilemma arose over Zionist participation in the struggle for Jewish rights in the diaspora. Herzl had opposed involvement in European politics on the grounds that the Jewish question was incapable of solution there and that Zionism should prepare for a total Jewish evacuation. In the brief political thaw after the Russian revolution of 1905, however, the Russian Zionists joined the "Union for the Attainment of Full Rights for the Jews in Russia," which called for a Jewish parliamentary bloc to work for the legal recognition of the Jews as a nonterritorial nationality in the tsarist empire. A similar development occurred in the Hapsburg empire as a result of the nationality struggles there. Commitment to the struggle for Jewish minority rights threatened to deflect Zionism from the goal of a Jewish homeland. A fourth issue arose as a result of a new wave of Jewish immigration to Palestine after 1904. Herzl had opposed "infiltration," but the rapid growth of the Jewish community in the land of Israel seemed to require that the movement become directly involved in practical measures to aid the new settlements, despite the evident hostility of the Turkish government. These last two issues, minority rights and the new settlements in Palestine, were connected to the rise of Jewish socialism.

Individual Jews were prominent in the socialist parties of Central Europe in the last quarter of the nineteenth century, but in Russia the attractions to young acculturated Jews of a universal socialist brotherhood were especially intense. By the turn of the century, Russified Jews were playing a conspicuous role in all the main radical movements: the revived Populist party (the Social Revolutionaries), anarchism (a force during the 1905 upheavals), and Marxism (the Social Democrats). Marxist socialism was especially compelling, because it purported to prove scientifically that a world-wide proletarian revolution would replace capitalism with an egalitarian and just society in which the coercive state would inevitably disappear. In the new age religious and ethnic differentiation would also vanish. Imbued with these ideas, some Russian Jewish socialists in the early nineties began to form small study circles of Jewish workers, teaching them Russian so that they could read revolutionary literature.[5]

Meanwhile, Jewish laborers in larger cities of the Pale, such as Vilna and Bialystok, began to form embryo labor unions and mutual aid associations and to organize strikes for better wages and working conditions. Between 1893 and 1895 several Jewish socialist intellectuals advocated abandoning small-scale propaganda for mass agitation in Yiddish, the language of the Jewish proletariat. The new frame of mind, that the Jewish proletariat should associate itself with the Russian labor

Drawing of Jewish recruits in the Russian army by the American Western artist Frederick Remington, 1894.

movement on the basis of partnership but not assimilation, led a group of Jewish socialists and workers, meeting in Vilna, to found the General Union (Bund) of Jewish Workers in Lithuania, Poland, and Russia. Organized in October 1897, the same year as the first Zionist Congress, the Bund quickly became Zionism's major competitor among the Jewish masses and one of the most effective branches of the Russian left. Bundist strikes, demonstrations, and mass protests played an important part in the political turbulence of 1903–1905. Bundist defense groups protected Jews during pogroms. Bundist agitators and writers educated a new generation of Jewish laborers to active political consciousness.

Like Zionism, the Bund in its formative years faced a series of tensions pulling in several directions. The question of its exact relationship to the Russian Social Democratic party (which the leaders of the Bund had helped to form in 1898) came to a head in 1903, when the Bund sought recognition as the sole representative of the Jewish workers in Russia. This proposal, which would have turned the party into a federation, was rejected by Social Democrats of varying views—especially by Lenin, the leader of the Bolshevik faction.[6] (In 1906, its automous status recognized, the Bund rejoined the Social Democratic organization.) Despite disagreement with the other Marxist socialists, the Bund remained committed to the primacy of the class struggle: The natural ally of the Jewish proletariat was the proletariat of other peoples, its principal enemy (apart from the tsarist regime), the capitalist class, including the Jewish bourgeoisie. As a consequence, the Bund found it difficult to define an "ideologically correct" relation to the Jewish people as a whole. Early Bundists followed the usual Marxist position that the Jews had survived in history as a distinct group only because of their unusual economic roles and legal status. (A thorough-going economic determinism, Marxism does not assign an independent causality to ideas or religious faith.) After the socialist revolution the Jews would inevitably assimilate because the economic substructure that maintained their identity would disappear.

At first the Bund proclaimed itself a Yiddish-speaking workers' movement. Only in 1901 did the Bund Congress agree that the term *nation* should be applied to the Jews, and even then it rejected the call for Jewish communal rights apart from political emancipation as individuals. In the next few years the goal of cultural and social autonomy became widely accepted in Russian Jewry as the only solution to the Jewish problem in a multinational state, and the Bund's leadership came to include Jews more deeply rooted in *Yiddishkeit* (the Ashkenazic folk ethos). As a result, in 1905 the chief Bundist theoretician, Vladimir Medem, proposed that, inasmuch as the Bund opposed oppression of any nationality, it should demand legal guarantees for the free development of Jewish culture. Medem qualified his position by a stance of "neutrality" as to whether Jewish identity would endure in the long run, which was to be left to the "laws of history." After 1907, when government repression and Jewish emigration led to a decline in Bundist political and economic activities, the Bund became involved in furthering Yiddish as the language of general education and Jewish literature. For the Bund, Yiddish was the language of the Jewish working class, and the working class was the sole legitimate representative of the people. The Bund remained hostile to Hebrew as the language of the modern Jewish renaissance, and it continued to oppose the Zionist movement as a dangerous form of "romantic," bourgeois nationalism drawing Jews away from the revolutionary struggle in East Europe.

During the political turmoil of the first few years of the twentieth century, several other Jewish socialist parties were formed in Eastern Europe. One was associated with the search for a Jewish homeland somewhere other than in Palestine. A second emphasized the attainment of extensive Jewish autonomous legal rights in Russia. A third combined Marxism with an affirmation of the centrality of the land of Israel on the grounds that only in the historic Jewish homeland could the Jews, freed from minority status and the pressures of an anti-Semitic environment, have a "normal" proletarian revolution. A fourth tendency based its ideology on personal fulfillment through pioneering agricultural labor.

The last two groups made Labor Zionism the most vital factor in the new wave of Jewish emigration to Palestine during the decade prior to World War I.

In 1881 the *yishuv* (the Jewish community in the land of Israel) numbered about 24,000 Sephardim and Ashkenazim, half of whom lived in Jerusalem. Almost all were pious traditionalists supported by charitable contributions raised in the diaspora. The first Zionist *aliyah* (wave of immigration) in the 1880s and 1890s resulted in about twenty agricultural settlements. As the Hovevei Zion were able to provide little material help, the settlers were forced to rely on generous financial aid and vexing supervision from Baron Edmond de Rothschild and his agents. Many became discouraged as a result of obstacles placed in their way by the Turkish government, the prevalence of malaria, and the backward economic conditions in the country. But early Zionist settlers, such as the Biluists, were an influential ideological precedent for the next generation.

The second aliyah (1904–1914) brought 40,000 Jews to Palestine, mostly idealistic youth despairing of the bleak situation in Russia after the failure of the revolution of 1905. The Marxist *Poalei Zion* (Workers of Zion) and the non-Marxist *Ze'irei Zion* (Young People of Zion) were dedicated to social and personal redemption through Zionism, and to the conviction that they must till the soil and do all the menial work them-

Founding ceremony in 1909 for the city of Tel Aviv, to be built on the site of these sand dunes. (Courtesy of the Zionist Archives, New York.)

selves rather than rely on hired Arab labor. Gradually the ideal of a cooperative farming community, the *kibbutz*, emerged. (The model, Deganyah, was established in 1910.) Although the Young Turk revolution in the Ottoman empire (1908) worsened political conditions for the yishuv, by 1914 there were 85,000 Jews in Palestine, 43 Jewish agricultural settlements, an association of Jewish armed watchmen to protect them, a new Jewish city (Tel Aviv, founded in 1909), a network of Jewish schools in which the language of instruction was Hebrew, a variety of modern Jewish political parties, mutual aid societies, and a periodical press. The ground had been laid for a modern Jewish homeland.

Jewish Migration and the Expansion of the American Diaspora

Since the mid-seventeenth century there had been a steady drift of Jews westward on the European continent, but the number who crossed the Atlantic to the New World was small until the nineteenth century. By 1776 there were about 2,500 Jews in the future United States; by 1820 about 4,000. Between 1840 and 1880 a quarter of a million Jews came to America, mainly from Germany, Bohemia, and Hungary, but also from Russia and Romania. After the traumatic pogroms of 1881–1882,

Jewish immigrants arriving at the Battery, New York, in the 1890s. (Courtesy of the Museum of the City of New York.)

Russian anti-Semitism and difficult economic conditions in East Europe led to an enormous increase. About 2,750,000 Jews left Eastern Europe between 1881 and 1914. Of these, 350,000 resettled in other parts of Europe: tens of thousands in Germany and France where they bolstered the numerical strength of these Jewries; and 200,000 in England where they increased the Jewish population more than threefold. East European Jews scattered over the globe. Among the more sizable migrations were the 40,000 that went to South Africa, 115,000 to Argentina,[7] 100,000 to Canada. But the most attractive land of all was the United States, to which 2 million East European Jews—85 per cent of the intercontinental migration—emigrated between 1881 and the outbreak of World War I.

This mass exodus produced striking changes in the social profile of American Jewry. The Sephardic Jews, who were the major force in the early eighteenth century, had lived in the coastal towns (the only towns of size at the time) where they had been merchant shippers, shopkeepers, and artisans. The German-speaking Jews who came in the mid-nineteenth century had spread throughout the continent. Starting out often as itinerant peddlers, they quickly became business proprietors in the growing cities of the midwest, south, and California. By 1880 the largest Jewish center, New York, contained 85,000 Jews, mostly of German derivation, including a few prominent Jewish bankers who had established their firms in the post-Civil War economic boom. The German Jews quickly Americanized themselves—and they Americanized their religion. In the sixties and seventies the majority of synagogues in the United States turned to Reform Judaism, a process aided by the arrival of several energetic and articulate European Reform rabbis. When efforts to create a broad federation of synagogues failed, the Reform temples joined together in the Union of American Hebrew Congregations in 1873. A Reform theological seminary, the Hebrew Union College in Cincinnati, was founded in 1875; a Reform rabbinic association, the Central Conference of American Rabbis, in 1889. Like European Reform, American Reform had its moderates and radicals, but the more extreme type of antitraditionalism (such as that of Samuel Holdheim) fell on fertile soil in the United States. Classical Reform reached its apex in the Pittsburgh Platform of 1885: Insisting that the Jews were only a religious association and not a national community, the Pittsburgh Platform portrayed Reform Judaism as a rational religion whose moral law pointed to the coming age of universal human brotherhood. Reform was closely attuned to the optimism of the American environment and to the efforts of American religious liberalism to stress that theology was fully compatible with the natural sciences and with the principle of historical evolution.

The social background of the East European Jews who arrived after 1881, combined with their arrival at a time when America was experiencing rapid industrialization, resulted in a much more diverse and ethnically distinct American Jewry by World War I. Almost two thirds of the new immigrants settled down in the big cities of the northeast, especially in crowded downtown neighborhoods such as the Lower East Side of New York City. There they found employment in manual labor of various kinds. Over half entered the ready-made clothing industry in which entrepreneurs, contractors, tailors, and seamstresses were mainly Jews. Wages were low, hours long, and working conditions poor in the small, unventilated, and dirty sweatshops. After 1900, when clothing factories grew larger and when experienced Jewish socialist leaders began to immigrate in larger numbers, a Jewish component in the American labor movement developed rapidly, especially through the International Ladies' Garment Workers Union and the Amalgamated Clothing Workers of America. (After considerable labor strife, these unions pioneered in methods of collective bargaining, arbitration, and welfare benefits for their members.) East European Jewish immigrants also organized societies of many kinds, such as the dozens of *landsmanshaftn* (associations of Jews from a particular locality in the old country), which maintained small Orthodox synagogues and provided sickness and burial insurance. A socialistically inclined Workmen's Circle (*Arbeter Ring*) fraternal order,

Hester Street in 1898, heart of the Jewish immigrant community on the Lower East Side of New York. (Courtesy of the Museum of the City of New York.)

formed in 1900, took over some of the mutual aid functions of the *landsmanshaftn* and sponsored lectures and educational programs in Yiddish. Free from tsarist political constraints, Yiddish literature, Yiddish theater, and Yiddish newspapers flourished in the Lower East Side. Although the East European Jewish immigrants were constantly augmented by new arrivals, signs of upward mobility were already present before 1914. Some of the more successful newcomers and especially the next generation, educated in public schools, found opportunities for advancement outside the proletariat and moved to middle-class neighborhoods, preparing the ground for the gradual fusion of the various elements of the Jewish population of the United States.

During the period between 1881 and 1914, however, a considerable social gap existed within American Jewry. Native-born Jews of German origin tended to view East European Jews as plebeian, noisy, and inclined toward either radicalism or Orthodoxy, even blaming them for the appearance of anti-Semitism in America at the end of the nineteenth century. "Downtown" Jews thought of the "uptowners" as haughty, cold, patronizing, and apologetic about their Jewishness. Nevertheless, a sense of *noblesse oblige* infused various efforts by the acculturated old leadership to defend Jewish interests and to speed the process of Americanization. In 1902 prominent members of the German Jewish establishment revived the Jewish Theological Seminary in New York (it had originally been organized by opponents of Reform in the late 1880s) to train rabbis espousing a modernized traditionalism like that of the Positive-Historical School in Germany. Under the leadership of the eminent scholar Solomon Schechter, the Seminary became the center of Conservative Judaism, which affirmed the need for adjustment to modern realities without breaking the continuity of Jewish law and tradition. For East European Jews, whose attachment to traditional rituals and the ethnic substance of Jewish life left them unmoved by classical Reform, Conservatism was an appealing synthesis of old and new, and it gradually influenced the transformation of Reform and Orthodox in a similar direction.[8]

The German Jewish elite was also active in founding settlement houses for the immigrants and furthering an extensive program of Jewish philanthropy. Beginning in the 1890s, federations of Jewish charities were established in the larger cities to coordinate the raising of funds for Jewish hospitals, homes for the aged, and other social services. Influential German Jews organized the American Jewish Committee in 1906 as a self-appointed quasi-ambassadorial group to influence the United States government on behalf of persecuted Jewish communities abroad. In 1913 the B'nai B'rith, a fraternal order organized in the United States by German Jews in 1843, set up an Anti-Defamation League to combat anti-Semitism. American Zionism was also affected by the encounter of German and East European Jews. Opposition to Zionism had been quite strong from Reform Judaism, from the American Jewish socialists influenced by the Bund, and from certain Orthodox rabbis. Although the initially small membership of the American Zionist movement was almost completely East European, however, many of its leaders came from the older German group. By World War I Zionism began to attract outstanding native-born figures, such as Louis D. Brandeis, the socially conscious and public-spirited lawyer who was the first Jew to serve on the Supreme Court. Brandeis and his associates added a distinctly American note into Zionism, rejecting the belief that the diaspora was a form of exile and also that Zionism raised a dangerous problem of dual loyalty for patriotic Jewish Americans. For Brandeis, American and Zionist ideals reinforced each other: The Jewish community in Palestine was both a refuge for the oppressed of Europe and a laboratory for social experimentation in which Jews could construct a model progressive and democratic society. In the 1920s there was to be a tension between the Brandeis group's concern that the yishuv be founded on sound financial methods and efficient budgetary controls, and the contrasting, more intensely ideological and collectivist goals of East European Zionism. But the efforts of Brandeis and others to bring non-Zionists into the philanthropic aspects of building the Jewish homeland were eventually to strengthen the Zionist project.

The emerging American Jewish community was unique not only for its size, but also for the degree of its acceptance by the general society. American society had taken shape without many of the forces that impeded the development of liberalism in Europe and that fed the reactionary backlash against it, such as a traditionalist peasantry, an entrenched nobility and gentry, an established clergy. The United States absorbed many ethnic and religious groups into a political system that, for all its imperfections, was solidly based on the "social contract" and civil liberties of the Enlightenment. Jews did not have to fight for their emancipation, leaving a pool of resentment and outrage in the wake. Separation of church and state and the respect accorded religion enabled Judaism to attain a recognized position denied it in Europe. Despite blatant inequalities in the case of the American blacks, despite the flare-up of social antagonisms during periods of economic crisis, American society possessed an openness and a tolerance unparalleled elsewhere. To be sure, toward the end of the nineteenth century Jews were excluded from many resorts and clubs, and populist orators played on a fear of sinister foreigners and unscrupulous bankers. After World War I informal quotas for Jewish students were instituted in colleges and universities, and it was a widespread practice not to employ Jews in basic industries and to discriminate against them in certain professions. However, the enormous absorptive capacity of the American economy offered vast opportunities

Lower East Side tenement apartment photographed in 1910, typical of the living conditions of Jewish immigrants after their arrival in America. (Courtesy of the Museum of the City of New York.)

for individual enterprise and talent, softening the impact of these barriers. And never was anti-Semitism adopted by a major political party.

American Jewry was also unique in the completely voluntary character of its institutions. How to identify as a Jew—even whether to do so—became a free personal choice to a degree unprecedented in Jewish history. A highly decentralized Jewish community, federated into overlapping and sometimes bickering associations of many kinds, broadened the base of individual participation but posed serious problems when the time came for effective joint action. And at the end of World War I, American Jewry, like America itself, was to be propelled into world leadership.

1914–1939: Coping with War and Depression, Nationalism and Imperialism

World War I and the Jews

In 1914 began a fateful clash between England, France, and Russia against Germany and Austria–Hungary, the first period of prolonged

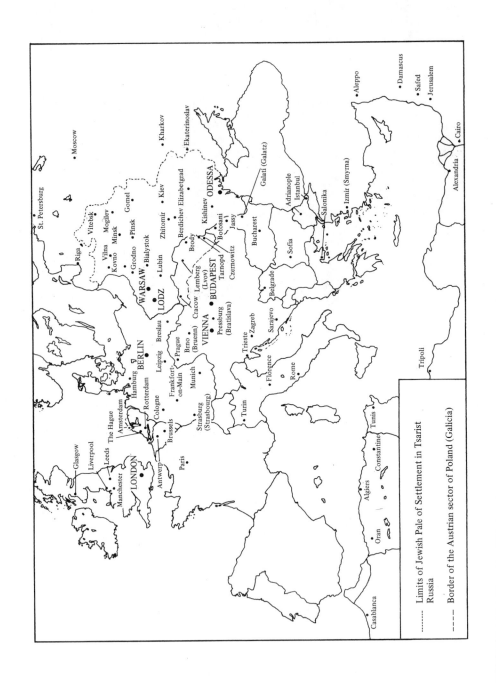

Limits of Jewish Pale of Settlement in Tsarist
Russia

Border of the Austrian sector of Poland (Galicia)

warfare on the European continent in a century and one which led to the end of European hegemony in the world. Tens of thousands of Jews fought on the sides of both the Allies and the Central Powers; hundreds of thousands of Jews were uprooted, wounded, or killed. In the west, after the initial German offensive, the main battlefields were limited to a ten-mile wide strip of northern France from the Alps to the sea where for three years the combatants fought a bloody war of attrition. The eastern battlefields ran through the Russian Pale of Settlement and Austrian Galicia. During 1915, almost 40 per cent of Russian Jewry in Poland and Lithuania passed under German control; this saved them from the brutal treatment accorded East European Jews by the Russian government and military. All Yiddish and Hebrew publications were banned by the Russians on the grounds that they might be used for spying. Whole communities were expelled from the front, resulting in a flight of Jewish refugees from the Pale to central Russia.

In March 1917, when the war was two-and-a-half years old, demoralization in the Russian army and bread riots in Petrograd (St. Petersburg) led to the overthrow of the tsar. One of the first actions of the Provisional Government was to abolish all the legal discriminations against Jews—the long-hoped-for emancipation at last (March 16, 1917). In November, further deterioration in the military situation, the inability of the Provisional Government to act decisively, and widespread agrarian unrest led to a second revolution, carried out by the Bolsheviks in the name of the Soviet (Council) of Workers and Soldiers' Deputies in the capital. Lenin immediately sued for peace and in March 1918 signed a treaty with Germany that left the Germans in control of Estonia, Latvia, Lithuania, Poland, and the Ukraine. But the German victory in Russia was short-lived. When America entered the war on the side of the Allies, the military balance on the western front decisively tipped. On November 11, 1918, an armistice was declared.

Fighting continued, however, in the east, where the Ukraine was in a state of almost complete chaos. In the early stages of the Russian Revolution of 1917 the Ukrainians had formed a separate government. In 1918 a German army occupied the Ukraine; when it was forced to withdraw, bitter civil war ensued. Vying for control were a Ukrainian

---

Larger Jewish Centers in Europe and the Mediterranean at the Beginning of the Twentieth Century. The densest Jewish population is still found in the Russian Pale of Settlement, in Austrian Galicia, and in northern Rumania, followed by Central Europe, and then by Western and Southern Europe, North Africa, and the Middle East. The political boundaries on this map are those on the eve of World War I. In the Pale of Settlement, most cities with an estimated Jewish population of over 20,000 are indicated; in Germany, Austria-Hungary and Romania, cities with over 10,000 Jews; elsewhere cities with over 5,000 Jews. The seven cities in large type each had over 150,000 Jews by 1914, an indication of the growing metropolitan concentration of Jews during this period.

army under Petlura, various anarchistic peasant bands, an anti-Bolshevik White Army under Denikin, and the Red Army of the Bolshevik government. The Red Army did attempt to suppress anti-Semitism in its ranks, but the other troops and gangs regularly massacred Jews. In 1920 further savagery accompanied an invasion of the Ukraine by the army of the newly established Polish government. Only at the end of 1920 did the fighting cease, leaving most of the Ukraine in Bolshevik hands. During the years of civil war and invasion, 2,000 pogroms had resulted in the death of 100,000–150,000 Jews.

The map of the Middle East had also changed at the end of the war, and the Zionist movement entered a new phase. On November 2, 1917, the British Foreign Secretary, Arthur James Balfour, sent a carefully worded letter to the British Zionist organization, affirming that "His Majesty's Government view with favor the establishment in Palestine of a national home for the Jewish people." This diplomatic break-through had concrete implications because during 1917 a British army based in Egypt occupied Palestine and Syria. (Ottoman Turkey had joined the Central Powers.) Besides their espousal of Zionism, the British also made extensive promises to the Sherif of Mecca, who threw his forces on the British side, and the British government had entered into secret agreements with the French concerning their respective spheres of influence. Final arrangements left the French in control of Syria and Lebanon, the British in control of Palestine (including Trans-Jordan) and Iraq. Authority to administer these areas was to derive from a mandate awarded by the League of Nations. In July 1922, the League of Nations, in approving the British mandate over Palestine, reaffirmed the Balfour Declaration. Twenty-five years after Herzl convened the First Zionist Congress, an internationally recognized legal status had been created for a Jewish home in the land of Israel.

Postwar Europe and America

World War I seemed to have been a victory for democracy and national self-determination, but the following two decades were marked by economic crisis, political instability, and rising dictatorship. Along with the normal burden of living in difficult and demoralizing times, a large proportion of Europe's Jews found themselves facing a renewed and even more virulent anti-Semitism.

Immediately after the war, westward migration recommenced, but in 1921 and 1924 restrictive laws were passed by the United States Congress, reducing the number of Jewish immigrants to a trickle. Other countries followed suit. Among the various factors responsible for the erection of these barriers was certainly anti-Semitism. Fear of "Jewish

Storming of the Winter Palace in Petrograd (now Leningrad) during the Communist revolution of November 1917. The Russian revolution brought about the emancipation of the Jews in Russia, but also the destruction of most Jewish communal and religious institutions.

Bolshevism" ran high in the Western countries in the twenties. The Communist leadership of Russia called for the violent overthrow of bourgeois governments and expropriation of the propertied classes. To the religious, Communism represented a militant antireligion with which no compromise was possible. Individuals of Jewish descent were conspicuous not only in the Communist party of the USSR (Trotsky, Kamenev, Zinoviev, and others) but in various abortive left-wing revolts in Germany and Hungary in 1919. The *Protocols of the Elders of Zion*, brought to Germany by Russian émigrés, won considerable credence even in England and the United States. Widespread enough in the twenties, in the thirties anti-Semitism was conspicuous everywhere. The New York stock market crash in 1929 had world-wide repercussions leading to a drastic decline in international trade and unprecedented unemployment. Anti-Semitic political agitators were active even in the most stable democracies.

Although worrisome, anti-Semitism in countries west of Germany did not jeopardize the political rights of Jews during the interwar period, and some Jews had important roles in government (Leon Blum, premier of France in the mid-thirties; Harold Laski, political theorist in the British Labor party; Jews in the New Deal administration of Franklin Delano Roosevelt). Shutting off the reservoir of East European immigration hastened the decline of the Jewish proletarian class and of the Yiddish cultural flowering. Jews in the West increasingly became a middle class and acculturated group. A sign of Jewish integration into the larger society was the large number of Jews or people of Jewish descent since 1900 who attained recognition in the arts, music, literature, the humanities, and science. To mention only a few: Sigmund Freud, Albert Einstein, Niels Bohr, Gustav Mahler, Arnold Schoenberg, Darius Milhaud, Kurt Weill, George Gershwin, Artur Schnabel, Jascha Heifetz, Myra Hess, Artur Rubinstein, Max Reinhart, Amedeo Modigliani, Marc Chagall, Emile Durkheim, Henri Bergson, Ludwig Wittgenstein, Edmund Husserl, Ernst Cassirer, Marc Bloch, Lewis Namier, Franz Kafka, Marcel Proust.

In East Central Europe the peace treaties after the war confirmed a new political map. The Austrian–Hungarian empire and the western borderlands of the tsarist empire were now divided into a tier of newly independent, often hostile nation-states. (The fragmentation of the area had started with the breakaway of the Balkan kingdoms from the Ottoman empire in the decades before World War I.) Because of intermingled settlement and residence patterns operating for centuries, every one of the new states had substantial minority populations. The largest numbers of Jews were to be found in reconstituted Poland (over 3 million), in diminished Hungary (445,000), and in expanded Romania (850,000). Significant Jewish populations were in Latvia (95,000), Lithuania (115,000), Czechoslovakia (375,000), Austria (191,000), Yugoslavia (68,000), Bulgaria (48,000), and Greece (73,000).[9]

The economic and political situation in most of these countries was very uncertain. The war caused enormous destruction of property, capital, and life. Large old markets were replaced by many small, competing economic units with limited resources and few viable industries; high protective tariffs further contributed to the economic stagnation of the area. In each case the government set out to promote the interests of the ruling nationality and to develop its own middle class at the expense of the minorities. Democratic parliamentary regimes established in these countries after the war were replaced, one by one, with rightist dictatorships. (The exception was Czechoslovakia, which had a prosperous economy, a liberal government, and a policy of respect for rights of its Jewish minority.)

Even though most of the new constitutions prohibited religious, racial, and national discrimination, the Jews, as the most vulnerable minority, could find almost no political allies. Jewish delegations had lobbied at the Paris peace talks in 1919 to assure that the treaties with the new states guarantee the cultural and religious rights of all minorities, but these stipulations remained a dead letter. In the Ashkenazic heartland (Lithuania, Poland, Czechoslovakia, Hungary, Romania) most Jews were distinctive in faith, customs, and language, but even where they had acculturated, they were still considered outsiders. Quotas were imposed on Jews in higher education and the professions. Jews were excluded from the bureaucracy, the state-controlled banks, and state-run business monopolies. Jewish firms were discriminated against, sometimes nationalized. In the thirties, anti-Semitic political parties were brought into the government, or ruling cliques supported boycotts and sweeping new anti-Semitic legislation. By the end of that decade, in Poland, Romania, and Hungary especially, the Jews were faced with economic disaster.

All these pressures notwithstanding, most of the countries of East Central Europe were not able to destroy the internal strength of Jewish culture. Jewish political parties, powerless to change government policy, competed actively for support within the Jewish communities. In interwar Poland, groupings included the *Agudat Israel* (the anti-Zionist Orthodox party), the *Mizrahi* (Orthodox Zionists), the General Zionists, the diaspora nationalists (*Folkspartei*), the Socialist Zionists, and the Bund. Extensive school systems in Hebrew and Yiddish were developed by some of these parties. Modern Jewish scholars continued to investigate the Ashkenazic Jewish past (especially at the Yivo Institute of Jewish Research founded in Vilna in 1925). Jewish youth movements, modern Hebrew and Yiddish literature and journalism, traditional yeshivot and Hasidic networks maintained the integrity and continuity of Jewish identity. The diversity and vitality of the modern Ashkenazic renaissance had not by any means run out when World War II began.

In the 1920s and 1930s more than 2.8 million Jews lived in the Union of Soviet Socialist Republics, a multinational federation officially instituted in 1922. Throughout the USSR, the Communist (formerly Bolshevik) party held a monopoly of political power in the name of the proletariat and peasantry. After the November 1917 revolution, the Communist regime set out systematically to eliminate any counterrevolutionary threat. Other political parties were dissolved; all private and civil organizations were destroyed or subjected to close supervision. The gentry and bourgeoisie that survived civil war, famine, and terror during the period of "War Communism" (1918–1920) had their property expropriated and found themselves disenfranchised. Inasmuch as the Marxist–Leninist ideology was scientific truth, the party launched a determined campaign against all other ideologies, including the Christian, Muslim, and Jewish religious traditions. A burst of Jewish self-organization following the March 1917 revolution was nipped in the bud. In mid-1919 Jewish com-

Leon Trotsky (1879–1940). Second in importance only to Lenin in the Communist Party until the mid-1920s, Trotsky organized the Red Army and directed its operations during the Russian Civil War. Himself of Jewish descent, he advocated assimilation of the Jews in a socialist society.

munal organizations were liquidated, except for synagogue committees; the Bund and other Jewish parties were repressed; in the mid-1920s the last nonpolitical activities of Zionist pioneering associations were prohibited. Impoverished Jews in the villages—religious functionaries, petty traders, and artisans—were labeled "superfluous" and deprived of civil rights. By the end of the 1920s all yeshivot had been closed and the printing of religious books discontinued.

Yet some new possibilities were now available for Russian Jews that had not existed under the tsarist regime. Jews flocked to the bigger Russian cities where they were able to find positions as managers and bureaucrats, for which the Communist government had a great need. Jews enrolled in large numbers in institutions of higher learning in order to qualify as professionals. With the adoption in 1921 of the "New Economic Policy" (a retreat from full communism that restored some features of a free market), opportunities opened up for private initiative. Jews were encouraged to establish farming villages in Belorussia, the Ukraine, and the Crimea, with the help of funds raised in the United States. In the late twenties an area of eastern Siberia (Birobidzhan) was set aside for Jewish colonization. When the Soviet government dropped the New Economic Policy in 1928, a brutal collectivization of agriculture undermined the impetus for Jewish farming, but a program of massive industrialization increased the flow of Jews into skilled labor, technology, science, and engineering.

In the 1920's the regime made tactical concessions to Jewish ethnic feelings. Under the supervision of Jewish sections of the Communist party (the *Yevsektsiia*, established late in 1918), Yiddish-speaking workers' councils and courts were set up in areas of large Jewish concentration; Yiddish schools, scholarly institutes, periodicals, publishing houses, and theaters were encouraged to create a secular, antireligious Yiddish Communist culture like that being developed for the other nationalities of the USSR. Also in the twenties the regime prohibited public manifestations of anti-Semitism (although Stalin was able to make adroit use of it after Lenin's death in 1924 in his struggle for control of the party against Trotsky). Once Stalin had consolidated his power as undisguised dictator of the USSR and launched a sweeping purge of the party apparatus and the repression of any source of dissent, most Jewish institutions were disbanded: the *Yevsektsiia* in 1930, almost all Jewish cultural programs during the Great Terror of 1934 to 1938. Along with millions of other Soviet citizens, most of the Jewish leadership were arrested by the secret police and either killed or sent to forced labor camps. By the eve of World War II, first as a by-product of the purge, and then, after the Stalin–Hitler pact, as a deliberate policy, Jews were completely removed from the party and the government. Therefore, the Jews of East Central Europe and the Jews of the Soviet Union had suffered different and contrasting agonies. The former had retained their religious and intellectual freedom, but fell victim to nationalistic fervor and anti-Semitism. The latter, although not subject to overt anti-Semitism as a political weapon, found that their religious and cultural traditions were being destroyed by a totalitarian form of socialism.

The Yishuv During the Interwar Period

Of all the Jewish communities that had obtained minority rights after World War I, only in Palestine were the Jews able to organize effectively as an autonomous body with a national assembly and executive council. Although valuable time and opportunity was lost because of Zionist inertia immediately after the issuance of the Balfour Declaration, The yishuv, together with the World Zionist Organization, and after 1929 the Jewish Agency for Palestine, developed a ramified set of institutions on cooperative principles despite the handicaps of limited financial resources, extreme fluctuations in aliyah, loss of the USSR as a source for immigration, and difficult relations with the Arabs.

Zionist pioneers disembarking at Haifa in 1923. (Courtesy of the Zionist Archives, New York.)

By 1929 the yishuv's population was 160,000; by 1939 a half million. At the end of the twenties 110 agricultural settlements existed; 233 at the end of the thirties. In 1939 about one fourth of the Jewish population of Palestine lived in cooperative farming communities; Tel Aviv had 150,000 Jews, Jerusalem 90,000, and Haifa 60,000. The Jewish-run Palestine Electric Corporation made possible the beginnings of industrialization, which was furthered by the *Histadrut* (the General Federation of Hebrew Workers). The Histadrut and the Hadassah Medical Organization developed public health facilities. The Hebrew University of Jerusalem was opened in 1925. In a conscious effort to negate the stereotype of the vulnerable and insecure diaspora Jew, the yishuv's model for the new generation was a self-assured, physically strong, Hebrew-speaking farmer or worker free from the psychological burden that conditions in Europe were thought to inflict.

The yishuv's chief political problem was its usually tense relationship with the British government and the Palestinian Arabs, which threatened to wreck the whole Zionist project. The interests of British imperialism hardly coincided with those of the yishuv. At the beginning of the twenties the territory east of the Jordan was administratively detached from Palestine and made a separate domain under the rule of Abdullah, a scion of the Hashimite family of Mecca, which had spearheaded the Arab revolt during World War I. As a result, Palestine was only 160 miles long and 70 miles wide and contained in the late thirties, besides the yishuv, about one million Arabs, many of whom were impoverished peasants, *fellahin*, dominated by a few landowning families. Arab riots in 1929, following a dispute concerning Jewish access to the Western ("Wailing") Wall of the ancient Temple site, led the British to announce a curtailing of Jewish immigration and purchase of land. (All the yishuv's land was brought from Arabs, the British commitment being only the maintenance of order and the recognition of Hebrew as an official language of the country.) The development of yishuv had transformed Palestine from one of the most backward to one of the most advanced Middle Eastern areas. For the Arabs, however, the Jewish home was a threat to their majority status, and the resulting intransigent stance of the Arab leadership frustrated various attempts by concerned Jews to lay the groundwork for a mutually satisfactory compromise.

By the late 1920s Labor Zionism was providing most of the yishuv's leadership. Various socialist and labor groups in Palestine had joined together in the Israel Labor party in 1930. A considerable right-wing opposition within the Zionist movement was highly critical of Chaim Weizmann, the president of the World Zionist Organization, who

Reforestation of barren terrain in the land of Israel, a continuing undertaking of the Jewish National Fund. (Courtesy of the Consulate General of Israel.)

was committed to close cooperation with the British. Vladimir Jabotinsky, the leader of the Union of Zionist Revisionists founded in 1925, insisted that the prime goal was the attainment of a fully independent Jewish state in the whole of Palestine; after several stormy Zionist congresses, the Revisionists seceded to form their own separate organization in the mid-thirties. Revisionists also began to withdraw from the Haganah, the militia of the yishuv, and to form their own separate military groups. Disagreeing with the yishuv's policy of self-restraint and reliance on defensive measures only, the Revisionists advocated active retaliation against Arab attacks.

In 1936 the Arab leadership of Palestine commenced an almost open war against Jews, British, and moderate Arabs, with the support of Syria, Iraq, and Egypt and with the encouragement of German and Italian agents. A six-month general strike was followed by a guerrilla revolt, repressed only at the end of 1938. In 1937 a British royal commission of investigation proposed that Palestine be partitioned into Jewish and Arab states and a British zone, which the Zionists accepted but the Arabs rejected. Finally in 1939 the British published a White Paper (a policy statement) announcing that there would be no partition, that Palestine would become independent in ten years, and that Jewish immigration would be limited to an additional 75,000, leaving the yishuv a perpetual minority. The British, afraid of losing the good will of the Arabs on the eve of another world war, had, in effect, decided to abandon their commitment to the idea of a Jewish homeland.

The Old Jewish Diasporas of Africa and Asia

A summary of the principal events of modern Jewish history inevitably focuses on Europe, Palestine, and America, but there was also a string of communities of the greatest antiquity, stretching across North Africa to central Asia and totaling more than one million Jews in the 1930s.[10] Most of these Jews in the nineteenth century were *dhimmis* (protected subjects under the "Pact of Omar" of Islamic governments) whose status ranged from tolerable to miserable. The process of their modernization was slower and more irregular than that of Jews in Eastern Europe and usually came as a result of direct European penetration.

French influence was strong in nineteenth-century North Africa. Algeria was conquered by France in 1830, and as a result of the efforts of the French Jewish statesman Adolphe Crémieux, most Algerian Jews were given French citizenship in 1870. French protectorates over Tunisia (1881) and over much of Morocco (1912) made it possible for some Jews in these lands also to acquire French citizenship. Although a small stratum of Sephardic and Italian Jewish merchant families in the Maghreb (western North Africa) had been in contact with Europe for centuries, most of the Jews there, until the coming of the French, lived in the villages of the Atlas Mountains and other isolated interior areas or in the crowded ghettos of the larger cities, where they were poverty-stricken artisans, craftsmen, and petty traders. In the 1860s the *Alliance Israélite Universelle* had begun to establish modern French-language schools for Jews in North Africa, the Balkans, and the Middle East. By the beginning of the twentieth century, Western secular patterns had penetrated among the old Jewish upper class and among much of the new middle class that was beginning to form.

The contact of eastern Jewish communities with the British began in India, where several waves of migration had deposited Jewish groups in the early Middle Ages in such localities as Cochin on the southwest coast and in villages south of Bombay.[11] After the seventeenth century, additional Jewish merchants from Iraq, Syria, Persia, and Europe settled in India. As the British strengthened their lines of communication to India, especially after the opening of the Suez Canal (1869), other Middle Eastern Jewish communities fell under British rule. The Jewries of Alexandria and Cairo expanded to play an active role in business and even in the government of British-controlled Egypt. The Jews of Iraq, one of the oldest and most learned communities of the Middle East, had been undergoing a renewal of their religious and Hebraic culture and a modernization of their careers and professions in the nineteenth century.

Sabbath services at a Jewish boys' school in Casablanca, Morocco. (Courtesy of Women's American ORT.)

Iraqi Jewish merchants developed far-flung trading ties throughout southern Asia. Under the British mandate, Jews played a crucial role in the educational, cultural, and economic life of Iraq and in the administration of the country.

Smaller Jewries fell under the control of Italy (Libya in 1911) and Spain (part of Morocco in 1912). The expansion of the Russian empire led to the incorporation at the beginning of the nineteenth century of the "Mountain Jews" of the Caucasus and the Jews of the ancient Christian kingdom of Georgia in the Transcaucasus, as well as of the central Asian emirate of Bukhara in the 1860s.[12] (Under Soviet rule the Georgian Jews were unusually successful in maintaining their religious traditions.)

Ottoman Turkey maintained its nominal independence from European rule in the age of imperial expansion, but Western influence was felt there too. The Sephardic Jews of the Ottoman-ruled cities of Salonika, Istanbul, and Izmir began to publish Ladino newspapers and translations of European literary works in the 1870s and 1880s. (Ladino is the Spanish dialect of the Sephardic Jews.) In 1913 the large Jewish community of Salonika passed under Greek rule. A bloody Greek-Turkish war after World War I led to the expulsion of the Greeks from Asia Minor and the establishment of a Turkish government determined to modernize the country as rapidly as possible. As a result, those Jews remaining in Turkey, half of whom lived in Istanbul, attained legal emancipation, but Turkish suspicion of minorities and strong pressure to adopt the Turkish language inhibited the effective development of Jewish and Hebrew education there.

The Jews of Persia had continued to live under oppressive, almost medieval conditions throughout the nineteenth century (pogroms, forced conversions, treatment by the Muslim clergy as ritually unclean), but a revival of Judeo-Persian literature began at the end of the century among Persian Jews in Jerusalem and then in Teheran. After the introduction in the mid-1920s of a modernizing regime in Persia (now renamed Iran), and with outside Jewish aid, the Iranian Jews began to construct a stronger network of cultural and educational institutions.

By the 1930s only a few Jewries had not been substantially affected by modern styles of life: the Kurdish Jews, the Jews of Yemen, and the Falashas of Ethiopia.[13] But modernization, as always, had its price. The development of Arab nationalism, socioeconomic tensions, the spread of pro-Nazi sentiment in the 1930s, and Arab hostility to Zionism were, in the long run, to have a fatal effect on Jewish existence in the Arab countries. In the nineteenth century, traditional yearnings for Zion brought considerable numbers of Jews from Yemen, Bukhara, Persia, and Georgia to Palestine. Branches of modern Zionism developed in Fgypt, Iran, and especially in Iraq in the 1920s and 1930s. After World

War II a large proportion of these Sephardic and eastern Jews were to join the yishuv as active participants in the mainstream of Jewish history.

Germany from Weimar Republic to Nazi Reich

After the abdication of the German emperor during the last days of World War I, a new constitution, written by a democratically elected assembly at Weimar, transformed Germany into a federal republic with a broad franchise and full civil liberties. From the start the new regime was faced by determined opposition on the extreme left and right. The German economy was in disarray, culminating in an inflation (1922–1923) that wiped out the savings of the middle class. The period 1924–1929 was one of greater stability, prosperity, and brilliant avant-garde intellectual flowering for the Weimar Republic. Then came the Great Depression. Between 1930 and 1932 German unemployment grew to over 6 million: One of every three Germans was without a job and German national income fell 43 per cent. As a result, the vote for the extremist parties, the Communists and the Nazis, soared. Faced with paralysis in the Reichstag, the government began to rule by presidential decree. After several ineffective conservative coalitions, the aging president, Field Marshall Paul von Hindenburg, appointed Adolf Hitler as chancellor (prime minister) of Germany on January 30, 1933, putting in control of one of the world's most highly industrialized nations a man whose personal identity, will to power, and political ideology revolved around the most extreme form yet of modern anti-Semitism.

Born and raised in Austria, Adolf Hitler (1889–1945) was a rootless, frustrated, unsuccessful artist who spent several years in Vienna, where he was much impressed by the anti-Semitic movement. Moving to Munich in 1913, he volunteered for the German army after the outbreak of war and fought on the western front. Returning to Munich in 1919 as one of many demobilized soldiers who maintained a loose connection with the army, he joined the tiny National Socialist German Workers' party, soon becoming its leader. The ideology of the Nazi party, formulated by Hitler between 1919 and 1924, combined extreme German nationalism, a few anticapitalist formulas, and racial anti-Semitism: The Jews were economic parasites and cultural degenerates alien to Europe; Germany lost the war because of a "stab in the back" by Jewish socialists, liberals, and pacifists (that the strikes and mutinies of the last month of the war directly caused the German defeat was widely believed by rightists); the Bolshevik take-over in Russia was part of the Jewish plan for world domination. (Fear of communism and an extreme sensitivity to the presence of Jews in the Communist movement was widespread in Europe and America, as noted earlier, and was thought by anti-

Typical front page of the Nazi newspaper **Die Stürmer,** showing anti-Semitic cartoon exposing Jewish ritual murder. The bottom line is a favorite Nazi slogan, "The Jews are our misfortune."

Semites to confirm the veracity of the *Protocols of the Elders of Zion.*) Hitler's fusion of anti-Semitism and anti-Communism was particularly potent, because it provided a handy justification for the belief that the Germans were entitled to a much greater *Lebensraum* (living space) in Eastern Europe. According to Hitler, inasmuch as the Jews had already taken over control of the inferior Slavs, the crusades against Communism ("Jewish Bolshevism") and against the Jewish race were one and the same. Hitler saw himself as the *Führer* (leader) of a ruthless, heroic war against an unclean, demonic, cancerous "international Jewry," which, were the Jews to win, would bring about the demise of humanity, whereas Aryan victory would leave the Germans in control of the vast *Reich* (empire) that its innate racial superiority merited. An unscrupulous demagogue able to exploit irrational fears and mob hysteria, he attracted a core of embittered and frustrated followers in the 1920s. And the Nazi party was able to make effective use of physical violence through the paramilitary storm troopers (the *Sturmabteilung* or SA), which attacked members of opposing parties and created a show of strength.

In the 1920s Hitler's movement was noisy and provocative, but a minor force in Germany. His one attempted *coup d'état* (November 1923 in Munich) was a failure. However, the depression won for the Nazis the financial backing of German industrialists fearful of Communist gains, the support of those strata yearning to bolster their shaky social position, and the enthusiasm of violence-prone youth. The Nazis received 810,000 votes in 1928; 6,380,000 in 1930, 14,000,000 in 1932 (37.4 per cent of the electorate). Their number of seats in the Reichstag in those years went from 12 to 107 to 230. In the election of March 5, 1933, when Hitler was chancellor and was able freely to use the SA to bully the opposition, the Nazis won 44 per cent of the total vote, indicating both the extent and the limit of their appeal.

Once in power the Nazi regime quickly adapted the totalitarian model of Soviet Communism and the Fascist example of Mussolini's Italy to its own racial goals. In March 1933, all civil liberties were rescinded and the government was given dictatorial powers. A "coordination" (*Gleichschaltung*) of social institutions led to their dissolution or absorption into a seemingly monolithic state structure. In the spring and summer of 1933, all political parties were liquidated, one by one. Strikes were outlawed and trade unions replaced by a government and employer-controlled "labor front." Public book burnings (May 1933) were followed by the arrest or flight of scientists, scholars, and artists of whom the government disapproved or who would not pay homage to the Nazi ideology. Pressure was applied to bring the churches under government direction or to neutralize their criticism. In June 1934 a purge of the SA eliminated the party's social radicals, paving the way for the expansion of the SS (the *Schutzstaffeln* or guard troops). Under Heinrich Himmler, the SS absorbed many of the police functions of the state, including the Gestapo or secret police, and it ran the concentration camps. After Hindenburg's death in August 1934 Hitler combined the roles of party chief and head of state as the supreme *Führer*. The army General Staff was brought under Hitler's full control in February 1938. Large sums of money were pumped into the economy through public works and rearmament, putting an end to unemployment. Hitler's foreign policy was a series of daring and provocative gambles to reverse the World War I settlement. In May 1936 the German army re-entered the Rhineland, in violation of the Treaty of Versailles. In 1937 the Germans and Italians gave considerable military support to Franco's forces in the Spanish Civil War. In March 1938 Hitler annexed Austria. In September 1938 the British prime minister, meeting with Hitler and the leaders of the French and Italian governments at Munich, agreed that Germany should control those areas of western Czechoslovakia with a large ethnic German (Sudeten) population. In March 1939, contrary to his promises, Hitler occupied Prague and extinguished the Czechoslovak state. In August 1939 he signed a non-

aggression pact with Stalin, secretly dividing Poland between them. On September 1, 1939, the Germans invaded Poland, and British and French declarations of war ensued. World War II had begun.

Nazi policies toward the Jews between 1933 and 1939 can be divided into three stages, reflecting Hitler's early dictum that anti-Semitism should be "rational" and not "emotional"—that the elimination of the Jews should be carried out by degrees and careful planning. The first two and a half years were marked by measures eliminating non-Aryans from the civil service, the legal and medical professions, and public cultural and educational institutions. The second stage began with the Nuremburg Laws of September 1935, which reduced Jews from citizens to second-class subjects (thus undoing the nineteenth-century emancipation). A purely racial definition of a Jew was introduced (anyone with a Jewish grandparent). All marriages and sexual relationships between Aryans and Semites were made crimes against "German blood and honor." The third stage began in 1938 when Jewish communal bodies were put under the control of the Gestapo and Jews ordered to register their foreign and domestic property. After the assassination of a German diplomat by a Jewish youth in Paris, a government-organized pogrom was launched throughout Germany (November 9–10, 1938) in which Jews were maltreated and murdered, Jewish shop windows smashed, and synagogues burned (*Kristallnacht*, "night of glass"). Many Jewish businesses and holdings were expropriated. By 1939, 300,000 of Germany's 500,000 Jews (as of 1930) had fled. Where to go was an agonizing problem, in view of the immigration restrictions prevailing throughout the world, including those imposed by the British in Palestine. Refusal of the Western democracies to admit more than a small number of Jewish refugees, despite an intergovernmental conference at Evian, France, in July 1938, indicated to the Nazis that nothing would be done, except for verbal protests, to oppose their Jewish policies.

1939–1945: The Holocaust of World War II

Beginning with the lightning conquest of Poland in 1939, the German armies soon occupied one country after another on the European continent: Denmark and Norway (April 1940), the Netherlands and Belgium (May 1940), France (June 1940). When the air war over England did not go according to plan, Hitler ordered preparations for the invasion of the USSR. In the spring of 1941 the Germans reinforced the Italian armies and extended their own control over the Balkans and North

News photo of the burning of a Berlin synagogue on **Krystallnacht,** Nov. 8–9, 1938, when most of Germany's synagogues were destroyed by the Nazis.

Roundup of Jews in Warsaw during World War II. (The Archives of the Yivo Institute of Jewish Research, New York.)

Africa. The German attack on Russia (June 22, 1941) brought them near Moscow and Leningrad by October; at the end of 1941 they had taken most of the Ukraine. In December 1941, after the Japanese attack on the American fleet at Pearl Harbor, the German and Italian governments declared war on the United States and the war became global. In 1942 the Germans recommenced their drive on Russia, stalled the previous winter by logistical difficulties and weather. The turning point of the war in the east was the successful Russian defense of Stalingrad in January 1943. By May 1943, the British and Americans had eliminated the Axis powers from North Africa; by the end of autumn the Allies had occupied Italy south of Rome. While the Russians were advancing into Poland and Romania, American and British troops landed on the coast of Normandy (June 6, 1944), and the liberation of France and Belgium began. Only after Hitler's suicide in Berlin at the end of April 1945 did the Germans surrender (May 7–8, 1945). When Japan accepted the Allied terms on September 2, 1945, World War II was over.

The war, which was all along Hitler's plan, provided an ideal setting for realizing his goals of depopulating the lands on which the greater Germanic *Reich* was to be constructed, enslaving the Slavs and other "inferior" groups, and effectuating a "Final Solution" of the Jewish question. Complete control of communications and transportation provided the needed cover of secrecy. Total mobilization of resources, including ruthless exploitation of what was called "human material," provided the general economic framework. The expansion of the SS into a state within the state provided the instrument, although the SS needed and received the cooperation of other branches of the German bureaucracy, the German army, and the Nazi puppet governments in the satellite countries. In October 1939 Hitler gave the SS *Reichsführer* Heinrich Himmler the additional position of "Commissar for the Strengthening of the German Nationhood," under which the administrative apparatus for the elimination of "undesirable" populations was constructed. The mentality of Himmler and his henchmen—pedantic fanaticism and brutal efficiency—was facilitated by an impersonal bureaucratic jargon that freed them from any residual moral inhibitions and at the same time concealed their real intentions from the victims ("evacuation," "resettlement," "transport," "actions," "special treatment," "final solution"—all with unspoken genocidal meanings). According to Himmler, mass murder was a glorious, historic task, to be carried out "bravely, without softening." "The SS man is to be guided by one principle alone: honesty, decency, loyalty, and friendship toward those of our blood and to no one else."[14] That there had to be an unequivocal solution to the Jewish problem meant that not only combatants but civilians, not only men but women and children, had to be killed so that no new generation of Jews

Jews lined up against the wall of the Warsaw ghetto. (The Archives of the Yivo Institute of Jewish Research, New York.)

could arise to threaten the Aryan "New Order." In 1943 Hitler's propaganda chief, Goebbels, noted in his diary that the Jews were being destroyed by "a rather barbarous procedure," but that "one must not allow sentimentality to prevail in these matters. The Jews would destroy us if we did not ward them off. It is a life and death struggle between the Aryan race and the Jewish bacillus."[15] Therefore, Himmler's inexorable statement: "The hard decision had to be taken—this people must disappear from the face of the earth."[16]

Immediately after the Germans occupied western Poland most of the Jewish leadership was interned or shot. During 1940 Polish Jews were ordered into walled ghettos and put to work in various enterprises vital to the German war effort. All Jews had to wear a yellow badge; if found outside without a special permit they were to be executed on the spot. Jewish councils were established to run the internal affairs of the ghettos under the supervision of the SS. During the first two and a half years of the war, the ghetto inhabitants managed to re-establish basic social, cultural, and educational programs under the most difficult conditions, including epidemics and widespread starvation. In the occupied areas of Western Europe, Jews not immediately sent to detention camps were ordered to register with the police to facilitate their eventual "evacuation."

The extermination plan was probably made final by Hitler and Himmler during preparations for the invasion of Russia (December 1940–February 1941). Two means of implementation were used: mobile armed SS units and annihilation camps. The SS "action groups" (*Einsatzgruppen*) were trained in May 1941 and sent to murder Jews, Soviet officials, and gypsies in occupied territory behind the German lines in the east. Local anti-Semites, especially Ukrainians, Lithuanians, and Moldavians, were encouraged to stage pogroms. Four *Einsatzgruppen*, about 3,000 officers and men, moved from locality to locality, rounding up Jews for "resettlement" and marching them outside the city or town, where they were forced to dig trenches or pits. The Jews were then stripped, machine-gunned, and buried. One of the largest single "actions" was the massacre of at least 34,000 Jews at Babi Yar outside Kiev at the end of September 1941. It is probable that between one and a half and two million Jews were killed by the *Einsatzgruppen* in occupied Russia in 1941–1942.

During the summer of 1941 orders were given for construction of the annihilation camps.[17] The techniques had already been tried out in a "euthanasia" operation devised several years earlier to eliminate "racially defective" (i.e., deformed) German children and the insane, of whom 70,000–100,000 were killed by poison gas until German public opinion forced the suspension of this program. "Euthanasia" functionaries were transferred to the Final Solution. On January 20, 1942, representatives of the SS, the Gestapo, and government ministries met in suburban Berlin

Last stages of the Warsaw ghetto uprising. (The Archives of the Yivo Institute of Jewish Research, New York.)

to arrange for extending the genocide to the satellite countries. (The surviving minutes of the Wansee Conference, so named from the street on which the meeting was held, make it one of the best documented events in the practical implementation of the Final Solution.)

The six death factories were all located in Polish territory. The first to be put into operation was at Chelmno, near Lodz, where 150,000–340,000 Polish Jews and some Soviet prisoners of war and gypsies were killed in camouflaged gas vans between December 1941 and spring 1943. The second was Belzec near Lvov and Lublin, where 600,000 Jews were liquidated by carbon monoxide poisoning between March 1942 and spring 1943. Sobibor, near Lublin, was used May 1942–October 1943 to kill about 250,000 Jews from east Poland, occupied Russia, Czechoslovakia, and Western Europe, in addition to many non-Jewish prisoners of war. The Majdanek concentration and extermination camp on the outskirts of Lublin was the scene of the death of at least 125,000 Jews in 1942–1943. In the Treblinka camp near Warsaw an estimated 800,000 Jews were gassed between July 1942 and October 1943. The largest of the camps was at Auschwitz, a small town in Galicia near the border of Upper Silesia, where one to two million Jews were killed by hydrogen cyanide gas (Zyklon B) January 1942–November 1944. To Auschwitz were sent Jews from all over occupied Europe: France, Belgium, Holland, Norway, Austria, Slovakia, Croatia, Italy, Yugoslavia, Greece, and Hungary. Auschwitz and Treblinka also served as forced labor camps. When the "transports" arrived, a small percent of the victims were selected to be worked to death in chemical and other factories built nearby. The rest of the men, women, and children, stripped of their clothing, were rushed with whips, dogs, and gunshots to "shower rooms." Nazi dignitaries watched the gassing through peepholes. Rings and gold fillings of the corpses were removed, women's hair cut off for industrial uses, and the bodies cremated or buried in nearby woods, often by squads of Jewish prisoners who were later killed.

The extermination process was carefully planned, using guile, lies, and terror to make organized resistance virtually impossible. Nevertheless, several Jewish ghetto and camp revolts took place, the most important of which was in the Warsaw ghetto. Beginning on April 19, 1943, several thousand poorly armed Jewish fighters held out for six weeks, forcing the SS to reconquer the district with massive military force, building by building.

During the "shipments," Himmler made only minimal short-term concessions on economic grounds. Large groups of Jews were being rounded up and sent to the camps, tying up much railroad equipment, months

Extermination camp incinerator. (The Archives of the Yivo Institute of Jewish Research, New York.)

after the Normandy landing. Two thirds of the extermination was carried out after 1942, when eventual German defeat was certain. Although the extermination program was known in the West by 1943, Allied military officials rejected pleas that the camps be bombed on the grounds that it would impede the war effort. It should be kept in mind that the unprecedented nature of the Holocaust—methodical murder of an entire civilian category of the population—precluded the formation of a quick and effective response by the victims or their friends.

Although precise statistics are not available because the Germans destroyed most of the documents connected with the Final Solution, in 1945 only 3.1 million Jews were left in Europe out of a population 9.2 million before the fighting. Of the 35 million Europeans killed during the war, 6 million were Jews. (Almost all these Jews were civilians.) In only a few lands did the extermination program run into obstacles. The Danes smuggled more than 6,000 Jews to neutral Sweden in October 1943. Certain governments allied with Germany did not turn over any or some of their native Jews (Finland, Bulgaria, Romania, Italy), but direct German occupation of southern France, northern Italy, and Hungary in the later stages of the war doomed many of the Jews there. Thousands of Jews joined the partisan movements. Other thousands were hidden at great risk by Christian friends and clergy. (On the other hand, many Polish and other peasants turned fleeing Jews over to the Nazis and some partisan movements refused to accept or aid the Jews.)

Seen in the perspective of modern European history, the Holocaust was the product of a long-range and complex set of circumstances, including chauvinistic nationalism throughout Europe, antidemocratic tendencies inherent in the creation of a German nation-state aspiring to great power status, the world economic crisis of the 1930s, technical possibilities afforded an advanced industrial state waging a war of conquest, and the power available to the absolute leader of a totalitarian party to realize his fantasies of omnipotence. Seen in the perspective of Jewish history, the Holocaust stands at the end of a chain going back much further: defects built into the emancipation process, Judeophobia built into medieval religion, the tragic dilemma of a people through whom ethical monotheism came to a humanity all too willing to hate and all too eager to destroy.

Jewish Social and Political Conditions After 1945

The State of Israel

Despite the White Paper of 1939, large numbers of the yishuv's Jews enlisted in the British army, and toward the end of the war the British

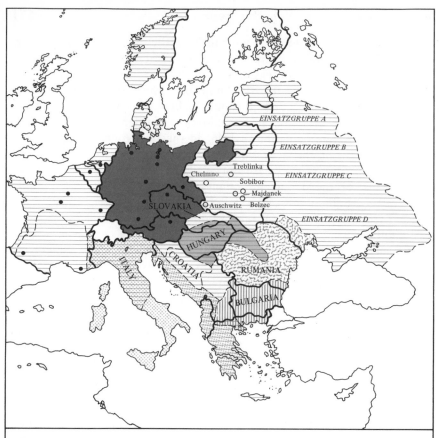

Key

— = International borders in 1937

█ = German Reich as of Sept. 1939, on outbreak of the war

▒ = Italy and areas of the Balkans and southern France occupied by Italy until its surrender in Sept. 1943, when the Germans occupied these areas and northern Italy

▒ = Hungary and areas occupied by it in 1939–41, until the Germans assumed direct control in March 1944

▥ = Bulgaria and areas ceded to it 1940–1941

▨ = Rumania and areas ceded to it 1939–1941

▱ = Areas occupied by German military during the course of the war, including the maximum extent of German penetration into the Soviet Union.

○ = Extermination camp.

● = Major concentration camp in western and central Europe

--- = Zones of occupation

Jewish boys being taught a trade in a displaced persons' camp after World War II.
(Courtesy of Women's American ORT.)

government finally allowed the formation of a Jewish Brigade to fight in Europe. The postwar aims of the Zionist movement were approved at a May 1942 Zionist meeting in New York: mass Jewish immigration to Palestine and the establishment of a Jewish commonwealth.

During the first year of peace 250,000 Jewish refugees made their way to Western Europe, where they were temporarily housed in displaced persons (DP) camps. Some were East European Jews who had tried to return to their former homes, only to encounter anti-Semitic hostility and violence. (The worst outbreak was a pogrom in the Polish town of

The Geography of the Holocaust. With some exceptions, the Nazis were able to elicit cooperation from allied and subject populations in carrying out the genocide. The per cent of Jews killed in a country mainly depended on if and when the German authorities took over direct control of the implementation of the Final Solution. The Nazis had a free hand in Poland and large sections of the USSR from the early stages of World War II. In November 1942 they occupied central and southern France, which had been until then ruled by a pro-Nazi French government at Vichy. In September 1943, the Germans occupied northern and central Italy and areas of the Balkans and southern France previously administered by Italy. In March 1944 they took over Hungary and adjacent areas given over to Hungarian rule. Because Bulgaria and Romania, also German allies, did not experience German rule during the last stages of the war, larger numbers of Jews escaped massacre in these areas when the fighting had ended in May 1945.

Kielce, June 1946.) The British persisted in refusing to allow the DP's to settle in Palestine. Even the formerly pro-Zionist British Labor party, when it came to power, continued the 1939 White Paper policy out of fear of antagonizing Arab governments. With the help of the yishuv and sympathizers in America and Europe, boatloads of DP's tried to reach Palestine illegally; the British intercepted many of them and sent the refugees to internment camps in Cyprus or returned them to Europe. Tension mounted in the yishuv. Beginning in the fall of 1945, underground Revisionist groups that had separated themselves from the Haganah launched attacks on British installations in Palestine. The British in turn attempted to repress the terrorists and the Haganah without success. Finally, in April 1947, the British government turned the question of Palestine's future over to the United Nations. On November 29, 1947, the General Assembly of the UN voted 33 to 13 in favor of partitioning Palestine between the Jews and the Arabs. The Soviet Union joined the United States in support of the partition resolution, which the Arab governments rejected completely.

On May 14, 1948, immediately after the British evacuation, the leaders of the yishuv assembled in Tel Aviv to proclaim the independence of the Jewish State:

> The land of Israel was the birthplace of the Jewish people. Here their spiritual, religious, and political identity was formed. Here they first achieved statehood, created a culture of national and universal significance, and gave to the world the eternal Book of Books.
>
> Exiled forcibly from its land, the people remained faithful to it in all the countries of the dispersion, never ceasing to pray and hope for return and restoration in it of their political freedom.
>
> Impelled by this historic and traditional attachment, Jews strove throughout every generation to re-establish themselves in their ancient homeland. In recent decades they returned in their masses. . . . They reclaimed the wilderness, revived the Hebrew language, built villages and cities, and established a vigorous and ever-growing community, with its own economic and cultural life, loving peace but knowing how to defend itself, bringing the blessings of progress to all the country's inhabitants, and aspiring toward independent statehood. . . .
>
> Accordingly, we, members of the People's Council, representatives of the Jewish people in the land of Israel and of the Zionist movement are here assembled on the day of the termination of the British Mandate over Palestine and, by virtue of our natural and historic right and on the strength of the resolution of the General Assembly of the United Nations, proclaim the establishment of a Jewish state in the land of Israel, to be known as the State of Israel.[18]

The previous November, just after the partition plan was adopted by the UN, irregular Palestinian Arab bands, financed by the Arab states,

Jerusalem during Israel's War for Independence, 1948. (Courtesy of the Zionist Archives, New York.)

began to attack Jewish settlements and neighborhoods. During this unde-clared war, the main goal of the Haganah was to keep roads open between the Jewish settlements, especially between the coastal plain and Jerusalem. Large numbers of Arabs living next to the Jews or in the battle zones fled, creating the future issue of the Palestinian refugees. As soon as the British troops departed and the State of Israel was proclaimed, the armies of Egypt, Transjordan, Lebanon, Syria, and Iraq entered the country. During May and June 1948 the Arab Legion of Transjordan seized the Old City of Jerusalem, including the Jewish Quarter, but the Israeli forces retained control of the heavily Jewish parts of the Galilee, the Jezreel Valley, the coastal plain, a corridor to Jerusalem, and a pocket of the Negev. Fighting was interrupted by temporary truces in late June to early July and in late July to October. By the end of Israel's war for inde-pendence in January 1949, the Israelis had also established themselves throughout the Galilee and the Negev, holding in all 8,000 square miles of Palestine, in contrast to the 6,200 square miles awarded them in the UN partition plan. Between February and July 1949 Israel and various Arab governments signed final truce agreements under UN supervision on the island of Rhodes. The Egyptians were left in control of the Gaza strip;

the Jordanians annexed the west bank of the Jordan and east Jerusalem. On May 11, 1949, Israel was admitted as a member of the United Nations.

Israel's first achievement was the "ingathering of the exiles" (the traditional phrase of the prayer book). At the end of 1947 the yishuv numbered 630,000; four years later Israel's Jewish population had doubled. Jews came from the DP camps in western Germany, from Bulgaria, Poland, and Romania, and from Arab lands. Most of the Jews of Yemen, Iraq, and Libya arrived in special airlifts, followed a few years later by large numbers from Morocco, Tunisia, and Egypt. Continued immigration and natural increase brought the total number of Jews in Israel in the late seventies to almost 3 million, approximately the population of Ireland or Uruguay or New Zealand. The result of the large influx from North Africa and the Middle East meant that by the end of the seventies half of Israel's Jews were of Sephardic or eastern extraction.

To absorb this population and to sustain the Zionist ideal of a "normal" Jewish nation-state meant overcoming the handicaps of limited natural resources, a small internal market, and persistent hostility of Israel's Arab neighbors. Progress was possible because of the thoroughly modern groundwork laid by the yishuv, because of a generally high educational level, which enabled the Israelis to use advanced technology and scientific planning, and because of considerable financial aid from the diaspora,

Yemenite Jews on their way to Israel in 1950. (Courtesy of the Zionist Archives, New York.)

from the United States government, and from the German reparations agreement of 1952. Israel has been able to advance without resort to coercion and while maintaining a democratic regime. The main governmental bodies are a cabinet of ministers and a parliament based on proportional representation for various party lists of candidates submitted to the electorate. The parties still substantially reflect the old groupings in the Zionist movement from before the establishment of the state. For the first twenty-nine years of the state's existence the central position in the ruling coalition was the Israel Labor party, until its replacement in 1977 by a nonsocialist alignment led by the political heir of the old Revisionist movement.

Internal tasks facing Israel are the complete integration of Jews from dozens of lands, whose languages and patterns of life differed greatly (some of whom had still been living a medieval existence in such places as Morocco, Yemen, Libya, and Persia shortly before they arrived), and the creation of a permanently prosperous economy through participation in a European or Middle Eastern integrated market. Solution to the latter seems to depend on an eventual resolution of the Israel-Arab impasse.

The overwhelming problem faced by Israel has been the refusal of Arab states to accept its legitimacy and enter into a permanent peace. Arab belligerence has a complex etiology: the reaction of a people that does not want to share its land with others who also claim title to it; the inability of Muslims to accept that a religious minority should gain sovereignty over a corner of the Islamic realm; the dilemma posed by the Palestinian refugees; the usefulness to the ruling Arab elites of focusing on hatred of a powerful and demonic enemy as a scapegoat for their difficulties in achieving stable and prosperous societies. Arab anti-Zionism has many of the attributes of Western anti-Semitism.

Besides resisting infiltration by Arab terrorists and an economic boycott organized by the Arab states, Israel has fought four major wars to preserve her security and viability (the Sinai Campaign of October–November 1956, the Six Day War of June 1967, a war of attrition along the Suez Canal in 1969–70, and the Yom Kippur War of October 1973). Technological and organizational skill, along with the overwhelming knowledge that they were fighting for the very existence of their country, enabled the Israelis to defend themselves successfully, open the Gulf of Aqaba to Israeli shipping, and enlarge the territory under their control. Unlike the Jews of the diaspora through many centuries and the Jews of Europe during World War II, they have possessed a geographical base and political sovereignty that made this possible. The overriding question at present for the Jewish state and for the Middle East is whether the Arab governments can convince themselves and their population to accept Israel's existence and whether arrangements can be negotiated to the satisfaction of all parties—Israel, the Palestinian Arabs, the Arab states, and

Modern farming techniques at Kibbutz Ein Gedi between the Judean desert and the Dead Sea. (Courtesy of the Consulate General of Israel.)

the interested powers—that will ensure tranquility, cooperation, and progress for the region as a whole.

The Diaspora

In the 1970s Israel contained slightly more than a fifth of the 14 million Jews in the world.[19] In 1975 the largest Jewish community, that of the United States, was estimated at 5.845 million. The United States and Canada (305,000) contained 43 per cent of the world's Jews. Latin America had an estimated 617,000 of which 300,000 lived in Argentina and 160,000 in Brazil; there are 72,000 Jews in Australia, 5,000 in New Zealand, and 118,000 in South Africa.

The Jewish population remaining in non-Communist Europe was estimated at about 1 million, the largest communities being in Great Britain (410,000) and France (550,000). Sephardic Jews now form the majority of French Jewry, as the result of an immigration from North Africa in the 1950s and 1960s of 225,000 Jews who had become French citizens during French rule there. The Jews of the Communist world are thought to number about 2.3 million, almost all in the USSR (2.151 million),

Hungary (80,000), and Romania (60,000). Jews have almost completely evacuated the Muslim states, although there remain about 30,000 in Morocco, 30,000 in Turkey, and 80,000 in Iran.

These figures indicate that the massive redistribution of Jews in the diaspora, a feature of modern Jewish history at least since the earlier half of the nineteenth century, has continued in the post-World War II era. Almost all Jews now live in the most advanced, industrialized countries, in contrast to the beginning of the modern era when most Jews lived in the backward economies of East Europe, North Africa, and western Asia. Even in the Soviet Union most Jews reside in the large metropolitan cities of Moscow, Leningrad, and Kiev, where the tsarist regime had tried to prevent them from settling in the nineteenth century.

Although poverty remains a problem among the elderly, the majority of Jews have become part of the middle class. The Jewish proletariat has declined steadily in recent decades and only in Israel are Jewish factory workers and farmers to be found in large numbers. Diaspora Jews are largely self-employed businessmen, white-collar workers, professionals, engineers, accountants, pharmacists, dentists, physicians, lawyers, journalists, teachers, scientists, artists, musicians, and writers. Diaspora Jews are rarely found in large-scale industry and banking, but they are present

The modern port of Haifa, photographed from the top of Mount Carmel. (Courtesy of the Consulate General of Israel.)

in such fields as retailing and wholesaling, real estate, the stock market, construction, communications, publishing, advertising, electronics, and computer technology. It has been argued that the occupational distribution of Jews, once thought to be abnormal, actually foreshadows an emerging postindustrial society, in which the service sector will predominate.

Almost all diaspora Jews have become acculturated, unless they refuse to do so in order to preserve an extremely traditional Orthodox way of life. The majority of Jews speak English; large numbers speak French, Spanish, and Russian. Yiddish survives as a second language, especially among the older generation in Russia, Argentina, and the United States, but except for students studying it in schools and universities, Yiddish seems to be fated to disappear. Hebrew has become the modern Jewish language, a basic component of diaspora Jewish education at home and during periods of study in Israel.

The lengthy history of Jewish emancipation has been concluded, but the history of Jew-hatred has probably not—because anti-Semitism still proves to be useful under certain circumstances. In South Africa, where there was considerable sympathy for the Nazis during World War II, the Jews have more recently been accepted in a white minority faced with the threat of racial upheaval, but in politically unstable Argentina, neo-Nazi groups have periodically attacked the Jews in print and physically.

In recent decades most persistent and systematic reinforcement of anti-Jewish stereotypes has been by the Soviet government, which since World War II has reverted to the contradictory old tsarist policy of wanting the Jews to assimilate while at the same time using them as scapegoats. Although Stalin was willing to support the establishment of the state of Israel in order to speed the ouster of the British from the Middle East, the last period of Stalin's life (1948–1953) is often known as the "Black Years" of Soviet Jewry. In 1952 the remaining group of outstanding Yiddish poets, playwrights, and novelists was executed. A show trial of Jewish Communists in Prague (the Slansky trial of 1952 arranged by the Soviet secret police) purported to uncover a plot by an international organization of Jewish capitalists and Zionists linked with American espionage agents to subvert the socialist system. In early 1953 the Soviet government announced the discovery of a conspiracy to murder Soviet leaders by Jewish physicians in Moscow in league with Israel, an American Jewish philanthropic agency, and the United States intelligence service. Although soon after Stalin died the "Doctors' Plot" was admitted to be a fabrication, Soviet authorities have subsequently been willing to exploit popular anti-Semitic feelings, such as blaming Jewish "economic criminals" for graft and other difficulties in the Soviet system. Official identity papers of Jews continue to indicate their "Jewish nationality,"

The Western Wall of the ancient Temple mount, the holiest Jewish site in Jerusalem. (Courtesy of the Consulate General of Israel.)

but they have been refused the opportunity to study Hebrew and Jewish history. They are confronted with considerable discrimination in higher education and careers, as part of a program to favor the dominant nationalities of the Soviet republics. Especially after 1967 a campaign against Zionism, partly the result of Soviet efforts to strengthen the government's influence in the Arab world, has identified the Israelis with the Nazis and the Jewish religion with racism. One result of these pressures has been a revival of Jewish nationalist sentiments among Soviet Jews. In recent years a fluctuating stream of Soviet Jews has been allowed, after considerable personal difficulties, to leave for Israel. It is possible that the Soviet government intends in this way to siphon off some of the dissident group that has called for greater freedom in the USSR.

Since World War II anti-Semitism has not been a problem in most Western countries, but anti-Zionism seems to have partly taken its place, especially the tendency to view the Israelis as the aggressors and the Arabs as the passive victims of the Middle Eastern stalemate and to consider Zionism a form of imperialism. Owing to the importance of Arab petroleum resources for the economies of the West and the resulting diplomatic leverage of certain Arab governments, the warm feelings for Israel seem to have weakened three decades after the Holocaust.

In the long run, even more serious for diaspora Jews in the West is assimilation and intermarriage, a by-product of successful acculturation and integration. The Jewish birthrate has declined to the point where most diaspora Jewries are numerically stationary, so that the loss through assimilation is not made up by an increase in other sectors of the Jewish population, as it was prior to World War II. The hallmark of cultural

The synagogue of the Technion, the Israel Institute of Technology, in Haifa. (Courtesy of the Synagogue Art and Architectural Library of the Union of American Hebrew Congregations.)

and religious identities in modern Western society is that they are freely chosen and subjectively appropriated. In order to pass on their heritage, American Jews since the war have expanded and developed synagogue religious instruction, all-day Jewish schools, summer youth camps, and theological seminaries and yeshivot. Jewish studies are now a recognized part of higher education. Jewish philanthropy is a means of active Jewish identification for many. Since World War II, Zionism has been a unifying bond in the diaspora, no longer merely one of several competing Jewish ideologies. The state of Israel has been in the diaspora a symbol of Jewish hope, dignity, and self-respect—and of the will-to-survive despite the Holocaust. In the context of history, however, the Jewish state is a means, but not the meaning, of being Jewish for most Jews in the diaspora and for many in the land of Israel. The search to define that meaning is the content of modern Jewish thought.

CHAPTER 15

Secular Jewish Thought in the Nineteenth and Twentieth Centuries

What are the perimeters of modern Jewish thought, defined with sufficient broadness to be comprehensive and with sufficient definiteness to be identifiably Jewish? There are acknowledged masterworks of Western civilization where the Jewish background of the author contributed a special ingredient and perspective, unstated and perhaps even unconscious (e.g., the novels of Franz Kafka and the psychoanalytic theories of Sigmund Freud). We will briefly return later in this chapter to the Jewishness of those who were Jewish in Spinoza's sense. For our purpose, however—that of tracing the amplification of a tradition—modern Jewish thought includes books explicitly concerned with the meaning and destiny of being Jewish. These books may have appeared in forms in which Jewish thought was previously cast or in forms new to the period after 1880, but they all take being Jewish with utmost seriousness and caring.

Indeed, what has Jewish thought consisted in? The scope of a Jewish book, the questions it seeks to answer, and the methods it uses to answer them have varied considerably. In every period of history there has been a variety of Jewish modes of expression, but certain issues have predominated. In its biblical stage, Jewish thought characteristically wanted to know what God required here and now, and how God was guiding events in the past, present, and future. In rabbinic Judaism, a dominant concern was what the sacred texts meant and how they applied to life. In medieval Jewish rationalism, thinkers informed about Islamic theology

Photograph of eminent Jewish writers of Odessa taken in 1908–1909. Seated from right to left: Rav Tsair (Chaim Tchernowitz), M. L. Lilienblum, Y. H. Ravnitsky, Ahad Ha-Am, Mendele Mocher Seforim, E. L. Lewinsky. Standing from right to left: Ber Borochov, Joseph Klausner, H. N. Bialik. (Courtesy of the Zionist Archives, New York.)

or Aristotelian philosophy or Neo-Platonic speculation asked how and to what extent the arguments of these intellectual systems were compatible with the fundamental pillars of revealed Torah, whereas medieval Jewish mystics and kabbalists asked what were the esoteric levels, hidden paths, and secret harmonies of the divine Torah, the heart and goal of creation. In the first century of modern Jewish thought, as the Enlightenment, Romanticism, and philosophical idealism penetrated Jewish circles, new issues were raised and new kinds of books were written: How was Judaism, as a particular religion, related to the universal discoveries of reason and scientific investigation? What was the true essence and core of Judaism that unfolded in the course of universal history and in juxtaposition with contrasting religions? In each successive phase old themes persisted but were supplemented by new modes of self-reflection; the scope, complexity, and context of the tradition expanded accordingly.

In the most recent century, it has become possible to separate, for the purposes of analysis and ideology, the peoplehood of the Jews from their religion, and, as a result, much Jewish thought has a pronounced secular character in the terminology it uses, the definitions of Jewish identity it employs, and the diagnosis of the Jewish future it offers. Secular Jewishness has been a response of Jews of non-religious temperament or personal philosophy who want to maintain being Jewish as a central personal concern. Although secular Jewishness flourished in a social environment where modernity was felt to be incompatible with commitment to organized religion, conceptions first proposed by Jewish secularists have been gradually absorbed by religious streams in contemporary Judaism. Moreover, both modern Jewish nationalism and Jewish socialism have a strong secular base. (However, Zionism, the most important form of Jewish nationalism, has a complex character and can be secular or religious; some of the most important Zionist thinkers will be discussed in this chapter and others in the next.) We will now examine the thought of men who had little or no interest in Jewish theological or metaphysical issues, who were primarily concerned with the political, sociological, or cultural facets of the Jewish situation, who drew on ancient Jewish hopes and symbols but recast them so that adherence to Jewish religious belief or action was no longer necessary, and who were notable champions of Jewish survival at a time when other Jews of similar background and philosophical commitments were not.

Two Early Nationalists: Moses Hess and Peretz Smolenskin

In the mid-nineteenth century, modern Jewish thought was still indebted to philosophical idealism for its vocabulary and analysis of the nature of Judaism. Moses Hess and Peretz Smolenskin represent the disengagement by some Jewish thinkers from the idealist approach and the emergence of a definition of Jewish identity influenced by Central and East European nationalism. As transitional figures moving toward an ideology based on the Jews as a social group, they were precursors of the fully developed Jewish nationalist movement of the end of the century.

Moses Hess (1812–1875) was born in Bonn to an Orthodox German Jewish family. Despite a traditional Jewish education in his early years, he drifted away from Judaism in his adolescence. Rejecting the opportunity to enter his father's business, Hess instead attended the University of Bonn. There he was captivated by left-wing interpreters of Hegel's philosophy, who pushed Hegel's dialectical thinking toward a radical criticism of all social and religious institutions. Hess became one of the first socialists in Germany; he introduced Friedrich Engels to Karl Marx and collaborated with them, before personal and ideological differences intervened. Most of his adult years were spent as a political émigré in Paris, except for a stay in Germany during the upheavals of 1848–1849 and again toward the end of his life.

Hess's early writings are important for his later views on Judaism. In these youthful works, he echoed the usual Christian opinion that Judaism's historical significance ended with the appearance of Jesus, but he occasionally spoke approvingly of the ethical and philosophical signifi-

Moses Hess, author of **Rome and Jerusalem,** containing the first secular proposal for a new Jewish commonwealth in the land of Israel. (Courtesy of the Zionist Archives, New York.)

cance of ancient Judaism and did not exhibit that Jewish self-denial and self-hate frequently found among assimilated Jewish socialists and communists. Hess's first book, *The Holy History of Mankind by a Young Spinozist* (1837), develops in an idiosyncratic way the Hegelian notion of the progressive self-revelation of the Absolute Spirit. According to Hess, three personal figures represent crucial turning points of human development: Adam symbolizes the moment when the ideal was first separated from the actual and the historical process began; Jesus represents the moment when the ideal was elevated above the actual and the spiritual realm recognized as supreme over the social; Spinoza produced the philosophy that theoretically restored the unity of the ideal and real, paving the way for the political and social revolutions of the modern age—revolutions that would, Hess felt, actualize that unity by eventually eliminating private property, putting an end to the use of physical coercion by the state, and abolishing the very existence of a ruling class. History will then culminate in a utopian communism where social justice and harmony will be fully attained.

In the 1840s and 1850s, still under the influence of Karl Marx, Hess turned away from philosophy to study economics, the natural sciences, and anthropology. By the 1860s, when he had rejected Marx's economic determinism, Hess's socialism became more gradualistic and moderate and, unlike Marx, he took a positive attitude toward the spread of liberal nationalism among the oppressed peoples of Europe. At the same time Hess also became interested in Jewish history and the condition of the Jews in Germany and in the East, a concern that was influenced in part by a friendship with Heinrich Graetz. The unification of Italy (1859–1861) suggested that the Jews of Eastern Europe could accomplish a similar national revival, resulting in his most important Jewish writing, *Rome and Jerusalem* (1862). Early in the book Hess recalls a previously suppressed loyalty to Judaism:

> A thought which I had stifled forever within my heart is again vividly present with me: the thought of my [Jewish] nationality, inseparable from the inheritance of my ancestors, the holy land, and the eternal city, the birthplace of belief in the divine unity of life and in the future brotherhood of all men.[1]

Hess's defense in *Rome and Jerusalem* of the legitimacy and even necessity of nations and especially of Jewish nationhood grows out of a reworking of the Hegelianism of his youth. The "cosmic" level of reality matures to produce "the organic," which in turn gives rise to "the social"; the whole evolutionary process will eventually lead to "the historical Sabbath," a messianic age of economic justice and national liberation for all mankind. Not humanity in general, however, but the nation provides the setting for a realization of ethical ideals. This insight was anticipated, according to Hess, in the Mosaic legislation and the prophetic books of the Bible, which envisioned a model society in the land of Israel as an example to the other nations. A re-established Jewish state in Palestine—a state founded on the triumph of productive labor, an end to social parasitism, and the unification of ethics and life—would serve as a bridge between three continents and a model for the suppressed peoples of Asia and Africa to emulate. Hess adopts the widespread concept of a Jewish "mission," but holds that economic and social conditions in the diaspora prevented the Jews from actualizing it. The Jews of Eastern Europe, who had maintained their traditional faith in the restoration of the Jewish kingdom, would be the main volunteers for the colonies out of which the restored Jewish commonwealth would emerge.

Hess's criticism of the illusions of the German Jews and especially of the Reformers follows from his rejection of abstract, idealist formulations in favor of the concrete, the social, and the national. The rationalistic theology of the Reformers, according to Hess, imitated the worst feature of Christianity: its tendency to separate the spiritual from the material, the ideal from the actual, the heavenly from the earthly. Christianity and Reform Judaism sundered that which the genius of biblical

Judaism had integrated. Furthermore, no religious reform that made Jewish worship more like Christian would ever win for Jews the respect of German Christians, because their dislike of Jews was so deeply ingrained as to be racial rather than theological. According to Hess the denial by German Jews of a Jewish nationality was a major obstacle to the very regeneration of Judaism that they espoused. Although he remained a secular, nonobservant Jew, he argued that Orthodoxy, transplanted to the renewed Zion, would lose its rigidity and become fertile again, producing the new institutions on which he pinned his hopes for mankind.

Largely ignored in his lifetime, Hess was later rediscovered to have been the first advocate of an ethical socialism in which the national renaissance of the Jewish people was a prominent feature.

In Eastern Europe the earliest major spokesman of modern Jewish nationalism was Peretz Smolenskin (c. 1840–1885). A child during the reactionary reign of Nicholas I, Smolenskin saw his brother kidnaped into the Russian army, lost his father at the age of 11, and spent a poverty-stricken youth at a yeshivah, in a Hasidic court, and finally in the city of Odessa where he earned his living as a Hebrew teacher and wrote articles and stories for the Hebrew press. In 1867 Smolenskin went to Vienna to study at the university; instead, he found employment as a typesetter, enabling him to establish a Hebrew journal (*Ha-Shahar, The Dawn*) destined to become the most important organ of the last decade of the Russian Haskalah. Smolenskin edited, printed, and distributed *Ha-Shahar* to subscribers in Eastern Europe and published most of his own essays and novels in its pages. His fiction remained generally faithful to the ideals of the Jewish Enlightenment, but his essays constituted a sharp criticism of the Haskalah and of the German Jewish Reformers, together with a groping for a new definition of Jewish identity.

According to Smolenskin, German Reform Judaism was a servile imitation of Christianity; it introduced division and sectarianism into the Jewish religion; it impeded Jewish progress by causing the traditionalists to be afraid of any change whatsoever. The roots of Jewry's incipient disintegration Smolenskin traced to Moses Mendelssohn, who had taught that Judaism was only a religion and that obedience to the revealed laws of the Bible was the sole requirement for a Jewish life. (Smolenskin was less interested in what Mendelssohn actually wrote than in attacking him as an example of Jewish cowardice and national self-denial.) Vehemently rejecting that Jewry was merely a religious association, Smolenskin insisted that the Jews were "a nation like all the nations," even though the source of their national unity was unique. Lacking a common territory, government, or spoken language, the Jews were a "spiritual nation," sustained by the Torah. Smolenskin draws extensively on the philosophical

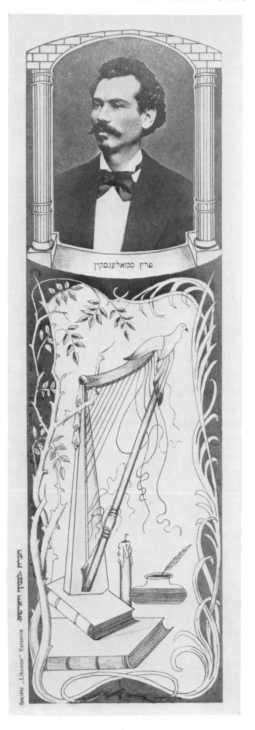

Bookplate of the Warsaw "Lebanon" Society, showing Peretz Smolenskin, early East European ideologue of Jewish nationalism and editor of the Hebrew journal **Ha-Shahar.** (Courtesy of the Zionist Archives, New York.)

terminology of the Galician maskil Nahman Krochmal in some of his formulations: The Jews were "an eternal nation." (Krochmal's phrase, *am olam*, was used by Smolenskin as the title of his influential essay of 1872.) The Torah was grounded in an imageless, infinite Spiritual Absolute. But Torah was not law: It was a flexible, evolving, organic national culture always adjustable to new historical conditions. Later in the 1870s Smolenskin began to use the notion of "national feeling" instead of Torah as the source of Jewish continuity.

The Mendelssohnian Haskalah and Reform Judaism, in Smolenskin's opinion, if successful, would result in the total disappearance of Judaism because these tendencies had abandoned two essential forces for Jewish unity: the Hebrew language and the hope for a collective redemption of the Jewish people. Although he acknowledged that the Jews should use in their daily lives the spoken language of the country in which they lived, he insisted that "without Hebrew there is no Torah, and without Torah there is no people of Israel." Hebrew must remain the medium in which Jewish children learn the Torah and in which Jewish scholarship transmits its findings. Similarly, although it was the duty of Jews to be loyal citizens of their respective governments, belief in the messianic ingathering of the Jewish people must be retained, despite its not being a practical possibility. If a Jew does not observe many of the religious laws of Judaism, he remained in Smolenskin's eyes a loyal member of his people as long as he hopes for Jewry's eventual redemption. Against the German Jewish Reformers Smolenskin reiterated that it was unworthy and unnatural to be embarrassed over one's ties to the Jewish people throughout the diaspora: Love of one's people, like love of one's family, is not incompatible with concern for humanity. Moreover, Jew-hatred was not religious in origin, but reflected gentile contempt for the fragmentation, disunity, and inferior status of the Jews as a group.

Because Smolenskin felt that Jewish nationhood was based on subjective feeling and cultural heritage, he has been called the forerunner of diaspora nationalism, which held that the Jews formed a unique national entity even though they remained a minority everywhere, without a homeland of their own. In the late 1870s Smolenskin's position came under attack in the pages of his own journal by Eliezer ben Yehudah, a young Russian Jew who later played an important role in the revival of Hebrew as a spoken language in Palestine. Ben Yehudah criticized Smolenskin's spiritual nationalism as too ethereal and impractical to respond effectively to the material suffering of the Jews and maintain the loyalty of the new generation. After the pogroms of 1881–1882 in Russia, Smolenskin admitted the validity of these charges. Despairing of the future of Jewry in the diaspora, he became an ardent supporter of Hibbat Zion in the last few years of his life.

The Founders of Zionism: Leon Pinsker and Theodor Herzl

Although Hess and Smolenskin recognized that hatred of the Jews was
not merely antiquated religious prejudice, they concerned themselves
with it only in passing. For Leon Pinsker (1821–1891) and Theodor Herzl
(1860–1905), the two most important figures in the establishment of the
Zionist movement, anti-Semitism was a crucial factor in the personal
awakening that led them to Jewish nationalism and that was, therefore,
the point of departure for their arguments in its behalf. One step further
removed from the traditional Judaism that Hess and Smolenskin had
absorbed in their childhoods, men like Pinsker and Herzl were especially
vulnerable to the upsurge of anti-Jewish sentiment among the European
populace in the 1880s and 1890s and were all the more sensitive to its
ominous implications.

The son of an eminent Haskalah authority on the Karaites, Leon

Leon Pinsker, Odessa physician, author of the Zion-
ist classic **Autoemancipation,**
leader of the Lovers of Zion
in Russia. (Courtesy of the
Zionist Archives, New York.)

Pinsker was given an up-to-date education and studied law and then medicine at the University of Odessa. (He realized quickly that there were no opportunities open to a Jewish lawyer in Russia at the time.) In the 1860s he was active in the promotion of Haskalah and Russification. The pogroms of 1881 renewed his concern with the Jewish question, leading to his pamphlet *Autoemancipation: A Warning to His Kinfolk by a Russian Jew* (1882). The acclaim that he received for this essay led to his becoming, against initial misgivings, head of the Hibbat Zion movement and chairman of its central executive committee in Odessa. Herzl's background was even more distant from Orthodoxy than Pinsker's. Herzl knew little of the Hebrew language, had no interest in religion, and was poorly acquainted with Jewish history and with the culture of East European Jews. The son of a successful Budapest businessman (Herzl was confirmed in a Budapest Reform temple), at the age of 18 he moved with his family to Vienna to study law. After graduation he decided on a career in literature, and became well known in Vienna during the early nineties for his theater pieces and newspaper essays. Growing social tensions and political instability of Europe, as expressed in Viennese anti-Semitism and the Dreyfus affair in France, convinced him that Jewish emancipation was not a success and that Jew-hatred was far more than an ephemeral aberration.

In *Autoemancipation,* Pinsker diagnosed anti-Semitism as a form of "demonopathy," an irrational fear of the stranger, exacerbated by the fact that the Jews were everywhere guests, nowhere hosts. Pinsker's explanation took seriously the anti-Semitic charge that the Jews were eternal aliens: Because Jews are viewed as a "ghost people" without a home of their own, their economic successes attract jealousy and resentment while their powerlessness makes them an ideal victim of popular violence. (In contrast to Graetz and Smolenskin, for Pinsker it was, therefore, a terrible defect that the Jews were a "spiritual nation.") Whereas Pinsker concentrated on the psychological factor in anti-Semitism, Herzl focused on the economic. In Herzl's seminal pamphlet, *The Jewish State* (1896), the "remote cause" of present-day Jew-hatred was medieval segregation of the Jews, which forced them to develop their financial acumen in order to keep alive. Once ghetto restrictions were dismantled, these acquired talents enabled Jews to compete successfully with gentiles and noticeably to better themselves. On the highest levels of society Christian aristocrats sometimes found it useful to marry children of well-to-do Jews, solving, as it were, the "Jewish problem" by intermarriage. But the Jewish prosperity that made this assimilation possible, at the same time intensified the fear of Jewish financial power among the Christian middle classes. Moreover, the growing surplus of university-educated Jews attracted to socialism and revolutionary ideas further exacerbated popular suspicions of Jews and hostility against them. The problem of anti-Semitism was therefore insolvable in the diaspora. Herzl, of course, did not imagine that emancipation, where it had been enacted, could be reversed, and he acknowledged that dislike of Jews in nineteenth-century Western and Central Europe was not as bloodthirsty as the medieval persecutions. But, he noted, "our sensitivity has increased, so that we feel no diminution in our suffering."[2] Hatred and prejudice are especially painful to the Jew who has adopted modern Western civilization and expected, in return, to be treated as a fellow human being. For Pinsker and Herzl one of the worst consequences of anti-Semitism was the damage it inflicted on Jewish self-esteem and dignity.

Both men had come to dismiss religion as the distinguishing feature of modern Jewry, but in one crucial respect they represented a continuation of a basic attitude of classical Reform Judaism: An activist, clear-cut cure of the abnormal Jewish situation required that drastic changes be put into effect immediately by the Jews themselves. One of the main themes of Pinsker's essay was that the Jews must take the initiative, in line with the maxim of the ancient sage Hillel, "If I am not for myself, who will be for me?" Instead of depending on the nonexistent good will of European rulers and peoples, the Jews had to emancipate themselves collectively (hence "autoemancipation") by finding a homeland of their own. Rational and clinical on the surface, Pinsker's essay betrays an underlying anguish, shame, and disillusionment. In contrast, Herzl, having arrived on his own at the conclusion that the Jewish question was a national one and required Jewish sovereignty somewhere on the globe, was seized by enthusiasm, optimism, and an almost messianic exhilaration. He saw the Jewish state as a major contribution to European stability: Once the idea was proposed, even the most anti-Semitic officials would realize that it was in their interest to solve the Jewish problem by cooperating with the Zionists. Evacuation from Europe could be accomplished with efficiency and minimal disruption. The agricultural and industrial structure of the new Jewish state would take advantage of the most recent technology. A seven-hour working day would defuse the danger of socialist agitation. In the new homeland religion would not be allowed to interfere with matters outside its proper purview. The secular society that Zionism would create somewhere (Herzl was not committed to Palestine) would lead the way toward solving the social and economic troubles plaguing contemporary Europe.

Although Herzl remained a liberal in his conception of the economy and government of the Jewish state, his imaginative flair and dramatic vision belong more to the *fin de siècle*'s fascination with the creative power of the human will than to sober Enlightenment liberalism. Desire and determination were to bring the Jewish state into being: "If you will it, then it will be." Coupled with his regal bearing, Herzl's audacious self-confidence reacted on the suffering Jews, especially in Eastern Europe,

Theodor Herzl, founder of the World Zionist Organization. Photo taken at the Sixth Zionist Congress, Basle, 1903, a year before his death.

to catalyze ancient Jewish messianic sentiments. But within the Zionist movement Herzl had his critics and opponents: An influential and articulate segment of East European Jewish secularists viewed Herzl's program with considerable misgivings.

Cultural Nationalism: Ahad Ha-Am and Simon Dubnow

For those who looked to Jewish nationalism to bring about a major Jewish cultural renaissance, Herzl's position seemed merely an imitation of commonplace European political formulas of the day. Although acutely aware of and affected by anti-Semitism, the leading East European spokesmen of Jewish cultural nationalism were searching for a bridge between the old and new: a synthesis of the traditional Jewish heritage in which they had been brought up and the secular outlook they had absorbed from the writings of the "critically thinking" Russian intelligentsia and admired French, English, and German figures. Not necessarily attracted to the revolutionary politics of the Russian radicals, this group of Jews did acquire their typical attitude that religion was a reactionary force and that human liberation was to be found through the natural and social sciences. Especially influential were the Russian critics Nicholas Chernyshevsky and Dmitry Pisarev, and Western Positivists, Utilitarians, and Social Darwinians, such as Auguste Comte, John Stuart Mill, and Herbert Spencer. Positivism inculcated a belief that theology and metaphysics were obsolete stages in the progress of the human mind toward a knowledge of the scientific laws governing phenomena, a belief that led to the agnostic position that one cannot know whether God exists or not. Utilitarianism provided the basis for a social ethics that avoided a transcendent source of value: The goal of human betterment was the greatest good for the greatest number; everybody was to count for one and nobody for more than one. Social Darwinism provided a way of unifying the scientific and the ethical: Mankind's history is governed by natural selection, so that the highest forms of social and cultural organization were those that had survived the most challenging circumstances. Applied to Judaism this approach led to a rejection of supernatural causation and a deliberate disregard of theology; it reinforced the primacy of justice and learning; it inculcated the conviction that understanding the evolutionary laws that enabled Judaism to survive in the past was a precondition for ensuring its survival in the future.

The foremost spokesman for cultural Zionism at the turn of the century was Asher Ginsberg (1856–1927), best known under his pen name Ahad Ha-Am (One of the People). Ginsberg's father was a devout hasid, a well-to-do merchant and leaser of estates who provided his son with a solid traditional upbringing. On his own Asher acquired the essentials of a modern education, including Russian, German, French, and English, but several half-hearted attempts to enter a Central European university ended in failure. When the May Laws forced his father off a leased estate in the mid-1880s, the Ginsbergs settled in Odessa. Almost immediately Asher became a member of the Hibbat Zion executive committee and an intellectual force among the illustrious circle of Jewish writers and thinkers living there. Beginning in 1889 and continuing for more than two decades, he published, under the name Ahad Ha-Am, essays on current ideological issues and topics in Jewish thought that became classics of modern Hebrew literature: polished, precise, economical in language; acute, forceful, ironic in style.[3] Among the Hovevei Zion, Ahad Ha-Am was the sharpest critic of the limited philanthropic activities of the movement. In the early nineties he became the moving figure of a short-lived but influential semisecret society, the *B'nei Mosheh* (Sons of Moses), whose members were required to pledge complete devotion to the cause of the Hebraic renaissance. In 1896 Ahad Ha-Am became director of the Hibbat Zion publishing house and editor of its new monthly, *Ha-Shiloah*, which he was determined to make the finest Hebrew literary journal of the time, on a level with the major European cultural journals. In 1903, overburdened by the demands on himself resulting from his exacting standards, he resigned these posts to enter the business world. As an employee of a Russian Jewish tea company, he moved to London in 1907, where he was not able to find the leisure or mental tranquility to write the systematic study of Jewish ethics that he promised to his friends. In 1922, Ahad Ha-Am retired to Tel Aviv. There he spent the last five years of his life, a revered figure among Zionist intellectuals.

If Herzl was the "secular messiah" of early Zionism, Ahad Ha-Am was its "agnostic rabbi."[4] The Jewish national movement was to be "a great, constructive national effort" of the Jewish people as a whole to cope with the post-ghetto situation. Hibbat Zion was a liberation of the tradition from subordination to the details of "the Book" (the Bible and the rabbinic law) so that Judaism could spontaneously confront the actualities of life.

> True Hibbat Zion is not merely part of Judaism, nor is it something added on to Judaism: it is the whole of Judaism. . . . It stands for a Judaism which shall have as its focal point the ideal of our nation's unity, its renascence, and its free development through the expression of universal human values in terms of its own distinctive spirit.[5]

Furthermore, Judaism could recover its inner freedom only in the land of Israel—the land where the Jewish people was born and where the Jewish right to reside was beyond question. Ahad Ha-Am is, therefore, identified with the doctrine of Zion as a "spiritual center" for modern Jewry:

Ahad Ha-Am (Asher Ginsberg), essayist, editor, philosopher of cultural Zionism. (Courtesy of the Zionist Archives, New York.)

A well-rounded and creative Jewish society in Palestine, freed from the pressures of conformity to a dominant gentile majority, would exert a spiritual effect on Jewry everywhere, radiating "to the great circumference, to all the communities of the diaspora, to inspire them with new life and to preserve the overall unity of our people."[6]

For Ahad Ha-Am the national rather than the religious character of Judaism was fundamental. The philosophical position of emancipated Western Jews that Judaism was a system of eternal religious verities he labeled "spiritual slavery under the veil of outward freedom." He was especially critical of the doctrine that the Jewish right to survive was dependent on a mission to teach ethical monotheism in the diaspora. Western Jews had been willing to efface their identity as a living people for the sake of political rights as individuals. The resulting loss of self-pride, Ahad Ha-Am insisted, was to be contrasted to the attitude of East European Jewry of his time, which he described as "inner freedom despite outer slavery," that is, strong Jewish ethnic loyalty in the face of the restrictive laws of the tsarist regime. Moreover, the Western notion implied that Jewishness was a rational decision made after a thorough investigation of religious and philosophical alternatives. This was, he felt, self-deception. Jewish feeling was a natural sentiment that needed no such justification.

Nobody asked us before we were born, Do you want to be Jews? Do you like the teachings of Judaism, the Torah of Judaism? Judaism introduced

us into its covenant without our knowledge or consent and gave us a completed Torah that preceded our own creation. . . . Why are we Jews?
How strange the very question! . . . Ask the tree why it grows! . . . It is
within us; it is one of our laws of nature. It has an existence and a con-
stancy of its own, like a mother's love for her children, like a man's love of
his homeland.[7]

Concern for the fate of one's people everywhere and respect for its historical memories was an emotion that all human beings experience, a tie
even more primary than one's rational, "abstract" duty to humanity at
large.

Jewish identity, therefore, committed one to no particular metaphysical doctrine, nor did it conflict with a scientific view of the cosmos. "I can
speak my mind concerning the beliefs and opinions which I have inherited
from my ancestors."[8] In place of theology and philosophical idealism,
Ahad Ha-Am turned to the social sciences, especially to the Darwinian
anthropology and social psychology of his time, to explain Judaism's
history. Like all organic entities, nations were collectivities with a powerful, primordial "will to live," which responded to the challenges of the
environment. Evolving national cultures were shaped by "innumerable
causes, some permanent and some transient, not in accordance with a
system laid down and defined at the onset."[9] The Jewish religion was a
result of the nation's instinct to adapt to its unique circumstances and to
survive the vicissitudes of history. Thus, for example, prophetic monotheism was accepted by the people during the Babylonian exile, according to Ahad Ha-Am, because it enabled them to reject the interpretation
that Israel's captivity was a victory of the Babylonian gods. Furthermore,
monotheism had the advantage of guaranteeing for the exiles in Babylonia that God would save his people not only in its own land but also
on foreign soil. During the medieval period, Ahad Ha-Am argued, the
ritual law of Judaism prevented the assimilation of the people and maintained its hope in an eventual return to the holy land. Hibbat Zion and
Zionism were a further instance of the principle that "the instinct of
self-preservation slumbers not nor sleeps in the nation's heart" (compare
Ps. 121:4).[10] Although intended as a scientific explanation for Jewish
existence, Ahad Ha-Am's "national will to live" takes on not a few of the
features of the religious attitude that Israel is an eternal people.

In Ahad Ha-Am's system, nations also have personalities: cultural configurations that distinguish one people from another and preserve inner
continuity. By means of this notion he returns to Jewish identity those
values that he was unable to affirm solely on religious grounds. In Judaism, historical evolution produced a culture that valued the spiritual
over military force. Of all ideals, Judaism gave greatest emphasis to the
prophetic idea of absolute justice. Ahad Ha-Am depicts the prophet of

Judaism as a "man of truth," a moral extremist who places righteousness ("truth in action") at the center of human life. The supreme Jewish prophet is the portrait of Moses in the Bible, whose importance in the national culture can never be affected by any archeological discovery because Moses was "created in the spirit of the Jewish people, and the creator creates in his own image."[11] It was this ethical imperative that rabbinic Judaism sought to put into practice through law. The evolving moral sense of the people led to the constant reinterpretation of certain biblical passages whose literal meaning offended later generations. In an essay dealing with the distinction between Judaism and Christianity, Ahad Ha-Am goes even further toward a rational defense of certain Jewish values, by arguing that the Jewish concept of justice is more objective and universal than the Christian emphasis on mercy. Whereas mercy gives the other person precedence over the self (an inverted egoism), justice demands that each individual be treated as fully equal. Even though his conception of the historical evolution of national cultures might imply a moral relativism, Ahad Ha-Am himself was convinced that the "moral law" is an objective standard of value. He did not hesitate to denounce any acts done in the name of Zionism that conflicted with "the great moral principles for which our people lived and for which it suffered and for which only [Jewry] thought it worthwhile to labor in order to become again a people in the land of its fathers."[12]

Ahad Ha-Am defends Jewishness as a natural fact explainable only through the "genetic method" of the social sciences. But he ends by reaffirming some of the key ideas of the Western Jewry whose ideology he had so sharply criticized: the primacy of prophetic ethics, the moral obligation of Israel to represent justice and righteousness, the task of creating a society that would be an example to all peoples. The crucial difference between Ahad Ha-Am and earlier nineteenth-century thinkers was that he, like Hess, turned away from what seemed to them empty abstractions toward a concrete Jewish community renewed in its ancient land, free to order its own life and realize its original moral vision.

A close friend of Ahad Ha-Am's, the Russian Jewish historian Simon Dubnow (1860–1941), used a similar evolutionary approach to arrive at a non-Zionist, diaspora nationalism according to which Jewish survival was not dependent on the attainment of a national home. Born in a small Belorussian market town, Dubnow refused to continue the study of Talmud after *bar mitzvah*, choosing instead to enter a Russian government school. In revolt against his family's traditional Judaism, he prepared privately to qualify for a Russian university, but was never able to gain admission. During an illegal stay in St. Petersburg in the early 1880s (the Russian capital was outside the Pale of Settlement and off limits for most Jews), Dubnow began writing for the Russian Jewish press,

Simon Dubnow, historian of Russian Jewry, author of the **World History of the Jewish People,** and proponent of diaspora Jewish nationalism. (Courtesy of the Jewish Publication Society of Amerca.)

soon acquiring a reputation as one of the most severe critics of Jewish literature and one of the most ardent advocates of Jewish cultural reform. Forced to return to his native town, he devoted himself to a study of Comte, Mill, Spencer, and other Western writers until, in 1887, he underwent a personal crisis that moderated his attraction to Positivism and cosmopolitan individualism. Realizing, as he said, that "abstract love for humanity" did not conflict with "concrete love for one's people," he decided that for him "the path to the universal lay through the national" —especially the researching and writing of Jewish history. Dubnow determined to become the first modern historian of the East European Jewish past, including the origins of the Hasidic movement and the kahal system of Jewish self-government. Moving to Odessa in 1890, he became closely associated with Ahad Ha-Am and his friends, but did not join the Hibbat Zion movement. In 1897 he began to publish a series of essays defining his own conception of Jewish nationalism. Collected as *Letters on Old and New Judaism* (1907), their impact extended beyond the small group that fully accepted his position and had especial influence on Yiddishists and the Jewish socialist Bund.[13]

For Dubnow, as for Ahad Ha-Am, a nation is a collective individual composed of common memories, a sense of kinship, and a desire to affirm a single destiny: "The consciousness of the nationality itself is the main criterion of its existence."[14] Like Smolenskin, Dubnow held that a nation can endure without the usual unifying attributes (land, language, state), if the subjective elements of its identity—a distinctive self-consciousness and the will to survive as a group—were sufficiently developed. Jewry was "the very archetype of the nation" because it had passed successfully through all stages of national evolution. From its primitive tribal origins the Jewish people had, like others, come to form a territorial-political entity, but later it had adjusted to loss of homeland by evolving novel institutions of self-government and by adapting its cultural forms to a wide range of diaspora conditions. From late antiquity to the present there has always been at least one creative Jewish center that exerted a spiritual hegemony over other branches (the Jewries of Babylonia, Spain, northwest Europe, Poland, and so on). Indeed, the Jews were a nation whose home was the globe: Dubnow's ten-volume magnum opus relating the people's past from its beginnings to the post-World War I era was entitled *The World History of the Jewish People*.[15] In particular, the Jews were one of the oldest groups resident on the European continent, being as much native Europeans as the peoples who attained their national consciousness subsequently (e.g., the Hungarians, the Poles, the Russians). Although Dubnow acknowledged that the revived Jewish community in Palestine would be a valuable new center, he opposed abandonment, physical or cultural, of Europe in order to recover Judaism's "eastern" roots.

The main issue between Ahad Ha-Am and Dubnow was "the negation or the affirmation of the diaspora." Ahad Ha-Am rejected the diaspora "subjectively": First, it was the hope of Jews throughout history to return to the land of Israel; second, an independent, modern Jewish culture could emerge only there and not in the diaspora. Ahad Ha-Am did not reject the diaspora "objectively" because he believed (against Herzl) that the diaspora would always exist and that a complete ingathering to Zion was impossible. Although Dubnow accepted Ahad Ha-Am's criticism of Herzlian Zionism, he opposed any negation whatsoever of the diaspora. Jewry outside of Zion was not a passive object that would survive only through the spiritual energy of the homeland. Each branch of the diaspora had its own needs; to remain alive it would have to maintain its own institutions and actively promote Jewish culture. His Jewry in Eastern Europe had a distinctive Yiddish folk culture that should be encouraged to develop alongside a Judaism that expressed itself in Russian and in Hebrew. (In contrast, Ahad Ha-Am opposed the modern cultivation of Yiddish, insisting that Hebrew alone was capable of drawing on the whole Jewish past and of winning for Judaism its rightful place as one of the great culture-bearers of world civilization.) Finally, Dubnow was far more optimistic than Ahad Ha-Am that diaspora Jewry could find the means to ensure its continuation. The kahal system of self-government, extensively developed in Poland from the fifteenth to the seventeenth centuries, should be reconstituted in the form of a secular, democratic communal body in which all parties, including Orthodox and Zionist, would participate on equal footing. Writing during the nationalist ferment of early twentieth-century Europe, Dubnow pointed to the evident intent of all Central and East European nationalities to win self-determination. The future of multinational states, such as Russia and Austria–Hungary, he was convinced, lay in a constitutional order leaving in the government's hands matters of general concern, while guaranteeing nationalities full autonomy in the realms of education and culture. Nationality would be personal, rather than territorial, permitting Jewry also to organize itself as a public entity. For Dubnow the right of minorities to cultural self-determination was the liberal principle of individual freedom applied to the collective individualities of which Jewry was one instance.[16]

Dubnow and Ahad Ha-Am were determined to make a place for secular, agnostic Jews as full members of the Jewish nation. One belonged to a nation by birth, by cultural heritage, by collective psychology. Nationality was a feeling; religion required intellectual assent. One might revere, as Ahad Ha-Am did, the "sancta" of the nation, its customs and symbols; one might experience in the solitude of nature, as Dubnow did, the impersonal beauty of cosmic unity; but the free-thinker could not be forced to accept metaphysical or religious doctrines not of his own choosing. To explain the inevitability of secular Judaism Dubnow proposed the following dialectic. The thesis was traditional Judaism, a stage when Jewish life was dominated by religious law and Jews had autonomy as a group but did not have civil rights as individuals. The antithesis was the Enlightenment, which liberated the mind from the fetters of tradition and fought for the political equality of man as man. However, the antithesis frequently led to loss of ethnic identity. The necessary synthesis was progressive cultural nationalism, combining commitments to personal dignity, civil equality, and intellectual freedom with an acknowledgment of the right of each group to live according to the inner law of its own identity. According to Dubnow, "Assimilation turned out to be in practice psychologically unnatural, ethically damaging, and practically useless."[17] First of all, pure cosmopolitanism was a fiction. Everyone, regardless of whether he admitted it, participated in a national culture: Through particularity lay the path to universality. Second, modern anti-Semitism demonstrated that Jews who try to "imitate other national types" only stir up scorn and resentment. Finally, it was morally repulsive for Jews to abandon their beleaguered people to gain the advantages of the majority. According to Dubnow, Jewish self-affirmation was an act of personal integrity and loyalty to a national individuality more than 3,000 years old, which was not aggressive, which respected (and gave birth to) some of the noblest values of the human race, and whose continued existence was in harmony with the finest rational ideals of humanitarian liberalism.

Extreme Rejectors of the Exile: Berdichevsky and the Socialist Zionists

Political and cultural Zionists differed mainly as to whether the "problem of the Jews" or the "problem of Judaism" had the higher priority. The former believed that Jewish vulnerability to anti-Semitism required the immediate redemption of the people from the abnormal condition of diaspora. The latter felt that Jewry was threatened by an internal crisis—a loss of morale, unity, and distinctiveness that could be reversed only by a flowering of Jewish cultural creativity in modern form. Despite this fundamental disagreement, Pinsker and Herzl, Ahad Ha-Am and Dubnow, remained gradualistic liberals on the economic and political structure of the renewed Jewish community and other issues. The ideological ferment in Eastern Europe at the turn of the twentieth century, however, produced more radical programs for the transformation of Jewry and Judaism.

One of Ahad Ha-Am's sharpest critics among the younger Hebrew writers was Micah Joseph Berdichevsky (1865–1921). Scion of a long chain of rabbis in the Ukraine, Berdichevsky lived after 1890 in Switzerland and Germany where he studied philosophy, wrote essays and short stories for the Hebrew press, and became a foremost collector and interpreter of Jewish folklore. Berdichevsky's defiant rejection of Ahad Ha-Am's synthesis of tradition and modernity and his dismissal of classical Jewish values made him a controversial and almost heretical figure, the *enfant terrible* of modern Hebrew letters.[18]

For Berdichevsky, liberation of the Jewish people from "the Book" had to be pushed much further than Ahad Ha-Am envisioned. "Among us, man is crushed by traditional customs, laws, doctrines, and judgments, for many things are bequeathed to us by our ancestors which deaden the soul and deny it freedom."[19] The talented individual had to be totally free to overthrow the stultifying burden of the past in order to pursue personal self-actualization and fulfill his creative passion. Berdichevsky remained within the Jewish orbit because he called on Jewry as a whole to show a similar boldness. The Jewish people would survive only if there was a complete "transvaluation of its values."[20] In place of bookish intellectualism and humble submission to the will of God, Berdichevsky

Micah Joseph Berdichevsky, Hebrew author, folklorist, and critic of traditional Jewish religiosity. (Courtesy of the Zionist Archives, New York.)

called for an enlarged Jewish capacity for self-initiated action, for a proud and vital assertion of physical power, for delight in nature and "wholeness of life"—qualities that he felt had been drained from the people by centuries of exile. That the Jews lived in exile was their own fault: It was Berdichevsky's opinion that they had fled their homeland in ancient times rather than fight to hold onto it. Tragically, in his opinion, the Jews had become in the course of history secondary to Judaism, Israel had become secondary to the Torah, and concrete material existence had become secondary to abstract spiritual essence. As a result, young Jews perceived Judaism as static, parochial, and passive. The first duty of the present generation, therefore, was "tearing down" in order to make room for the free exercise of the will. Berdichevsky demanded that his readers decide whether they were "the last Jews"—the end of a long tradition of submissive piety—or "the first Hebrews," still able to be a dynamic, creative nation.

For all his extreme language, however, Berdichevsky did not entirely reject the Jewish past. He extolled certain earlier heterodox forms of Judaism as examples of that vitalism he wished to resurrect. He praised the heroism of the zealots during the Roman–Jewish wars and admired the intense individuality of the Hasidic rabbis. He discerned, buried in occasional biblical allusions, traces of an imaginative mythology and a glorious worship of nature that was repressed when the people was forced to accept the rule of "the Book" after the Babylonian exile. History contained many Judaisms. There was no authoritative, conclusive pattern to which the present had to conform: Judaism was what a Jew thinks and feels. Therefore, the new generation was free to determine for itself the relevant content of its "Hebrew humanism."

Berdichevsky produced no well-formulated ideology: His writings are lyrical and impulsive outbursts against the denial of life. For him there can be no Ahad Ha-Amist resolution of the tension between the old and new, only a self-propelled move forward in a modern age of continuous crisis. But—here Berdichevsky was closer to Ahad Ha-Am than to Herzl—the Jewish crisis was cultural rather than political: The question of values remained the heart of his people's predicament. Despite his preference for material existence as against spiritual essence, Berdichevsky remained as much a learned, urban intellectual as those he opposed. However, not individualism but collectivism was to trigger the most compelling image of the secular Jewish idealist. The closest embodiment of a new, heroic style of Jewish living was the pioneering socialist movement that crystallized during the second aliyah to Palestine, after 1904, seeking Jewish regeneration through renewed contact with the land.[21]

Nahman Syrkin (1868–1924) was the first theoretician of socialist Zionism, according to which there had to be a territorial solution to the Jewish question in the form of a cooperative society based on economic justice and productive labor. The Zionist dream would succeed only if the Jewish commonwealth were based on socialist values, but, conversely, Zionism alone could end the distorted economic situation of the Jewish proletariat. Against most socialists (including those of Jewish extraction) at the turn of the twentieth century, Syrkin and the other Labor Zionists insisted that the triumph of socialism throughout Europe would not end anti-Semitism. Jew-hatred was not merely the by-product of capitalist exploitation: It was only an instance of the common occurrence of the strong hating the weak. And there was no reason to believe that ethnic rivalries would cease with the socialist revolution.

Syrkin's ideology was quite similar to that of Moses Hess, whom he greatly admired. Socialism and nationalism flowed from moral imperatives; the end of economic exploitation and the liberation of all oppressed nations were complementary goals. Jewish survival could be ensured only if the East European masses, deeply rooted in Jewish ethnic values, refused to emulate the assimilated Western Jewish bourgeoisie, whose pursuit of individual enrichment led, Syrkin believed, to ethical bankruptcy. The Russian Jewish working class was morally obligated to participate in the struggle to overthrow the brutal tsarist regime; its main goal, however, was to solve the Jewish problem through concerted action to advance the Zionist cause. Indeed, Syrkin argued, Zionism could be one of the first realizations of socialism in history because "what is utopian in other contexts is a necessity for the Jews."

For Syrkin, as for many other Labor Zionists, socialist values were not alien to ancient Judaism; they were a rediscovery in the modern context of the biblical concern for social justice found in the prophetic visions of the messianic age and in the Mosaic legislation protecting the widow, orphan, and slave and restoring social equality in the Sabbatical and Jubilee years. Socialist Zionism was also a manifestation of deep-seated longings of the traditionalist Jewish masses in Eastern Europe. Through a socialist Jewish homeland "the messianic hope, which was always the greatest dream of exiled Jewry, will be transformed into political action."[22] Syrkin was opposed to the "petrified rule of the rabbis" (he did, though, have moments of pantheistic exaltation), but his Zionism was yet another attempt to confront modernity head-on while maintaining a conscious link to the Jewish past.

A second form of left-wing Zionism was the Poalei Zion ideology of Ber Borochov (1881–1917), based on the dialectical materialism of Karl Marx and a rejection of the "sentimental" ethical utopianism of Hess and Syrkin. As most Marxists at the turn of the century were cosmopolitan internationalists, young Borochov in 1905–1906 had first to defend the principle that nationalism was not per se reactionary. Borochov proposed that alongside the "relations of production" as the primary cause of the formation of classes and of conflict, Marxist socialism should acknowledge the importance of the geographical "conditions of production" that brought nations into being. Nations existed long before modern social classes, he argued, because a common past could give rise to a feeling of common kinship. Such sentiments of national unity, quite real in their effect, were not "spiritual" because they had material causes in earlier times. Marxists must realize that nations would not fade away after the proletarian revolution. According to Borochov, the validity of each form of nationalism depended on the social class whose economic interests it reflected. The nationalism of the landowning gentry and the bourgeoisie was reactionary and chauvinistic; the nationalism of the proletariat was legitimate and defensive. Proletarian nationalism furthered the economic interests of the nation's workers, forced sometimes to compete with other nations, by defending the "strategic base" (the homeland) on which the working class supported itself.

From this analysis Borochov drew specific implications for the Jews. Socialization of the means of production alone would not solve the Jewish question because the Jewish proletariat would continue to be pressed into an increasingly narrow, stunted, and marginal place in dias-

Ber Borochov, ideologist of the Workers of Zion, who sought to synthesize Marxism and Zionism. (Courtesy of the Zionist Archives, New York.)

pora society. Earlier the Jews had been financially useful to the ruling classes of European society, but now they were superfluous, excluded from basic industries from which a normal proletariat emerges. Emigration, such as to America, was not the answer, because in the course of time the same cycle of discrimination and anti-Semitism would be repeated: Jewish workers would find themselves resented as intruders by the gentile majority. Zionism, Borochov concluded, was a "therapeutic" movement of national liberation creating in Palestine a strategic base that would eventually lead to a Jewish socialist society.

Syrkin's ideology had emphasized ethical freedom and moral idealism; Borochov adhered to the Marxist principle that socialism must be modeled on the deterministic laws of natural science. Concentration of the Jewish masses in Zion, according to Borochov, was a *"stychic* process," a result of elemental, spontaneous, and unconscious factors not dependent on human willing. His followers were convinced that normalization of the material conditions of Jewish existence was an inevitable result of the dialectical laws of history. Religion was, of course, "the opiate of the masses" (the Marxist phrase); human desire alone could not create a just society if the objective forces of history were not headed in that direction. As a result, Marxist Zionism became one of the most determinedly antireligious forms of Jewish secularism to emerge in the early twentieth century.[23]

The Ideal of a Secular Jewish Culture; Its Relationship to Jewish Literature and Historiography

Whereas premodern civilizations are marked by a pervasive reverence for the holy and acknowledgment of the formal authority of the divine, modernity has emancipated most realms of public and private life from religious supervision and sacred values, placing great confidence in man's capacity to understand the world and to shape his own destiny. Secular Jewish thought was brought into being not only by the specific dangers facing Jewry since the late nineteenth century (anti-Semitism and assimilation), but by the secularization process as it has affected all peoples: Traditionalist societies everywhere have been on the decline. What has happened to Jewish secularism since its heyday at the turn of the century? Twentieth-century events have revealed the strengths and exposed the weaknesses of the ideologies of Herzl and Ahad Ha-Am. That there is a sovereign state of Israel, Herzl's dazzling vision, is only the most conspicuous Jewish adaptation to the secular modern world of nation-states. The segment of the Jewish people residing in Israel now has a voice in world politics and can enter into diplomatic negotiations with other governments, undertake economic and social planning, and if necessary, conduct military operations. (The absence of a Jewish state was painfully evident in the Holocaust.) The establishment of Israel has not, however, meant the complete normalization of the Jewish people that Herzl envisioned. The complexities of Israel's relationship to the diaspora and the special hatred with which it has been singled out in the international arena testify to that. Nevertheless, there is now available a new form of Jewish identity: the person who is Jewish by birth according to rabbinic law and an Israeli citizen according to international law. This type of secularist may not have felt any need consciously to appropriate his Jewish heritage. For many "free-thinking" Israelis, however, and for most secular Jews in the diaspora, the Ahad Ha-Amist notion of a Jewish cultural identity has not lost its appeal. That Israel can provide a congenial setting for realizing this aspiration remains a major justification for there being a Jewish state.

Regardless of whether a Jew is an Israeli or not, what does Jewish cultural identity entail? It is easiest to say what it is not. The Jewish cultural secularist[24] rejects the inevitability of the "non-Jewish Jew": the notion that the modern Jewish intellectual must find the Jewish tradition too old-fashioned and constricting to hold his interest and attention. Isaac Deutscher, a lifelong Marxist scholar, used the phrase "non-

Sigmund Freud (1856–1939), pioneer in the psychology of the unconscious and of psychoanalysis, in a photograph taken in Vienna in 1936. Although not an observant Jew, Freud was a member of a B'nai B'rith lodge in Vienna and was fascinated by the origins and character of Jewry. (Courtesy of the Leo Baeck Institute.)

Jewish Jew" approvingly to describe such figures as Spinoza, Heine, Marx, Trotsky, and Freud, who found their fulfillment in larger, more cosmopolitan loyalties. On the contrary, for Jewish secularists, a broad-minded, humanitarian concern for mankind is fully compatible with and even strengthened by an explicit Jewish identification. Indeed, they argue, immersion in Jewish culture provides a humanistic education unique in certain respects. Thus Marvin Lowenthal, in an essay entitled "On Jewish Humanism," wrote

> For a Jew, an absorption in the Jewish experience as a means of acquiring a humanistic attitude offers peculiar advantages. Because it is the experience of his own people, because he has himself, no matter how far he may think he is from being a Jew, relived fragments of it and shared it as a living thing and not as a matter of books, records, and monuments, because of all this he can more quickly and sympathetically enter into the Jewish experience of the past. . . . The cry for justice, the search for social adjustment, the sense and hope of an international unity to be ultimately set over petty patriotisms and side by side with these, a burning loyalty to a group—these are, even if imperfectly, shared in every Jew's individual life. When he encounters these humanizing elements in Jewish culture, they are not something foreign to be digested as best one can, but something native that will simply bring to fuller flower what is already living within him.[25]

As we saw in the case of Dubnow, the Jewish secularist frequently argues that true cosmopolitanism is reached through the medium of a national culture. A contemporary of Dubnow's, the Yiddish writer Isaac Leib Peretz, proposed the formulation: "Jewishness is the universal spirit as it is embodied in the Jewish soul."[26] The Yiddishist secular tradition, which matured parallel to the Hebraic, reveres moral seriousness, decency, responsibility to others, devotion to learning, passion for justice, faith in the dignity of the individual and in the perfectibility of humanity, as all being components of the Jewish cultural ideal.

Secular Jewish thinkers are not necessarily hostile or even indifferent to religion. To be sure, there are certain anti-religious forms of modern Jewish secularism, reflecting the impact of Positivism and Marxism. At its most extreme this militant secularism takes on the character of a counter-religion, claiming absolute or scientific truth and offering a comprehensive plan for secular salvation. But Western secularity is more often marked by a skeptical attitude toward inclusive and total views of reality, an attitude that may be inimical to certain attributes of traditional religion, but not to all. Many Jewish culturalists admit to having personal religious sentiments. Indeed, it was frequent for socialist Jews, like Hess and Syrkin, to find in the philosophy of Spinoza virtually a theology: a cosmic and moral tranquility, which they believed was a valid expression of Judaic monotheism in harmony with the methods and findings of natural science. Thus Chaim Zhitlovsky, a prominent figure of the Yiddishist and Jewish socialist movements in Russia and later in America, spoke of Jewish religious philosophy as having "attained its highest level in Spinoza's pantheism." And Albert Einstein, an active Zionist, made the often-quoted remark: "I believe in Spinoza's God, who reveals himself in the orderly harmony of what exists. . . ."[27]

The historian treats Judaism, like all religions, as an evolving product of the human mind. From this Jewish secularists drew the conclusion that contemporary Jewish self-affirmation is both the recognition of a social fact and a personal remembering of something ancient, revered, and familial. The secularists insist, however, that being Jewish does not require one to observe any Jewish religious practice. And they jealously guard their freedom to reject any received idea, however central it may have been to Judaism. Ben Halperin writes of the secular Zionist:

That he is a secular and not a religious Jew means that he has not experienced such a religious commitment to Jewish culture as would make it, for him, not only a profound but a most personal revelation of God. This does not mean he is unable to appreciate the expressions of an urge toward divinity in it and in other religious cultures. Nor does it mean that his relation to Jewish religious culture is a neutral or indifferent one. Certainly as a

Albert Einstein (1879–1955), physicist, Nobel Prize winner for his theory of relativity, and a German Jewish refugee in the United States. A committed Jew, Einstein was an ardent supporter of Zionism. (Courtesy of the Zionist Archives, New York.)

culture, if not as a religion, it has an intimate personal meaning for him, and there is no collective tradition in which he is more disposed to find expressions of divinity that speak to him personally . . . [But] he cannot accept a Jewish religious ideology simply because he is a Jew, for he will only be converted as a human before God.[28]

These are the borders that a secularist Jew places around his Jewishness. What are the cultural media for the transmission of a humanistic Jewish education to the next generation? Yiddishists and Hebraists looked especially to Jewish literature and to Jewish historiography for new Jewish content. Some remarks on these forms of modern Jewish self-exploration will point up the dilemmas that Jewish secularism now faces.

By the late nineteenth century, imaginative writing in Hebrew and Yiddish had fulfilled one of the most desired goals of the maskilim. The most important Jewish writers of Eastern Europe—Mendele Mocher Seforim, David Frischmann, Sholem Aleichem, Isaac Leib Peretz, Hayyim Nahman Bialik, to mention only the acknowledged masters—produced a body of writing highly skillful and artistic, fully modern and yet deeply rooted in Jewishness, combining the critical distance and objective stance of the Haskalah with the compassion and respect for the integrity of

Jewish life that accompanied the Jewish nationalist awakening. Mendele and Sholem Aleichem, for example, used realism, irony, and satire in order to depict the virtues and limitations of the intense Jewish milieu in which they were brought up and in order to convey the humble heroism, impracticality, and resilience of typical shtetl figures. Such achievements as Bialik's lyrics and his poems of reproof and wrath, Peretz's Hasidic stories and symbolic dramas, Frischmann's biblical tales, freed Jewish literature from Haskalah didacticism and slavish dependence on biblical style, while using Jewish cultural materials creatively and imaginatively. They gave the Hebrew and Yiddish languages new flexibility and depth, drawing on the Bible, medieval Jewish poetry, rabbinic and Hasidic literature, on distinctively Jewish ways of posing issues and resolving them, and on the characteristic inflections of everyday Jewish speech in Eastern Europe. This generation of writers quickly became classic and revered exemplifications of the Ahad Ha-Amist cultural ideal of the East European Jewish secularists.

Even before World War I, however, when Hebrew and Yiddish literature were rooted in the same environment and still overlapped, Jewish writers sought to break out, to experiment with Neo-Romanticism, impressionism, and symbolism (Peretz) or to discover sources of new spiritual energy in natural beauty, the physical passions, and the joy of living (Berdichevsky and others, especially the poet Saul Tchernichovsky). The impetus of Jewish writers to move out into broader literary currents became even more pronounced after World War I. Yiddish retained its main homes in Poland, Lithuania, the USSR, and immigrant America, whereas Hebrew authors increasingly concentrated in Palestine. Even though Hebrew and Yiddish literature separated, there were parallel developments in the two bodies of writing. Jewish poets turned to modernist, sophisticated forms and colloquial, even slangy, language to produce complex fusions of traditional Jewish symbols with personal, introspective longing (Peretz Markish, Itzik Manger, Jacob Glatstein, Aaron Zeitlin, and many others in Yiddish; Abraham Shlonsky, Nathan Alterman, Uri Zvi Greenberg, and many others in Hebrew). Writers of Yiddish fiction depicted strata of the shtetl that had previously been overlooked (the Jewish underworld, the Jewish revolutionary), explored the ferment of big city Jewish life in Eastern Europe and America, wrote family novels chronicling the transition to modernity during several generations, and focused on elements of experience ignored by the classical writers, such as sexuality and the demonic (I. J. Singer, Scholem Asch, Joseph Opatoshu, Isaac Bashevis Singer, and others). Hebrew literature found new themes in ancient and medieval Jewish messianism, in the Jewries of the Middle East, and above all, in the life of the Jewish pioneer in Palestine whose social radicalism and Zionist idealism symbolized a desperate Jewish determination to recover from diaspora abnormality

The flowering of the Yiddish theater in New York: Lazar Freed, Celia Adler, and Maurice Schwartz in Sholem Aleichem's **Stempenyu,** the Yiddish Art Theater, 1927. (Courtesy of the Museum of the City of New York.)

(Joseph Hayyim Brenner, Judah Burla, Hayyim Hazaz, Abraham Kabak, and others).

The modern Jewish predicament had other effects too. Changes in Jewish life and the broadened purview of Jewish literature during the interwar period produced not only moments of hope and enthusiasm, but also of doubt and despair: doubt that the Jews could overcome a growing rent between old and new; despair resulting from a nostalgic sense of loss at the fading away of traditional Jewish spirituality. (Such themes can be found in the writings of the great twentieth-century Hebrew master and Nobel laureate S. Y. Agnon.) World War II and the establishment of the Jewish state had a profound impact, the full implications of which are not yet clear. For Yiddish writers, the future of the language, the memory of the Holocaust and the world Hitler and Stalin destroyed, the tragic fate of the Jews in history, all became obsessive themes. In Israel, Hebrew writers who have grown up after the independence of the state have increasingly abandoned the ideological certainties of pioneering Zionism and turned to explore the malaise of the contemporary urban setting. Even more important, they have sought to redefine their own personal connection to the Jewish experience. The relative decay into which Jewish socialism has fallen in recent decades has created a moral crisis in the heart of Israeli society, like that in the West as a whole—but it has also opened up new possibilities for regaining direct contact with some of the primary symbols of Judaism. Intimations of this occurred in the wake of the 1967 war, which brought about a momentary experience of Jewish self-affirmation and salvation, and a direct confrontation with the uniqueness of the Jewish people among the nations.

While Jewish literature in Yiddish and Hebrew mirrored the tensions and agony of the onslaught of modernity on the Jewish people since 1880, Jewish writers in Western languages were bringing Jewish themes, styles of thought, and modalities of feeling into other literatures: Russian, German, French, Italian, Hungarian, Polish, and especially English. American Jewish writing has become an important indicator of the entrance of Jews into the American mainstream. Ranging from popular, best-selling novels (often a symptom of changing Jewish identity among authors and their public) to avant-garde renditions of Jewish materials in poetry and prose, American Jewish writing by the 1960s had become a recognized branch of American literature. Beginning with the portrayal of the immigrant experience (Abraham Cahan's *The Rise of David Levinsky*) and of a "second generation" growing up in heavily ethnic neighborhoods seeking to break away from immigrant parents (Henry Roth's *Call It Sleep* and Daniel Fuch's trilogy set in the Williamsburg section of Brooklyn), Jewish writers after World War II went on to highly individualistic portraits of human estrangement and alienation and the partial recovery of traditional symbols as sources of meaning and inner strength (the work of Saul Bellow, Bernard Malamud, and others). Imaginative Jewish fiction has become a means whereby American culture has recognized the presence of the Jewish heritage in its midst and absorbed some of its distinctive features.[29]

This incomplete sketch of modern Jewish literature is intended as background to our original question: What is the relationship between imaginative Jewish writing and the Jewish secular ideal? Without doubt, an enrichment, but a problematic one. The best literature is an end in itself; it avoids sentimentalism and clichés and refuses to be propaganda for nationalist or socialist ideologies. Militant Jewish secularism, such as the glorification of the heroic revolutionary or of the Jewish pioneer, have reflected profound but passing moments in recent Jewish history and literature. As we have seen, secularity does not necessarily mean the end of religion; some of the best twentieth-century literature has revealed the anguish of spiritual emptiness in an industrial society and the search for a transcendent ground of human freedom and dignity. Indeed, many of the most important questions of recent Jewish religious thought have first been played out on the pages of Jewish novels and poetry, before they found adequate expression in theology. Literary critics such as Simon Halkin and Irving Howe have pointed out the religiosity in much Hebrew and Yiddish writing—frequently an unorthodox religiosity which raises issues of doubt and affirmation without resolving them, but which blurs the secularists' sharp distinction between Jewishness and religious commitment.[30]

The future of Jewish literature as a component of secular Jewish culture also raises the question of what makes writing "Jewish." The best literature draws on the deepest roots of the author's world, and if these roots lack Jewish substance, the Jewishness of the writing becomes superficial and trite. Jewish literature is the writer's response to the modern Jewish predicament—if he has truly internalized and not merely exploited

Habimah, the first professional Hebrew theater, founded in Moscow in 1917 and now the National Theater of Israel, in a production of H. Leivick's **The Golem,** one of the earliest plays in its repertoire. (Courtesy of the Zionist Archives, New York.)

Jewish resources and situations. (This is a question for the most discerning literary criticism to determine.) Whether secular Jewish culture in the diaspora and in Israel can continue to provide rich Jewish content remains to be seen. We will return to this issue at the end of the chapter.

Like Jewish literature, Jewish historiography has broadened and become more complex in the twentieth century.[31] Simon Dubnow already represented a considerable departure from the *Wissenschaft des Judentums* of mid-nineteenth-century Germany: a shift of emphasis from religious literature and thought to the social institutions of the Jewish people and the situation of the Jewish masses. In Eastern Europe after the turn of the century, scholars inspired by the ideals of Jewish nationalism (some of whom were Dubnow's students and disciples) continued to research the past of Polish and Russian Jewry, collect Jewish folklore, and undertake the scientific study of Yiddish, now recognized as an independent language, not merely a "jargon." Socialism sensitized Jewish historians to class tensions and conflict of interest within the Jewish communities of the Middle Ages and the modern period, and made them more fully aware of the socioeconomic factor behind Jewish sectarian movements. The founding of the Hebrew University in Jerusalem created a major center of Jewish research in Palestine; amateurs and professionals in the yishuv began to recover tangible traces of their distant ancestors in the land (buildings, inscriptions, objects of daily use), and archeology emerged as an Israeli national passion. The Stalinist repressions and the Holocaust in large measure destroyed the flourishing Jewish studies of interwar Europe. But scholars in Israel, America, and elsewhere have continued to absorb recent trends in Western historiography and the social sciences, to reshape the established biblical, rabbinic, and other disciplines, and to expand newer fields such as Jewish demography, local and regional Jewish history, Jewry law, Jewish economic history, Jewish-gentile relations, eastern Jewries, popular religion, and nonconformist elements in Jewish history.

Modern Jewish historiography has liberated the student from a static, narrow conception of Judaism and Jewry based on any one particular historical setting: The totality of Jewish history is more diverse and more intimately related to the changing context of world history than previously imagined. The inclusiveness of Jewish history, however, has created problems for the secular Jewishness espoused by Ahad Ha-Am and Dubnow, who believed that they had found in the concept of evolution and in a "national will to survive" the verification of their humanist values. In subsequent Jewish historical writing, detailed economic, legal, and social analysis of contingent factors and long-range trends have been more useful than an evolutionary will to survive in analyzing the reasons for the rise and decline of a branch of the Jewish diaspora. At the same time, modern Jewish historiography has brought out the decisive importance of religion in maintaining the separateness of the Jewish people, at least in the premodern world: Not just a vague and unconscious Jewish "life force" but a set of mental and emotional attitudes and a structured world picture motivated Jewish resistance to assimilation and dissolution. Scholars who are themselves not religious, or who do not intend in their historical writing to defend Jewish theology as such, have emphasized the primacy of religious symbols and beliefs in Jewish survival (exile and redemption according to Yitzhak Baer and Benzion Dinur, classical Jewish monotheism according to Yehezkel Kaufmann, the Kabbalah as a vitalizing spiritual phenomenon according to Gershom Scholem—to mention only a few men writing from the perspective of twentieth-century Zionism). Contrary to the old evolutionary scheme, it now appears that the Jewish past has a dialectical character, that it contains many internal tensions and polarities: messianism and halakhah, rationalism and mysticism, folk tradition and intellectual elitism, holy land and diaspora, internal and external causation, and so on. Within the totality there are cycles and continuities, surprises and discontinuities, all of which become apparent the more distance and perspective modern scholarship attains.

Through modern Jewish literature and historical writing, Jewish self-consciousness has gathered to itself new insights and depths. But these forms of artistic imagination and scholarly knowledge are autonomous realms. By themselves they do not ensure the survival of secular Jewish identity because they are not able—nor do they wish—to provide the sense of personal obligation that is necessary if a Jew is to attach himself to his tradition more actively than as a biographical fact. One of the most telling features of Jewish secularism is that it is most dear to those who received a traditional religious upbringing at home and in school and who then cut themselves off from it for the sake of new mental horizons, while at the same time conserving an emotional tie to their first world. They sought, therefore, to separate tradition, on the one hand, and belief and value, on the other, even though sometimes they were able to bring together the two sides rather closely. But what of a new secular generation raised without a direct relationship in childhood to the tradition? Sometimes a more extreme rebellion, a call for even greater liberation. Sometimes the opposite: the desire for a more personal tie with Judaism, a search for existential meaning in it. The careful distinction between tradition and value tends to dissolve, and the result may be a new religiosity, quite different from the old.

Secular Jewish identity will continue among Jews whose deep Jewish involvement is accompanied by refusal to commit themselves to a religious definition of Jewishness. But recent cultural trends indicate, at the very least, that religious needs persist or re-emerge. We will, therefore, complete our survey of Jewish thought with an account of some twentieth-century Jewish theologies that take their departure from post-traditional modes of philosophical and religious thought.

CHAPTER 16

Twentieth-Century Jewish Religious Thought

Diverse Tendencies and Representative Figures: An Overview

Since 1900 Jewish philosophy has become more variegated than ever before. Traditional Judaism not only produced articulate modern defenders but attracted young secular Jews searching for their spiritual roots. Reform, Neo-Orthodox, and Conservative approaches continued to develop, sometimes with major modifications of their nineteenth-century positions. Before discussing key figures in twentieth-century Jewish philosophy—Cohen, Rosenzweig, Buber, Kaplan, and Heschel—we will survey religious tendencies before World War II in Eastern and Central Europe, the land of Israel, and America, pausing briefly to describe several important men for whom limited space prevents more extended treatment.

In late tsarist Russia the rabbinate continued to write in the time-honored talmudic and moralistic literary forms and East European orthodoxy showed some signs of an inner religious revival. One of the most saintly rabbis of the mitnagedic (non-Hasidic) Orthodox was Israel Meir Ha-Kohen (1838–1933), author of many halakhic and ethical treatises. (He is usually known as the Hafetz Hayyim, from the title of his book on the laws of slander, gossip, and talebearing.) The Hafetz Hayyim was associated with one wing of the *musar* (ethics) movement, founded

720

The ancient synagogue of Peki'in in the Galilee, a village which has had a Jewish population from before the first century CE to the present. (Courtesy of the Consulate General of Israel.)

by Rabbi Israel Lipkin Salanter in the 1840s, which had spread to many Lithuanian yeshivot by 1900. In the yeshivot, *musar* teachers sought to counteract the corrosive effects on traditional piety of Enlightenment and modernity through regular study of moral treatises, daily meditation, and self-examination, in order to inculcate constant self-criticism, subdue vanity, overcome preoccupation with worldly matters, and advance toward spiritual perfection. Hasidic rabbis also continued to maintain a following among the East European Jewish masses in pre-World War I Russia as well as in Poland, Romania, and Hungary up to the Holocaust. In 1912 mitnagedic and Hasidic rabbis joined with German and Hungarian Orthodox leaders to form the *Agudat Israel* (League of Israel) party to combat secularist ideologies, especially Zionism. By the 1920s and 1930s the Agudat Israel constituted a political and social force in the Polish Jewish communities and maintained an extensive network of Jewish schools for girls as well as boys. (The Agudat Israel was, of course, not opposed to settlement by Jews in the holy land, but rejected the Zionist ideal of a secular Jewish society that would not conform to the halakhah.)

In the decade before World War I, Hasidic spirituality began to interest certain philosophically sophisticated Central European Jewish writers who rejected positivism and Marxist materialism. Martin Buber (to be discussed later in this chapter) was only one of several who discovered in Hasidism an orientation to life and to God that they could appropriate into their own personal religious quest. Another revered figure of this type in interwar Poland was Hillel Zeitlin (1871–1942), poet, journalist, and essayist. Zeitlin's early monographs and essays had been marked by a philosophical pessimism mixed with humanitarian sympathies; as he gravitated to Orthodoxy, he found in the teachings of the Hasidic masters a path leading the lonely and despairing individual to fervent repentance and renewed messianic hope. Judaism, he insisted, was essentially mystical and not rationalistic. (Clad in prayer shawl and *tefillin*, Zeitlin was killed by the Nazis on the way from the Warsaw ghetto to the extermination camp of Treblinka—a modern incarnation of the traditional Jewish martyr dying for the sanctification of God's name.)

If East European Orthodoxy was showing signs of vitality in the last decades before the Holocaust (in the Soviet Union, of course, the lack of religious freedom made this impossible), German Jewry of the same period witnessed renewal of Jewish philosophy of religion. The three most important figures—Hermann Cohen, Franz Rosenzweig, and Martin Buber—were thoroughly trained in classical philosophy. Apart from Cohen, Rosenzweig, and Buber, who were not rabbis (they will be treated separately later in the chapter), German Jewry in the twentieth century also produced several eminent rabbinic theologians. Leader of the small, closely knit Frankfort Neo-Orthodoxy was Isaac Breuer (1883–1946). In his many articles and books, Breuer continued to espouse Samson Raphael Hirsch's position that the Jewish people was a suprahistorical entity under the direct sovereignty of God and that the Torah was an inexhaustible, eternally valid communication of content from God to man. (Breuer was active in the Agudat Israel and settled in Palestine in the mid-1930s.) Among the liberal rabbis of Germany, outstanding was Leo Baeck (1873–1956), who studied at the Breslau Jewish Theological Seminary and then at the Berlin *Hochschule für die Wissenschaft des Judentums* where he was ordained. From 1912 Baeck held a rabbinical position in Berlin and taught at the *Hochschule*, with the exception of a stint as German army chaplain during World War I. When the Nazis came to power in 1933, he was elected president of the overall body representing German Jews in the Third Reich. Refusing to leave Germany, Baeck was interned in the concentration camp of Theresienstadt in 1943; he survived the Holocaust to become one of the most eminent Jewish spiritual figures of the immediate post-World War II era, continuing to write and teach in England and America.

Baeck's first and most influential book, *The Essence of Judaism* (first edition 1905, second and expanded edition 1922) originated as a polemic against the position that Judaism was only a preparation for the ethical perfectionism represented by Jesus. On the contrary, according to Baeck, Judaism is the clearest instance of the "classical" type of religion characterized by a realistic but hopeful ethical optimism and a firm commitment to man's moral freedom. In his essay "Romantic Religion," Baeck contrasts classical religion with a tendency in Christianity, beginning with Paul, to emphasize complete dependence on divine grace, mystical union with God, and faith alone at the expense of works, which resulted, Baeck argued, in passive indifference to the struggle against evil in the world. Baeck did not identify Judaism only with the ethical: "The commandment," the never-ending duty to realize the good, emerges out of "the mystery" that is God. Jewish religious consciousness preserves a necessary tension between the finite and the infinite, existence and the ideal, the human and the transcendent. In glimpsing the divine mystery, man recognizes that he is created; in apprehending the divine commandment, he becomes conscious that he is expected to create. Baeck's last book, completed after World War II (*This People Israel: The Meaning of Jewish Existence*), shifts from a definition of the essence of Judaism to the inner meaning of Jewish history—a path of repeated rebirth in which Israel must reformulate and reapply God's demand to an ever-changing present.

All these strands of European Jewish thought have been absorbed by the newer Jewries of the land of Israel and America, albeit in quite different ways. Several eminent European scholars who settled in Jerusalem in the 1920s and 1930s (Samuel Hugo Bergman, Julius Guttmann, Ernst Simon, Leon Roth, and others) continued the academic philosophical tradition that reached its height in German Jewry. But the most influential spiritual figures in the yishuv came from Eastern Europe, such as the venerated mentor of the *halutzim*, or "pioneers," Aaron David Gordon (1856–1922). A Russian Jew who arrived in Palestine in 1904 when he was almost fifty, Gordon was inspired not only by Jewish sources but by Tolstoi, Dostoievski, and the Russian populists, especially their idealization of the peasant life. Rejecting the impersonal and dehumanizing effects of industrialization and mass, urban society, Gordon saw in small Zionist agricultural communities a primary means for inner Jewish redemption as individuals and as a people. (His non-Marxist, agrarian socialism is sometimes called the "religion of labor.") Gordon's religiosity is expressed through a mystical bond between man and nature. Rational knowledge may be a necessary tool for physical survival, but man grasps the immediacy of life in its fullness only through intuition. Gordon acknowledged that for the secular pioneers traditional religious forms and rituals may have lost their meaning, but the deepest content of religion—the organic unity and purposiveness of the cosmos—remains eternally available for rediscovery. For Gordon, nations, as well as human

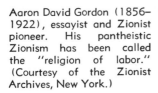

Aaron David Gordon (1856–
1922), essayist and Zionist
pioneer.   His   pantheistic
Zionism has been called
the "religion of labor."
(Courtesy of the Zionist
Archives, New York.)

beings, are natural phenomena, products of the interaction of a society
with its physical environment. To his readers and followers, therefore,
Gordon held out the hope that Jewry could experience moral rebirth
in the homeland—a rebirth that would make the Jewish people, in
Gordon's phrase, an "incarnation" of the ideal humanity.

Within Orthodoxy in Palestine, a similar mystical Zionism was the
hallmark of Abraham Isaac Kook (1865–1935). Emigrating from Russia
to Palestine in 1904, Kook became the rabbi of Jaffa, and in 1921, the
Ashkenazic Chief Rabbi of the yishuv. In contrast to the Agudat Israel
in Europe and the extreme traditionalists in the holy land, Kook was
distinctly impressed by the ethical idealism of the young Jewish socialists,
who, in building the Jewish national home, were aiding the divine plan.
Redemption is the central theme of Kook's writings. Drawing on the
Kabbalah, Kook insisted that there was no real separation between the
religious and the secular. Holiness, an intensified form of life itself and
the ceaseless impetus to perfection, is the ever-present task to transmute
coarse and earthly aspects of existence to higher planes of being. Social
and scientific progress have intrinsic value as long as they are not divorced

Abraham Isaac Kook in 1914. A mystic and a religious Zionist, Kook (1865–1935) was later Ashkenazic Chief Rabbi of Palestine. (Courtesy of the Zionish Archives, New York.)

from the spiritual. Kook endorsed the Darwinian view of evolution as compatible with a cosmic process in which all souls, fragments of the one world soul and refractions of God's unitive being, yearn to discover and return to God. Like Judah Halevy, whose philosophy he admired, Kook was convinced that Israel had a special genius for holiness and that the renewal of the Jewish bond to the land was an important stage in mankind's advance to universal harmony.

Neither Gordon's nor Kook's mysticism generated large-scale religious movements in the yishuv, where the contrast (sometimes the sharp disagreement) between secularism and traditionalism is still a feature of Israeli life. In America, the distinction between secularist and religionist was less important in the long run than that between Reform, Conservatism, and Orthodoxy, each of which had a sizable membership and extensive network of congregational federations, rabbinical bodies, and institutions of higher Jewish learning. Nevertheless, although the dividing lines between the three movements remained evident, all gradually developed more traditionalist and more liberal wings on such issues as adjustment of Jewish practice to the contemporary situation and the theology most suited to religion in a secular age. During the first half of the twentieth century, the various strands of European Jewish religious thought were absorbed and reshaped in the American environment, to produce new emphases and points of view.

One of the most important figures of Reform Judaism at the turn of the century was Kaufmann Kohler (1843–1926). Kohler came to the United States from Germany in 1867 and served as rabbi of several Reform temples until he became president of the Hebrew Union College in Cincinnati in 1903. A prodigious scholar, Kohler was the author of *Jewish Theology Systematically and Historically Considered* (1917). Acknowledging that Judaism had a communal aspect and distinctive rituals and ceremonies, Kohler nevertheless saw as its core a universal set of ethical and religious truths, proclaimed by the biblical prophets and evolving in the course of history toward greater clarity. Kohler was both a believer in a personal God and a rationalist: Revelation and religious intuition were indispensable, but the validity of Judaism lay not in its source but in its content. The Bible does not inspire because it is holy, it is holy because it inspires. Man's ethical conscience is the main proof for God's existence, and the moral law is the principal message of Judaism. Kohler was opposed to Zionism because, to him and other classical Reformers, it was a retreat to an obsolete and particularistic Jewish nationalism. Just before World War I, however, and especially in the twenties and thirties, younger Reform rabbis took an increasingly positive attitude toward the idea of Jewish peoplehood and the rebirth of the Jewish homeland (Stephen S. Wise, Abba Hillel Silver, Judah Magnes, and others). At the same time, they became involved in concrete issues of social justice in the United States, arguing that Reform's commitment to the prophetic tradition mandated active concern for the rights of organized labor, the blacks, and the poor. (The next generation of Reform rabbis, who took on the task of formulating a new Jewish theology after World War II, will be discussed at the end of the chapter.)

In American Conservative Judaism the major contemporary of Kaufmann Kohler was Solomon Schechter (1847–1915). Born in Romania, for two decades a prominent scholar of Judaica at Oxford University, Schechter was invited in 1901 to become president of the Jewish Theological Seminary of America in New York. Unlike Kohler, Schechter believed that the Jewish religion was not reducible to a logically formulated system of principles but was the ongoing manifestation of the religious consciousness of "catholic Israel" (catholic in the sense of all-inclusive). For Schechter, Judaism was a consensus emerging from the study of

Leo Baeck (1873–1956), leading German liberal rabbi and theologian, Holocaust survivor. In this photograph he is being awarded a honorary degree by Rabbi Stephen S. Wise, President of the Jewish Institute of Religion, April 12, 1948. (Courtesy of the Leo Baeck Institute and Whitestone Photo, New York.)

Torah over many centuries. In *Some Aspects of Rabbinic Theology* (1909), he defined talmudic Judaism as a complicated arrangement of checks and balances, rather than a fixed scheme of salvation: Indeed, the health of a religion was to have a theology without being conscious of it. Schechter eloquently defended the joy of Jewish observance of the law and the "applied holiness" exemplified by the great spiritual figures of the Jewish past, lovingly described in his *Studies in Judaism* (3 volumes, 1896–1924). Because of the centrality of Jewish peoplehood in the Conservative movement, it was not painfully caught up in the dispute between anti-Zionism and Zionism that troubled early twentieth-century Reform and European Orthodoxy. The Conservatives did develop their own divergent tendencies in the 1930s and 1940s, however, between those who called for greater flexibility and innovation in response to the challenges of modern science and democracy, and others who emphasized the need for a firm commitment to the Jewish legal and theological mainstream (as we shall see later in our more lengthy discussion of Mordecai Kaplan and Abraham Heschel).

American Orthodoxy, although united in its devotion to a supernaturally revealed Torah and to the normative status of the *Shulhan Arukh* and its regulations, also came to embrace a wide gamut of religious styles. Transplanted East European traditionalism was preserved by yeshivot of the Old World, Lithuanian type founded in various American cities, and German Neo-Orthodoxy established roots in New York in the 1930s. (Hasidic groups have also settled in the Northeast since World War II.) The major focus of modern American Orthodoxy has been the Rabbi Isaac Elhanan Theological Seminary of Yeshiva University in New York. A persistent disagreement within Orthodoxy has revolved around whether it should cooperate with non-Orthodox movements in the Jewish community in order to preserve the unity of the people or whether it should adamantly refuse to recognize the legitimacy of secular, Reform, and Conservative forms of Jewishness and avoid joint activities with them. Although a few traditional rabbis continued to warn against the dangers of secular learning, modern Orthodoxy in America has become increasingly able, since the 1930s, to present its position in contemporary theological terms. (Two of the most important Orthodox theologians, Joseph Soloveitchik and Eliezer Berkovits, will be discussed in the last part of this chapter.)

The next sections will concentrate on five men who stand out by having published a body of writing recognized as modern classics. Highly original thinkers, they also represent the impact on Judaism of four of the most influential philosophical or theological tendencies in twentieth-century Europe and America—Neo-Kantianism, existentialism, religious naturalism, and Protestant Neo-Orthodoxy. An examination of these men indicates some of the methodological and substantive dilemmas facing Jewish religious thought in recent decades.

Hermann Cohen's Neo-Kantian Philosophy of Judaism

The man who stood at the borderline between the nineteenth and twentieth-century liberal philosophies of Judaism—perfecting the former in such a way as to point to the new departures of the latter—was Hermann Cohen (1842–1918), a towering figure in modern Jewish rationalism. Born in the small German town of Coswig (his father was a Hebrew teacher and cantor), Cohen received a Jewish education at home and a general education in a *gymnasium*. Intending to become a rabbi, he attended the Breslau Jewish Theological Seminary, but soon left to study science, mathematics, and philosophy at the University of Berlin. Little more than ten years after receiving his doctorate, Cohen was appointed full professor at the University of Marburg (1876), a signal honor for a Jew at that time. Cohen made Marburg one of the great centers of German academic philosophy. He wrote three distinguished books on Kant's thought, followed by a series of volumes on the philosophical foundations of the natural sciences, ethics, and art. Unlike most modern Jewish thinkers, Cohen achieved eminence in professional philosophy before he made his most important contribution to Judaism. When anti-Semitism made its conspicuous appearance, around 1880, in German politics, Cohen began to publish articles defending the ethical teachings of Judaism and the value of Jewish religious survival. Against German intellectuals who looked on Judaism as a particularistic anachronism that a Jew would have to drop as he entered the mainstream of German culture, Cohen insisted on the affinity between Judaism and "Germanism," that is, between a purified, rational Judaism and his conception of German civilization as a central force in the progressive movement of the human mind toward moral freedom and intellectual autonomy. Retiring from Marburg in 1912, Cohen moved to Berlin to lecture at the *Hochschule für die Wissenschaft des Judentums* and to devote himself to an examination of religion's relation to philosophy. In 1915 he published *The Concept of Religion in the System of Philosophy*. His major Jewish work, *Religion of Reason Out of the Sources of Judaism* (1919), was issued after his death. In 1924 over sixty of his shorter essays on Jewish subjects were collected and published in three volumes (*Jüdische Schriften* [*Jewish Writings*]).

Cohen's position represents the most rigorous and original example of the reformulation of Jewish religious belief in accordance with the philosophy of Immanuel Kant (1724–1804). A brief digression on Kant's philosophy, one of the greatest in Western intellectual history, is necessary at this point in order to indicate what Cohen took from Kant and where he departed from him.

Like all forms of philosophical idealism, Kant's "critical" idealism places great emphasis on the activity of the mind as determining what is real. Unlike the most extreme forms of speculative idealism, which view all reality as a manifestation of mind, however, he sought a compromise between thoroughgoing rationalism and empiricist skepticism. Kant distinguished between reality as known to experience—the phenomena—and an ultimate reality that lies beyond all possible experience—the noumena or things-in-themselves. Phenomena are known only insofar as they conform to the essential structure of consciousness; noumena are unknowable, although their existence is a necessary presupposition of philosophy. In Kant's system, man's knowledge is saved from a complete skepticism, at the cost of being limited to the world of phenomena and therefore to the structuring activity of the mind. What the mind supplies can be divided into three levels: the "perceptual forms" of space and time, without which sense experience is impossible; the basic "categories of the understanding" (such as causality and substance) by which we understand phenomenal experience; the three "regulative principles" of God, world, and self through which reason unifies knowledge into a coherent whole. "Ideas" are much more than subjective notions in Kant's philosophy, for he believes that God, world, and self cannot be affirmed or denied on empirical grounds, yet are necessary elements in a complete account of the phenomenal world.

The three great issues of metaphysics—the existence of God, human freedom, and personal immortality—are, according to Kant, insoluble by speculative reason, but their validity can be affirmed through an analysis of the ethical life. (Kant calls this realm the "practical" reason, in contrast to the "pure" reason, which deals with scientific and mathematical truth.) The basis of ethics is the "categorical imperative" or the "moral law": The various formulations of this principle state that one's ethical maxims must be universalizable (applicable to everyone in a similar situation), respectful of man as an end in himself (not merely as a means), and self-legislating (adhering to the sovereignty of reason and independent of any other authority). Freedom of the will cannot be scientifically demonstrated, but is required logically because freedom makes morality possible. ("You can because you ought.") Kant felt that the practical reason had to postulate immortality because man's obligation to be virtuous required that he have infinite time in another world to strive toward "the highest good." The highest good is the union of virtue and happiness, which in turn requires a being (God) who is perfectly good in order to want to unite virtue and happiness, and sufficiently powerful to be able to do so. The core of rational religion, therefore, is ethics, and the ideas of God, freedom, and immortality are reliable articles of moral faith about things unknowable in themselves. The Kantian system was particularly attractive to liberal Jewish religious philosophers because it involved no submission to revealed dogmas, such as the Trinity or the Incarnation, and because the primacy of the moral law reinforced the ethical element of prophetic Judaism.

In the first half of the nineteenth century, Kantian idealism had given way to the speculative systems of Hegel and others, which in turn had been superseded by positivism and philosophical materialism at mid-century. In the late 1860s Kantian critical idealism was revived as a starting point for investigations into the philosophical underpinnings of science and the humanities. Cohen, in his Marburg period, was a leading figure in this Neo-Kantian movement. Although generally adhering to the Kantian method, he advocated several crucial changes in it. First, Cohen interpreted the notion of the noumena not as an unknowable reality, but as a symbol of man's unending task to refine his knowledge through the interplay of rational analysis and empirical research (his model being mathematical physics). Dropping the Kantian distinction between the receptivity of sense perception and the spontaneous activity of the understanding, Cohen viewed thought not as an organizing of the given, but as a purely creative act of the mind. Second, in his ethical theory, Cohen dismisses the concept of personal immortality as an unfortunate compromise with morality as an end-in-itself. The philosophical function of the idea of God is to guarantee the progressive realization of man's ethical task in the natural world. Only the idea of God provides the ground for the belief that man's moral obligation can indeed be actualized in reality. Cohen was an idealist in the ordinary as well as the philosophical meaning of the word. He was passionately committed to the ethical goals of socialism and to international peace: that the working-man should be protected against economic exploitation and that war must be eliminated through a global confederation of nations.

Of all modern Jewish thinkers, Cohen comes closest to Maimonides' effort in the Middle Ages to redefine the principles of Judaism according to a severely rational method: Only those aspects of Judaism can be taken with utmost intellectual seriousness that are compatible with reason. In Cohen's last great work, *Religion of Reason Out of the Sources of Judaism*, the Jewish faith measures up very well to this standard, for Cohen feels that he can show that its basic ideas (God, creation, revelation, holiness, atonement, messianism, and so on) are vital elements in a scientific and ethical world view. To be sure, traditional Jewish teachings have to be sifted critically. Some are radically changed. (Like Maimonides, Cohen sought to eliminate any trace of anthropomorphism from the Jewish notion of God.) The reverse occurs as well: Cohen is led to revise substantially some of his earlier assumptions concerning religious truth. The result was the most important presentation in modern Jewish philosophy of the conviction that Judaism represents a progressive, universally valid manifestation of mind's intellectual and moral creativity.

Like Maimonides' *Guide for the Perplexed, Religion of Reason* has two levels: the construction of a philosophical system and the interpretation of copious quotations from Jewish sources to show that they are in line with the religion of reason. Although Cohen generally remains within the Neo-Kantian framework, he preserves a great deal of Jewish piety in this book. The two levels are harmonized by his conviction that there is a definite connection between the principles of critical ideal-

Hermann Cohen, foremost Jewish Neo-Kantian philosopher; a drawing by Max Libermann. (Courtesy of the Leo Baeck Institute, New York.)

ism and the faith of absolute monotheism, Kantianism being "a philosophy whose truth is its methodology" and Judaism being "a religion whose truth is its God." To call God an "idea" is to pay Him the highest compliment possible in Cohen's vocabulary:

> What the *idea* as ethical reality means positively, and as such is able to achieve for actuality, becomes most clear in man's love for God, on the basis of God's love for man. The power of the idea to realize itself is nowhere so clear as in the love for the idea. *How is it possible to love an idea?* To which one should retort: how is it possible to love anything but an idea? Does one not love, even in the case of sensual love, only the idealized person, only the idea of the person?[1]

According to Cohen, the essential feature of Jewish monotheism is not God's numerical oneness, but His uniqueness: The difference between

God and the world is not merely quantitative but qualitative. (That God's transcendent being can be grasped only by the mind, Cohen interprets as the meaning of the biblical prohibition of idols.) God is the source of everything in the phenomenal world: In the Kantian terminology, the idea of God is the precondition for scientific causality. Because Cohen believes that the universe is eternal and did not come into existence at an initial moment of time, the idea of creation—the relation between God and the world—means constant renewal and permanence in change, as in the prayer book's phrase that "God renews daily the work of creation."

Like creation, revelation is not limited to a particular historical event. For Cohen, revelation means nothing less than that man is the bearer of reason. Cohen's conception of revelation is spelled out in his interpretation of the biblical "spirit of holiness." The spirit of holiness is the moral quality common to God and man, present in each in a different way. God's holiness is that He is the "archetype" of ethical action. Man's holiness is his task to emulate the divine archetype by actualizing ethics in the world. It is essential that the divine and the human be brought into relationship without blurring the crucial distinction between them. Cohen emphatically rejects any pantheism, such as Spinoza's, which fuses God, nature, and man into a monistic unity, because pantheism eliminates the gap between what is and what ought to be, thus destroying the meaning of ethics. Man's task is to bring about the good that at present exists only in God and not yet in the world.

To characterize the reciprocity between God and man, Cohen employs the term *correlation*, which is the key to his philosophy of Judaism. As he develops the implications of this relation, Cohen discovers that he can retain features of religion that he had previously dissolved into the universal principles of ethics. Ethical monotheism correlates man with God in three ways unique to religion: the concepts of fellowman, the individual, humanity.

It was monotheism that first discovered the concept of the "fellowman," or *Mitmensch* in contrast merely to the "other man," or *Nebenmensch*, the distinction being that fellowman implies consciousness of a common humanity between the self and the other, together with the moral obligation of sympathy. The biblical injunction "Love your neighbor as yourself" Cohen interprets as "Love the fellowman because he is like you." Cohen notes that for the prophets, the suffering of the poor and the oppressed is guiltless suffering, eliciting not blame but pity and requiring specific improvements in social life. In the concept of the fellowman, religion achieves what philosophical ethics cannot originate from its own resources: the idea of the God of social love, an archetype for human compassion and for concrete activities in behalf of the exploited.

Second, it is religion and not philosophy that correlates the individual and God through the process of atonement for sin. Religion's concept of the intimate relationship of the person, in his singularity, to God comes to the fore in confession of wrongdoing and repentance before God. Unlike the undeserved suffering of the poor, the suffering of the penitent has a positive significance: Deeming oneself deserving of suffering is a step in the individual's moral self-transformation, a sign of earnest regretfulness. The rituals and prayers of Yom Kippur, the Day of Atonement, are a model for that self-purification which makes man worthy of God's forgiveness. Cohen is sharply critical of the Christian view that Christ acts as mediator in the creation of the new, redeemed human self and that Christ's death is a vicarious atonement for the sins of mankind. God does not collaborate in man's moral self-purification. God's role is not causal but teleological: Repentance is the responsible and free action of man, for which God's forgiveness remains the goal. Nevertheless, in postulating a forgiving God, Cohen expands quite definitely his earlier notion that the idea of God functions solely as universal reason's guarantee that there is a link between the natural and the moral realms.

The third correlation between man and God in monotheism is the prophetic idea of humanity, "a creation of thought absolutely unique in the entire world of the spirit." Prophetic messianism goes beyond philosophical ethics in that it postulates a future in which war is eliminated and the unity of humanity fully recognized. This goal elevates man's consciousness beyond the limits of the past and present, revealing an ideal that it is man's task to actualize. According to Cohen, immortality should be interpreted in line with this messianic vision. Stripped of mythological and supernatural elements—as well as of the notion of individual reward and punishment—immortality is a living-on of the individual in the historical continuity of people and humanity. The only fitting compensation for the good act is its contribution to mankind's infinite task of self-perfection. In connection with his discussion of messianism, the Jewish people is seen as the symbol for the eventual unity of humanity. Recalling Isaiah 53, Cohen portrays Israel as the servant of God, who willingly suffers because he knows the value of his historical destiny for the moral education of all peoples.

Israel is preserved for its messianic task through law and through prayer. For Cohen, Jewish law is implicitly ethical even when not explicitly so: Religious rituals and ceremonies are signs or memorials for spiritual perfection. The degree of social isolation from non-Jews that observance of the law entails (such as prohibitions against mixed marriage and eating of nonkosher food) strengthens the people as a community of believers and preserves Israel for its mission. For this reason, Cohen rejects Zionism: Jews must remain citizens of their respective states in the diaspora and full participants in general culture because the Jews are a spiritual association that must survive for the sake of pure monotheism. As the "language of the religious correlation between man and God," prayer makes the messianic future present in the assembly of Israel, reinforcing and fortifying the power of religious ideals. Through reaffirmed confidence in the loving God of forgiveness and reconciliation, prayer arms the individual against the dangers of insincerity and self-deception, and enables him to overcome the despair resulting from a realization of his finitude.

Religion of Reason concludes with the "ways to morality": the virtues of truthfulness and modesty, justice, courage, and faithfulness, and *shalom*. *Shalom* is the infinite perfection of the human race and the peace of soul that removes hatred from the heart. "Peace is the sign of eternity and also the watchword for human life, in its individual conduct as well as in the eternity of its historical calling. In this historical eternity the mission of messianic mankind is completed."[2] Whoever loves peace cannot fear death, for the peace of death is not the end of life but its goal on man's way to eternity.

Cohen's *Religion of Reason* is permeated by nineteenth-century optimism, epitomized by his faith in human perfectibility. (Cohen's calm acceptance of death also stands in decided contrast to the anxiety of personal finitude found in certain twentieth-century philosophies.) Several areas of his thought have been sharply disputed since the 1920s. First, his ethereal view of the Jewish people as willing sufferers for the sake of mankind's advance has been attacked for its lack of realism about modern anti-Semitism, especially in his beloved Germany. Secondly, his sublimation of God into an idea also appears excessively abstract, losing much of its power if one does not accept the Neo-Kantian framework. To be sure, in *Religion of Reason* and other late writings Cohen went far beyond his earlier belief that religion was merely the historical source of the values that philosophy constructs into a coherent and autonomous system. In Cohen's mature view, the God of religion is intimately related to the individual. Yet the God of forgiveness remains an idea—a postulate of the practical reason, which exists solely in the realm of thought and has no actuality. (For Cohen, actuality implies participation in the spatial-temporal manifold of perceptual existence.) Much of subsequent twentieth-century Jewish religious thought went far beyond Cohen's tentative step from the general to the particular, by locating the living presence of God more specifically in concrete human existence. Even when his system was rejected as a whole, however, the spiritual quality of *Religion of Reason* and Cohen's other Jewish writings has been widely admired. In several of his most original notions, especially that the relation between God and man is one of correlation, he anticipated thinkers in the next generation who sought to describe the structure of Jewish religious experience in quite different ways.

The Emergence of Jewish Existentialism: Franz Rosenzweig and Martin Buber

The two most important figures in the overthrow of the idealist interpretation of Judaism were close friends and collaborators in the 1920s, who laid the groundwork for a new approach to Jewish theology that is still being pursued. Franz Rosenzweig and Martin Buber diverged considerably on issues affecting Jewish action, but shared certain points of departure that warrant their being treated under the same heading.

Franz Rosenzweig (1886–1929) was born in Cassel, Germany, to an affluent, cultured family; although affiliated with the Jewish community, his parents observed few Jewish rituals and Franz was given a superficial and perfunctory Jewish education. In 1905 his university training began with the study of medicine, then shifted to history and philosophy. (Rosenzweig's doctoral dissertation on Hegel's political doctrines, completed in 1914 and published in 1920, is an important scholarly work on the subject.) In the summer of 1913, under the influence of several young Jewish friends who had converted to Christianity, Rosenzweig gave up what he called his "philosophical relativism" and was on the verge of following their example. Soon afterwards, however, he attended Yom Kippur services in a small traditional synagogue in Berlin, where he discovered that he could find religious fulfillment in Judaism. During the rest of the 1913–1914 academic year, he remained in Berlin, studying Jewish texts and developing a close and warm friendship with Hermann Cohen.

Rosenzweig spent most of World War I in the German army on the Balkan front. During those years an erudite and searching theological correspondence with the friends mentioned earlier paved the way for his major work, *The Star of Redemption*, begun on army postal cards and letters to his mother and completed upon his return home. (It was published in 1921.) Immediately after the war, Rosenzweig married, rejected an academic career, and settled in Frankfort-on-Main where he founded the *Freies Jüdisches Lehrhaus* (Independent House of Jewish Learning) as a center for a new type of adult Jewish education for acculturated, marginal Jews in search of their roots. The *Lehrhaus* attracted a group of outstanding Jewish intellectuals, many of whom later achieved prominence in Jewish and humanistic studies (Nahum Glatzer, Gershom Scholem, Leo Strauss, Erich Fromm, and others). Shortly before the birth of his son in 1922, Rosenzweig learned that he had con-

Franz Rosenzweig, Jewish existentialist; a drawing by Ludwig Jonas. (Courtesy of the Leo Baeck Institute, New York.)

tracted a disease that was to paralyze first his limbs, then his whole body, and finally his power of speech. With the aid of his wife and friends and using a specially constructed typewriter, he continued a wide correspondence, wrote a number of important essays, translated and commented on the poems of Judah Halevy, and, together with Martin Buber, began a new German translation of the Bible, which sought to convey the living spiritual experience that had shaped the Hebrew text. He died in 1929 at the age of 43.

If Hermann Cohen was the Maimonides of modern Jewish philosophy, Rosenzweig was its Judah Halevy. Cohen, like Maimonides, was highly aware of the philosophical implications of science. Rosenzweig, like Halevy, was a man of unusual poetic sensitivity who disengaged religion from rationalistic philosophy and placed primary emphasis on the experience of revelation.

The Star of Redemption is not a philosophy of Judaism but a journey from philosophy to theology to religion. Part I criticizes philosophy's pretensions to reduce the universe to a simple underlying essence, such as the Hegelian consciousness-in-general. The attempt to explain the manifold of existence by a single principle flies in the face of everyday reality as intuited by common sense. At best, philosophy can apprehend three distinct essences: world, man, and God, each with its own separate nature, part rational, part irreducibly given. Together these essences form independent constituents of a "pre-world" and must be brought into relationship by concepts derived from outside rational speculation.

How this can be done is the subject of Part II of the *Star*. Theology complements philosophy, supplying the connections between world, man, and God through the three "miraculous facts" of creation, revelation, and redemption. Like Cohen, Rosenzweig views as everpresent possibilities the relationship between God and world (creation), between God and man (revelation), and between man and world (redemption).

Of the three dimensions of existence, the most crucial in Rosenzweig's system is revelation. In revelation God addresses the individual in unpredictable moments of love, breaking down the barrier of man's inner isolation and loneliness. All that God gives the individual is His presence, but the experience of divine love takes the form of a command to love God in return. Rosenzweig here distinguishes between a commandment, which is personally addressed to the individual, and a law, which is a universally binding obligation. Revelation does not result in laws but in commandments: demands spontaneously internalized by the individual in the love relationship. Creation—the world's awakening to its creature-liness—is a second fundamental relationship that theology supplies to philosophy. Creation means the dependence of all individual objects and of the world as a whole on God's active power. The third relationship, redemption, is the turning toward others of one who has experienced revelation. Through redemption, the isolation of human beings from each other is overcome, because out of love between God and the individual arises the commandment to love the fellowman, also a creation of God. In the course of history, redemption permeates the world with deeds of love, bringing about its gradual "ensoulment" and the eventual unification of world and man with God.

Rosenzweig's themes of creation, revelation, and redemption draw on Cohen's concept of correlation but with certain important differences. Whereas to Cohen, revelation is the exercise of reason, to Rosenzweig it is the experience of love; the messianic age as an infinite moral task in Cohen, is in Rosenzweig a cosmic process of total redemption similar to that of the Kabbalah. The two triads of Rosenzweig's philosophical-theological synthesis are seen as interlocking triangles, forming a symbolic star of David—the star of the title.

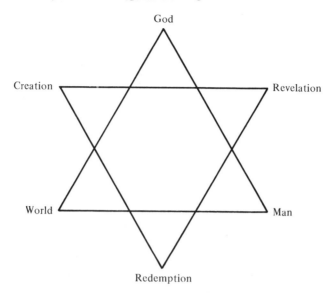

Part III of the *Star* considers what Rosenzweig calls "sociology": a description of Judaism and Christianity in relation to the eternal kingdom of God. Although separate forms of religious life, both traditions are authentic communities of love through which eternity enters the stream of time. Judaism is the "eternal life," Christianity the "eternal way." According to Rosenzweig, the religious calendar and liturgy of the Jews commemorates the rhythm of creation-revelation-redemption, placing the community outside history. Possessing a direct bridge to God, Jewish existence anticipates the eventual redemption of all. Moreover, the Jewish holy land, holy language, and holy Torah are removed from the vicissitudes of time. Because the individual Jew enters the covenant by birth, the continuity of the people is not contingent on conversion of non-Jews: Jewry's task is to be, not to missionize. In contrast, Christianity, always on the way from the first to the second coming of Christ, has a different character and historical role. Every Christian, through baptism, is a convert from paganism. Christianity bears witness to the truth by conversion of the gentiles, bringing the masses into its covenant for the sake of the redemption of the world. In this discussion, Rosenzweig is not concerned primarily with the beliefs of the religions, but with the concrete religious experience that each community of faith offers its members. By asserting that Judaism and Christianity have distinct authentic vocations, Rosenzweig sharply departs from the approach of nineteenth-century Jewish thinkers and of Cohen and Leo Baeck in the twentieth century, who contrasted the doctrines of the two religions in order to defend the superior reasonableness of Judaism. Rosenzweig's position is very much the product of his earlier argument to Christian friends that the Christian needs a mediator to the Father, but the Jew does not. (Perhaps Rosenzweig also intended in this way to defend the legitimacy of Jewish survival in the face of Christianity's historical success.)

The Star of Redemption is a difficult, passionate, and youthful book (he was in his early thirties when he wrote it) which, ironically, is heavily indebted to the Hegelian thinking that its author so severely criticizes. This debt can be seen especially in his overall intent to unfold the evolution of human consciousness. Greek civilization, to Rosenzweig the highest expression of paganism, is aware of God, world, and man only in isolation: The Greeks viewed the world as an infinite, self-subsistent cosmos without beginning or end; the mythic gods of the Greeks were unconcerned with the cosmos and man, except for arbitrary acts of interference; the hero of Greek tragic drama remained isolated by his character and fate, dependent only on himself. Biblical faith takes the leap of bringing world, man, and God into correlation. Out of biblical faith emerge Judaism and Christianity, two partial truths destined to be absorbed into the one divine truth at the end of time. Whereas Rosenzweig initially asserts the irreducible complexity of existence, he ends by positing as the goal of history a final, pantheistic absorption of all souls into God.

Rosenzweig's fatal paralysis and premature death prevented him from fully developing his theology after he became more knowledgable in the Jewish tradition. Judging from his later essays, he would have discarded what he called his "conceptual crutches" and moved toward an explicit religious existentialism. The term *existentialist* is used for a diverse group of thinkers, Christian, Jewish, and atheist, who criticize traditional Western philosophy's preoccupation with unchanging, universal, and rational features of being as overlooking the concrete and personal nature of human existence. Unlike things with a fixed essence, the peculiarity of human existence is its inescapable limits, anxieties, and discontinuities; the whole self, not just the disengaged mind, faces continual possibilities of action and decision. Existentialism has been traced to various nineteenth-century writers, pre-eminently Soren Kierkegaard, the biting and profound Danish critic of Hegel's claim to have constructed an all-inclusive philosophical system. *The Star of Redemption* already contains proto-existentialist tendencies, but these became more pronounced in Rosenzweig's writings of the 1920s, especially in his essay, "The New Thinking."

A first existentialist element in Rosenzweig's anti-idealist "new thinking" is that "earthly truth" begins, not with a theory of knowledge, but with "the experience of factuality." With some hesitation he defined his position as absolute empiricism, "the attitude that claims to know nothing more of the divine [and the terrestrial] than what it has experienced—but really to know this, in the teeth of [classical] philosophy."[3] Philosophy must start by accepting the world as it is apprehended by common sense: by what human beings really experience. Second, all thinking is inescapably rooted in the concrete, unique situation of the thinker and is done in the face of eventual death. For Rosenzweig and other existentialists, traditional philosophy is based on the self-deception that a thinker can rise above this situation:

> Man, chilled in the full current of life, sees . . . death waiting for him. So he steps outside of life. He escapes from the inevitability of death into the paralysis of artificial death. We [the spokesmen for the "new thinking"] have released him from his paralysis, but we are unable to prevent his death; no physician can do that. By teaching him to live again, we have taught him to move towards death; we have taught him to live, though each step he takes brings him closer to death. . . .[4]

The new thinking is a therapy to awaken the self from the pretense of detachment and impersonal inquiry into a confrontation with the time-bound nature of free choice. According to Rosenzweig and his colleagues, traditional reasoning is in the nature of a monologue, whereas that thinking appropriate to human existence is an open dialogue in which truth is discovered through the encounter of two selves.

A third existentialist aspect is that what matters most is not "the hopelessly static truths like those of mathematics," but convictions that can be justified only in actual living.

> From those most unimportant truths, such as "two times two are four," on which people are apt to agree without making more than a minimum use of their brains (a little less for the multiplication table through ten, a little more for the theory of relativity), the way leads over those truths for which a man is willing to pay, on to those that he cannot verify save at the cost of his life, and finally to those that cannot be verified until generations upon generations have given up their lives to that end.[5]

Truth is not an object grasped by the mind but a commitment of the whole self.

In Rosenzweig's later writings, an authentic Jewish life means that everything that happens to a Jew, happens "in a Jewish way." For the marginal Jew seeking a path from the periphery of Jewishness into the center, Rosenzweig wanted to develop at the Frankfort *Lehrhaus* a modern method of Jewish learning that would avoid the aloof, academic scholarship of *Wissenschaft des Judentums*. Jews would confront the classical texts in order to discover what the text says to them now. Although Rosenzweig did not deny the findings of biblical criticism, to him not the literary origins but the religious destiny of the Bible was crucial for a Jewish learning that would perpetuate Judaism and increase the substance of the tradition binding the centuries together.

On the issue of Jewish law, Rosenzweig rejected both Neo-Orthodox and liberal positions. Not feeling obligated to the totality of Jewish law as expounded by traditional rabbinic authorities, he agreed with the liberals that Judaism had created the law and was not identical to it, and that Judaism was recreated anew in every generation. But carrying out the commandments was crucial to living Jewishly. Although he became increasingly observant, he insisted that he could follow only those laws which took on for him the character of commandments. The laws should be put to the test of practice, but one reserved the right of personal decision: The quest to appropriate the law involved an open-minded, serious encounter with tradition. When asked whether he observed a certain practice, Rosenzweig was said to have replied, "Not yet."

Finally, a word about Rosenzweig's relationship to Zionism. He and Hermann Cohen had rejected Zionism for undermining the uniquely nonpolitical, spiritual nature of the Jewish people; both saw the diaspora as necessary for the future historical role of Judaism. In the twenties, however, Rosenzweig came to appreciate the realistic need to safeguard Jewish physical survival in the face of rampant anti-Semitism, and he admired the urge to authentic Jewish existence among many young Zionists. But this did not alter his view of redemption, which remained eschatological—not an episode in history but an event beyond it.

The existentialist tendency in Rosenzweig's thought is even more pronounced in Martin Buber (1878–1965). Born in Vienna, Buber spent his childhood and youth in Polish Galicia (before World War I a province of Austria–Hungary) at the home of his grandfather, Solomon Buber, an authority on the midrashic literature, and in Lvov where Martin attended a secular secondary school. At the Universities of Vienna and Berlin, Buber studied philosophy and art history, receiving a doctorate in 1904 at Berlin for a dissertation on mysticism. While still a student he was active in the newly founded Zionist movement and a member of the Democratic Fraction critical of Herzl's autocratic manner and exclusive preoccupation with diplomacy. In 1904 Buber temporarily withdrew from Zionist affairs to devote himself to Jewish studies, especially Hasidism, but in 1909 he resumed his participation in Jewish journalism and Zionist cultural activities in Germany. In 1924 Buber became professor of Jewish philosophy and ethics at the University of Frankfort-on-Main and began to work closely with Rosenzweig on their Bible translation. When the Nazis came to power, he became head of the revived Frankfort *Lehrhaus* and director of adult Jewish education for

German Jewry. Forced to leave Germany in 1938, he became professor of social philosophy at the Hebrew University in Jerusalem. After World War II he directed an institute that trained adult education teachers for new immigrants to Israel and he lectured extensively in Europe and America. In the last decades of his life, Buber was one of the most widely respected spiritual figures in the West, and the influence of his ideas was evident not only in Jewish and Christian theology but in such secular fields as psychiatry and education.

The classic text for Buber's "philosophy of dialogue" is his short, poetic, almost oracular book *I and Thou* (1923). For Buber, there are two primary attitudes that the self may take up vis-à-vis the world. The first he calls the I–It, in which the I observes, studies, or uses something else, the self remaining detached from the other and the resulting experience or knowledge objectified according to the coordinates of space and time and the laws of causality. The second, radically different, posture Buber calls the I–Thou. The I–Thou is an encounter between two subjects in which each stands "over against" (*gegenüber*) the other, fully engaged to the point of loss of self-awareness and reserve. Unlike the I–It, the

Martin Buber, educator, philosopher, and social thinker. (Courtesy of the Zionist Archives, New York.)

I–Thou is characterized by spontaneity, mutuality, and total presentness. The I addresses the Thou and is addressed by the Thou; they confront each other freely, intensely, immediately. Whereas in the realm of the I–It one can initiate and plan one's maneuvers and actions, the I–Thou cannot be predetermined or controlled. If and when an I–Thou encounter will occur and what will transpire cannot be predicted in advance, although one can hold oneself open, hoping that it will happen, ready to respond with one's whole being.

In developing the dichotomy of I–It and I–Thou, Buber warns that, as a writer, he can only point to the I–Thou but not describe it. The I–Thou is not an "experience," experience being an I–It category implying a distance between subject and object. The I–Thou is not a "feeling," for a feeling can be explained psychologically. The I–Thou encounter is a basic dimension of human existence in the world and the key to what Buber calls the realm of "relation." It has the character of a dialogue, even though no physical speaking or hearing may take place and even though the I may interact with a natural object like a tree, or with a "spiritual form" like a great work of literature. The I–Thou cannot be demonstrated philosophically because logic is the instrument of the I–It. The reality of the I–Thou is established only by entering into it.

According to Buber, man must move back and forth between the I–It and I–Thou modes of being. From the I–It comes that refinement of knowledge and understanding that man requires in order to deal effectively with the world. But an overwhelming augmentation of the I–It in modern civilization, in the will-to-power and the will-to-profit, threatens to eclipse the I–Thou almost totally. Living in the I–It alone constitutes, for Buber, the main source of evil in human existence. A fully human life cannot be lived without the I–Thou dimension, for "All actual living is encounter."[6] A restored balance between I–Thou and I–It is necessary for the recovery of meaning and fulfillment in private and social life.

God is brought into Buber's philosophy of dialogue through the concept of an "eternal Thou," a living center of Thou-ness "in which the extended lines of relations intersect." God is the only Thou that can never become an It, the being that confronts us "immediately and first and always, and legitimately can only be addressed, not asserted."[7] The eternal Thou is the inclusive and unifying ground for the particular Thous, a ground that makes mutual relationship possible in the world. The I–Thou encounter with God is not an experience of unity with the divine, as this is usually understood in mysticism. One cannot flee from the world to find God, nor is it necessary to do so, because there is nothing in which God cannot be found. Although at the beginning of his literary career, Buber was a student of Western mysticism and mentions having had private moments of mystical exaltation, he came to feel that the desire to encounter God in this manner was an inadmissible escapism: God is met through all things with which one enters into relation—and only through them.[8]

Interpreters of Buber's *I and Thou* disagree on whether his conception of God is closer to theism or pantheism; Buber himself, desiring to keep his philosophy to a minimum, did not seek to resolve all the intellectual issues inherent in the notion of an eternal Thou. For Buber, theology and religious doctrine are inadequate and dubious substitutes for the direct encounter that is living religiosity. No dogmatic or systematic formulation of the contents of faith should replace a receptivity to the self-revealing —and at times self-concealing—God. Faith brings "holy insecurity," a state of affirmation and hope that does not completely expunge doubt. One of the most problematic features of Buber's post-World War II thought was his notion of "the eclipse of God," which, he felt, occurred in certain dark historical hours like the Holocaust. Consistent with his refusal to explain abstractly what cannot be resolved in real living, Buber did not offer a rationale for dispelling this barrier between God and man, but exhorted his readers not to close off the possibility of renewed divine-human encounter by adopting some fashionable ideology that dismisses this hope as illusory.

Like Rosenzweig, Buber believed that revelation is eternally possible. Revelation is a "presence as strength," not the transmitting of communicable content. After an encounter with God, the individual finds his specific situation outwardly unchanged but enriched with new meaning. In *I and Thou*, Buber explains that after the immediacy of revelation one must turn to ordinary, everyday existence to actualize one's unique opportunities in the here-and-now:

> That you need God more than anything else, you know at all times in your heart. But don't you know also that God needs you—in the fullness of his eternity, you? How would man exist if God did not need him, and how would you exist? You need God in order to be, and God needs you—for that which is the meaning of your life.[9]

I and Thou makes no reference to Judaism as such, but Buber applied his philosophy of dialogue to the Bible, Hasidism, and Zionism in many writings. In his biblical studies, Buber sought to formulate a fully modern alternative to the scholarship that analyzes Scripture as an ancient document of only historical interest. Using existentialist categories of interpretation in order to penetrate to the original experience underlying the biblical sagas, he wrote, "The human substance is melted by the spiritual fire which visits it, and there now breaks forth from it a word, a statement, which is human in its meaning and form, human conception and human speech, and yet witnesses to Him who stimulated it and to His will."[10] For Buber, the Bible is a record of man's response to encountering the divine—a record of encounters that are in principle open to everyone but which took an exceptional form in ancient Israel. Thus Moses glimpses in a natural event God's power and presence (the "burning bush" of Ex. 3:1–4:17), leading Moses to place himself wholly in the service of the eternal Thou who called personally to him. Moses becomes the leader of a people who has experienced deliverance from slavery, bringing them to Sinai where they enter into relationship with Him "who will always be present for them" (Buber's interpretation of *Ehyeh Asher Ehyeh* in Ex. 3:14). At Sinai, Israel resolves to make itself a holy nation by dedicating to God not merely its cult, but every aspect of its worldly existence. Israel and God assume a covenantal responsibility that requires repeated and spontaneous renewal throughout history. In Buber's interpretation, the biblical covenant is not a legal contract but a tie similar to a marriage vow, linking two parties in a relation of mutual trust. Buber traces Israel's encounters with God and its understanding of their meaning through subsequent periods of biblical history with special attention to the classical prophets. Each prophet rediscovers the divine in an actual historical situation, forcing him to shatter the congealed, dogmatic expectations of the people and confront them with hidden options open to them in the present. Likewise, Buber insists that the revelational significance of much of the Bible is accessible to later generations: Modern man can regain access to the biblical encounters with God and can appropriate their significance by allowing himself to be addressed by the text and responding to this address.

In later Jewish history, according to Buber, Hasidism represents one of the greatest moments of return to the immediacy of faith. (Buber's interest in Hasidism goes back to his childhood visits with the Galician hasidism, and his renditions of Hasidic tales and essays on aspects of Hasidism have been one of the most important channels by which the Western public has become informed of this religious movement.) Scholars have pointed out that Buber frequently read his own existentialist predilections into Hasidism, to which Buber responded that he never intended to write a detached, comprehensive description but to offer himself as a "filter" for certain remarkable Hasidic insights and achievements.

In Hasidism, Buber saw a new form of the prophetic protest against mistaking obedience to set patterns of religious behavior for living encounter with God, as in Hasidism's concern for praying and observing the commandments with the greatest possible fervor, intention, and devotion. Even more important, Hasidism created genuine communities by transforming the Kabbalah from esoteric knowledge of divine secrets into a blueprint for hallowing the everyday. (For Buber, all distinctions between holy and profane are provisional, the profane being only the "not yet sanctified.") Hasidism awakened its followers to wholeness of life in the here-and-now, to "joy in the world as it is, in life as it is, in every hour of life in this world, as that hour is."[11] The great Hasidic masters, according to Buber, taught that each man's task is not to repeat another's, but to realize his personal, never-recurring potentialities; that one can find his way to God only by unifying his soul and binding together the diverse elements within him; that one must start with oneself but not remain self-preoccupied.

> The Hasidic teaching is the consummation of Judaism. And this is its message to all: *You yourself must begin.* Existence will remain meaningless to you if you yourself do not penetrate into it with active love and if you do not in this way discover its meaning for yourself. Everything is waiting to be hallowed by you; it is waiting to be disclosed in its meaning and to be realized in it by you. For the sake of this your beginning, God created the world. He has drawn it out of himself so that you may bring it closer to Him. Meet the world with the fullness of your being and you shall meet Him. . . .[12]

On the crucial Jewish issues of law and Zionism, Buber's views differ sharply from Rosenzweig's. Rosenzweig held that one should approach the halakhah with the same openness to being personally addressed that the two men advocated with respect to the classical texts of Judaism. Buber, however, insisted that Judaism for him could never take the form of objectively defined laws and rituals, because these jeopardize the risk and freedom of actual living. For Buber, the individual's active participation in the whole is attainable through Zionism, a movement about which Rosenzweig had considerable misgivings. Although Buber opposed the political realism of Herzl and others for whom Zionism was a means for the sociopolitical normalization of the Jewish people, he saw in the ethical-spiritual stream of Zionism (Moses Hess, Ahad Ha-Am, Rav Kook, and especially Aaron David Gordon) a renewal of the eternal tie between people and land and a revitalization of the biblical covenant. For Buber, the kibbutzim were experiments in cooperative living that avoided the modern dangers of extreme individualism and monolithic collectivism. Creation of a community in which people could enter into direct, personal relations with each other was an indispensable means for a recovery of the I–Thou in contemporary life, and this was the crucial mission of the modern Jewish commonwealth.[13]

The philosophies of Rosenzweig and Buber resulted from the desire of two acculturated, modern Jews to reappropriate Judaism as the meaning of their lives. They found quite inadequate the formulas of nineteenth-century religious liberalism, especially the effort to define, with the help of philosophical idealism, an objective essence of Jewish belief. Even more important was their rejection of positivist and materialist positions that denied the realness of subjective (for them, intersubjective) religious experience. There was no going back to that naïve faith that modern scientific and historical knowledge had undermined, but the meticulous scholarship of *Wissenschaft des Judentums* provided no adequate grounding for living religion. In the new existentialist orientation of twentieth-century philosophy they found a diagnosis of the human situation and a way to recover the depths of the divine–human encounter that would, they felt, restore the personal relevance of Judaism and the vitality of the Jewish people.

Two Styles of Jewish Religious Thought in America: Mordecai Kaplan and Abraham Heschel

Of the many Jewish religious thinkers in the United States since the era of Kaufmann Kohler and Solomon Schechter, the two described in this section stand out by virtue of having produced extensive bodies of writing that have gained them recognition throughout American Jewry. Mordecai Kaplan represents a stream of twentieth-century religious thought quite distinct from philosophical idealism and religious existentialism. Drawing on social psychology, philosophical pragmatism, religious naturalism, and cultural Zionism, Kaplan's position calls for a rational and democratic reformulation of Jewish religious identity in harmony with a modern scientific world view. Abraham Joshua Heschel, in contrast, has combined an intimate, firsthand knowledge of Hasidism with existentialist and other European philosophical approaches in a poetic and mystical evocation of the traditional structures of Jewish consciousness.

Kaplan was born in 1881 in the small town of Svencionys, in the Lithuanian district of the Jewish Pale of Settlement in tsarist Russia. At the age of eight he came to the United States with his family. Kaplan's early religious education was traditional, but he attended public school and Columbia University where he absorbed a modern critical approach to religion and to the Bible. After ordination from the Jewish Theological Seminary in 1902, Kaplan served as rabbi of an Orthodox synagogue in New York until, in 1909, he was appointed dean of the newly established Teachers Institute of the Seminary and soon afterwards also made professor of homiletics, midrash, and philosophies of religion. During his more than fifty years on the faculty of the Seminary he attracted a devoted student following and, at the same time, maintained an extensive involvement in Jewish communal activities. In 1917 he became leader of the first synagogue to incorporate a broad range of cultural and recreational activities into its program. After a split developed in the congre-

Mordecai Kaplan, founder of the Jewish Reconstructionist movement in America. (Courtesy of the Society for the Advancement of Judaism.)

gation over his innovative views, he and his supporters left to organize the Society for the Advancement of Judaism (1922), a New York synagogue and Jewish center based on Kaplan's position that worship was only one of the functions that a congregation should foster. His first major book, *Judaism as a Civilization* (1934), contained a detailed criticism of existing Jewish movements and a call for the "reconstruction" of Jewish life, leading him and his associates, the following year, to publish *The Reconstructionist*, a journal of Jewish affairs that has made considerable impact on the leadership of non-Orthodox American Jewry. In the 1940s and 1950s the Jewish Reconstructionist Foundation issued a series of new liturgical texts: a Passover Haggadah and prayer books for the Sabbath, the high holy days, and the festivals. In 1968 the Foundation opened the Reconstructionist Rabbinic College in Philadelphia with a curriculum arranged according to priorities that the movement felt were not adequately espoused by other forms of American Judaism. Thus, in Kaplan's later years, Reconstructionism was transformed from an ecumenical position cutting across Jewish denominational lines to a small separate movement.

As previously noted, the starting point for Kaplan's position is his critical evaluation of the main tendencies of American Jewry, especially their inadequate view of Judaism as a totality. According to Kaplan,

Reform rightly recognized the evolving character of Judaism but ignored the social basis of Jewish identity and the organic culture of the people. At the other extreme, Neo-Orthodoxy recognized that Judaism was a complete way of life and provided a substantial Jewish education for children (something noticeably lacking in Reform), but considered the Jewish religion to be timeless and static. Congenial to Kaplan was Conservatism's commitment to the scientific study of the Jewish past, its sympathy for Zionism, and its concern for the unity of the Jewish people. However, Kaplan eventually came to feel that the Conservative movement remained too closely bound by the traditional methods and contents of the halakhah and was not adequately responding to new conditions and needs. (According to Kaplan, Jewish law is to be respected but it has "a vote and not a veto," so that precedent must, at times, give way to deliberate enactment.) The solution of the present-day confusion was a definition of Judaism as "an evolving religious civilization."

The practical side of Kaplan's position called for the re-establishment of a network of all-embracing, "organic" Jewish communities around the world that would ensure the self-perpetuation of Jewish identity and further secular as well as religious components of the Jewish heritage (art, music, philanthropy, and so on). Membership should be strictly voluntary, leadership would be democratically elected, and private religious beliefs would not be infringed upon, because diversity in modern Jewish life must be cherished. (Kaplan is a strong advocate of cultural and religious pluralism, and he maintains that American Jews should participate fully and creatively in both Jewish and American civilizations.) To clarify the international status of Jewry, Kaplan proposed a world-wide Jewish assembly that would adopt a formal covenant defining the Jews as a transitional people, the hub of which was Zion and the spokes the branches of the diaspora. In this formulation Kaplan synthesized Simon Dubnow's conception of an autonomous, global Jewry with Ahad Ha-Am's insistence on the land of Israel as the spiritual center of modern Jewish culture.

Despite his affinity with ideologies such as Dubnow's and Ahad Ha-Am's, however, Kaplan is not a secularist: Religion, the concretization of the collective self-consciousness of the group, is an essential dimension of a civilization and a necessary component of an authentic and satisfying modern Jewishness. The religion of a group is manifested in "sancta," spiritual symbols such as persons, places, events, and writings, which inspire feelings of reverence, commemorate what the group feels is most valuable, provide continuity through the flux of history, and fortify the collective conscience of a people. Kaplan felt a deep attachment to Jewish sancta and Jewish religious literature. In order to hold the loyalty of a new generation of Jews educated in scientific and democratic principles, however, the Jewish tradition must expunge authoritarianism, dogmatic claims of infallibility, and recourse to supernatural revelation. (By supernaturalism Kaplan meant God as a substantive, anthropomorphic entity and miracles as the divine suspension of the laws of nature.) The most important personal function of religion is to answer the question, "What shall man believe and do in order to experience that life, despite the evil and suffering that mar it, is extremely worthwhile?"[14] Religion is the pursuit of salvation, which Kaplan defines in a humanistic, this-worldly way:

> When religion speaks of salvation it means in essence the experience of the worthwhileness of life. When we analyze our personal experience of life's worthwhileness we find that it is invariably based on specific ethical experiences—moral responsibility, honesty, loyalty, love, service. If carefully pursued, this analysis reveals that the source of our ethical experience is found in our willingness and ability to achieve self-fulfillment through reciprocity with others. This reciprocity in turn is an expression of a larger principle that operates in the cosmos in response to the demands of a cosmic force, the force that makes for creativity and interdependence in all things.[15]

In Kaplan's frequently reiterated statement, "God is the Power that makes for salvation" or as he sometimes puts it, "God is the sum of the animating, organizing forces and relationships which are forever making a cosmos out of chaos."[16] For Kaplan, the idea of God must be viewed not metaphysically but functionally, in terms of its effects on human life. "We learn more about God when we say that love is divine than when we say God is love. A veritable transformation takes place. . . . Divinity becomes relevant to authentic experience and therefore takes on a definiteness which is accompanied by an awareness of authenticity."[17] Belief in God stems not from the intellect but from the will-to-live, reflecting the faith that there is enough in the world for man's needs, although not for man's "greeds and lusts." Divinity is that coordinating, integrating factor in nature that makes possible the actualization of justice, truth, and compassion on earth.

Various ambiguities and contradictions in Kaplan's idea of God have been pointed out by his critics, especially that his reference to God as "the sum of forces" calls into question God's unity, and that he refers to God sometimes as a "power," sometimes as a "process." Whether a divine aspect of the cosmos is as empirically evident as Kaplan assumes has also been challenged. In response, Kaplan acknowledges the necessity of faith, but he feels that man's "salvational behavior" indicates the influence of a cosmic Godhood, as the behavior of the magnetic needle indicates the magnetism of the earth's poles. Kaplan has proposed that Godhood is a "trans-natural," "super-factual," and "super-experiential" transcendence not infringing on the laws of nature, but constituting a potentiality that transforms the elements of nature into organic wholes greater than the sum of their parts. Kaplan's position also implies that God, as one aspect of a pluralistic universe, is limited in power and that nature contains forces that can thwart God. He admits that natural evil cannot be explained theologically, but moral and social evils (hatred, poverty, war) represent the failure of men to attain complete awareness of the cosmic source of value and to transform the world accordingly.

Kaplan holds that his position is compatible with historic Judaism because of his emphasis on the primacy of peoplehood and Zion and because the divine in Judaism has always been identified with moral value and cosmic purpose. He does insist that the traditional notion of the Jews as a chosen people should be eliminated from Jewish theology and from the liturgy, because no reinterpretation of chosenness, however innocuous, can completely dispel the implication that some nations are superior to others. Instead, Kaplan proposes that every people freely take on a "vocation" by dedicating itself to those universal values that its history has clarified, thus contributing to the growing richness of human life through "ethical nationhood" and the ideal of a peaceful humanity.

Abraham Joshua Heschel (1907–1972), a descendant of two important Hasidic dynasties, was born in Warsaw. After receiving a thorough Jewish education in Poland, Heschel entered the University of Berlin where in 1934 he received his doctorate for a study of the biblical prophets. (Heschel used the phenomenological method, a movement originated by Edmund Husserl about 1905, which seeks to describe what is actually present to the human consciousness, apart from considerations of objective reality and subjective response. The phenomenological approach is crucial to Heschel's later writings.) In 1937 Heschel became Martin Buber's successor at the *Jüdisches Lehrhaus* in Frankfort and head of adult Jewish education in Germany, but the following year he and other Polish Jews were deported by the Nazis. After stays in Warsaw and London, in 1940 he came to the United States to teach at the Hebrew Union College. In 1945 Heschel became Professor of Ethics and Mysticism at the Jewish Theological Seminary in New York and began to publish a series of works, ranging from studies on the piety of East European Jewry and the inward character of Jewish observance, to religious symbolism, Jewish views of humanity, and contemporary moral and political issues. Before his untimely death, Heschel had become highly respected among American religionists of many faiths not only for his writings but also for his active role in the civil rights and peace movements of the 1960s and in the Jewish-Christian dialogue.

Heschel's literary style is unique among modern Jewish religious authors. (Significantly, his earliest book, published in Warsaw in 1933, was a collection of Yiddish poems.) Remarkable juxtapositions of the

Abraham Joshua Heschel, scholar and theologian. (Courtesy of the Jewish Theological Seminary of America, New York.)

concrete and the abstract, suggestive similes and metaphors, striking aphorisms and extended images, concepts from classical and existentialist philosophy, are all used to evoke the numinous quality of the divine and the capacity for human self-transcendence. Heschel's aim is to shock modern man out of his complacency and awaken him to that spiritual dimension fading from the contemporary consciousness. Because he stresses now one and now another polarity of the religious experience and because of the rich cumulative impact of his style, Heschel's point of view does not lend itself to paraphrase or brief summary. The following remarks are limited to a few characteristic themes.

In Heschel's view, the basic intuition of reality takes place on a "preconceptual" level; a disparity always remains between what we encounter and how we can express our encounter in words. The great achievements of art, philosophy, and religion are brought forth in moments when the individual senses more than he can say. "In our religious situation we do not comprehend the transcendent; we are present at it, we witness it. Whatever we know is inadequate; whatever we say is an understatement. . . . Concepts, words must not become screens; they must be regarded as windows."[18]

How can modern man regain a personal awareness of God? A universally accessible feeling is the experience of the sublime—for example, in the presence of the grandeur of nature. A sense of the sublime entails wonder and "radical astonishment." Astonishment is radical because it embraces not only what one sees but the very act of seeing and the very self that is astonished at its ability to see.

> Wonder goes beyond knowledge. We do not doubt that we doubt, but we are amazed at our ability to doubt, amazed at our ability to wonder. . . . We are amazed not only at particular values and things but at the unexpectedness of being as such, at the fact that there is being at all.[19]

The individual confronts the "ineffable," that which cannot ever be expressed in words. Heschel insists that the ineffable is not a psychological state but an encounter with a mystery "within and beyond things and ideas."[20] The divine is "within" because the self is "something transcendent in disguise." The divine is "beyond" because it also is

> a message that discloses unity where we see diversity, that discloses peace where we are involved in discord. . . . God means: No one is ever alone; the essence of the temporal is the eternal; the moment is an image of eternity in an infinite mosaic. God means: Togetherness of all beings in holy otherness.[21]

In these passages Heschel's position is a form of *panentheism:* a term coined in the early nineteenth century, but which is, of late, becoming more widely used in philosophy. Panentheism—literally, the all-in-God— is the belief that God's being includes and permeates the universe, but that God is more than the universe. (*Panentheism*, which preserves a dimension of divine transcendence, is usually distinguished from *pantheism*, in which God is completely identified with the totality of the world.)

A second experience that, according to Heschel, awakens the individual to the presence of God is a pervasive, underlying anxiety that he calls "the need to be needed." Religion entails the certainty that something is asked of man and that he is not a mere bystander in the cosmos. When the individual feels the challenge of a power, not born of his will, that robs him of self-sufficiency by a judgment of the rightness or wrongness of his actions—then God's concern for his creatures is grasped.

> Unless history is a vagary of nonsense, there must be a counterpart to the immense power of man to destroy, there must be a voice that says NO to man, a voice not vague, faint, and inward, like qualms of conscience, but equal in spiritual might to man's power to destroy.[22]

For Heschel it is the Bible—particularly the prophets—that provides a primary model for authentic spirituality. Biblical revelation is not a mystical act of seeking God but an awareness of being sought and reached by Him: The prophets bear witness to an event that they formulate in their own words, but the event itself is God's reaching out. It is not propositional truths about God or general norms and values that the prophets transmit but the "divine pathos" (*pathos*—from a Greek root denoting emotion, feeling, passion). The divine pathos is God's outraged response to man's sin and His merciful response to man's suffering and anguish. Heschel does not actually attribute "pathos" to God's metaphysical essence, but sees it as a corrective to a conception of monotheism that restricts the scope of God's knowledge to universal principles only. The classical tradition of religious philosophy, shaped by the Aristotelian notion of God as the "unmoved mover," assumed that God's perfection did not permit Him to be affected by what happens in history. "The divine pathos alone is able to break through this rigidity and create new dimensions for the unique, the specific, and the particular."[23] Biblical prophecy conveys God's dynamic attentiveness to man—the realization that God is moved by and intimately affected by man's actions.

> We must continue to ask: What is man that God should care for him? And we must continue to remember that it is precisely God's care for man that constitutes the greatness of man. To be is to stand for, and what man stands for is the great mystery of being His partner. God is in need of man.[24]

In contrast to traditional religious philosophy, Heschel's view of biblical prophecy has been described as "the displacement of subjectivity from humanity to God."[25] The usual subject-object relationship (man the subject, God the object of human knowledge) is reversed: Human reality is presented from the point of view of a God who cares for and enters man's life. In Heschel's phrase, "The Bible is not man's theology, but God's anthropology."[26] According to Heschel, the divine pathos generates "prophetic sympathy," a willingness to align oneself to God's purpose and actively to realize His will, which lies at the heart of Jewish religious living.

Along with "radical astonishment" and reappropriation of the prophetic consciousness, a third mode of apprehending God's presence is the life of holiness. A few of Heschel's aphorisms convey his rejection of a utilitarian, sociological approach to Jewish observance (such as Kaplan's) and his supracognitive, mystical feeling for halakhah. The halakhah sharpens men's sympathy to the ineffable: "To perform deeds of holiness is to absorb the holiness of deeds." "A Jew is asked to take a leap of action rather than a leap of thought. He is asked . . . to do more than he understands in order to understand more than he does." Whereas the term *ceremony* merely expresses what we think, mitzvah expresses what God wills: a mitzvah is "a prayer in the form of a deed." Heschel is among those Jewish theologians who insist, in opposition to Kantianism, that the Jew is required to adhere to a heteronomous law, a law impossible of being generated by man's mind alone. The commandments are tasks with which God confronts us in particular moments as "points of eternity in the flux of temporality." Jewish observance can be described only in polarities: on the one hand, stability, repetitiveness, and regularity, but on the other hand, inwardness, spontaneity, freedom. Jewish law answers the question, what does God ask of man now, but the question itself must be kept continually alive. Intention, as well as action, is crucial; an exaggerated concern for legality and discipline Heschel labels "religious behaviorism." Intention is "not the awareness of being commanded but the awareness of Him who comands; not of a yoke we carry but of a will we remember; the awareness of God rather than the awareness of duty."[27]

For Heschel, Jewish survival is a spiritual act. God's concern with man is expressed in Judaism through the idea of a covenant imposing a mutual, correlative responsiveness on man and God both, because God needs man for the attainment of his ends in the world. Unlike Kaplan, Heschel holds to the idea of a chosen people, chosenness meaning responsibility, not superiority. "The significance of [the term "chosen people"] is genuine in relation to God rather than in relation to other peoples. It signifies not a quality inherent in the people but a relationship between the people and God."[28] Chosenness is a "kinship with ultimate reality" requiring a self-transcendence of the people as a whole, as well as of the individual.

> There is a price to be paid by the Jew. He has to be exalted in order to be normal. In order to be a man, he has to be more than a man. To be a people, the Jews have to be more than a people.[29]

Heschel stands in that stream of modern Jewish thought which emphasizes the limitations of reason to grasp the full significance of the religious life. His approach has been called "devotional philosophy" (Maurice Friedman), a religious rhetoric (Arthur A. Cohen), mystical apologetics (Edward K. Kaplan)—all honored and accepted types of religious writing. Heschel himself characterized his method as "depth theology," the attempt to rediscover the questions to which religion is the answer. Of the figures considered in this chapter Heschel perhaps is closest to the Neo-Orthodox tendency in modern Protestant thought (Karl Barth, Reinhold Niebuhr, and others), sharply critical of liberal religion's assumption that man can perfect himself by his own unaided efforts and motivated, above all, by the aim to recover biblical faith as an inward dynamic process. Whereas Protestant Neo-Orthodoxy turns for inspiration to Luther and the other theologians of the reformation, in Heschel traditional Hasidic piety finds its authentic modern voice.

Concluding Remarks: Some Features of Recent Jewish Theology

Like every living religion, Judaism is a frame of reference for apprehending the ultimate and for participating in a community formed by and constantly re-forming a sacred tradition. Jewish thought is an effort to present Jewish teaching in a theoretically consistent manner. Each such effort eventually passes into history where it awaits the historian, but the articulation remains a perpetual task if Judaism is still to be a viable spiritual form. According to Hermann Cohen, the philosopher of religion undertakes the "conceptual idealization" of a tradition, systematizing and purifying its basic orientation:

> It is neither the historian's task nor does he have the competence to define essence. He may acknowledge that some phenomena are of merely secondary importance; but as far as his research is concerned, he cannot regard any of them as non-essential. Only philosophy of religion can accept the responsibility to decide what is and what is not essential in any given religion.[30]

Likewise, one of the outstanding existentialist theologians of contemporary Judaism, Emil Fackenheim, acknowledges that a definition of the structure of Judaism remains crucial.

> An existentialist commitment open to any content would raise the spectre of anarchism. And since this spectre is also raised by an historical positivism prepared to identify as Judaism whatever Jews past or present may have happened to believe, there is practical value, as well as theoretical validity, in the display of an inner logic within Judaism, which dispels anarchy and sets limits.[31]

Recent Jewish thinking often calls itself theological, rather than philosophical, although the distinction is not clear-cut, inasmuch as both philosophy and theology order the contents and structure of the Jewish religion and reflect on Jewish faith with an eye to its truthfulness. In the past, Jewish philosophy usually sought to correlate Judaism with a specific philosophical system so as to demonstrate the rational basis of Jewish beliefs about God, man, and world. As we have seen, Jewish philosophers used Aristotelianism and Neo-Platonism in the Middle Ages and Hegelianism and Kantianism in the nineteenth and early twentieth centuries. Jew-

Synagogue ark doors, carved in black walnut by Milton Horn for Temple Isaiah of Forest Hills, New York. (Courtesy of the Synagogue Art and Architectural Library of the Union of American Hebrew Congregations.) The Hebrew text and the motif is Ehyeh Asher Ehyeh, "I am that I am," God's name as explained to Moses at the burning bush in Exodus 3:14.

ish theology also makes use of certain contemporary philosophies, either explicitly or implicitly. But the term *theology* implies a more definite stance within the tradition and a more self-confident, forthright, and determined commitment to the integrity of Jewish faith.

Why has theology become a conspicuous and self-conscious concern in American Jewry, especially since World War II? Several historical factors may be responsible. First, Jewish religious spokesmen can no longer take for granted that the majority of their congregants have such a deep awareness of Jewish religious living that the fundamentals of faith may be approached in a fragmentary, ad hoc manner. Addressing the Jew uncertain of why he feels definitely committed to Jewishness, recent Jewish theology seeks to show him that an apparent commitment to secular ethics or ethnicity is actually drawn from deeper religious roots. Furthermore, how to explain the meaning of Jewish religiosity requires a coherent and comprehensive grounding in theological method. Second, Judaism in America has acquired a greater general recognition since World War II; Jewish thinkers participate in interfaith dialogue where they

The chapel of Brandeis University, Waltham, Mass., Max Abramovitz, architect. (Courtesy of the Synagogue Art and Architectural Library of the Union of American Hebrew Congregations.)

must speak of the common ground between Judaism and Christianity and of the crucial differences between them, clarification of which is a theological subject. Third, theology, rather than philosophy, is the common category, because academic philosophy at present, with certain exceptions, is not so amenable to correlation with religion as was nineteenth-century philosophical idealism. Finally, and perhaps most important, the older forms of liberal religious thought prevalent in Europe before World War I and in America before World War II have come under severe criticism among Jewish and Christian theologians for being inadequate to the situation of religion in the twentieth century and for conceding too much of religion's authentic substance to supposed universal principles that were actually temporary and questionable nineteenth-century attitudes. Theology has been, therefore, a symbolic term for sweeping away the previous identification of modern Judaism with rationalism.

Before describing some aspects of contemporary Jewish theology, a word should be said about the changed intellectual and emotional climate that has tended to discredit the older religious liberalism. The cataclysmic release of cruel and barbaric impulses within enlightened and technologically advanced nations, accompanied by grandiose self-glorification and brutal dehumanization, has made to appear superficial and naïve the rational, optimistic tone of much nineteenth-century religious writing, both Jewish and Christian. (For Jews it is perhaps an understatement to say that the Holocaust calls for utter realism about the human potentialities for evil.) As a result, few thinkers have fully retained that belief in human perfectibility and the inevitability of progress that was once supposed to accompany the growth of modern science and historical knowledge. And the twentieth-century West has witnessed a disorienting loss of cultural consensus and a bewildering proliferation of specialized knowledge, rendering the construction of a coherent world view far more difficult than ever before. Especially ominous is the threat posed by a vastly increased power over nature that can easily be employed to destroy bodies and manipulate minds—and has been. In place of the former liberal confidence that divine providence is working itself out in the historical process, there has been a renewed conviction that the heart of religion is a transcendent God who judges history, and not infrequently condemns what He sees. Whereas the old confidence fostered the assuredness that religious liberalism had risen once and for all above the inherent limitations of traditional faith, twentieth-century theology has gained new insight into supposedly obsolete concepts, such as idolatry (the worship of the self) and sin (the utter failure to be responsible). For many people, to be sure, traditional religious loyalties have dissipated under the impact of secularity. But religionists argue that secular substitutes, such as utopian ideologies, psychoanalysis, and the exploration of sensuality (however valuable), still leave a spiritual vacuum that can be filled only by faith's commitment to an ultimate source of being and value and by a personal core of meaning and integrity that lies at the center of religion at its most profound.

For some Jewish thinkers, the result has been the formulation of positions that are called "postliberal": not an abandonment of all features of religious liberalism, such as the historical criticism of texts and the autonomy of the individual, but the effort to recover lost dimensions of reli-

Temple Beth Shalom of Elkins Park, Penn., Frank Lloyd Wright, architect. (Courtesy of the Synagogue Art and Architectural Library of the Union of American Hebrew Congregations.)

gious faith. Many of the most productive and articulate Jewish theologians since World War II have developed further the Jewish existentialism pioneered by Rosenzweig and Buber. As we have seen, existentialists reject the effort to reduce reality to a rational, unified system of metaphysical essences. Instead, they emphasize personal relatedness and dialogue as primary modes of being; they conceive of human existence as subjective, time-bound, and paradoxical; they insist that no man is an uncommitted spectator and that faith is not a matter of the intellect alone but an expression of the whole individual, who must make specific, unavoidable choices in his life. Jewish religious existentialists have criticized the idealist and naturalist forms of Jewish philosophy for, in effect, reducing God to a changing human concept, and for making the philosopher, rather than the self-revealing, commanding Presence, the arbiter of Jewish religious truth. Buber has been especially influential in offering an alternative to the notion of revelation as a human act akin to poetic imagination, as well as to the fundamentalist position that in revelatory moments man is a passive recipient of God's word. For the existentialists, the Bible is a diary of man's actual encounters with the divine Thou, encounters that require both human readiness to be addressed and a decisive self-disclosure of God in the moment. For all these reasons, the existentialists view the present hallmark of authentic Judaism as a combination of personal religious experience and visibly recognizable Jewish religious action.

For Emil Fackenheim (b. 1916), a liberal existentialist theologian, the most serious challenge to contemporary religion is the "subjectivist reductionism" of modern empiricism that defines every claim to an experience of the divine Presence as a mere feeling. Empiricism's methodological dogmatism does not refute religious faith; it merely explains it away. Fackenheim suggests that for the modern believer there can be an "immediacy after reflection"—a renewed faith even after exposure to reductionist analysis—out of which the individual can find the stubbornness to remain a witness to God. Addressing himself to the Jewish tradition, Fackenheim has recently proposed that there are historic "root experiences," public memories of the saving Divine Presence, such as the biblical exodus, and of the commanding Divine Presence at Sinai—public memories which the Jew relives in moments of worship.

A redefinition of faith and revelation are issues common to Judaism and Christianity, but there are theological concerns that are definitely Jewish, especially the religious status of Jewish law and peoplehood. The position of Jewish theologians on the halakhah is the main issue where denominational lines between Orthodoxy, Conservatism, and Reform are still determinative. The Orthodox insist on the absolute centrality of religious law as interpreted by authentic halakhic methods according to a consensus of the leading talmudic authorities. The Conservatives take a more creative approach, allowing for deliberate changes and reinterpretation of laws according to present needs and understandings. Reform has tended toward a conception of non-halakhic or posthalakhic Judaism, a Judaism of commandments and observances, not of law. Particularly influential among existentialist theologians in the Reform movement has been Franz Rosenzweig's view that a modern Jew who cannot accept the whole body of laws will find that some particular laws are meaningfully directed to his situation, thereby combining the values of disciplined piety with personal freedom. Emil Fackenheim suggests that appropriating the Torah existentially may even require rejection of a particular ancient response to revelation "because the divine challenge demands of his life a different total response. Thus new commandments are given even as ancient ones lose their reality."[32] The subjectivism of this position does not satisfy either the Orthodox insistence on the binding nature of the law or the Conservative affirmation of halakhic continuity, but it does represent a significant departure from the older liberal attitude that the commandments embodies general and timeless ethical values.

One of the most important presentations of a theology of halakhah has been found in several influential essays written by Joseph Dov Soloveitchik (b. 1903), the esteemed mentor of modern Orthodoxy in America. Using both Neo-Kantian and existentialist themes, Soloveitchik contrasts man as worker, investigator, and dominator of nature with man, open to wonder and awe, concerned with the source of natural and of human existence. Out of the depth of his solitude and in humble surrender, the "lonely man of faith" meets God in the covenantal community. For Soloveitchik, a life lived according to the classic halakhic tradition makes redemptiveness manifest in a complex structure of intellection and revealed norms that enables man to achieve his full status as a self-determined being.

Eugene Borowitz (b. 1924), one of the major Reform exponents of Jewish existentialism, has suggested that these, at present, incompatible views of halakhah can be subsumed under the overarching biblical conception of covenant. For Borowitz, the primary commitment is the wish to serve God as a member of the people. Even though a Jew may feel that traditional patterns require revision or innovation, the bond that unites him to all Jews is far greater than the disputes separating him from the Orthodox. For Borowitz, the covenantal situation provides a key to interpreting and integrating the universalistic and the folk elements of Jewish identity, because covenant embraces both God and Israel as responsible agents, holding in equilibrium God's demands and Israel's needs, humanitarian duties to the world at large and particular obligations to the people. Even apart from the covenant theology espoused by Borowitz and others, however, Jewish religious thought in recent decades has insisted on the religious importance of *klal Yisrael* (the whole of the people of Israel), in place of the more apologetic and defensive universalism that was the

The synagogue of the Hebrew University in Jerusalem, designed by Heinz Rau and David Resnik. (Courtesy of the Synagogue Art and Architectural Library of the Union of American Hebrew Congregations.)

hallmark of Jewish religious liberalism up to and including Hermann Cohen.

Placing peoplehood at the heart of Jewish faith poses, in the most extreme manner, the question of the religious meaning of the Holocaust. In the 1960s Auschwitz, as symbol and fact, became the subject of a theological discussion inaugurated by Richard Rubenstein (b. 1924). Rubenstein argued that the Holocaust decisively and irrevocably demolished the Jewish belief in a God of history, leaving the Jew in "a cold, silent, unfeeling cosmos, unaided by a purposeful power beyond [his] own resources."[33] Rubenstein affirmed the value of Jewish identity and of religious ritual on existentialist and psychoanalytic grounds, but in place of the theistic God he proposed a devouring Nothingness out of which man has been thrust and into which he returns at death. In contrast, Emil Fackenheim has suggested that there has occurred, in fact, an intense reaffirmation of Judaism out of the Holocaust, disclosing a divine imperative not to hand Hitler a posthumous victory by destroying Jewish hope and faith. Fackenheim believes that no theological explanation is possible for the Holocaust, but that there was a religious response by Jewry world-wide, confirming God's presence in history. A third position is that of the Orthodox thinker, Eliezer Berkovits (b. 1900), who insists that the Holocaust does not pose unprecedented problems for Jewish faith. Berkovits points to the biblical concept of the "hiddenness of God" (Psalm 44). Paradoxically, man's moral freedom requires both God's redemptive acts and moments of His apparent withdrawal. For Berkovits, the continued existence of the people of Israel, in the face of an experience of suffering over many centuries, is an important proof of God's ultimate power. A number of other theological responses to the Holocaust have also been proposed, including the observation that the very act of designating the Holocaust an unmitigated evil entails the affirmation of an absolute moral standard by which it is judged.

The other great event of recent Jewish history—the establishment of the State of Israel—poses special problems for interreligious dialogue, because the Jewish State, for many Jews, has religious significance as an intimation of salvation after the Holocaust and as a symbol of the eternality

The House of the Book of the Brandeis-Bardin Institute, Brandeis, California, Sidney Eisenshtat, architect.

of the Jewish people. Eliezer Berkovits has been one of the theologians most committed to the eschatological, as well as the historical, dimension of the Jewish return to Zion, in which he sees a vindication of God's redemptive action.

The positions briefly sketched in this section reflect, on the whole, those theologians for whom religious faith is nonrational (not irrational), and who hold that Judaism has a self-validating claim to truth. Determinedly rationalist tendencies still have their exponents, and it is possible that new forms of Jewish critical rationalism will emerge in the future, for Judaism has been an intellectual as well as an existential quest for meaning. The aim of Maimonidean philosophy, to show that the philosophical presuppositions of science are compatible with the philosophical presuppositions of Judaism, remains to be fully explored in view of recent remarkable advances in such fields as cosmology, subatomic physics, and molecular biology. Thus, the metaphysics of Alfred North Whitehead has inspired in Christian thought the approach known as process theology, emphasizing the primacy of events, of selfhood, and of organic wholeness in nature, and of God as supremely real, yet responsive to and growing with the creative becoming of the cosmos. Even apart from this particular system of thought, the biblical theme of God as creator may offer the possibility of a new Jewish theology of nature as a reservoir of dynamic potentialities of which human existence is one emergent actuality. That other major theme of Judaism, messianic fulfillment, may also stimulate a reformulated conception of Torah and mitzvot (and halakhah) as ideal ends according to which present reality is to be shaped. Combined with existentialist insights, the result would be an enriched, integrated Jewish theology that does justice to the Maimonidean conviction of the unity of truth, to human subjectivity and natural purposiveness, to the fragile and the eternal, to God as the source of created order and God as ground of future order that is to be brought about by the moral will of his creatures.

The course of modern Jewish thought—indeed of all Jewish thought—demonstrates that every theology is provisional and that Judaism remains contemporary only through confronting a perplexing and changing present. Without the desire to conserve and assimilate the gift of the past, there is no genuine Jewish identity and no genuine human identity. Without the horizon of messianic purpose, there is no existentially appropriated, unifying self-dedication to the reality of God, Torah, and Israel. Holding on to a continuity always in danger of being lost but always available for renewal, a tradition more than thirty-two centuries old perseveres.

Notes

Chapter 1. The History of Israel from Its Origins to the Sixth Century BCE

1. The geographical area currently called the Middle East (modern-day Egypt, Israel, Syria, Lebanon, Iraq, the Arabian peninsula, and adjacent lands) is usually known as the Near East in scholarship dealing with the ancient period, a convention we have followed in this book.

2. For the Greek term *Ioudaïsmos*, see 2 Maccabees 2:21, 8:1, 14:38.

3. *Israel* is also used in biblical times for the northern of the two kingdoms. Currently a citizen of the state of Israel is an Israeli, a secular term that can refer to a person of Jewish, Muslim, or Christian extraction.

4. For an early use of *Yehudi* as a term for a member of the people as a whole, rather than for one of its tribes, see Esther 2:5, 5:13.

5. We will use the terms *Bible* and *biblical* in referring to the Jewish Scriptures, except when discussing Christianity, where *Old Testament* is at times less confusing.

6. James B. Pritchard, editor, *The Ancient Near East: An Anthology of Texts and Pictures* (Princeton, N.J.: Princeton University Press, 1958), p. 231.

7. The geographical term *Palestine* was derived in Roman times from the name *Philistia*.

8. *Genesis* (The Anchor Bible), introduction, translation, and notes by E. A. Speiser (Garden City, N.Y.: Doubleday & Company, Inc., 1964), p. xlviii, p. li.

9. William Foxwell Albright, *Yahweh and the Gods of Canaan: A Historical Analysis of Two Contrasting Faiths* (Garden City, N.Y.: Doubleday & Company, Inc., 1968), pp. 164, 206, 244.

10. On Akhenaton, see John Bright, A *History of Israel,* 2nd edition (Philadelphia: The Westminster Press, 1972), p. 108; and Yehezkel Kaufmann, *The Religion of Israel,* trans. and abridged by Moshe Greenberg (Chicago: University of Chicago Press, 1960), p. 226. Part One of Kaufmann's book contains his important contrast between paganism and Israelite religion.

11. George E. Mendenhall, "Biblical History in Transition," in G. Ernest Wright, editor, *The Bible and the Ancient Near East: Essays in Honor of William Foxwell Albright* (Garden City, N.Y.: Doubleday & Company, Inc., 1965), p. 40.

12. Robert H. Pfeiffer, *Introduction to the Old Testament* (New York: Harper & Row, Publishers, 1948), p. 474.

13. The Most High (*El Elyon*) was originally a title for a Canaanite deity, but came to be appropriated for YHVH. Our discussion of the emergence of monotheism is greatly indebted to Professor Matitiahu Tsevat's article, "God and the Gods in Assembly: An Interpretation of Psalm 82," in *Hebrew Union College Annual,* Vols. XL–XLI (1969–1970), pp. 123–37. The translation of Deut. 32:89 is Tsevat's. Like most modern biblical scholars, Tsevat emends the text of Deut. 32:8 according to the ancient Greek translation and the Dead Sea scrolls Hebrew text to restore the original meaning "sons of God (*El*)." Sons of God are premonotheistic divine beings (see Gen. 6:2).

14. The translation is from Tsevat, "God and the Gods in Assembly," pp. 125–26.

15. Some of the expressions that imply the perspective of a writer living long after the death of Moses include mention of the Philistines in the Pentateuch, although they did not appear in Canaan until after the Israelite invasion (Gen. 21:32, Gen. 26:1, Ex. 13:17); reference to the city of Dan, although it acquired this name much later (compare Gen. 14:14 with Judg. 18:29); the statement "these are the kings who reigned first in Edom, before any king reigned over the Israelites" (Gen. 36:31); a reference to the later king of the Amalekites (compare Num. 24:7 with 1 Sam. 15:8). Narratives repeated several times in the Pentateuch include the patriarchal wife-sister stories (Gen. 12:10–20, Gen. 20, Gen. 26:1–11); Hagar's ejection from Abraham's household (Gen. 16 and 21); the naming of Beersheba (Gen. 21:25–34), of Bethel (Gen. 28:1–17 and 35:1–15), of Esau (Gen. 25:25 and 25:30), and of Israel (Gen. 32 and 35). The stories of the manna and the quail are related in Exodus 16 and Numbers 11; the decalogue is given in Exodus 20 and Deuteronomy 5. Contradictions in the Pentateuch

include the specification of one altar (Deut. 12) versus many (Ex. 20:24–25), and the remark that YHVH's name was not known before the time of Moses (Ex. 6:3) even though it is widely used in the stories of the patriarchs in Genesis. Composite narratives include the story of the flood (Gen. 6–9) where conflicting details on the duration of the flood and the number of animals taken aboard the ark reflect the conflation of two sources. In the sale of Joseph in Genesis 37, in one place Midianites, in another place Ishmaelites buy Joseph, and there is a contradiction as to whether Reuben or Judah came to Joseph's defense. In Genesis 15:13 a period of 400 years is given as elapsing between the death of Joseph and the birth of Moses; Exodus 6:16–20 relates that four generations passed between the entrance of Jacob and his family into Egypt and the exodus.

Chapter 2. The Biblical Heritage: Narratives, Law, and Pre-exilic Prophecy

1. On ancient Near Eastern religion, see Thorkild Jacobsen, *The Treasures of Darkness: A History of Mesopotamian Religion* (New Haven: Yale University Press, 1976), especially pp. 3–5. For this section I am much indebted to Jacobsen's book and to Yehezkel Kaufmann, *The Religion of Israel*, chapter III.

2. That aspect of biblical poetry known as parallelism refers to the following pattern: The first part of a poetic line is repeated or modified in the later part through the use of identical or synonymous words to heighten the impact or extend the meaning of the verse. There are many variations, such as using synonyms, antitheses, inversions of word order, and elaboration of the thought further in the second or third line, all of which bring additional meaning to the complete statement. For illustrations see O. Eissfeldt, *The Old Testament, An Introduction*, trans. by Peter R. Ackroyd (New York: Harper & Row, Publishers, 1965), pp. 57–58. For Canaanite precedents, see Michael David Coogan, editor and translator, *Stories from Ancient Canaan* (Philadelphia: The Westminster Press, 1978), p. 15.

3. Martin Noth, *Exodus, A Commentary* (The Old Testament Library), trans. by J. S. Bowden (Philadelphia: The Westminster Press, 1962), p. 18. On biblical style also see E. A. Speiser, *Genesis* (The Anchor Bible), pp. xxiv–xxxiv, and his discussions of specific stories. Among the commentaries used in the following discussion are those by Gerhard Von Rad and Umberto Cassuto on Genesis. Valuable insight into the character of biblical writing can be gained from Erich Auerbach, *Mimesis: The Representation of Reality in Western Literature*, trans. by Willard Trask (Princeton, N.J.: Princeton University Press, 1953), chapter 1.

4. On "Enuma Elish," see Jacobsen, *Treasures of Darkness*, pp. 168–91. Jacobsen offers a structural analysis of the Babylonian epic developing the theme that Marduk's assumption of permanent kingship in the divine assembly

reflects the political transformation of Mesopotamian society, as well as the tensions inherent in the transfer of familial authority from father to son.

5. Besides the commentaries of Speiser and Von Rad, analyses of the biblical and Mesopotamian flood stories are found in Alexander Heidel, *The Gilgamesh Epic and Old Testament Parallels* (Chicago: University of Chicago Press, 1946, 1969) and in Tikva Frymer-Kensky, "The Atrahasis Epic and Its Significance for Our Understanding of Genesis 1–9," *Biblical Archeologist*, Vol. 40, No. 4 (December 1977), pp. 147–55.

6. A seminal study on this subject is G. E. Mendenhall, "Ancient Oriental and Biblical Law, in *The Biblical Archeologist*, Vol. XVII, No. 2 (1954), pp. 26–46, and "Covenant Forms in Israelite Tradition," *The Biblical Archeologist*, Vol. XVII, No. 3 (1954), pp. 50–76. A recent work is Moshe Weinfeld, *Deuteronomy and the Deuteronomic School* (Oxford: The Clarendon Press, 1972), which deals with the impact of the Assyrian treaties. See also Delbert R. Hillers, *Covenant: The History of a Biblical Idea* (Seminars in the History of Ideas) (Baltimore: The Johns Hopkins University Press, 1969).

7. The lateness of the priestly source in the Pentateuch is still, perhaps, the prevailing opinion among scholars. See, for example, Otto Eissfeldt, *The Old Testament: An Introduction*, pp. 204–208. There is another position that argues for the antiquity of the priestly material and suggests that P was redacted either before or at the same time as Deuteronomy, that is, before the Babylonian exile. Yehezkel Kaufmann, *The Religion of Israel*, pp. 175–200, and Moshe Weinfeld, *Deuteronomy and the Deuteronomic School*, pp. 179–89. Weinfeld proposes that P and D existed concurrently as separate traditions and that D decisively modified priestly assumptions and legal requirements.

8. Comparisons of biblical and Mesopotamian law are found in Shalom M. Paul, *Studies in the Book of the Covenant in the Light of Cuneiform and Biblical Law* (Supplements to Vetus Testamentum, Vol. XVIII) (Leiden: E. J. Brill, 1970) and in Roland de Vaux, *Ancient Israel*, 2 vols. (New York: McGraw-Hill Book Company, 1961), Part II, chapter 10. These parallels are found in biblical case law in conditional or "if . . . then" statements that apply a ruling to a specific situation. It is now common to distinguish between casuistic (case) law, on the one hand, and apodictic law, which takes the form of a direct divine command, on the other hand. Biblical apodictic law has no parallel in the Mesopotamian codes, but there are similar expressions in Hittite and other vassal treaties.

9. An instance of the biblical concern to preserve the continuity of each family is the institution of levirate marriage, the obligation of a man to marry the wife of a deceased brother to provide him with a male heir (Deut. 25:5–10). See Speiser, *Genesis*, p. 300, on Genesis 38, a narrative illustration of its importance. The book of Ruth, which has as one of its themes the importance of family loyalty (in this case that between a mother

and her daughter-in-law), conveys details concerning land redemption and levirate marriage somewhat different from those in the Pentateuchal codes.

10. Numbers 19, the rite of the red heifer, contains a purification ritual that in postbiblical Judaism becomes the epitome of a law accepted as a divine commandment whose details cannot be explained rationally. On the purification rites in general, see de Vaux, *Ancient Israel*, II, pp. 460–64.

11. The most important passages are Exodus 23:12–17, Exodus 34:18–24, Leviticus 23, Deuteronomy 16. Additional passages on the Sabbath are Exodus 31:12–17 and 35:1–3; on Passover, Exodus 12:1–27 and Numbers 9:1–14; on the Day of Atonement, Leviticus 16. This discussion of the festivals and other sacred days is indebted to De Vaux, *Ancient Israel*, II, chapters 16–18.

12. For an account of a supposed Israelite New Year festival and criticism of this theory, see de Vaux, *Ancient Israel*, II, pp. 502–506. A moderate defense of the New Year as a celebration of covenant renewal and divine kingship over nature is found in Walter Harrelson, *From Fertility Cult to Worship* (Garden City, N.Y.: Doubleday & Company, Inc., 1970), chapter 4.

13. Albright, *Yahweh and the Gods of Canaan*, p. 212.

14. See Kaufmann, *The Religion of Israel*, p. 365.

15. On the importance of the religious metaphors of marital fidelity and jealousy as part of the bond between Israel and its God, see Gerson D. Cohen, "The Song of Songs and the Jewish Religious Mentality," in *The Samuel Friedland Lectures, 1960–66* (New York: The Jewish Theological Seminary of America, 1966), especially pp. 4–10.

16. See S. R. Driver, *An Introduction to the Literature of the Old Testament* (New York: Meridian Books, 1956), pp. 227–28. Driver's book, first published in 1897, contains many valuable insights on the style and contents of biblical writings.

17. I am grateful to Professor Matitiahu Tsevat's suggestions for the translation of these two epigrammatic verses.

18. Many scholars feel that the End of Days passage in Isaiah 2:2–4, repeated in Micah 4:1–4, is by neither the historical Isaiah nor Micah, but is an anonymous oracle of the postexilic period, when the ultimate future became a pronounced theme in the prophetic literature. Also attributed to prophecy after 587 are Isaiah 11:1–9 and, somewhat less frequently, Isaiah 9:1–6 (Heb. 9:2–7), two oracles on the future righteous king. (See O. Eissfeldt, *The Old Testament: An Introduction*, pp. 318–19; Ernst Sellin and Georg Fohrer, *Introduction to the Old Testament*, trans. by David E. Green [Nashville: Abingdon Press, 1968], pp. 370–71.) Other commentators, however, point out that the phraseology of these passages is characteristically Isaianic, as is the combination of concern for Zion and for the whole world. (Y. Kaufmann, *The Religion of Israel*, p. 386; also G. W. Anderson, *The History and Religion of Israel* [London: Oxford University Press, Inc., 1966], pp. 121–22). We have not felt that the evidence

requires that these passages be treated as secondary and transferred to the later period; the openness of classical prophecy to alternative futures permits a single prophet to evoke images both of disaster and of universal happiness.

In view of the importance of Isaiah 9 and 11 for later Judaism and Christianity, it should be noted that the term *Messiah* does not appear in them; since the messianic doctrine is a postbiblical notion, we have avoided the term *messianic age* in speaking of what the text calls the End of Days. (Isaiah 2:2–4 describes this ideal without any reference to a specific ruler.) Another passage, Isaiah 7:10–17, contains the famous prediction that the "young woman" will conceive and bear a son Immanuel, whose name means "God-is-with-us"; in its context this passage does not concern the End of Days, but reassures a frightened Judean king that God will soon frustrate the plans of his enemies.

19. The first view is represented by Gerhard von Rad, *Studies in Deuteronomy* (Studies in Biblical Theology, No. 9) (London: SCM Press, 1953), p. 66. See also G. W. Anderson, *The History and Religion of Israel*, p. 127, and E. Sellin–G. Fohrer, *Introduction to the Old Testament*, pp. 174–77. The opposing view, that the Deuteronomic movement was a force that undermined many old sacral traditions and that it was a product of a class of scribes and sages, is taken by Moshe Weinfeld, *Deuteronomy and the Deuteronomic School*, pp. 54–58, 161–64, 177–78. Although not agreeing with Weinfeld on all matters, the discussion of Deuteronomy in the next section has profited greatly from his book.

20. Habakkuk 2:4 in its context contrasts the wicked (possibly the Chaldeans), who will fail, with the righteous, who will survive through faithfulness to God.

21. On Jeremiah's relation to Deuteronomy, see Weinfeld, *Deuteronomy and the Deuteronomic School*, pp. 46, 160, 198, and 207; Weinfeld holds that Jeremiah supported the Deuteronomic movement but felt that the reform was not being carried out wholeheartedly. Sheldon H. Blank (*Jeremiah, Man and Prophet* [Cincinnati: Hebrew Union College Press, 1961] pp. 189–92) concludes that Jeremiah may have hesitated at first, but probably did not endorse the Deuteronomic program in the end.

22. On the Deuteronomic oration as a literary form, see Weinfeld, *Deuteronomy and the Deuteronomic School*, p. 52, where he compares it to a similar device used by the Greek historians Herodotus and Thucydides.

Chapter 3. The Biblical Heritage: Later Developments and Other Streams of Thought

1. See Moshe Greenberg, "Prolegomena" to C. C. Torrey, *Pseudo-Ezekiel and the Original Prophecy* (New York: Ktav Publishing House, Inc., 1970), pp. 20–23.

2. On assimilation into pre-exilic Israel and on the Samaritans, see Y. Kaufmann, *The Religion of Israel*, pp. 300–301; on the religion of the Jews of Elephantine, pp. 148–49. For other views of these difficult historical problems, see John Bright, *History of Israel*, pp. 380–403 and G. W. Anderson, *History and Religion of Israel*, pp. 158–68, 176–78. Both authors discuss the complicated chronology of Ezra and Nehemiah.

3. The Psalms are divided by the final editors into five groups, perhaps in imitation of the five books of the Pentateuch (1–41, 42–72, 73–89, 90–106, 107–150). The Temple Levitical guilds that may have composed some of the psalms are also mentioned in 1 Chronicles 15:19, 2 Chronicles 29:30, Ezra 2:41, Nehemiah 12:41–46. There is almost no explicit reference in the psalms to details of the sacrificial system, but the titles of some contain technical terms that seem to refer to music directions, and psalms 92, 98, and 150 refer to musical instruments in the body of the poem.

   Examples of the various categories into which modern scholars have divided the psalms are these:

   a. Hymns (e.g., psalms 145–150).
   b. Personal laments (e.g., 3, 6, 13), which make up about one third of the Psalter. In communal laments the people asks God to come to its aid in a time of national crisis (e.g., 79, 80).
   c. Personal or communal thanksgiving songs (e.g., 107, 116, 124, 136).
   d. Enthronement hymns proclaiming the kingship of YHVH (e.g., 47, 93, 96 through 99).
   e. Songs recited by the king or on his behalf (2, 20, 21, 72, 101, 110, 132, 144). Psalm 45 is a poem celebrating a king's wedding.
   f. Poems in praise of Jerusalem and its Temple (46, 48, 76, 84, 87, 122).
   g. Pilgrimage hymns, probably used in processions to the Temple (15, 24).
   h. History poems, surveying some phases of YHVH's guidance of Israel during its early existence (78, 105, 106, 135, 136).
   i. Psalms expressing utter confidence in YHVH (16, 23, 121, 131).
   j. Wisdom poems: meditations instructing the reader in conduct pleasing to God (34, 36, 73, 91, 119). Some are not actually psalms, since they do not address God; they belong to the wisdom literature described in the next section (Ps. 1, 37, 49, 112, 127, 128, 133).

   Many psalms fall into more than one of these overlapping classes or contain a mixture of forms.

4. Some psalms employ archaic, premonotheistic concepts, antedating an explicit denial of gods other than YHVH. (Compare 89:5–10 and Ps. 82, in which other deities still have some existence attributed to them, with 115:3–8 and 135:15–18 where idolatry is denounced.) Psalms 18 and 20 resemble ancient Israelite victory songs.

5. Instances of how psalms were applied to everyday situations can be seen in the Bible itself. Hannah recites a psalm in 1 Sam. 2:1–10 and Jonah in 2:1–9; in both cases a single detail made the whole poem appropriate to the circumstances of the suppliant.

6. Parallels have been discovered between Israelite wisdom books and those of Egypt and Mesopotamia. (Some materials in chapters 22–24 of Proverbs were probably directly taken from an Egyptian text, "The Instruction of Amen-em-Opet.")

7. A brief description of Proverbs' contents: After a series of odes that warn against a life given over to folly and that praise wisdom as a pious, reasonable guide (chaps. 1–9), the core of Proverbs contains several collections of short exhortations. Chapters 10:1 to 22:16 and chapters 25–29 are attributed to Solomon; 22:17–24:22 and 24:23–24:34 are simply entitled "Words of the Wise." The final chapters (30–31) contain several appendices, including numerical enigmas and a portrait of the ideal wife. The isolated maxims in 10:1–22:16 are probably the most ancient materials in the book.

8. Most scholars feel that the speeches of Elihu in chapters 32–37 are later additions to the book, along with the poem on wisdom in chapter 28 and the passages on Behemoth and Leviathan in 40:15–41:34.

9. Walter Eichrodt, *Man in the Old Testament*, trans. by K. and R. Gregor Smith (London: SCM Press Ltd., 1951), p. 59.

10. Nahum N. Glatzer, editor, *The Dimensions of Job: A Study and Selected Readings* (New York: Schocken Books, Inc., 1969), p. 85.

11. Yehezkel Kaufmann, *The Religion of Israel*, pp. 336–38.

12. Martin Buber, *At the Turning* (New York: Farrar, Strauss & Giroux, Inc., 1952), pp. 61–62.

13. Glatzer, *The Dimensions of Job*, pp. 125–26.

14. Matitiahu Tsevat, "The Meaning of the Book of Job," *Hebrew Union College Annual*, Vol. 37 (1966), pp. 73–106.

15. Ibid., p. 105.

16. Rabbi Jack Bemporad has suggested that 40:8–14 could be read as a moral imperative: It is man's task to "tread down the wicked" and actualize justice in society. He also proposes that Job be seen as a symbol for suffering Israel, a continuation of Second Isaiah's servant passages. See his essay, "Man, God, and History," especially pp. 44–48, in Jack Bemporad, editor, *A Rational Faith: Essays in Honor of Rabbi Levi A. Olan* (New York: Ktav Publishing House, 1977).

17. Roth in Glatzer, *The Dimensions of Job*, p. 74.

18. Robert Gordis upholds the view that the bulk of the material is pre-exilic (*The Song of Songs, A Study, Modern Translation and Commentary* [New York: The Jewish Theological Seminary of America, 1954], pp. 23–24). Pointing to the influence of Hellenism and treating the Song of Songs in the larger context of biblical theology is Gerson D. Cohen, "The Song of Songs and the Jewish Religious Mentality" in *The Samuel Fried-*

land Lectures 1960–66 (New York: The Jewish Theological Seminary of America, 1966), especially p. 16 and note 15 on pp. 20–21. On the dating of the various works mentioned here see Otto Eissfeldt, *The Old Testament, An Introduction:* p. 470 on a fourth-century dating for Job, p. 490 on a third-century date for the Song of Songs, pp. 446–51, on the pre-exilic origin of many of the psalms and a fourth to second-century date for the final compilation of the books, pp. 473–75 on a similar dating for Proverbs (with some material in Proverbs dated to Hellenistic times). Y. Kaufmann, *The Religion of Israel,* argues for a pre-exilic date for Job, pp. 334–38.

19. The title of the book, Koheleth, is usually rendered "The Preacher," but more likely implies someone who addresses an assembly (Heb., *kahal*), hence "Speaker" or "Orator." Posing as King Solomon buttresses the author's claim in chapters 1–2 that he has exhausted all that wisdom, pleasure, and wealth can provide, and that they are devoid of intrinsic significance. "Solomon" could say this; a mere speaker before the assembly or a teacher would hardly have been convincing. Later in the book the author drops his royal stance. Although the book probably belongs to the Hellenistic era, parallels can be found in the wisdom literature of other peoples in the ancient Near East.

20. Georg Fohrer and Ernest Sellen, *Introduction to the Old Testament,* pp. 340–41 on Ecclesiastes and Gilgamesh. Elias Bickerman, *Four Strange Books of the Bible: Jonah, Daniel, Koheleth, Esther* (New York: Schocken Books, Inc., 1967), pp. 145–57. Martin Hengel, *Judaism and Hellenism* (Philadelphia: Fortress Press, 1974), trans. by John Bowden, I, pp. 115–30. Robert Gordis, *Koheleth: The Man and His World* (New York: Bloch Publishing Co., Inc., 1955), pp. 39–42, 51–58. *Proverbs and Ecclesiastes* (The Anchor Bible), introduction, trans. and notes by R. B. Y. Scott (Garden City, N.Y.: Doubleday & Company, Inc., 1965), pp. 191–96. In "Some Philosophical Aspects of Koheleth," *Dimensions,* Fall 1966, pp. 15–19, Jack Bemporad suggests the Ecclesiastes was actually a Jew who set out to criticize the notion, so pervasive in Greek thought, of eternal cycles of time, decay, and dissolution.

21. According to the preface, Ben Sira's book was written in Hebrew and translated into Greek by his grandson in Alexandria, Egypt, around 130 BCE. Although the book was excluded from the Hebrew canon, the Greek translation was preserved by the Christian Church. Ancient Hebrew manuscripts of parts of Ben Sira were discovered at the end of the nineteenth and in the present century.

22. Among the other tales preserved from the last centuries BCE are the books of Tobit and Judith. Tobit is the story of a charitable Israelite exiled to Nineveh, whose son, in a series of adventures and with the help of the angel Raphael, restores the family's fortunes, marries a virtuous maiden, and cures his father's blindness; the book also contains a collection of wise maxims in the spirit of Proverbs and Ben Sira. Judith is a resolute and beautiful Jewish widow who rescues her village and her people from in-

vaders, by enticing and then decapitating Holofernes, an enemy general. After meeting her, a pagan exclaims, "Who can despise these people, who have women like these among them?" (10:19). Three other tales about the figure of Daniel, not included in the biblical book of that name, have survived: Daniel establishing the innocence of Susanna, who has falsely been accused of adultery; Daniel exposing the fakery of the idol Bel; Daniel demonstrating that a serpent worshipped by the Babylonians was not divine.

23. Jonah the son of Amittai is mentioned in 2 Kings 14:25 as having lived during the reign of Jeroboam II, but almost all biblical scholars date the book of this name to postexilic times (except for Y. Kaufmann, *The Religion of Israel*, pp. 282–86). Although a narrative and not a book of oracles, Jonah is included in the *Nevi'im* of the Hebrew Bible, not in the *Ketuvim*.

24. When Esther was translated by a Jew into the Greek language in the early first century BCE, the absence of an overt religious element in the Hebrew version led to the inclusion in the Greek version of several passages of prayer and an explicit religious moral that drove home the providential aspect of the story of Purim.

25. See Elias Bickerman, *From Ezra to the Last of the Maccabees: Foundations of Postbiblical Judaism* (New York: Schocken Books, Inc., 1962), pp. 93–111; Victor Tcherikover, *Hellenistic Civilization and the Jews*, trans. by S. Appelbaum (Philadelphia: Jewish Publication Society of America, 1959), pp. 175–203; Martin A. Cohen, "The Hasmonean Revolution Politically Considered: Outline of a New Interpretation," *Journal of the Central Conference of American Rabbis*, Vol. XXII, No. 4 (Fall 1975), pp. 13–34.

26. Several accounts have survived of the tumultuous events in Judea during the 170s and 160s, preserved in Greek and not included in the Bible. The First Book of Maccabees was originally composed in Hebrew by an unknown author and narrates the military and political events from about 175 to 135 BCE, when the Judeans won their complete independence. Second Maccabees, an abridgement of a five-volume history of the period written in Greek by Jason of Cyrene (Jason's work has not survived), contains more miraculous touches than 1 Maccabees and greater detail in the preliminaries leading up to the revolt. 2 Maccabees ends its account in 164 BCE. A third version, mainly drawn from the previous two, is contained in Josephus's *Jewish Antiquities*.

27. On the Hellenistic aspect of Jewish apocalyptic, see John J. Collins, "Cosmos and Salvation: Jewish Wisdom and Apocalyptic in the Hellenistic Age," *Journal of Religion*, Vol. 17, No. 2 (November 1977), pp. 121–42. Also on Daniel see the following: Louis F. Hartman and Alexander A. Di Lella, *The Book of Daniel: A New Translation with Introduction and Commentary* (The Anchor Bible) (Garden City, N. Y.: Doubleday & Company, Inc., 1978); D. S. Russell, *The Method and Message of Jewish*

Apocalyptic (Philadelphia: Westminster Press, 1964); and Martin Hengel, *Judaism and Hellenism*, Vol. I, pp. 175–218.

Chapter 4. The Hellenistic Diaspora and the Judean Commonwealth to 70 CE

1. Much insight into Jewish life in Hellenistic and Roman Egypt has been culled from papyrus documents, preserved in the dry Egyptian climate, which have come to light in recent archeological investigations. Apart from references in Latin literature, information about the Jews in ancient Rome has been supplemented by inscriptions found in Jewish underground burial chambers (catacombs) outside Rome, rediscovered in the seventeenth century.

2. On the complex question of Jewish civic rights in the Hellenistic-Roman diaspora, see Victor Tcherikover, *Hellenistic Civilization and the Jews*, which is the source of much of the information in this section.

3. Josephus is also the author of a short autobiographical defense of his conduct during the early stages of the Jewish revolt against the Romans (he was one of the generals), before he went over to the Roman side and became an adviser of Vespasian, the commander and soon-to-be Roman emperor. Besides this work, entitled *The Life*, he also wrote *Against Apion*, defending Judaism against the pagan Jew-haters of his time. *Against Apion* will be discussed in the final section of Chapter 5. All quotations from the writings of Josephus in this chapter and the next are taken from the Loeb Classical Library edition: H. S. T. Thackeray, R. Marcus, A. Wikgren, and L. H. Feldman, editors and translators, *Josephus*, 9 vols. (Cambridge: Harvard University Press, 1926–1965). A standard method of citation specifies the division ("book") of the treatise with Roman numerals, followed by the line with Arabic.

Chapter 5. Varieties of Judaism in the Late Second Temple Period

1. The Septuagint generally adheres closely to the Hebrew original, so that a comparison of the Hebrew and Greek is an important factor in biblical scholarship. Proverbs, Job, and Jeremiah, however, diverge considerably from the Hebrew. The reconstruction of the development of the present version of the Septuagint is a scholarly discipline of great complexity.

2. The term *Apocrypha* was used by Protestant Bible translators for Septuagint material not found in the Hebrew text. The Apocrypha contains the book of Ben Sira described in Chapter 3, the stories of Tobit and Judith, additional chapters of Esther and Daniel, two supplements to the book of Jeremiah (letters attributed to Jeremiah and his scribe, Baruch), a prayer expressing the repentance of the wicked biblical king Manasseh, an alter-

native account, with additional material, of the period from Josiah to Ezra (the book of 1 Esdras, sometimes called 3 Ezra). Also in the Apocrypha are 1 and 2 Maccabees (histories of the revolt) and 2 Esdras (an apocalyptic work). Of particular importance for Hellenistic Jewish thought is the Wisdom of Solomon. Incidentally, the term *Apocrypha* ("hidden away") is a misnomer; these chapters and books were not deliberately suppressed by the Jewish authorities but dropped out of circulation when the Jewish canon became fixed toward the end of the first century CE. Besides the Apocrypha, there are various other Hellenistic works, such as 4 Maccabees and the *Letter of Aristeas*, which have survived from this period.

3. On Hellenistic-Jewish literature, in addition to works by Wolfson, Goodenough, Guttmann, Lewy, and others mentioned in the bibliography at the end of the book, I am grateful for notes supplied by Rabbi Jack Bemporad.

4. Quotations from the *Letter of Aristeas* are taken from the translation in R. H. Charles, editor, *Apocrypha and Pseudepigrapha of the Old Testament*, Vol. II (Oxford: The Clarendon Press, 1913), pp. 83–122.

5. Quotations from 4 Maccabees are taken from the translation in R. H. Charles, editor, *Apocrypha and Pseudepigrapha of the Old Testament*, Vol. II, pp. 653–685.

6. The quotations from Philo in this section are from the Loeb Library edition: F. H. Colson and Ralph Marcus, editors and translators, *Philo*, 10 volumes and 2 supplementary volumes (Cambridge, Mass.: Harvard University Press, 1929–1962). The Arabic number refers to the line, the Roman refers to the book where a treatise has been divided into such.

7. Some of the other passages in which Josephus discusses these groupings are *War* I, 110–14; II, 159–66; *Antiquities* XIII, 171–73; XVIII, 14–17. On the edition of Josephus used, see Chapter 4, note 3.

8. For these and some other aphorisms attributed to Hillel, see Pirkei Avot (Sayings of the Fathers), 1:12–14; 2:4–7.

9. Representing the first point of view is Ephraim Urbach, *The Sages, Their Concepts and Beliefs*, trans. by Israel Abrahams (Jerusalem: The Magnes Press, 1975) I, chapter XVI. The second position, that the Pharisees accomplished a revolution in Judaism beginning in the Maccabean period, is advocated by Ellis Rivkin. See his *A Hidden Revolution: The Pharisees' Search for the Kingdom Within* (Nashville, Tenn.: Abingdon Press, 1978) and his *The Shaping of Jewish History* (New York: Charles Scribner's Sons, 1971), chapter III. The third position is represented by Morton Smith's essay "Palestinian Judaism in the First Century" in Moshe Davis, editor, *Israel: Its Role in Civilization* (New York: Harper & Row, Publishers, 1956), pp. 67–81, and by the research of Jacob Neusner; see, for example, the summary of his position in *From Politics to Piety: The Emergence of Pharisaic Judaism* (Englewood Cliffs, N.J.: Prentice-Hall, Inc., 1973).

10. Information on the Essenes can be found in Josephus, *War* II, 119–61 and *Antiquities* XVIII, 18–22. As we shall see later, most scholars identify the Qumran sect and the Dead Sea scrolls with the Essenes. A treatise attributed to Philo ("Every Good Man Is Free") contains a chapter on the Essenes. The Roman writer Pliny describes an Essene sect near the Dead Sea in his *Natural History* 5:73. These various descriptions of the movement have been gathered together in Y. Yadin, *The Message of the Scrolls*, (New York: Simon & Schuster, Inc., 1957), chapter 18.

11. That Qumran was Essene rests on two assumptions disputed by some scholars: that the scrolls were indeed the library of the Qumran community and that the differences between the group that produced the scrolls and the Essenes as described by Josephus are trivial. The rule books of the scrolls and the references in Josephus both describe groups that held goods in common, were concerned with ritual purity, engaged in frequent immersions, required periods of probation and oaths of secrecy for new members, and had separated themselves from the general society. On the other hand, Josephus does not report that the Essenes gave pre-eminence to priests or to a Teacher of Righteousness. Also he portrays them as pacifists and submissive to kings and other rulers—whereas the scrolls indicate a high degree of militancy. (Perhaps the difference is a reflection of changes in the mood of the movement over the course of its long history.) G. R. Driver and Cecil Roth have suggested that the scrolls were not Essene but the work of Zealot groups occupying Qumran, who survived the war against the Romans. Most scholars, however, have come to accept the scrolls as Essene and view the Qumran community as closely fitting Pliny's description mentioned in the previous note.

12. Mark 1:3–6 and Matthew 3:2. The New Testament is interested in John only as the direct precursor of Jesus, but John's followers remained a distinct group even after Jesus' death (see Acts 19:1–7). John the Baptist is also mentioned in Josephus, *Antiquities* XVIII, 116–19, where it is related that he was put to death by a Herodian prince who feared that the enthusiasm shown by John's followers might lead to sedition, unlike the story in Mark 6:17–28 that John's execution was Salome's doing.

13. See also *Antiquities* XVIII, 4–10 and *War* II, 118.

14. On Menahem: *War* II, 433–48; on Eleazar ben Jair, *War* VII, 323–401; on those who refused after the war to acknowledge the legitimacy of the Roman victory despite torture, *War* VII, 417–19.

15. Josephus's terminology can sometimes be confusing. After the outbreak of the war he calls the "fourth philosophy" by the name *Sicarii*, but they are apparently to be distinguished from the general term *sicarii*, designating terrorists that appeared in the Judean cities in the late 40s CE who used a dagger (*sica*) to assassinate Jewish collaborators, including a high priest. On the Zealots see *War* IV, 161; VII, 268–74. The name may be derived from Num. 25:11, and there are some scholars who apply the term *Zealot*

to the whole revolutionary tendency in the first century. A balanced treatment of the various groups and the problems posed by Josephus's account of them is found in David M. Rhoads, *Israel in Revolution, 6–74* CE (Philadelphia: Fortress Press, 1976), especially chaps. IV and V.

16. The term *Pseudepigrapha*, sometimes used as a title for collections of these writings assembled in recent centuries, can be misleading to the general reader because pseudepigraphical writings are also found in the Bible and in the Apocrypha (such as the books ascribed to Solomon). Moreover, not all noncanonical books from this period are pseudepigraphical; many of the Dead Sea scrolls are not.

17. Among the other pseudepigraphical works surviving from this time are these:
2 or Slavonic Enoch (in distinction from 1 Enoch previously described, preserved in an Ethiopian translation).
2 Baruch, preserved in Greek (1 Baruch, previously described, has been preserved in a Syriac translation).
The Assumption of Moses; the Martyrdom of Isaiah; the Life of Adam and Eve; the Biblical Antiquities (falsely ascribed to Philo in the Middle Ages); the Temple Scroll (discovered in 1967 and now included among the Dead Sea Scrolls).
For more information on these and other works see the following:
Leonhard Rost, *Judaism Outside the Hebrew Canon: An Introduction to the Documents*, trans. by David E. Green (Nashville: Abingdon Press, 1976); and Otto Eissfeldt, *The Old Testament: An Introduction*, Part Four.

18. The translation of the Psalms of Solomon used is that of R. H. Charles, editor, *Apocrypha and Pseudepigrapha of the Old Testament*, Vol. II, pp. 625–52. The verses quoted are on pp. 649–51.

19. 1 Enoch, in Charles, *Apocrypha and Pseudepigrapha of the Old Testament*, Vol. II, pp. 163–281; the verses cited are on pp. 264–65.

20. The translation of 2 Esdras is that of the Apocrypha, Revised Standard Version.

21. Like the narrative books of the Old Testament, the gospels of the New Testament are the interpretation, by religious men, of God's saving acts in history and were not intended to be objective historical records in the modern sense. Some of the historiographical difficulties can be seen by comparing Mark, Matthew, and Luke with each other (called the "synoptic gospels" because they follow the same overall summary or outline) and by comparing the synoptic gospels with the Gospel of John, which radically differs in its presentation of the general sequence of events. See, for example, the analysis in Howard Clark Kee, *Jesus in History: An Approach to the Study of the Gospels*, 2nd edition (New York: Harcourt Brace Jovanovich, Inc., 1977). The gospels contain what is probably surmise (what the High Priest and the Roman governor said to Jesus during his interrogation), legend or what in the rabbinical tradition is called ag-

gadah (the story of Jesus' birth in Bethlehem, the city of David), and information about Jesus that is undoubtedly historical (some, but not all of the parables and teachings ascribed to him). The historiographical problem is not unlike that of extracting from the texts of Old Testament narratives a reliable picture of ancient Israel, as discussed in Chapter 1 of this book.

22. The scholarly literature on the question of the "historical Jesus," especially on his trial and crucifixion, is immense. In addition to books mentioned in our Suggestions for Further Reading, see the following biblographical surveys: Reginald H. Fuller, *The New Testament in Current Study* (New York: Charles Scribner's Sons, 1962), especially chap. 3; Charlotte Klein, *Anti-Judaism in Christian Theology* (Philadelphia: Fortress Press, 1978), chap. 5; F. E. Talmage, editor, *Disputation and Dialogue: Readings in the Jewish Christian Encounter* (New York: Ktav Publishing Co., 1975), pp. 363–76. (Talmage's selection covers the gamut of Jewish-Christian relations from ancient to contemporary times.) Some additional studies are the following: E. Bammel, editor, *The Trial of Jesus* (Studies in Biblical Theology, Series II, No. 13) (Naperville, Ill.: Allenson, 1970); John Bowker, *Jesus and the Pharisees* (Cambridge, England: Cambridge University Press, 1973); S. G. F. Brandon, *The Trial of Jesus of Nazareth* (New York: Stein and Day, 1968); Joel Carmichael, *The Death of Jesus* (New York: Dell Publishing Co., 1967); Ellis Rivkin, "Beth Din, Boulé, Sanhedrin: A Tragedy of Errors," *Hebrew Union College Annual*, Vol. XLVI (1975), pp. 181–99; Gerard Sloyan, *Jesus on Trial: The Development of the Passion Narratives and Their Historical and Ecumenical Implications* (Philadelphia: Fortress Press, 1973); Morton Smith, *Jesus the Magician* (New York: Harper & Row, 1978), especially pp. 36–43; Paul Winter, "The Trial of Jesus," *Commentary*, September 1964, pp. 35–41.

23. Paul's letters are the earliest documents of the New Testament, dating from the 50s and 60s. Because they focus almost exclusively on the crucifixion and resurrection as a redemptive event of unparalleled significance, they contain little information about Jesus himself. The seven Pauline epistles that most scholars accept as authentic are 2 Thessalonians, Galatians, 1 and 2 Corinthians, Romans, Philippians, and Philemon; most were written for Christian groups that Paul had founded or had directly influenced, and deal with specific issues that arose in his absence. The New Testament contains other epistles attributed to Paul whose authenticity has been challenged by modern scholarship. Biographical details concerning Paul contained in Acts conflict, in part, with information drawn from his undoubted epistles and seem to be a later attempt to harmonize his point of view with that of other leading apostles, especially Peter.

24. *Against Apion* also contains a summary of current anti-Jewish libels and accusations (Book I), an explication of the Jewish idea of God combining biblical and philosophical concepts (II, 190–92), and typical Jewish criticisms of paganism (I, 200–204 and II, 239–49).

25. Tacitus, *The Histories,* trans. by Kenneth Wellesley (Baltimore: Penguin Books, 1964), pp. 273–74.

Chapter 6. The Efflorescence of Rabbinic Judaism, Second to Seventh Centuries

1. *The Fathers According to Rabbi Nathan,* trans. by Judah Goldin (New Haven: Yale University Press, 1955), p. 34.

2. On the rabbis at Yavneh (Jabneh) see the following: Jacob Neusner, *First-Century Judaism in Crisis: Yohanan ben Zaccai and the Renaissance of Torah* (Nashville, Tenn.: Abingdon Press, 1975), pp. 155–98; Solomon Zeitlin, *The Rise and Fall of the Judean State,* Vol. 3 (Philadelphia: The Jewish Publication Society of America, 1978), pp. 155–222. Among the important early sources on the Sanhedrin at Yavneh is Mishnah Rosh Hashanah 4:1–4. On the period of reconstruction after the revolt see S. W. Baron, *A Social and Religious History of the Jews,* 2nd edition, Vol. 2 (New York: Columbia University Press, 1952), chap. 11, pp. 89–128; the rest of volume 2 of Baron's history is a valuable synthesis of the period under consideration in this chapter.

3. Eusebius, *The History of the Church,* trans. by G. S. Williamson (Baltimore: Penguin Books, 1965), pp. 154–55.

4. An argument that Hadrian's decrees were the result, not the cause of the war, and that they were enforced as martial law in order to weaken the morale of the Jews during the fighting is found in Hugo Mantel, "The Causes of the Bar Kokhba Revolt," *Jewish Quarterly Review,* Vol. LVIII, No. 3 (1968), pp. 224–42; No. 4, pp. 274–91. This article surveys the limited written and archeological evidence for the revolt. On the recent discoveries in the Judean caves relating to Bar Kokhba see Yigael Yadin, *Bar Kokhba* (New York: Random House, Inc., 1971).

5. Jacob R. Marcus, editor, *The Jew in the Medieval World* (New York: Harper & Row Torchbook, 1965), p. 5.

6. On the history of the Jews in Persia during late antiquity, I am indebted to Jacob Neusner, *A History of the Jews of Babylonia,* 5 vols. (Leiden: E. J. Brill, 1966–1970); a shorter version is his *There We Sat Down: Talmudic Judaism in the Making* (Nashville, Tenn.: Abingdon Press, 1972). A collection of his papers on this topic is *Talmudic Judaism in Sasanian Babylonia: Essays and Studies* (Leiden: E. J. Brill, 1978). On the question of the rabbis' lack of authority over the local synagogues, pp. 87–107; on their relations with the exilarch, pp. 108–135. Also see David M. Goodblatt, *Rabinical Instruction in Sasanian Babylonia* (Leiden: E. J. Brill, 1975).

7. Jacob Neusner, "Transcendance and Worship Through Learning: The Religious World-View of Mishnah," *Journal of Reform Judaism* (formerly the *Journal of the Central Conference of American Rabbis*), Vol. XXV, No.

2 (Spring 1978), pp. 15–29. A more detailed analysis is found in Neusner's "Form and Meaning in Mishnah," *Journal of the American Academy of Religion,* Vol. XLV, No. 1 (March 1977), pp. 27–54.

8. Some other midrashic works dating from the middle or late period are these:

a. Later books included in the families mentioned, such as Midrash Rabbah on Exodus, Numbers, Deuteronomy, and the other scrolls; the *Pesikta Rabbati* on the Pentateuchal and prophetic lessons for the festivals; other works included in the category of Midrash Tanhuma.

b. Large midrashic collections on Proverbs, Samuel, and Psalms.

c. Aggadic books that are not compilations of the teachings of many sages, but unified works by a medieval author who, in the pseudepigraphical tradition, attributed his book to an ancient authority. Two important books of this kind, dating from the period when Jews lived under Muslim rule, are the *Tanna de-ve-Eliyahu* or *Seder Eliyahu* (*Order of Elijah*), a didactic and moralistic work; the *Pirkei de Rabbi Eliezer* (*Chapters of Rabbi Eliezer*), which contains many apocalyptic and eschatological interpretations of Pentateuchal tales.

d. Two thirteenth-century medieval anthologies containing midrashic interpretations of biblical verses: the *Yalkut Shimoni,* covering the whole Bible and drawing on more than fifty midrashic books, many of which have disappeared; the *Midrash ha-Gadol,* which excerpts passages from lost early midrashim on the Pentateuch and the scrolls.

e. A number of minor tractates added to the talmudic literature in later times, which provide additional material for existing Mishnah tractates or which bring together scattered references on specific topics. These include *Avot de-Rabbi Nathan* (an elaboration of the Mishnah tractate Pirkei Avot), and fourteen other works that deal with such matters as proselytes, Torah scrolls, ritual objects of other kinds, laws of mourning and good manners.

9. The main sources of rabbinic literature available in English translation (from which the extracts in this and the following section are taken) are the following: the complete translation of the Babylonian Talmud in 18 volumes done under the editorship of Isidore Epstein (London: Soncino Press, 1935–1948); the complete translation of the Midrash Rabbah in 10 volumes done under the editorship of H. Freedman and Maurice Simon (London: Soncino Press, 1939; New Compact Edition in 5 volumes, 1977); *The Minor Tractates of the Talmud,* 2 volumes, trans. under the editorship of A. Cohen (London: Soncino Press, 1965); *The Mishnah,* trans. by Herbert Danby (London: Oxford University Press, 1933); *Mekilta de-Rabbi Ishmael,* trans. and edited by Jacob B. Lauterbach, 3 vols. (Philadelphia: Jewish Publication Society of America, 1949); *The Midrash on Psalms,* trans. by William G. Braude, 2 vols. (New Haven: Yale University Press, 1959); *Pesikta Rabbati: Discourses for Feasts, Fasts, and Special Sabbaths,* trans. by William G. Braude, 2 vols. (New Haven: Yale University Press, 1968); *Pesikta de-Rab Kahana,* trans. by William G. Braude and Israel J. Kap-

stein (Philadelphia: Jewish Publication Society of America, 1975); *The Fathers According to Rabbi Nathan* (*Avot de-Rabbi Natan*), trans. by Judah Goldin (New Haven: Yale University Press, 1955). The *Fathers According to Rabbi Nathan* is also found in the Soncino edition of the *Minor Tractates of the Talmud;* the tractate Pirkei Avot is found in the Mishnah. A useful selection of midrashim is C. G. Montefiore and H. Loewe, editors, *A Rabbinic Anthology* (first published 1938), reprinted in 1970 by Schocken Books.

10. In this section all works are cited according to the units into which the text is divided in the various English translations listed in the previous note. (The *Mekhilta* is cited according to the volume and page number of the Lauterbach edition.) Tractates of the Babylonian Talmud are preceded by the abbreviation B. T.; of the Jerusalem Talmud by J. T. The volumes of the Midrash Rabbah are abbreviated Gen. R., Ex. R., and so forth. For the *Sifra*, *Sifrei*, and the Jerusalem Talmud, which have not been fully translated into English, reference is made where possible to the *Rabbinic Anthology*.

11. Max Kadushin, *Organic Thinking* (New York: Jewish Theological Seminary of America, 1938); *The Rabbinic Mind* (New York: Jewish Theological Seminary of America, 1952). On the general features of rabbinic thought see Julius Guttmann, *Philosophies of Judaism*, trans. by David W. Silverman (New York: Holt, Rinehart and Winston, 1964), pp. 30–43. Important books on rabbinic theology by Solomon Schechter, George Foot Moore, and E. E. Urbach will be listed in our Suggestions for Further Reading. A major work on the folklore and midrashic exegesis of biblical stories and personalities is Louis Ginzburg, *Legends of the Jews*, 7 vols. (Philadelphia: Jewish Publication Society of America, 1961); this is also available in a one-volume abridgement, *Legends of the Bible* (1956).

12. *Rabbinic Anthology*, p. 104.

13. On the rabbinic names for God and related concepts see the following: A. Mormorstein, *The Old Rabbinic Doctrine of God*, Vol. 1: *The Names and Attributes of God* (first published 1927), Vol. 2: *Essays in Anthropomorphism* (first published 1937); both volumes reprinted by Ktav Publishing Co., New York, 1968.

14. By the late Second Temple period the pronunciation of YHVH as Yahveh had passed out of general usage and was restricted to the High Priest on the Day of Atonement, eventually to be dropped completely after 70 CE. As mentioned in Chapter 1, YHVH was pronounced Adonai (Lord) in prayer and study.

15. Early sources speak only of a single *yetzer* against whose urgings one must struggle; later the terms *good* and *evil* were applied to the concept of the *yetzer*.

16. *Rabbinic Anthology*, p. 203.

17. Ibid., p. 276.

18. Ibid., p. 157.

19. Ibid., p. 105.

20. On this principle see Solomon Schechter, *Aspects of Rabbinic Theology* (New York: Schocken Books, Inc., 1961), pp. 215–16, and Samuel Atlas, "Rights of Private Property and Private Profit," *Yearbook of the Central Conference of American Rabbis*, Vol. LIV (1944), pp. 212–56, especially p. 219. Atlas' article contrasts several basic principles of Jewish law with Roman. On the relationship of Jewish ethics and law to each other, see Moshe Silberg, "Law and Morals in Jewish Jurisprudence," *Harvard Law Review* (1961), pp. 306–31.

21. On the antipathy to the taking of interest on loans from fellow-Jews in biblical and talmudic times and the practical and theoretical limitations on this ban, see the article by Haim H. Cohen, "Usury," in the *Encyclopedia Judaica*, Vol. 16, pp. 27–33. The money economy of Sassanian Babylonia spurred the development of devices in rabbinic law to permit investment and credit, a tendency that continued in medieval and early modern times, so that restrictions on the taking of interest were eventually dropped. On the history of the concept of usury in general see Benjamin Nelson, *The Idea of Usury: From Tribal Brotherhood to Universal Otherhood*, 2nd edition (Chicago: University of Chicago Press, 1969). (See also Chapter 7, note 24.)

22. *Rabbinic Anthology*, p. 337.

23. Ibid., pp. 269–70.

24. For other rabbinic viewpoints on these themes, see Solomon Schechter, "The Doctrine of Divine Retribution in Rabbinic Literature" in his *Studies in Judaism: A Selection* (Philadelphia: Jewish Publication Society of America, 1958), pp. 105–22, and Henry Slonimsky, "The Philosophy Implicit in the Midrash" in his *Essays* (Chicago: Quadrangle Books, 1967), pp. 11–84.

25. *The Daily Prayer Book*, trans. by S. Singer (New York: Bloch Publishing Co., 1962), pp. 80–81.

26. *Rabbinic Anthology*, p. 600.

27. *Gehinnom* (sometimes *Gehenna*) takes the place of the biblical *Sheol* as the term for the netherworld; the name is derived from the Valley of Ben Hinnom outside Jerusalem where, in biblical times, children were made to pass through fire for the god Moloch (2 Kings 23:10, Jer. 7:32). On some of the folklore see B. T. Ta'anit 10a for its immeasurable vastness, B.T. Hag. 13b for the fiery stream that pours down from the angels onto the wicked in *Gehinnom*, *Pesikta de Rav Kahana* (Piska 9:1) for *Gehinnom* as an abyss of darkness.

28. Relevant also to the Jewish situation is E. R. Dodds, *Pagan and Christian in an Age of Anxiety: Some Aspects of Religious Experience from Marcus Aurelius to Constantine* (Cambridge, Eng.: Cambridge University Press, 1965). On the Dura synagogue and other aspects of Jewish art, Cecil Roth, editor, *Jewish Art: An Illustrated History* (New York: McGraw-Hill Book Company, 1961), pp. 191–246. A major scholarly effort to bring together and analyze all this material is Erwin R. Goodenough, *Jewish Symbols in the Greco-Roman Period* (Bollingen Series XXXVII), 12 volumes (New York: Pantheon Books, Inc., 1953–1965), especially Vol. 12, *Summary and Conclusions*. See also Morton Smith, "The Image of God: Notes on the Hellenization of Judaism, with Especial Reference to Goodenough's Work on Jewish Symbols," *Bulletin of the John Rylands Library* 40 (1958), pp. 473–512. On the magic bowls a recent article is Charles D. Isbell, "The Story of the Aramaic Magical Incantation Bowls," *Biblical Archeologist* Vol. 41, No. 1 (March 1978), pp. 5–16. (An instance of talmudic discussion of demons is B. T. Hagigah 16a.) On Torah as a source of supernatural power: Jacob Neusner, *Talmudic Judaism in Sasanian Babylonia: Essays and Studies* (Leiden: E. J. Brill, 1976), pp. 53–60. (On the secret twelve-letter and forty-two-letter names of God, B. T. Kiddushin 71a; on the ability of some rabbis to work miracles, B. T. Sanhedrin 65b, 67b.) The *hekhalot* and related literature are discussed by Gershom Scholem in *Jewish Gnosticism, Merkavah Mysticism, and the Talmudic Tradition* (New York: The Jewish Theological Seminary of America, 1965). It has been argued that the term *Jewish Gnosticism* is misleading, because these works show no hatred for the world as is found in much Gnostic literature; see the remarks by Hans Jonas in J. Philip Hyatt, editor, *The Bible in Modern Scholarship* (Nashville, Tenn.: Abingdon Press, 1965), pp. 286–93, and generally his *The Gnostic Religion*, 2nd edition revised (Boston: Beacon Press, 1958, 1963). Also on the subject of the *hekhalot* works, Morton Smith, "Observations on Hekhalot Rabbati," in Alexander Altmann, editor, *Biblical and Other Studies* (Cambridge, Mass.: Harvard University Press, 1963), pp. 142–60. (Talmudic examples are B. T. Hagigah 12b–14b.)

29. Abraham Menes, in *Jewish People Past and Present* (New York: Jewish Encyclopedic Handbooks, 1948), Vol. II, p. 109.

Chapter 7. Medieval Jewry to 1500

1. Koran quotations in this chapter are from *The Koran*, trans. by N. J. Dawood, 4th ed. (Baltimore: Penguin Books, 1974).

2. Yemen had been the home of the ancient civilization of Sheba in biblical times; King Solomon was said to have had close diplomatic and economic ties with Sheba.

3. Muhammad accuses the Jews of considering Ezra to be the son of God (Sura 9:30), a charge without any basis in the Jewish tradition. Although

Muhammad accepted the virgin birth and ascension to heaven of Jesus and considered Jesus a true messenger prophet, he rejected the Christian view that Jesus was divine (Sura 5:17 and 5:73).

4. According to the Koran, Abraham and Ishmael had made a pilgrimage to Mecca where they established the shrine of the Kaaba, but the Arabs had lapsed into paganism afterwards. Linking the Arabs to Ishmael and maintaining that he, rather than Isaac, was the more important son of Abraham, strengthens Muhammad's appropriation of the biblical tradition. There is no evidence that the Arabs traced their ancestry to Ishmael before Muhammad's time.

5. Other Jewish laws found in the Koran are the prohibition on eating pork, blood, and carcasses. (Muhammad rejected the other dietary laws as a divine punishment inflicted on the Jews alone.) Muhammad also established a Muslim parallel to Jewish communal worship, but changed the main day of public prayer to Friday and rejected the principle of abstaining from work on the Sabbath.

6. The messiahship of Jesus, the cause of most of the differences between Judaism and Christianity, made it possible and indeed necessary in the long run for the two religions to separate. As Islam did not have to undergo this divorce, it could evolve along the same structural lines as Judaism.

7. The Judaism of the Khazars has been much discussed but the historical evidence is very limited. Only the ruling class of the Khazars became Jews, and the orthodoxy of their Judaism is somewhat doubtful. The Khazar state had disappeared by the end of the tenth century, but legends and rumors about the Khazars survived in Jewish sources long after.

8. On the shift here to the term *Middle East,* see Chapter 1, note 1.

9. B. Halper, ed. and trans., *Post-Biblical Hebrew Literature: An Anthology* (Philadelphia: Jewish Publication Society of America, 1921), pp. 64–67.

10. Twelfth-century sources describe Anan as a disgruntled candidate for exilarch, said to have rallied his followers to him when a younger brother was chosen exilarch in his place. The veracity of this report has been challenged, especially by Leon Nemoy (*Karaite Anthology* [New Haven: Yale University Press, 1952], pp. 3–11), who feels that the most that one can say with certainty about Anan is that he was a learned Jew from a prominent family, who lived for a while in Persia and then founded his own sect in Baghdad. Fragments of Anan's *Book of Precepts* use talmudic and midrashic modes of interpretation to come to practical conclusions different from those of the rabbis.

11. Interested in theology as well as law, Benjamin espoused a theory that attempted to avoid an anthropomorphic depiction of God (that is, a representation of God as having human characteristics). Accordingly, the world was made by an angel created by God, and the law was revealed

and the prophets inspired through a created angel. Attacks on superstitious and anthropomorphic views of rabbinic Jews became common in Karaite polemics. Anthropomorphism was an important issue also in medieval Jewish philosophy, as we shall see in the next chapter.

12. Leon Nemoy, ed. and trans., *The Karaite Anthology*, pp. 113–115.

13. Best known of the Jerusalem Karaites are the biblical exegete and translator, Jephet ben Ali, and two philosophers, Joseph al-Basir and Yeshua ben Yehudah.

14. Exactly how were the emergence and growth of Karaism consequences of the character of Rabbanite Judaism during the eighth and ninth centuries? Various theories have been proposed to explain the social and ideological sources of Karaite dissidence: that the Judaism of Anan and his followers may have drawn on ancient customs, not accepted in talmudic law, practiced by sectors of eastern Jewry, especially in Persia; that Karaite separatism from the gentiles may have been a quietistic version of the hope for redemption found in more violent form in the Jewish messianic movements immediately preceding it; that the Karaites were a collection of scholarly intellectuals seeking to break away from the aegis of the rabbinical academies in order to interpret the law on their own; that Karaite law reflected and even sanctified the poverty of disadvantaged echelons of Jewish society and their opposition to a Rabbanite elite seen as being all too comfortable with the Islamic state. For more information on these interpretations of the limited information available to the modern historian, see Leon Nemoy's introduction to his *Karaite Anthology*, Salo Baron, *A Social and Religious History of the Jews,* 2nd edition, Vol. V, chap. XXVI, and especially the analysis and further bibliography in Martin A. Cohen, "Anan ben David and Karaite Origins," *The Jewish Quarterly Review,* Vol. LXVIII (1978), No. 3, pp. 139–45 and No. 4, pp. 224–34. Two important discussions in Hebrew are Raphael Mahler, *Ha-Karaim* [The Karaites], trans. from the Yiddish by Ephraim Shemueli (Merhavya: Sifriyat ha-Poalim, 1949) and H. H. Ben-Sasson, *Perakim be-toldot ha-Yehudim bimei ha-benayim* [Chapters on Jewish History in the Middle Ages] (Tel Aviv: Am Oved, 1962), chap. 9.

15. The Lithuanian village of Troki, not far from Vilna, was a center of Polish Karaism until World War II. In the nineteenth century, the Crimean Karaites cut themselves off from the Jewish people in order to exempt themselves from the legal disabilities of the Jews in tsarist Russia. The Egyptian Karaites continued to have close ties with rabbinic Jews, and many of them moved to Israel in the 1950s.

16. The Shiite tendency dates to the power struggle soon after Muhammad's death, when certain groups insisted that the caliphate should remain in Muhammad's family through his son-in-law Ali. (*Shi'a* means "party," that is, party of Ali.) The Shiites became a distinct wing of Islam—actually a collection of religious movements with political aspirations and distinctive religious practices and beliefs that were different from the majority

(Sunni) form of Islam. Because they were Shiites, the Fatimid dynasty did not follow the form of Islam predominant among their Muslim subjects. On the whole, the Fatimids were favorably disposed to the Jews. (For the main exception, when the Jews were persecuted by a Fatimid ruler, see note 18 of this chapter.) Several other Shiite dynasties, especially in early modern Persia, were among the harshest persecutors of Jews in Islamic history.

17. The work of creating a uniform text of the Hebrew Bible may have begun before the Muslim conquests, but it was probably spurred by a standardizing and vocalizing of the text of the Koran undertaken by Muslim scholars. For some time there circulated several systems of Hebrew vocalization. (Vocalization is the adding of vowel points to the ancient texts, which consist mainly of consonants.) There was also a Babylonian system but the Tiberian version, soon generally accepted as standard, was famous for its clarity and accuracy. The texts established there by the scholarly families of Ben Asher and Ben Naphtali (who may have had Karaite sympathies) became normative, and yet another unifying factor for the diaspora. The Masoretes also developed the cantillation marks by which the Torah is chanted (these marks served as punctuation), and they entered many small scholarly emendations of the biblical text where they felt it had been transmitted inaccurately.

18. In the early eleventh century Jews and Christians of the Fatimid realm were subject to a brief but devastating persecution by the Caliph al-Hakim (ruled 996–1020). When the persecution was called off, Jewish life was restored and Egyptian Jewry remained secure for another century and a half. (This caliph became the spiritual force behind the formation of the Middle Eastern sect known as the Druses.) Egyptian Jewry under the Fatimids and under their successors, the Ayyubids, is quite well documented, as a result of the discovery of the Cairo *Genizah*, a storehouse for old Jewish documents in the synagogue of Old Cairo. Not only did the *Genizah* findings bring to light many manuscripts of Jewish literary works in the early twentieth century when they were first published, but in recent years the materials have been used to assemble a remarkable portrait of the economic, social, and religious life of the Jews in the Mediterranean during those centuries. See Jacob Mann, *The Jews in Egypt and in Palestine under the Fatimid Caliphs*, 2 volumes, first published 1920–22 (reprinted, New York: Ktav Publishing Co., 1970) and his *Texts and Studies in Jewish History and Literature*, 2 volumes, first published 1931–35 (reprinted, New York: Ktav Publishing Co., 1972). A major work of recent scholarship is S. D. Goitein, *A Mediterranean Society: The Jewish Communities of the Arab World as Portrayed in the Documents of the Cairo Genizah*, 3 volumes (Berkeley and Los Angeles: University of California Press, 1967–1978).

19. The outstanding grammarians and poets of the generation of Hisdai ibn Shaprut were Menahem ben Jacob ibn Saruq and Dunash ibn Labrat. (The scientific study of Hebrew grammar was of great cultural importance be-

cause it made possible a more natural and idiomatic Hebrew style, which was a necessary groundwork for the creation of great poetry.) Their philological studies were continued in the early eleventh century by Judah Hayyuj and Jonah ibn Janah. Outstanding writers of the age of Samuel ibn Nagrela were Solomon ibn Gabirol, one of the great poets and the first important Jewish philosopher on Spanish soil, and Bahya ibn Pakuda, author of an influential ethical treatise. In the interim between the Almoravides and Almohades were such great writers as the poet Moses ibn Ezra (c. 1055–af. 1135), the poet and philosopher Judah Halevy (c. 1075–1141), the poet and biblical exegete Abraham ibn Ezra (1089–1164), the philosopher and chronicler Abraham ibn Daud (c. 1110–1180). (For more information on some of these figures, see Chapter 8.)

20. There were several waves of Jewish settlement in medieval India. Tenth-century inscriptions from the city of Cochin in southwest India testify to an active Jewish community (which has survived to the present). Documents from the Cairo *Genizah* indicate the important commercial ties between Jews of the Mediterranean and a string of Jewish settlements on India's western coast from the tenth to twelfth centuries. Other Jewish groups from Iraq, Persia, and Europe continued to settle in India in succeeding centuries. The Jewish settlement in the Chinese city of Kaifeng was established by Jews from Persia or India after 1127; they were experts in the production of cotton fabric. This Jewish community had a long history and produced a unique synthesis of Chinese and Jewish culture; descendants were still found there at the beginning of the twentieth century.

21. These include a Hebrew chronicle on the history of the Jews during the Second Temple period, called Jossiphon (loosely based on the writings of Josephus); a commentary on the mystical work known as *Sefer Yetzirah;* medical treatises by Shabbatai Donolo, the first known European Jewish author; the family chronicle of Ahimaaz ben Paltiel, to which historians owe much of their information on the Jews in southern Italy from the ninth to the mid-eleventh centuries.

22. The most eminent eleventh-century Jewish scholar in Rome was Nathan ben Yehiel, who wrote the *Sefer he-Arukh*, a talmudic dictionary that contains a large number of otherwise lost geonic sources and rabbinical opinions from Kairouan, Provence, and the Rhineland.

23. Julius Hoexter and Moses Jung, editors, *Source Book of Jewish History and Literature* (London: Shapiro, Vallentine and Co., 1938), pp. 116–17.

24. Many medieval Christian theologians continued to hold that all interest on loans was morally abhorrent, a view also found in biblical and talmudic literature. (See also Chapter 6, note 21.) But Christian views of "usury" were not static, nor were Jewish. The more positive attitude of medieval Jews was a practical necessity (moneylending being one of the few economic roles open to them in northern society in the high Middle Ages), but it also represents an early indication of new economic theories about

compensation for risk that became apparent in Europe at the end of the medieval period. On this subject see J. T. Noonan, *The Scholastic Analysis of Usury* (Cambridge, Mass.: Harvard University Press, 1957).

25. Theodore Morrison, editor and trans., *The Portable Chaucer* (New York: Viking Press, 1949), pp. 182–85.

26. The blood libel and host desecration tales were projections of a Christian viewpoint onto the Jews, in order to depict them as enemies of the Christian religion—fiends who enjoyed inflicting pain on Christians, just as they had supposedly enjoyed tormenting Jesus before his crucifixion. That Jews wanted to torture the wafer of the Host only made sense if one believed that Jesus was really present in the Host. Similarly, the idea of blood being used in the making of matzah is a reflection of the Christian conception of the Eucharist, namely, that the consecrated elements become the body and blood of Christ. However, the accusation of Jewish ritual slaughter can also be traced to pre-Christian Hellenistic enemies of the Jews; the Christians of pagan Rome were also the object of such charges.

27. Solomon Grayzel, *The Church and the Jews in the Thirteenth Century*, revised edition (New York: Hermon Press, 1966), pp. 105–107.

28. Ibid., p. 127.

29. Jews were recalled to France in 1315 by the government to collect debts owed them, with a substantial percentage going to the king. Only a small number actually returned. They were expelled again in 1322, recalled in 1359, and finally expelled in 1394. Certain areas of modern-day France, then still outside the borders of the kingdom, such as the County of Provence, were not affected by the expulsion for another century. Only in the papal territories around the city of Avignon did a few Jewish communities survive continuously through the Middle Ages into modern times.

30. The massacres of 1298 are known in Jewish history as the Rindfleisch persecutions, after the German nobleman who first instigated them. The slaughter of 1336–1338 is known as the *Armleder* persecutions, from the leather arm bands worn by the rioting peasants. During the Black Death, there were certain areas where the governments were effective in limiting the number of outbursts against Jews (Castile, Sicily, the papal states, Bohemia, Hungary, Poland). The story that the Jews poisoned the wells first appeared during a wave of massacres of Jews in southern France (the Shepherd's persecution) in 1321–1322, when it was rumored that the Jews had formed a conspiracy with the lepers to kill Christians.

31. The extent to which the Spanish Conversos before the establishment of the Spanish Inquisition practiced Judaism in secret has been the subject of dispute among Jewish historians. Ellis Rivkin has warned against the use of inquisitional documents for evidence of secret Judaism, because confessions were extracted by torture and psychological pressure: "The Utilization of Non-Jewish Sources for the Reconstruction of Jewish History," *Jewish Quarterly Review* (New Series), XLVIII (October 1957),

pp. 183–203. Support for this view is found in B. Netanyahu, *The Marranos of Spain from the Late Fourteenth to the Early Sixteenth Century According to Contemporary Christian Sources* (New York: American Academy for Jewish Research, 1966). A defense of the Judaism of the Marranos is Haim Beinart, *Anusim bedin ha-inkvizitsia* (Tell Aviv: Am Oved, 1965). On Beinart's and Netanyahu's conflicting views and a possible resolution see Michael A. Meyer, "How Jewish Were the Marranos?" *Reconstructionist*, Apr. 5, 1968, pp. 25–29. On the Spanish Inquisition in general see the following: Henry Kamen, *The Spanish Inquisition* (New York: New American Library, 1965), Cecil Roth, *The Spanish Inquisition* (New York: W. W. Norton & Co., Inc., 1937). That Marranos in Spain and especially in Portugal in the sixteenth and seventeenth centuries did retain Jewish consciousness is indicated by the steady flight to lands where Marranos reverted to Judaism. For a defense of the view that there existed a clandestine Judaism at this time in the Iberian peninsula, see Yosef Hayim Yerushalmi, *From Spanish Court to Italian Ghetto: Isaac Cardoso, A Study in Seventeenth-Century Marranism and Jewish Apologetics* (New York: Columbia University Press, 1971), especially pp. 21–42. For information on New Christians in Spain who tried to hide their Jewish ancestry and yet remained a definable social group see Ruth Pike, *Aristocrats and Traders: Sevillian Society in the Sixteenth Century* (Ithaca, N.Y.: Cornell University Press, 1972). The later history of the Marranos will be described in Chapter 10.

Chapter 8. Medieval Jewish Theology and Philosophy

1. For the origins of philosophy in general and for the first appearance of Jewish philosophy, see "Diaspora Judaism and Greek Philosophy" in Chapter 4.

2. Leon Roth, "Is There a Jewish Philosophy?" in Raymond Goldwater, editor, *Jewish Philosophy and Philosophers* (London: The Hillel Foundation, 1962), p. 11. Roth prefers the term *philosophy of Judaism* to *Jewish philosophy*. Whereas philosophy in general is a questioning of the widest aspects of human experience, the philosophy of Judaism is a study of certain ideas held by the Jewish tradition; the ideas of Judaism may be of universal importance, but this is a matter for philosophical inquiry to demonstrate.

3. An *accident* is a technical term in Aristotle and in medieval philosophy for a quality that does not belong to a thing because of that thing's essential nature, but occurs as an effect of other causes. Accidents come and go, so to speak, accidentally.

4. *Incorporeal* is also an important medieval term, referring to a being that has no material (that is, corporeal) body.

5. A. Altmann, trans., in *Three Jewish Philosophers* (New York: Harper & Row, 1965), p. 113.

6. The phrase *dogmatic rationalist* is taken from Samuel Atlas, "The Contemporary Relevance of the Philosophy of Maimonides," *Yearbook of the Central Conference of American Rabbis* LXIV (1954), pp. 194–95, where the "dogmatic rationalism" of the Kalam is contrasted with the "critical rationalism" of Maimonides. Our summary of Saadiah's theological book omits the concluding chapter, usually considered a separate treatise, on the mode of life that best satisfies man's needs and develops his powers.

7. The term *Aristotelianism* refers to a stream of thought more complex than that conveyed by the necessarily simplified summary in this chapter. First, one must distinguish between the philosophy of Aristotle himself (384–322 BCE) and the interpretations given his ideas by medieval commentators, who saw him not as a pioneer in defining philosophical and scientific topics but as an encyclopedic synthesizer of knowledge already in large measure assembled. Second, medieval Aristotelianism depended on the availability at different times of Aristotle's writings, the history of the transmission and translation of which is complex. Some were translated into Arabic from the Greek or from Syriac translations by Nestorian Christians in the East around the ninth century CE, a program of translation encouraged and patronized by Abbasid caliphs; it was through these Arabic versions and the commentaries to them by Muslim philosophers that Aristotle was known to the Jews up to the time of Maimonides. In the twelfth and thirteenth centuries, Aristotelian texts and commentaries on them were gradually translated into Hebrew and into Latin in southern Italy and especially in Christian Spain. (The availability of Aristotle in Latin stimulated medieval Christian Aristotelianism at the University of Paris and elsewhere.) Third, much medieval Aristotelian thought was actually a fusion of Aristotle with Neo-Platonic ideas, because two Neo-Platonic works were erroneously considered part of the Aristotelian corpus: the *Theology of Aristotle*, made up of passages from the *Enneads* of the third-century CE philosopher Plotinus, and the *Liber de Causis*, derived from the fifth-century CE Neo-Platonist Proclus. For more information on these topics see the following: Richard Walzer, *Greek Into Arabic: Essays in Islamic Philosophy* (Cambridge, Mass.: Harvard University Press, 1962), Etienne Gilson, *History of Christian Philosophy in the Middle Ages* (New York: Random House, 1955), Majid Fakhry, *A History of Islamic Philosophy* (New York: Columbia University Press, 1970), David Knowles, *The Evolution of Medieval Thought* (New York: Random House, 1962). The two standard works on Jewish philosophy are Julius Guttmann, *Philosophies of Judaism* (New York: Holt, Rinehart, and Winston, 1964), especially pp. 134–43 on Aristotelianism, and Isaac Husik, *A History of Medieval Jewish Philosophy* (New York: Meridian Books, 1958), pp. xxviii–xxxiv on Aristotelianism. In preparing this chapter I am also grateful for materials supplied by Rabbi Jack Bemporad.

8. David Goldstein, editor and trans., *The Jewish Poets of Spain* (Baltimore: Penguin Books, 1971), p. 128.

9. Ibid., pp. 131, 133.

10. As mentioned in the previous chapter, the Khazars were a Turkish people living in the vicinity of the Volga, whose royalty converted to Judaism in the ninth century. This episode was well known in Spain, and Halevy found it an ideal setting for the expression of his beliefs. See Chapter 7, note 7.

11. *The Kuzari*, H. Hirschfeld, trans. (New York: Schocken Books, 1964), p. 44.

12. The Jewish sage departs at the end of the book to settle in Jerusalem where, as Halevy says, "the invisible and spiritual presence" of God can be found, and where the ultimate redemption will occur—when Israel yearns sufficiently for its stones and dust. An appropriate conclusion, in view of Halevy's final pilgrimage to Zion.

13. Halevy does follow the example of the philosophers on the question of divine attributes. He accepts the principle that Scripture must be interpreted so as to remove all possible taint of anthropomorphism from God, and advances a theory of the attributes of the biblical God of revelation that avoids this danger.

14. Maimonides also wrote an enumeration of the 613 divine laws (the *Book of the Commandments*), many responsa (two of the most important are a letter to the Yemenite Jews on dealing with religious persecution and a messianic pretender there, and an epistle against astrology), and various medical treatises.

15. This warning has been the subject of much scholarly research and varied interpretation. Some scholars, such as Julius Guttmann, feel that the deliberate contradictions are few, obvious, and relatively easy to spot. Others, such as Shlomo Pines and Leo Strauss, believe that there is a hidden level of intention in the *Guide*. Our summary, by and large, follows Guttmann's approach. The reader may also want to consult the introductions by Pines and Strauss in *The Guide of the Perplexed*, translated by Shlomo Pines (Chicago: University of Chicago Press, 1963); Isadore Twersky, editor, *A Maimonides Reader* (New York: Behrman House, Inc., 1972); Leon Roth, *The Guide for the Perplexed: Moses Maimonides* (London: Hutchinson's University Library, 1948); the article by Samuel Atlas on Maimonides' contemporary relevance, cited in note 4 of this chapter; Isaac Husik's summation of the *Guide* in his *History of Medieval Jewish Philosophy;* Israel Zinberg's discussion of Maimonides' elitism in Vol. 1, chap. 6 of his *History of Jewish Literature*, translated by Bernard Martin, (Cleveland: Case Western Reserve University Press, 1972).

16. A more technical wording: Inasmuch as everything moves from potentiality to actuality because of an outside agent, there must be an ultimate incorporeal agent that is always actual—that exists perpetually in one and the same state. This Being, in which there is no potentiality, a Being that is separate from matter and that exists intrinsically and essentially, is God.

17. *The Guide of the Perplexed*, trans. by Shlomo Pines (Chicago: University of Chicago Press, 1963), p. 137.

18. Ibid., pp. 327–29.

19. Ibid., p. 526.

20. Ibid., p. 638, with a slight change in the wording of the biblical citation.

21. See Hans Jonas, "Jewish and Christian Elements in Philosophy," in his *Philosophical Essays* (Englewood Cliffs, N.J.: Prentice-Hall, Inc., 1974).

Chapter 9. Medieval Jewish Mysticism and Kabbalah

1. Gershom Scholem, *Major Trends in Jewish Mysticism* (New York: Schocken Books, 1954), p. 8.

2. Ibid., p. 206.

3. G. Scholem, editor, *Zohar: The Book of Splendor, Basic Readings from the Kabbalah* (New York: Schocken Books, 1963), p. 27.

4. Ibid., p. 29.

5. Louis Jacobs, editor, *Jewish Ethics, Philosophy, and Mysticism* (New York: Behrman House, 1969), p. 115.

6. The Zohar also contains a different configuration of divinity, one not involving the sefirot but modeled on the symbolism of the old *shiur Komah* material that described God in highly anthropomorphic terms. In these Zohar passages the divine powers are visualized as features of a human face, especially the hair and beard. There are three such divine structures: *Atika Kadisha* (the Ancient Holy One), *Arikh Anpin* (the Long-Faced One), and *Ze'eir Anpin* (the Short-Faced One). This symbolism was not central to the Franco-Spanish Kabbalah, but became important in the sixteenth century.

7. *The Zohar*, trans. by Harry Sperling and Maurice Simon, 5 volumes (London: Soncino Press, 1933), Vol. IV, p. 98.

8. *Zohar*, Sperling and Simon, trans., Vol. I, p. 135.

9. Ibid., Vol. I, pp. 83–84.

10. Ibid., pp. 231–32.

11. Scholem, *Zohar: The Book of Splendor*, pp. 34–35.

12. Ibid., pp. 44–45.

13. Ibid., p. 33.

14. *Zohar*, Sperling and Simon, trans., Vol. V, p. 176.

15. Ibid., Vol. IV, pp. 224–25.

16. Criticism of the Jewish leadership on these grounds can be seen especially in the later strata of the Zohar. See Yitzhak Baer, *A History of the Jews in Christian Spain*, Vol. 1 (Philadelphia: The Jewish Publication Society of America, 1961), chap. 6.

Chapter 10. Jews and Judaism in the Early Modern Period (Sixteenth to Mid-Eighteenth Centuries)

1. The Jews of Persia had enjoyed rather good relations with the Mongol Il Khans who ruled the area in the thirteenth and fourteenth centuries, a time marked by the emergence of Judo-Persian literature, including poetry and biblical translation. During the reign of the Safavid dynasty (1502–1736), however, the Jewish situation was, on the whole, grim. The dominant Shiite clergy considered the Jews ritually unclean, and there were persecutions and forced conversion (especially in the 1650s). During the Safavid period some Persian Jews settled in central Asia (Afghanistan and Turkestan), where Bukhara became a lively cultural center. The degrading circumstances of Persian Jewry began to improve only at the end of the nineteenth century.

2. *The Authorized Daily Prayer Book*, trans. by S. Singer (London: Eyre and Spottiswoode, 1962), pp. 146–47.

3. Solomon Schechter, *Studies in Judaism: A Selection* (Philadelphia: The Jewish Publication Society of America, 1958), pp. 262–63.

4. The most famous of Luria's disciples was Hayyim Vital (1542–1620). Vital's voluminous work *Etz Hayyim* (*Tree of Life*) and his other writings transmit many quotations from Luria, with lengthy explanations by Vital. Vital's works did not circulate widely until after his death, by which time Luria's ideas were already being studied through writings of other kabbalists. Isaac Luria's life is known through the work of a Moravian kabbalist who settled in Safed after 1600 and composed letters that relate legends circulating about Luria there. These letters were published as the *Shivhei ha-Ari* (*Praises of the Ari*), a form of pious biography that was imitated by the admirers of other charismatic personalities.

5. The formation of the *kelippot* involves very complex speculation, treated differently in the various versions of the Lurianic Kabbalah. In some systems, the deepest root of the *kelippot* are explained as the residue of the Ayn Sof left in the vacuum after *tzimtzum*, indicating that the source of the *kelippot* existed even before the breaking of the vessels. (In a frequent metaphor, this residue of the divine light is like a few drops of oil left in a bowl when it is emptied.) As the notion of the shattering of the sparks penetrated the popular imagination, it was interpreted as a divine catastrophe, but among the kabbalistic writers it was not chaotic, but a process that followed definite laws. It is sometimes described as a carefully planned occurrence to prepare the way for reward and punishment in the lower worlds that were to emerge later in the cosmic drama. Other interpreters

explain the breaking of the vessels as a catharsis whereby impure elements were ejected from the divine, or even as a catharsis of the very roots of Stern Judgment, which had crystallized in the hidden recesses of the Ayn Sof and were purged from God's nature.

6. The doctrine of the *partzufim* was based in part on certain passages in the Zohar that present a system of the divine structure quite different from that of sefirot. See Chapter 9, note 6.

7. As mentioned in the previous chapter, the earlier Kabbalah had limited reincarnation to souls that committed certain heinous sins; in the Lurianic Kabbalah it becomes a universal law of existence.

8. The biography of Shabbatai Zevi by Gershom Scholem supersedes previous accounts of Shabbateanism: *Sabbatai Sevi: The Mystical Messiah*, trans. by R. J. Zwi Werblowsky (Princeton, N.J.: Princeton University Press, 1973). The brief summary of Shabbatai Zevi's life given in this chapter does not do justice to the wealth of detail that Scholem has reconstructed. Although Scholem seeks to rehabilitate Shabbateanism as an outpouring of Jewish spirituality (albeit an ambiguous one), his account of Shabbatai's personality is based on a diagnosis that he was a typical manic-depressive, whose emotional cycle was regularly repeated regardless of external circumstances. A criticism of this diagnosis is Y. Tishbi, *Netivei emunah u'minut* (Paths of Faith and Heresy), (Jerusalem: Sifriyat Makor, 1964), pp. 235–75. Tishbi acknowledges that Shabbatai experienced sweeping changes of mood, but suggests that there was more premeditation and conscious purpose behind his actions than Scholem allows for, including Shabbatai's willingness to condone brutality to promote his messianic revolution. Although this is the best documented messianic movement in Jewish history, gaps and problems of interpretation remain, for example, in connection with the immediate social, political, and economic conditions of the Jewish communities in the Ottoman empire. On Shabbatean theology, see Scholem's *Major Trends in Jewish Mysticism*, chap. 8, and his *Kabbalah* (New York: Quadrangle/The New York Times Book Company, 1974), pp. 244–86. Scholem's *The Messianic Idea in Judaism and Other Essays in Jewish Spirituality* (New York: Schocken Books, Inc., 1971) also contains several important essays on Shabbatean themes.

9. The Doenmeh survived as a group into the early twentieth century, although, unlike the Marranos, they did not re-identify with the Jewish people. The exchange of populations that took place after the Greco-Turkish fighting following World War I forced the Doenmeh to leave Salonika. Afterwards the group dissolved. (See Scholem, *Kabbalah*, "The Doenmeh," pp. 327–32.)

10. Jacob Frank and the Frankists have been studied both in connection with the rise of Hasidism and with the later history of the Frankish families in nineteenth-century Warsaw. See Bernard D. Weinryb, *The Jews of Poland* (Philadelphia: The Jewish Publication Society of America, 1972), chap. 11. Scholem feels that the Shabbateans and the Frankists were in revolt

against the medieval character of Jewish life, and as such they later played an important role in the rise of the Jewish Enlightenment and the Reform movement in Central Europe in the nineteenth century. (See Scholem, *Kabbalah*, 287–309; "Redemption Through Sin," in *The Messianic Idea in Judaism.*) Weinryb argues that Frank did not possess a coherent ideology but a jumble of ideas reflecting his changes of mood or situation, and that Scholem has exaggerated the numbers and cohesiveness of the Frankist group.

11. On the Sephardic and Marrano element in Shabbateanism, see Weinryb, *The Jews of Poland*, chapter 10, especially pp. 210–11. Weinryb also feels that Scholem has inflated the impact of Shabbatai Zevi on the Jews of Poland by relying on a few descriptions from a later time.

12. Poland and Lithuania came under the same ruler after 1386, although they remained administratively separate. (The grand duke of Lithuania was also king of Poland.) As a result of the Union of Lublin (1569) they were more closely integrated, although Poland and Lithuania still remained legally distinct. At this time the Ukraine passed from Lithuanian to Polish control.

13. Nathan Hanover, *The Abyss of Despair*, trans. by Abraham J. Mesch (New York: Bloch Publishing Co., 1950), pp. 111–15.

14. The founders of rabbinical scholarship in Poland were Jacob Pollack from Bavaria (c. 1460–c. 1522), who established the first Polish yeshivah in Cracow, and his pupil Shalom Shakhna (c. 1500–1558) of Lublin. Beginning in the next generation and lasting over a century, Poland produced a number of scholars the equal of Joseph Caro. Shalom Shakhna's greatest pupil was Moses Isserles (c. 1525–1572), head of the yeshivah at Cracow, author of a theological work (*Torat ha-Olah*) drawing on Maimonides and the Kabbalah, and commentator to the writings of Joseph Caro. Isserles' notes to the *Shulhan Arukh*, specifying where Ashkenazic practice differed from Sephardic, made the *Shulhan Arukh* suitable as a code for Ashkenazic Jewry. Solomon Luria (1510–1574) was the author of a commentary to the Talmud which traces, with great clarity and the avoidance of pilpul, the discussion of talmudic issues by medieval authorities up to Luria's time. The following generation of rabbis produced other talmudic commentaries, which became basic texts in advanced rabbinics (the works of Meir of Lublin [1558–1661] and Samuel Edels [1555–1631]). Mordecai Yaffe (c. 1535–1612), a student of Isserles and Luria, was the author of an immense work that contained, as one part, his own code of Jewish law. Yaffe's code competed with the *Shulhan Arukh* for some time as the basic textbook of halakhah in the yeshivot. Also critical of the growing preponderance of the *Shulhan Arukh* was Joel Sirkes (1561–1640), rabbi of Cracow and head of its yeshivah. The eventual acceptance of the *Shulhan Arukh* as the standard code was helped by two seventeenth-century commentaries tracing Caro's sources and explaining his decisions: those of Shabbatai Cohen (1621–1662) and David ben Samuel Halevy (1586–1667). For more in-

formation on these and other figures, see Moses A. Shulvass, *Jewish Culture in Eastern Europe: The Classical Period* (New York: Ktav Publishing House, Inc., 1975).

15. The four lands were the four main provinces of Poland: Great Poland, Little Poland, Polish or Red Russia (Podolia and Galicia), and Volhynia. For a while the kehillot of Lithuania were also represented in the Council of the Four Lands, but Lithuanian Jewry separated to form its own council in 1623.

16. Other aspects of Jewish culture in Poland included Yiddish secular and religious tales for women. Especially popular was the translation of the Torah into Yiddish, with the addition of legends and moral principles, by Joseph Ashkenasi (1550–1628). This work, called the *Tzena Urena*, was first published in 1622 and went through many editions. In the early sixteenth century there were signs of interest among the Polish rabbinate in philosophy, and a few Polish Jews had a knowledge of scientific thought as a result of connections between Poland and Italy, but these fields did not become major concerns of Polish Jewish culture at the time. The Kabbalah of Safed made its appearance in seventeenth-century Poland, but the Ashkenazic kabbalists were less interested in speculative systems than in practical piety. Thus the basic orientation of the Hasidei Ashkenaz remained important in Polish Judaism, despite the adoption of kabbalistic concepts and terms.

17. The Cossacks were former peasants who fled across the borders of Russia and Poland to establish encampments of warriors in the still-wild steppes of the southeastern Ukraine. In the early seventeenth century they had been employed as troops by the Polish government to defend the borderlands against the Tatars. In Ukrainian history, the revolt of 1648 is a national war for liberation; in Polish and Jewish history it is a tragedy.

18. Hanover, *The Abyss of Despair*, pp. 43–44.

19. It is necessary to keep in mind that the terms *hasid* ("pious person") and *Hasidism* (*hasidut*, "piety") recur in Jewish history for various religious tendencies that have no direct connection to each other.

20. *The Autobiography of Solomon Maimon*, trans. by J. Clark Murray (London: The East and West Library, 1954), pp. 81–82.

21. *Toldot Yaakov Yosef* (New York: Israel Rev, Publisher, 1954–55), p. 74a. The Hasidic doctrine of God's immanence has wrongly led some writers to describe Hasidism as a form of pantheism. Although Hasidic doctrine emphasized God's omnipresence, it did not teach that all existing things are part of God. Like the Kabbalah in general, Hasidism defined reality as a unified spiritual system and yet it maintained that the souls of human beings have a fully independent existence apart from God.

22. *The Autobiography of Solomon Maimon*, pp. 171–72.

23. Jacob Joseph of Polonnoye, *Toldot Yaakov Yosef*, p. 48b.

24. Ibid., p. 32a.

25. One of the more influential metaphysical works appearing during the Italian Renaissance, the *Dialoghi* was not merely a work of a Jew adopting a non-Jewish form of thought, but a weaving together of general and Jewish Neo-Platonic themes, including kabbalistic materials which themselves had earlier developed out of Neo-Platonic as well as other sources. (I owe this observation to a comment by Professor Joseph L. Blau.)

26. For example, Elijah Levita (c. 1468–1549), a German Jew who settled in Italy and taught Hebrew grammar to several important Christian humanists, published valuable studies on the system of accents and vowel points in the Masoretic text of the Bible. It was Levita who first recognized that this system did not date from biblical times, but was introduced after the close of the Talmud. (Levita, also one of the first scholars to take an interest in the Yiddish language, wrote entertaining romances in Yiddish.)

    Apropos of Renaissance Jewish historiography, the sixteenth century was also an important period in the writing of Jewish historical chronicles by Sephardic Jews who sought to trace the causation and to explore the theological implications of the expulsions from the Iberian peninsula. (Two of the most valuable such works were Solomon ibn Verga's *Shevet Yehudah* (*Staff* or *Tribe of Judah*), published in 1554, probably in Adrianople, and Samuel Usque's *Consolaçam as Tribulaçoens de Israel* (*Consolation for the Tribulations of Israel*), published in Ferrara, 1553. The latter has been edited and translated into English from the Portuguese by Martin A. Cohen (Philadelphia: The Jewish Publication Society of America, 1965).

27. The term *ghetto* originally designated the section of Venice to which Jewish residence was restricted. In 1516 this area, near the iron foundry (*getto* or *ghetto*), was surrounded by walls and gates and declared the only place in which Jews could settle. Although the term becomes synonymous with the walled-in, impoverished Jewish quarter of Central European cities, ironically this was not the case in Venice, where Jews continued to intermingle socially with non-Jews even after Counter Reformation measures had been adopted almost throughout Italy. Seventeenth and eighteenth-century Leghorn (Livorno) was another exception, because the dukes of Tuscany wanted to attract Sephardic merchants in order to build up the importance of the port.

28. One major Hebrew writer emerged in eighteenth-century Padua: Moses Hayyim Luzzatto (1707–1746). Luzzatto wrote kabbalistic works, lyric poems, allegorical dramas, and a much beloved ethical treatise, *Mesillat Yesharim* (*The Path of the Upright*). Luzzatto is now recognized by Hebrew literary critics as one of the most important Jewish authors of the early modern period. He was subjected to bitter attacks by the rabbis of Padua for his supposed Shabbatean leanings.

29. There is a tie between the Jewish studies of the Renaissance humanists and the beginnings of the Protestant Reformation. Between 1510 and 1520, Johannes Reuchlin (1455–1522), a German humanist and Hebrew scholar

who had been introduced to the Kabbalah by Pico della Mirandola, became embroiled in controversy concerning the supression of Jewish books that attracted widespread attention. A Jewish convert, Johannes Pfefferkorn, had denounced Jewish practices and called for the destruction of the Talmud. Reuchlin and the German humanists opposed Pfefferkorn and his allies, the Dominican theologians of Cologne. A by-product was the satirical classic, *Letters of Obscure Men* (published in 1515 and 1517), which ridiculed scholastic philosophers and monks and helped undermine popular support for the Roman Catholic Church in Germany on the eve of Martin Luther's defiance of the pope.

30. Among the many *Hofjuden* of the seventeenth and eighteenth centuries, especially famous were Samuel Oppenheimer (1630–1703), the Court Jew of the Austrian Hapsburgs, who had connections with Jewish contractors and agents throughout Central Europe, and Samson Wertheimer (1658–1724), who succeeded him as Court Jew in Vienna. (Oppenheimer's entourage became the core of the re-established Jewish community in Vienna in 1676, after the Jews had been expelled from there in 1670.) Joseph Oppenheimer (c. 1699–1738), Court Jew of the Duke of Wuerttemberg, was put in charge of the financial affairs of the duchy in 1733. He lived the life of a typical European nobleman of the time, but after the death of his duke, his enemies contrived to have him hanged for embezzlement. A striking figure who had little respect for religion in the time of his glory, Jew Suess (as he was known) became determined, after his downfall, to die as a Jewish martyr.

31. The outstanding Jewish writer of the seventeenth-century Amsterdam community was Manasseh ben Israel (1604–1657), of a Portuguese Marrano family, who made a name for himself as a preacher and theologian, published defenses of Judaism to the Christians, was a friend of Rembrandt's, and participated in efforts to enable Jews to resettle in England.

Chapter 11. The European State and the Jews, 1770–1880

1. The population figures in this chapter are only guesses, but offer a rough notion of the relative distribution of Jews in the world at that time. Outside Christian Europe there were about 600,000 Jews living under Muslim rule around 1800 and 5,000–10,000 in the Western hemisphere. The estimates are based on Simon Dubnow, *History of the Jews*, trans. by Moshe Spiegel, Vol. IV (South Brunswick, N.J.: Thomas Yoseloff, Publisher, 1971), pp. 447–92, and on Salo Baron, "Population," *Encyclopedia Judaica*, Vol. 13, pp. 866–903.

2. In this zone of European Jewry are included the 200,000 Jews of Prussia and other German states, the 150,000 under Hapsburg rule (70,000 in Bohemia and Moravia, 80,000 in Hungary, and about 1,000 in Austria), and the 40,000 in Italy. The 30,000 Jews of Alsace and Lorraine also fall into this group because these areas were incorporated into France from the Holy Roman Empire only in the later seventeenth century.

3. Joseph II issued separate edicts for the Jews of Bohemia-Moravia, Hungary, and Galicia. (Galicia was the former Polish territory annexed by the Hapsburgs in 1772.) Although an important precedent, his reform involved only a limited equalization of Jewish status; the fixed quotas for permitted marriages, the protection tax, and of course the ineligibility of Jews for government positions were not touched.

4. Raphael Mahler, editor, *Jewish Emancipation: A Selection of Documents* (New York: The American Jewish Committee, 1941), p. 26.

5. Significantly the debts of the Jewish communal organizations were not assumed by the state, as were the debts of the Christian churches.

6. The "July Monarchy" of the new king, Louis Philippe, equalized the status of the Jewish religion in law by agreeing to pay the salaries of the consistories' rabbis, as it did those of the Christian clergy (1831). The last remaining legal difference, a special Jewish oath, was abolished in France in 1846.

7. English Jews were admitted to Parliament only in 1858. Full political emancipation of the Jews took so long in England because the English constitution was not an explicit written document, but a body of traditional practices and legal formulas built up over several centuries. At the beginning of the nineteenth century English Jews were limited by those measures which affected all nonmembers of the established Church. When, however, Protestant dissenters and Catholics in 1828–1829 were permitted to hold public office without being in communion with the Church of England, the Jews were left in an anomalous position. Over a period of almost thirty years the House of Commons debated whether men who could not take an oath "on the true faith of a Christian" should be allowed to sit in Parliament—where they would vote on the affairs of the Church of England. During this period other barriers were falling and Jews were allowed to enter the legal profession (1833), to be elected sheriff (1835), and to hold all municipal offices (1845). In 1858 Lionel Rothschild was finally allowed to take his seat in the House of Commons. In 1871 a new oath formula permitted members of the Jewish religion to enter the universities of Oxford and Cambridge and the last significant handicap was abolished. Cecil Roth, the historian of English Jewry, notes that the integration of Jews into English society was "a gradual acceptance based on common sense rather than on doctrine, consolidating itself slowly but surely, and never outstripping public opinion" (*The History of the Jews of England*, 2nd edition [London: Oxford University Press, 1949], p. 267). On the continent large segments of the population remained hostile to the principle of Jewish emancipation even after it was enacted into constitutional law, which fed anti-Semitism.

The position of the Jew in American law has not been discussed in this chapter, because equality of all citizens and full freedom of religion was established in the United States constitution, reflecting the high degree of social acceptance and Jewish integration even in the colonial period. A few states did retain the theoretical requirement that only a Christian be eligible for public office (Maryland until 1824, North Carolina until 1868).

8. During the Polish partitions, Prussia occupied the westernmost part of Poland around the city of Posen, Austria occupied the southern area known as Galicia, and Russia the Ukraine, Lithuania, and Belorussia (White Russia). After defeating Prussia and Austria, Napoleon combined some of their Polish lands in the Duchy of Warsaw, a French satellite. Most of the Duchy of Warsaw was turned over by the Congress of Vienna to Russia as a semiautonomous province (sometimes called Congress Poland). The Jews of Posen and surrounding areas who remained under Prussian rule received equal rights after 1848. The Jews of the Austrian province of Galicia were emancipated in 1867. As we shall see in Chapter 14, the Jews of Russia were emancipated in 1917.

Chapter 12. First Encounters with Modern Thought, from Spinoza to Krochmal

1. Uriel Acosta, *A Specimen of Human Life* (New York: Bergman Publishers, 1967), pp. 18–19.

2. A Theological-Political Treatise, in *The Chief Works of Benedict de Spinoza*, trans. by R. H. M. Elwes, Vol. 1 (New York: Dover Publications, 1951), p. 189.

3. Ibid., p. 265.

4. On the Improvement of the Understanding, in *The Chief Works of Benedict de Spinoza*, trans. by R. H. M. Elwes, Vol. 2 (New York: Dover Publications, 1951), p. 1.

5. The doctrine that extension and thought are parallel aspects of the one infinite God-or-nature is Spinoza's attempt to overcome Descartes' dualism in which mind and matter are realities virtually independent of each other. Bridging this gap was a central issue of seventeenth-century rationalism and of much subsequent European philosophy.

6. Ethics, in *Chief Works of Spinoza*, Vol. 2, pp. 270–71.

7. Ibid., p. 72.

8. Peter Gay, *The Enlightenment: An Interpretation*, Vol. 1 (New York: Random House, 1966), p. 3.

9. *Nathan the Wise*, trans. by Bayard Quincy Morgan (New York: Frederick Ungar Publishing Co., 1955), p. 52.
   At first Mendelssohn supported himself as a tutor for the children of a Berlin Jew who owned a silk factory. Later he became bookkeeper of the enterprise and finally a partner. In 1762 Mendelssohn married, and in the following year was finally granted by the Prussian government the status of "extraordinary protected Jew" in recognition of his fame. However, be-

cause Mendelssohn was a Jew, the king refused to ratify his election to the Prussian Royal Academy of Sciences. The Mendelssohns became an eminent German banking and artistic family (the composed Felix Mendelssohn-Bartholdy was a grandson). Most of Mendelssohn's children converted to Christianity after their father's death.

10. In 1769 Mendelssohn became embroiled in a dispute with Johann Caspar Lavater, a Swiss pastor and author who had visited Mendelssohn earlier in the decade. In the introduction to his German translation of a defense of the historical truth of Christianity, Lavater challenged Mendelssohn either to refute Christianity or to do "what good sense, love of truth, honesty would enjoin upon you"—to convert. The resulting exchange of views attracted wide attention. Mendelssohn was forced to defend his intellectual integrity: "If my decision, after all these years of study, had not been entirely in favor of my religion, I would certainly have found it necessary to make my convictions known publicly. I fail to see what could have kept me tied to a religion that is so severe and generally despised had I not, in my heart, been convinced of its truth" (*Jerusalem and Other Jewish Writings*, edited and translated by Alfred Jospe [New York: Schocken Books, 1969], p. 115). In the name of enlightened philosophy and of Judaism he rejected Lavater's proselytizing zeal: Righteous men of all faiths will merit salvation; the revealed laws of Judaism are binding only on the Jews, all other nations being enjoined by God to observe the moral laws of the religion of nature and of reason. Lavater apologized for his audacity, but again asked how Mendelssohn could possibly support the validity of Judaism against Christian arguments. Mendelssohn's published Postscript to his exchange with Lavater makes use of the traditional Jewish principle that the Mosaic law was a public revelation before the whole people of Israel, and that its certainty is not based on miracles witnessed only by a few—as was the case with Jesus. See Michael Meyer, *The Origins of the Modern Jew* (Detroit: Wayne State University Press, 1967), pp. 27–32; *Jerusalem and Other Jewish Writings*, pp. 113–22; Eva Jospe, editor and trans., *Moses Mendelssohn: Selections from His Writings* (New York: Viking Press, 1975), pp. 128–30.

11. *Jerusalem and Other Jewish Writings*, p. 57.

12. Ibid., pp. 44, 37.

13. Ibid., p. 61.

14. Ibid., pp. 64–65.

15. Ibid., pp. 68–69.

16. Ibid., p. 89.

17. Ibid., p. 102.

18. Ibid., p. 106.

19. Ibid., pp. 104–105.

20. Ibid., p. 109.

21. The resulting exchange of views, called the *Pantheismusstreit* (pantheism controversy), spread beyond Jacobi and Mendelssohn to involve Herder, Goethe, and many others. One result was that Spinoza finally became generally recognized as a thinker of great suggestiveness and profundity.

22. *Jerusalem and Other Jewish Writings*, p. 67.

23. See the remarks on Moses Hayyim Luzzatto in Chapter 10, note 20.

24. On Schelling's influence on Krochmal, see Julius Guttmann, *Philosophies of Judaism*, pp. 321–44. An important essay on Krochmal's relation to German idealist philosophy is Simon Rawidowicz, "Was Nachman Krochmal a Hegelian?" in his *Studies in Jewish Thought*, edited by Nahum N. Glatzer (Philadelphia: The Jewish Publication Society of America, 1974), pp. 327–84. Notable is the almost total absence of the Hegelian dialectic in Krochmal's philosophy of history. In general, Krochmal left an incomplete, programmatic sketch for a philosophy of Judaism rather than a finished, polished system. The bulk of the *Guide for the Perplexed of our Time* consists not in metaphysical speculation but in a presentation of the inner pattern of Jewish history and in detailed studies of the historical problems arising when one seeks to understand Jewish literature accordingly.

25. Most of the historical studies included in the later part of the *Guide* are not directly related to his schematization of Jewish history, but are suggestive in their own right and had considerable impact on Jewish scholarship. His dating of various biblical books sometimes daringly departs from the traditional view. Krochmal's view of the halakhah as an evolving process of conceptual clarification and logical deduction made him one of the pioneers in the historical understanding of Jewish law. His treatment of the aggadah as a means for popular edification, intended primarily to inspire the masses to piety and morality, constituted an important attempt to place this type of Jewish literature in a proper historical perspective. Krochmal was also interested in Hellenistic Jewish philosophy, in Gnosticism, and in the Kabbalah. In order to formulate a philosophy of Jewish history, he had to undertake preliminary research in all these subjects, which had in his day only begun to be explored scientifically.

Chapter 13. The Question of Jewish Religious Reform in Nineteenth-Century Germany

1. Samson Raphael Hirsch, *The Nineteen Letters on Judaism*, trans. by Bernard Drachman (New York: Feldheim, 1960), p. 24.

2. Ibid., p. 54.

3. Ibid., p. 65.

4. Ibid., p. 113.

5. Ibid., p. 107.

6. Heinrich Graetz, *The Structure of Jewish History and Other Essays*, edited and translated by Ismar Schorsch (New York: The Jewish Theological Seminary of America, 1975), p. 63.

7. *Judaism Eternal: Selected Essays from the Writings of Samson Raphael Hirsch*, edited and translated by I. Grunfeld (London: Soncino Press, 1956), Vol. II, p. 216.

8. W. Gunther Plaut, editor, *The Rise of Reform Judaism: A Sourcebook of Its European Origins* (New York: World Union for Progressive Judaism, 1963), p. 57.

9. The second synod also authorized the use of the organ in Sabbath worship.

10. The third conference discussed, but left to the discretion of individual rabbis and congregations, changes in mourning practice, in marriage law, and in the position of women in Jewish religious ritual.

11. While in Frankfort, in addition to his other duties, Geiger delivered several series of popular lectures on the history of Judaism, which provide a convenient summary of his views. See *Das Judentum und sein Geschichte* (1864–1871), translated into English by Charles Newburgh as *Judaism and Its History* (New York: Bloch Publishing Co., 1911).

12. *Judaism and Its History*, p. 24.

13. Max Wiener, editor, *Abraham Geiger and Liberal Judaism* (Philadelphia: The Jewish Publication Society of America, 1962), p. 84.

14. *Judaism and Its History*, p. 29.

15. Ibid., p. 25.

16. Ibid., p. 47.

17. *Abraham Geiger and Liberal Judaism*, pp. 156–57.

18. See *Judaism and Its History*, p. 213.

19. Ibid., p. 160.

20. Ibid., p. 392.

21. Plaut, *The Rise of Reform Judaism*, p. 123.

22. David Philipson, *The Reform Movement in Judaism* (New York: Ktav Publishing Co., 1967), p. 66.

23. Ibid., p. 205.

24. Heinrich Graetz, *History of the Jews* (Philadelphia: The Jewish Publication Society of America, 1895), pp. 680–81.

25. Graetz, *The Structure of Jewish History and Other Essays*, p. 65.

26. Ibid., p. 65.

27. Ibid., p. 84.

28. Ibid., p. 95.

29. Ibid., p. 96.

30. Ibid., p. 122.

31. Ibid., p. 124.

32. Michael A. Meyer, editor and trans., *Ideas of Jewish History* (New York: Behrman House, 1974), p. 230.

33. Ibid., p. 237. It should be noted that in the mid-nineteenth century the term *race*, which Graetz uses here, was not yet irrevocably wedded to the idea of superior or inferior inbred characteristics; race could be used for a social body of common descent, a fellowship based on familial ties and spiritual traditions such as Jewry.

34. *The Structure of Jewish History and Other Essays*, p. 301.

Chapter 14. The Onslaught of Modernity: Jewish History from 1880 to the Present

1. Quoted in Paul W. Massing, *Rehearsal for Destruction: A Study of Political Anti-Semitism in Imperial Germany* (New York: Harper & Row, 1949), p. 9.

2. See also the confrontation at this time between Heinrich von Treitschke and Heinrich Graetz, described in Chapter 13.

3. Before 1880 a number of rabbis, journalists, and writers, including several Christians, advanced more or less practical proposals for the return of the Jews to Zion and the creation of a modern Jewish state there (Yehudah Alkalai, Zvi Hirsch Kalischer, Moses Hess, Eliezer ben Yehudah). Some of them will be discussed in Chapter 15. Although their impact was limited, they put into circulation ideas that were to form the basis of the ideology of Hibbat Zion (Love of Zion), to be described in this section. Another important precedent was the formation in Romania in 1880, when political conditions for the Jews deteriorated there, of societies for the settlement of Jews in Palestine.

4. The name *Bilu* comes from the initial letters of Isaiah 2:5, "House of Jacob, come and let us go." A similar group, also imbued with the populist and Haskalah idealization of agricultural labor, went off to America with this goal in mind but it was not able to survive.

5. There was a prehistory to Jewish socialism, as to Jewish nationalism. The first to advocate spreading socialist ideals among the Jewish public in its own language was Aaron Liebermann of Vilna, who left Russia in the 1870s to found a small Jewish socialist group in London and who published the first Jewish socialist journal in Hebrew in the late 70s for yeshivah students in Lithuania. Liebermann and his associates had only limited impact because the Jewish proletariat was still quite small.

6. The assimilated Jews in the Russian S.D. party voted against the Bund's proposal. This episode was an important one in the development of Russian Marxism: When the Bund walked out, Lenin's faction was left in the majority, hence its name Bolshevik (majority), in contrast to the more moderate wing (the Menshevik or minority), opposed to Lenin's centralism.

7. Argentina was the setting for an ambitious attempt to settle impoverished Russian Jews in farming communities. This program, financed by the Belgian philanthropist Baron Maurice de Hirsch, was inaugurated in the early 1890s and peaked at 20,000 Jewish farmers by the mid-1920s. Most of them eventually moved to the larger Argentine cities.

8. In 1913 the Conservative movement formed the United Synagogue of America and in 1919 the Rabbinical Assembly. About that time a modern wing of Orthodoxy emerged: The R. Isaac Elhanan Theological Seminary, founded in 1897, became part of Yeshiva University of New York, a ramified institution of higher learning that was developed between 1912 and 1928. Reform Judaism in the 1930s became more moderate and less dogmatic, taking a more positive stance on the value of traditional rituals and Jewish ethnicity.

9. Independent Finland and Estonia had small Jewish communities, whereas Belorussia and the Ukraine, where many Jews lived, remained under Communist control and were part of the USSR.

10. Jewish population figures, difficult to determine accurately, are even more uncertain for these countries, but the following estimates for the 1930s give a general notion of the relative numbers of Jews in Africa and Asia: Morocco (200,000), Algeria (115,000), Tunisia (60,000), Libya (25,000), Egypt (65,000), Syria and Lebanon (25,000), Iraq (90,000), Yemen and Aden (50,000), Turkey (80,000), Iran (75,000), India (25,000), non-Ashkenazic Jews in the USSR, 85,000 (Georgia, 35,000; Mountain Jews, 25,000; Bukharan Jews, 25,000), the Falashas of Ethiopia (15,000). These figures are based on articles in the *Encyclopedia Judaica* for the various lands as well as the general article on "Population."

11. Some of the oldest Jewish groups in India had forgotten most of the Jewish tradition, only to rediscover their heritage through contact with Jewish merchants in the seventeenth century. The Bene Israel, almost completely Indianized in their language and culture, enlisted in native British regiments in the eighteenth century and came to play a role in the economy of Bombay.

12. The Mountain Jews in the nineteenth century were still hunters and farmers who spoke Judeo-Tat, an Iranian dialect containing Hebrew and Caucasian expressions. Also in the Persian-Jewish orbit were the Jews of Afghanistan, of Bukhara, and some of the Jews of India.

13. Kurdish Jews lived mainly in northern Iraq and western Iran and were among the most agricultural of all the old Jewish communities. The Jews of Yemen possessed an old, intense Hebrew tradition and had been in close contact with Eastern centers of Jewish learning in the Middle Ages; by the modern period they had been reduced to an inferior social position in a very conservative Islamic state, although jewelry-making and other traditional artisan skills did insure them a special niche. The Falashas, a black ethnic-religious group who live as farmers and craftsmen in villages of northern Ethiopia, base their Judaic tradition on the Ethiopian translation of the Scriptures. Scholars who have studied their culture are divided on the question of whether the Falashas are indeed descendants of ancient Jews.

14. Quoted in Karl Dietrich Bracher, *The German Dictatorship*, trans. by Jean Steinberg (New York: Praeger Publishing Co., 1970), p. 422.

15. Quoted in Erich Goldhagen, "Pragmatism, Function, and Belief in Nazi Anti-Semitism," *Midstream*, December 1972, p. 55.

16. Quoted in Erich Goldhagen, "Albert Speer, Himmler, and the Secrecy of the Final Solution," *Midstream*, October 1971, p. 46.

17. Besides these special killing centers, a large network of other transit, concentration, and forced labor camps were set up through Europe, where Jews and others died of mistreatment, shooting, malnutrition, disease, and bizarre medical experiments. Some of the most infamous were Dachau, near Munich; Buchenwald, near Weimar; Bergen-Belsen, in northwest Germany near Hanover.

18. Proclamation of the State of Israel by the Provisional Council, May 14, 1948. See "Declaration of Independence, Israel" in *Encyclopedia Judaica* (Jerusalem: Keter Publishing Company, 1971), Vol. 5, cols. 1451-55.

19. The following estimates, with some changes, are based on the *American Jewish Yearbook*, Vol. 77, Morris Fine and Milton Himmelfarb, editors (New York: The American Jewish Committee, and Philadelphia: The Jewish Publication Society of America, 1976). Although these figures do not take into account the degree or types of Jewish identity in the different countries, they do convey the changing distribution of world Jewry. There is disagreement as to the number of Jews in Argentina (400,000 or more according to some authorities) and the USSR. The *American Jewish Yearbook* reports that there are 2.68 million Soviet Jews, but the lower figure given in this chapter seems to reflect the census of 1970. See Richard Cohen, editor, *Let My People Go! Today's Documentary Story of Soviet Jewry's Struggle to Be Free* (New York: Popular Library, 1971), p. 167.

Chapter 15. Secular Jewish Thought in the Nineteenth and Twentieth Centuries

1. Moses Hess, *Rome and Jerusalem,* trans. by Meyer Waxman (New York: Bloch Publishing Co., 1943), p. 43.

2. Theodor Herzl, *The Jewish State,* trans. by Harry Zohn (New York: Herzl Press, 1970), p. 109.

3. Ahad Ha-Am's collected essays were published in the four volumes of *At the Crossroads* (Vol. 1, 1895; Vol. 2, 1903; Vol. 3, 1904; Vol. 4, 1913). His only other major literary legacy was his collected letters, edited and published by him in the 1920s in Palestine.

4. The phrase *agnostic rabbi* is from Arthur Hertzberg in his *The Zionist Idea: A Historical Analysis and Reader* (Garden City, N.Y.: Doubleday and Co., 1959).

5. Ahad Ha-Am, *Essays, Letters, Memoirs,* trans. and edited by Leon Simon (Oxford: East and West Library, 1946), p. 63.

6. *The Zionist Idea,* p. 267.
   Ahad Ha-Am's rejection of Herzl was based on several arguments. Ahad Ha-Am felt that the idea of a complete ingathering was impossible: Palestine would never be the home of most of the Jews in the world because the natural increase in the diaspora would offset the smaller numbers who would immigrate to the national home. Furthermore, Ahad Ha-Am viewed political Zionism as imitative of non-Jewish nationalism in its aspiration that the Jews become a normal nation like any other. Judaism would always remain unique, abnormal, and misunderstood. Zionism could not avert the physical suffering of the Jews, but it could cure the decline of Jewish morale by creating a modern Jewish style of life that would inculcate self-respect and maintain cultural unity throughout the diaspora. Therefore, the quality of Jewish life in Zion was more important than the number of Jews there.

7. Ahad Ha-Am, "Three Steps," in David Hardan, editor, *Sources of Contemporary Jewish Thought,* No. 1 (Jerusalem: World Zionist Organization, 1970), pp. 53–54.

8. *Selected Essays of Ahad Ha-Am,* trans. by Leon Simon (Philadelphia: The Jewish Publication Society of America, 1962), p. 194.

9. Ibid., p. 238.

10. Ahad Ha-Am, *Ten Essays on Zionism and Judaism,* trans. by Leon Simon (New York: Arno Press, 1973), p. 132.

11. *Selected Essays of Ahad Ha-Am,* p. 309.

12. See Leon Roth, "Back to, Forward from Ahad Ha-Am?" *Conservative Judaism,* XVII, 1–2 (Fall 1962–Winter 1963), p. 23.

13. Dubnow left Odessa in 1903; after a stay in Vilna he settled in St. Petersburg in 1906, where he taught at a private institute of Jewish studies and edited the scholarly quarterly of the Jewish Historico-Ethnographic Society. Through World War I and the revolutionary years he labored on his *World History of the Jewish People*. A political liberal, he left the USSR in 1922 for Berlin where he published the German and Hebrew translations of most volumes of his history. (The Russian original was published in the 1930s.) When Hitler came to power in 1933, Dubnow moved to Riga; there he was shot during the evacuation of the ghetto in 1941. In addition to a vast number of articles and specialized studies and his magnum opus, he wrote a pioneering history of Hasidism (original Russian version, 1888–1893; Hebrew revision, 1930–1932), a *History of the Jews of Poland and Russia* (published in English by the Jewish Publication Society of America, 1916–1920), and an autobiography (Vols. 1–2, 1934–35; Vol. 3, 1940, reprinted 1957). Dubnow's diaspora nationalism was congenial to the Bund, but he rejected Marxism as dogmatic and as divisive of the Jewish people. His ideology became the program of a small political group (the *Folkspartei*) between 1907 and 1917 in Russia and later in interwar Poland.

14. Simon Dubnow, *Nationalism and History*, edited by Koppel S. Pinson (Philadelphia: The Jewish Publication Society of America, 1958), p. 98.

15. Although Dubnow admired and was influenced by Graetz's *History of the Jews*, he turned away from his mentor's emphasis on religious thought and martyrdom ("thinking and suffering") in order to focus on the people and its communal life. Moreover, rather than narrate the history of the Jews century by century as though it were a single entity, Dubnow treated each major diaspora center separately, carefully locating the minor centers in their orbit around the more influential ones.

16. The minority rights provisions of the Versailles treaties with the successor states of East Central Europe were an exemplification of what Dubnow had in mind. Intense nationalism of the ruling peoples and rampant anti-Semitism in the interwar period prevented these arrangements from being carried out.

17. *Nationalism and History*, pp. 134–35.

18. Berdichevsky is included as an extreme instance of a tendency in modern Jewish literature. With less rebellious vehemence and polemical overstatement, many of his ideas were expressed by other Jewish writers of the early twentieth century and, indeed, his criticisms of Judaism can be traced to the Haskalah.

19. Hertzberg, *The Zionist Idea*, p. 299.

20. Because of this phrase and because Berdichevsky frequently cited the German-Swiss philosopher Friedrich Nietzsche, he has often been called a Jewish Nietzschean. This term is misleading, because Berdichevsky's posi-

tion on the transvaluation of Jewish values was in the process of formation well before he came to know Nietzsche's writings.

21. A principal spokesman of the Zionist "religion of labor," Aaron David Gordon, will be discussed in Chapter 16.

22. Marie Syrkin, *Nachman Syrkin: Socialist Zionist* (New York: Herzl Press, 1961), p. 284.

23. In the last years of his life, Borochov moved to a greater appreciation of the roles of will and desire in solving the Jewish problem, but he is best known for the earlier, deterministic position that attempted to remain as close as possible to dialectical materialism. A further contrast between Syrkin and Borochov: Syrkin, although a great Yiddish orator, was thoroughly committed to the Hebrew revival, whereas Borochov and the left wing of the Poalei Zion remained loyal to Yiddish. Borochov published important research in Yiddish philology.

24. Among the important exponents of Jewish cultural identity of Ahad Ha-Am's generation are Isaac Leib Peretz and Chaim Zhitlovsky. More recently there were Chaim Greenberg, Maurice Samuel, and Horace Kallen. The *Menorah Journal*, especially during the 1920s, when it was a monthly, provided an important forum for writers on this theme, which has been continued by *Commentary*, *Midstream*, and other magazines. A compendium of selections is to be found in Saul L. Goodman, editor, *The Faith of Secular Jews* (New York: Ktav Publishing House, Inc., 1976). The line is often impossible to draw between a secular writer with a sensitivity to religion and a religious author who writes in an informal way, not attempting a systematic exposition of his belief.

25. *The Menorah Treasury*, Leo W. Schwartz, editor (Philadelphia: The Jewish Publication Society of America, 1964), pp. 72, 76.

26. *The Faith of Secular Jews*, pp. 130–31.

27. Ibid., pp. 152, 195.

28. Ben Halpern, *The American Jew* (New York: Theodor Herzl Foundation, 1956), pp. 157–58.

29. The literary criticism of Irving Howe, especially Part IV of his *World of Our Fathers: The Journey of East European Jews to America and the Life They Found and Made* (New York: Simon & Schuster, 1976) is a portrayal of this psychological transformation with its various implications.

30. Simon Halkin, *Modern Hebrew Literature: Trends and Values* (New York: Schocken Books, Inc., 1950) chaps. 10 and 11; Irving Howe and Eliezer Greenberg, editors, *A Treasury of Yiddish Poetry* (New York: Holt, Rinehart and Winston, 1969), pp. 52–61.

31. A list of twentieth-century Jewish historians whose work has implications outside the specific area of their expertise would be very long. At the top, certainly, is Salo Baron, the eminent American Jewish historian whose

Social and Cultural History of the Jews, in the revised, expanded second edition, now runs to 16 volumes. Other outstanding figures include Israel Zinberg (history of Jewish literature), Julius Guttman (history of Jewish philosophy), Raphael Mahler (the Marxist interpreter of Jewish history), Harry Wolfson (Jewish, Christian, and Muslim philosophy from Philo to Spinoza), Shlomo Goitein (Jews in the Arab environment), Ellis Rivkin (Jewish history in relationship to general political and economic developments), Jacob Neusner (Judaism in late antiquity), Jacob Katz, Shmuel Ettinger, H. H. Ben-Sasson, J. L. Talmon (the last four of the Hebrew University of Jerusalem).

Chapter 16. Twentieth-Century Jewish Religious Thought

1. *Religion of Reason Out of the Sources of Judaism*, trans. by Simon Kaplan (New York: Frederick Unger, 1972), p. 160.

2. Ibid., p. 462.

3. *Franz Rosenzweig: His Life and Thought*, Nahum N. Glatzer, editor (Philadelphia: The Jewish Publication Society of America, 1953), p. 207.

4. Franz Rosenzweig, *Understanding the Sick and Healthy*, N. N. Glatzer, editor (New York: Noonday Press, 1953), p. 90.

5. *Franz Rosenzweig: His Life and Thought*, p. 206.

6. *I and Thou*, trans. by Walter Kaufmann (New York: Charles Scribner's Sons, 1970), p. 62.

7. Ibid., pp. 123, 129.

8. Late in life Buber explained that he developed his I–Thou philosophy quite independently of Hermann Cohen and others, and some Buber scholars deny any connection between Buber and Cohen in this regard. Although for Cohen correlation takes place in the realm of ideas and for Buber I–Thou occurs in the heart of existence, the nonreductive emphasis in both their positions indicates a considerable resemblance between Cohen's concept of correlation and Buber's I–Thou.

9. *I and Thou*, p. 130.

10. Martin Buber, *Eclipse of God* (New York: Harper & Row, 1952), p. 17.

11. Martin Buber, *Tales of the Hasidim: The Early Masters*, trans. by Olga Marx (New York: Schocken Books, 1947), p. 3.

12. Martin Buber, *At the Turning* (New York: Farrar, Straus and Giroux, 1952), p. 44.

13. In Palestine Buber became active in a Jewish group advocating a binational Arab-Jewish commonwealth to resolve the tensions between the two peoples in mutual recognition and good will. (There was no significant Arab participation in this group.)

14. See Mordecai Kaplan, "The Meaning of God for the Contemporary Jew," in Alfred Jospe, editor, *Tradition and Contemporary Experience* (New York: Schocken Books, 1970), p. 66.

15. Ibid., p. 70.

16. Mordecai Kaplan, *The Meaning of God in Modern Jewish Religion* (New York: Reconstructionist Press, 1962), p. 76.

17. "The Meaning of God for the Contemporary Jew," p. 73.

18. Abraham Heschel, *God in Search of Man* (Philadelphia: The Jewish Publication Society of America, 1956), p. 116.

19. Ibid., p. 12.

20. Abraham Heschel, *Man Is Not Alone* (Philadelphia: The Jewish Publication Society of America, 1951), p. 127.

21. Ibid., p. 109.

22. *Between God and Man: An Interpretation of Judaism.* Selections from the writings of Abraham J. Heschel, Fritz A. Rothschild, editor (New York: The Free Press, 1959), p. 75.

23. Ibid., p. 120.

24. Ibid., p. 151.

25. See Edward K. Kaplan, "Mysticism and Despair in Heschel's Religious Thought," *Journal of Religion*, Vol. 57, No. 1 (January 1977), p. 41.

26. *Between God and Man*, p. 112.

27. For quotations in this paragraph, see ibid., pp. 164, 81, 194, 86, 165.

28. *God in Search of Man*, pp. 425–26.

29. *The Earth Is the Lord's* and *The Sabbath* (New York: Harper & Row Torchbook, 1966), p. 64.

30. *Reason and Hope: Selections From the Jewish Writings of Hermann Cohen*, Eva Jospe, editor and trans. (New York: W. W. Norton, 1971), p. 88.

31. Emil L. Fackenheim, *Quest for Past and Future* (Boston: Beacon Press, 1968), p. 13.

32. *The Condition of Jewish Belief, A Symposium Compiled by the Editors of Commentary Magazine* (New York: Macmillan Publishing Co., 1969), p. 53.

33. Ibid., p. 199.

Suggestions for Further Reading

The following bibliography is a selection of classic studies and recently published books, which, in turn, will direct the reader to the many other important works of scholarship omitted for lack of space. Some English translations of sources are also included, supplementing those mentioned in the notes. In some instances books on related subjects are grouped together and listed approximately according to the order in which the topic is discussed in the chapter.

General and Introductory Books

BIBLIOGRAPHICAL SURVEYS AND REFERENCE WORKS

Adams, Charles J., editor. *A Reader's Guide to the Great Religions.* 2nd edition. New York: The Free Press, 1977. See the bibliographical essays by Judah Goldin on early and classical Judaism (pp. 283–320) and by Seymour Cain on medieval and modern Judaism (pp. 321–44).

Bibliographical Essays in Medieval Jewish Studies (The Study of Judaism, Vol. II). New York: Anti-Defamation League of the B'nai B'rith, 1976. (Surveys of the Jews in Western Europe, the Church and the Jews, the Jews under Islam, medieval Jewish religious philosophy, medieval Jewish mysticism, minor midrashim.)

Encyclopedia Judaica. 16 volumes. Jerusalem: Keter Publishing House, Ltd., 1972.

Finkelstein, Louis, editor. *The Jews: Their History, Culture, and Religion.* 3rd edition. New York: Harper & Row, Publishers, 1960. (Articles on many phases of the Jewish past and of Jewish literature.)

Jewish Encyclopedia. 12 volumes. New York: Funk & Wagnalls, Inc., 1901–1905.

The Jewish People, Past and Present. 4 volumes. New York: Jewish Encyclopedic Handbooks, 1945–1955. (Based on a projected Yiddish-language encyclopedia, the first three volumes contain much information on East European Jewry; Volume 4 commemorates the tercentenary of Jewish life in America.)

Shunami, Shlomo, editor. *Bibliography of Jewish Bibliographies.* 2nd edition. Jerusalem: Magnes Press, 1965.

The Study of Judaism: Bibliographical Essays. New York: Anti-Defamation League of the B'nai B'rith, 1972. (Bibliographical surveys of Judaism in New Testament times, rabbinic sources, Judaism on Christianity and Christianity on Judaism, modern Jewish thought, the contemporary Jewish community, the Holocaust.)

Werblowsky, R. J. Zwi, and Wigoder, Geoffrey. *Encyclopedia of the Jewish Religion.* New York: Holt, Rinehart and Winston, 1966.

SURVEYS OF JEWISH HISTORY AND LITERATURE

Baron, Salo Wittmayer. *A Social and Religious History of the Jews.* 2nd edition. 16 volumes to date. New York: Columbia University Press, 1952–1976.

Ben-Sasson, H. H., editor. *A History of the Jewish People.* Cambridge, Mass.: Harvard University Press, 1976. (First published in Hebrew in 1969.)

Margolis, Max L., and Marx, Alexander. *A History of the Jewish People.* Philadelphia: Jewish Publication Society of America, 1927.

Rivkin, Ellis. *The Shaping of Jewish History: A Radical New Interpretation.* New York: Charles Scribner's Sons, 1971.

Silver, Daniel Jeremy, and Martin, Bernard. *A History of Judaism.* 2 volumes. New York: Basic Books, Inc., Publishers, 1974.

Waxman, Meyer. *A History of Jewish Literature.* 2nd edition. 5 volumes. New York: Thomas Yoseloff, Publisher, 1960.

Zinberg, Israel. *A History of Jewish Literature.* Trans. from the Yiddish by Bernard Martin. 12 volumes. Vols. 1–3. Cleveland, Ohio: Case Western Reserve, 1972–73. Vols. 4–12, New York: Ktav Publishing House, 1974–1978.

COLLECTIONS OF ESSAYS ON JEWISH HISTORY AND LITERATURE

Ben-Sasson, H. H., and Ettinger, S., editors, *Jewish Society Throughout the Ages.* New York: Schocken Books, Inc., 1969. (A collection of studies first published in the *Journal of World History,* Vol. XI, No. 1–2 [1968].)

Goldin, Judah, editor. *The Jewish Expression*. New York: Bantam Books, Inc., 1970. (Essays on the Jewish tradition from the biblical period to the post-World War II era, by eminent scholars.)

Gross, Nachum, editor. *Economic History of the Jews*. New York: Schocken Books, Inc., 1975. (A collection of articles by Salo W. Baron, Arcadius Kahan, and others from the *Encyclopedia Judaica*.)

Wagner, Stanley M., and Breck, Allen D., editors. *Great Confrontations in Jewish History*. Denver: University of Denver Department of History, 1977. (A group of essays on six major phases of Jewish history.)

JEWISH HISTORIOGRAPHY

Baron, Salo W. *History and Jewish Historians: Essays and Addresses*. Philadelphia: Jewish Publication Society of America, 1964. (Includes essays on Maimonides' historical outlook, on Azariah dei Rossi, Jost, Graetz, and Steinschneider.)

Meyer, Michael A., editor. *Ideas of Jewish History*. New York: Behrman House, Inc., 1974.

INTRODUCTIONS TO THE JEWISH RELIGION

Jacobs, Louis. *A Jewish Theology*. New York: Behrman House, Inc., 1973.

Katz, Steven T. *Jewish Ideas and Concepts*. New York: Schocken Books, Inc., 1977. (Based on material from the *Encyclopedia Judaica*.)

Neusner, Jacob. *The Way of Torah: An Introduction to Judaism*. 2nd edition. Encino, Calif.: Dickenson Pub. Co., Inc., 1974.

Roth, Leon. *Judaism: A Portrait*. New York: The Viking Press, Inc., 1961.

Steinberg, Milton. *Basic Judaism*. New York: Harcourt Brace Jovanovich, Inc., 1947.

Wouk, Herman. *This Is My God: The Jewish Way of Life*. Garden City, N.Y.: Doubleday & Company, Inc., 1968.

Chapter 1. The History of Israel from Its Origins to the Sixth Century BCE

HISTORICAL SURVEYS AND STUDIES

Albright, William Foxwell. *From the Stone Age to Christianity: Monotheism and the Historical Process*. 2nd edition. Garden City, N.Y.: Doubleday & Company, Inc., 1959.

————. *Yahweh and the Gods of Canaan: A Historical Analysis of Two Contrasting Faiths*. Garden City, N.Y.: Doubleday & Company, Inc., 1968.

Alt, Albrecht. *Essays on Old Testament History and Religion.* Trans. by R. A. Wilson. Garden City, N.Y.: Doubleday & Company, Inc., 1967.

Anderson, G. W. *The History and Religion of Israel.* London: Oxford University Press, 1966.

Bright, John. *A History of Israel.* 2nd edition. Philadelphia: Westminster Press, 1972.

De Vaux, Roland. *Ancient Israel.* Vol. 1: *Social Institutions.* Vol. 2: *Religious Institutions.* New York: McGraw Hill Book Company, 1961. (First published in French in 1958–1960.)

Hayes, John. H., and Miller, J. Maxwell, editors. *Israelite and Judean History.* Philadelphia: Westminster Press, 1977.

Mazar, Benjamin, editor. *The Patriarchs* (World History of the Jewish People, Vol. 2). New Brunswick, N.J.: Rutgers University Press, 1970.

————. *The Judges* (World History of the Jewish People, Vol. 3). New Brunswick, N.J.: Rutgers University Press, 1971.

Mendenhall, George E. *The Tenth Generation: The Origins of the Biblical Tradition.* Baltimore: The Johns Hopkins University Press, 1973.

Miller, J. Maxwell. *The Old Testament and the Historian* (Guides to Biblical Scholarship, Old Testament Series). Philadelphia: Fortress Press, 1976.

Noth, Martin. *The History of Israel.* 2nd edition. Trans. from the German by P. R. Ackroyd. New York: Harper & Row, Publishers, 1960.

————. *The Old Testament World.* Trans. by Victor I. Gruhn. Philadelphia: Fortress Press, 1966.

Speiser, E. A., editor. *At the Dawn of Civilization: A Background of Biblical History* (World History of the Jewish People, Vol. 1). New Brunswick, N.J.: Rutgers University Press, 1964.

Wellhausen, Julius. *Prolegomena to the History of Ancient Israel.* New York: Meridian Library, 1958. (First published in German in 1878.)

Wright, G. Ernest, editor. *The Bible and the Ancient Near East: Essays in Honor of William Foxwell Albright.* Garden City, N.Y.: Doubleday & Company, Inc., 1965. (See especially "Modern Study of Old Testament Literature" by John Bright and "Biblical History in Transition" by George E. Mendenhall.)

SURVEYS OF BIBLICAL LITERATURE

Driver, S. R. *An Introduction to the Literature of the Old Testament.* New York: Meridian Books, 1956. (First published in 1897.)

Eissfeldt, Otto. *The Old Testament: An Introduction.* Trans. from the German by P. R. Ackroyd. New York: Harper & Row, Publishers, 1965.

Fohrer, Georg, and Sellin, Ernest. *Introduction to the Old Testament.* Trans. by David Green. Nashville, Tenn.: Abingdon Press, 1968.

Pfeiffer, Robert H. *Introduction to the Old Testament.* New York: Harper & Row, Publishers, 1948.

West, James King. *Introduction to the Old Testament: "Hear, O Israel."* New York: Macmillan Publishing Co., Inc., 1971.

GEOGRAPHY AND ARCHEOLOGY

Aharoni, Yohanan. *The Land of the Bible: A Historical Geography.* Trans. from the Hebrew by A. F. Rainey. Philadelphia: Westminster Press, 1967.

———. and Avi-Yonah, Michael. *The Macmillan Bible Atlas.* New York: Macmillan Publishing Co., Inc., 1968.

The Biblical Archeologist Reader, Vol. 1, David Noel Freedman and Ernest G. Wright, editors. Garden City, N.Y.: Doubleday & Company, Inc., 1961.

The Biblical Archeologist Reader, Vol. 2, Edward F. Campbell, Jr., and David Noel Freedman, editors. Garden City, N.Y.: Doubleday & Company, Inc., 1964.

The Biblical Archeologist Reader, Vol. 3, Edward F. Campbell, Jr., and David Noel Freedman, editors. Garden City, N.Y.: Doubleday & Company, Inc., 1970.

Dever, William G., and Paul, Shalom, editors. *Biblical Archeology.* New York: Quadrangle Books/The New York Times Book Co., 1973. (Based on articles in the *Encyclopedia Judaica.*)

Freedman, David Noel, and Greenfield, Jonas C., editors. *New Directions in Biblical Archeology.* Garden City, N.Y.: Doubleday & Company, Inc., 1969.

Pritchard, James. *Archeology and the Old Testament.* Princeton, N.J.: Princeton University Press, 1958.

———, editor. *The Ancient Near East: An Anthology of Texts and Pictures.* Princeton, N.J.: Princeton University Press, 1958.

———. *The Ancient Near East,* Vol. 2: *A New Anthology of Texts and Pictures.* Princeton, N.J.: Princeton University Press, 1975.

Chapter 2. The Biblical Heritage: Narratives, Law, and Pre-Exilic Prophecy

GENERAL WORKS

Fohrer, Georg. *History of Israelite Religion.* Trans. from the German by David E. Green. Nashville, Tenn.: Abingdon Press, 1972.

Frankfort, H., Frankfort, H. A., Wilson, John A., and Jacobsen, Thorkild. *Before Philosophy: The Intellectual Adventure of Ancient Man.* Baltimore: Penguin Books, 1951. (Originally published in 1946.)

Kaufmann, Yehezkel. *The Religion of Israel: From Its Beginnings to the Babylonian Exile.* Trans. from the Hebrew and abridged by Moshe Greenberg. Chicago: University of Chicago Press, 1960.

Ringgren, Helmer. *Israelite Religion.* Trans. from the German by David E. Green. Philadelphia: Fortress Press, 1966.

INDIVIDUAL BIBLICAL BOOKS

Cassuto, U. *Commentary on the Book of Genesis.* 2 volumes. Part I: *From Adam to Noah.* Part II. *From Noah to Abraham.* Trans. from the Hebrew by Israel Abrahams. Jerusalem: Magnes Press, 1961–1964. (First published in Hebrew in 1944–1949.)

Sarna, Nahum M. *Understanding Genesis: The Heritage of Biblical Israel.* New York: Schocken Books, Inc., 1970.

Speiser, E. A., trans. and editor. *Genesis* (The Anchor Bible). Garden City, N.Y.: Doubleday & Company, Inc., 1964.

Von Rad, Gerhard. *Genesis: A Commentary* (Old Testament Library). Trans. from the German by John H. Marks. Philadelphia: The Westminster Press, 1961.

Cassuto, U. *A Commentary on the Book of Exodus.* Trans. by Israel Abrahams. Jerusalem: Magnes Press, 1967. (First published in Hebrew in 1951.)

Greenberg, Moshe. *Understanding Exodus.* New York: Behrman House, Inc., 1969.

Other commentaries on biblical books that have appeared in the Anchor Bible series, published by Doubleday, include these: Judges (Robert G. Boling), Ruth (Edward F. Campbell, Jr.), Lamentations (Delbert R. Hillers), Esther (Carey A. Moore), Song of Songs (Marvin H. Pope), 1 Chronicles (Jacob M. Myers), 2 Chronicles (Jacob M. Myers), Ezra and Nehemiah (Jacob M. Myers), Job (Marvin H. Pope), Psalms 1–50 (Mitchell Dahood), Psalms 50–100 (Mitchell Dahood), Psalms 101–150 (Mitchell Dahood), Proverbs and Ecclesiastes (R. B. Y. Scott), Second Isaiah (John L. McKenzie), Jeremiah (John Bright), Daniel (Alexander A. Di Lella and Louis F. Hartman).

Other commentaries on biblical books that have appeared in the Old Testament Library series, published by Westminster Press, include these: Exodus (Martin Noth, and also a separate commentary by Brevard S. Childs), Leviticus (Martin Noth), Numbers (Martin Noth), Deuteronomy (Gerhard Von Rad), Joshua (J. Alberto Soggin), 1 and 2 Samuel (Hans Wilhelm Hertzberg), 1 and 2 Kings (John Gray), Psalms (Artur Weiser), Proverbs (William McKane), Isaiah 1–12 (Otto Kaiser), Isaiah 13–39 (Otto Kaiser), Isaiah

40–66 (Claus Westermann), Ezekiel (Walther Eichrodt), Daniel (Norman W. Porteous), Hosea (James L. Mays), Amos (James L. Mays), Micah (James L. Mays).

SPECIAL TOPICS AND THEMES IN BIBLICAL THOUGHT

Adar, Zvi. *The Biblical Narrative.* Trans. from the Hebrew by Misha Louvish. Jerusalem: Department of Education and Culture of the World Zionist Organization, 1959.

Boman, Thorleif. *Hebrew Thought Compared with Greek.* Trans. by Jules L. Moreau. Philadelphia: Westminster Press, 1960.

Buber, Martin. *The Prophetic Faith.* Trans. from the Hebrew by Carlyle Witton-Davies. New York: Macmillan Publishing Co., Inc., 1949.

Eichrodt, Walther. *Man in the Old Testament.* Trans. by K. and R. Gregor Smith. London: S C M Press, 1951.

Heidel, Alexander. *The Babylonian Genesis: The Story of Creation.* 2nd edition. Chicago: University of Chicago Press, 1951.

————. *The Gilgamesh Epic and Old Testament Parallels.* 2nd edition. Chicago: University of Chicago Press, 1949.

Heschel, Abraham Joshua. *The Prophets.* New York: Harper & Row, Publishers, 1962.

Paul, Shalom. *Studies in the Book of the Covenant in the Light of Cuneiform and Biblical Law* (Supplements to Vetus Testamentum, Vol. XVIII). Leiden: E. J. Brill, 1970.

Scott, R. B. Y. *The Relevance of the Prophets.* Rev. edition. New York: Macmillan Publishing Co., Inc., 1969.

Weinfeld, Moshe. *Deuteronomy and the Deuteronomic School.* Oxford: The Clarendon Press, 1972.

Whybray, R. N. *The Succession Narrative: A Study of 2 Samuel 9–20 and 1 Kings 1–2.* London: S C M Press, 1968.

Chapter 3. The Biblical Heritage: Later Developments and Other Streams of Thought

GENERAL WORKS

Bickerman, Elias. *From Ezra to the Last of the Maccabees: Foundations of Postbiblical Judaism.* New York: Schocken Books, Inc., 1962. (The two parts were first published separately in 1947 and 1949.)

Blenkinsopp, Joseph. *Prophecy and Canon: A Contribution to the Study of Jewish Origins.* Notre Dame, Ind.: University of Notre Dame Press, 1977.

Hanson, Paul D. *The Dawn of Apocalyptic*. Philadelphia: Fortress Press, 1975.

Hengel, Martin. *Judaism and Hellenism: Studies in Their Encounter in Palestine During the Early Hellenistic Period*. 2 volumes. Trans. from the German by John Bowden. Philadelphia: Fortress Press, 1974.

Kaufmann, Yehezkel. *The Babylonian Captivity and Deutero-Isaiah*. (Vol. IV, chaps. 1 and 2, of his *History of the Religion of Israel*.) Trans. from the Hebrew by C. W. Efroymson. New York: Union of American Hebrew Congregations, 1970.

————. *History of the Religion of Israel: From the Babylonian Captivity to the End of Prophecy*. (The whole of Vol. IV.) Trans. by C. W. Efroymson. New York: Ktav Publishing House, Inc., 1978.

Schalit, Abraham, editor. *The Hellenistic Age: Political History of Jewish Palestine from 332 BCE to 67 CE* (World History of the Jewish People, Vol. 6). New Brunswick, N.J.: Rutgers University Press, 1972.

Smith, Morton. *Palestinian Parties and Politics That Shaped the Old Testament*. New York: Columbia University Press, 1971.

WISDOM LITERATURE

Rankin, O. S. *Israel's Wisdom Literature: Its Bearing on Theology and the History of Religion*. New York: Schocken Books, Inc., 1969. (First published in 1936.)

Scott, R. B. Y. *The Way of Wisdom in the Old Testament*. New York: Macmillan Publishing Co., Inc., 1971.

Von Rad, Gerhard. *Wisdom in Israel*. Nashville, Tenn.: Abingdon Press, 1972.

Chapter 4. The Hellenistic Diaspora and the Judean Commonwealth to 70 CE

Avi-Yonah, Michael, editor. *The Herodian Period* (World History of the Jewish People, Vol. 7). New Brunswick, N.J.: Rutgers University Press, 1975.

Dodd, C. H. *The Bible and the Greeks*. London: Hodder & Stoughton, 1935.

Hadas, Moses. *Hellenistic Culture: Fusion and Diffusion*. New York: Columbia University Press, 1959.

Josephus. *The Jewish War*. Trans. by G. A. Williamson. Baltimore: Penguin Books, 1970. (The complete translation of Josephus's works in the Loeb Classical Library, 9 vols., is by H. St. J. Thackeray, Ralph Marcus, and Louis H. Feldman, 1926–1965.)

Leon, Harry J. *The Jews of Ancient Rome*. Philadelphia: Jewish Publication Society of America, 1960.

Mantel, Hugo. *Studies in the History of the Sanhedrin.* Cambridge, Mass.: Harvard University Press, 1965.

Rhoads, David M. *Israel in Revolution, 6–74* CE: *A Political History Based on the Writings of Josephus.* Philadelphia: Fortress Press, 1976.

Safrai, S., and Stern, M. *The Jewish People in the First Century: Historical Geography, Political History, Social, Cultural, and Religious Life and Institutions.* 2 volumes. Philadelphia: Fortress Press, 1974–1976.

Sandmel, Samuel. *Judaism and Christian Beginnings.* New York: Oxford University Press, 1978.

Schürer, Emil. *The History of the Jewish People in the Age of Jesus Christ* (*175* BC–AD *135*). A new English edition revised and edited by Geza Vermes and Fergus Millar, Vol. 1. Edinburgh: T. and T. Clark, 1973.

Smallwood, E. Mary. *The Jews under Roman Rule, from Pompey to Diocletian* (Studies in Judaism in Late Antiquity, XX). Leiden: E. J. Brill, 1976.

Tcherikover, Victor. *Hellenistic Civilization and the Jews.* Trans. from the Hebrew by S. Appelbaum. Philadelphia: Jewish Publication Society of America, 1959.

Yadin, Yigael. *Masada: Herod's Fortress and the Zealots' Last Stand.* New York: Random House, Inc., 1966.

Zeitlin, Solomon. *The Rise and Fall of the Judean State.* Vol. 1: *332–37* BCE. Vol. 2: *37* BCE–*66* CE. Vol. 3: *66* CE–*120* CE. Philadelphia: Jewish Publication Society of America, 1962–1978.

Chapter 5. Varieties of Judaism in the Late Second Temple Period

PHILO

Goodenough, Erwin R. *An Introduction to Philo Judaeus.* 2nd edition. Oxford: Basil Blackwood, 1962.

Lewy, Hans, editor. *Philo: Selections.* In *Three Jewish Philosophers.* New York: Harper Torchbook, Harper & Row, Publishers, 1965. (The complete translation of Philo's work in the Loeb Classical Library, 10 vols. and 2 supplementary vols., is by F. H. Colson, G. H. Whitaker, and Ralph Marcus, 1929–1962.)

Wolfson, Harry Austryn. *Philo: Foundations of Religious Philosophy in Judaism, Christianity, and Islam.* 2 volumes. Cambridge, Mass.: Harvard University Press, 1947.

———. *Religious Philosophy: A Group of Essays.* New York: Atheneum Publishers, 1965. (Contains essays on Philo, the Church fathers, and Spinoza, developing the theme that medieval philosophy was inaugurated by Philo and demolished by Spinoza.)

PHARISAIC JUDAISM

Guttmann, Alexander. *Rabbinic Judaism in the Making: The Halakhah from Ezra to Judah I.* Detroit, Mich.: Wayne State University Press, 1970.

Lauterbach, Jacob Z. *Rabbinic Essays.* Cincinnati, Ohio: Hebrew Union College Press, 1951. (Contains essays on the Pharisees, on Midrash and Mishnah, on the ethics of the halakhah, on Jesus in the Talmud.)

Neusner, Jacob. *Early Rabbinic Judaism: Historical Studies in Religion, Literature, and Art* (Studies in Judaism in Late Antiquity, XIII). Leiden: E. J. Brill, 1975.

————. *From Politics to Piety: The Emergence of Pharisaic Judaism.* Englewood Cliffs, N.J.: Prentice-Hall, Inc., 1973.

Rivkin, Ellis. *A Hidden Revolution: The Pharisees' Search for the Kingdom Within.* Nashville, Tenn.: Abingdon Press, 1978.

THE DEAD SEA SCROLLS

Rabin, Chaim. *Qumran Studies.* New York: Schocken Books, Inc., 1975. (First published in 1957.)

Vermes, G., editor and trans. *The Dead Sea Scrolls in English.* 2nd edition. Baltimore, Md.: Penguin Books, 1975.

————. *The Dead Sea Scrolls: Qumran in Perspective.* London: Collins, 1977.

Yadin, Yigael. *The Message of the Scrolls.* New York: Simon & Schuster, Inc., 1957.

PSEUDEPIGRAPHA; APOCALYPTICISM

Charles, R. H., editor. *The Apocrypha and Pseudepigrapha of the Old Testament in English.* 2 vols. Oxford: Clarendon Press, 1913.

Charlesworth, James H. *The Pseudepigrapha and Modern Research.* Missoula, Mont.: Scholars Press for the Society of Biblical Literature, 1976. (Bibliographies and brief introductions to the current state of research on the Pseudepigrapha.)

Russell, D. S. *The Method and Message of Jewish Apocalyptic, 200 BC–AD 100.* Philadelphia: Westminster Press, 1964.

Schmithals, Walter. *The Apocalyptic Movement: Introduction and Interpretation.* Trans. from the German by John E. Steely. Nashville, Tenn.: Abingdon Press, 1975.

JUDAISM AND EARLY CHRISTIANITY

Aulen, Gustaf. *Jesus in Contemporary Historical Research*. Trans. from the Swedish by Ingalil H. Hjelm. Philadelphia, Pa.: Fortress Press, 1976.

Brandon, S. G. F. *Jesus and the Zealots: A Study of the Political Factor in Primitive Christianity*. New York: Charles Scribner's Sons, 1967.

Kee, Howard Clark. *Jesus in History: An Approach to the Study of the Gospels*. 2nd edition. New York: Harcourt Brace Jovanovich, Inc., 1977.

Ruether, Rosemary Radford. *Faith and Fratricide: The Theological Roots of Anti-Semitism*. New York: Seabury Press, Inc., 1974.

Sandmel, Samuel. *A Jewish Understanding of the New Testament*. Augmented edition. New York: Ktav Publishing House, Inc., 1974.

———. *We Jews and Jesus*. New York: Oxford University Press, 1965.

Sanders, E. P. *Paul and Palestinian Judaism: A Comparison of Patterns of Religion*. Philadelphia: Fortress Press, 1977.

Stendahl, Krister. *Paul Among Jews and Gentiles*. Philadelphia: Fortress Press, 1976.

Vermes, Geza. *Jesus the Jew: A Historian's Reading of the Gospels*. London: Collins, 1973.

Chapter 6. The Efflorescence of Rabbinic Judaism, Second to Seventh Centuries

HISTORICAL STUDIES AND MONOGRAPHS

Avi-Yonah, M. *The Jews of Palestine: A Political History from the Bar Kokhba War to the Arab Conquest*. Trans. by Basil Blackwell. New York: Schocken Books, Inc., 1976.

Finkelstein, Louis. *Akiba: Scholar, Saint, and Martyr*. Cleveland, Ohio: William Collins & World Publishing Co., Inc., 1962. (First published in 1936.)

Goodenough, Erwin R. *Jewish Symbols in the Greco-Roman Period*. (Bollingen Series XXXVII.) 12 volumes. New York: Pantheon Books, Inc., 1953–1965.

Lieberman, Saul. *Greek in Jewish Palestine*. New York: Feldheim, 1965. (First published in 1942.)

———. *Hellenism in Jewish Palestine*. New York: Ktav Publishing House, Inc., 1962. (First published in 1950.)

Neusner, Jacob. *There We Sat Down: Talmudic Judaism in the Making*. Nashville, Tenn.: Abingdon Press, 1972.

———. *First-Century Judaism in Crisis: Yohanan ben Zakkai and the Renaissance of Torah.* Nashville, Tenn.: Abingdon Press, 1975.

———. *Talmudic Judaism in Sasanian Babylonia: Essays and Studies.* (Studies in Judaism in Late Antiquity, XIV.) Leiden: E. J. Brill, 1976.

Parkes, James. *The Conflict of the Church and the Synagogue: A Study in the Origins of Antisemitism.* New York: Meridian Books, 1961. (First published in 1934.)

Yadin, Yigael. *Bar-Kokhba: The Rediscovery of the Legendary Hero of the Last Jewish Revolt Against Imperial Rome.* New York: Random House, Inc., 1971.

LITERATURE AND THOUGHT

Cohen, A. *Everyman's Talmud.* New York: Schocken Books, Inc., 1975. (First published in 1949.)

Elizur-Epstein, B., editor and trans. *A Chapter of Talmud: Bava Mezia IX.* Jerusalem: Department of Torah Education and Culture in the Diaspora of the World Zionist Organization, 1963.

Ginzberg, Louis. *The Legends of the Jews.* 7 volumes. Philadelphia: Jewish Publication Society of America, 1909–1938.

———. *On Jewish Law and Lore.* New York: Meridian Books, 1962. (Contains articles on the Palestinian Talmud, on the significance of the halakhah for Jewish history, on allegorical interpretation of Scripture.)

———. *Students, Scholars, and Saints.* New York: Meridian Books, 1958. (Originally published in 1928; contains articles on the religion of the Pharisees and on Jewish thought in the halakhah.)

Gold, Ze'ev. *Lessons in Talmud: Tractate Berachoth 1–5b.* Jerusalem: Department for Torah Education and Culture in the Diaspora of the World Zionist Organization, 1956.

Goldin, Judah, editor and trans. *The Living Talmud: The Wisdom of the Fathers.* New York: Mentor Books, 1957.

Kadushin, Max. *The Rabbinic Mind.* New York: Jewish Theological Seminary of America, 1952.

Mielziner, Moses. *Introduction to the Talmud.* 4th edition. New York: Bloch Publishing Co., Inc., 1968.

Montefiore, C. G., and Loewe, H., editors. *A Rabbinic Anthology.* New York: Schocken Books, Inc., 1974. (Originally published in 1938.)

Moore, George Foot. *Judaism in the First Centuries of the Christian Era: The Age of the Tannaim.* 3 volumes. Cambridge, Mass.: Harvard University Press, 1927–1930.

Neusner, Jacob. *Invitation to the Talmud: A Teaching Book*. New York: Harper & Row, Publishers, 1973.

Schechter, Solomon. *Aspects of Rabbinic Theology*. New York: Schocken Books, Inc., 1961. (First published in 1909.)

Spiegel, Shalom. *The Last Trial: On the Legends and Lore of the Command to Abraham to Offer Isaac as a Sacrifice*. Trans. from the Hebrew by Judah Goldin. New York: Random House, Inc., 1967.

Steinsaltz, Adin. *The Essential Talmud*. Trans. from the Hebrew by Chaya Galai. New York: Basic Books, Inc., Publishers, 1976.

Strack, Hermann L. *Introduction to the Talmud and Midrash*. Trans. from the 5th German edition. Philadelphia: Jewish Publication Society of America, 1931.

Urbach, Ephraim E. *The Sages: Their Concepts and Beliefs*. 2 volumes. Trans. from the Hebrew by Israel Abrahams. Jerusalem: Magnes Press, 1975.

JEWISH LAW

Cohen, Boaz. *Jewish and Roman Law*. 2 volumes. New York: United Synagogue Books, 1966.

Elon, Menachem, editor. *The Principles of Jewish Law*. Jerusalem: Keter, 1975. (Articles from the *Encyclopedia Judaica*.)

Herzog, Isaac. *The Main Institutions of Jewish Law*. 2 volumes. London: Soncino Press, 1965–1967. (First published 1936–1939).

Horowitz, George. *The Spirit of Jewish Law: A Brief Account of Biblical and Rabbinic Jurisprudence with a Special Note on Jewish Law and the State of Israel*. New York: Central Book Co., Inc., 1963.

Lewittes, Mendell. *The Nature and History of Jewish Law*. New York: Yeshiva University Department of Special Publications, 1966.

Chapter 7. Medieval Jewry to 1500

HISTORICAL STUDIES AND MONOGRAPHS

Abrahams, Israel. *Jewish Life in the Middle Ages*. New York: Atheneum Publishers, 1969. (First published in 1896.)

Agus, Irving A. *The Heroic Age of Franco-German Jewry*. New York: Yeshiva University Press, 1969.

Ankori, Zvi. *Karaites in Byzantium: The Formative Years, 970–1100*. New York: Columbia University Press, 1959.

Ashtor, Eliyahu. *The Jews of Moslem Spain*. 2 volumes to date. Trans. from the Hebrew by Aaron Klein and Jenny Machlowitz Klein. Philadelphia: Jewish Publication Society of America, 1973–1979.

Baer, Yitzhak. *A History of the Jews of Christian Spain.* 2 volumes. Trans. by Louis Levensohn, Hillel Halkin, S. Nardi, and H. Fishman. Philadelphia: Jewish Publication Society of America, 1961.

Baron, Salo Wittmayer. *The Jewish Community: Its History and Structure to the American Revolution.* 3 volumes. Philadelphia: Jewish Publication Society of America, 1948.

Casper, Bernard M. *An Introduction to Jewish Bible Commentary.* New York: World Jewish Congress, 1960.

Chasan, Robert. *Medieval Jewry in Northern France: A Political and Social History.* Baltimore, Md.: The Johns Hopkins University Press, 1973.

Dunlop, D. M. *The History of the Jewish Khazars.* New York: Schocken Books, Inc., 1967. (First published 1954.)

Finkelstein, Louis. *Jewish Self-government in the Middle Ages.* New York: Feldheim, 1964. (First published in 1924.)

Freehof, Solomon B. *The Responsa Literature.* Philadelphia: Jewish Publication Society of America, 1955.

Goiten, S. D. *Jews and Arabs: Their Contacts Through the Ages.* New York: Schocken Books, Inc., 1964.

————. *A Mediterranean Society: The Jewish Communities of the Arab World as Portrayed in the Documents of the Cairo Geniza.* 3 volumes. Berkeley and Los Angeles: University of California Press, 1967–1978.

————, editor. *Religion in a Religious Age (Proceedings of Regional Conferences Held at the University of California, Los Angeles, and Brandeis University in April 1973).* Cambridge, Mass.: Association for Jewish Studies, 1974. (Talks and comments on medieval Jewish religious life.)

Grayzel, Solomon. *The Church and the Jews in the XIIIth Century.* Rev. edition. New York: Hermon Press, 1966. (First published 1933.)

Hailperin, Herman. *Rashi and the Christian Scholars.* Pittsburgh, Pa.: University of Pittsburgh Press, 1963.

Katz, Jacob. *Exclusiveness and Tolerance: Studies in Jewish-Gentile Relations in Medieval and Modern Times.* New York: Schocken Books, Inc., 1962.

Kisch, Guido. *The Jews in Medieval Germany: A Study of Their Legal and Social Status.* Chicago: University of Chicago Press, 1949.

Lowenthal, Marvin. *The Jews of Germany: A Story of Sixteen Centuries.* Philadelphia: Jewish Publication Society of America, 1938.

Mann, Jacob. *Texts and Studies in Jewish History.* Introduction by Gerson D. Cohen. New York: Ktav Publishing House, Inc., 1972. (Originally published 1931–1935; research and essays especially on the Geonic period.)

Newman, Abraham A. *The Jews in Spain: Their Social, Political, and Cultural Life.* 2 volumes. Philadelphia: Jewish Publication Society of America, 1942.

Parkes, James. *The Jew in the Medieval Community: A Study of His Political and Economic Situation.* New York: Hermon Press, 1976. (First published in 1938.)

Rankin, O. S. *Jewish Religious Polemic.* Edinburgh: Edinburgh University Press, 1956.

Richardson, H. G. *The English Jewry Under Angevin Kings.* London: Methuen & Co., Ltd., 1960.

Roth, Cecil. *A History of the Jews in England.* 2nd edition. London: Oxford University Press, 1949.

———, editor. *The Dark Ages: Jews in Christian Europe, 711–1096* (World History of the Jewish People, Vol. 11). New Brunswick, N.J.: Rutgers University Press, 1966.

Sharf, Andrew. *Byzantine Jewry: From Justinian to the Fourth Crusade.* London: Routledge and Kegan Paul, 1971.

Synan, E. M. *The Popes and the Jews in the Middle Ages.* New York: Macmillan Publishing Co., Inc., 1965.

Talmadge, Frank. *David Kimhi: The Man and the Commentaries.* Cambridge, Mass.: Harvard University Press, 1976.

Trachtenberg, Joshua. *The Devil and the Jews: The Medieval Conception of the Jews and Its Relation to Modern Antisemitism.* New York: Meridian Books, 1961. (First published in 1943.)

———. *Jewish Magic and Superstition: A Study in Folk Religion.* New York: William Collins & World Publishing Co., Inc., 1961. (First published in 1939.)

Twersky, Isadore. *Rabad of Posquières: A Twelfth-Century Talmudist.* Cambridge, Mass.: Harvard University Press, 1962.

Zimmels, H. J. *Ashkenazim and Sephardim: Their Relations, Differences, and Problems as Reflected in the Rabbinic Responsa.* London: Oxford University Press, 1958.

TRANSLATIONS OF MEDIEVAL JEWISH LITERATURE

(See also the philosophical and mystical works listed under the following chapters. Medieval works are listed in chronological order.)

Goldstein, David, editor and trans. *The Jewish Poets of Spain.* Baltimore, Md.: Penguin Books, 1971.

Eidelberg, Shlomo, editor and trans. *The Jews and the Crusades: The Hebrew Chronicles of the First and Second Crusades.* Madison, Wisc.: University of Wisconsin Press, 1977.

Marcus, Jacob R., editor. *The Jew in the Medieval World, A Source Book: 351–1791*. New York: Harper Torchbooks, Harper & Row, Publishers, 1965. (First published 1938.)

Nemoy, Leon, editor and trans. *Karaite Anthology: Excerpts from the Early Literature*. New Haven: Yale University Press, 1952.

Abraham bar Hayya (11th century). *The Meditation of the Sad Soul*. Trans. by Geoffrey Wigoder. New York: Schocken Books, Inc., 1969.

Solomon Ibn Gabirol (c. 1020–1058). *The Kingly Crown*. Trans. by Bernard Lewis, London: Vallentine-Mitchell, 1961.

Rashi (Solomon ben Isaac, 1040–1105). *The Pentateuch with Rashi's Commentary*. 2 volumes. Trans. by M. Rosenbaum and A. M. Silbermann. London: Shapiro, Vallentine, 1946.

Abraham Ibn Ezra (1089–1164). *The Commentary of Ibn Ezra on Isaiah*. Edited and trans. by M. Friedländer. (First published, London, 1873.) Reprinted, New York: Feldheim, n.d.

Joseph Kimhi (c. 1105–1170). *The Book of the Covenant*. Trans. by Frank Talmadge. Toronto: The Pontifical Institute of Medieval Studies, 1972.

Abraham Ibn Daud (c. 1110–1180). *Sefer Ha-Qabbalah: The Book of Tradition*. Edited and trans. by Gerson D. Cohen. Philadelphia: Jewish Publication Society of America, 1967.

Judah al-Harizi (1170–1235). *The Tahkemoni*. 2 volumes. Trans. by Victor Emanuel Reichert. Jerusalem: R. H. Cohen, 1965–1973.

Benjamin of Tudela (second half of the twelfth century). *The Itinerary of Benjamin of Tudela*. Trans. by Marcus Nathan Adler. (First published London, 1907.) Reprinted New York: Feldheim, n.d.

Joseph ben Meir ibn Zabara (second half of the twelfth century). *The Book of Delight*. Trans. by Moses Hadas. New York: Columbia University Press, 1932.

Berechiah ha-Nakdan (late twelfth to early thirteenth centuries). *Fables of a Jewish Aesop: The Fox Fables of Berechiah ha-Nakdan*. Trans. by Moses Hadas. New York: Columbia University Press, 1967.

Epstein, Morris, editor and trans. *Tales of Sendebar*. Philadelphia: Jewish Publication Society of America, 1967. (Popular stories and legends in a version probably from the twelfth or thirteenth century.)

Immanuel ben Solomon Romi (c. 1261 to after 1328). *Tophet and Eden (Hell and Paradise): In Imitation of Dante's Inferno and Paradiso*. Trans. by Hermann Gollancz. London: University of London, 1921.

Berger, David, editor and trans. *The Jewish-Christian Debate in the High Middle Ages: A Critical Edition of the Nizzahon Vetus* [*Old Book of Polemic*]. Philadelphia: Jewish Publication Society of America, 1978. (From thirteenth-century Germany.)

Sefer Ha-Yashar: The Book of the Righteous (thirteenth century). Edited and trans. by Seymour J. Cohen. New York: Ktav Publishing House, Inc., 1973.

Jonah ben Abraham of Gerona (c. 1200–1263). *Shaarei Teshuvah: The Gates of Repentance.* Trans. by Shraga Silverstein. Jerusalem and New York: Feldheim, 1967.

Orchot Tzaddikim: The Ways of the Righteous (probably fifteenth century). Trans. by Seymour J. Cohen. Jerusalem and New York: Feldheim, 1969.

Chapter 8. Medieval Jewish Theology and Philosophy

GENERAL AND HISTORICAL STUDIES

Agus, Jacob Bernard. *The Evolution of Jewish Thought, From Biblical Times to the Opening of the Modern Era.* London and New York: Abelard-Schuman, 1959.

Blau, Joseph L. *The Story of Jewish Philosophy.* New York: Random House, Inc., 1962.

Guttmann, Julius. *Philosophies of Judaism: The History of Jewish Philosophy from Biblical Times to Franz Rosenzweig.* Trans. by David W. Silverman. New York: Holt, Rinehart and Winston, 1964.

Husik, Isaac. *A History of Medieval Jewish Philosophy.* Philadelphia: Jewish Publication Society of America, 1958. (First published in 1916.)

Katz, Steven T., editor. *Jewish Philosophers.* New York: Bloch Publishing Co., Inc., 1975. (Based on articles in the *Encyclopedia Judaica.*)

Silver, Daniel Jeremy. *Maimonidean Criticism and the Maimonidean Controversy, 1180–1240.* Leiden: E. J. Brill, 1965.

INDIVIDUAL PHILOSOPHERS (in order of discussion in the chapter)

Saadia Gaon. *The Book of Beliefs and Opinions.* Trans. by Samuel Rosenblatt. New Haven: Yale University Press, 1948.

————. *Book of Doctrines and Beliefs.* Edited, trans., and abridged by Alexander Altmann. In *Three Jewish Philosophers.* New York: Harper Torchbook, Harper & Row, Publishers, 1965. (First published in 1945.)

Bahya ben Joseph ibn Pakuda. *The Book of Direction to the Duties of the Heart.* Trans. from the original Arabic by Menahem Mansoor. London: Routledge and Kegan Paul, 1973.

————. *Duties of the Heart*. 2 volumes. Trans. from the Hebrew version of Judah ibn Tibbon by Moses Hyamson. New York: Bloch Publishing Co., Inc., 1925–1947. (Reprinted by Boys Town Jerusalem Publishers, 1962.)

Judah Halevy. *The Kuzari: An Argument for the Faith of Israel*. Trans. from the Arabic by Hartwig Hirschfeld. New York: Schocken Books, Inc., 1964. (First published in 1905.)

Moses Maimonides. *The Guide of the Perplexed*. Trans. by Shlomo Pines. Chicago: University of Chicago Press, 1963.

Goodman, Lenn Evan, editor and trans. *Rambam: Readings in the Philosophy of Maimonides*. New York: The Viking Press, Inc., 1976.

Guttmann, Julius, editor. *Maimonides: The Guide of the Perplexed*. Trans. and abridged by Chaim Rabin. London: East and West Library, 1952.

Twersky, Isadore, editor. *A Maimonides Reader*. New York: Behrman House, Inc., 1972.

Roth, Leon. *The Guide for the Perplexed: Moses Maimonides*. London: Hutchinson's Universal Library, 1948.

Wolfson, Harry A. *Crescas' Critique of Aristotle: Problems of Aristotle's Physics in Jewish and Arabic Philosophy*. Cambridge, Mass.: Harvard University Press, 1929.

Husik, Isaac, editor and trans. *Sefer ha-Ikkarim (Book of Principles) by Joseph Albo*. 4 volumes. Philadelphia: Jewish Publication Society of America, 1929–1930.

Chapter 9. Medieval Jewish Mysticism and Kabbalah

GENERAL AND HISTORICAL STUDIES

Scholem, Gershom. *Major Trends in Jewish Mysticism*, 3rd edition. New York: Schocken Books, Inc., 1954. (Originally published 1941.)

————. *Kabbalah*. New York: Quadrangle/The New York Times Book Co., 1974. (Based on his articles in the *Encyclopedia Judaica*.)

————. *The Messianic Idea in Judaism and Other Essays on Jewish Spirituality*. New York: Schocken Books, Inc., 1971.

————. *On the Kabbalah and Its Symbolism*. Trans. by Ralph Manheim. New York: Schocken Books, Inc., 1965.

Jacobs, Louis, editor. *Jewish Mystical Testimonies*. New York: Schocken Books, Inc., 1977.

Weiner, Herbert. *9 1/2 Mystics: The Kabbalah Today*. New York: Collier Books, 1969.

TRANSLATIONS (in order of discussion in the chapter)

Singer, Sholom Alchanan, trans. *Medieval Jewish Mysticism: Book of the Pious.* Northbrook, Ill.: Whitehall, 1971. (A translation of the first 161 of the 1173 sections of the *Sefer Hasidim.*)

Gaster, Moses, editor and trans. *Ma'aseh Book: Book of Jewish Tales and Legends.* 2 volumes. Trans. from the Judeo-German. Philadelphia: Jewish Publication Society of America, 1934. (A collection of stories published in the seventeenth century, containing tales about Samuel the hasid [no. 158–no. 165] and Judah the hasid [no. 166–no. 183].)

The Zohar. Trans. by Harry Sperling, Maurice Simon, and Paul P. Levertoff. 5 volumes. London: Soncino Press, 1933–1934.

Rosenberg, Roy A., trans. *The Anatomy of God: The Book of Concealment, The Great Holy Assembly and the Lesser Holy Assembly of the Zohar, with the Assembly of the Tabernacle.* New York: Ktav Publishing House, Inc., 1973.

Zohar: The Book of Splendor. Selections edited by Gershom Scholem. New York: Schocken Books, Inc., 1963.

Chapter 10. Jews and Judaism in Early Modern Times

GENERAL WORKS AND MONOGRAPHS

(Also see Roth, *History of the Jews of England;* Lowenthal, *The Jews of Germany;* Baron, *The Jewish Community*, listed in Chap. 7.)

Barzilay, Isaac E. *Between Reason and Faith: Anti-Rationalism in Italian Jewish Thought, 1250–1650.* The Hague: Mouton, 1967.

Cohen, Martin A. *The Martyr: The Story of a Secret Jew and the Mexican Inquisition in the Sixteenth Century.* Philadelphia: Jewish Publication Society of America, 1973.

Feingold, Henry L. *Zion in America: The Jewish Experience from Colonial Times to the Present.* New York: Hippocrene Books, Inc., 1974.

Kamen, Henry. *The Spanish Inquisition.* New York: New American Library, 1965.

Katz, Jacob. *Tradition and Crisis: Jewish Society at the End of the Middle Ages.* New York: The Free Press, 1961.

Marcus, Jacob R. *The Colonial American Jew, 1492–1776.* 3 volumes. Detroit: Wayne State University Press, 1970.

Netanyahu, B. *Don Isaac Abravanel: Statesman and Philosopher.* Philadelphia: Jewish Publication Society of America, 1953.

———. *The Marranos of Spain.* New York: American Academy for Jewish Research, 1967.

Roth, Cecil. *A History of the Marranos.* Philadelphia: Jewish Publication Society of America, 1932.

——. *A Life of Menassah ben Israel.* Philadelphia: Jewish Publication Society of America, 1934.

——. *The Spanish Inquisition.* New York: W. W. Norton & Company, Inc., 1964. (First published in 1937.)

——. *The House of Nasi: Dona Gracia.* Philadelphia: Jewish Publication Society of America, 1947.

——. *The House of Nasi: The Duke of Naxos.* Philadelphia: Jewish Publication Society of America, 1948.

——. *The Jews in the Renaissance.* Philadelphia: Jewish Publication Society of America, 1950.

——. *History of the Jews of Venice.* New York: Schocken Books, Inc., 1975. (First published in 1930.)

Scholem, Gershom. *Sabbatai Sevi: The Mystical Messiah, 1626–1676.* Trans. by R. J. Zwi Werblowsky. Princeton, N.J.: Princeton University Press, 1973.

Shulvass, Moses A. *Jewish Culture in Eastern Europe: The Classical Period.* New York: Ktav Publishing House, Inc., 1975.

Stern, Selma. *The Court Jew: A Contribution to the History of the Period of Absolutism in Central Europe.* Trans. by Ralph Weiman. Philadelphia: Jewish Publication Society of America, 1950.

——. *Josel of Rosheim: Commander of Jewry in the Holy Roman Empire of the German Nation.* Trans. by Gertrude Hirschler. Philadelphia: Jewish Publication Society of America, 1965.

Weinryb, Bernard D. *The Jews of Poland: A Social and Economic History of the Jewish Community in Poland from 1100 to 1800.* Philadelphia: Jewish Publication Society of America, 1973.

Werblowsky, R. J. Zwi. *Joseph Karo: Lawyer and Mystic.* Philadelphia: Jewish Publication Society of America, 1977. (First published in 1962.)

Yerushalmi, Yosef Hayim. *From Spanish Court to Italian Ghetto: Isaac Cardoso.* New York: Columbia University Press, 1971.

TRANSLATIONS OF JEWISH LITERATURE FROM THE EARLY MODERN PERIOD

(Works are listed in chronological order.)

Usque, Samuel (sixteenth century). *Consolation for the Tribulations of Israel.* Trans. from the Portuguese and edited by Martin A. Cohen. Philadelphia: Jewish Publication Society of America, 1965.

Joseph b. Joshua Ha-Kohen (1496–1578). *The Vale of Tears*. Trans. from the Hebrew by Harry S. May. The Hague: Nijhoff, 1971.

Cordovero, Moses (1521–1570). *The Palm Tree of Deborah*. Trans. from the Hebrew by Louis Jacobs. London: Vallentine, Mitchell, 1960.

Hanover, Nathan (died 1683). *The Abyss of Despair*. Trans. from the Hebrew by Abraham J. Mesch. New York: Bloch Publishing Co., Inc., 1950.

Glückel of Hameln (1645–1724). *The Memoirs of Glückel of Hameln*. Trans. by Marvin Lowenthal. New York: Schocken Books, Inc., 1977. (Originally published in 1933.) Also trans. by Beth-Zion Abrahams. New York: Thomas Yoseloff, 1963.

Luzzatto, Moses Hayyim (1707–1747). *Mesillat Yesharim: The Path of the Upright*. Trans. by Mordecai M. Kaplan. Philadelphia: Jewish Publication Society of America, 1966. (First published in 1936.)

HASIDISM

(See also Scholem, *Major Trends in Jewish Mysticism*, and Weiner, *9 1/2 Mystics*, listed under Chap. 9, and Ettinger, "The Hassidic Movement—Reality and Ideals" in Ben-Sasson and Ettinger, *Jewish Society Throughout the Ages*, listed in the opening section of this bibliography.)

Ben-Amos, Dan, and Mintz, Jerome R., editors and trans. *In Praise of the Baal Shem Tov (Shivei ha-Besht): The Earliest Collection of Legends About the Founder of Hasidism*. Bloomington: Indiana University Press, 1970.

Band, Arnold, editor and trans. *Nahman of Bratslav: The Tales*. New York: Paulist Press, 1978.

Dobh Baer of Lubavitch (1773–1827). *Tract on Ecstasy*. Trans. by Louis Jacobs. London: Vallentine, Mitchell, 1963.

Dresner, Samuel H. *The Zaddik: The Doctrine of the Zaddik According to the Writings of Rabbi Yaakov Yosef of Polnoy*. New York: Schocken Books, Inc., 1974. (First published in 1960.)

Jacobs, Louis. *Seeker of Unity: The Life and Works of Aaron of Starosselje [1766–1828]*. New York: Basic Books, Inc., Publishers, 1966.

———, editor. *Hasidic Prayer*. New York: Schocken Books, Inc., 1973.

Rabinowitsch, W. Z. *Lithuanian Hasidism from Its Beginnings to the Present Day*. Trans. from the Hebrew by M. B. Dagut. London: Vallentine, Mitchell, 1970.

Wiesel, Elie. *Souls on Fire: Portraits and Legends of Hasidic Leaders*. Trans. from the French by Marion Wiesel. New York: Random House, Inc., 1973.

Chapter 11. The European State and the Jews, 1770–1880

GENERAL SURVEYS

(See also Roth, *History of the Jews of England;* Lowenthal, *The Jews of Germany;* Feingold, *Zion in America,* listed in Chaps. 7 and 10.)

Sachar, Howard Morley. *The Course of Modern Jewish History*. Updated and expanded edition. New York: Dell, 1977.

Elbogen, Ismar. *A Century of Jewish Life*. Trans. by Moses Hadas. Philadelphia: Jewish Publication Society of America, 1960. (Covers the period from 1848 to the outbreak of World War II.)

Chazan, Robert, and Raphael, Marc Lee, editors. *Modern Jewish History: A Source Reader*. New York: Schocken Books, Inc., 1974.

INDIVIDUAL COUNTRIES AND PERIODS

Albert, Phyllis Cohen. *The Modernization of French Jewry: Consistory and Community in the Nineteenth Century*. Hanover, N.H.: University Press of New England, 1977.

Dawidowicz, Lucy S., editor. *The Golden Tradition: Jewish Life and Thought in Eastern Europe*. New York: Holt, Rinehart and Winston, 1966.

Dubnow, Simon. *History of the Jews in Russia and Poland*. Trans. from the Russian by I. Friedlaender. New York: Ktav Publishing House, Inc., 1973. (Originally published in three volumes, 1916–1918.)

Greenberg, Louis. *The Jews in Russia*. New York: Schocken Books, Inc., 1976. (Originally published in 2 volumes, 1944–1951.)

Hertzberg, Arthur. *The French Enlightenment and the Jews*. New York: Columbia University Press, 1968.

Jick, Leon A. *The Americanization of the Synagogue, 1820–1870*. Hanover, N.H.: University Press of New England, 1976.

Katz, Jacob. *Out of the Ghetto: The Social Background of Jewish Emancipation, 1770–1870*. Cambridge, Mass.: Harvard University Press, 1973.

Kobler, Franz. *Napoleon and the Jews*. New York: Schocken Books, Inc., 1975.

Levitats, Isaac. *The Jewish Community in Russia, 1772–1844*. New York: Octagon Books, Inc., 1970. (First published in 1943.)

Meyer, Michael. *The Origins of the Modern Jew: Jewish Identity and European Culture in Germany, 1749–1824*. Detroit: Wayne State University Press, 1967.

Patterson, David. *Abraham Mapu: The Creator of the Modern Hebrew Novel*. London: East and West Library, 1964.

————. *The Hebrew Novel in Czarist Russia.* Edinburgh: Edinburgh University Press, 1964.

Roskies, Diane K., and Roskies, David G., editors. *The Shtetl Book.* New York: Ktav Publishing House, Inc., 1975.

Spiegel, Shalom. *Hebrew Reborn.* Cleveland, Ohio: William Collins & World Publishing Co., Inc., 1962. (First published 1930.)

Zborowski, Mark, and Herzog, Elizabeth. *Life Is with People: The Culture of the Shtetl.* New York: Schocken Books, Inc., 1962. (First published 1952.)

Chapter 12. First Encounters with Modern Thought, from Spinoza to Krochmal

GENERAL SURVEYS

(See also Blau, *The Story of Jewish Philosophy;* Guttmann, *Philosophies of Judaism;* and Katz, *Jewish Philosophers,* listed in Chap. 8.)

Blau, Joseph L. *Modern Varieties of Judaism.* New York: Columbia University Press, 1964.

Jacob, Walter. *Christianity Through Jewish Eyes: The Quest for Common Ground.* Cincinnati, Ohio: Hebrew Union College Press, 1974.

Rotenstreich, Nathan. *Jewish Philosophy in Modern Times: From Mendelssohn to Rosenzweig.* New York: Holt, Rinehart and Winston, 1968.

INDIVIDUAL THINKERS (in order of discussion in the chapter)

Acosta, Uriel. *A Specimen of Human Life.* New York: Bergman Publishers, 1967.

Roth, Leon. *Spinoza, Descartes, and Maimonides.* New York: Russell and Russell, Publishers, 1963. (First published in 1924.)

————. *Spinoza.* London: George Allen & Unwin Ltd., 1929.

Strauss, Leo. *Spinoza's Critique of Religion.* Trans. by E. M. Sinclair. New York: Schocken Books, Inc., 1965.

Wolfson, Harry Austryn. *The Philosophy of Spinoza.* New York: Meridian Books, 1958. (First published in 1934.)

Maimon, Solomon. *The Autobiography of Solomon Maimon.* Trans. by J. Clark Murray. London: East and West Library, 1954.

Mendelssohn, Moses. *Jerusalem and Other Jewish Writings.* Trans. by Alfred Jospe. New York: Schocken Books, Inc., 1969.

Jospe, Eva., editor and trans. *Moses Mendelssohn: Selections from His Writings.* New York: The Viking Press, Inc., 1975.

Altmann, Alexander. *Moses Mendelssohn: A Biographical Study*. Philadelphia: Jewish Publication Society of America, 1973.

Rosenbloom, Noah H. *Luzzatto's Ethico-Psychological Interpretation of Judaism: A Study in the Religious Philosophy of Samuel David Luzzatto*. New York: Yeshiva University Department of Special Publications, 1965.

Chapter 13. The Question of Jewish Religious Reform in Nineteenth-Century Europe

GENERAL SURVEYS AND STUDIES

(See also the books on Jewish philosophy by Blau, Guttmann, Jacob, Rotenstreich, and Katz listed in Chaps. 8 and 12.)

Agus, Jacob B. *Modern Philosophies of Judaism*. New York: Behrman House, Inc., 1941.

Davis, Moshe. *The Emergence of Conservative Judaism: The Historical School in Nineteenth-Century America*. Philadelphia: Jewish Publication Society of America, 1965.

Katz, Jacob, editor. *The Role of Religion in Modern Jewish History (Proceedings of Regional Conferences of the Association for Jewish Studies Held at the University of Pennsylvania and the University of Toronto in March–April 1974)*. Cambridge, Mass.: Association for Jewish Studies, 1975.

Petuchowski, Jakob J. *Prayerbook Reform in Europe: The Liturgy of European Liberal and Reform Judaism*. New York: World Union for Progressive Judaism, 1968.

Philipson, David. *The Reform Movement in Judaism*. New York: Ktav Publishing House, Inc., 1967. (First published in 1907.)

Plaut, Gunther W., editor. *The Rise of Reform Judaism: A Sourcebook of Its European Origins*. New York: World Union for Progressive Judaism, 1963.

———. *The Growth of Reform Judaism: American and European Sources Until 1948*. New York: World Union for Progressive Judaism, 1965.

INDIVIDUAL THINKERS (in order of discussion in the chapter)

Marcus, Jacob R. *Israel Jacobson: The Founder of the Reform Movement in Judaism*. Cincinnati, Ohio: Hebrew Union College Press, 1972.

Hirsch, Samson Raphael. *The Nineteen Letters on Judaism*. Trans. by Bernard Drachman. New York: Feldheim, 1960.

———. *Horeb: A Philosophy of Jewish Laws and Observances*. 2 volumes. Trans. by I. Grunfeld. London: Soncino Press, Ltd., 1962.

Rosenbloom, Noah H. *Tradition in an Age of Reform: The Religious Philosophy of Samson Raphael Hirsch*. Philadelphia: Jewish Publication Society of America, 1976.

Geiger, Abraham. *Judaism and Its History*. Trans. by Charles Newburgh. New York: Bloch Publishing Co., Inc., 1911.

Petuchowski, Jakob J., editor. *New Perspectives on Abraham Geiger*. New York: Hebrew Union College Press, 1975.

Weiner, Max, editor. *Abraham Geiger and Liberal Judaism: The Challenge of the Nineteenth Century*. Trans. by Ernst J. Schlochauer. Philadelphia: Jewish Publication Society of America, 1962.

Graetz, Heinrich. *The Structure of Jewish History and Other Essays*. Trans. and edited by Ismar Schorsch. New York: Jewish Theological Seminary of America, 1975.

Chapter 14. The Onslaught of Modernity: Jewish History from 1880 to the Present

(See also Sachar, *Course of Modern Jewish History;* Elbogen, *A Century of Jewish Life;* Dubnow, *History of the Jews in Russia and Poland;* Greenberg, *The Jews in Russia;* Feingold, *Zion in America;* Chazan and Raphael, *Modern Jewish History: A Source Reader;* and Dawidowicz, *Golden Tradition*, listed in Chap. 11.)

SURVEYS ON SPECIAL TOPICS

Ben-Zvi, Itzhak. *The Exiled and the Redeemed*. Philadelphia: Jewish Publication Society of America, 1961. (On the ancient Jewish communities in Muslim lands and other topics.)

Chouraqui, André N. *Between East and West: A History of the Jews of North Africa*. Trans. by Michael M. Bernet. Philadelphia: Jewish Publication Society of America, 1968.

Lowenthal, Marvin. *A World Passed By: Scenes and Memories of Jewish Civilization in Europe and North Africa*. New York: Behrman House, Inc., 1938.

Patai, Raphael. *Tents of Jacob: The Diaspora—Yesterday and Today*. Englewood Cliffs, N.J.: Prentice-Hall, Inc., 1971.

Wischnitzer, Mark. *To Dwell in Safety: The Story of Jewish Migration Since 1800*. Philadelphia: Jewish Publication Society of America, 1948.

GENERAL WORKS ON ANTI-SEMITISM

Bernstein, Herman. *The Truth About "The Protocols of the Elders of Zion": A Complete Exposure*. New York: Covici–Friede, 1935.

Cohn, Norman. *Warrant for Genocide: The Myth of the Jewish World-Conspiracy and the Protocols of the Elders of Zion*. New York: Harper & Row, Publishers, 1966.

Leschnitzer, Adolf. *The Magic Background of Modern Anti-Semitism: An Analysis of the German-Jewish Relationship*. New York: International Universities Press, Inc., 1956.

Parkes, James. *Anti-Semitism: A Concise World History*. New York: Quadrangle/The New York Times Book Co., 1964.

Pinson, Koppel S., editor. *Essays on Antisemitism*. New York: Conference on Jewish Relations, 1946.

Poliakov, Léon. *The History of Anti-Semitism*. 3 volumes. Trans. from the French by Richard Howard. New York: Vanguard Press, Inc., 1965–1976.

ANTI-SEMITISM AND ZIONISM IN FRANCE AND GERMANY

Byrnes, Robert R. *Antisemitism in Modern France: The Prologue to the Dreyfus Affair*. New Brunswick, N.J.: Rutgers University Press, 1950.

Liptzin, Solomon. *Germany's Stepchildren*. New York: Meridian Books, 1961. (First published in 1944.)

Marrus, Michael. *The Politics of Assimilation: A Study of the French Jewish Community at the Time of the Dreyfus Affair*. London: Oxford University Press, Inc., 1971.

Massing, Paul W. *Rehearsal for Destruction: A Study of Political Anti-Semitism in Imperial Germany*. New York: Harper & Row, Publishers, 1949.

Mosse, George L. *Germans and Jews*. New York: Grosset & Dunlap, Inc., 1970.

Poppel, Stephen M. *Zionism in Germany, 1897–1933: The Shaping of a Jewish Identity*. Philadelphia: Jewish Publication Society of America, 1977.

Pulzer: Peter G. J. *The Rise of Political Anti-Semitism in Germany and Austria*. New York: John Wiley & Sons, Inc., 1964.

Reinharz, Jehuda. *Fatherland or Promised Land: The Dilemma of the German Jew, 1893–1914*. Ann Arbor: University of Michigan Press, 1975.

Schorsch, Ismar. *Jewish Reactions to German Anti-Semitism, 1870–1914*. New York: Columbia University Press, 1972.

Tal, Uriel. *Christians and Jews in Germany: Religion, Politics, and Ideology in the Second Reich, 1870–1914*. Trans. from the Hebrew by Noah Jacobs. Ithaca, N.Y.: Cornell University Press, 1975.

ZIONISM AND ISRAEL

Halpern, Ben. *The Idea of the Jewish State*. Rev. edition, Cambridge, Mass.: Harvard University Press, 1969.

Laqueur, Walter. *A History of Zionism.* New York: Schocken Books, Inc., 1976.

———, editor. *The Israel-Arab Reader: A Documentary History of the Middle East Conflict.* New York: Bantam Books, Inc., 1969.

Sachar, Howard M. *A History of Israel.* New York: Alfred A. Knopf, Inc., 1976.

Schweid, Eliezer. *Israel at the Crossroads.* Trans. by Alton Meyer Winters. Philadelphia: Jewish Publication Society of America, 1973.

Spiro, Melford E. *Kibbutz: Venture in Utopia.* New edition. Cambridge, Mass.: Harvard University Press, 1975.

Stein, Leonard. *The Balfour Declaration.* New York: Simon & Schuster, Inc., 1961.

Vital, David. *The Origins of Zionism.* London: Oxford University Press, 1975.

Weisbord, Robert G. *African Zion.* Philadelphia: Jewish Publication Society of America, 1968.

Weizmann, Chaim. *Trial and Error.* New York: Harper & Row, Publishers, 1949.

EAST EUROPEAN JEWRY

Baron, Salo W. *The Russian Jews Under Tsar and Soviets.* 2nd edition. New York: Macmillan Publishing Co., Inc., 1975.

Fishman, William J. *Jewish Radicals: From Czarist Shtetl to London Ghetto.* New York: Random House, Inc., 1974.

Gitelman, Zvi Y. *Jewish Nationality and Soviet Politics: The Jewish Sections of the C.P.S.U., 1917–1930.* Princeton, N.J.: Princeton University Press, 1972.

Heller, Celia. *On the Edge of Destruction: Jews of Poland Between the Two World Wars.* New York: Columbia University Press, 1977.

Janowsky, Oscar I. *The Jews and Minority Rights, 1898–1919.* New York: AMS Press, 1966. (First published in 1933.)

Kochan, Lionel, editor. *Jews in Soviet Russia since 1917.* 3rd edition. London: Oxford University Press, 1978.

Korey, William. *The Russian Cage: Anti-Semitism in Russia.* New York: The Viking Press, Inc., 1973.

Mendelssohn, Ezra. *Class Struggle in the Pale: The Formative Years of the Jewish Workers' Movement in Tsarist Russia.* London: Cambridge University Press, 1970.

Nedava, Joseph. *Trotsky and the Jews.* Philadelphia: Jewish Publication Society of America, 1972.

Patkin, A. L. *The Origins of the Russian-Jewish Labour Movement*. London: F. W. Cheshire, 1947.

Samuel, Maurice. *Blood Accusation: The Strange History of the Beiliss Case*. Philadelphia: Jewish Publication Society of America, 1966.

Tager, Alexander. *The Decay of Czarism: The Beiliss Trial*. Philadelphia: Jewish Publication Society of America, 1935.

Tobias, Henry J. *The Jewish Bund in Russia, from Its Origins to 1905*. Stanford, Calif.: Stanford University Press, 1972.

Vago, B., and Mosse, G. L., editors. *Jews and Non-Jews in Eastern Europe, 1918–1945*. New York and Toronto: Halstead Press, 1974.

GERMAN JEWRY; THE HOLOCAUST

Bracher, Karl Dietrich. *The German Dictatorship: The Origins, Structure, and Effects of National Socialism*. Trans. from the German by Jean Steinberg. New York: Praeger Publishing Co., 1970.

Dawidowicz, Lucy S. *The War Against the Jews, 1933–1945*. New York: Holt, Rinehart and Winston, 1975.

————, editor. *A Holocaust Reader*. New York: Behrman House, Inc., 1976.

Friedlander, Albert H., editor. *Out of the Whirlwind: A Reader of Holocaust Literature*. Garden City, N.Y.: Doubleday & Company, Inc., 1968.

Hilberg, Raul. *The Destruction of the European Jews*. New York: Quadrangle/New York Times Book Co., Inc., 1961.

Jäckel, Eberhard. *Hitler's Weltanschauung*. Trans. from the German by Herbert Arnold. Middletown, Conn.: Wesleyan University Press, 1972.

Levin, Nora. *The Holocaust: The Destruction of European Jewry, 1933–1945*. New York: Schocken Books, Inc., 1973.

Trunk, Isaiah. *Judenrat: The Jewish Councils in Eastern Europe Under Nazi Occupation*. New York: Stein & Day, Publishers, 1972.

Weinreich, Max. *Hitler's Professors: The Part of Scholarship in Germany's Crimes Against the Jewish People*. New York: Yivo, 1946.

AMERICAN JEWRY

Agar, Herbert. *The Saving Remnant: An Account of Jewish Survival*. New York: The Viking Press, Inc., 1960. (On the American Jewish Joint Distribution Committee.)

Blau, Joseph L. *Judaism in America: From Curiosity to Third Faith*. Chicago: University of Chicago Press, 1976.

Cohen, Naomi W. *American Jews and the Zionist Idea*. New York: Ktav Publishing House, Inc., 1975.

———. *Not Free to Desist: A History of the American Jewish Committee, 1906–1966*. Philadelphia: Jewish Publication Society of America, 1972.

Glazer, Nathan. *American Judaism*. Rev. edition. Chicago: University of Chicago Press, 1972.

Halpern, Ben. *The American Jew: A Zionist Analysis*. New York: Theodor Herzl Foundation, 1956.

Howe, Irving. *World of Our Fathers: The Journey of East European Jews to America and the Life They Found and Made*. New York: Simon & Schuster, Inc., 1976.

Liebman, Charles S. *The Ambivalent American Jew*. Philadelphia: Jewish Publication Society of America, 1973.

Morse, Arthur D. *While Six Million Died: A Chronicle of American Apathy*. New York: Hart Publishing Co., 1975.

Neusner, Jacob. *American Judaism: Adventure in Modernity*. Englewood Cliffs, N.J.: Prentice-Hall, Inc., 1972.

———, editor. *Understanding American Judaism: Toward the Description of a Modern Religion*. Vol. 1: *The Rabbi and the Synagogue*. Vol. 2: *Sectors of American Judaism*. New York: Ktav Publishing House, Inc., 1975.

Poll, Solomon. *The Hasidic Community of Williamsburg: A Study in the Sociology of Religion*. New York: Schocken Books, Inc., 1969.

Rischin, Moses. *The Promised City: New York's Jews, 1870–1914*. New York: Corinth Books, 1964.

Rosenberg, Stuart E. *The Search for Jewish Identity in America*. Garden City, N.Y.: Doubleday Anchor Books, Doubleday & Company, Inc., 1965.

Sklare, Marshall. *America's Jews*. New York: Random House, Inc., 1971.

———. *Conservative Judaism: An American Religious Movement*. New edition. New York: Schocken Books, Inc., 1972.

Tcherikower, Elias. *The Early Jewish Labor Movement in the United States*. Trans. by Aaron Antonovsky. New York: Yivo, 1961.

Urofsky, Melvin I. *American Zionism from Herzl to the Holocaust*. Garden City, N.Y.: Doubleday Anchor Books, Doubleday & Company, Inc., 1976.

Chapter 15. Secular Jewish Thought in the Nineteenth and and Twentieth Centuries

ANTHOLOGIES

Goodman, Saul L., editor. *The Faith of Secular Jews*. New York: Ktav Publishing House, Inc., 1976.

Hertzberg, Arthur, editor. *The Zionist Idea: A Historical Analysis and Reader.* Garden City, N.Y.: Doubleday & Company, Inc., 1959.

INDIVIDUAL THINKERS (in order of discussion in the chapter)

Hess, Moses. *Rome and Jerusalem: A Study in Jewish Nationalism.* Trans. by Meyer Waxman. New York: Bloch Publishing Co., Inc., 1943. (First published in English translation in 1918.)

Berlin, Isaiah. *The Life and Opinions of Moses Hess.* Cambridge, Eng.: W. Heffer & Sons, Ltd., 1959.

Weiss, John. *Moses Hess: Utopian Socialist.* Detroit, Mich.: Wayne State University Press, 1960.

Pinkser, Leo. *Road to Freedom: Writings and Addresses.* New York: Scopus Publishing Company, 1944.

Herzl, Theodor. *The Jewish State (Der Judenstaat).* Trans. by Harry Zohn. New York: Herzl Press, 1970.

———. *Zionist Writings.* 2 volumes. New York: Herzl Press, 1973–1975.

Bein, Alex. *Theodore Herzl: A Biography.* Trans. from the German by Maurice Samuel. New York: Atheneum Publishers, 1970. (First published in English translation in 1941.)

Elon, Amos. *Herzl.* New York: Holt, Rinehart and Winston, 1975.

Simon, Leon, trans. *Selected Essays of Ahad Ha-Am.* New York: Meridian Books, 1962. (First published in English translation in 1912.)

———, translator. *Achad Ha-Am: Ten Essays on Zionism and Judaism.* New York: Arno Press, Inc., 1973. (First published in English translation in 1922.)

———, editor and trans. *Ahad Ha-Am: Essays, Letters, Memoirs.* London: East and West Library, 1946.

Kohn, Hans, editor. *Nationalism and the Jewish Ethic: Basic Writings of Ahad Ha-Am.* New York: Schocken Books, Inc., 1962.

Simon, Leon. *Ahad Ha-Am, Asher Ginsberg: A Biography.* Philadelphia: Jewish Publication Society of America, 1960.

Dubnow, Simon. *Nationalism and History: Essays on Old and New Judaism.* Edited by Koppel S. Pinson. Philadelphia: Jewish Publication Society of America, 1958.

Syrkin, Marie. *Nachman Syrkin, Socialist Zionist: A Biographical Memoir and Selected Essays.* New York: Herzl Press, 1961.

Gordon, A. D. *Selected Essays.* Trans. by N. Teradyon and A. Shohat. New York: Arno Press, Inc., 1973. (First Published in English translation in 1938.)

Borochov, Ber. *Nationalism and the Class Struggle*. Edited by Moshe Cohen, with an introduction by Abraham G. Duker. New York: Young Poale Zion Alliance of America, 1937.

MODERN JEWISH LITERATURE

Alter, Robert. *After the Tradition: Essays on Modern Jewish Writing*. New York: E. P. Dutton & Co., Inc., 1971.

———. *Defenses of the Imagination: Jewish Writers and Modern Historical Crisis*. Philadelphia: Jewish Publication Society of America, 1977.

Halkin, Simon. *Modern Hebrew Literature: Trends and Values*. New York: Shocken Books, Inc., 1950.

Madison, Charles A. *Yiddish Literature: Its Scope and Major Writers*. New York: Frederick Ungar Publishing Co., Inc., 1968.

Rabinovich, Isaiah. *Major Trends in Modern Hebrew Fiction*. Trans. from the Hebrew by M. Roston. Chicago: University of Chicago Press, 1968.

(Also see Patterson, *Mapu and The Hebrew Novel*, listed in Chap. 11; Schweid, *Israel at the Crossroads*; and Howe, *World of Our Fathers*, listed in Chap. 14.)

Chapter 16. Twentieth-Century Jewish Religious Thought

GENERAL WORKS AND ANTHOLOGIES

(See the books by Guttmann, Blau, Rotenstreich, Jacob, Katz, and Agus on Jewish philosophy and theology listed under Chaps. 8, 12, and 13.)

Bergman, Samuel Hugo. *Faith and Reason: An Introduction to Modern Jewish Thought*. Trans. and edited by Alfred Jospe. New York: Schocken Books, Inc., 1963.

Berkovits, Eliezer. *Major Themes in Modern Philosophies of Judaism*. New York: Ktav Publishing House, Inc., 1974.

Kaufman, William E. *Contemporary Jewish Philosophies*. New York: Behrman House, Inc., 1976.

Martin, Bernard, editor. *Great Twentieth-Century Jewish Philosophers: Shestov, Rosenzweig, Buber, with Selections from Their Writings*. New York: Macmillan Publishing Co., Inc., 1970.

Noveck, Simon, editor. *Great Jewish Thinkers of the Twentieth Century*. New York: B'nai B'rith Department of Adult Jewish Education, 1963.

INDIVIDUAL THINKERS (in order of discussion in the chapter)

Kohler, Kaufmann, *Jewish Theology Systematically and Historically Considered*. Cincinnati, Ohio: Riverdale Press, 1943. (First published 1917.)

Bentwich, Norman. *Solomon Schechter: A Biography*. Philadelphia: Jewish Publication Society of America, 1938.

——, editor. *Solomon Schechter: Selected Writings*. Oxford: East and West Library, 1946.

Eckman, Lester. *The History of the Musar Movement, 1840–1945*. New York: Shengold Publishers, Inc., 1975.

——. *Revered by All: The Life and Works of Israel Meir Kagan—Hafets Hayyim (1838–1933)*. New York: Shengold Publishers, Inc., 1974.

Chafetz Chaim (Israel Meir Kagan). *Ahavath Chesed: Kindness as Required by God*. Trans. by Leonard Oschry. Jerusalem and New York: Feldheim, 1967.

Kook, Abraham Isaac. *The Lights of Penitence, The Moral Principles, Lights of Holiness, Essays, Letters, and Poems*. Trans. by Ben Zion Bokser. New York: Paulist Press, 1978.

Agus, Jacob B. *High Priest of Rebirth: The Life, Times, and Thought of Abraham Isaac Kuk*. New York: Bloch Publishing Co., Inc., 1946.

Baeck, Leo. *The Essence of Judaism*. Trans. from the German by Irving Howe. New York: Schocken Books, Inc., 1948.

——. *Judaism and Christianity*. Essays by Leo Baeck trans. and introduced by Walter Kaufmann. Philadelphia: Jewish Publication Society of America, 1958.

——. *This People Israel: The Meaning of Jewish Existence*. Trans. by Albert H. Friedlander. New York: Holt, Rinehart and Winston, 1964.

Friedlander, Albert H. *Leo Baeck: Teacher of Theresienstadt*. New York: Holt, Rinehart and Winston, 1968.

Baker, Leonard. *Days of Sorrow and Pain: Leo Baeck and the Berlin Jews*. New York: Macmillan Publishing Co., Inc., 1978.

Cohen, Hermann. *Religion of Reason Out of the Sources of Judaism*. Trans. by Simon Kaplan. New York: Frederick Ungar Publishing Co., Inc., 1972.

Jospe, Eva., trans. and editor. *Reason and Hope: Selections from the Jewish Writings of Hermann Cohen*. New York: W. W. Norton & Company, Inc., 1971.

Rosenzweig, Franz. *The Star of Redemption*. Trans. by William H. Hallo. New York: Holt, Rinehart and Winston, 1970.

Glatzer, Nahum N. *Franz Rosensweig: His Life and Thought*. Philadelphia: Jewish Publication Society of America, 1953.

Buber, Martin. *I and Thou*. Trans. by Walter Kaufmann. New York: Charles Scribner's Sons, 1970.

————. *Hasidism and Modern Man*. Edited and trans. by Maurice Friedman. New York: Harper & Row, Publishers, 1966. (First published in 1958.)

————. *The Origin and Meaning of Hasidism*. Edited and trans. by Maurice Friedman. New York: Harper & Row, Publishers, 1966. (First published in 1960.)

Herberg, Will, editor. *The Writings of Martin Buber*. New York: Meridian Books, 1956.

Friedman, Maurice S. *Martin Buber: The Life of Dialogue*. Chicago: University of Chicago Press, 1955.

Diamond, Malcolm L. *Martin Buber: Jewish Existentialist*. New York: Harper & Row, Publishers, 1968. (First published in 1960.)

Brown, James. *Kierkegaard, Heidegger, Buber, and Barth: Subject and Object in Modern Theology*. New York: Collier Books, 1963. (First published in 1955.)

Kaplan, Mordecai M. *Judaism as a Civilization: Toward a Reconstruction of Jewish Life*. New York: Thomas Yoseloff, Publisher, 1957. (First published in 1934.)

————. *The Meaning of God in Modern Jewish Religion*. New York: Reconstructionist Press, 1962. (First published in 1937.)

————. *The Purpose and Meaning of Jewish Existence: A People in the Image of God*. Philadelphia: Jewish Publication Society of America, 1964.

Cohen, Arthur, and Kaplan, Modecai M. *If Not Now, When? Conversations Between Mordecai Kaplan and Arthur A. Cohen*. New York: Schocken Books, Inc., 1973.

Heschel, Abraham Joshua. *Man Is Not Alone: A Philosophy of Religion*. Philadelphia: Jewish Publication Society of America, 1951.

————. *The Insecurity of Freedom: Essays on Human Existence*. New York: Schocken Books, Inc., 1972.

————. *God in Search of Man: A Philosophy of Judaism*. Philadelphia: Jewish Publication Society of America, 1956.

————. *Between God and Man: An Interpretation of Judaism*. Selections from the writings of Abraham J. Heschel, edited by Fritz A. Rothschild. New York: The Free Press, 1959.

RECENT JEWISH RELIGIOUS THOUGHT

Berkovits, Eliezer. *Faith After the Holocaust*. New York: Ktav Publishing House, Inc., 1973.

————. *Crisis and Faith*. New York: Sanhedrin Press, 1976.

Borowitz, Eugene B. *A New Jewish Theology in the Making.* Philadelphia: Westminster Press, 1968.

————. *How Can a Jew Speak of Faith Today?* Philadelphia: Westminster Press, 1969.

Cohen, Arthur A. *The Natural and the Supernatural Jew: An Historical and Theological Introduction.* New York: Pantheon Books, Inc., 1962.

The Condition of Jewish Belief: A Symposium Compiled by the Editors of Commentary *Magazine.* New York: Macmillan Publishing Co., Inc., 1969. (First appeared in *Commentary,* August 1966.)

Fackenheim, Emil L. *Quest for Past and Future: Essays in Jewish Theology.* Boston: Beacon Press, 1968.

————. *God's Presence in History: Jewish Affirmations and Philosophical Reflections.* New York: Harper Torchbook, Harper & Row, Publishers, 1972. (First published in 1970.)

————. *Encounters Between Judaism and Modern Philosophy: A Preface to Future Jewish Thought.* New York: Basic Books, Inc., Publishers, 1973.

————. *The Jewish Return to History: Reflections in the Age of Auschwitz and a New Jerusalem.* New York: Schocken Books, Inc., 1978.

Herberg, Will. *Judaism and Modern Man: An Interpretation of the Jewish Religion.* New York: Farrar, Straus & Giroux, Inc., 1951.

Martin, Bernard, editor. *Contemporary Reform Jewish Thought.* New York: Quadrangle/The New York Times Book Co., 1968.

Rubenstein, Richard L. *After Auschwitz: Radical Theology and Contemporary Judaism.* New York: The Bobbs-Merrill Co., Inc., 1966.

Scholem, Gershom. *On Jews and Judaism in Crisis: Selected Essays.* New York: Schocken Books, Inc., 1976. (Especially "Reflections on Jewish Theology," pp. 261–97.)

Steinberg, Milton. *Anatomy of Faith.* Edited by Arthur A. Cohen. New York: Harcourt Brace Jovanovich, Inc., 1960. (Steinberg's theological essays.)

Wiesel, Elie. *A Jew Today.* Trans. from the French by Marion Wiesel. New York: Random House, Inc., 1978.

Index